BRUNNER-ROUTLEDGE PSYCHOSOCIAL STRESS SERIES
Charles R. Figley, Ph.D., Series Editor

HANDBOOK OF STRESS, TRAUMA, AND THE FAMILY

DON R. CATHERALL, Ph.D.

Brunner-Routledge
Taylor & Francis Group

Published in 2004 by
Brunner-Routledge
270 Madison Avenue
New York, NY 10016

Published in Great Britain by
Brunner-Routledge
27 Church Rd.
Hove, East Sussex, BN3 2FA

Brunner-Routledge is an imprint of the Taylor & Francis Group.

Transferred to Digital Printing 2006

10 9 8 7 6 5 4 3 2 1

Library of Congress Cataloging-in-Publication Data

Handbook of stress, trauma and the family / edited by Don R. Catherall.
 p. cm. — (Brunner-Routledge psychosocial stress series)
Includes bibliographical references and index.
 ISBN 0-415-94754-5 (hbk.)
 1. Post-traumatic stress disorder—Handbooks, manuals, etc. 2. Psychic trauma—
Handbooks, manuals, etc. 3. Posttraumatic stress disorder—Patients— Family
relationships—Handbooks, manuals, etc. 4. Psychic trauma—Patients— Family
relationships—Handbooks, manuals, etc. 5. Family—Psychological aspects—Handbooks,
manuals, etc. I. Catherall, Donald Roy, 1946-II. Title. III. Series.

RC552 .P67H355 2004
616.85'21—dc22

2003024677

Contents

PART II: RESEARCH

PART III: PRACTICE

Models of Assessment

Models of Family Treatment

About the Editor

Don R. Catherall, Ph.D., is Clinical Associate Professor, Feinberg School of Medicine, Northwestern University, and former Executive Director of the Phoenix Institute. Dr. Catherall has specialized in the areas of relationship problems and traumatization for more than two decades. He is the author of *Back From the Brink: A Family Guide to Overcoming Traumatic Stress*, as well as numerous articles on families and traumatic stress.

Contributors

Marianne Amir, Ph.D. (Deceased)
Ben-Gurion University of the Negev (Israel)

Zev Apel, Ph.D.
Bar Ilan University (Israel)

Kathryn Basham, Ph.D., LICSW
Smith College, Northampton, Massachusetts (USA)

Don R. Catherall, Ph.D.
Feinberg School of Medicine
Northwestern University, Evanston, Illinois (USA)

Victoria M. Follette, Ph.D.
University of Nevada, Reno, Nevada (USA)

Jane F. Gilgun, Ph.D. LCSW
University of Minnesota, St. Paul, Minnesota (USA)

Steven Gold, Ph.D.
Nova Southeastern University, Fort Lauderdale, Florida (USA)

Mandra L. Rasmussen Hall, M.A.
University of Nevada, Reno, Nevada (USA)

Chrys J. Harris, Ph.D.
Family & Therapy Trauma Center
Greer, South Carolina (USA)

Steven M. Harris, Ph.D.
Texas Tech University
Lubbock, Texas (USA)

Summer Sherburne Hawkins, M.S.
Fox Chase Cancer Center and Drexel University
Philadelphia, Pennsylvania (USA)

Stevan E. Hobfoll, Ph.D.
Kent State University, Kent, Ohio (USA)
KSU-SUMMA Health System Center for the Treatment and Study of Traumatic Stress
St. Thomas Hospital, Akron, Ohio (USA)

Lee Hyer, Ed.D., A.B.P.P.
University of Medicine and Dentistry of New Jersey
Newark, New Jersey (USA)

David Read Johnson, Ph.D.
Post Traumatic Stress Center
New Haven, Connecticut (USA)

Susan M. Johnson, Ed.D.
University of Ottawa (Canada)

Erin R. Kraftcheck, M.A.
York University, Toronto (Canada)

Noel R. Larson, Ph.D.
Meta Resources Institute for Psychotherapy and Training
St. Paul, Minnesota (USA)

Jay Lebow, Ph.D.
Northwestern University, Evanston, Illinois (USA)

Rachel Lev-Wiesel, Ph.D.
Ben-Gurion University of the Negev (Israel)

James W. Maddock, Ph.D.
University of Minnesota, St. Paul, Minnesota (USA)

Sharon L. Manne, Ph.D.
Fox Chase Cancer Center
Philadelphia, Pennsylvania (USA)

Aphrodite Matsakis, Ph.D.
Silver Springs Vet Center
Silver Springs, Maryland (USA)

Monica McGoldrick, ASCW, Ph.D. (Hon.)
Multicultural Family Institute
Highland Park, New Jersey (USA)

Lise A. McLewin, M.A.
York University, Toronto (Canada)

Dennis Miehls, Ph.D.
Smith College, Northampton, Massachusetts (USA)

Robert T. Muller, Ph.D., C.Psych.
York University, Toronto (Canada)

Briana Nelson, Ph.D.
Kansas State University
Manhattan, Kansas (USA)

Erin O'Hea, Ph.D.
University of Medicine and Dentistry of New Jersey
Newark, New Jersey (USA)

Luis E. Oliver, Ph.D.
Saint Paul University
Ottawa (Canada)

David H. Olson, Ph.D.
University of Minnesota, Roseville, Minnesota (USA)

Claire Rabin, Ph.D.
Tel Aviv University (Israel)

Lube Rafalson, M.S.
University of Medicine and Dentistry of New Jersey
Newark, New Jersey (USA)

Kathleen Newcomb Rekart, B.A.
Northwestern University, Evanston, Illinois (USA)

Rory Remer, Ph.D.
University of Kentucky, Lexington, Kentucky (USA)

Rebecca J. Ribar, B.A.
University of Wisconsin at Milwaukee, Wisconsin (USA)

John Rolland, M.D.
University of Chicago
Chicago, Illinois (USA)

Dani Rowland-Klein, B.Sc. Psych. (Hons), Dip.Fam.Ther., M.Clin.Psych.
Waverly Action for Youth Services, New South Wales (Australia)

Jeremiah A. Schumm, M.A.
Kent State University, Kent, Ohio (USA)

Kami L. Schwerdtfeger, Ph.D.
Kansas State University
Manhattan, Kansas (USA)

Karen Stoiber, Ed.D.
University of Wisconsin at Milwaukee, Wisconsin (USA)

Glade L. Topham, Ph.D.
Oklahoma State University, Stillwater, Oklahoma (USA)

Ana-Maria Vranceanu, B.A.
Kent State University, Kent, Ohio (USA)

Gregory A. Waas, B.A.
University of Wisconsin at Milwaukee

Froma Walsh, Ph.D.
University of Chicago, Chicago, Illinois (USA)

Valerie E. Whiffen, Ph.D., C.Psych.
University of Ottawa (Canada)

Series Editor's Foreword

As "peacekeeping" in Iraq continues, military personnel join their families for a few weeks of rest and recuperation (R&R) before returning to their units to serve out their one-year tour of duty. All families and family members know how hard it is to wait for their loved ones to return home and to let them go back into harm's way. These dramas have occurred thousands and thousands of times across the US. They represent the irony of viewing stress and trauma through a family lens.

Families often account for both causes and consequences of stress and trauma. We all know this as family members. In the first book in this Series, *Stress Disorders among Vietnam Veterans: Theory, Research, and Treatment* (Figley, 1978), it was noted that the interpersonal consequences of highly stressful or traumatic events are not fully understood, even at a theoretical level. Yet, these consequences are real and dangerous.

Don Catherall's *Handbook of Stress, Trauma and the Family* will become a well-referenced classic that is bound to remain timeless. It is a remarkable synthesis of a number of important knowledge streams that have never before been presented in one book. This handbook joins a distinguished list in the Psychosocial Stress Book Series. Consistent with the purpose of the series, to generate and disseminate new knowledge about the causes and consequences of stress in psychosocial contexts, it is a collection of new knowledge and existing knowledge in one useful package.

On the following pages I provide some additional contextual and historic background for appreciating the contributions of this groundbreaking book.

Trauma and families have always existed and co-existed. Yet the serious study of families affected by stress can be dated back only to 1949. In that year Ruben Hill (1949) published *Families Under Stress*. Hill's other important contribution here focused on how families behave in response to disasters (Hill & Hansen, 1965). In the former book Hill presented his findings of how the returning World War II veteran and his or her family adjusted to the absence but especially the reunion. Although another family sociologist, Willard Waller, wrote about the phenomenon (Waller, 1944), curiously there was little mention of the distress of family members.

Although the evolution of family sciences and family therapy emerged since Hill's work, this book serves as a vital extension of our understanding of how stress is manifested and processed within intimate systems. This handbook incorporates modern "systemic" thinking by attending to the relational dynamics. Traditional family systems theory attending to the stress of the family members was limited mostly to Bowen's (1985) notion of anxiety as an indicator of relational conflict rather than caused by an external stressor.

In this essential work, Dr. Catherall assembles an extraordinary array of experts in both traumatology (the study of trauma) (Figley, 1988), and famology (the study of families) (Burr & Lee, 1982)—illustrating how each field informs the other. Both fields emerged separately. With few exceptions, famologists, especially systems-oriented family therapists, see PTSD as a symptom maintained by the dysfunctional family system. There is little need to attend to the how and why of the traumatic event because symptom maintenance is the real issue. In contrast, traumatologists most often attend to the individual and his or her symptoms-related causes and consequences. There is little need to attend to the family except to enlist them in a program of assessment and treatment unless they caused the trauma. The exception is when family members are viewed as being traumatized either because of a specific, primary trauma agent or because they were traumatized secondarily (i.e., secondary or vicarious stress) that may lead to either burnout (Figley, 1998) or compassion fatigue (Figley, 1995, 2002). It should be pointed out that these latter works do indeed address the systemic costs of caring. Be that as it may, traumatologists are often blind to familial consequences and famologists are often blind to the traumatic consequences.

Dr. Catherall and his authors, as beautifully illustrated throughout this work, capably bridge and contribute to both fields of study. The book is organized by function: theoretical issues, research issues, and practice issues. Because the readership is especially interested in the latter issues and because it is so complex, the handbook includes practice chapters divided among issues of assessment, treatments for families, and treatments for couples. As a result, each chapter takes the reader to a far higher level of sophistication and understanding of the topic, as compared to most other available books.

As we read in the newspaper about a military serviceman or servicewoman being home on R&R, this handbook will remind us of the complexities of both traumatology and famology. It will also provide a treasure trove of resources for helping these families now and when they come home for good. May we all pray for that day.

Charles R. Figley, Ph.D., Series Editor
Director, Florida State University Traumatology Institute,
Tallahassee, Florida

REFERENCES

Bowen, M. (1985). *Family therapy in clinical practice*. New York: Jason Aronson.

Burr, W., & Lee, G. K. (1982). *Famology: A new discipline*. Minneapolis, MN: National Council on Family Relations.

Figley, C. R. (Ed.) (1978). *Stress disorders among Vietnam veterans: Theory, research, and treatment*. New York: Brunner-Mazel.

Figley, C. R. (1988). Toward a new field of traumatic stress studies. *Journal of Traumatic Stress*, 1(1) 3–11.

Figley, C. R. (Ed.) (1995) *Compassion fatigue: Coping with secondary traumatic stress disorder in those who treat the traumatized*. New York: Brunner/Mazel.

Figley, C. R. (Ed.) (2002) *Treating compassion fatigue*. New York: Brunner-Routledge.

Hill, R. (1949). *Families under stress*. New York: Harper & Row.

Hill, R., & Hansen, D. (1965). The family in disaster. In G. Baker & D. S. Chapman (Eds.), *Man and society in disaster*, pp. 37–51. New York: Basic Books.

Waller, W. (1944). *The veteran comes back*. New York: Dryden.

Preface

When I was an undergraduate at the University of Texas, I took an independent study under Dr. Ray Hawkins. I was working with children at the time and I was interested in different ways of thinking about how to help them. Ray had me read some unusual and interesting authors, such as Jay Haley. After I had completed my reading, Ray asked me to summarize what I had learned. I thought about it and finally said that it seemed that mental health was all about relationships. Ray smiled and nodded, and my interest in the role of relationships was formed.

In graduate school, I had the extraordinary fortune to work with Bill Pinsof at the Family Institute of Chicago. Bill took an interest in my growth as a psychologist and gave me the most valuable thing any senior professional can ever offer a novice—a mentoring relationship. Bill Pinsof taught me to think like a researcher, to write like a scholar, and to do family therapy like a hunting dog that won't let go once he finds the scent. He also taught me flyfishing.

In the early 1980s, I met Charles Figley, who shared my interest in the role of relationships but also was doing everything possible to expand interest in the new field of traumatic stress. As I was to discover, when Charles is interested in an area, it soon becomes a major field of study. Charles continues to open doors and invite me to explore new dimensions of traumatology.

These psychologists opened my eyes to the mental health implications of the interpersonal world. Throughout my career, my interest has been divided between two passions—traumatic stress and relational systems. In recent years, the mental health field has begun to actively explore the relationship between these two seemingly disparate areas (primarily because of Charles Figley's tireless efforts). But the body of that knowledge has been spread thinly across the literature. Now much of it is gathered here in your two hands.

Don R. Catherall, Ph.D.

Introduction

DON R. CATHERALL

Stress and trauma have been impinging on families throughout history, yet the relationship between families and the influence of stress and trauma is a recent field of study. The mental health field has spent much of its history focused on individuals as the fundamental unit of humanity, thus attention to the impact of stress and trauma was originally focused on individuals. But no individual can even become a human being without the benefit of human society, and the fundamental unit of human society is the family, in all its various forms.

STRESS AND TRAUMA

Stress and trauma are relatively new areas of focus. Until the 1980s, societal recognition of the psychological impact of traumatic experience repeatedly disappeared and reappeared, paralleling the cycles of intrusion and denial that characterize the experience of many traumatized individuals (Shalev, Galai, & Eth, 1993). The fractured history of professional interest still affects our efforts to achieve a comprehensive view of all aspects of the trauma phenomenon. For example, trauma and dissociation have developed into separate fields of study, even though the two are so clearly related (van der Kolk, Herron, & Hostetler, 1994).

The impact of trauma long has been recognized by astute clinicians, but the idea of stress as a general state that can be produced by a variety of experiences did not exist until the middle of the 20th century. In 1936, medical researcher Hans Selye first observed that a variety of "diverse nocuous agents"—toxic substances, cold, heat, infection, trauma, hemorrhage, nervous irritation, and others—produced a very similar response, including loss of weight and appetite, diminished muscular strength, and absence of ambition (1936, 1982). He called this response a biologic stress syndrome; eventually it became known as the *general adaptation syndrome*

(1952, 1982). Part of Selye's unique contribution was his recognition that this response could be provoked (a) by emotional events as well as physical events and (b) not only by distressing events but also by positive events, such as the experience of intense joy. He contended that anything that disrupted the body's homeostatic equilibrium and required alterations in bodily resources (e.g., the production of stress hormones) in order to re-achieve homeostasis constituted a stressor.

Today, stress is frequently viewed as a negative but Selye actually had a more comprehensive view of stress. He distinguished eustress, the pleasant stress of fulfillment, from distress and contended it could be experienced without the damaging consequences of distress (Selye, 1974). Indeed, he has argued that the popular view that people are stressed by working too much still misses the point. He felt the more important issue was satisfaction with life and that people suffer because they have "no particular taste for anything, no hunger for achievement" (Selye, 1982, p. 14).

The focus on stress in this volume is on distress and the effects of going into the general adaptation syndrome—first into an alarm state, then a state of resistance, and finally into a state of exhaustion. Selye noted that most people go through the first two stages many times in the course of their lives as they learn to adapt. It is remaining in the third stage that causes the serious damage.

FAMILY

The history of the family in the field of mental health is rather complicated. For one thing, the term "family therapy" is used to refer to two different aspects of psychotherapy—*orientation* and *context*. Orientation refers to the theories of problem formation and problem resolution that inform a particular approach; context refers to the interpersonal structure of an approach; i.e., who is directly involved in the treatment (Pinsof, 1995). Failure to allow for this distinction creates confusion; some clinicians espouse a family therapy orientation even when working in an individual therapy context, while other clinicians espouse an individual orientation even when meeting with entire families. To do justice to this complexity, we must consider both orientation and context and clearly distinguish which we are talking about.

The term "family therapy" usually is intended to include couple therapy, but sometimes the two are differentiated, with the term "couple therapy" used for marital or cohabiting couples or for two individuals from different families who are involved in a relationship, while the term family therapy is reserved for work with members of different generations (e.g., parent and child) or for members of the same family even if they are of the same generation (e.g., siblings). In the early days of couple treatment, the problems were seen as largely individual and the therapy was primarily adjunctive to individual therapy. Now there is considerable evidence to suggest that couple therapy is a productive avenue for treating a variety of individual problems, as well as the only form of treatment that has been found effective for problems among couples (Johnson & Lebow, 2000; Lebow, 2000; Lebow & Gurman, 1995).

Similarly, family therapy has evolved into greater legitimacy. Several decades ago, it was most often viewed as an adjunct to individual treatment, and the problems were viewed as existing within the individual. Now family therapy has been shown to be an effective form of treatment for a variety of individual problems, with the corresponding view that many individual problems may be reactions to dynamics in the family (Sprenkle, 2000).

Throughout their history, family and couple therapies have refined the art of communication. Therapists have behaved as teachers and coaches, actively helping individuals discuss their relationships and resolve their conflicts. The activity level of therapists in these conjoint therapies is typically much higher than in individual therapies. And family therapists have employed an array of approaches that go far beyond the usual confines of talk therapy. The use of interventions such as genograms, homework, rituals, family sculpting, the one-way mirror, the consulting team, paradoxical injunctions, and a vast array of structured communication tasks mark the field of family and couple therapy as especially innovative and open to trying new approaches. This volume continues that tradition with several new techniques and ways of thinking about the problems encountered when stress and trauma impinge on families and couples.

STRESS, TRAUMA, AND THE FAMILY

Charles Figley and Hamilton McCubbin edited the first, and foremost, work in the area of stress, trauma, and the family. Their two-volume series focused on the concept of coping—Volume I was on coping with normative transitions and Volume II was on coping with catastrophes (McCubbin & Figley, 1983; Figley & McCubbin, 1983). Helping families learn to cope effectively remains the primary goal of intervening with families dealing with stress and trauma. The primary criterion distinguishing functional families from dysfunctional families is the effectiveness of their coping strategies. Dysfunctional strategies include: (a) ineffective problem solving (failing to effectively identify stressors and being blame-oriented rather than solution-oriented), (b) poor communication (indirect, closed communication patterns and intolerance for idiosyncratic expressions and behavior), (c) structural defects (lack of cohesion, rigidity of roles and tendency to view problems as centered in an individual rather than family-centered), (d) poor resource utilization, and (e) problem-producing strategies of violence and drug usage (Figley, 1983; Catherall, 1998).

A distinguishing feature of the relationship between families and stress or trauma is its bidirectional nature. Family support can moderate the impact of trauma on a family member, even as the impact of a traumatized member can traumatize a family. This is an area that is ripe for research so that we can better understand both processes—the ways in which the traumatization of one member affects other members of a family and the ways in which social support can moderate the impact of trauma on an individual. The research in both areas is examined in this volume—from the impact of traumatic stress on marital intimacy (chapter 7) and the quality of life among survivors' loved ones (chapter 8) to a comprehensive review of the overall relationship between social support and traumatic stress (chapter 11).

The notion that people involved with a trauma survivor can develop their own symptoms of traumatic stress first appeared in the literature in a classic paper by Sarah Haley (1974) in which she described how she was affected by working with traumatized veterans. This was before the diagnosis of PTSD had even been conceived. By the 1980s, we had both the diagnosis and a beginning awareness that the effects of traumatic stress could somehow be transmitted to people who were not themselves exposed to the traumatic event. But, just as it was difficult to introduce the concept of traumatization into the existing psychiatric nosology, the concept of secondary stress needed the support of research and widespread clinical acceptance. Much of the research on family stress is classified according to stressor type, such as families dealing with cancer or troubled adolescents. But the notion of secondary stress ignores the original source of the stress and instead focuses on the route through which the effects are transmitted. Figley (1989b) identified four ways in which a family system can be traumatized.

1. *Simultaneous effects*—All members of the family are directly affected by the traumatic event, such as in natural disasters and auto accidents.
2. *Vicarious effects*—Other family members are traumatized vicariously when they learn that one family member(s) has experienced an emotional traumatic event.
3. *Secondary traumatic stress*—Other family members are traumatized by being exposed to the experience of the traumatized member. Kishur (1984) originally labeled this as chiasmal effects, but the modern term is secondary traumatic stress and the associated disorder is secondary traumatic stress disorder (Figley, 1995).

4. *Intrafamily trauma*—Family members are traumatized by other family members, as in cases of abuse.

Discussion of how the traumatization of one member of a family affects other members abounds in this volume. The impact of trauma spreads in families. Other family members may develop their own trauma symptoms, the functioning of the entire family may be affected and, sometimes, the effects of traumatization are so powerful that they are transmitted across generations, even to children who were not born when the trauma occurred. This phenomenon of *secondary traumatization* has become a major source of interest among those who work with trauma and families; it is addressed from a variety of perspectives in this volume.

Attachment is another area of interest that has grown rapidly in the past few years. Early life trauma, neglect, or other forms of stress wreak havoc on the developing child's attachment relationships, and going through life with an insecure attachment puts a person at greater risk for being traumatized. Quality of attachment is discussed in many of the chapters in this volume; some of the latest and most intriguing research appears in chapter 10.

ORGANIZATION OF THIS HANDBOOK

This handbook is divided into three parts—theory, research, and practice—with the third part divided into sections on assessment, family treatment, and couple treatment. Since theory is intrinsic to both research and practice, discussion of theory is not confined to the first part. The research chapters necessarily discuss theory and the theoretical bases for many of the treatment approaches are embedded in the practice chapters. This melding of the three areas occurs throughout the volume; research and practice are built on theory even as theory is derived from research and practice. This volume was constructed with the expectation that readers would already have a basic knowledge of psychology and some familiarity with the topic area. Hence, we have not spent a lot of time on background material, such as recitations of the DSM symptom criteria for Post Traumatic Stress Disorder. My goal was to start off at a level of sophistication that would permit this gathering of leading authors in the field to expand on their topics unimpeded.

PART I, THEORY

Part I contains six chapters that delve into some of the current theoretical questions. Please note these are only a partial exposure to the prevalent theories in the field; the practice chapters are rich in specific theories of treatment. In chapter 1, Aphrodite Matsakis introduces one of the core ideas in this volume, that the effects of trauma affect everyone in the family, not just the individual trauma survivor. Matsakis, author of numerous books aimed at helping trauma survivors and their families, delineates the many pathways through which this effect is seen. In chapter 2, Jeremiah Schumm, Ana-Maria Vranceanu, and Stevan Hobfoll present Hobfoll's Conservation of Resources theory. This theory provides a means of conceptualizing stress that transcends the type of stressor and allows us to make predictions about families' ability to cope successfully.

In chapter 3, Rory Remer examines the experience of the partner of the trauma survivor, someone who has a strong feeling of responsibility for the survivor's well-being, yet lacks the blood ties of other relatives. Remer suggests the use of Chaos Theory as a way of understanding and coping with this experience. In chapter 4, Lee Hyer, Luba Rafalson, and Erin O'Hea look at the stress of aging and offer a model for helping aging individuals and their families achieve maximal adaptation to the inevitable losses and changes that accompany aging. Similarly, in chapter 5, John Rolland examines what happens when a family has to deal with chronic illness. He has developed a model that allows for the interaction between the family, the type of disease, and the phase of the disease process. In chapter 6, Dani Rowland-Klein examines the intrapsychic processes that underlie the intergenerational transmission of trauma. Her transcripts from interviews with adult children of Holocaust survivors provide a vivid description of the everyday manifestation of these processes. This is the last chapter in the Theory section, but its organization around a research study could easily be the first chapter in the Research section.

PART II, RESEARCH

Part II is composed of six chapters containing comprehensive reviews of research on three powerful aspects of the relationship between families and stress and trauma. These include: (a) the secondary traumatization of loved ones as a result of their involvement with the survivor, (b) the role of attachment quality in determining risk of traumatization, and (c) the role of social support in coping with stress and trauma. The section ends with a review of the research on the effectiveness of marital and family therapy for stress and trauma.

Three chapters examine aspects of secondary traumatization in various elements of the family. In chapter 7, Valerie Whiffen and Luis Oliver examine the question of whether trauma has a direct negative impact on marital intimacy, or whether it is the PTSD of the individual survivors which creates marital problems. They conclude that the symptoms of PTSD create the majority of marital problems. In chapter 8, Marianne Amir and Rachel Lev-Wiesel examine the impact of survivors' sharing their traumatic memories with their loved ones. They conclude that the secondary symptoms of the spouse may be more the result of living with the anger, hostility, and paranoia of a difficult person than the result of empathic connection with the pain of a suffering person. In chapter 9, Briana Nelson Goff and Kami Schwerdtfeger examine the impact on the family system when children are traumatized, and here it appears that the secondary traumatization of parents may indeed be more the result of their empathy than the difficult problems between spouses.

The concept of secondary traumatic stress includes various routes by which others can be affected, including being exposed to the symptomatic survivor as well as vicariously sharing the survivor's experience as a result of learning of it. The latter route is based on the listener's empathic connection, which is the mechanism proposed by McCann and Pearlman (1990) in their concept of vicarious traumatization, originally conceived as an inevitable risk for therapists working with trauma clients. The exact nature of the mechanism of transmission of secondary traumatic stress has been a subject of some dispute, but these three research chapters, combined with Rowland-Klein's research/theory chapter, suggest that routes differ according to the nature of the relationship: (a) marital partners may be more affected by the problems of living with symptomatic spouses, (b) parents may be more vulnerable to feeling their children's pain, and (c) children may be more vulnerable to feeling their parents' pain, as well as identifying with their parents' traumas, defenses, and worldview.

In the past decade, the significance of attachment security has become widely recognized as a key variable affecting vulnerability to a vast array of psychological problems. In chapter 10, Robert Muller, Erin Kraftcheck, and Lise McLewin examine the research on attachment. Muller's research highlights the importance of positive versus negative view of self in determining an individual's vulnerability to traumatization. The other key variable that has long been recognized as a major factor in protecting individuals from traumatization is social support. In chapter 11, Summer Sherburne Hawkins and Sharon Manne review what is known about social support. Drawing on their work with families of cancer victims and examining the vast literature, they document the complexity of the support relationship, concluding that effective support must be matched to the specific stressor involved.

Finally, in chapter 12, Jay Lebow and Kathleen Newcomb Rekart review the research literature on the use of couples and family therapy with people who have been traumatized. There is little research, and thus only limited support, for the use of couples and family therapy in the treatment of PTSD. Lebow and Rekart emphasize that dramatic confrontations of the trauma survivor have not been effective; the involvement of spouses and family members is most useful when it is organized around efforts to understand and differentiate from the problem and promote engagement in treatment.

PART III, PRACTICE

Part III, Practice, contains three sections: The first section contains three chapters on different models of assessment; the second section contains five chapters on models of family treatment; and the third section contains five chapters on models of couples treatment.

Section A, Models of Assessment. The assessment of couples and families experiencing stress and trauma is a challenge. The assessment must capture the complexities of family relationships, identifying where and how the stressors affect the system, and be able to produce a comprehensive picture that will be useful to the clinician. The three models discussed in this section each achieve such a picture, but in some very different ways. The section contains a pure theory-based model, a model for identifying strengths, and a model for identifying exactly where and how stressors are affecting the system.

In chapter 13, Steven Harris and Glade Topham describe the Bowen Family Systems approach to assessment, which emphasizes the family's level of differentiation and capacity to manage chronic anxiety. This model is founded on Murray Bowen's systemic theories about the centrality of interpersonal variables and is less interested in the nature of the stressor. In chapter 14, Jane Gilgun presents a strengths-based approach to assessing children and families that examines risks and assets equally. Asset variables such as good relationships, an emotionally expressive atmosphere, embeddedness in the community, and a healthy approach to sexuality cluster with psychological factors, such as secure attachment, to greatly enhance the resilience of individuals and families. In chapter 15, David Olson presents his MASH model of assessment, which builds on his earlier Circumplex model (Olson, Russell, & Sprenkle, 1989), which examined family cohesion, flexibility, and communication. The MASH model captures the complex, recursive relationships between stress, coping, system variables, and adaptation as they occur at the levels of the individual, the couple, the family, and in the work world.

Section B, Models of Family Treatment. Five chapters describe family treatment models. The first two chapters both address intrafamilial abuse, but highlight the value of Pinsof's distinction between family *orientation* to treatment and family *context* of sessions. In chapter 16, Steven Gold uses a family orientation, but the context is the individual treatment of adult survivors of abuse. Gold's contextual therapy contends that the ineffective family environment surrounding the abuse means that survivors still need to acquire core interpersonal and intrapersonal skills and abilities, and that processing the abuse memories is contraindicated until these fundamental failures of the family are addressed. In chapter 17, James Maddock and Noel Larson discuss what must be done when intervening with the family when children are young and the abuse is still occurring. Their emphasis is systemic in both orientation and context; they argue that it is imperative to preserve the family as a functional system, noting the damage that comes from separating perpetrators from the rest of the family.

In chapter 18, Froma Walsh and Monica McGoldrick discuss the challenges that arise when a family deals with loss. Their 1991 book on this topic helped shift the field from a pathological view to a greater recognition of loss as a normative transition in the family life cycle. Here they present a systemic framework for determining where and how to intervene and enhance family resiliency.

In chapter 19, Chrys Harris discusses the issues encountered and how to intervene when a family is in crisis. He notes the crisis itself often is not as great a problem as the family's perception of the crisis and the difficulties they may have accepting alternative routes to coping. Ultimately, he seeks to help the family establish a unified healing theory that will work for the entire group. In chapter 20, Karen Callan Stoiber, Rebecca Ribar, and Gregory Waas discuss a cost-efficient approach to intervening with families facing various stressors and crises. Multiple family groups are used to enhance family strengths and coping resources rather than to remediate family deficits. This model is ideal for families living in high risk contexts; its non-pathologizing approach is oriented toward building resilience.

Section C, Models of Couples Treatment. Many therapies that start out with whole families end up as couples treatment. The centrality of the marital partners, and their influence as a parental dyad, often make the couple the fundamental unit of change in a family system. As Remer emphasized in chapter 3 and Whiffen and Oliver showed in chapter 7, the marital relationship has a unique vulnerability to traumatic stress. This section contains five chapters on the treatment of couples affected by stress and trauma, ranging from comprehensive models to explicit interventions. In chapter 21, Claire Rabin and Zev Apel discuss the value of psychoeducation with couples. In an innovative example of the treatment of couples stress, they present their work with couples in which one member has been imprisoned. Echoing the concerns of Maddock and Larson in chapter 17, they emphasize the harm done by social systems that separate people from their families. In chapter 22, Dennis Miehls and Kathryn Basham present a model of couples therapy with trauma survivors that is founded on object relations theory. They stress the importance of working with the process of projective identification and offer a structured, phase-oriented approach that allows couples to reach a level where they can safely examine their projective identification process.

In chapter 23, Susan Johnson presents her emotionally focused couples therapy for trauma survivors. Johnson developed emotionally focused couples therapy (1996) and then went on to apply it to trauma survivor couples (Johnson, 2002). Her emphasis is on attachment injuries and helping couples recognize and respond to these fundamental injuries to the attachment relationship. In chapter 24, David Read Johnson examines how a partner's past trauma can be present, but invisible, in the current relationship. When some event triggers the survivor's shame associated with the traumatic event (a critical interaction), Johnson provides an intervention that allows the couple to recognize the impact of the past trauma and use it to deepen their connection. Finally, in chapter 25, Mandra Rasmussen Hall and Victoria Follette offer an example of modern behavior therapy that focuses on accepting the self and one's traumatic history and changing only what can be changed. Follette's Acceptance and Commitment Therapy emphasizes the centrality of avoidance among trauma survivors and uses examples of interactive shame and withdrawal much like David Read Johnson's critical interactions.

FINAL COMMENT

Psychologists have often used human figure drawings in their battery of assessment techniques. A person's perception of stress and his or her capacity to manage it was portrayed when he or she drew a Person in the Rain. Sometimes the central moment of a trauma can be captured in a drawing, but psychologists have understood that these drawings are subjective. They provide an avenue for the person to project his or her own personal meanings into the picture. Then it becomes the evaluator's task to understand that personal meaning within the context of this one person and his or her life. That task becomes even more difficult as we try to consider the complexities of families.

This volume is filled with theories, techniques, and ways of understanding people and their families—what Rory Remer refers to as maps. But its richness is a dim reflection of the actual range of different kinds of people, families, sources of stress, and traumas that we encounter in our work. As in assessing the individual, our capacity to understand is aided by our tools but also depends in large part on our willingness to let our clients teach us. I once had a young boy draw a person in the rain with no umbrella, usually regarded as an indication that he felt he had no protection against the stressful elements in his life. Yet when we talked, I learned that his mother was carrying his umbrella for him because he enjoyed walking in the rain.

Never before have so many different tools for working with families and stress and trauma been assembled in one volume. My goal with this edited volume was synergistic: to bring the thoughts of these gifted researchers, theorists, and clinicians together in hopes of achieving a new level of understanding and appreciation of issues such as attachment, the role of social support, the ways in which the effects of trauma are transmitted among members of families, and the value of focusing on strengths and fostering resilience. I hope this book spurs new research and theory, and helps many clinicians to help many families with many kinds of stress and trauma.

REFERENCES

Catherall, D. R. (1998). Treating traumatized families. In C. R. Figley (Ed.), *Burnout in families: The systemic cost of caring* (pp. 187–215). New York: CRC Press.

Figley, C. R. (1983). Catastrophes: An overview of family reactions. In C. R. Figley & H. I. McCubbin (Eds.), *Stress and the family, Vol. II: Coping with catastrophe* (pp. 3–20). New York: Brunner/Mazel.

Figley, C. R. (1984). Treating post-traumatic stress disorder: The algorithmic approach. *Newsletter of American Academy of Psychiatry and Law, 9,* 25–26.

Figley, C. R. (1987). Post-traumatic family therapy. In F. Ochberg (Ed.), *Post-traumatic therapy* (pp. 83–109). New York: Brunner/Mazel.

Figley, C. R. (1989a). *Treating stress in families.* New York: Brunner/Mazel.

Figley, C. R. (1989b). *Helping traumatized families.* San Francisco: Jossey-Bass.

Figley, C. R. (1995). *Compassion fatigue: Coping with secondary traumatic stress disorder in those who treat the traumatized.* New York: Brunner/Mazel.

Figley, C. R., & McCubbin, H. I. (1983). *Stress and the family, Vol. II: Coping with catastrophe.* New York: Brunner/Mazel.

Haley, S. (1974). When the client reports atrocities: Specific treatment considerations of the Vietnam veteran. *Archives of General Psychiatry, 30,* 191–196.

Johnson, S., & Lebow, J. (2000). The "coming of age" of couple therapy: A decade review. *Journal of Marital & Family Therapy, 26,* 23–38.

Johnson, S. M. (1996). *The practice of emotionally focused marital therapy: Creating connection.* New York: Brunner/Mazel (now Taylor & Francis).

Johnson, S. M. (2002). *Emotionally focused couple therapy with trauma survivors: Strengthening attachment bonds.* New York: Guilford.

Kishur, G. R. (1984). Chiasmal effects of traumatic stressors: The emotional costs of support. Masters thesis, Purdue University, West Lafayette, Indiana.

Lebow, J. L. (2000). What does the research tell us about couple and family therapies? *Journal of Clinical Psychology, 56,* 1083–1094.

Lebow, J. L., & Gurman, A.S. (1995). Research assessing couple and family therapy. *Annual Review of Psychology, 46,* 27–57.

McCann, I. L., & Pearlman, L.A. (1990). Vicarious traumatization: A framework for understanding the psychological effects of working with victims. *Journal of Traumatic Stress, 3,* 131–149.

McCubbin, H. I., & Figley, C. R. (1983). *Stress and the family, Vol. I: Coping with normative transitions.* New York: Brunner/Mazel.

Olson, D. H., Russell, C., & Sprenkle, D. H. (Eds.) (1989). *Circumplex model of marital and family system.* Newbury Park, CA: Sage Publications.

Pinsof, W. M. (1995). *Integrative problem-centered therapy: A synthesis of family, individual, and biological therapies.* New York: Basic Books.

Selye, H. (1936). A syndrome produced by diverse nocuous agents. *Nature, 138,* 32.

Selye, H. (1952). *The story of the adaptation syndrome.* Montreal: Acta.

Selye, H. (1974). *Stress without distress.* Philadelphia: Lippincott.

Selye, H. (1982). History and present status of the stress concept. In L. Goldberger & S. Breznitz (Eds.), *Handbook of stress: Theoretical and clinical aspects* (pp. 7–17). New York: The Free Press.

Shalev, A. Y., Eth, S., & Galai, T. (1993). Levels of trauma: A multidimensional approach to the treatment of PTSD. *Psychiatry, 56,* 166–177.

Sprenkle, D. H. (2003). Effectiveness research in marriage and family therapy: Introduction. *Journal of Marital and Family Therapy, 29,* 85–96.

van der Kolk, B. A., Herron, N., & Hostetler, A. (1994). The history of trauma in psychiatry. *Psychiatric Clinics of North America, 17,* 583–600.

Walsh, F., & McGoldrick, M. (Eds.). (1991). *Living beyond loss: Death in the family.* New York: Norton.

Part I

THEORY

1

Trauma and Its Impact on Families

APHRODITE MATSAKIS

In Greek, trauma means *wounding*. Life-threatening events—whether they be fires or floods, sexual assaults, or terrorist attacks—wound the mind, the body, and the soul. Assumptions about personal invulnerability are shattered (Janoff-Bulman & Wortman, 1977). Cherished spiritual beliefs are challenged. Under conditions of prolonged or otherwise severe trauma, the person's biochemistry (Friedman, 1991; Kolb, 1987; McDonagh-Coyle et al., 2001; Murberg, 1996; van der Kolk, 1988, 1996) may be permanently altered, as is the ability to give and receive love (Herman, 1992; Jordan et al., 1992; Matsakis, 1994a, 1996a, 1996b, 1998b). (See also chapters 3, 4, and 11 in this volume.) Just as in novels and the movies, trauma seldom affects the individual alone.

Based on Freud's emphasis on *liebe* (love) and *arbeit* (work), a simple working definition of mental health is the ability to love, work, and play. Yet when a traumatized individual develops more than a 30-day acute stress reaction and goes on to acquire a longer term and more devastating traumatic reaction (such as posttraumatic stress or a dissociative, depressive, or somatic disorder), that person's ability to pursue meaningful work and to develop and maintain safe and loving relationships is severely impaired (Kates, 1999; Sheehan, 1994; Spasojevic, Heffer, & Snyder, 2000; Williams & Williams, 1987; Matsakis, 1994a, 1994b). Unfortunately, at the very time survivors need people the most, their symptoms can lead to alienation, hostilities, and a host of misunderstandings for all involved including coworkers, neighbors, grandparents, and other members of the extended family.

Although not all survivors develop posttraumatic stress disorder (PTSD), the interpersonal repercussions of PTSD are the focus of this chapter. However, due to the overlap between the symptoms of PTSD and those of other possible reactions, such as a dissociative, somatic, or depressive disorder (Cascardi & O'Leary, 1992; Feeny, Zoeller, & Foa, 2000; Tampke and Irwin, 1999; van der Kolk & Fisler, 1995; Zoellner, Fitzgibbons, & Foa, 2000), many of the observations made regarding PTSD may also apply to instances where survivors develop a different traumatic reaction. Exceptions include those interpersonal problems that stem directly from the unique feature of PTSD: the PTSD cycle—states of hyperarousal alternating with states of numbing. Either state can result in mental and emotional disorganization, leaving survivors feeling out-of-control, even terrified, unless they have ways of managing them.

Extreme states of numbing or hyperarousal can be dangerous. When intrusive thoughts, flashbacks, panic attacks, or other forms of hyper-arousal occur while driving, cooking, or working with children or machinery, accidents can result. In addition, the feelings of helplessness and confusion engendered by being unable to modulate the PTSD cycle are reminiscent of the powerlessness and disorientation experienced during the original trauma. Hence the symptoms of PTSD are retraumatizing in themselves (Matsakis, 1994a, 1996a). Under such circumstances, survivors have difficulty in being present to others. In response, others can feel angered, rejected, or helpless and can easily decide that the survivor is "impossible," "antisocial," or "crazy."

A common way survivors try to circumvent the PTSD cycle is by avoiding interpersonal and other situations that might stimulate it. Abraham Kardiner, who worked with shell-shocked World War I veterans, wrote that traumatization (what we now call PTSD) is similar to schizophrenia in that the person withdraws from the world (Kardiner & Spiegel, 1947). Since the ego can not handle the anxiety generated by the trauma in addition to the anxieties of normal life, a diminished interest in the world and a decline in personal functioning can follow (Matsakis, 1994a, 1996b). Indeed, it is more often the avoidant symptoms of PTSD, rather than the survivor's reminiscences, that create negative marital and family dynamics.

Survivors frequently report that they seek relief from the PTSD cycle (and the clinical depression that frequently attends those with severe or chronic PTSD) through addiction. Alcohol, excess food, and certain street drugs can have a suppressant effect on the nightmares, night terrors, and panic attacks of hyperarousal as well as mitigating effects on depressive and numbing symptoms. Survivors are at high risk for developing clinical depression or substance abuse problems or both (or for exacerbating preexisting ones); this has been found in numerous populations, from combat veterans to victims of family violence and sexual assault (Courtois, 1998; Herman, 1992; Kates, 1999; Jelinek & Williams, 1984; Keane, Caddell, Martin, Zimering, & Fairbank, 1983; Lacoursiere, Godfrey, & Ruby, 1980; Matsakis, 1994a; McLeod et al., 2001; van der Kolk, 1988, 1996).

For example, in a national sample, Hankin et al. (1999) found that symptoms of depression were three times higher, and rates of alcohol abuse were two times higher among women Veterans Administration (VA) outpatients who reported sexual assault while in the military. Hence, any discussion of the interpersonal effects of trauma must take into account the fact that a substantial number of families have a loved one with more than one diagnosis. When substance abuse exists, it, alone, can ravage a family's emotional and financial stability.

The "consequence of PTSD" hypothesis views substance abuse as a form of self-medication for the symptoms of PTSD and depression; however, there are at least two other hypotheses regarding the frequency of the dual diagnoses of alcohol abuse and PTSD (McLeod et al., 2001). The "shared stressor" hypothesis holds that addiction and PTSD are the results of a shared stressor, while the "shared vulnerability" hypothesis suggests that environmental or genetic factors or both create vulnerability to both PTSD and alcohol.

As researchers and clinicians have observed, strong marital or family ties and community support can serve as a buffer, if not a life-saver, for trauma survivors (van der Kolk, 1996; Herman, 1992; Matsakis, 1998a, 1998b). One of the most critical factors in determining whether a traumatized person will develop a long-term traumatic reaction (as opposed to a short-term stress reaction) is the quality of the individual's attachment system—his or her ability to derive comfort and hope from others. This requires that there are persons who are able to provide such assistance and that, furthermore, the traumatized individual is able and willing to receive it.

IMPACT ON SIGNIFICANT OTHERS

Despite the observed buffering effects of supportive others, there is no lack of evidence for the negative impact of trauma on family and intimate relationships. Separation, divorce, marital dissatisfaction, and emotional instability in children are common (Carroll, Foy, Cannon, & Zwier, 1991; Herman, 1992; Kates, 1999; Kulka et al., 1990; Matsakis, 1996b; Matsakis, 2001; Scaturo & Hayman, 1991; Sheehan, 1994; Vogel & Marshall, 2001; Williams & Williams, 1987).

Some survivors may function well at work or when focused on specific projects. However, at home, their mood swings, irritability, depression, memory problems, emotional numbing, and difficulties with conflict-resolution and life-span transitions eventually manifest themselves and affect the entire family, even toddlers (Daniele, 1994; Scaturo & Hayman, 1991; Taft, King, King, Leskin, & Riggs, 1999; Vogel & Marshall, 2001). Family members describe having to "walk on eggshells" so as not to increase the suffering of a loved one who is already distressed. They may also fear irritating an already irritable person and risk becoming the object of that person's rage reactions or rejections.

THE THREAT OF SUICIDE

It is well established that persons with PTSD and depression, especially if comorbid with substance abuse, are high suicide risks, especially during anniversaries of the trauma or in response to major losses, such as the death of a child or loss of a job (Hendlin & Haas, 1984; Kates, 1999; Matsakis, 1994a, 1996b). Family members who are aware of this suicide potential, or whose survivor has threatened or attempted suicide in the past, may be especially cautious in their interactions. "I edit everything I say to him so as not to upset him. I don't want him going off on me or, worse, going into a slump because of something I said or did," explains the wife of a firefighter. "He's threatened suicide a few times. If he does it, I know it won't be my fault. But I don't want to be the one who pushes him over the edge."

The author has worked with dozens of spouses and young adult children of survivors who refrained from leaving their unhappy home because they feared the survivor might act on a suicide threat. In many instances, it was as hard for the clinician as for the family member to determine whether the threat was manipulative or sincere. In the author's experience, sometimes the departure of a disgruntled family member did precipitate a suicide attempt or parasuicidal behavior, such as driving while intoxicated, having sexual relationships with HIV-infected persons, or not taking needed medications. There were cases of completed suicides and parasuicidal behaviors which were ultimately lethal. According to Kates (1999), more police officers die as the result of PTSD than in the line of duty.

FULFILLMENT OF FAMILY ROLES

Partners frequently describe their trauma survivor as either a "part-time" lover or as a controlling or suffocating one, as either a nonexistent parent or as an overly protective or inconsistent one (Courtois, 1988; Matsakis, 1994b, 2000). Parents with combat histories or histories of child abuse may have difficulties disciplining children. Some employ the harsh methods of discipline inflicted upon them in the past. Others are so fearful of repeating their past, they avoid disciplining their children altogether. Adult survivors of child abuse who were severely punished, then later indulged, by their abuser may repeat this pattern as parents (Courtois, 1988). Any of these disciplinary methods can lead to conflicts with the other parent and deleterious effects on the children.

When the trauma survivor's symptoms do not permit, or they severely limit, the ability to sustain gainful employment, others in the family must shoulder the economic burden. In instances observed by the author, this can create resentments and possible guilt about harboring such resentments. The husband of a car accident survivor explains, "Of course I mind having to work overtime to make ends meet. Who wouldn't? What I can't stand is when she damns me and anyone else who isn't in constant pain like she is. Yet when I remember that her tantrums are not her fault and see her bravely trying to go on, I feel guilty for blaming her and sometimes even hating her for ruining my life."

INTERGENERATIONAL EFFECTS

The effects of trauma can ripple down to future generations (Barocas & Barocas, 1973; Epstein, 1979; Figley, 1995; Freyberg, 1980; Rosenheck & Fontana, 1998). "Will I ever be able to love again?" were the first words uttered by the son of a combat veteran as he barged into my office. "I don't care about my nightmares and panic attacks, but will I be able to feel again? To love others and to let them love me?"

This young man had internalized his father's traumas to the point of reenacting them in highly dissociative states. Although he was the sole object of his father's adoration, in the name of "initiating" his son into manhood, the father treated him harshly. After the young man married, his attachment to his father continued to dominate his life. He felt he had to tolerate his father's ongoing emotional abuse and intrusions into his marriage so as not to see his father psychologically disintegrate. As Kerr and Bowen (1988) would have predicted, just as the young man began to make therapeutic progress, the father insisted that he terminate therapy—and he did.

PARENTIFICATION OF CHILDREN

The multigenerational impacts of trauma are diverse. Studies of the children of Holocaust survivors, veterans of World War II and the Vietnam conflict, and other trauma survivors show that one or more children often assume caretaker roles with respect to either (a) the traumatized parent or (b) the more functional but extremely stressed nontraumatized spouse (Brende & Goldsmith, 1991; Rosenheck & Nathan, 1985; Rosenheck, 1986; Sigal, 1976; Sigal & Rakoff, 1971). As these "parentified" children grow into adolescence, they view their troubled parent as being misunderstood and rejected by others. They fear that if they start their own lives, no one will be available to care for the parent. In cases observed by the author, often the children's perceptions are accurate: there is no one else to help. Even when they do leave home, their loyalty to the parent can remain paramount. Some never marry or leave home.

Some of these family angels, however, become devils. Children who have nursed traumatized parents through their nightmares and flashbacks and stayed home from school to watch over them can do an about-face upon becoming adolescents or young adults. In my clinical experience it was not unusual for family angels, whether male or female, to run away from home, acquire an addiction, or pursue a promiscuous life style as a way of rebelling against their caretaker role (Matsakis, 1996a).

Children can develop low self-esteem and anger as a result of the emotional instabilities in the home or the afflicted parent's emotional distancing or both, which children tend to experience as rejection, even if there is no overt abuse. Like their nontraumatized parent, they can have both empathy for and anger toward their trauma-survivor parent. This creates inner turmoil, which is yet another source of anger, depression, and low self-esteem.

Even in elementary school, children from PTSD-afflicted homes may displace their anger onto siblings, classmates, or others. Alternatively, they may internalize it in the form of depression, preadolescent and adolescent substance abuse or eating disorders, and somatic complaints. Concentration and learning problems and social phobia have also been found (Matsakis, 1996b).

FAMILY SYSTEM DYNAMICS

In some families, the traumatized family member becomes the family scapegoat. Children join other family members in blaming nearly all the family's problems on the survivor's symptoms which they label as self-pity or excuses. In other homes, the family is organized around supporting and protecting the survivor. This usually requires family members to put aside some of their own goals and needs, even when the family is wealthy. Ultimately, family members begin to restrict their social contacts and outside activities and can become almost as isolated as the survivor. If the survivor receives effective treatment and becomes stronger, some family members rejoice. Others, however, may feel threatened by the survivors' growth and turn against them.

In some families, coalitions are formed, one grouping being for and the other against the victim. Once again, ambivalence toward the survivor is common: An intense empathy for the survivor's pain (and any physical injuries) may be coupled with resentment at the burdens imposed by the survivor's dysfunctions. Siblings, as well as adults, may feel jealous of the attention given to the survivor (especially when their needs are not being met), as well as guilt for harboring such jealousy. Survivors themselves have displayed patterns of insecure, anxious, avoidant, overly dependent, or ambivalent attachment (Courtois, 1988; Jordan et al., 1992; Muller, Sicoli, & Lemieux, 2000; Zoeller, Foa, & Bridigi, 1999). Some survivors alienate themselves from their families in varying degrees, even to the point of becoming virtual hermits.

There are no set patterns. The impact of trauma on relationships depends on a host of factors, including the nature and severity of the trauma and any resulting medical, financial, and psychological repercussions; the strengths and resiliency of the survivor and the family; available community and cultural supports; the nature and degree of subsequent stressors; and socioeconomic and cultural factors.

THE SURVIVOR'S PARTICIPATION IN FAMILY LIFE

Recovery does not mean forgetting the trauma or permanently erasing all of its effects, but rather an increase in the ability to invest one's psychic energies in the present, rather than the past. A major source of interpersonal problems for survivors, whether they suffer from PTSD, depression, or a dissociative disorder, is the limited psychic energy they have available for relationships. The sources of this lack of psychic energy include (1) living in two worlds: the world of the trauma and the present-day world; (2) unprocessed or unresolved emotions and issues pertaining to the trauma, especially unresolved grief; (3) medical problems caused by the trauma and medical, financial, and psychological problems caused by addiction; (4) feelings of low self-worth and lack of assertiveness; and (5) survivor guilt.

In the case of PTSD, additional factors contribute to the limited psychic energy: (6) time and energy spent managing triggers and trigger reactions; (7) the symptoms of untreated depression; (8) dissociation, depersonalization, and derealization; (9) reenactment and revictimization

(Merrill et al., 1999; Herman, 1992); and (10) relationships with those who died during the trauma. Not all of these reasons, however, apply to all trauma survivors.

Compounding interpersonal tensions are the survivor's feelings of betrayal, difficulties with trust, and cognitive mindsets appropriate for traumatic, but not for nontraumatic, situations. These mindsets include all-or-nothing thinking, perfectionism, denial of personal difficulties, and continuation of survival tactics (Matsakis 1994a, 1996a). While all of the above-mentioned factors are relevant, the following will focus on the effects of the PTSD cycle and of guilt.

THE PTSD CYCLE

The life-threatening nature of trauma gives rise to physical emergency responses whose function is survival. Included in these responses are the *"three Fs"*—fight, flight, and freeze as illustrated in Figure 1.1. Since the organism cannot tolerate a protracted state of hyperarousal, a numbing or *"shut-down"* period usually follows. In the "freeze" mode, some individuals also experience dissociation and derealization. Posttrauma reminders of the trauma (triggers) can activate the stress-related emotional and physiological symptoms.

Triggers can be internal or external. When survivors are triggered by their loved ones, not only can survivors feel guilty, but their sense of being "damaged goods" is also confirmed. Many on my case load have expressed resentment, if not fury, at having to experience and cope with triggers. "I can't stand having to do all these coping techniques just to get through the day," is a common complaint.

Even more distressing to survivors are feelings of jealousy and anger toward those whose lives are not being disrupted by the PTSD cycle. The presence of these feelings can contribute to the need to create distance from others so that one's unacceptable feelings do not become transparent or expressed. "Only a monster mother would get mad at her own children because they weren't traumatized like she was," an incest survivor states.

External triggers include any current danger or current stress such as financial, medical, or marital problems. Normal life transitions, such as the birth, growth, and eventual departure of children, the death of a parent, and one's own aging process are also triggers (Scaturo and Hayman, 1991; Danieli, 1994). Other triggers include any sight, smell, sound, touch, or action on the part of others that reminds the trauma survivor of the trauma. The trigger may not be reminiscent of the actual past danger, but of something associated with that danger.

For many trauma survivors, crowded places such as playgrounds, malls, concerts, traffic jams, parades, or even large social gatherings are

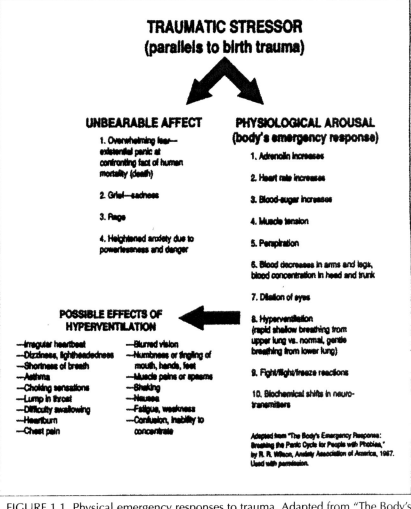

FIGURE 1.1. Physical emergency responses to trauma. Adapted from "The Body's Emergency Response: Breaking the Panic Cycle for People with Phobias," by R. R. Wilson, Anxiety Association of America, 1967. Used with permission.

triggers. The trauma may or may not have occurred in such places, but the large number of people, the noise level, and the presence of uncontrolled movements may be similar to the uncontrolled, unpredictable actions of people during the trauma. At the very least, such situations can result in sensory overload. Fearing the resulting PTSD cycle, the survivor may avoid normal family experiences such as going shopping or to movies and attending family (and other) functions such as weddings, funerals, and graduations. Some survivors absent themselves from, or limit the time spent at, their children's birthday parties or school events to protect themselves from becoming overstimulated or numb (Herman, 1992; Matsakis, 1996b, 1999, 2000; van der Kolk, 1988, 1996).

Sometimes an inflection or feeling in a person's voice can be a trigger. A child's, spouses's, or coworker's anger may be relatively mild, but to former victims of family violence, the anger can sound like thunder and feel like a major life threat. Logically, the survivor may know that the other person is simply irritated, not furious, and that there is no danger. But on an emotional and physiological level, the survivor is now on guard and waiting for an outburst of violence. To avoid being triggered, survivors may avoid or minimize contact with others, which impedes marital and family communications.

"Even a simple debate over a television show can get out of hand. He flares up, or he walks out of the room," the wife of a police officer explains. Yet the officer's avoidance stems not only from his fear of being triggered but also from his desire to protect his family from his reactions to them. "I know I hurt my family by over-reacting or under-reacting, but if I stay away, that hurts them too," the officer stated. "It hurts me to see their hurt. It also hurts to be so angry or numb inside that their hurt doesn't touch me."

The survivor's avoidant behavior and hyperactivity in relationships make problem-solving difficult, often leaving important marital and family issues unresolved (Bloom & Llye, 2001; Carroll et al.,1991; Parson, 2001; Scaturo & Hayman, 1991; Williams & Williams, 1987; Taft et al., 1999). An atmosphere of chaos, frustration, anger, and hopelessness can then develop in the home, creating even more triggers for the survivor. Others then respond negatively to the survivor's trigger reactions, further increasing the negative emotions in the home, which further triggers the survivor and leads to additional frustration and anger in others, and so forth. Thus, a negative, ever-escalating, self-perpetuating cycle is created.

Additional complexities arise if the family is a dual trauma family, that is, if more than one person has a trauma history. Without a keen awareness of each other's triggers and an ability to handle their own, family members inevitably trigger one another. This can result in hostility, paranoia, regression, and emotional instability in the home, thus recreating the emotional climate of the original trauma (Matsakis, 1994b).

The interpersonal consequences of autonomic hyperarousal and those produced by the numbing or increased opioid response are not identical, yet there is some overlap. Common to both are concentration problems ("I can't remember what my son just told me"); memory problems ("My wife gets mad because I can't remember to take my antidepressants"); and difficulties differentiating present from past realities, with an overfocus on any potential triggers in the environment ("All I could focus on was my supervisor's one tiny complaint, not the promotion and awards he gave me. Suddenly I was back with my ex-husband who always criticized me before a beating, and I wanted to spit in his face").

Other consequences of the PTSD cycle include the depletion of biological and psychological resources necessary to moderate affect and experience a wide range of emotions; fears that having to do something new (or to meet someone new) will be disorganizing or cause a shut down; difficulties in organizing behavior to achieve a goal; difficulties in staying focused on a conversation or social interaction; retreating from others because of the energy and effort required to control arousal or numbing; sexual dysfunctions and rage reactions (Matsakis, 1998a; van der Kolk, 1988, 1996). These consequences, some of which have been shown to have a biological basis (Glover, 1992; Kardiner & Spiegel, 1947; Kolb, 1987; van der Kolk, 1988, 1996), have obvious implications for interpersonal relationships at home and in the community and workplace.

The physiology of trauma is far more complex than the simple hyper-arousal-numbing model presented here. PTSD has been found to be associated with changes in the endogenous opioid system; the sleep cycle; levels of neurotransmitters and neurohormones; the hypothalamic-pituitary-adrenocortical axis, and other biological changes (Friedman, 1991; van der Kolk, 1996). Today's ongoing research promises an even greater understanding of the physiology of trauma.

Guilt

Trauma is the breeding ground not only for survivor guilt but also for many other types of guilt, such as competency guilt and "superman" or "superwoman" guilt (Kubany & Manke, 1995; Kubany, 1994; Kubany, 1997). Strong feelings of guilt can inhibit and harm relationships in the following ways (Matsakis, 1998b):

1. A deep feeling that positive supportive relationships are not deserved.
2. A fear of intimacy based on fear that (a) guilty secrets will be revealed or that (b) once the other person discovers the truth about one's thoughts, actions, or feelings during the trauma, one will be rejected.
3. Guilt-related addictions and compulsions which take away time and energy that could be invested in relationships and also that directly interfere with them.

4. Permitting oneself to be exploited (financially, sexually, emotionally, or vocationally) as an expression of unworthiness or a form of
   penance or atonement.
5. Overgiving and overprotectiveness in relationships.
6. Lack of assertiveness: The feeling that others are more important
   and that one does not deserve to have one's needs met.
7. Alienating or distancing from others by not returning calls, frequent
   cancelling or not keeping dates and promises, fighting over trivia,
   irritability, and verbal or physical abuse or both.
8. Ending relationships because they are becoming too intimate or loving.

The pathos of the situation is that at the very time that survivors need
people the most, their traumatic reactions strain their relationships.
Negative responses from others generate hostility and negative self-eval-
uations, which only intensify the damaging effects of trauma on the survivor (Herman, 1992; Ullman & Filipas, 2001). The emotional world of
survivors who are lovingly embraced by their family or community (on a
sustained, not a temporary, basis) differs vastly from that of those who
are stigmatized and ostracized. When attachment systems remain relatively intact after a trauma, survivors more readily begin to trust the
world—and their therapist.

THE PEOPLE IN THE SUPPORT SYSTEM

Although empirical research is needed to validate the following, in my
30 years of clinical experience, survivors with a support system, such as a
12-Step program, a religious affiliation, or a few sympathetic relatives or
friends, tend to attend sessions more regularly, be more compliant
with medical directives, have fewer medical problems associated with
trauma (Kimmerling, Clum, & Wolfe, 2000; Wagner, Wolfe, Rotnitsky,
Proctor, & Erickson, 2000; Williams & Siegel, 1989), and make more rapid
gains in therapy. Furthermore, family members and friends who were
able to stay meaningfully connected with survivors seem to have less
intense feelings of helplessness and anger toward them.

There is ample evidence that those who care about the survivors can
also bear their pain (Figley, 1995; McNeil, Hatcher & Reubin, 1988; Miles
& Demi, 1992; Muphy et al., 1999; Ochberg, 1988). Like the survivor, they
can also feel anger that the trauma occurred, feel helpless in not being
able to make the scars disappear, undergo a grieving process, and feel
that life has betrayed and cheated them. One of the Greek words for love
is *ponesi*, or experiencing another's pain as if it were one's own. To do so
is considered a normal, if not an admirable, part of caring for someone

else, even nonrelatives. Yet family members who make sacrifices for the survivor are often labeled as needy, controlling, codependent, enmeshed, or just as mentally ill as the survivor, while relatives who are intolerant of the survivor's limitations are often characterized as cold, self-centered, narcissistic, weak, or rigid. Spouses have been accused of deliberately or unconsciously selecting disturbed partners because they themselves were equally mentally unfit or because they desired to hold the power in the relationship. While such hypotheses remain to be proven, they certainly do not apply to couples who were together prior to the trauma or to those who are bound by religious principles.

Undoubtedly, there are family members with emotional problems, even to the point of meriting a diagnosis. In families where there is abuse and addiction and insufficient action is taken by family members to protect themselves, underlying personal dynamics certainly must be considered. Furthermore, living with or even treating someone with a severe traumatic reaction can create symptoms in the other person.

Devoted family members might be viewed quite differently in collectivist cultures or groups where selfhood is defined in terms of belonging to and fulfilling obligations toward a group. Individualist societies such as ours define selfhood in terms of individual self-actualization, self-esteem, and liberty (Myers, 2001). In Asian, African, middle-eastern, southern Mediterranean, and other cultures where loyalty to the family or community traditionally is considered more important than personal growth, self-sacrifice for the sake of a traumatized family member would probably not be described in pejorative terms such as enmeshment, symbiosis, overidentification, or infantile dependency. The individual who pursues personal growth at the expense of taking care of a needy family member may risk ostracism and economic or social forms of punishment in such societies.

In countries with histories of famine, civil war, or foreign occupation, trauma tends to be viewed in a different light (de Vries, 1996; Terheggen, Strobe, & Kleber, 2001). Sympathetic labels such as *misfortunados* ("unfortunate ones" in Spanish) or *atihi* ("unlucky ones" in Greek) are more widespread than psychiatric labels, and there is more cultural tolerance for long-term grief reactions. In addition, there are cultural supports for survivors and their families in the form of literature, drama, song, and communal or religious rituals, which help to legitimate the pain and struggles of survivors and their families, thus reducing social stigma. Except in cases of communal disasters such as the Oklahoma City bombing, our society tends to convey the message that having long-term traumatic reactions is shameful or that standing by someone who does is a sign of psychological deficiency.

CONCLUDING COMMENTS

Much of this chapter has focused on the difficulties inherent in forming and maintaining relationships posttrauma. Yet survivors can have fulfilling relationships. Treatment approaches such as those described in this volume can improve the survivor's functioning, bring families together, and even make them stronger. Once initial hurdles have been crossed, survivors and their families can have even more rewarding relationships because they have taken the time to communicate feelings, values, and personal limitations to one another.

In instances where survivors have been able to accept their pain and grow from it, their loving feelings toward family members, friends, and other loved ones are usually intensified. Having been traumatized has taught them the value and necessity of human connection and human love. In my experience, it is relationships, rather than work or external forms of success, that can take top priority among such survivors, and their relationships are helped, not hurt, by the realization that life is full of loss and pain and that past events affect the present. Through therapy or other means of recovery, survivors and their families can acquire the invaluable ability to make positive use of frustration, fear, anger, and pain.

REFERENCES

Barocas, H., & Barocas, C. (1973). Manifestations of concentration camp effects on the second generation. *American Journal of Psychiatry, 130*, 820–821.

Bloom, A. D., & Lyle, R. (2001). Vicariously traumatized: Male partners of sexual abuse survivors. In B. J. Brothers (Ed.), *The abuse of men: Trauma begets trauma* (pp. 9–28). Binghamton, NY: Hawthorne.

Brende, J., & Goldsmith, R. (1991). Post traumatic stress disorder in families. *Journal of Contemporary Psychology, 2*, 115–124.

Caroll, E. M., Foy, D. W., Cannon, B. J., & Zwier, G. (1991). Assessment issues involving the families of trauma victims. *Journal of Traumatic Stress, 4*, 25–40.

Cascardi, M., & O'Leary, K. D. (1992). Depression symptomatology, self-esteem, and self-blame in battered women. *Journal of Family Violence, 7*, 249–259.

Courtois, C. (1988). *Healing the incest wound: Adult survivors in therapy.* New York: Norton.

Danieli, Y. (1994). As survivors age: Part 1. *Clinical Quarterly.* Menlo Park, CA: The National Center for Post-Traumatic Stress Disorder.

deVries, M. W. (1996). Trauma in cultural perspective. In B. A. van der Kolk, D. Pelcovitz, S. Roth, F. Mandel, A. McFarlane, & J. Herman, *Dissociation, somatization, and affect dysregulation: The complexity of adaptation to trauma* (pp. 393–416). New York: Guilford.

Epstein, H. (1979). *Children of the Holocaust.* New York: Putnam.

Feeny, N., Zoeller, L., & Foa, E. (2000). Anger, dissociation, and post traumatic stress disorder among female assault victims. *Journal of Traumatic Stress, 13*, 89–100.

Figley, C. (1995). *Systematic traumatology: Family therapy with trauma survivors.* Presentation at the Maryland Psychological Association, Rockville, MD.

Freyberg, J. T. (1980). Difficulties in separation and individuation as experienced by offspring of Nazi holocaust survivors. *American Journal of Orthopsychiatry, 50,* 87–95.

Friedman, M. J. (1991). Biological approaches to the diagnosis and treatment of PTSD. *Journal of Traumatic Stress, 4,* 67–92.

Glover, H. (1992). Emotional numbing: A possible endorphin-mediated phenomenon associated with post-traumatic stress disorders and other allied psychopathologic states. *Journal of Traumatic Stress, 5,* 643–676.

Goodman, L., Salyes, M., Mueser, K., Rosenberg, S., Swartz, M., & Essock, S. (2001). Recent victimization in women and men with severe mental illness: Prevalence and correlates. *Journal of Traumatic Stress, 14,* 615–632.

Hankin, C., Skinner, K., Sullivan, L., Miller, D., Frayne, S., & Tripp, T. (1999). Prevalence of depressive and alcohol abuse symptoms among women VA outpatients who report experiencing sexual assault while in the military. *Journal of Traumatic Stress, 12,* 601–612.

Hendlin, H., & Haas, A. P. (1984). Suicide and guilt as manifestations of PTSD in Vietnam combat veterans. *American Journal of Psychiatry, 148,* 589–591.

Herman, J. (1992). *Trauma and Recovery: The aftermath of violence-from domestic abuse to political terror.* New York: Basic Books.

Janoff-Bulman, R., & Wortman, C. B. (1977). Attributions of blame and coping in the "real world": Severe accident victims react to their lot. *Journal of Personality and Social Psychology, 35,* 351–363.

Jelinek, J., & Williams, T. (1984). PTSD and substance abuse in Vietnam veterans: Treatment problems, strategies, and recommendations. *Journal of Substance Abuse Treatment, 1,* 87–97.

Kardiner, A., & Speigel, H. (1947). *The traumatic neuroses of war.* New York: Paul Hoeber.

Kates, A. (1999). *Cop shock: Surviving posttraumatic stress disorder (PTSD).* Tucson, AZ: Holbrook Street.

Keane, T., Caddell, J. M., Martin, B., Zimering, R. T., & Fairbank, J. A. (1983). Substance abuse among Vietnam veterans with PTSD. *Bulletin of the Society of Psychologists in Addictive Behavior, 2,* 117–122.

Kerr, M., & Bowen, M. (1988). *Family evaluation: An approached based on Bowen Theory.* New York: Norton.

Kimerling, R., Clum, G., & Wolfe, J. (2000). Relationships among trauma exposure, chronic posttraumatic stress disorder symptoms, and self-report health in women: Replication and extension. *Journal of Traumatic Stress, 13,* 115–128.

Kolb, L. C. (1987). A neuropsychological hypothesis explaining post-traumatic stress disorders. *American Journal of Psychiatry, 144,* 989–995.

Kubany, E. (1994). A cognitive model of guilt typology in combat-related PTSD. *Journal of Traumatic Stress, 7,* 3–19.

Kubany, E. (1997). Thinking errors, faulty conclusions, and cognitive therapy for trauma-related guilt. *National Center for Post Traumatic Stress Disorder Quarterly, 7,* 6–8.

Kubany, E., & Manke, F. (1995). Cognitive therapy for trauma-related guilt: Conceptual bases and treatment outlines. *Cognitive and Behavioral Practice, 2,* 27–62.

Kulka, R., Schlenger, W., Fairbank, J., Jordan, B., Marmar, C., & Weiss, D. (1990). *Trauma and the Vietnam war generation: Report of findings from the national Vietnam veterans readjustment study.* New York: Brunner/Mazel.

Lacoursiere, R. B., Godfrey, K. E., & Ruby, L. M. (1980). Traumatic neurosis in the etiology of alcoholism: Vietnam combat and other trauma. *American Journal of Psychiatry, 137,* 966–968.

Matsakis, A. (1994a). Dual, triple, and quadruple trauma couples: Dynamics and treatment issues. In M. B. Williams & J. Sommer, Jr. (Eds.), *Handbook of post-traumatic therapy* (pp. 78–93). Westport, CT: Greenwood.

Matsakis, A. (1994b). *Post-traumatic stress disorder: A complete treatment guide.* Oakland, CA: New Harbinger.

Matsakis, A. (1996a). *I can't get over it: A handbook for trauma survivors* (Rev. ed.). Oakland, CA: New Harbinger.

Matsakis, A. (1996b). *Vietnam wives: Women and children facing the challenge of living with veterans with post-traumatic stress disorder* (Rev. ed.). Lutherville, MD: Sidran Foundation.

Matsakis, A. (1998a). *Managing client anger: What to do when clients are angry with you.* Oakland, CA: New Harbinger.

Matsakis, A. (1998b). *Trust after trauma: A guide to relationships.* Oakland, CA: New Harbinger.

Matsakis, A. (2000). *Emotional claustrophobia.* Oakland, CA: New Harbinger.

Matsakis, A. (2001). The abuse of men: Trauma begets trauma. In B. J. Brothers (Ed.), *The Impact of the abuse of males on intimate relationships* (pp. 29–40). Binghamton, NY: Hawthorne.

McDonagh-Coyle, A., McHugo, G., Matthew, F., Schnurr, P., Zafert, C., & Descamps, M. (2001). Psychophysiological reactivity in female sexual abuse survivors. *Journal of Traumatic Stress, 14,* 667–684.

McLeod, D. S., Koenen, K. C., Meyer, J. M., Lyons, M. J., Eisen, S., & True, W. (2001). Genetic and environmental influences on the relationship among combat exposure, posttraumatic stress disorder symptoms, and alcohol use. *Journal of Traumatic Stress, 14,* 259–276.

McNeil, D. E., Hatcher, C., & Reubin, R. (1988). Family survivors of suicide and accidental death. *Suicide and Life-Threatening Behavior, 18,* 137–148.

Merrill, L., Newell, C., Thomsen, C., Gold, S., Milner, J., Koss, M., & Rosswork, S. (1999). Childhood abuse and sexual revictimization in a female navy recruit sample. *Journal of Traumatic Stress, 12,* 211–226.

Miles, M. S., & Demi, A. S. (1992). A comparison of guilt in bereaved parents whose children died by suicide, accident, or chronic disease. *Omega Journal of Death and Dying, 24,* 203–215.

Muller, R., Sicoli, L., & Lemieux, K. (2000). Relationship between attachment style and posttraumatic stress symptomatology among adults who report the experience of childhood abuse. *Journal of Traumatic Stress, 13,* 32–332.

Murberg, M. (Ed.). (1996). *Catecholamine function in PTSD: Emerging concepts.* Washington, DC: American Psychiatric Press.

Murphy, S., Braun, T., Tillery, L., Cain, K., Johnson, C., & Beaton, R. (1999). PTSD among bereaved parents following the violent deaths of their 12–28 year old children: A longitudinal prospective analysis. *Journal of Traumatic Stress, 12,* 272–292.

Myers, D. (2001). *Exploring Psychology* (5th ed.). New York: Worth.

Ochberg, F. M. (Ed.) (1988). *Post-trauma theory and victims of violence.* New York: Brunner/Mazel.

Parson, E. R. (2001). Intertraumatic Dissociative attachment: Treating trauma-based interactions in couples. In B. J. Brothers (Ed.), *The abuse of men: Trauma begets trauma* (pp. 69–112). Binghamton, NY: Hawthorne.

Rosenheck, R. (1986). Impact of posttraumatic stress disorder of World War II on the next generation. *The Journal of Nervous and Mental Disease, 174,* 319–327.

Rosenheck, R., & Fontana, A. (1998). Transgenerational effects of abusive violence on the children of Vietnam combat veterans. *Journal of Traumatic Stress, 11,* 731–742.

Rosenheck, R., & Nathan, P. (1985). Secondary traumatization in the children of Vietnam veterans with post-traumatic stress disorder. *Hospital and Community Psychiatry, 36,* 538–539.

Scaturo, D., & Hayman, P. (1991). The impact of combat trauma across the family life cycle: Clinical considerations. *Journal of Traumatic Stress, 5,* 273–288.

Sheehan, P. L. (1994). Treating intimacy issues of traumatized people. In M. B. Williams & J. Sommers, Jr. (Eds.), *Handbook of post-traumatic therapy* (pp. 94–105). Westport, CT: Greenwood.

Sigal, J. J. (1976). Effects of paternal exposure to prolonged stress on the mental health of the spouse and children. *Canadian Psychiatric Association Journal, 16,* 393–397.

Sigal, J. J., & Rakoff, V. (1971). Concentration camp survival: A pilot study of effects of the second generation. *Canadian Psychiatric Association Journal, 21,* 169–172.

Spasojevic, J., Heffer, R., & Snyder, D. (2000). Effects of posttraumatic stress and acculturation on marital functioning in Bosnian refugee couples. *Journal of Traumatic Stress, 13,* 205–218.

Taft, C., King, L. A., King, D. A., Leskin, G., & Riggs, D. (1999). Partner's ratings of combat veterans PTSD symptomatology. *Journal of Traumatic Stress, 12,* 327–334.

Tampke, A., & Irwin, H. (1999). Dissociative processes and symptoms of posttraumatic stress in Vietnam veterans. *Journal of Traumatic Stress, 12,* 725–738.

Terheggen, M., Stroebe, M., & Kleber, R. (2001). Western conceptualizations and Eastern experiences: A cross-cultural study of traumatic stress reactions about Tibet refugees in India. *Journal of Traumatic Stress, 14,* 391–404

Ullman, S., & Filipas, H. (2001). Predictors of PSD symptom severity and social reactions in sexual assault victims. *Journal of Traumatic Stress, 14,* 369–390.

van der Kolk, B. A. (1988). The biological response to psychic trauma. In F. Ochberg (Ed.), *Post traumatic therapy and victims of violence.* New York: Brunner/Mazel.

van der Kolk, B. A. (1996). The body keeps score: Approaches to the psychobiology of posttraumatic stress disorder. In B. A. van der Kolk, A. C. McFarlane, & L. Weisath (Eds.), *Traumatic stress: The effects of overwhelming experience on mind, body, and society* (pp. 214–242). New York: Guilford.

van der Kolk, B. A., & Fisler, R. (1995). Dissociation and the fragmentary nature of traumatic memories: Overview and exploratory study. *Journal of Traumatic Stress, 8,* 505–525.

van der Kolk, B. A., McFarlane, A. C., & Weisath, L. (Eds.). (1996). *Traumatic stress: The effects of overwhelming experience on mind, body, and society.* New York: Guilford.

van der Kolk, B. A., Pelcovitz, D., Roth, S., Mandel, F., McFarlane, A., & Herman, J. (1996). Dissociation, somatization, and affect dysregulation: The complexity of adaptation to trauma. *American Journal of Psychiatry, 153,* 83–93.

Vogel, L., & Marshall, L. (2001). PTSD symptoms and partner abuse: Low income women at risk. *Journal of Traumatic Stress, 14,* 560–584.

Wagner, A., Wolfe, J., Rotnitsky, A., Proctor, S., & Erickson, D. (2000). An investigation of the impact of posttraumatic stress disorder on physical health. *Journal of Traumatic Stress, 13,* 41–57.

Williams, C., & Williams, T. (1987). Family therapy for Vietnam veterans. In T. Williams (Ed.), *Post-traumatic stress disorders: A handbook for clinicians* (pp. 75–92). Cincinnati, OH: Disabled American Veterans.

Williams, J., & Siegel, J. (1989). Marital disruption and physical illness: The impact of divorce and spouse death on illness. *Journal of Traumatic Stress, 2,* 555–562.

Wilson, R. R., (1987). *The body's emergency response: Breaking the panic cycle for people with phobias.* Washington, DC: Anxiety Association of America.

Zoellner, L., Fitzgibbons, L., & Foa, E. (2000). Exploring the roles of emotional numbing, depression, and dissociation in PTSD. *Journal of Traumatic Stress, 13,* 489–498.

Zoellner, L., Foa, E., & Bridigi, B. (1999). Interpersonal friction and PTSD in female victims of sexual and nonsexual assault. *Journal of Traumatic Stress, 12,* 689–700.

2

The Ties That Bind: Resource Caravans and Losses Among Traumatized Families

JEREMIAH A. SCHUMM, ANA-MARIA
VRANCEANU, AND STEVAN E. HOBFOLL

In order to develop and implement interventions for families who have experienced trauma, it is important to have a theoretical framework that provides a way of understanding all aspects of the trauma process. Conservation of Resources (COR) theory (Hobfoll, 1988, 1989, 1998) provides a means for understanding the impact of trauma on the family and for preventing resource loss, maintaining existing resources, and gaining resources necessary for the family to cope with that impact.

Interpersonal resources such as social support allow for the provision and exchange of resources outside the individual. Although interpersonal resources can facilitate families' abilities to cope with trauma, social networks can also have a negative impact, acting as a channel by which the effects of trauma are spread throughout the family unit and contributing to *resource loss spirals*, a key corollary of COR theory. Interpersonal trauma originating from within the family (e.g., child or spousal abuse) can cause particularly long-lasting loss spirals in interpersonal domains of familial resources. Indeed, intrafamilial trauma often results in revictimization of the victim, which then serves to maintain the momentum of resource loss spirals.

ELEMENTS OF FAMILY STRESS THEORY   *"resourses"*

The study of family stress can be traced back to the seminal work of Hill (1949) on separation and reunion during and after World War II. Hill and others (Caplan, 1964; Jahoda, 1958) were interested in how individuals and families successfully coped with stressful demands throughout their lifetime (Hobfoll & Spielberger, 1992). A central theme from this work was that psychosocial resources help buffer the negative impact of stressful demands. They also realized that stressful demands could outweigh the existing resources of individuals and families and cause negative sequelae (see also Hobfoll, 1989; Lazarus & Folkman, 1984). Family trauma thus can be viewed as major challenges to the psychosocial resources of family members and the family system.

ABC-X Model of Family Stress

In order to provide a perspective for COR theory (Hobfoll, 1998, 1989, 1988) in the context of trauma and the family, we will outline the principles of the ABC-X model (Hill, 1949) and its contribution for understanding the impact of trauma on the family.

The event. The A factor in Hill's theory refers to the stressor or traumatic event. Hill defined stress as events that create change within the family system; all forms of change were postulated to be stressful. However, research has suggested that not all changes are, in fact, stressful (Thoits, 1983). COR theory differs substantively from the ABC-X model on this point as it posits that only undesirable changes (losses) are stressful. Indeed, positive changes act as stress buffers, limiting stressors' negative sequalae (Billings, Folkman, Acree, & Moskowitz, 2000; Cohen & Hoberman, 1983).

The resources. The B factor refers to the resources or strengths that individuals or families use to combat demands (Hill, 1949). McCubbin and Patterson (1983) subsequently incorporated family resources into their double ABC-X model in a more complex and sophisticated manner, suggesting that not only are psychosocial resources important in combating the demands of trauma, but psychosocial resources are themselves transformed in the stress process. Likewise, COR theory views transformation of resources as central to the stress and coping process because traumas cause rapid challenges to coping resources. This is critical because the availability of resources determines, in large part, the efficacy with which individuals, families, and communities can cope with trauma.

Perception of stress. The C factor in the ABC-X model involved the perception of the impact of trauma, which determines the meaning of such events to family members. This cognitive factor has received much weight in transactional models of stress and coping (e.g., Lazarus & Folkman, 1984). Consistent with Lazarus and Folkman's transactional model (1984), COR theory assumes that idiosyncratic perceptions of stress are more important in low to moderately stressful situations as opposed to highly stressful situations such as those involving trauma. However, COR theory differs from appraisal-based models of stress and coping in attributing more importance to the objective qualities of environmental stressors and shared social perceptions, and places less importance on the idiosyncratic (individualistic) perceptions of major stressor events.

The resulting crisis. The X factor in the ABC-X model can be conceptualized as the stress outcome or crisis following the trauma and coping process. McCubbin and Patterson (1983) emphasized this factor by suggesting that trauma can have residual effects on the family by its recurrent demands. This principle is also central to COR theory; it suggests that the impact of trauma can be long-lasting and branch out into a web of additional challenges to individuals and families.

Conservation of Resources Theory

COR theory (Hobfoll, 1988, 1989, 1998) builds on the conceptual strength of the ABC-X model by emphasizing factors that are important for developing interventions, with particular emphasis on resource loss. In contrast to homeostatic models of stress, COR theory does not view change in itself as the cause of stress. Instead, it predicts that stress will occur when there is (a) loss of valued resources, (b) threat of loss of valued resources, or (c) failure to gain resources after investment.

The nature of resources. COR theory views resources and strengths of individuals and families as important in buffering the effects of trauma. It describes four general resource categories. Resources can be categorized as (a) object resources (e.g., car, house), (b) personal resources (e.g., self-esteem), (c) energy resources (e.g., time invested driving children to activities), and (d) condition resources (e.g., familial relationships). Although COR theory distinguishes among categories of resources, these categories are viewed as part of a caravan of resources that bridge levels of the individual, the family, and the community (Hobfoll, 1998). Resources possessed by individuals, families, and communities can be pooled for protection of individuals. However, losses within one category of the resource caravan or at different social levels (e.g., individual, family) can also negatively affect the availability of resources in other categories. Change within a single resource category can occur but, consistent with a caravan concept, the aggregate of resources tends to travel together over time (Baltes, 1997). This interdependence of resources among individuals increases the importance of condition resources such as social support for families coping with traumatic events.

Objective losses versus perception. COR theory emphasizes the role of the environment over the role of cognitive perceptions in the stress and coping process. It does not view perceptions as unimportant; perceptions play a major role affecting reactions to minor and midlevel stressors (Lazarus & Folkman, 1984). However, traumas are of such high magnitude that they are universally perceived as stressful. Thus, efforts to understand trauma and coping are best served when the primary focus is on understanding the environment and the ecological context of the trauma. For example, virtually everyone would appraise experiences such as combat or rape as stressful. Appraisals are important but of secondary impact.

The concept of loss spirals. Consistent with the X factor in the ABC-X model (Hill, 1949), COR theory proposes that resource losses have residual consequences, and the impact of losses is cumulative. Specifically, multiple losses often result in resource loss spirals whereby resource loss broadens across people's resource reservoirs, gains momentum, and causes losses to occur more rapidly. Further, loss cycles are more likely to occur among families which are already depleted in their resources. This occurs because such families are less likely to have the resources necessary to withstand circumstances that initially threaten or result in resource loss. Thus, preventing or halting loss spirals should be the primary concern of interventions focused on trauma and the family.

In addition to the idea of loss spirals, COR theory proposes that gain spirals also occur, and individuals and families persistently seek to increase availability of resources in order to cope with challenges to their resource pools. However, gain cycles are predicted to occur at much slower rates than loss cycles and have less psychological and social impact.

INTERPERSONAL RESOURCES, TRAUMA, AND THE FAMILY

Interpersonal relationships provide a primary avenue through which individuals obtain emotional and functional support and exchange and share resources in the context of trauma. Social support has a buffering effect both in the context of nontraumatic but highly stressful life events and in the context of traumatic, life-threatening stressors. Trauma often causes resource loss spirals, which can exacerbate reactions of individuals and families. Social roles and efforts to preserve the family in the context of trauma can have paradoxically detrimental effects upon individuals. Interpersonal traumas initiated from within the family are especially detrimental as they are caused by the same individuals upon whom the victims must rely for support.

The Concept of Social Support as a Coping Resource

Social support is an omnibus metaconstruct that contains many subunits including social attachments, social assistance, and the perception of social aid (Vaux, 1988). As such, social support should be viewed as a multiple resource that involves different aspects of social interaction (Monnier & Hobfoll, 1997). Social support acts as the figurative glue in holding together caravans of resources; it provides a bridge for individuals to engage the coping resources of their communities and families.

Social support systems are themselves coping resources. In the context of large-scale traumas, such as natural disasters or terrorist attacks, individuals and families are functionally reliant upon one another for providing immediate avenues to safety. Individuals and families also utilize the functional aspects of social support post disaster for reestablishing object resources, such as homes, or energy resources, such as money. In addition, the emotional ties of individuals, families, and communities are important coping resources in the context of stressful circumstances.

Empirical Evidence for Social Support as a Coping Resource

A cohesive, supportive family life provides family members with the means to cope with effects of stress by allowing individuals to feel connected to one another and to transfer personal resources among one another. A large body of research acknowledges the importance of familial social support in a variety of stressful situations (e.g., Burt, Cohen, & Bjork, 1988; Kazak, 1989; Wilcox, 1986; Woodall & Mathews, 1989).

The importance of familial social support is increasingly evident in instances of extreme stress. Solomon, Mikulincer, Freid, and Wosner (1987) found that familial support was related to lower levels of PTSD (posttraumatic stress disorder) at 1-year follow-up in a sample of 383 Israeli soldiers who suffered combat stress reactions. Although a severe traumatic event such as combat often leads to psychological damage immediately after the event, family ties are important factors in determining recovery and adjustment post trauma. Strong relationships with family members help offset the resource losses associated with the traumatic event at each stage of victims' reactions, leading to better psychological outcomes.

Of course, social support comes from outside the family as well; interpersonal resources act as a bridge for individuals and families to access coping resources from higher order collective structures, such as groups, communities, and tribes (Hobfoll, 1998). Support from family, friends, and community becomes key in coping with traumatic events because such situations can result in rapid loss of resources. In meta-analyses of a large number of studies, Brewin, Andrews, and Valentine (2000) found that trauma severity and lack of social support were among the strongest predictors of adjustment and PTSD symptomatology in a variety of military and civilian samples. Although there are multiple factors implicated in the response of individuals to traumatic events, social support emerges consistently and reliably as a vital coping resource and a strong contributor to posttrauma adjustment.

Personal resources. Since resources are interdependent and part of a caravan, strong personal resources often co-occur with strong social resources. Likewise, absence of personal resources is typically linked with absence of social resources. By personal resources, we particularly emphasize *self-esteem* (Rosenberg, 1965), *self-efficacy* (Bandura, 1997), and *optimism* (Carver & Scheier, 1998). Having strong personal resources allows individuals and families to create and sustain close ties and to be more capable of effectively mobilizing and benefiting from social support, thereby contributing to their ability to manage the challenges and demands imposed by traumatic events.

In contrast, those lacking personal resources have less support available to them and are also less likely to engage in behaviors that will lead to mobilizing and deriving benefit from social support. Dougall, Hyman, Hayward, McFeeley, and Baum (2001) studied the effects of personal resources such as optimism on social support, coping, and adjustment following traumatic stress in a sample of 159 rescue and recovery workers. They found that a more optimistic disposition was positively related to adjustment at 2, 6, 9, and 12 months after the crash. Although optimism was directly predictive of adjustment, this relationship was in part due to individuals higher in optimism being more likely to seek and obtain greater levels of social support.

Social support and resource caravans. Personal resources not only determine whether individuals will possess support in times of need, but higher levels of personal resources also predict higher levels of satisfaction with support when support is provided. Hobfoll, Nadler, and Leiberman (1986) obtained evidence for this idea when longitudinally evaluating satisfaction with support in a sample of 113 Israeli women following the outcome of both normal and medically complicated pregnancies. Results revealed that women reporting greater intimacy with their spouses and friends also reported better satisfaction with the support provided. In addition, they found that self-esteem was significantly and positively related to satisfaction with support. These results support the notion that personal and social resources are interconnected entities. This is extremely important because satisfaction

Good gets better +
Bad gets worse.

with social support may be a key ingredient in its overall effectiveness (Barrera, 1986; Sarason, Sarason, & Shearin, 1986).

Overall, these studies highlight the centrality of individual and familial resources in battling the demands inherent in traumatic events. Individuals lacking personal resources react negatively to stress or trauma in part because they lack social support and in part because they are unable to engage in support-seeking behaviors when potential support is available. The studies also illustrate the coexistence of resources in a caravan, as well as the interdependence of resources at the individual, familial, and community level. A sense of self-efficacy, self-esteem, and optimism are likely to be linked to high availability of social support from family members and the community, whereas low self-efficacy, low self-esteem, and low optimism are likely to be associated with poor social support, less adequate coping styles, and overall poor adjustment to the demands posed by traumatic events.

Social interactions and stress exacerbation. Although social support can act as a buffering agent in times of stress, it is not always beneficial. In studying women's reaction to the mobilization of their loved ones in the Israeli Defense Force during the Israel–Lebanon War, Hobfoll and London (1986) found that, contrary to predictions, women with greater social support (measured in terms of intimacy and received support) were more likely to experience psychological distress than women with less social support. Moreover, the women high in mastery and self-esteem were more negatively affected by greater social support. In this situation, rather than acting as a resource, social support interactions served as a "pressure cooker" (Hobfoll & London, 1986) and increased the emotional demand of the situation. At time of crises, women high in mastery and self-esteem found themselves enmeshed in social ties that made demands on them. They were forced into the role of caregiver, feeling obligated to engage in nearly constant social supportive interactions. Women with more intimate relationships were more exposed to the sorrows of others, and the results were draining. The demands of caring for others or feeling obligated to attend to others' needs also made these women more vulnerable to the effects of war rumors and uncertainty, further increasing the emotional pressure of the situation.

Being supportive listeners for the other members of their support network may have constituted a form of stress contagion (Riley & Eckenrode, 1986) or secondary traumatic stress (Figley, 1986) for these women, suggesting that provision of support based on role expectancy may interfere with individuals being able to utilize resources to their personal benefit in the context of traumas shared by the family or group.

Westman and Vinokur (1998) found compelling evidence for such crossover effect of stress between partners in a sample of 354 male Vietnam veterans, nonveterans, and their wives or committed partners.

They noted a positive correlation between depressive symptoms within couples. This was due both to common stressors experienced as a couple, as well as crossover effects of stressors uniquely experienced by each member of the couple. The crossover effect, which originated from stressors experienced by one but not both partners, occurred via *social undermining*, defined as displays of negative affect and negative evaluations of the partners by the initially stressed individuals. In this way, the initial distress experienced by one partner was passed onto the other partner via negative interpersonal exchanges.

Crossover effect was also observed by Waysman, Mikulincer, Solomon, and Weisenberg (1993), who assessed family environment and psychosocial adjustment of 212 wives of Israeli veterans of the 1982 Israel–Lebanon War. They found that families of veterans experiencing high levels of distress due to combat were more likely to be conflict oriented and less likely to be expressive. This style of family interactions led to higher levels of distress among the veterans' wives, suggesting that traumatic events, such as wars, not only affect those directly experiencing such events but also can deplete the resources of families (see Figure 2.1). The effects could be bidirectional: either the impact of the veterans' trauma spilled over into family resources (such as cohesiveness and expressiveness), or an impaired family environment (represented by low cohesiveness and expressiveness and high conflict) could have affected the veterans' reaction to the combat stressor. In either case, the study demonstrates the imperative role of family environment and social resources in recovery after war.

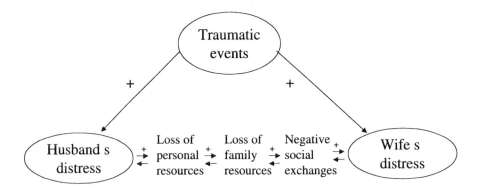

FIGURE 2.1. Distress from the trama victim can spread throughout families, causing losses in supportiveness and cohesiveness and increased levels of psychological distress for all family members. Preexisting low levels of supportiveness and cohesiveness mean fewer resources and greater distress for all family members.

Social Support and Resource Loss Spirals

Although social support may buffer or negatively affect reactions to trauma, it is itself taxed and depleted as a result of stressful and traumatic events or both. Indeed, social support is not static, and loss spirals in resources such as social support have long-lasting consequences (Kaniasty & Norris, 2001; Norris & Kaniasty, 1996). In a study of nontraumatic life events among a community and clinical sample of individuals (Holahan, Moos, Holahan, & Cronkite, 1999, 2000), personal and interpersonal resource loss, including family cohesion and expressiveness, were directly predictive of depressive symptoms over a course of years. More important, life events only affected depression to the extent psychosocial resources were depleted. These findings support COR theory's view that resources such as social support are malleable, and resource losses are the key component driving the negative effects of changes in life events (Hobfoll, 1988, 1989).

Research suggests that losses in social support can also mediate the impact of traumatic events. Consistent with COR theory's prediction that loss spirals often result from traumatic events, Kaniasty and Norris (1993; Norris & Kaniasty, 1996) studied the impact of natural disasters such as hurricanes and floods in a sample of 222 older adults and two independent samples of 498 and 404 victims interviewed before and after the occurrence of the traumatic event. LISREL analyses indicated that natural disasters led to deterioration of social resources including perceived social support, social embeddedness, and received social support. This deterioration in social support, in turn, led to higher levels of distress among families. Thus, loss of social support, the figurative glue, led to further loss of other resources within the caravan and contributed to the propagation of loss spirals. Also, individuals lacking social resources prior to the disaster were less likely to benefit from the provision of support after the disaster, suggesting that families with inadequate pools of existing resources benefit less from provision of social support, even when such support is provided.

These findings highlight the impact of social support losses following traumatic events and suggest that such losses can be especially detrimental for individuals already lacking in coping resources. Whether loss of social support occurred after the traumatic event or erosion of support was already occurring prior to the event, victims of disaster should be encouraged to continue the routine of their social activities. By sustaining social contacts, individuals, families, and communities can better interact, exchange, and transfer resources, leading to better recovery outcomes after the traumatic event.

Research by King, King, Foy, Keane, and Fairbank (1999) provides a telling picture of the relationship between functional problems such as

PTSD and caravans of resources across individuals' life spans, i.e., before, during, and after traumatic events. Among a sample of 1,632 Vietnam veterans, King et al. (1999) studied the relationships among (a) prewar risk factors such as familial relationships and instability, (b) war zone factors such as exposure to atrocities, (c) postwar resiliency-recovery factors such as hardiness and structural and functional social support, and (d) PTSD (see Figure 2.2). Separate structural equation models for male and female veterans indicated that resources at each time period (prewar, war zone, and postwar) were predictive of PTSD for both groups, suggesting that resources across the life span can affect clinical trauma reactions. They also found that prewar risk factors such as family instability were related to lower levels of adulthood resources such as social support. This suggests that early losses in resources in the domain of interpersonal relationships are fairly stable and continue to deteriorate across time. These results are consistent with COR theory's prediction that resources tend to travel in lifelong caravans, and that losses in childhood increase individuals' vulnerabilities later in life by increasing the likelihood that individuals will experience ongoing resource loss spirals. This study also highlights the value of preventing resource loss spirals among individuals and families in order to prevent later resource erosion and vulnerability to traumatic stressors.

The detrimental effects of trauma may be transmitted across generations from parents to children via the mechanism of loss spirals

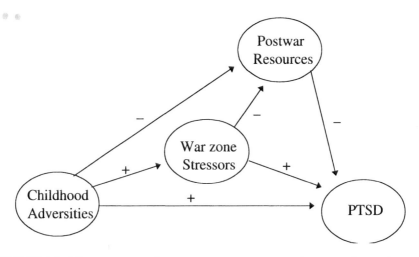

FIGURE 2.2. Lifespan perspective on resource caravans and resource losses. Losses initiated in childhood can snowball into resource loss spirals later in life, leaving individuals ill-equipped to handle challenges presented by new traumas. Adapted from King et al. 1999.

(Lomranz, 1990). For example, among a sample of women with breast cancer, the psychological distress was higher in a group of second-generation Holocaust survivors than it was among women whose parents were not in the Holocaust (Baider et al., 2000). The offspring of Holocaust victims may have inherited a depleted resource caravan lacking in hardiness, optimism, self-efficacy, and other such vital protective resources.

In summary, social support is a vital resource for families dealing with negative life events of varying severity, from daily hassles to traumatic events. Social support helps individuals, families, and communities exchange resources and prevent loss spirals. Resources are interconnected; strong personal resources increase the likelihood that individuals can benefit from social support, and families with strong interpersonal ties are more likely to benefit from the buffering effects of social support in times of need. However, social support provision is not always a positive coping resource, and well-intentioned attempts at providing support can sometimes spread the effects of psychological distress among families and communities. Thus, social support can either serve as a coping resource and means of exchanging resources or as a conduit by which the effects of trauma spread throughout families and communities.

Interpersonal Trauma From Within the Family

Interpersonal trauma is often initiated from within the very networks and families which victims rely upon for support. Domestic violence is by definition perpetrated by family members, and the childhood sexual abuse of girls is more often perpetrated by a family member (Finkelhor, Hotaling, Lewis, & Smith, 1990). The entire social fabric of the family can become compromised as the family network becomes characterized by the complicated roles of perpetrator, victim, silent partner, abuse witness, and those who pretend that nothing has occurred. Each of these roles and their constellation undermine the functions of social support and the self-esteem of the victim.

Interpersonal trauma within the family has the potential for activating profound resource loss cycles that can have devastating lifetime impact. Familial interpersonal trauma results in loss spirals within key interpersonal domains. The individuals whom victims would hope to rely upon for support and nurturance are often the perpetrators. Further, in examples of abuse by one parent, the second parent may be submissive or ineffectual and also compromised as a support provider (Elliott & Carnes, 2001).

Victims are likely to experience both immediate and long-term interpersonal loss spirals (see Figure 2.3). The existing social network of

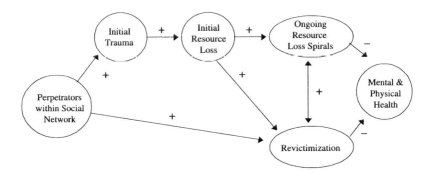

FIGURE 2.3. Perpetrators within victims' social support networks are likely to produce recurrent trauma and revictimization. Such perpetrators deteriorate interpersonal resources of victims by straining relationships within existing support networks and by decreasing victims' abilities to initiate and maintain healthy relationships later in life.

victims is likely to be destroyed or, at the very least, severely strained, and victims are set up for future interpersonal resource deterioration. In their classic empirical review of the effects of childhood sexual abuse, Browne and Finkelhor (1986) conclude that childhood sexual abuse is associated with a variety of long-term sequelae including problems in victims' abilities to relate to others (e.g., lower levels of trust), hostility toward families of origin, and sexual problems. In a more recent empirical review, Briere and Runtz (1993) conclude that victims of such abuse are more likely to have difficulties relating to others in adulthood and are more likely to be diagnosed with personality disorders. The interpersonal nature of childhood abuse, rape, or partner violence is likely to erode both current and future interpersonal resources.

Victims of interpersonal trauma also appear to be more sensitized to the effects of later stressors and less able to use support. In a 2-year prospective study, Hammen, Henry, and Daley (2000) found that adolescent girls who previously experienced childhood adversity, such as being the victim of abuse and witnessing violence within the family, were more likely to become depressed during times of low stress than girls who did not experience such adversity. Among a sample of African American and Latina adolescents ($N = 265$), Osborne and Rhodes (2001) examined the effects of sexual victimization on social support and psychological distress. They found that prior sexual victimization was positively related to depression and anxiety and moderated the impact of levels of social support on both measures of psychological distress. In deconstructing the interaction terms, results suggested that sexually victimized individuals derived benefit from social support only at low levels of stress.

Interpersonal trauma can have an eroding effect on interpersonal domains of coping resources. Among women seeking assistance from a battered women's shelter, Mitchell and Hodson (1983) found that levels of interpersonal violence were inversely related to interpersonal coping resources, such as contact with friends and family and the number of individuals within women's support networks. Partner violence appears to lead to lower social support for victims; the likelihood that individuals will not respond favorably to victims' request for assistance increases with the levels of violence. This may occur because the social ties of victims and their partners overlap, thereby increasing the pressure on individuals in this support network to take sides (e.g., Hirsh, 1980).

Ineffectual interpersonal resources resulting from childhood abuse are also associated with a decreased ability to negotiate preventative health behaviors. In a study of Native American women ($N = 160$), Hobfoll et al. (2002) found that women who were physically or emotionally abused or both as children were at five times greater risk for contracting sexually transmitted diseases than women who did not experience such abuse. The abusive experiences probably compromised the women's interpersonal resources, such as assertiveness, which are necessary for negotiating with their partners. Negotiation is a highly complex interpersonal skill, essential for engaging partners in safer sex behaviors; childhood abuse may introduce an early developmental barrier for cultivating such skills. Abused women also displayed higher levels of anger and depressive mood. This distress likely contributed to negative interactions between the women and their partners and further eroded the women's abilities to negotiate safer sex.

The resource caravan concept views resources as long strands, interconnected, and moving forward in time (Hobfoll, 1998). Seen this way, family-based trauma not only has immediate and long-term impact on victims, it compromises the entire caravan of resources upon which they rely. Given the key role of social in this caravan, victims remain vulnerable to new events and less capable of benefiting from others' attempts to offer nurturance.

Recurrent Violence: Reinitiating the Loss Spiral

Interpersonal trauma originating from within the family not only splinters resources of families but often ignites chains of violence that further deplete existing resources. In an empirical review, Appel and Holden (1998) conclude that spousal violence often occurs in conjunction with abuse toward children within families. They note that such violence patterns can become sequential (e.g., spousal violence leads to violence toward children) or bidirectional (e.g., familial members begin to engage

Other book says
no . . .

in reciprocal acts of violence). In this way, family units are thrown into a violence-laden loss spiral.

Once the cycle of violence has been initiated, individuals are at greater risk of experiencing revictimization and further resource erosion (Neumann, Houskamp, Pollock, & Briere, 1996) (see Figure 2.3). In a sample of recent rape victims ($N = 117$), Nishith, Mechanic, and Resick (2000) found childhood sexual abuse was a risk factor for adulthood rape, which, in turn, led to PTSD among women. These results suggest that childhood abuse can lead to long-term, negative consequences in the form of similar interpersonal traumas in adulthood. Not only are victims depleted of current coping resources but the nature of interpersonal trauma halts the progression of victims' resource caravans by decreasing their abilities to augment resources through developing healthy relationships and a sense of self-worth.

Trauma originating from within the family also interferes with families' abilities to maintain their cohesive structure. In a sample of 179 mother–daughter pairs, McCloskey and Bailey (2000) found that daughters of mothers who themselves reported being sexually abused in childhood were 3.4 times more likely to report sexual abuse than daughters of mothers without such abuse histories. Daughters of mothers who were both sexually abused and who used drugs were 23.7 times more likely to be sexually abused. The drug-using mothers had even fewer resources to protect their daughters due to the draining financial, personal, and interpersonal consequences of their drug use. Cross-generational revictimization was often occurring because of the continued contact with the same family members who were involved in the mothers' abuse.

In conclusion, intrafamilial trauma initiates cyclical chains that result in future trauma and reverberates throughout the family structure. Such traumatic events are all the more damaging because the individuals with whom victims would expect to join in order to maintain and build caravans of coping resources are often the abuse perpetrators or enablers. While victims are attempting to move forward in developing caravans of coping resources, the individuals to whom they turn for support are sabotaging their efforts by laying the potential for future abuse. In this way, chains of revictimization continue to fragment resources of families, leading to interpersonal loss spirals that continue across lifetimes and even generations.

SUMMARY

COR theory (Hobfoll, 1988, 1989, 1998) provides researchers and clinicians a framework by which the impact of traumatic events on families can be conceptualized. According to COR theory, individuals, families, and communities seek to maintain coping resources in order to offset the effects of challenges to resource reservoirs. Social support is a particularly important resource because it is the vehicle for the exchange of resources outside the individual and the figurative glue that binds resources of families and communities. However, social support is a multifaceted construct, and not all efforts at social support provision are effective in allowing families to exchange and increase resource reservoirs. In some circumstances, social ties might, in fact, act as a conduit for transmitting the negative effects of trauma throughout families and communities.

COR theory asserts that traumatic events can result in loss spirals among resources such as social support, especially among those with already depleted coping resources. Due to the interpersonal nature and meaning of interpersonal traumas such as childhood abuse, such traumas have especially detrimental and long-lasting effects for victims and their families. As these traumas are often initiated from within the social support network of the victim, such events tear at the fabric that binds together families' coping resources. These forms of trauma are also likely to engage victims and their families in long-term resource loss spirals while increasing the potential for victims to reexperience similar forms of trauma.

ACKNOWLEDGMENT

Support for this project was provided by NIH Grant # 2 ROI MH 45669-09A2.

REFERENCES

Appel, A. E., & Holden, G. W. (1998). The co-occurrence of spouse and physical child abuse: A review and appraisal. *Journal of Family Psychology, 12,* 578–599.

Baider, L., Peretz, T., Hadani, P. E., Perry, S., Avramov, R., & De-Nour, A. K. (2000). Transmission of response to trauma? Second-generation Holocaust survivors' reaction to cancer. *American Journal of Psychiatry, 157,* 904–910.

Baltes, P. B. (1997). On the incomplete architecture of human ontogeny: Selection, optimization, and compensation as foundation of developmental theory. *American Psychologist, 52,* 366–380.

Bandura, A. (1997). *Self-efficacy: The exercise of control.* New York: W. H. Freeman.

Barrera, M., Jr. (1986). Distinctions between social support concepts, measures, and models. *American Journal of Community Psychology, 14,* 413–445.

Billings, D. W., Folkman, S., Acree, M., & Moskowitz, J. T. (2000). Coping and physical health during caregiving: The roles of positive and negative affect. *Journal of Personality and Social Psychology, 79,* 131–142.

Brewin, C. R., Andrews, B., & Valentine, J. D. (2000). Meta-analysis of risk factors for posttraumatic stress disorder in trauma-exposed adults. *Journal of Consulting and Clinical Psychology, 68*, 748–766.

Briere, J., & Runtz, M. (1993). Childhood sexual abuse: Long-term sequelae and implications for psychological assessment. *Journal of Interpersonal Violence, 8*, 312–330.

Browne, A., & Finkelhor, D. (1986). Impact of child sexual abuse: A review of the research. *Psychological Bulletin, 99*, 66–77.

Burt, C. E., Cohen, L. H., & Bjorck, J. P. (1988). Perceived family environment as a moderator of young adolescents' life stress adjustment. *American Journal of Community Psychology, 16*, 101–122.

Caplan, G. (1964). *Principles of preventive psychiatry.* New York: Basic Books.

Carver, C. S., & Scheier, M. F. (1998). *On the self-regulation of behavior.* New York: Cambridge University Press.

Cohen, S., & Hoberman, H. M. (1983). Positive events and social supports as buffers of life change stress. *Journal of Applied Social Psychology, 13*, 99–125.

Dougall, A. L., Hyman, K. B., Hayward, M. C., McFeeley, S., & Baum, A. (2001). Optimism and traumatic stress: The importance of social support and coping. *Journal of Applied Social Psychology, 31*, 223–245.

Elloitt, A. N., & Carnes, C. N. (2001). Reactions of nonoffending parents to the sexual abuse of their child: A review of the literature. *Child Maltreatment, 6*, 314–331.

Figley, C. R. (1986). Traumatic stress: The role of family and social support system. In C. R. Figley (Ed.), *Trauma and its wake, Vol. II. Traumatic stress theory, research, and intervention* (pp. 39–54). New York: Brunner/Mazel.

Finkelhor, D., Hotaling G., Lewis, I. A., & Smith, C. (1990). Sexual abuse in a national survey of adult men and women: Prevalence, characteristics, and risk factors. *Child Abuse and Neglect, 14*, 19–28.

Hammen, C., Henry, R., & Daley, S. E. (2000). Depression and sensitization to stressors among young women as a function of childhood adversity. *Journal of Consulting and Clinical Psychology, 68*, 782–787.

Hill, R. (1949). *Families under stress: Adjustment to the crisis of war, separation, and reunion.* New York: Harper & Row.

Hirsch, B. A. (1980). Natural support systems and coping with major life changes. *American Journal of Community Psychology, 8*, 159–172.

Hobfoll, S. E. (1988). *The ecology of stress.* New York: Hemisphere.

Hobfoll, S. E. (1989). Conservation of resources: A new attempt at conceptualizing stress. *American Psychologist, 44*, 513–524.

Hobfoll, S. E. (1998). *Stress, culture, and community: The psychology and philosophy of stress.* New York: Plenum.

Hobfoll, S. E., Bansal, A., Schurg, R., Young, S., Pierce, C. A., Hobfoll, I., & Johnson, R. (2002). The impact of perceived child physical and sexual abuse history on Native American women's psychological well-being and AIDS risk. *Journal of Consulting and Clinical Psychology, 70*, 252–257.

Hobfoll, S. E., & London, P. (1986). The relationship of self-concept and social support to emotional distress among women during war. *Journal of Social and Clinical Psychology, 4*, 189–203.

Hobfoll, S. E., Nadler, A., & Leiberman, J. (1986). Satisfaction with social support during crisis: Intimacy and self esteem as critical determinants. *Journal of Personality and Social Psychology, 51*, 296–304.

Hobfoll, S. E., & Spielberger, C. D. (1992). Family stress: Integrating theory and measurement. *Journal of Family Psychology, 6*, 99–112.

Holahan, C. J., Moos, R. H., Holahan, C. K., & Cronkite, R. C. (1999). Resource loss, resource gain, and depressive symptoms: A ten-year model. *Journal of Personality and Social Psychology, 77*, 620–629.

Holahan, C. J., Moos, R. H., Holahan, C. K., & Cronkite, R. C. (2000). Long-term posttreatment functioning among patients with unipolar depression: An integrative model. *Journal of Consulting and Clinical Psychology, 68*, 226–232.

Jahoda, M. (1958). *Current concepts of positive mental health*. New York: Basic Books.

Kaniasty, K., & Norris, F. H. (1993). A test of the social support deterioration model in the context of natural disaster. *Journal of Personality and Social Psychology, 64*, 395–408.

Kaniasty, K., & Norris, F. H. (2001). Social support dynamics in adjustment to disasters. In. S. R. Sarason and S. Duck (Eds.), *Personal relationships: Implications for clinical and community psychology* (pp. 201–224). New York: John Wiley & Sons.

Kazak, A. E. (1989). Families of chronically ill children: A systems and social-ecological model of adjustment and challenge. *Journal of Consulting and Clinical Psychology, 57*, 25–30.

King, D. W., King, L. A., Foy, D. W., Keane, T. M., & Fairbank, J. A. (1999). Posttraumatic stress disorder in a national sample of female and male Vietnam veterans: Risk factors, war-zone stressors, and resilience-recovery variables. *Journal of Abnormal Psychology, 108*, 164–170.

Lazarus, R. S., & Folkman, S. (1984). *Stress, appraisal, and coping*. New York: Springer.

Lomranz, J. (1990). Long-term adaptation to traumatic stress in light of adult development and aging perspectives. In M. A. P. Stephens, J. H. Crowther, S. E. Hobfoll, & D. L. Tennenbaum (Eds.), *Stress and coping in later-life families* (pp. 99–121). Washington, DC: Hemisphere.

McCubbin, H. I., & Patterson, J. M. (1983). The family stress process: the double ABCX model of adjustment. *Marriage and Family Review, 6*, 7–37.

McCloskey, L. A., & Bailey, J. A. (2000). The intergenerational transmission of risk for child sexual abuse. *Journal of Interpersonal Violence, 15*, 1019–1035.

Mitchell, R. E., & Hodson, C. A. (1983). Coping with domestic violence: Social support and psychological health among battered women. *American Journal of Community Psychology, 11*, 629–654.

Monnier, J., & Hobfoll, S. E. (1997). Crossover effects of communal coping. *Journal of Social and Personal Relationships, 14*, 263–270.

Neumann, D. A., Houskamp, B. M., Pollock, V. E., & Briere, J. (1996). The long-term sequelae of childhood sexual abuse in women: A meta-analytic review. *Child Maltreatment, 1*, 6–16.

Nishith, P., Mechanic, M. B., & Resick. P. A. (2000). Prior interpersonal trauma: The contribution to current PTSD symptoms in female rape victims. *Journal of Abnormal Psychology, 109*, 20–25.

Norris, F. H., & Kaniasty, K. (1996). Received and perceived social support in times of stress: A test of the social support deterioration deterrence model. *Journal of Personality and Social Psychology, 71*, 498–511.

Osborne, L. N., & Rhodes, J. E. (2001). The role of life stress and social support in the adjustment of sexually victimized pregnant and parenting minority adolescents. *American Journal of Community, 29*, 833–849.

Riley, D., & Eckenrode, J. (1986). Social ties: Sub-group differences in costs and benefits. *Journal of Personality and Social Psychology, 51*, 770–778.

Rosenberg, M. (1965). *Society and adolescent self-image*. Princeton, NJ: Princeton University Press.

Sarason, I. G., Sarason, B. R., & Shearin, E. N. (1986). Social support as an individual difference variable: Its stability, origins, and relational aspects. *Journal of Personality and Social Psychology, 5*, 845–855.

Solomon, S., Mikulincer, M., Freid, B., & Wosner, Y. (1987). Family characteristics and posttraumatic stress disorder: A follow-up of Israeli combat stress reaction casualties. *Family Process, 26*, 383–394.

Thoits, P. A. (1983). Dimensions of life events that influence psychological distress: An evaluation and synthesis of the literature. In H. B. Kaplan (Ed.), *Psychological stress* (pp. 33–103). San Diego: Academic Press.

Vaux, A. (1988). *Social support: Theory, research, and intervention.* New York: Praeger.

Waysman, M., Mikulincer, M., Solomon, Z., & Weisenberg, M. (1993). Secondary traumatization among wives of posttraumatic combat veterans: A family typology. *Journal of Family Psychology, 7,* 104–118.

Westman, M., & Vinokur, A. D. (1998). Unraveling the relationship of distress levels within couples: Common stressors, empathic reactions, or crossover via social interaction? *Human Relations, 51,* 137–156.

Wilcox, B. L. (1986). Stress, coping, and the social milieu of divorced women. In S. E. Hobfoll (Ed.), *Stress, social support, and women* (pp. 171–200). Beverly Hills, CA: Sage.

Woodall, K. L., & Mathews, K. A. (1989). Familial environment associated with type A behaviors and psychophysiological responses to stress in children. *Health Psychology, 8,* 403–426.

3

The Partner's Experience: Learning to Cope With Chaos

RORY REMER

You can choose your friends, but you can't choose your family.

Blood is thicker than water.

Trauma victims, by definition, have suffered through an extraordinary life event causing physical or psychological sequelae or both. They need help to cope and recover—to become survivors. This aid usually comes from professionals and the victims' social support networks. However, the impact of trauma does not stop with these primary victims; it takes its toll on the supporters as well. These people are secondary victims. The consequences to the secondary victims have only recently been recognized. Attempts to learn about their reactions, to characterize their responses, and to formulate effective interventions for their benefits are increasingly emerging.

Of all the support network members—parents, children, friends, other family members, and trauma workers—partners bear a special burden. They usually are the closest people to the victims, yet have the most tenuous ties (of all family members, at least). This contradictory circumstance, plus the continual, intimate contact of day-to-day living tends to wear on partners, provoking both interpersonal and intrapsychic crises. These pressures can result in dissolution of the relationship—something that is less likely with blood relationships (after all, partners are not blood relatives). So what exactly produces these pressures? How are they different from the day-to-day demands on any relationship? And what can be done to ameliorate the situation?

The focus of this chapter is on partners' healing. We will look at how the healing process parallels that of the victims, and we will examine a model of healing from trauma, particularly human-induced trauma (Remer, 1984). We will consider the need for models (maps) of the problem and possible intervention, and their relation to a coordinating metamap, with chaos theory (ChT) being nominated for the latter position.

SECONDARY VICTIMS

A secondary trauma victim, or potential victim, is anyone in the social support network of a trauma victim, including family members, partners, friends, and even therapists, who can suffer vicarious traumatization or compassion fatigue (Figley, 1989, 1997; Pearlman & Mac Ian, 1995). A secondary victim (or secondary survivor) is anyone on whose personal resources (e.g., time, energy, and emotional support) a trauma victim draws because of the trauma suffered. Social support networks extend far beyond the individual traumatized—the *primary victim* (Remer & Elliott, 1988a, 1988b). The toll of traumas on primary victims is staggering; the total impact on secondary victims is mind-boggling.

The needs of secondary victims have received considerably less attention than those of primary victims. Secondary victims are usually recognized not for their own problems, but rather as needing help in order to provide resources necessary for primary victim healing or because their actions and reactions can interfere with that healing process (e.g., van der Kolk, McFarlane, & Weisaeth, 1996).

Secondary victims have problems of their own; many are linked in some way to the primary victim, but many are distinct. Since many of the problems of secondary victims relate to the primary victim and primary victim healing, most attention has been focused on relational (interpersonal) problems, but individual (intrapsychic) and systemic (cultural, societal, and familial) level difficulties are also present. Secondary victims need help in understanding their own complex healing processes—even if they do not label them as such—as well as the healing process of primary victims and how these processes interact. Whether recognized as problematic or not, *all* victims need to be aware of their biases, tendencies, and personal issues that influence and, at times, interfere with productive adaptation. They need to comprehend the difficulties they face and develop strategies and skills to address the demands of the situation.

Focus on Partners

What makes partner situations different from that of other secondary victims? Partners are usually the ones with the first and the most contact with the primary victims, and they feel the most responsible. This condition places a very heavy burden, a continual and perhaps inevitable one, on the partner. Additionally, partners fall into a kind of no-man's-land—they are not blood relations, yet they have stronger ties to victims than friends and acquaintances. The question of what the partner commitment means—the choice to stay in the relationship or not—is a perpetual undercurrent. Blood relations are motivated to hang in there through the toughest of times. Nonfamily can supply support or not, as they choose. The force of the commitment that partners make to each other usually promotes ambivalence that contributes to the stress. The 50% divorce rate in the general population is evidence of the power of this ambivalence. And, although the secondary victim seems the obvious candidate for a bailout, in my experience, just as many primary victims leave the relationships.

MODELS OF TRAUMA VICTIM HEALING

Models developed to characterize trauma victims' healing processes, both primary and secondary, have been labeled processional stage models—suggesting certain obstacles or tasks must be faced, if not overcome, before others can be addressed, but also possessing a quality of nonlinearity (looping) indicating that movement is not smooth or gains necessarily complete. The processes are similar and parallel.

Primary survivors. To imply that one specific model can convey the healing of every trauma survivor is misleading. Most people understand that each survivor, as an individual, has a somewhat different healing process. Beyond the individual difference issue, the type of trauma from which the survivor is healing (e.g., human vs. nature induced) influences the variations of the general healing process (Whetsell, 1990).

The model presented here (Remer, 1984; Worell & Remer, 1992) not only shares the majority of the salient aspects of the other prominent models (e.g., Burgess & Holmstrom, 1979a; 1979b; Figley, 1985a; Scurfield, 1985; Sutherland & Sherl, 1970), but because of its unique initial stage, anticipates some of the differences seen as a result of the type of trauma without addressing each type specifically. The model addresses the nonlinearity and nonindependence of the healing process. The adjacent stages are not mutually exclusive (see Figure 3.1). This distinction is important because complexity, and some confusion, results. This complexity is not a weakness of the model; on the contrary, these overlaps and mixings allow the

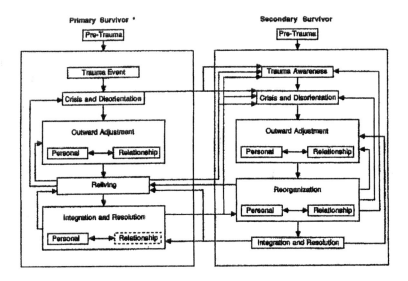

* Adapted from R. Remer (1984)

FIGURE 3.1. Schematic of the healing process of secondary survivors. Adapted from *Stages in Coping With Rape*, by R. Remer, 1984, unpublished manuscript, University of Kentucky at Lexington.

model to represent reality more accurately—from a chaos theory perspective. The hallmarks of both primary and secondary survivors' healing processes are chaotic patterns—complexity, nonlinearity, and nonindependence—and consequent reactions.

Remer (1984) portrays the survivor's healing process in six stages: (a) pretrauma, (b) trauma event, (c) crisis and disorientation, (d) outward adjustment, (e) reliving, and (f) integration and resolution. The unique feature of this model is the pretrauma stage, which allows a deeper understanding of the healing process. Note the recycling involved in the last four stages (in particular, the final three), which may occur simultaneously or recursively. Specific attention should be directed to the possible consequences of these overlaps (see Remer, 1990, for more details).

Secondary survivors. The secondary survivor healing process, while intertwined with, and in many ways parallel to, that of primary victims (Ferguson, 1993; Remer, 1997; Remer & Ferguson, 1995, 1997), has unique aspects. Parallels are intentional and designed to provide a comprehensive view of the secondary victims' healing process because the general adjustment in healing can be viewed similarly for both primary and secondary victims.

As an example of nonindependent and nonlinear systems, the model is divided into six different stages (see Figure 3.1). The stages are: (a) pretrauma, (b) trauma awareness, (c) crisis and disorientation, (d) outward adjustment, (e) reorganization, and (f) integration and resolution. The first two stages occur in a linear fashion perforce. The last four can, and almost invariably do, overlap and recycle.

The right side of Figure 3.1 provides a schematic of the healing process of secondary survivors; the left side outlines that of primary survivors. The interfaced flow charts indicate the complexities that can be expected in the recovery process of the secondary survivor. The essence of each stage is presented here.[1]

The *pretrauma stage* accounts for the context, environment, and learning of victims (deVries, 1996; Gold, 2000). In many instances, large portions of the backgrounds (schemata and patterns) of the primary and secondary victims will be shared. Clinical experience has shown that the more similar the socialization of the primary and secondary victims (e.g., sharing the same ethnic background), the more likely their pretrauma patterns will be similar (self-affine). Of course, secondary victims may still vary greatly in the background shared with the primary victims. Often trauma uncovers previously unnoticed discrepancies in the backgrounds which, when significant, cause problems in the coordination of primary and secondary survivor healing. The pretrauma stage influences not only the flow of the healing process but also each of the subsequent stages.

The *trauma awareness stage* would seem to be straightforward but is not. How, how much, and how soon secondary victims become aware of primary victims' traumas depends on the healing process of the primary victims. Inclusion of trauma awareness obviates the need to distinguish between those recently traumatized and those further along in the healing process. As more details of the trauma are learned and more of the effects felt, this stage may be revisited again and again, leading to crisis and disorientation.

As with more general models of adjustment (Kubler-Ross, 1969; Piaget & Inhelder, 1969), the trauma must be faced once it is recognized. During this period, marked by chaos, shock, denial, and confusion, the secondary victim will be off balance and out of touch—the hallmarks of *crisis and disorientation*. Length and degree of disorientation will depend on a number of factors—environmental, intrapsychic, and interpersonal—and their interaction; much of this confusion will be directly related to pretrauma experiences and resultant schemata–conserves.

---

1. For a more comprehensive exposition, particularly with regard to their interaction and nonlinearity, and including examples of typical reactions of secondary survivors, see Remer and Ferguson (1995, 1997).

Outward adjustment occurs once the immediate crisis has passed. Secondary victims often attempt to employ previously successful coping mechanisms to reestablish pretrauma patterns. To the extent that these mechanisms are effective, seeming outward adjustment will prevail. As with the primary victim, this outward adjustment is necessary in order to marshal the resources of the secondary victim (and of relationships) to face the next stage of the healing process: system self-organization indicative of deeper adjustment and healing. Outward adjustment, as the name implies, may be a brief, superficial return to what was the *status quo* prior to awareness of the traumatic event.

Outward adjustment occurs on two levels: personal and relationship. On the personal/intrapsychic level, the individual defense mechanisms will dominate; on the relationship level, established role patterns will prevail. These two levels interact significantly as indicated in Figure 3.1. Outward adjustment can continue for some time as long as *both* the personal and relationship aspects coordinate to maintain the facade. Often, role structures—familial rules or sex role socialization—will act in accord with the pretrauma stage patterns and expectations (conserves/ strange attractors) to attain the temporary adjustment, particularly in closed systems. However, when significant change produces chaos at *either* the personal or interpersonal level (most often in the form of a shift in the healing process of the primary victim), outward adjustment will disintegrate and the healing process will move into the next stage.

Reorganization (self-organization of the systems) occurs on the same two levels: personal and relationship. As the result of the secondary traumatic impact, input must be integrated at several levels: cognitive, emotional, behavioral, and interactional. On the personal/intrapsychic level, the defenses that block the process of necessary adaptation will have to be addressed and overcome (McCann, Sakheim, & Abrahamson, 1988); on the interpersonal relationship level, new interaction patterns will have to be developed and implemented. Reorganization on both levels must be coordinated to be effective. Here again the pretrauma stage will have a significant impact, making the required modifications more or less easily achieved. The more spontaneous, flexible, and resourceful all parties can be, the more effective and rapid the reorganization.

The more complete the reorganization, at least at a particular level of trauma awareness, the more likely the healing will be to move into the final stage. However, the reorganization, if only partially successful, may lead to recycling to one of the previous stages. Reorganization, if successful but not complete, may provoke further disclosures. In an environment of increased trust, the primary victim may experience further trauma awareness, that is, the healing processes will recycle to the trauma awareness stage for both types of survivors. Unsuccessful reorganization, particularly if retraumatization is the result, may trigger further reliving of the catastrophic event by the primary victim. Again this will lead to further trauma awareness, but of a kind certain to have a negative effect on both the secondary and primary victims and their relationship.

If reorganization at either or both levels is unsuccessful to some degree, another crisis may be precipitated and the healing process will recycle back to the crisis and disorientation stage. Since reorganization takes a significant amount of personal and interpersonal energy, another period of gathering resources may be required; thus a cycle through another stage of outward adjustment may begin. Another possible effect of reorganization is the triggering of the secondary victims' own unresolved traumas, obviously complicating matters. Once sufficient reorganization has occurred and enough resources are available to *all* individuals for intrapsychic change and to system members for relationship change, the process can move on.

The *integration and resolution stage*, in a sense, is no different for the secondary victim than it is for the primary victim. Integration indicates having accepted the trauma and made it a part of the secondary survivors' patterns of dealing with life at cognitive, emotional, behavioral, and interpersonal levels. Resolution does not mean a finished product but rather the ability to see more clearly the ongoing aspects of the healing process and their continuance, perhaps forever. Just as with the primary survivor, the secondary survivor must be prepared to continue the process indefinitely as new aspects of the primary survivor's trauma come to light. The hallmark of this stage is making positive meaning from the experience. The difference between this stage and previous ones is that, when these new memories, insights, and other aspects emerge, the process tends to revert to the reorganization stage, rather than throwing the whole process back into total chaos (crisis and disorientation). In a new round of reorganization, the new information is dealt with and worked through more quickly and effectively. In fact, the only way of distinguishing between this stage and outward adjustment is by observing how the process proceeds.

Though possibly disheartening, the healing process is without an endpoint. The secondary survivor should be prepared to recycle again and again, whenever necessary, in order to maintain the sense of healing on both an intrapsychic and an interpersonal level. In any event, self-organization of the system will occur in one form or another, whether the new patterns meet the expectations of those involved or not.

PERSPECTIVE ON INTERDEPENDENCE AND INTERCONNECTEDNESS

A distinctive feature of the secondary survivor healing process is its dependence on the healing process of the primary survivor. Unlike the primary survivor, the secondary victim awaits cues from the primary survivor to which to react. The complex interconnectedness of the two processes—the aspects of nonlinear, nonindependent systems contributing to chaos—can be seen in Figure 3.1. Although the relationship aspect is important in the primary survivor healing process, predominantly because of the need for support and resources from the secondary survivors (the support network), primary survivors have to focus on their own personal/intrapsychic healing first. However, the explicit interaction between the personal and interpersonal aspects of adjustment is often underemphasized for primary survivors.

Secondary survivors, on the other hand, must attend not only to their own personal adjustment but also to the vicissitudes of the primary victim healing and to the impact of those fluctuations on the relationship. Many effective secondary survivors are keenly aware of the impact of the trauma on both the primary survivor and on the relationship. In fact, in many ways, they may be too attuned. A relationship is not a relationship unless it is maintained by both those involved. While the secondary survivor healing process has been portrayed as reliant on and reactive to the healing process of the primary survivor, little has been said about the ongoing role relationship dynamics in the overall healing (self-organization) process of the entire social support network.

One of the main issues involved in dealing with primary and secondary victims is how to mesh their healing processes. Familiarity with a number of perspectives on interconnected processes would be useful to both practitioners and victims. Most helpful are chaos (dynamical systems, nonlinear, and nonindependent systems) theory and the concept of interdependence (see Remer, 1990).

Conceptualizations of the healing process that take the perspective of the primary victim frequently fail to address the importance of the relationship. The relational considerations—the interplay, the give and take, and the balance—are necessary for the resources to be available for the adjustment of all affected, not just the primary survivor.

Primacy of the primary victim's healing. The primary victim is and must be the focal point of the healing process if the relationship is to survive. Relationship healing is unlikely unless primacy is given to the healing of the primary victim. But exactly what does primacy mean?

If by primacy we mean that the primary victim would have to heal entirely before the healing of any secondary victims could begin, the relationships would most likely break up before healing could occur, which is already too often the case with partners. Therapeutic intervention must support the healing of the primary victim and the secondary victims at the same time, somehow finding a balance between the requirements of both. Interventions must negotiate the interdependence of the healing processes and prevent or eliminate, as much as possible, any tendencies toward codependency. Furthermore, given the ambiguity of partners' commitments, the question of primacy—or how long that primacy is required—underlies the entire healing process.

The dance of interconnectedness, which perpetually takes its lead from the process of the primary victim, almost appears to be a form of codependency. When trauma awareness leads to crisis, the focus must be on the primary victim if that person is to survive and remain part of the relationship. However, like a dance, the partnership must develop a subtle communication that makes the flow, the movement, collaborative. Different partners develop different patterns, and may dance very different dances. Codependent type actions can be part of the dance without the overall pattern being one of codependency—enabling can have positive connotations and effects in addition to the better known negative ones. Learning the dance and changing the pattern over time is not easy to accomplish but can be very gratifying to all involved.

Consequences of primary victim primacy: Suggestions for intervention. After a severe trauma, the primary victim will be in great need of support. Even the most resourceful person will be stretched to cope without additional help—a functional social support network. Secondary victims will have to support and supply resources for the healing of the primary victim while, at the same time, not attempting to draw on the resources of the primary victim. In the initial phases of healing, little (if any) reciprocity or balance can be expected in relationships between the primary and secondary victims. This situation will also be the case during other stages of healing, such as in particularly disturbing times when the incident is relived.

When these difficulties are encountered, secondary victims must put some of their needs aside to support the primary victim. Secondary victims will have to look elsewhere for the resources to meet their own needs. Indeed, even the pursuit of alternative resources for secondary victims' needs may have to be delayed if the process of doing so disrupts the healing of the primary victim, at least through the initial critical phases of the healing process. In the long run, however, a return to some semblance of an interdependent pattern must occur. The resources of all individuals in the support network cannot be indefinitely subordinated to the primary victim. The relationships will eventually break down if some balance, or reciprocity, is not restored. The dissolution of any relationship may not be welcome, but it may be the only viable alternative if optimal healing is to occur and the system is to self-organize. This alternative should not be denied (by the therapist or the victims) when considered by those involved.

The restoration of balance, or the establishment of a new balance involving a new pattern of interaction, often necessitates therapeutic intervention. New methods of negotiating the give and take in the relationships may be necessary—for example, learning how to encounter appropriately. The healing process of both primary and secondary victims will last a very long time, if not a lifetime, and any expectation that the original relationship patterns can be functionally reestablished is unrealistic. Expectations should be that new patterns will have to be implemented in the place of the old ones.

The difficulty in establishing a balance between the demands of secondary and primary survivors increases geometrically with the number of people involved. In addition, many secondary victims are also primary victims in their own right, either by virtue of experiencing the same traumatic events with the primary victim or because many primary victims gravitate to other primary victims to form relationships (e.g., abuse victims). The circularity (nonindependence and mutual influence) of healing interactions escalates the complexity of coordinating multiple healing processes.

Secondary victims often seek some indication of how long the healing process will take. Any normative estimates—either of the amount of time required or of the healing process overall—are nothing more than blind guesses. No norms are possible since the process is nonlinear and usually cyclical; stages can be encountered more than once and under varying conditions, and the movement through the patterns is unpredictable. As Figley says: " ... [it] can last as little as a month or as long as a lifetime" (1993, p. 2).

The need for maps. Traumatic events are varied, and individuals differ in regard to their personalities, histories, backgrounds, and life circumstances. The mix of all these influences makes the situations complex, requiring ways to organize and communicate information; that is, there should be maps to guide interventions and help both clients and therapists grasp their intents. Models and theoretical perspectives can provide these cognitive maps.

Maps—to be worthwhile—must be communicable, usable, and heuristic. Accordingly, both victims and professionals must readily understand maps of the healing process; they must lead to effective actions, and they must allow for their own adaptation.

Some useful maps. Many perspectives have proved useful for addressing the repercussions of traumatic events (e.g., Figley, 1985a, 1985b; van der Kolk et al., 1996). Some are general theories and models of adaptation—for example, loss (Kubler-Ross, 1969), cognitive development and learning (Mounoud, 1976; Piaget, 1976; Piaget & Inhelder, 1969), or general systems (von Bertalanffy, 1968). Others are specific to the area of trauma—for example, sexual assault (Remer, 1984) or child sexual abuse (Chard, Weaver, & Resick, 1997). To deal with secondary victim healing, maps that aid in addressing the four levels already mentioned—behavioral, affective, cognitive, and relational—are essential.

Looking again at Figure 3.1, one is struck immediately by its complexity. In fact, it is multiple-complex, having at least three characteristics that can generate patterns of complexity. First, many influences (variables) are included. Second, it is recursive (recycling). Third, it has embedded aspects and, less obviously, it itself is embedded in larger patterns (e.g., societal, cultural). Both primary and secondary victims need help in coping with the complexity and the interconnectedness of the processes involved in healing from trauma. The maps employed must accommodate multiple perspectives. They must also be mutually enhancing; that is, when superimposed (overlaid), they should bring essential features into starker relief, not obscure or muddle them.

An overarching framework—a metatheory—is needed to provide an encompassing perspective and guide the coordination of interventions. Chaos theory meets that demand, as well as supplying its own additional framing of a problem.

TRAUMA AND CHAOS THEORY

Traumatic events wreak havoc in the lives of both primary and secondary victims. If the events do not have these effects then those involved are not victims and the events are neither traumatic nor chaotic—possibilities that do occur. The impact of these events can produce severe, sometimes violent, disruptions in the patterns of these lives that must be addressed to return to some semblance of stability.

The impacts of traumatic events are often described as total chaos. The popular connotation of the term chaos is a completely disorganized, unpredictable, and disjointed situation. From a more disciplined, scientific perspective this description is not accurate. Chaos, as opposed to havoc, not only has a pattern and type of predictability to it, but also possesses the property of self-organization (which is why the term *havoc* is more appropriate when referring to the impact of trauma). This distinction is essential to making meaning from the experience. Chaos Theory (ChT) is a perspective that promotes an understanding of patterns and how they are changed, as well as suggesting ways to influence the reorganization.

The impact of trauma can destroy the life patterns of both primary and secondary victims, but in most cases, some degree of the pattern remains, if only because the victim systems attempt to reassert established patterns. However, survivors (and society at large) need to understand and accept that the patterns have irrevocably altered, lest they struggle against the changes—usually to the detriment of the healing process.

Because these systems are dynamical—nonlinear and nonindependent—the patterns of interaction they produce are chaotic in nature (Butz, 1997; Butz, Chamberlain, & McCown, 1997).

ChT is a perspective on human dynamical systems that has its origins in the mathematical and physical study of nonlinear, nonindependent, and dynamical systems (Briggs & Peat, 1989; Gleick, 1987; Lorenz, 1993) and fractal geometry (Falconer, 1990). The main ChT concepts and terms of use in treating trauma victims are: (a) phase space, (b) strange attractors and their basins, (c) self-affinity, (d) fractalness, (e) unpredictability, (f) bifurcation/cascade, and (g) self-organization. Their utility is in the sense they can convey about the ebb and flow of life—human patterns of behavior, thought, emotion, and interpersonal interaction.

Reality is the sum total of all the different kinds of patterns of experience—the territory. Since we cannot attend to all of reality at once, we focus on some subset (phase space) that provides a representation (mapping) of the patterns of life we need to address at any particular time. Patterns are developed and maintained around focal points (attractors). When the patterns reach chaos—and, fortunately, all patterns do not—the attractors are different than what we usually expect (strange attractors). These patterns are unpredictable in two ways: Although patterns can be identified, small changes in initial position can lead to huge differences in later positions; and, because of nonlinearity, nonindependence, and, often though not necessarily, multiple influences, control is an impossibility. However, the patterns are contained within boundaries (basins) and as the perspective on the patterns shifts from level to level, both the patterns themselves and processes that produce them are similar (self-affinity). Often a branching (bifurcation) occurs, disrupting the pattern and adding complexity. Should the added complexity proliferate beyond the capability for orderly adjustment (bifurcation cascade), particularly to the point of becoming chaotic, a new pattern will be established incorporating the new influences, yet also resembling the previous pattern (the system evidences self-organization). Still, the new pattern will never replicate the old exactly and where patterns meet, their boundaries are rarely, if ever, perfectly meshed (fractalness).

Traumatic events usually produce huge disruptions in life patterns at multiple levels—personal, familial, social (support network), and even societal. ChT provides a means for making some sense of the disruptions and changes in the patterns. Sociatry, an approach to healing larger social systems (Remer, 2000), not only helps in understanding the impacts of these disruptions, but also can afford means for influencing the production of new more functional patterns.

APPLICATIONS AND INTERVENTIONS

Let's make a shift at this point. Imagine you are the partner of a trauma victim. Your relationship is not new—say 5 years old—and you consider it solid. Suddenly one day your partner starts acting funny, talking less, sleeping poorly, and generally acting rather distracted. When you ask what's wrong, you get replies like "Oh, nothing," "Oh, what were you saying?" "Just leave me alone," and "You should know." This pattern continues for a few weeks. Suppose you think back and recall that these changes started shortly after your partner had been inadvertently knocked down by a purse snatcher being pursued by the police. What are you experiencing? What do you need or want and why?

You are probably confused, concerned, hurt, frustrated, and disconcerted (likely among a host of other feelings and thoughts). You probably need explanations and other information. Why? Probably because you desire some kind of control over the situation.

Control requires predictability. If one message comes through from all that has been presented above, predictability is the one thing you do not and cannot have. You can try what has worked in the past (as if you have not already been doing so); you can apply new strategies. In either case results are sometimes positive, sometimes negative, sometimes even positive for a while and still your partner's reactions are unpredictable. So, where do you go from here?

People in these circumstances are the ones we see coming to therapy. What do we have to offer and how do we go about offering?

First and foremost, we must be willing to encounter the chaos with our clients, to offer some sense of reassurance that they are not alone in their confusion or ambivalence. The job of the therapist is to help the partners and partnership plot a course (or more accurately, possible courses) through uncharted and turbulent territory. We, clients and therapist together, must choose the appropriate focus (phase space) for the demands of the moment, while considering what has been learned from the past (other mappings and mapping processes) and what may lie ahead. The task will seem daunting, so normalizing it *and* the attendant chaotic experience are essential. Reframing—shifting the paradigm—to expectations consistent with the lack of prediction and concomitant lack of control, is both a starting point and a goal. Supplying the ChT perspective—at whatever level is comprehensible, acceptable, and usable—can provide some structure to which to cling.

From that base other aspects of their lives (other subterritories and their mappings) can be addressed and explored, in turn as needed. Because of the multitude of factors involved in treating the secondary survivor and interfacing such treatment with those of the primary survivor and the relationship, some structure to facilitate coordination is helpful. Viewing intervention from two dimensions—treatment goals and therapeutic milieu—is useful and facilitates a balancing of efforts and timing of interventions. Crossing three levels of goals (education, awareness and personal development, and skill acquisition) with three categories of milieu (individual, conjoint, and group therapy) produces a grid (see Figure 3.2) of possible areas needing attention and approaches to supplying direction and resources. (See Remer and Ferguson, 1995, 1997 for further details about this tool.)

What might be done in the situation with which you are faced as the secondary survivor above? One obvious area of concern is the emotional upheaval being experienced. Maybe you are not comfortable dealing with anger, hurt, or even expressing feelings in general—perhaps your family was not prone to such expressions. Through examination of the situation, you become aware that you do not recognize and handle feelings when they arise and that this pattern seems to be problematic in many instances with your partner (and probably with others). You decide to learn more about the effects of cultural, familial, and gender-role messages (education), to look at your own discomfort with

		Treatment Goals		
		Education about Trauma	Awareness/ Personal Development	Skill Acquisition
M I L I E U	Individual Therapy	1	1/2	3
	Conjoint Therapy		3*	2
	Group Therapy	2	2/1	1

Numbers in cells indicate order of effectiveness:

1 = most effective
2 = 2nd most effective
3 = 3rd most effective

* Conjoint therapy contraindicated except for recycling

FIGURE 3.2. Schematic for choice of appropriate therapeutic intervention for partners: Treatment goals by therapy approach.

expression of emotion (personal awareness and development), and to learn how to identify and express your feelings more directly and constructively (skill acquisition). To meet these goals you believe that first you must look at your personal issues (individual therapy), then find an acceptable place to practice your skills (group therapy), and then bring the new patterns into your relationship (conjoint therapy).

Sounds like a good plan, no? However, the other aspects (e.g., recognition that this incident has probably triggered a reexperiencing of a trauma for your partner) of the distressing pattern you are encountering are not independent of your emotional facility (the interface between primary and secondary healing processes). Nor is separating the milieus likely to be effective since changes in patterns in one area are going to precipitate reactions in others (e.g., in group therapy, learning what other partners experience in their relationships will affect your expectations of your own). Each focus will offer choices and combinations of approaches.

Knowledge of the healing processes' interface and an acceptance of the journey is essential; they not only constitute another educational intervention, but serve as markers of awareness and personal development. A grasp, at the metalevel, of the nature of the dynamical systems involved and their implications provides a metamap helpful in remembering: (a) the map is not the territory; (b) the message is not what is sent, but what is received; (c) you see what you look for; (d) easier said than done; and (e) do what you can do and trust in the process—little changes can make great differences.

What of the other dimensions of the problem presented (e.g., trust issues, family transmission of attitudes and patterns of behavior, feelings of having gotten involved in more than you bargained for) and where they might lead? As many variations and paths exist as there are clients and sessions. If you are feeling overwhelmed by the challenges, disconcerted by feelings of impotence and frustration, then welcome to the chaos of dealing with trauma victim healing. You are a secondary victim. I hope this chapter can help you, and your clients, become secondary survivors.

SOME FINAL THOUGHTS: SHIFT IN PERSPECTIVE FROM 1988 TO THE PRESENT

The biggest change in my thinking since 1988 when I first published an article on working with partners of trauma victims has been a personal paradigm shift from *logical positivism* and its belief in and emphasis on control, to ChT and the belief that control is illusive if not illusory. With this switch have come the seemingly contradictory stances that people pretty much do the best they can do (systems self-organize), yet we may have more influence than we think we have if we are willing to give our best shots (little changes can have great impacts). With this acceptance has come a degree of calm and freedom. I try to convey that shift to those partners (and others) with whom I work.

ChT, with the emphasis on patterns, has also produced some insight into the somewhat paradoxical nature of the impact of trauma on partner relationships. These posttrauma patterns are both self-affine and fractal. In some ways these interactions are little different from what they were prior to the trauma. In other words, many of the problems were present before the trauma (Gold, 2000). Now, however, awareness is heightened; the trauma has focused attention on them. That focus, while seemingly a minor change, can have major ramifications. At least the patterns will be somewhat different from what they were previously—if only because a degree of awareness will be present. Despite all desire to the contrary, this impact is irreversible.

Although I often employ many of the tools (interventions) I learned as a social learning/behavioral therapist early in my career, I am less constrained by the tenets (e.g., the belief that I have to be, or can be, an objective observer). The flexibility that both ChT and sociatry encourage—including the use of less traditional interventions like action-oriented techniques (Kellerman & Hudgins, 2000)—offer a broader armamentarium and adaptability to the dictates of the clients' circumstances. In particular, the focus on spontaneity is more positive, heartening, and productive than a strict pathology or problem orientation, thereby energizing therapy for both clients and me.

REFERENCES

Briggs, J., & Peat, F. D. (1989). *Turbulent mirror.* New York: Harper & Row.

Burgess, A. W., & Holmstrom, L. L. (1979a). Adaptive strategies and recovery from rape. *American Journal of Psychiatry, 136,* 1278–1282.

Burgess, A. W., & Holmstrom, L. L. (1979b). *Rape: Crisis and recovery.* Bowie, MD: Robert J. Brady Co.

Butz, M. R. (1997). *Chaos and complexity: Implications for psychological theory and practice.* Washington, DC: Taylor & Francis.

Butz, M. R., Chamberlain, L. L., & McCown, W. G. (1997). *Strange attractors: Chaos, complexity, and the art of family therapy.* New York: Wiley.

Chard, K. M., Weaver, T. L., & Resick, P. A. (1997). Adapting cognitive processing therapy for child sexual abuse survivors. *Cognitive and Behavioral Practice, 4,* 31–52.

deVries, M. W. (1996). Trauma in cultural perspective. In B. A. van der Kolk, A. C. McFarlane, & L. Weisaeth (Eds.), *Traumatic stress: The effects of overwhelming experience on mind, body, and society* (pp. 398–413). New York: Guilford.

Falconer, K. (1990). *Fractal geometry: Mathematical foundations and applications.* New York: Wiley.

Ferguson, R. A. (1993). *Male partners of female survivors of childhood sexual abuse: An inquiry into the concept of secondary victimization.* Unpublished doctoral dissertation, University of Kentucky, Lexington.

Figley, C. R. (Ed.). (1985a). *Trauma and its wake: Vol. I. The study and treatment of post traumatic stress disorder.* New York: Brunner/Mazel.

Figley, C. R. (Ed.). (1985b). *Trauma and its wake: Vol. II. Traumatic stress theory, research, and intervention.* New York: Brunner/Mazel.

Figley, C. R. (1989). *Helping traumatized families.* San Francisco: Jossey-Bass.

Figley, C. R. (1993). Compassion stress: Toward its measurement and management. *Family Therapy News,* February, 3–6.

Figley, C. R. (Ed.). (1997). *Burnout in families: The systemic cost of caring.* Delray Beach, FL: St. Lucie Press.

Gleick, J. (1987). *Chaos: Making a new science.* New York: Viking Penguin.

Gold, S. N. (2000). *Not trauma alone: Therapy for child abuse survivors in family and social context.* Philadelphia: Brunner-Routledge.

Kellerman, P. F, & Hudgins, M. K. (Eds.). (2000). *Psychodrama and trauma: Acting out your pain.* London: Jessica Kingsley.

Kubler-Ross, E. (1969). *On death and dying.* New York: Macmillan.

Lorenz, E. N. (1993). *The essence of chaos.* Seattle, WA: University of Washington Press.

McCann, I. L., Sakheim, D. K., & Abrahamson, D. J. (1988). Trauma and victimization: A model of psychological adaptation. *The Counseling Psychologist, 16,* 531–595.

McFarlane, A. C., & van der Kolk, B. A. (1996). Trauma and its challenge to society. In B. A. van der Kolk, A. C. McFarlane, & L. Weisaeth (Eds.), *Traumatic stress: The effects of overwhelming experience on mind, body, and society* (pp. 24–46). New York: Guilford.

Mounoud, P. (1976). The development of systems of representation and treatment in the child. In B. Inhelder & H. Chipman (Eds.), *Piaget and his school* (pp. 166–185). New York: Springer-Verlag.

Pearlman, L. A., & Mac Ian, P. S. (1995). Vicarious traumatization: An empirical study of the effects of trauma work on trauma therapists. *Professional Psychology: Research and Practice, 26,* 558–565.

Piaget, J. (1976). Biology and cognition. In B. Inhelder & H. Chipman (Eds.), *Piaget and his school.* New York: Springer-Verlag.

Piaget, J., & Inhelder, B. (1969). *The psychology of the child.* New York: Basic Books.

Remer, P. (1984). *Stages in coping with rape.* Unpublished manuscript, University of Kentucky at Lexington.

Remer, R. (1990). *Secondary victim/Secondary survivor.* Unpublished manuscript, University of Kentucky at Lexington.

Remer, R. (2000). Sociatric interventions with secondary victims of trauma: Producing secondary survivors. In P. F. Kellerman & M. K. Hudgins (Eds.), *Psychodrama and trauma: Acting out your pain* (pp. 316–341). London: Jessica Kingsley.

Remer, R., & Elliott, J. E. (1988a). Characteristics of secondary victims of sexual assault. *International Journal of Family Psychiatry, 9*(4), 373–387.

Remer, R., & Elliott, J. E. (1988b). Management of secondary victims of sexual assault. *International Journal of Family Psychiatry, 9*(4), 389–401.

Remer, R., & Ferguson, R. (1995). Becoming a secondary survivor of sexual assault. *Journal of Counseling and Development, 7,* 407–414.

Remer, R. (1997, August). A support group for secondary survivors of sexual assault. In J. Robinson (Chair), *Men's support groups—Current issues.* Symposium conducted at the meeting of the American Psychological Association, Chicago, IL.

Remer, R., & Ferguson, R. (1997). Treating traumatized partners: Producing secondary survivors. In C. R. Figley (Ed.), *Burnout in families: The systemic cost of caring* (pp. 137–167). Delray Beach, FL: St. Lucie Press.

Scurfield, R. (1985). Post-trauma stress assessment and treatment: Overview and formulations. In C.R. Figley (Ed.), *Trauma and its wake: The study and treatment of post traumatic stress disorder* (pp. 219–255). New York: Brunner/Mazel.

Sutherland, S., & Sherl, D. J. (1970). Patterns of response among victims of rape. *American Journal of Orthopsychiatry, 10,* 503–511.

van der Kolk, B. A., McFarlane, A. C., & Weisaeth, L. (Eds.). (1996). *Traumatic stress: The effects of overwhelming experience on mind, body, and society.* New York: Guilford.

von Bertalanffy, L. (1968) *General system theory.* New York: George Braziller.

Whetsell, M. S. (1990). *The relationship of abuse factors and revictimization to the long-term effects of childhood sexual abuse in women.* Unpublished doctoral dissertation, University of Kentucky, Lexington.

Worell, J., & Remer, P. (1992). *Feminist perspectives in therapy: An empowerment model for women.* New York: Wiley.

4

Selected Optimization With Compensation: Older Adults Adjusting to Change

LEE HYER, LUBA RAFALSON, AND ERIN L. O'HEA

People are always "adjusting," especially as a result of aging. As adjustments occur, there is either a meaningful accommodation or problems ensue. When stress and loss transpire, a *learned dependence* may result where the older person downwardly adjusts and settles for a lower life satisfaction. We will address the issue of more resources being devoted to the management of decline and loss at later life, and consider how the aging person can maintain control by applying core psychological strategies in later life.

A unidimensional view of later life cannot incorporate the multiple aspects of aging. A life span perspective views behaviors as the result of the assimilation and accommodation of the whole person and the social environment (Baltes P., & Baltes, 1990). Explicating the parameters of this process is a mean task and is just the beginning. It involves the multicausality, multidimensionality, and multifunctionality of the dynamics of a fluid system. Biological, sociocultural, and psychological factors interact to form the person's response. As ineluctable decline progresses, the person accommodates by downwardly adjusting. In this context the savvy elder accommodates by compensation to a lesser level of adjustments, a so-called *dependency-support script*. This is not a negative correction but, rather, a compensatory must.

In this chapter we consider the dynamic of accommodation and downward adjustment (the understandable and positive effects in the process of change due to aging), borrowing from the selection, optimization, and compensation (SOC) model of aging. This model has been used to conceptualize how people with cognitive, behavioral, physical, and affective deficits continue to function and become active managers of their lives. We consider the SOC model of change to be a meaningful representation of accommodation to life change as individuals age.

OVERVIEW

The population of the U.S. over age 65 is projected to grow from 35 million to 70 million by 2030. At that time one in five Americans will be 65 or older (Gerontological Society of America, 2000). Although people are living longer, healthy life expectancy (number of healthy years after age 65) has remained at about 12 years. Heart disease, stroke, and cancer continue to account for 60% of deaths among those 65 and older. In fact, older people have as many chronic diseases as ever but experience less disability as health care now provides better management of chronic problems. The gap between life span and healthy life span has narrowed. Interestingly, 70% of physical decline that occurs with aging is related to modifiable factors, including smoking, poor nutrition, lack of physical activity, injuries from falls, and failure to use preventative services (Abeles et al., 1998). In sum, older people live longer and enjoy it more but have many years of adaptation to endure as a result of health issues alone.

Aging is not a medical disease; it is a gradual and natural process, a period of life evaluation and increased freedom and a period associated with physical decline and concerns about health and loss (Keller, Leventhal, & Larson, 1989). In an important study, Steverink, Westeroff, Bode, and Dittmana-Koli (2001) showed that a description of the aging experience is best captured by physical decline, social loss, and diminished continuous growth (Steverink et al., 2001). These components are influenced by subjective health, higher income, loneliness, and degree of hope, as well as by just being older.

Mental health is a marker of older individuals' increased needs. Approximately 20% of older Americans experience mental disorders that are beyond the problems of the natural decline caused by aging. This is due largely to system constraints that prevent a collaborative model of care, poor mental health practices among primary care physicians, and attitudes among the elderly themselves (Blumenthal, 2003). The fundamental problem is undertreatment; older adults are not screened or diagnosed well and hence not treated. Almost 70% of older people who are depressed are missed in primary care clinics and only 3% receive out-patient care in a mental health clinic (American Psychiatric Association, 2000). Those with physical problems are at greater risk for mental health problems, and vice versa. The unique contribution of mental illness, especially depression, is greater than that of medical conditions in relation to dysfunction, poor health perception, and well-being (Ormel et al., 1998). This applies regardless of whether the first episode of mental illness occurs before or after the age of 65. There are long periods of satisfaction and relative health, but there is a downward spiral that inevitably occurs and an adjustment that is required. What we need to know is how this process is best negotiated and what the variables are that assist it.

STRESS AND ALTERED ADAPTATION

Stress in later life is distinctive; it can best be considered as falling along a continuum. One may argue that there exists small stress (e.g., the vagaries of aging and hassles), moderate stress (e.g., health, losses, caregiving, etc.), and large stress (e.g., trauma). Small stressors consist of minor frustrations that cause the person to feel boxed into a corner and experience internal conflict. These are the so-called hassles and discomforts that exist at high rates at later life (Hyer & Sohnle, 2001). Stress at moderate levels is pervasive and often compelling; the older person must rearrange a lifestyle, as occurs in the common situation of caregiving (Lyons, Zarit, Sayer, & Whitlach, 2002). Stress at high levels usually involves trauma. These large stressors can be very detrimental, but research has demonstrated that older people tend to respond well and do not seem to be more affected by trauma than other age groups. When the impact of trauma on an older individual is great, distinctive treatment may be in order, but the vast majority of stressors are of the small or moderate kind, requiring older persons to accommodate to them on their own (Hyer & Sohnle, 2001).

In general, older people experience more stress associated with losses of health, spouse/friends, and roles. There is now considerable evidence that stress has an impact on the aging experience. Older people who move, divorce, act as caregivers, experience a recent loss, or experience a major physical illness have more stress and less immune competence (DeAngeles, 2002). In addition, stress models show that age is a mediator in the unfolding of stress, along with the key coping variables related to aging, especially social support and attitudes about perceived control.

In older adults the relationship between stressors and depression or trauma is similar to that in younger groups, especially if social support or physical health is compromised. Over 60% of depressed older adults, for example, have experienced a negative life event the year before depression. Acute and chronic stressors, poor health, death or serious illness of a loved one, relocation, and caregiving are associated with increased rates of depression and a poor response to trauma (Wolfe, Morrow, & Fredickson, 1996). Perhaps the best formulation of mental health problems among the elderly is that there exists a biopsychosocial disorder triggered by stressors, including the mental illness itself (Geriatric Psychiatry Alliance, 1996).

At present, there is much we do not know about how the actions of individual (personalities) impact or moderate the changing process of aging. We do know that people respond to the same stressful situation in different physiological and psychological ways, depending on how they appraise it. Each person self-regulates by sensing current states and comparing the sensation to some reference value. In effect, the person makes adjustments and copes. Thus, personality influences the way in which an individual copes with change. The external coping mechanism of social support and the internal one of perceived control are particularly relevant in later life.

We seek a model to describe adjustment in decline, and coping mechanisms represent the methods of operation for such a process. A lack of competence decreases behavioral choices, while environmental factors influence the development and maintenance of competence. In long-term care facilities, for example, better functioning residents adopt a dependency-support script. In this way dependency becomes highly functional and adaptive. With an understanding of the SOC model and better coping skills, the older person is more able to accommodate and retain well-being.

SELECTION, OPTIMIZATION, AND COMPENSATION (SOC)

Literature on aging is awash with theories. In response to the loss-deficit model of aging, there was an early push to convince people in the scientific community that aging was a positive experience. Rowe and Kahn (1987) suggested that successful aging is seen in one who exhibits minimal disease and disability or in one who exhibits high levels of physical functioning. However, three major theories have predominated: disengagement, activity, and continuity. Each focuses on the person growing old. *Disengagement theory* highlights withdrawal as a coping mechanism as one gets older and loses roles; *activity theory* emphasizes the maintenance of activity for high levels of life satisfaction; and *continuity theory* holds that individuals must feel a sense of continuity with the past to be happy. Supplementing these are theories of competence—*ecological* (Lawton & Nahemow, 1973) and *person-environment* (Kahana, 1982)—that address the best match between the person and the environment. Competence theories presume that optimal functioning occurs when environmental demands are accounted for (Putnam, 2002).

Theories of the aging individual within the social system explain the relationship between the aging individual and society. *Social exchange, age stratification*, and *modernization theories* focus on the structure of society and the roles available to older adults; all assume that a change in resources can upset the relationship between an older person and society. More recent social system theories focus on the power differential between the older person and society (Putnam, 2002). The objective of these theories is to explicate the decline process according to different sociological mechanisms.

The life span model is more optimistic; in fact, the *maturity/specific challenge model* of aging (Knight & Satre, 1996) highlights the advantages of the changes experienced by aging individuals. Old age is seen as a mature time—one that has sociocultural and personal circumstances that require considerable effort and resources. It is argued that the performance of older people is sufficient for most tasks including those related to therapy and normal adjustment, despite the existence of cognitive deficits, especially in memory and fluid intelligence tasks (Knight & Satre, 1999). Moreover, older adults utilize emotions in more integrated and complex ways (Carstensen & Turk-Charles, 1994) and utilize intelligence in more wise and deliberative ways (Thornstam, 1996). Therefore, it may be argued that the potential for continual growth toward maturity throughout the life span is frequently actualized. The continual growth involves cognitive complexity and the development of areas of experiential competence in work, family, and relationships. However, it may be that older people change by rediscovering their skills and not by learning them for the first time.

Paul and Margaret Baltes (1980, 1990) proposed a model that views successful aging as doing the best with what one has. Their holistic model allows for problems, disease, and loss. The emphasis is on coping and a positive view of the inevitable. The model proposed three strategies of adaptively responding to everyday demands and functional decline in later life: *selection, optimization*, and *compensation* (SOC). The application of the SOC strategies is associated with better functioning. They also require the use of resources. The more resources the aging individual has, the better they can engage in the use of SOC. The SOC model is one of adaptive development, a framework for the understanding of the processes of developmental regulation over the life span.

Selection: Selection is defined as active or passive reduction of the number of activities, goals, or domains in order to focus on those areas that are most important in one's life. It is perhaps best if the person selects *emotionally meaningful experiences* (Carstensen, Isaacowitz, & Charles, 1999). Perceptions of a limited future were found to be associated with prioritizing generative and emotionally meaningful goals (Lang & Carstensen, 2002). Furthermore, in the context of aging, selection appears to relate to the reduction in the diversity of activities. A focus on the most preferred activities occurs. In effect, when confronted with loss, the successful older person selects the most meaningful choices.

Compensation: Compensation refers to the use of new and alternative means to reach a goal or to maintain a desired state once a loss has occurred. People may intensify or expand routines once a functional loss has happened. Again, the process of compensation is most successful when there are resources available.

Optimization: Optimization is defined as the enhancement and refinement of the means to utilize one's resources in a selected domain. It refers to adaptive processes or strategies where no direct or indirect aging losses have occurred and where an actual amelioration or maximization of means can be found. Investing more time and effort in specific tasks or activities that provide meaning and less in others that are less salient is most reflective of optimization.

Selection at later life is largely made to ease loss-based problems and includes focusing on the most important goals, reconstructing a goal hierarchy, adapting of standards, and searching for new goals. Optimization involves distinct means-action: attentional focus, seizing the right moment, persistence, acquiring new skills, practice of skills, time allocation, and modeling successful others. Compensation is the means used to counter the loss: substitute means, use external aids, use therapeutic intervention, acquire new skills and resources, increase effort and energy, increase time allocation, and activate unused skills (Freund & Baltes, 1998).

The SOC theory has some empirical support. Lang, Reickmann, and Baltes (2002) found that resource-rich participants demonstrated more indications of SOC in everyday activity and were more likely to survive after 4 years as compared to resource-poor people. The resource-rich people were more active in everyday life. In effect, older people with more resources were more resistant to the negative effects of aging, and those with fewer resources were more vulnerable. Brandstadler and Greve (1994) proposed that older adults use a combination of active, assimilative strategies and passive, accommodative strategies. This *dual process model* asserts that advancing age results in a shift away from active adjustment strategies more to accommodating of personal preferences to fit situational constraints, making fewer psychological demands on the person's resources. Older adults who replace lost activities may be viewed as successfully accommodating to losses by shifting from a blocked activity to a different one. If the present activity level becomes unfeasible, accommodative strategies should allow for a change in focus to alternatives.

In a key study, Duke, Leventhal, Brownlee, and Leventhal (2002) assessed 250 older adults longitudinally to examine activity loss and replacement as a consequence of an important illness episode. They found that reductions in activity were predicted by physical factors. Replacing lost activities was facilitated by social support and optimism, and inhibited by a belief in the need to conserve physical resources. Older adults who replaced lost activities had a higher positive affect level 1 year after illness onset than those who did not replace them. The beneficial use of accommodative strategies in coping with chronic illness was endorsed. Notably, physical incapacity was less important for activity replacement than social factors such as optimism and conservation of resources, both of which affected motivation to seek alternatives.

Older people must manage their own aging process. This self-regulated dependency then becomes an integral part of successful aging (Baltes & Wahl, 1990). SOC proposes that dependency or other forms of performance productions have adaptive value. The older person has several choices: (a) give up the activities hampered by functional loss; (b) compensate for them by searching for a means to maintain activities; or (c) become increasingly dependent in the weakened domains to free energy for other more personal areas. In option (c), the person recognizes the loss and delegates control to others as a form of proxy control. Only option (a) causes problems.

The model highlights the possible adaptive potential of lowered performance where behavioral dependency can be adaptive. The effective coordination of the three processes (SOC) ensures successful management of aging losses and reduction of resources. Selection requires that the age-related loss is identified and that proxies take on a high priority. The selection process often involves a convergence of environmental demands, individual motivations, skills, and biological capacities. Compensation becomes important when life tasks require a capacity beyond that of the current skills. Losses of various sorts apply. Optimization ensures that it is also possible to maintain high levels of functioning in old age in some selected domains through practice and acquisition of new bodies of knowledge and technology. In this way dependency becomes self-selected and the outcome of active selection and compensation.

Similar processes may also apply to emotions. Socioemotional selectivity theory (Carstensen & Turk-Charles, 1994), a variant of SOC, posits that older adults prioritize the goal of emotional regulation. With age, adults want more satisfying emotional contact. Consequently, older adults prune their social ties to weed out unsatisfying relationships and to retain satisfying ones. Perhaps it is no accident that the amount and duration of positive emotion increase, and negative affect decreases with age.

AGING MEDIATORS

There are many examples of older people altering their outlook to maintain adequate life satisfaction. Several studies have documented the substantial role of psychological factors in the developmental processes of disability, especially internal and external resources that are most reflective of the aging experience (Jang, Haley, Small, & Mortimer, 2002). We believe that the combination of the coping mechanisms of social support and perceived control, as well as optimism, allows for a meaningful adjustment (according to the SOC model) to the realities of the problems of aging.

Social Support

Social support is commonly considered a coping resource, a social fund from which people may draw when handling stressors (Thoits, 1995). Social support is typically viewed within the context of a stress and coping framework. Stress arises when an individual appraises a situation as threatening or otherwise demanding. Social support may serve (a) to attenuate or prevent the stress appraisal response or (b) to modulate the experience of stress and the onset of negative outcomes such as psychological distress and negative health behaviors. As a result of either mechanism, an individual deals with a stressful situation effectively and positive outcomes result (Cohen & Syme, 1985).

Cohen and colleagues proposed a distinction between structural and functional support measures (Cohen, 1988; Cohen & Syme, 1985). *Structural* refers to measures describing the existence of, and interconnections between, social ties (e.g., marital status, number of relationships, or number of relations who know one another). *Functional* measures assess whether interpersonal relationships serve particular functions such as the provision of affection, feelings of belonging, or material aid (Cohen, 1988). Greater structural and functional social support have been linked to reduced morbidity and mortality in the general population (see review by Berkman,

1995). Based on evidence from studies examining relationships between social support and physiological processes, a common sympathetic-adrenergic mechanism has been proposed connecting social support to long-term health outcomes (Uchino, Cacioppo, & Kiecolt-Glaser, 1996). Moreover, in a rigorously controlled study, greater social network diversity has been shown to predict reduced susceptibility to the common cold (Cohen, Doyle, Skoner, Rabin, & Gwaltney, 1997). Social support is clearly an important variable to consider when examining not only psychological but health outcomes.

In a recent study, Walter-Ginzburg, Blumenstein, Chetrit, and Modan (2002) set out to determine those aspects of social networks that were most significantly associated with 8-year, all-cause mortality among the old-old in Israel. They randomly selected 1,340 individuals aged 75 to 94, stratified by age, gender, and place of birth. After controlling for sociodemographics and measures of health, cognitive status, depressive symptoms, and physical function, the measures of social engagement that explicitly involved others were associated with a lower risk of mortality. The hypothesis that those with larger network structures would show reduced risk of mortality was not supported. Moreover, none of the measures of the functioning (supportiveness) of the social network (frequency of contact with children and perceived instrumental support) were found to be associated with risk of mortality. In short, neither social network size nor supportiveness of the network appeared to be related to survival in the old-old population in Israel. Social support findings in older individuals do not appear to mirror those in younger adults, but by taking older adults' goals into account, socioemotional selectivity theory may be able to explain these findings.

Socioemotional selectivity theory: One of the most reliable findings in social gerontology is that the rates of social interaction decline with age. This finding has been replicated in many cultures (see review by Fung, Carstensen, & Lang, 2001). Traditionally, the decline has been interpreted as an inevitable loss associated with the aging process, due either to a process of mutual emotional distancing between aging people and societies, as in disengagement theory, or to physical and social barriers that bar older people from desired social interactions, as in activity theory. However, socioemotional selectivity theory has recast the decline as an adaptive response to perceived limitations on time left in life (Carstensen et al., 1999).

Socioemotional selectivity theory contends that two broad classes of social goals operate throughout life but their relative salience and importance change as a function of place in the life cycle. One class is characterized by the *pursuit of knowledge*—seeking information about the self and social world. Knowledge seeking is highly salient during the early years of life when stores of knowledge are limited and the future is viewed as largely open-ended. Knowledge seeking gradually becomes less salient as a function of experience and also because of an increasingly limited future. The second class of social motives concerns *emotional gratification*. Examples of these social motives include efforts to feel good, derive emotional meaning from life, deepen intimacy, and maintain a sense of self. In late life, when many of life's lessons have been learned and future-oriented strivings are less relevant, emotional goals remerge as highly salient (Carstensen et al., 1999).

Because social partners differ in the types of goals they fulfill for the individual, evidence of these goals is found in social network composition. During life stages in which information seeking is at its peak, social networks are replete with relatively novel social partners. During life stages in which emotional goals are more important, a drop occurs in peripheral social partners, but emotionally close social partners are retained. Carstensen and her colleagues argue that rather than reflect age-related loss, the relatively smaller social networks of older people reflect their preferences for emotionally close social partners and their relative disinterest in peripheral ones (Carstensen et al., 1999).

Considerable empirical evidence exists to support the socioemotional selectivity theory. A reanalysis of longitudinal data from the Child Guidance Study found that rates of interaction with acquaintances and satisfaction with them declined from early to middle adulthood (Carstensen, 1992). Across the same period, however, interaction rates and satisfaction with three groups of emotionally close partners— spouses, parents, and siblings—were all maintained or increased. This pattern of findings suggests that decline in social contacts appears to occur relatively early in life, too early for age-related losses to be the cause. Moreover, reductions are limited primarily to acquaintances.

The selective reduction of social partners appears to continue well into old age. The Berlin Aging Study and a similar cross-validation study (Lang & Carstensen, 2002; Lang, Staudigner, & Carstensen, 1998) found that very old people consistently had smaller social networks than did the young-old, but the difference was accounted for by the number of peripheral social partners. Very old persons had fewer peripheral social partners than the young-old but as many emotionally close social partners. A study of African Americans and Europeans found that older people had similar number of very close social partners and fewer peripheral social partners as compared to younger people across a wide age range (Fung et al., 2001). Moreover, the authors found that the percentage of very close social partners was negatively correlated with happiness among young adults but not among older age groups, even after controlling for perceived health, educational level, and marital status.

These findings challenge the accepted notion that remaining socially active and involved in broad social networks is essential for successful aging. When emotional satisfaction is the primary social goal, limiting social contacts to more emotionally close social partners may be a good strategy for successful aging, particularly in view of the undeniable physical and cognitive declines that accompany aging. This pattern may be an example of selective optimization with compensation in the social domain (Fung et al., 2001). Individuals who age successfully may compensate for age-related social barriers and optimize their social interactions by concentrating their limited time and energy on the few social partners who are best able to satisfy their primary social needs.

Socioemotional selectivity theory predicts age-related changes in exchanges of emotional support based on the premise that older adults prioritize the goal of emotional regulation (Keyes, 2002). Adults prune their social ties to weed out unsatisfying (and retain satisfying) social relationships as they age. Exchange theory suggests that adults achieve emotional regulation by establishing equitable or balanced exchanges of emotional support. Keyes (2002) found that, with age, adults spent less time engaging in acts of emotional support and less time receiving emotional support. Although adults of all ages gave more support than they received, the discrepancy between hours of emotional support given and received became more balanced with age. Compared with equal exchanges, unequal exchanges predicted worse emotional well-being profiles among individuals over the age of 55.

In conclusion, it appears that socioemotional selectivity theory, which is a specific case of the SOC model, holds considerable explanatory power for the structure and function of social support in older individuals. It remains to be seen whether applying the SOC model to the study of dispositional optimism and pessimism in older adults will explain some of the inconsistent findings.

Personal Control

A sense of control is an important factor in successful aging and emotional well-being. This applies to both negative outcomes and positive outcomes (Kunzmann, Little, & Smith, 2002). Roberts, Dunkle, and Hang (1994) showed that a great sense of control significantly altered the negative impact of stress and protected emotional well-being.

Personal control is synonymous with the concept of *locus of control* (LOC) (Rotter, 1966) and has been defined as "the belief that one can determine one's own internal states and behavior, influence one's environment, and/or bring about desired outcomes" (Wallston,

Wallston, Smith, & Dobbins, 1987, p. 5). Perceptions of control can be accurate or inaccurate, but even if totally based on false perceptions, these perceptions can have a strong impact on behaviors as well as psychological and medical outcomes (Rodin, 1990).

As a global personality trait, high internal locus of control has been related to greater life satisfaction, more positive self concept, better ratings of health status, and greater participation in activities among the elderly (Eizenmann, Nesselroade, Featherman, & Rowe, 1998; Seeman & Lewis, 1995). For example, high levels of internal control beliefs have been linked with low levels of mortality and fewer activity limitations in older medically ill patients (Seeman & Lewis, 1995). Low levels of internal control have predicted decreased exercise and greater levels of depression in older medical patients (Weaver & Gary, 1996). High internal locus of control has even been found to be protective against the occurrence of morbidity (Van den Akker, Buntinx, Metsemakers, van der Aa, & Knottnerus, 2001). Finally, greater levels of choice and internal control were found to be associated with better well-being, less reliance on facility services, and greater participation in community activities among residents of residential care settings (Langer & Rodin, 1976; Timko & Moos, 1989).

Personal control interacts with coping strategies to influence adjustment to life stress among the elderly. Problem-focused or active coping strategies have often been found to correlate with high internal perceived control, while emotion-focused or passive coping strategies tend to correlate with lower levels of perceived personal control. Melding (1995) demonstrated better adjustment to coping with chronic pain in elderly patients with high perceived control beliefs when they also used active coping strategies. Fry and Wong (1991) examined elderly patients' preferred coping style and matched coping skills training intervention with these preferences. Individuals who preferred problem-focused coping and received a matched type of intervention reported reduced pain and anxiety and better satisfaction and adjustment compared to individuals who used emotion-focused coping. Finally, Pinard and Landreville (1998) found that individuals who use escape and avoidance coping strategies, which are often correlated with lower levels of perceived control, have poorer psychological adaptation to their living arrangements than those who use a more active approach (i.e., seeking social support from friends and family) to cope with aging related stress.

Whether personal control is viewed as a personality trait, as a moderator of coping strategies, or as a complex multidimensional construct, perception of control among the elderly is an important contributing factor to maintaining and increasing rewarding life events while minimizing negative ones. The degree to which older individuals perceive personal control can affect their psychological and physical well-being.

Among older- and oldest-old (the frail elderly) the operative issue may involve altering control or at least keeping the illusion of control, which may involve the application of secondary control and a higher dependence on the environment and on accommodation to problems. Schultz and Heckhausen (1996) equate successful aging with the development and maintenance of primary control, which is achieved through control-related processes that optimize selection and failure compensation functions. Primary control is directed outward and targets the external world; secondary control targets the self and attempts to achieve changes within the individual. Both can involve cognition and action but primary control always involves action. The ratio of gains to losses becomes less favorable with age and secondary control becomes more important.

There are four control processes that involve selection and compensation. First, optimal development is enhanced by diversity of opportunity and choice. Second, selection regulates the choice of action goals so that diversity is maintained. Third, the person must compensate for and cope with failure. Compensation is essential in order to maintain, enhance, and remediate competencies and motivational resources after failure experiences. Fourth, the person must manage trade-offs across domains and sequential life phases and recognize that resources must be juggled to maintain balance.

As individuals age, their primary control may decrease, but their secondary control may become more stable and malleable. Thus, elderly individuals who continue to place great import on primary control may experience poorer adjustment to the aging process than those persons who shift their paradigms and gradually place a greater emphasis on secondary control. When conceptualized in this manner, poor adjustment (e.g., general distress, depression, anxiety) may be seen to result from frustration associated with continuing to attempt to exert control on aspects of one's life that are no longer in one's realm of control. Individuals may adjust poorly to the changes associated with aging because they continue to place a high priority on controlling their environment, while individuals who accept the declining control that comes with aging and focus on their ability to control their own behaviors and internal states may demonstrate successful adjustment to aging.

Although this view seems obvious, the concept of personal control as a multidimensional construct has not been widely researched among the aging. Further research is needed to determine if individuals indeed view personal control as multidimensional and if certain types of personal control are instrumental in determining adjustment among the elderly.

Dispositional Optimism

Finally, dispositional optimism must be considered because it is clinically relevant and has a conceptual connection to perceived control. Dispositional optimism has been defined as the generalized expectation that one will have good outcomes in life even if one is presently facing adversity (Carver & Scheier, 2001). An optimistic outlook has been linked to psychological and physical well-being in younger and middle-aged adults (Carver & Scheier, 2001). Studies linking optimism with adaptive outcomes suggest that optimists do not respond to stressful situations with less distress than pessimists simply because they are more cheerful. Optimists differ from pessimists both in their stable coping tendencies and in the kinds of coping responses that they generate spontaneously when confronting stressful situations (Carver & Scheier, 1999). Optimists tend to use more problem-focused coping strategies and, when problem-focused coping is not possible, optimists turn to adaptive emotion-focused coping strategies such as acceptance, use of humor, and positive reframing (Carver & Scheier, 1999).

Several studies have examined the costs and benefits of optimism and pessimism across the life span, and the findings are mixed (Isaacowitz & Seligman, 1998; Isaacowitz & Seligman, 2002; Norem & Chang, 2001; Robinson-Whelen, Kim, MacCallum, & Kiecolt-Glaser, 1997; Schulz, Bookwala, Knapp, Scheier, & Williamson, 1996). Isaacowitz and Seligman (1998) report that among older adults, a realistically pessimistic perspective is associated with better adaptation to negative life events in contrast to the typical findings with younger participants in the sample groups. Robinson-Whelen et al. (1997) found little evidence of the power of positive thinking in predicting anxiety, stress, depression, and self-appraised health among a group of older people composed of caregivers and noncaregivers. However, they did find that dispositional pessimism significantly predicted outcomes in the expected direction.

Schulz et al. (1996) followed 238 cancer patients receiving palliative radiation treatment for 8 months (during which 70 patients died) and studied the independent effects of pessimism, optimism, and depression on mortality. They found that the endorsement of a pessimistic life orientation is an important risk factor for mortality among middle-aged (ages 30 to 59) but not older individuals. The pessimism of the older individuals may reflect a coping strategy that has become adaptive in the face of declining ability to control important life outcomes such as health.

The basic tenet of the cognitive style approach to the study of emotion and aging is that constructs involving the lenses through which individuals understand their environment may predict who gets happier and sadder over time, especially in the face of stressful life events. Isaacowitz and Seligman (2002) found that a more optimistic explanatory style for health-related events predicted more depressive symptoms over time among community-dwelling older adults. Thus, an extremely optimistic explanatory style may in some cases be maladaptive. As expected, the authors found that higher levels of dispositional optimism predicted better affective functioning, whereas higher levels of dispositional pessimism were related to worse affective profiles over time.

An optimistic explanatory style and dispositional optimism were not correlated with each other in the beginning of the study. Isaacowitz and Seligman (2002) speculate that one way in which they might produce opposite effects would be if dispositional optimists are sensitive to situational constraints and can transition from problem-focused to emotion-focused coping when the situation they face cannot be changed. It is possible that dispositional optimism involves this flexible coping style, whereas an optimistic explanatory style demands active attempts to fix the problem and control the environment. This explanation suggests that optimistic individuals are more likely to engage in selection, optimization, and compensation due to the greater flexibility of their coping strategies.

Postscript: Goals and Personality

Since individuals apply coping strategies in the context of their goals or their personalities, examination of personality or goals may explain some of the contradictory findings of the effects of dispositional optimism and pessimism on physical and psychological outcomes in older adults, just as it did in Segerstrom's (2001) study of optimism, goal conflict, and stressor-related immune change.

There is evidence that this interactive process of personality in relationship to goals and adjustment may be positive at later life. Block and Block (1980) noted that two personality dimensions, ego-control and ego-resiliency, are moderately consistent across the life span. More recent research has demonstrated that personality at the trait level is reasonably consistent (McRae & Costa, 1990) but develops uniquely well into adulthood (Viallant, 1977). It now appears that individuals may be open to new experiences well into old age. In older age it is most likely that, when there are losses, resources are devoted to maintenance and recovery (resilience) and that this can be creative.

The influence of interaction between the coping mechanisms of support, control, personality, and goals is complex. Interactions of the person's behavior and the environment are almost always present. People are self-organizing, proactive, self-reflecting, and self-regulating and are not just reactive to external events (Bandura, 1999). Perhaps the most parsimonious and realistic view of human actions is that the person is neither driven by global traits nor automatically shaped by the environment. Change is not random; it is guided by a personality system which mediates the relationship between types of situations and the cognitive/affective behavior patterns of the person (Mischel & Shoda, 1999). Thus, there are predictable, characteristic patterns of variation in the person's behavior across situations and age. Organisms self-organize and do so naturally, consistently, and holistically.

The transition to old age is accompanied by an increased awareness of what one cannot do in the context of what one can do. This awareness influences the type of goals selected in late life. Since the central task of later life is facing decline, one's possibilities adjust accordingly. The adjustment process is a function of health, identity (personal characteristics), and attachment (social relationships and positive contacts). The elderly are not just seeking to avoid undesirable outcomes or maintain the current status. The desire for new experiences continues into old age. And with the younger old, there is the presence of motivation for change. Smith and Freund (2002) showed that 72% of participants added new domains of hope and 53% added new fears.

CONCLUSION

We noted at the beginning that as aging unfolds, the person must adjust. Evidence suggests that this adjustment is not a singular event but continues over a lifetime as debility changes. Evidence also suggests that adjustment can be for better or worse. The main path to aging adjustment or disability is shaped by imbedded risk factors (such as behavioral, psychological, and biological) and mediated, we believe, by the coping mechanisms as applied in the SOC model. These involve lifestyle and behavioral actions as well as appropriate psychosocial attitudes.

Age itself is largely an empty variable. It is not the passage of time alone but various biological and social events that occur with the passage of time that have relevance for change. People continuously revise their choices in life (SOC) and do so best by application of the coping mechanisms of support and control. The application of selection, optimization, and compensation is associated with better functioning. These components also require the use of resources; the more, the better. Importantly, we have advocated that social support and control (as well as dispositional optimism) allow for the best unfolding of SOC. We have also intimated that older individuals apply these coping strategies in the context of their goals or their personality, often for the better.

We conclude with a summary of what occurs in therapy. Recent evidence suggests that identifiable internal and external events influence and re-create conditions for positive or negative outcomes in therapy. Much of what goes on involves an attempt to shift people's focus to watch themselves more closely in their daily lives. In this way, change is a function of having people respond differently to new situations or new contingencies. Older people do benefit from this therapy contract—really an SOC understanding of problem as influenced by age. Optimism-generating, support-assisting, and control-enhancing interventions make a difference in this context. The enhancement of a sense of control and modification of the environment make a difference in several settings, even in long-term care facilities. Increasing social networks and creating control appropriately maximize satisfaction and assist in protection from psychological distress.

REFERENCES

Abeles, R., Cooley, S., Deitch, I., Harper, M., Hinrichsen, G., Lopez, M., & Molinari, V. (1998). *What practitioners should know about working with older adults.* Washington, DC: American Psychological Association.

American Psychiatric Association. (2000). *Handbook of psychiatric measures.* Washington, DC: American Psychiatric Association.

Baltes, M., & Wahl, H. (1990). The dependency-support script in institutions: Generalization to community settings. *Psychology and Aging, 7,* 409–417.

Baltes, P., & Baltes, M. (1980). Plasticity and variability in psychological aging: Methodological and theoretical issues. In G. E. Gorski (Ed.), *Determining the effects of aging in the central nervous system* (pp. 41–46). Berlin: Shering.

Baltes, P., & Baltes, M. (1990). *Successful aging: Perspectives from the behavioral sciences.* Cambridge, U.K.: Cambridge University Press.

Bandura, A. (1999). Social cognitive theory of personality. In L. Pervin & O. John (Eds.), *Handbook of personality: Theory and research.* New York: Guilford.

Berkman, L. F. (1995). The role of social relations in health promotion. *Psychosomatic Medicine, 57,* 245–254.

Block, J., & Block, J. (1980). The role of ego control and ego resiliency in the organization of behavior. In W. A. Collins (Ed.), *Minnesota symposium on child psychology.* Hillside, NJ: Erlbaum.

Blumenthal H. T. (2003). The aging-disease dichotomy: True or false. *Journal of Gerontology, SBA,* 138–145.

Brandstadler, J., & Greve, W. (1994). The aging self: Stabilizing and protecting processes. *Developmental Review, 14,* 52–80.

Carstensen, L., Isaacowitz, D., & Charles, S. (1999). Taking time seriously: A theory of socioemotional selectivity. *American Psychologist, 54,* 165–181.

Carstensen, L., & Turk-Charles, S. (1994). The salience of emotion across the life span. *Psychology and Aging, 9,* 259–264.

Carstensen, L. L. (1992). Social and emotional patterns in adulthood: Support for socioemotional selectivity theory. *Psychology and Aging, 7,* 331–338.

Carver, C. S., & Scheier, M. F. (1999). Optimism. In C. Snyder (Ed.), *Coping: The psychology of what works.* New York: Oxford Univeristy Press.

Carver, C. S., & Scheier, M. F. (2001). Optimism, pessimism, and self-regulation. In E. C. Chang (Ed.), *Optimism and pessimism: Implications for theory, research, and practice* (pp. 13–30). Washington, DC: American Psychological Association.

Cohen, S. (1988). Psychosocial models of the role of social support in the etiology of physical disease. *Health Psychology, 7,* 269–297.

Cohen, S., Doyle, W. J., Skoner, D. P., Rabin, B. S., & Gwaltney, J. M. (1997). Social ties and susceptibility to the common cold. *Journal of the American Medical Association, 277,* 1940–1944.

Cohen, S., & Syme, S. L. (1985). *Social support and health.* Orlando, FL: Academic Press.

Contrada, R., Cather, C., & O'Leary, A. (1999). Personality and health: Disposition and processes in disease susceptibility and adaptation to illness. In L. Pervin & O. John (Eds.), *Handbook of personality: Theory and research* (pp. 576–605). New York: Guilford.

Duke, J., Leventhal, H., Brownlee, S., Leventhal, E. A. (2002). Giving up and replacing activities in response to illness. *Journal of Gerontology, 57B,* 367–376.

Eizenmann, D. R., Nesserloade, J. R., Featherman, D. L., & Rowe, J. W. (1998). Intraindividual variability in perceived control in an older sample. The MacArthur successful aging studies. *Psychology and Aging, 12,* 489–502.

Freund, A., & Baltes, P. (1998). Selection, optimization, and compensation as strategies of life management: Correlations with subjective indicators of aging. *Psychology and Aging, 13,* 431–543.

Fry, P. S., & Wong, P. T. (1991). Pain management training in the elderly: Matching interventions with subjects' coping styles. *Stress Medicine, 7,* 93–98.

Fung, H. H., Carstensen, L. L., & Lang, F. R. (2001). Age-related patterns of social networks among European American and African Americans: Implications for socioemotional selectivity across the life span. *International Journal of Aging and Human Development, 52,* 185–206.

Geriatric Psychiatry Alliance. (1996). *Diagnosis and treatment of late-life depression: Making a difference.* Washington, DC: American Association of Geriatric Psychiatry.

Gerontological Society of America. (2000). *The state of aging and health in America.* Washington, DC: Merck Institute of Aging and Health.

Hyer, L., & Sohnle, S. (2001). *Trauma among older people: Issues and treatment.* Philadelphia: Brunner-Routledge.

Isaacowitz, D. M., & Seligman, M. E. P. (1998). *Prevention of depression in older adults: Theory, methodology, and pitfalls.* Paper presented at the Annual Meeting of the American Psychological Association, San Francisco.

Isaacowitz, D. M., & Seligman, M. E. P. (2002). Cognitive style predictors of affect change in older adults. *International Journal of Aging and Human Development, 54,* 233–253.

Jang, Y., Haley, W., Small, B., & Mortimer, J. (2002). The role of mastery and social resources in the associations between disability and depression in later life. *The Gerontologist, 42,* 807–813.

Kahana, E. (1982). A congruence model of person-environment interaction. In P. Lawton, P. Windley, & T. Byerts (Eds.), *Aging and environment: Theoretical approaches* (pp. 97–121). New York: Springer.

Keller, M. L., Leventhal, E. A., & Larson, B. (1989). Aging: The lived experience. *International Journal of Aging & Human Development, 29,* 67–82.

Keller, M., Leventhal, H., Prohaska, T. R., & Leventhal, E. A. (1989). Beliefs about aging and illness in a community sample. *Research in Nursing and Health, 12,* 247–255.

Keyes, C. L. M. (2002). The exchange of emotional support with age and its relationship with emotional well-being by age. *Journal of Gerontology: Psychological Sciences, 57B,* 518–525.

Knight, B., & Satre, D. (1996). Cognitive behavioral psychotherapy with older adults. *Clinical Psychology: Science and Practice, 6,* 188–203.

Kunzmann, U., Little, T., & Smith, J. (2002). Perceiving control: A double edge sword in old age. *Journal of Gerontology: Psychological Sciences, 57B,* 484–492.

Lang, F., & Carstensen, L. (2002). Time counts: Future time perspective, goals, and social relationships. *Psychology and Aging, 17,* 125–139.

Lang, F., Reickmann, N., & Baltes, M. (2002). Adapting to aging losses: Do resources facilitate strategies of selection, compensation, and optimization in everyday functioning. *Journal of Gerontology, 57B,* 501–509.

Lang, F. R., Staudinger, U. M., & Carstensen, L. L. (1998). Perspective on socioemotional selectivity in late life: How personality and social context do (and do not) make a difference. *Journal of Gerontology: Psychological Sciences, 53,* 21–30.

Langer, E. J., & Rodin, J. (1976). The effects of choice and enhanced personal responsibility for the aged: A field experiment in an institutional setting. *Journal of Personality and Social Psychology, 37,* 191–198.

Lawton, P., & Nahemow, L. (1973). Ecology and the aging process. In C. Eisdorfer & P. Lawton (Eds.), *The psychology of adult development and aging.* Washington, DC: American Psychological Association.

Lyons, K., Zarit, S., Sayer, A., & Whitlach, C. (2002). Caregiving as a dyadic process: Perspectives from caregiver and receiver. *Journal of Gerontology, 57B,* 195–205.

McRae, R., & Costa, P. (1990). *Personality in adulthood.* New York: Guilford.

Melding, P. S. (1995). How do older people respond to chronic pain? A review of coping with pain and illness in elders. *Pain Reviews, 2,* 65–75.

Mischel, W., & Shoda, Y. (1999). Integrating dispositions and processing dynamics with a unified theory of personality: The cognitive-affective personality system. In L. Pervin & O. John (Eds.), *Handbook of personality: Theory and research.* New York: Guilford.

Norem, J. K., & Chang, E. C. (2001). A very full glass: Adding complexity to our thinking about the implications and applications of optimism and pessimism research. In E. C. Chang (Ed.), *Optimism and pessimism: Implications for theory, research, and practice* (pp. 347–367). Washington, DC: American Psychological Association.

Ormel, J., Kempen, G., Deeg, D., Brilman, E., van Sonderven, E., & Relyveld, J. (1998). Functioning, well-being, and health perception in late middle-aged and older people: Comparing the effects of depressive symptoms and chronic medical conditions. *Journal of the American Geriatrics Society, 46,* 39–48.

Pinard, C., & Landreville, P. (1998). Adaptation strategies, depressive symptoms, anxiety, and well-being among aged persons living in an institutional setting. *Canadian Journal on Aging, 17,* 40–58.

Putnam, M. (2002). Linking aging theory and disability models: Increasing the potential to explore aging with physical impairment. *The Gerontologist, 42,* 799–806.

Roberts, B. L., Dunkle, R., & Hang, M. (1994). Physical, psychological, and social resources as moderators of the relationship of stress to mental health of the very old. *Journal of Gerontology, 49,* 535–543.

Robinson-Whelen, S., Kim, C., MacCallum, R. C., & Kiecolt-Glaser, J. K. (1997). Distinguishing optimism from pessimism in older adults: Is it more important to be optimistic or not to be pessimistic? *Journal of Personality and Social Psychology, 73,* 1345–1353.

Rodin, J. (1990). Control by any other name: Definitions, concepts, and processes. In J. Rodin, C. Schooler, & K. W. Schaie (Eds.), *Self-directedness: Cause and effects throughout the life course.* Hillsdale, NJ: Erlbaum.

Rotter, J. B. (1966). Generalized expectancies for internal vs. external control of reinforcement. *Psychological Monographs, 80,* 1–28.

Rowe, J. W., & Kahn, R. L. (1987). Human aging: Usual and successful. *Science, 237,* 143–149.

Schultz, R., & Heckhausen, J. (1996). A life span model of successful aging. *American Psychologist, 51,* 702–714.

Schulz, R., Bookwala, J., Knapp, J., Scheier, M., & Williamson, G. M. (1996). Pessimism, age, and cancer mortality. *Psychology and Aging, 11,* 304–309.

Seeman, M., & Lewis, S. (1995). Powerlessness, health, and mortality: A longitudinal study of older men and mature women. *Social Science and Medicine, 41,* 486–517.

Segerstrom, S. C. (2001). Optimism, goal conflict, and stressor-related immune change. *Journal of Behavioral Medicine, 24,* 441–467.

Smith, J., & Freund, A. (2002). The dynamics of possible selves in old age. *Journal of Gerontology, 57,* 492–501.

Steverink, N., Westeroff, G., Bode, C., & Dittmana-Koli, F. (2001). The personal experience of aging, individual resources, and subjective well-being. *Journal of Gerontology, 56B,* 364–373.

Thoits, P. A. (1995). Stress, coping, and social support processes: Where are we? What next? *Journal of Health and Social Behavior, Extra Issue,* 53–79.

Thornstam, L. (1996). Gerotranscendence: A theory about maturing into old age. *Journal of Aging and Identity, 1,* 37–50.

Timko, C., & Moos, R. H. (1989). Choice, control, and adaptation among elderly residents of sheltered care settings. *Journal of Applied Psychology, 8,* 636–655.

Uchino, B. N., Cacioppo, J. T., & Kiecolt-Glaser, J. K. (1996). The relationship between social support and physiological processes: A review with emphasis on underlying mechanisms and implications for health. *Psychological Bulletin, 119,* 455–531.

Van den Akker, M., Buntinx, F., Metsemakers, J. F., van der Aa, M., & Knottnerus, J. A. (2001). Psychosocial patient characteristics and GP-registered chronic morbidity: A prospective study. *Journal of Psychosomatic Research, 50,* 95–102.

Viallant, G. (1977). *Adaptation to life.* Boston: Little Brown.

Walter-Ginzburg, A., Blumenstein, T., Chetrit, A., & Modan, B. (2002). Social factors and mortality in the old-old in Israel: The CALAS study. *Journal of Gerontology: Social Sciences, 57B,* 308–318.

Weaver, G. D., & Gary, L. E. (1996). Correlates of health-related behaviors in older Black adults: Implications for health promotion. *Family Community Health, 19,* 43–57.

Wolfe, R., Morrow, J., & Fredickson, B. (1996). Mood disorders in older adults. In L. Carstensen, B. Edelstein, & L. Dornbrand (Eds.), *The practical handbook of clinical gerontology* (pp. 274–303). New York: Sage.

5

Families and Chronic Illness: An Integrative Model

JOHN S. ROLLAND

Illness, disability, and death are universal experiences in families. Chronic and life-threatening conditions confront all of us with some of life's greatest challenges. The impact of a diagnosis of cancer reverberates throughout the family system, leaving no one untouched. The quality of life deteriorates for some families and family members, whereas others are resilient and thrive (Weihs, Fisher, & Baird, 2001). We need conceptual models that guide both clinical practice and research, and allow a dynamic, open communication between these disciplines. What is most wanted is a comprehensive way to organize our thinking about all the complex interactions between the biological illness, family, individual family members, and professionals involved in providing care. We need models that can accommodate the changing landscape of interactions between these parts of the system over the course of the illness and the changing seasons of the life cycle.

Families enter the world of illness and disability without a psychosocial map. Appropriate clinical intervention, family education, and national policies to support these families are severely lacking. To master the challenges, families need, first, a psychosocial understanding of the condition in system terms. This means learning the expected pattern of practical and emotional demands over the course of the disorder, including a timeline for disease-related developmental tasks associated with different phases of the disorder. Second, they need a systemic understanding of themselves as a functional unit. Third, an appreciation of the individual, couples, and family life cycles helps them stay attuned to the changing fit between the demands of a chronic disorder and emerging developmental issues for the family unit and each member. Finally, families need to understand the beliefs and multigenerational legacies that guide their constructions of meanings about health problems and their relationship to caregiving systems and health care providers.

In order to organize this complex landscape in a manner useful to families and clinical practice, we need a conceptual framework that can serve as a guide for families coping with major illness.

OVERVIEW OF FAMILY SYSTEMS–ILLNESS MODEL

With chronic disorders, a biopsychosocial orientation should be conceptualized from a systems perspective, with the family as the interactive focal point. The unfolding of a chronic disorder is best viewed in developmental context, involving the intertwining of three evolutionary threads: the illness, the individual, and family development.

The family systems–illness model (Rolland, 1984, 1987a, 1987b, 1990, 1994a, 1994b, 1998, 2002) provides a useful framework for evaluation, formulation, and intervention with families dealing with chronic illness and disability. The model is based on a strength-oriented perspective viewing family relationships as a resource and emphasizing the possibilities for resilience and growth—not just their liabilities and risks (Walsh, 1996, 1998).

The model addresses three dimensions: (a) psychosocial types of illness and disability, (b) major developmental phases in their natural history, and (c) key family system variables (Figure 5.1). It attends to the expected psychosocial demands of a disorder through its various phases, family systems dynamics that emphasize family and individual life cycles, multigenerational patterns, and belief systems (Figure 5.2). The model emphasizes the goodness of fit between the psychosocial demands of the disorder over time and the strengths and vulnerabilities of a family.

PSYCHOSOCIAL TYPES OF ILLNESS

The standard disease classification is based on purely biological criteria, clustered to establish a medical diagnosis and treatment plan, rather than the psychosocial demands on patients and their families. I have proposed a different classification schema that provides a better

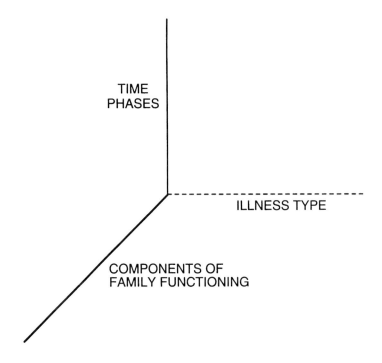

FIGURE 5.1. Three-dimensional model: illness type, time phase, family functioning. Note: From "Chronic Illness and the Life Cycle: A Conceptual Framework," by J. S. Roland, 1987, *Family Process*, 26, no. 2, 203–221.

link between the biological and psychosocial worlds, clarifying the relationship between chronic illness and the family (Rolland, 1984, 1987a, 1994). Chronic conditions can be grouped according to key biological similarities and differences with distinct psychosocial demands for the patient and family. The clinical manifestation of the full spectrum of illness and disabilites presents an enormously diverse range of expected psychosocial demands. This typology defines meaningful and useful categories with similar psychosocial demands for a wide array of chronic illnesses affecting individuals across the life span. Illness patterning can vary in terms of onset, course, outcome, incapacitation, and the level of uncertainty about its trajectory.

Onset: Illnesses can be divided into those that have either an acute clinical onset, such as strokes, or gradual onset, such as Alzheimer's disease. For acute onset illnesses, affective and practical changes are compressed into a short time, requiring more rapid mobilization of crisis management skills. Families need to be helped to tolerate highly charged emotional situations, exchange roles flexibly, problem solve efficiently, and utilize outside resources.

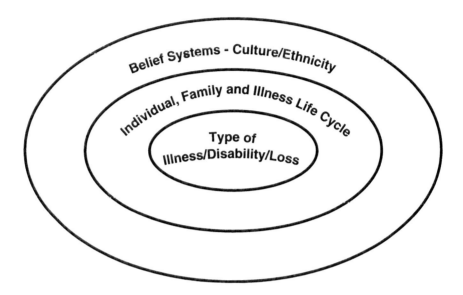

FIGURE 5.2.   Family Systems—Illness Model. Note: From *Families, Illness and Disability: An Integrative Treatment Model*, by J. S. Roland, 1994, New York: Basic Books. Adapted with permission.

Course: The course of chronic diseases can take three general trajectories: progressive, constant, or relapsing or episodic. With a *progressive* disease such as metastatic cancer, disability worsens in a stepwise or gradual way. The family must live with perpetual symptoms, the prospect of continual role change as the disease progresses, growing strain and exhaustion, few periods of relief, and new caretaking and financial challenges over time.

With a *constant* course illness an initial event is followed by a stable biological course, as after a single heart attack or spinal cord injury. Typically, after an initial period of recovery, there persists a clear-cut deficit or limitation. The family is faced with a semipermanent change that is stable and predictable over a considerable time span. The potential for family exhaustion exists without the strain of new role demands over time.

A *relapsing* or *episodic* course illness, like disc problems and asthma, are distinguished by the alternation of stable low symptom periods with periods of flare-up or exacerbation. Families are strained by both the frequency of transitions between crisis and noncrisis, and the ongoing uncertainty of when a recurrence will occur. This requires family flexibility to alternate between two forms of family organization. The wide psychological discrepancy between periods of normalcy versus flare-up is particularly taxing and is unique to relapsing conditions.

Outcome: The extent to which a chronic illness leads to death or shortens one's life span has profound psychosocial impact. The continuum ranges from illnesses that do not typically affect the life span, such as disc disease or arthritis, to those that are progressive and usually fatal, such as metastatic cancer. An intermediate, more unpredictable category includes both illnesses that can shorten the life span such as cardiovascular disease, and those with the possibility of sudden death such as hemophilia. Crucial factors are family members' initial expectation of whether or not a disease is likely to cause death and the degree to which they experience anticipatory loss (Rolland, 1990).

Incapacitation: Disability can involve impairment of cognition (e.g., dementia), sensation (e.g., blindness), movement (e.g., stroke with paralysis), stamina (e.g., cardiovascular disease), disfiguring conditions (e.g., severe burns, mastectomy), and those associated with social stigma (e.g., AIDS) (Olkin, 1999). The extent, kind, and timing of incapacitation will affect the degree of family stress. For instance, the combined cognitive and motor deficits caused by a major stroke necessitate greater family role reallocation than a spinal cord injury in a person who retains his cognitive abilities. With some illnesses, like stroke, disability is often worst at the beginning. For progressive diseases, like Alzheimer's disease, disability looms as an increasing problem in later phases of the illness, allowing a family more time to prepare for anticipated changes. This allows an opportunity for the ill member to participate in disease-related family planning while still cognitively able (Boss, 1999).

By combining the kinds of onset, course, outcome, and incapacitation into a grid format, we generate a typology that clusters illnesses according to similarities and differences in patterns that pose differing psychosocial demands (Figure 5.3).

Level of uncertainty: The predictability of an illness and the degree of uncertainty about the specific way or rate at which it unfolds overlay all other variables. For illnesses with highly unpredictable courses such as multiple sclerosis, family coping and future planning are hindered by anticipatory anxiety and ambiguity about what is to come and how much time they have before the condition worsens. Families who are able to put long-term uncertainty into perspective are best prepared to avoid the risks of exhaustion and dysfunction.

TIME PHASES OF ILLNESS

Too often, discussions of coping with cancer tend to approach illness as a static state and fail to appreciate the dynamic unfolding of the illness process over time. The concept of time phases provides a way for clinicians to think longitudinally and to understand chronic illness as an

	INCAPACITATING		NONINCAPACITATING	
	Acute	**Gradual**	**Acute**	**Gradual**
FATAL Progressive Relapsing		Lung cancer with CNS metastases AIDS Bone marrow failure Amyotrophic lateral sclerosis	Acute leukemia Pancreatic cancer Metastatic breast cancer Malignant melanoma Lung cancer Liver cancer	Cystic fibrosis*
			Incurable cancers in remission	
POSSIBLY FATAL/ SHORTENED LIFE SPAN Progressive Relapsing		Emphysema Alzheimer's disease Multi-infarct dementia Multiple sclerosis (late) Chronic alcoholism Huntington's chorea Scleroderma		Juvenile diabetes* Malignant hypertension Insulin-dependent adult-onset diabetes
Constant	Angina	Early multiple sclerosis Episodic alcoholism	Sickle cell disease* Hemophilia*	Systemic lupus erythematosis*
	Stroke Moderate/severe myocardial infarction	P.K.U. and other congenital errors of metabolism	Mild myocardial infarction Cardiac arrhythmia	Hemodialysis treated renal failure Hodgkin's disease
NONFATAL Progressive		Parkinson's disease Rheumatoid arthritis Osteoarthritis		Non insulin-dependent adult-onset diabetes
Relapsing	Lumbosacral disc disorder		Kidney stones Gout Migraine Seasonal allergy Asthma Epilepsy	Peptic ulcer Ulcerative colitis Chronic bronchitis Irritable bowel syndrome Psoriasis
Constant	Congenital malformations Spinal cord injury Acute blindness Acute deafness Survived severe trauma & burns Posthypoxic syndrome	Nonprogressive mental retardation Cerebral palsy	Benign arrhythmia Congenital heart disease	Malabsorption syndromes Hyper/hypothyroidism Pernicious anemia Controlled hypertension Controlled glaucoma

FIGURE 5.3. Categorization of chronic illnesses by psychosocial type.
* = Early
Note: From "Toward a Psychosocial Typology of Chronic and Life- Threatening Illness," by J. S. Rolland, 1984, *Family Systems Medicine,* 2, pp. 245–262. Adapted with permission of Family Process Inc.

ongoing process with landmarks, transitions, and changing demands. Each phase has its own psychosocial developmental tasks that require significantly different family strengths, attitudes, or changes from a family. To capture the core psychosocial themes in the natural history of chronic disorders, three major phases can be described: crisis, chronic, and terminal (Figure 5.4 & Table 5.1).

Crisis phase: The crisis phase includes any symptomatic period before diagnosis and the initial period of readjustment and treatment plan. This initial period of socialization to chronic illness holds a number of key developmental tasks for the patient and family (Moos, 1984), which include creating a meaning for the disorder that preserves a sense of mastery; grieving the loss of the pre-illness family identity; acceptance of permanency of the condition; undergoing short-term crisis reorganization while developing family flexibility in the face of uncertainty and threatened loss; learning to live with illness-related symptoms and treatments; and forging a working relationship with professionals and institutional settings.

During this initial crisis period, health professionals have enormous influence over a family's sense of competence and their approach to these developmental tasks. Initial meetings and advice given at the time of diagnosis can be thought of as a framing event. Because family members are so vulnerable at this point, clinicians need to be sensitive in their interactions and aware of messages conveyed by their behavior. Who is included or excluded (e.g., patient) from a discussion can be interpreted by the family as a message conveying how the family should communicate for the duration of the illness. For instance, if a clinician meets with parents separately from adolescents to give them information about a cancer diagnosis and prognosis, the parents may assume they

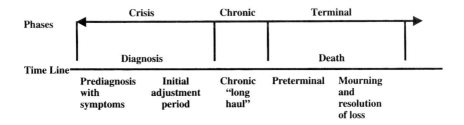

FIGURE 5.4. Time line and phases of illness.
Note: From *Families, Illness, and Disability: An Integrative Treatment Model,* by J. S. Rolland, 1994, New York: Basic Books. Adapted with permission.

TABLE 5.1
Time Phases of Illness Developmental Tasks

Crisis Phase

1. Families understanding themselves in systems terms
2. Psychosocial understanding of illness
    (a) in practical and emotional terms
    (b) in longitudinal and developmental terms
3. Family appreciation of developmental perspective (individual, family, illness life cycles)
4. Crisis reorganization
5. Creating meaning that promotes family mastery and competence
6. Defining challenge in "we" terms
7. Accepting permanence of illness and disability
8. Grieving loss of family identity before chronic disorder
9. Acknowledging possibilities of further loss while sustaining hope
10. Developing flexibility to ongoing psychosocial demands of illness
11. Learning to live with symptoms
12. Adapting to treatments and health care settings
13. Establishing functional collaborative relationship with health care providers

Chronic Phase

1. Maximizing autonomy for all family members given constraints of illness
2. Balancing connectedness and separateness
3. Minimizing relationship skews
4. Mindfulness to possible impact on current and future phases of family and individual life cycles

Terminal Phase

1. Completing process of anticipatory grief and unresolved family issues
2. Supporting the terminally ill member
3. Helping survivors and dying member live as fully as possible with time remaining
4. Beginning the family reorganization process

Note: From *Families, Illness, and Disability: An Integrative Treatment Model,* by J. S. Rolland, 1994, New York: Basic Books. Adapted with permission.

were being instructed implicitly to protect their adolescent from any discussion of the illness.

Chronic phase: The chronic phase can be marked by constancy, progression, or episodic change. It has been referred to as "the long haul" or the "day-to-day living with chronic illness phase." Salient issues include pacing and avoiding burnout; relationship skews between the patient and other family members; sustaining autonomy and preserving or redefining individual and family developmental goals within the constraints of the illness; and sustaining intimacy in the face of threatened loss. Family effort to maintain the semblance of a normal life is a key task of this period. If the illness is fatal, this is a time of living in limbo. For certain highly debilitating but not clearly fatal illnesses, such as a massive stroke, the family can feel saddled with an exhausting problem without end. Encouraging maximal autonomy for *all* family members in the face of protracted adversity helps offset these trapped, helpless feelings. For instance, customary patterns of intimacy for couples become skewed by discrepancies between ill and well spouse or caregiver. Emotions often remain underground and contribute later to survivor guilt. As one young husband lamented about his wife's cancer, "It was hard enough two years ago to absorb that, even if Ann was cured, her radiation treatment would make pregnancy impossible. Now I find it unbearable that her continued uncertain battle with cancer makes it impossible to go for our dreams like other couples our age." Psychoeducational family interventions that normalize such emotions related to threatened loss can help prevent cycles of blame, shame, and guilt. Also, when physicians inquire about and validate the psychosocial burden of caregivers, especially well spouses, they help prevent the physical burden of the patient from becoming the only currency in family relationships. This approach facilitates families seeing a chronic disorder as a "we" problem (rather than solely the domain of the patient), a major contributor to dysfunctional family dynamics when living with a serious illness.

Terminal phase: In the terminal phase of an illness the inevitability of death becomes apparent and dominates family life. The family must cope with issues of separation, death, mourning, and family reorganization beyond the loss (Walsh & McGoldrick, 2004). Families adapt best to this phase when they are able to shift their view of mastery from controlling the illness to a successful process of letting go. Optimal coping involves emotional openness as well as dealing with the myriad of practical tasks. Families can be helped to see this phase as an opportunity to share precious time together, acknowledge the impending loss, deal with unfinished business, say goodbyes, and begin the process of family reorganization. The patient and key family members need to decide about such things as a living will, involvement of hospice, wishes about a funeral, and provision for the surviving family members.

Critical transition periods link the three time phases during which families reevaluate the fit of their previous life structure with new illness-related developmental demands. Unfinished business can complicate or block movement forward. Families can become permanently frozen in an adaptive structure that has outlived its utility (Penn, 1983). For example, the usefulness of pulling together in the crisis phase can become maladaptive and stifling in a long chronic phase.

Clinical Applications

In sum, the time phases (crisis, chronic, and terminal) can be considered broad developmental periods in the natural history of chronic disease. Each period has certain basic tasks independent of the type of illness. Each type of illness has specific supplementary tasks. The psychosocial demands of any condition can be thought about in relation to each phase of the disorder and to different components of family functioning (e.g., communication, problem solving, role flexibility).

The model clarifies research design and treatment planning. Goal setting is guided by awareness of the components of family functioning most relevant to particular types or phases of an illness. Sharing this information with the family and deciding on specific goals provides a better sense of control and realistic hope to the family. This process empowers families in their journey of living with chronic conditions. Also, this knowledge educates the family about warning signs that should alert them to call on a family therapist at appropriate times for brief, goal-oriented treatment.

This framework can guide periodic family consultations and psychosocial checkups as salient issues and priorities surface and change over time. Preventively oriented family psychoeducational or support groups for patients and their families (Gonzalez, Steinglass, & Reiss, 1989; Steinglass, 1998) can be designed to deal with different types of conditions (e.g., progressive, life-threatening, relapsing). Also, brief psychoeducational modules timed for critical phases of an illness enable families to digest manageable portions of a long-term coping process. Modules can be tailored to particular phases of the illness and to family coping skills necessary to confront disease-related demands. This provides a cost-effective preventive service that also can identify high-risk families.

The model also informs evaluation of general functioning and illness specific family dynamics such as the interface of the illness with individual and family development; the family's multigenerational history of coping with illness, loss, and other adversity; the family's health or illness belief system; the meaning of the illness to the family; social support and use of community resources; and the family's capacity to manage illness-related crises or perform home-based medical care. At a larger systems level, the model provides a lens for clinicians to analyze shifts in relationships between health care institutions, professionals, the patient, and family members.

FAMILY LEGACIES, LIFE CYCLES, AND BELIEF SYSTEMS

Multigenerational Legacies of Illness, Loss, and Crisis

A family's current behavior, and therefore its response to illness, cannot be adequately comprehended apart from its history (Bowen, 1978; Carter & McGoldrick, 1998; Framo, 1992; Walsh & McGoldrick, 2004). Clinicians can use historical questioning and can construct a genogram and timeline (McGoldrick, Gerson, & Schellenberger, 1999) to gain an understanding of a family's organizational shifts and coping strategies as a system in response to past stressors, and more specifically, to past illnesses. Such inquiry helps explain and predict the family's current style of coping, adaptation, and creation of meaning. A multigenerational assessment helps to clarify areas of strength and vulnerability. It also identifies high-risk families burdened by past unresolved issues and dysfunctional patterns that cannot absorb the challenges presented by a serious condition.

A chronic illness-oriented genogram focuses on how a family organized around past stressors and tracks the evolution of family adaptation over time. It shows how a family organized as an evolving system specifically around previous illnesses and unexpected crises. A central goal is to bring to light areas of consensus and learned differences (Penn, 1983) that are sources of cohesion and conflict. Patterns of coping, replications, discontinuities, shifts in relationships (i.e., alliances, triangles, cutoff), and sense of competence are noted. These patterns are transmitted across generations as family pride, myths, taboos, catastrophic expectations, and belief systems (Walsh & McGoldrick, 2004). In one case involving a husband diagnosed with basal cell carcinoma, the oncologist discussed a favorable prognosis, yet the wife believed her husband would die from this skin cancer. This resulted in increased marital discord and ultimately a couple's consultation. In the initial interview, when asked about prior experiences with illness and loss, the wife revealed that her own father had died tragically of a misdiagnosed malignant melanoma. This woman had a catastrophic fear based on both sensitization to cancer (particularly any related to the skin) and the possibility of human error by health professionals. Had the oncologist inquired about prior experiences at the time of diagnosis, earlier intervention would have been facilitated.

It is also useful to inquire about other forms of loss (e.g., divorce, migration), crisis (e.g., lengthy unemployment, rape, a natural disaster), and protracted adversity (e.g., poverty, racism, war, political oppression). These experiences can provide transferable sources of resilience and effective coping skills in the face of a serious health problem (Walsh, 1998).

Illness Type and Time Phase Issues

Whereas a family may have standard ways of coping with any illness, there may be critical differences in their style and success in adaptation to different types of diseases. It is important to track prior family illnesses for areas of perceived competence, failures, or inexperience. Inquiry about different types of illness (e.g., life-threatening versus non–life-threatening) may find, for instance, that a family dealt successfully with non–life-threatening illnesses but reeled under the weight of metastatic cancer. Such a family might be well equipped to deal with less severe conditions, but it might be particularly vulnerable if another life-threatening illness were to occur.

Tracking a family's coping capabilities in the crisis, chronic, and terminal phases of previous chronic illnesses highlights legacies of strength as well as complication in adaptation related to different points over the course of the illness. One man grew up with a partially disabled father with heart disease, and witnessed his parents successfully renegotiate traditional gender-defined roles when his mother went to work while his father assumed household responsibilities. This man, now with heart disease himself, has a positive legacy about gender roles from his family of origin that facilitated a flexible response to his own illness. Another family with a member with chronic kidney failure functioned very well in handling the practicalities of home dialysis. However, in the terminal phase, their limitations with emotional expression left a legacy of unresolved grief. Tracking prior illness experiences in terms of time phases helps clinicians see both the strengths and vulnerabilities in a family, which counteracts the assignment of dysfunctional labels that emphasize the difficult periods. Clinicians need to ask specifically about positive family-of-origin experiences with illness and loss that can be used as models to adapt to the current situation.

For any significant illness in either adult spouse's family of origin, a clinician should try to get a picture of how those families organized to handle the range of disease-related affective and practical tasks. What role did each play in handling these tasks and did they emerge with a strong sense of competence or failure? Such information can help to anticipate areas of conflict and consensus and similar patterns of adaptation. Hidden strengths, not just unresolved issues, can remain dormant in a marriage and suddenly reemerge when triggered by a chronic illness in the current family unit.

While many families facing chronic disease have healthy multigenerational family patterns of adaptation, any family may falter in the face of multiple superimposed disease and nondisease stressors that impact in a relatively short time. With progressive, incapacitating diseases or the concurrence of illnesses in several family members, a pragmatic approach that focuses on expanded or creative use of supports and resources outside the family is most productive.

Interface of Individual, Family, and Illness Development

When a condition is chronic, the dimension of time becomes a central reference point. The family, as well as each member, faces the formidable challenge of focusing simultaneously on the present and the future, which includes mastering the practical and emotional tasks of the immediate situation while charting a course for dealing with the complexities and uncertainties of their problem in an uncertain future. This task is facilitated by placing the unfolding chronic condition in a developmental framework that integrates the three evolutionary threads—illness, individual, and family development (Rolland, 1987a, 1994). It is essential to consider the interaction of individual and family development. A chronic disorder will influence the development of the affected person and various family members in distinct ways, depending on a number of factors including age of onset of the illness, the core commitments in the affected person and each family member's life at that time, and the stage of the family life cycle. Life-cycle models can facilitate thinking proactively about the timing and nature of strains on the family unit and each member over the course of a major health problem.

Life cycle and *life structure* are central concepts for both family and individual development. Life cycle means there is a basic sequence and unfolding of the life course within which individual, family, or illness uniqueness occurs. Life structure refers to the core elements (e.g., work, childrearing, caregiving) of an individual's or family's life at any phase of the life cycle.

Illness, individual, and family development have in common the notion of phases, each with its own developmental tasks. Carter and McGoldrick (1998) have divided the family life cycle into six phases where marker events (e.g., marriage, birth of first child, adolescence, children leaving home) herald the transition from one phase to the next. Also, the family life cycle can be viewed as oscillating between phases where family developmental tasks require intense bonding or relatively higher cohesion, as in early childrearing, versus phases such as families with adolescents, during which the external family boundary is loosened, often emphasizing personal identity and autonomy (Combrinck-Graham, 1985). Levinson (1986), in his description of individual adult development describes how individuals' and families' life structures can move between periods of life structure transition and building and stability. Transition periods are sometimes the most vulnerable because previous individual, family, and illness life structures are reappraised in light of new developmental tasks that may require major discontinuous change rather than minor alterations. The primary goal of a life structure building and maintaining period is to form a life structure and to enrich life within it based on the key choices an individual or family made during the preceding transition period.

These unifying concepts provide a base to think about the fit among illness, individual, and family development. Each phase in these three kinds of development pose tasks and challenges that move through periods of being more or less in sync with each other. The model distinguishes (a) the phases of the family life cycle, particularly the kind and degree of cohesion required; (b) the alternation of transition and life structure building and maintaining periods in the family and individual life cycles; and (c) periods of higher and lower psychosocial demands requiring relatively greater and lesser degrees of family cohesion over the course of a chronic condition.

Generally, illness and disability tend to push individual and family developmental processes toward transition and increased cohesion. Analogous to the addition of a new family member, illness onset sets in motion an inside-the-family-focused process of socialization to illness. Symptoms, loss of function, the demands of shifting or acquiring new illness related roles, and the fear of loss through death all require a family to focus inward.

The need for family cohesion varies enormously with different illness types and phases. The tendency for a disease to pull a family inward increases with the level of disability or risk of progression and death. Progressive diseases over time inherently require a greater cohesion than constant course illnesses. The ongoing addition of new demands as an illness progresses keeps a family's energy focused inward, often impeding or halting the natural life-cycle evolution of other members. After an initial period of adaptation, a constant-course disease (without severe disability) permits a family to get back on track developmentally. Relapsing illnesses alternate between periods of drawing a family inward and periods of release from the immediate demands of disease. But the on-call nature of many such illnesses keeps part of the family focus inward despite asymptomatic periods, hindering the natural flow between phases of the family life cycle.

In clinical assessment, a basic question is: What is the fit between the psychosocial demands of a condition, family and individual life structures, and developmental tasks at a particular point in the life cycle? Also, how will this fit change as the course of the illness unfolds in relation to the family life cycle and the development of each member?

From a systems viewpoint, at the time of diagnosis it is important to know the phase of the family life cycle and the stage of individual development of all family members, not just the ill member. Chronic disease in one family member can profoundly affect developmental goals of another member. For instance, an infant's disability can be a serious roadblock to the parents' preconceived ideas about competent childrearing, or a life-threatening illness in a young married adult can interfere with the well spouse's readiness to become a parent. Also, family members frequently do not adapt equally to chronic illness. Each member's ability to adapt, and the rate at which he or she does so, is related to his or her own developmental stage and role in the family (Ireys & Burr, 1984). When family members are in tune with each other's developmental processes while promoting flexibility and alternative means to satisfy developmental needs, successful long-term adaptation is maximized.

By adopting a longitudinal developmental perspective, a clinician will stay attuned to future developmental transitions. Imagine a family in which the father, a carpenter and primary financial provider, has a heart attack. Dad's rehabilitation is uneventful, includes appropriate life style modifications, and a return to work. The oldest son, aged 15, seems relatively unaffected. Two years later, his father experiences a second heart attack, leaving him disabled. His son, now 17, has dreams of going away to college. The specter of financial hardship and the perceived need for a man in the family creates a serious dilemma of choice for the son and the family, which surfaces with precipitously declining academic performance and alcohol abuse. In this case, there is a fundamental clash between developmental issues of separation and individuation and the ongoing demands of a progressive, life-threatening type of heart disease on the family. Further, there is a resurgence of fears of loss fueled not only by the recurrence, but also its timing with a major life-cycle transition for the oldest son. The son may fear that if he were to move away, he might never see his father alive again. This case demonstrates the potential clash between simultaneous transition periods: the illness transition to a more disabling, progressive, and life-threatening course; the adolescent son's transition to early adulthood; and the family's transition from living with teenagers to the launching young adults stage. At the time of initial diagnosis, inquiry about anticipated major transitions over the next 3 to 5 years and discussing them in relation to the specific kind of heart disease and its related uncertainties would help avert a future crisis.

The timing of chronic illness in the life cycle can be normative (e.g., expectable in relation to chronological and social time) or non-normative (e.g., "off-time"). Coping with chronic illness and death are considered normally anticipated tasks in late adulthood, whereas their occurrence earlier is out of phase and developmentally more disruptive (Neugarten, 1976). For instance, chronic diseases that occur in the childrearing period can be challenging because of their potential impact on family financial and childrearing responsibilities. The actual impact will depend on the type of illness and pre-illness family roles. Families governed by flexible gender-influenced rules about who is the financial provider and caregiver of children will tend to adjust better.

For instance, when a parent develops cancer during the childrearing phases of the life cycle, a family's ability to stay on course is severely taxed. For more serious and debilitating forms of cancer, the impact of the illness is like the addition of a new infant member, one with special needs that will compete with those of the real children for potentially scarce family resources that are diminished by parental loss. Moreover, in two-parent families, the well parent must juggle childrearing demands with caregiving to the spouse (Rolland, 1994b).

With chronic disorders, an overarching family goal is to deal with the developmental demands of the illness without family members sacrificing their own or the family's development as a system over time. It is important to determine whose life plans were cancelled, postponed, or altered, and when plans put on hold and future developmental issues will be addressed. In this way, clinicians can anticipate life-cycle nodal points related to autonomy within versus subjugation to the condition. Family members can be helped to strike a healthier balance with life plans that resolve feelings of guilt, over-responsibility, and hopelessness and find family and external resources to enhance freedom, both to pursue personal goals and provide needed care for the ill member.

HEALTH BELIEFS

At the time of a medical diagnosis, a primary developmental challenge for a family is to create a meaning for the illness experience that promotes a sense of competency and mastery (Kleinman, 1988; Rolland, 1987a, 1994a, 1997, 1998; Wright, Watson, & Bell, 1996; Wynne, Shields, & Sirkin, 1992).

Since serious illness is often experienced as a betrayal of our fundamental trust in our bodies and belief in our invulnerability (Kleinman, 1988), creating an empowering narrative can be a formidable task. Health beliefs help us grapple with the existential dilemmas of our fear of death, our tendency to want to sustain our denial of death, and our attempts to reassert control when suffering and loss occur. Beliefs serve as a cognitive map guiding decisions and action; they provide a way to approach new and ambiguous situations for coherence in family life, facilitating continuity between past, present, and future (Antonovsky & Sourani, 1988; Reiss, 1981). Our inquiry into, and curiosity about, family beliefs is perhaps the most powerful foundation stone of collaboration between families and health professionals (Wright et al., 1996).

In the initial crisis phase, it is useful for clinicians to inquire about key family beliefs that shape the family's narrative and coping strategies. This includes tracking beliefs about: (a) normality; (b) mind–body relationship, control, and mastery; (c) meanings attached by a family, ethnic group, religion, or the wider culture to symptoms (e.g., chronic pain) (McGoldrick, Giordano & Pearce, 1996; Griffith & Griffith, 1994), types of illnesses (e.g., life-threatening), or specific diseases (e.g., leukemia); (d) assumptions about what caused an illness and what will influence its course and outcome; (e) multigenerational factors that have shaped a family's health beliefs and response to illness (Seaburn, Lorenz, & Kaplan, 1992); and (f) anticipated nodal points in illness, individual, and family development when health beliefs will be strained or need to shift. A clinician should also assess the fit of health beliefs within the family and its various subsystems, as well as between the family, health care system, and wider culture (Rolland, 1998).

Beliefs About Normality

Family beliefs about what is normal or abnormal, as well as the importance members place on conformity and excellence in relation to the average family, have far-reaching implications for adaptation to chronic disorders. Family values that allow having a problem without self-denigration have a distinct advantage, enabling one to seek outside help and yet maintain a positive identity in the face of chronic conditions. Families who define help-seeking as weak and shameful undercut this kind of resilience. Essentially, problems are to be expected with chronic disorders, and the use of professionals and outside resources is necessary; beliefs that pathologize this normative process add insult to injury.

Two excellent questions to elicit these beliefs are, "How do you think other average families would deal with a similar situation to yours?" And, "How would a healthy family ideally cope with your situation?" Families with strong beliefs in high achievement and perfectionism are prone to apply standards in a situation of illness where the kind of control they are accustomed to is impossible. Particularly with untimely conditions that occur early in the life cycle, there are additional pressures to keep up with normative socially expectable developmental milestones of age-peers or other young couples. The fact that life-cycle goals may take longer or need revision requires a flexible belief about what is normal and healthy. This kind of flexibility helps sustain hope.

The Family's Sense of Mastery Facing Illness

It is important to determine how a family defines mastery or control in general and in situations of illness. Mastery is similar to the concept of health locus of control (Lefcourt, 1982) which can be defined as the belief about influence over the course and outcome of an illness. It is useful to distinguish whether a family's beliefs are based on the premise of internal control, external control by chance, or external control by powerful others.

An internal locus of control orientation means that individuals or families believe they can affect the outcome of a situation. In illness, such families believe they are directly responsible for their health and have the power to recover from illness (Wallston & Wallston, 1978). An external orientation entails a belief that outcomes are not contingent upon the individual's or family's behavior. Families that view illness in terms of chance believe that when illness occurs it's a matter of luck and that fate determines recovery. Those who see health control as in the hands of powerful others view health professionals, God, or sometimes powerful family members as exerting control over their bodies and illness course.

A family may adhere to a different set of beliefs about control when dealing with biological as opposed to typical day-to-day issues. Therefore, it is important to assess both a family's basic value system and beliefs about control for illnesses in general, chronic and life-threatening illness, and finally the specific disease facing the family. For instance, regardless of the actual severity or prognosis in a particular case, cancer may be equated with death or no control because of medical statistics, cultural myth, or prior family history. On the other hand, families may have enabling stories about a member or friend who, in spite of cancer and a shortened life span, lived a full life centered on effectively prioritizing the quality of relationships and goals. Clinicians can highlight these positive narratives as a means to help families counteract cultural beliefs that focus exclusively on control of biology as defining success.

A family's beliefs about mastery strongly affect the nature of its relationship to an illness and to the health care system. Beliefs about control can affect treatment compliance and a family's preferences about participation in their family member's treatment and healing process. Families that view disease course and outcome as a matter of chance tend to establish marginal relationships with health professionals, largely because their belief system minimizes the importance of their own or the professional's impact on a disease process. Also, poor minority families may receive inadequate care or lack insurance or access, leading to a fatalistic attitude and lack of engagement with health care providers who may not be trusted to help. Just as any psychotherapeutic relationship depends on a shared belief system about what is therapeutic, a workable accommodation among the patient, family, and health care team in terms of these fundamental values is essential. Families that feel misunderstood by health professionals are often reacting to a lack of joining at this basic value level. Too often, their healthy need to participate was ignored or preempted by a professional needing unilateral control.

The goodness of fit between family beliefs about mastery can vary dependent on the time phase of the condition. For some disorders, the crisis phase involves protracted care outside the family's direct control.

This may be stressful for a family that prefers to tackle its own problems without outside control and interference. The patient's return home may increase the workload but allow members to reassert more fully their competence and leadership. In contrast, a family guided more by a preference for external control by experts can expect greater difficulty when their family member returns home. Recognition of such normative differences in belief about control can guide an effective psychosocial treatment plan tailored to each family's needs and affirming rather than disrespecting their core values.

In the terminal phase, a family may feel least in control of the biological course of the disease and the decision-making regarding the overall care of the dying member. Families with a strong belief about being involved in a family member's health care may need to assert themselves more vigorously with health providers. Effective decision making regarding the extent of heroic medical efforts or whether a patient will die at home, an institution, or hospice requires a family and provider relationship that respects the family's basic beliefs.

With illness and disability, we must be cautious about judging the relative usefulness of positive illusions (Taylor, 1989) or minimization versus direct confrontation with, and acceptance of, painful realities. Often both are needed. The healthy use of minimization or selective focus on the positive, timely uses of humor should be distinguished from the concept of denial, regarded as pathological. The skilled clinician must thread the needle supporting both the usefulness of exaggerated hope and the need for treatment to control the illness or a new complication. There is greater incentive for a family to confront denial of an illness or its severity both when there is hope that preventive action or medical treatment can affect the outcome and when an illness is entering a terminal phase. Yet, coping with an arduous, uncertain course may require families to acknowledge the condition itself even as they minimize treatment risks or the likelihood of a poor outcome.

Family Beliefs About the Cause of an Illness

When a significant health problem arises, all of us wonder, "Why me (or us)?" and "Why now?" We invariably construct an explanation or story that helps organize our experience. With limits of current medical knowledge, tremendous uncertainties persist about the relative importance of a myriad of factors, leaving individuals and families to make idiosyncratic attributions about what caused an illness. A family's beliefs about the cause of an illness need to be assessed separately from its beliefs about what can affect the outcome. It is important to ask each family member for his or her explanation. Responses will generally reflect a combination of medical information and family mythology. Beliefs might include punishment for prior misdeeds (e.g., an affair), blame of a particular family member ("Your drinking made me sick!"), a sense of injustice ("Why am I being punished?"), genetics (e.g., cancer runs on one side of the family), negligence by the patient (e.g., smoking) or by parents (e.g., sudden infant death syndrome), or simply bad luck.

Optimal family narratives respect the limits of scientific knowledge, affirm basic competency, and promote the flexible use of multiple biological and psychosocial healing strategies. In contrast, causal attributions that invoke blame, shame, or guilt are particularly important to uncover. Such beliefs make it extremely difficult for a family to cope and adapt in a functional way. With a life-threatening cancer, a blamed family member is implicitly, if not explicitly, held accountable if the patient dies. Frequently decisions about treatment then become confounded and filled with tension. A mother who feels blamed by her husband for their son's leukemia may be less able to stop a low-probability experimental treatment than the angry, blaming husband. A husband who believes his drinking caused his wife's coronary and subsequent death may increase self-destructive drinking in his profound guilt.

Belief System Adaptability

Because illnesses vary enormously in their responsiveness to psychosocial factors, both families and providers need to make distinctions between beliefs about their overall participation in a long-term disease process, their beliefs about their ability to control the biological unfolding of an illness, and the flexibility with which they can apply these beliefs. Families' experience of competence or mastery often depends on their grasp of these distinctions. Optimal family and provider narratives respect the limits of scientific knowledge, affirm basic competency, and promote the flexible use of multiple biological and psychosocial healing strategies.

A family's belief in their participation in the total illness process can be thought of as independent from whether a disease is stable, improving, or in a terminal phase. Sometimes, mastery and the attempt to control biological process coincide, as when a family tailors its behavior to help maintain the health of a member with cancer in remission. This might include changes in family roles, communication, diet, exercise, and balance between work and recreation. Optimally, when an ill family member loses remission as the family enters the terminal phase of the illness, participation as an expression of mastery is transformed to a successful process of letting go that eases suffering and allows palliative care to be provided.

Families with flexible belief systems are more likely to experience death with a sense of equanimity rather than profound failure. The death of a patient whose long, debilitating illness has heavily burdened others can bring relief as well as sadness to family members. Since relief over death goes against societal conventions, it can trigger massive guilt reactions that may be expressed through such symptoms as depression and family conflict. Clinicians need to help family members accept ambivalent feeling they may have about the death as natural.

Thus, flexibility both within the family and the health professional system is a key variable in optimal family functioning. Rather than linking mastery in a rigid way with biological outcome (survival or recovery) as the sole determinant of success, families can define control in a more holistic sense with involvement and participation in the overall process as the main criteria defining success. This is analogous to the distinction between curing the disease and healing the system. Healing the system may influence the course and outcome, but a positive disease outcome is not necessary for a family to feel successful. This flexible view of mastery permits the quality of relations within the family or between the family and health professional to become more central to criteria of success. The health provider's competence becomes valued from both a technical and caregiving perspective not solely linked to the biological course (Reiss & Kaplan De-Nour 1989).

Ethnic, Religious, and Cultural Beliefs

Ethnicity, race, and religion strongly influence family beliefs concerning health and illness (McGoldrick et al., 1996; Walsh, 1999; Zborowski, 1969). Significant ethnic differences regarding health beliefs typically emerge at the time of a major health crisis. Health professionals need to be mindful of the belief systems of various ethnic, racial, and religious groups in their community, particularly as these translate into different behavioral patterns. Cultural norms vary in such areas as the definition of the appropriate sick role for the patient; the kind and degree of open communication about the disease; who should be included in the illness caregiving system (e.g., extended family, friends, professionals); who is the primary caretaker (almost always wife, mother, or daughter/daughter-in-law); and the kind of rituals viewed as normative at different stages of an illness (e.g., hospital bedside vigils and healing and funeral rituals) (Imber-Black, Roberts, & Whiting, 2003; Imber-Black, 2004). This is especially true for minority groups (e.g., African-American, Asian, Hispanic, etc.) that experience discrimination or marginalization from prevailing white Anglo culture. Illness provides an opportunity to encourage gender role flexibility and shift from defining one female member as the caregiver to a collaborative caregiving team that includes male and female siblings and adult children.

Clinicians need to be mindful of these cultural differences between themselves, the patient, and the family as a necessary step to forging a workable alliance that can endure a long-term illness (Seaburn, Gunn, Mauksh, Gawinski, & Lorenz, 1996). Disregarding these issues can lead families to wall themselves off from health providers and available community resources—a major cause of noncompliance and treatment failure. For example, traditional Navajo culture holds that thought and language have the power to shape reality and control events (Carrese & Rhodes, 1995). In other words, language can determine reality. From the Navajo world view, discussing the potential complications of a serious illness with a newly diagnosed Navajo patient is harmful and increases the likelihood that such complications will occur. This belief system clashes dramatically with those of health professions (backed by powerful legal imperatives) that mandate sharing possible complications or promoting advance directives. Carrese and Rhodes in their study give one example of a Navajo daughter describing how the risks of bypass surgery were explained to her father: "The surgeon told him that he may not wake up, that this is the risk of every surgery. For the surgeon, it was very routine, but the way that my Dad received it, it was almost like a death sentence, and he never consented to the surgery."

Sometimes, professionals may need the flexibility to suspend their need to prevail, especially in relation to family and cultural beliefs that proscribe certain standard forms of medical care (e.g., blood products for Jehovah's Witnesses). This requires an acceptance that the patient, not the physician, retains final responsibility for decisions about his or her body.

Fit Among Clinicians, Health Systems, and Families

It is a common but unfortunate error to regard the family as a monolithic unit that feels, thinks, believes, and behaves as an undifferentiated whole. Clinicians should inquire both about the level of agreement and tolerance for differences among family members regarding their beliefs and between the family and health care system. Is the family rule that members must agree on either all or some values? Or are diversity and different viewpoints acceptable? How much do they feel the need to stay in sync with prevailing cultural or societal beliefs, or family tradition?

Family beliefs that balance the need for consensus with diversity and innovation are optimal and maximize permissible options. If

consensus is the rule, then individual differentiation implies disloyalty and deviance. If the guiding principle is "We can hold different
viewpoints," then diversity is allowed and the family is more open to
novel and creative forms of problem solving that may be needed in a
situation of protracted adversity. Families also need open communication and effective conflict resolution when members differ on major
health care and treatment decisions.

To assess the fit between the family and health care team, the same
questions concerning beliefs asked of families are relevant to the medical
team:

1. What are their attitudes about their own and the family's ability to
   influence the course and outcome of the disease?
2. How does the health team see the balance between theirs versus the
   family's participation in the treatment process?
3. If basic differences in beliefs about control exist, how can these differences be reconciled?

Because of the tendency of most health facilities to disempower
individuals and thereby foster dependence, utmost sensitivity to family
values is needed to create a therapeutic system. Many breakdowns in
relationships between noncompliant or marginal patients and their
providers can be traced to natural disagreements at this basic level that
were not addressed.

Normative differences among family members' health beliefs may
emerge into destructive conflicts during a health crisis, as in the
following case:

When Stavros H., a first-generation Greek-American, became ill
with heart disease, his mother kept a 24-hour bedside vigil in his hospital room so she could tend to her son at any hour. His wife, Dana,
from a Scandinavian family, greatly resented the "intrusive" behavior
of her mother-in-law, who in turn criticized Dana's emotional cold-
ness and relative lack of concern. Stavros felt caught between his war-
ring mother and wife and complained of increased symptoms.

In such situations, clinicians need to sort out normative cultural
differences from pathological enmeshment. In this case, all concerned
behaved according to their own cultural norms. In Greek culture, it is
normal to maintain close ties to one's family of origin after marriage, and
it is expected that a mother would tend to her son in a health crisis. A son
would be disloyal not to allow his mother that role. This sharply differs
with Northern European traditions of the wife. Each side pathologizes
the other, creating a conflictual triangle with the patient caught in the
middle. The clinician who affirms normative multicultural differences

promotes a transformation of process from blaming or pathologizing to one of accommodating different equally legitimate cultures.

It is common for differences in beliefs or attitude to erupt at any major life-cycle or illness transition. For instance, in situations of severe disability or terminal illness, one member may want the patient to return home, whereas another prefers long-term hospitalization or transfer to an extended care facility. Since the chief task of patient caretaking is usually assigned to the wife or mother, she is the one most apt to bear the chief burdens in this regard. Sometimes a family is able to anticipate the collision of gender-based beliefs about caregiving with the potential overwhelming demands of home-based care for a dying family member. If it can flexibly modify its rules, this family would avert the risk of family caretaker overload, resentment, and deteriorating family relationships.

The murky boundary between the chronic and terminal phase highlights the potential for professionals' beliefs to collide with those of the family. Physicians can feel bound to a technological imperative that requires them to exhaust all possibilities at their disposal regardless of the odds of success. Families may not know how to interpret continued lifesaving efforts, assuming real hope where virtually none exists. Health care professionals and institutions can collude in a pervasive societal wish to deny death as a natural process truly beyond technological control (Becker, 1973). Endless treatment can represent the medical team's inability to separate a general value placed on controlling diseases from their beliefs about participation (separate from cure) in a patient's total care.

CONCLUSION

Facing the risks and burdens of chronic illness or disability, the healthiest families are able to harness that experience to improve the quality of life. Families can achieve a healthy balance between accepting limits and promoting autonomy. For conditions with long-range risks, families can maintain mastery in the face of uncertainty by enhancing their capacities to acknowledge the possibility of loss, sustain hope, and build flexibility into family life-cycle planning that conserves and adjusts major goals and helps circumvent the forces of uncertainty.

A serious illness, such as cancer, and a brush with death provides an opportunity to confront catastrophic fears about loss. This can lead to family members developing a better appreciation and perspective on life that results in clearer priorities and closer relationships. Seizing opportunities can replace procrastination for the right moment or passive waiting for the dreaded moment. Serious health conditions, by emphasizing life's fragility and preciousness, provide families with an opportunity to heal unresolved issues and develop more immediate, caring relationships. For diseases in a more advanced stage, clinicians should help families emphasize quality of life by defining goals that are attainable more immediately and that enrich their everyday lives.

As the genetic revolution unfolds, families and clinicians are facing unprecedented complex clinical and ethical challenges (Miller, McDaniel, Rolland, & Feetham, in press). Families will increasingly be able to choose genetically informed knowledge of their future health risks or fate. Some key questions include: Which individuals and families will benefit by genetic risk screening and knowledge of their health risks or fate? How can we best help family members reach decisions about whether to pursue predictive testing? Who are the relevant family members to include in these decisions? Spouses or partners? Extended family? Our societal fixation on "the perfect, healthy body" could meld seamlessly with technology and eugenics, forcing families living with disability, illness, or genetic risk to further hide their suffering in order to demonstrate the value of their lives and avoid increased stigmatization (Rolland, 1997; 1999).

Also, clinicians need to consider their own experiences and feelings about illness and loss (McDaniel, Doherty, & Hepworth, 1997). Awareness and ease with our own multigenerational and family history with illness and loss, our health beliefs, and our current life-cycle passage will enhance our ability to work effectively with families facing serious illness.

Living well with the strains and uncertainties of illness can be a monumental challenge. The family systems–illness model offers a way to address this challenge and make the inevitable strains more manageable. Attending to the psychosocial demands of different kinds of conditions over time within a multigenerational life cycle and belief system context can provide a strength-based framework—a common language that facilitates collaborative, creative problem solving, and quality of life for families facing illness, disability, and loss.

REFERENCES

Antonovsky, A., & Sourani, T. (1988). Family sense of coherence and family adaptation. *Journal of Marriage and the Family, 50,* 9–92.

Becker, E. (1973). *The denial of death.* New York: Free Press.

Boss, P. (1999). *Ambiguous loss: Learning to live with unresolved grief.* Boston: Harvard University Press.

Bowen, M. (1978). Theory in the practice of psychotherapy. In *Family therapy in clinical practice.* New York: Jason Aronson.

Carrese, J., & Rhodes, L. (1995). Western bioethics on the Navajo reservation: Benefit or harm. *Journal of the American Medical Association, 274,* 826–829.

Carter, E. A., & McGoldrick, M. (Eds.). (1998). *The expanded family life cycle: Individual, family, and social perspectives* (3rd ed.). New York: Allyn & Bacon.

Combrinck-Graham, L. (1985). A developmental model for family systems. *Family Process, 24,* 139–150.

Framo, J. (1992). *Family-of origin therapy: An intergenerational approach.* New York: Brunner/Mazel.

Gonzalez, S., Steinglass, P., & Reiss, D. (1989). Putting the illness in its place: Discussion groups for families with chronic medical illnesses. *Family Process, 28,* 69–87.

Griffith, J., & Griffith, M. (1994). *The body speaks.* New York: Basic Books.

Imber-Black, E. (2004). Rituals and the healing process. In F. Walsh & M. McGoldrick (Eds.), *Living beyond loss: Death in the family* (2nd ed.) (pp. 305–358). New York: Norton.

Imber-Black, E., Roberts, J., & Whiting, R. (Eds.). (2003). *Rituals in families and family therapy* (2nd ed.). New York: Norton.

Ireys, H. T., & Burr, C. K. (1984). Apart and a part: Family issues for young adults with chronic illness and disability. In M. G. Eisenberg, L. C. Sutkin, & M. A. Jansen (Eds.), *Chronic illness and disability through the life span: Effects on self and family* (pp. 184–209). New York: Springer.

Kleinman, A. (1988). *The illness narratives: Suffering, healing, and the human condition.* New York: Basic Books.

Lefcourt, H. M. (1982). *Locus of control* (2nd ed.). Hillsdale, NJ: Erlbaum.

Levinson, D. J. (1986). A conception of adult development. *American Psychologist, 41,* 3–13.

McDaniel, S., Hepworth, J., & Doherty, W. (Eds.). (1997). *The shared experience of illness: Stories of patients, families, and their therapists.* New York: Basic Books.

McGoldrick, M., Gerson, R., & Schellenberger, S. (1999). *Genograms in family assessment* (2nd ed.). New York: Norton.

McGoldrick, M., Giordano, J., & Pearce, J.K. (1996). *Ethnicity and family therapy* (2nd ed.). New York: Guilford.

Miller, S., McDaniel, S., Rolland, J., & Feetham, S. (Eds.) (in press). *Individuals, families, and the new genetics.* New York: Norton.

Moos, R. (Ed.). (1984). *Coping with physical illness: Vol. 2. New Perspectives.* New York: Plenum.

Neugarten, B. (1976). Adaptation and the life cycle. *The Counseling Psychologist, 6,* 16–20.

Olkin, R. (1999). *What psychotherapists should know about disability.* New York: Guilford.

Penn, P. (1983). Coalitions and binding interactions in families with chronic illness. *Family Systems Medicine, 1,* 16–25.

Reiss, D. (1981). *The family's construction of reality.* Cambridge, MA: Harvard University Press.

Reiss D., & Kaplan-DeNour, A. (1989). The family and medical team in chronic illness: A transactional and developmental perspective. In C. N. Ramsey, Jr. (Ed.), *Family systems in family medicine* (pp. 435–445). New York: Guilford.

Rolland, J. S. (1984). Toward a psychosocial typology of chronic and life-threatening illness. *Family Systems Medicine, 2,* 245–263.

Rolland, J. S. (1987a). Chronic illness and the life cycle: A conceptual framework. *Family Process, 26,* 203–221.

Rolland, J. S. (1987b). Family illness paradigms: Evolution and significance. *Family Systems Medicine, 5,* 467–486.

Rolland, J. S. (1990). Anticipatory loss: A family systems developmental framework. *Family Process, 29,* 229–244.

Rolland, J. S. (1994a). *Families, illness, and disability: An integrative treatment model.* New York: Basic Books.

Rolland, J. S. (1994b). In sickness and in health: The impact of illness on couples' relationships. *Journal of Marital and Family Therapy, 20,* 327–349.

Rolland, J. S. (1997). The meaning of disability and suffering: Socio-political and ethical concerns. *Family Process, 36,* 437–440.

Rolland, J. S. (1998). Beliefs and collaboration in illness: Evolution over time. *Families, Systems, and Health* (formerly *Family Systems Medicine)*, 16(1/2), 7–27.

Rolland, J. S. (1999) Families and genetic fate: A millennial challenge. *Families, Systems, and Health, 17*(1), 123–133.

Rolland, J. S. (2002). Managing chronic illness. In M. Mengel, W. Holleman, & S. Fields (Eds.), *Fundamentals of clinical practice: A textbook on the patient, doctor, and society* (2nd ed.). New York: Plenum.

Seaburn, D., Gunn, W., Mauksh, L., Gawinski, A., & Lorenz, A. (Eds.). (1996). *Models of collaboration: A guide for mental health professionals working with physicians and health care providers.* New York: Basic Books.

Seaburn, D., Lorenz, A., & Kaplan, D. (1992). The transgenerational development of chronic illness meanings. *Family Systems Medicine, 10,* 385–395.

Steinglass, P. (1998). Multiple family discussion groups for patients with chronic medical illness. *Families, Systems, and Health,* 16(1, 2), 55–71.

Taylor, S. (1989). *Positive illusions: Creative self-deception and the healthy mind.* New York: Basic Books.

Wallston, K. A., & Wallston, B. S. (1978). Development of the Multidimensional Health Locus of Control (MHLC) Scales. *Health Education Monographs,* 6(2), 160–170.

Walsh, F. (1996). The concept of family resilience: Crisis and challenge. *Family Process, 35,* 261–283.

Walsh, F. (1998). *Strengthening family resilience.* New York: Guilford.

Walsh, F. (Ed.). (1999). *Spiritual resources in family therapy.* New York: Guilford.

Walsh, F., & McGoldrick, M. (Eds.). (2004). *Living beyond loss: Death in the family,* 2nd ed. New York: Norton.

Weihs, K., Fisher, L., & Baird, M. (2001). *Families, health, and behavior.* Commissioned report, Institute of Medicine, National Academy of Sciences.

Wright, L. M., Watson, W. L., & Bell, J. M. (1996). *Beliefs: The heart of healing in families and illness.* New York: Basic Books.

Wynne, L., Shields, C., & Sirkin, M. (1992). Illness, family theory, and family therapy: I. Conceptual issues. *Family Process, 31,* 3–18.

Zborowski, M. (1969). *People in pain.* San Francisco: Jossey-Bass.

6

The Transmission of Trauma Across Generations: Identification With Parental Trauma in Children of Holocaust Survivors

DANI ROWLAND- KLEIN

"The parents, the actual victims in these cases, are not conspicuously broken people. ... Yet their children, all of whom were born after the Holocaust, display severe psychiatric symptomatology. It would almost be easier to believe that they, rather than their parents, had suffered the corrupting, searing hell." (Epstein,1979)

This statement appeared in the earliest published writing on children of Holocaust survivors in 1966 by Vivian Rakoff. He describes three case studies of adolescents and notes that they share striking features that are different from his other adolescent patients. Since then, there have been a number of papers written on the sequelae of Nazi persecution on the offspring of survivors, the "second generation."

Classical psychoanalytic theory has provided the dominant context for research into the transmission of trauma with largely clinical–descriptive studies and case histories. There has been a tendency to pathologize and overgeneralize from clinical samples, with conceptualization of the second generation as a "homogenous group of vulnerable individuals" (Solkoff, 1992, p. 343). Although investigators continue to describe a constellation of common features of pathology, there is increasing recognition and acknowledgment of common strengths among the second generation. This chapter explores the intergenerational transmission of trauma through a qualitative research study with a nonclinical sample of postwar children of Holocaust survivors. An object relations framework (which emphasizes the interactional relationship between parent and child) is used to explain and understand the process of transmission. Transmission to the second generation is defined as the presence of (a) generalized anxiety, fear, and wariness of others, and (b) a sense of having personally experienced concentration camp incarceration associated with (c) vivid Holocaust-related imagery, as well as (d) reverse parenting and enmeshment. Considering the evidence of these phenomena, I propose a mechanism through which unconscious transmission may have occurred. Conscious transmission of Holocaust knowledge in this Jewish sample is also acknowledged.

To understand the impact of the Holocaust on the second generation, it is necessary to consider the massive psychic trauma parents suffered as a result of surviving Hitler's "Final Solution." Torture, as practiced in the Nazi camps, was not carried out for purposes of extracting information. Rather, physical pain and psychological degradation were inflicted as acts of gratuitous punishment. Although there were differences in the intensity and duration of cruelties (depending on type of camp and time during the war), the goal of captivity was clear and consistent: to break the psychological, physical, and spiritual resistance of Jewish inmates and to stigmatize and depersonalize them in such a grotesque manner as to facilitate their extermination (Solkoff, 1992a).

Given the horror of their experiences, it is not surprising that survivors carry physical and emotional scars long after their liberation. The literature often refers to the survivor's syndrome to capture the psychological consequences (Chodoff, 1963; Niederland, 1968). Symptoms include cognitive and memory disturbances, depression and survivor guilt, chronic anxiety related to fear of renewed persecution, and phobic fears. There are frequently sleep disturbances (insomnia, nightmares, and anxiety dreams related to persecution) and psychosomatic manifestations (Kaminer & Lavie, 1994). There is evidence of loss of childhood memories and unique changes in perception of personal identity and object relations. Furthermore, this impact is said to frequently lead to personality changes affecting interpersonal relations, including parenthood (Steinberg, 1989).

Early writers had difficulty explaining the heterogeneity of the survivors' clinical presentation. However, more recent views emphasize the influence of other variables such as post-Holocaust experiences, immigration, extent of familial and financial losses, and developmental phase during the Holocaust. Certainly preexisting strengths which may have facilitated their survival play a role in their post-Holocaust recovery (Steinberg, 1989).

THE SECOND GENERATION

"The children of survivors show symptoms which would be expected if they had actually lived through the Holocaust. ... The children come to feel that the Holocaust is the single most critical event that has affected their lives although it occurred before they were born." (Bergmann & Jucovy, 1990, p. 331)

By the mid-1970s, it was widely accepted that characteristics of Holocaust survivors were likely to appear in their children even though the children had never been inside a concentration camp (Epstein, 1979). Chronic deprivation or distortions in the psychological environment may have impaired survivors' capacity for human relations, thus hampering their ability to form healthy parent–child relationships, leading to maladaptive behavior in the second generation (Berger, 1988).

Initial research focused on the psychopathological aspect of this population with agreement on many of the clinical features of the survivor's child (Steinberg, 1989). Survivors' children have presented with symptoms resembling those of their parents, including depression, anxiety, phobias, guilt, and separation problems (Steinberg, 1989; Hass, 1990) and similar dream imagery and environmental misperception (Steinberg, 1989). Separation problems are among the most prevalent features described. Characteristics of the survivor parent–child relationship may contribute to these symptoms as children are typically overprotected by their parents and encouraged to view the world as a dangerous place, with the family as the only shield from danger. They are also perceived as possible replacements for the family's lost relatives and past world (Steinberg, 1989; Hass, 1990). Finally, children's depressive symptoms have been attributed to anger turned inward since expression of aggression is generally not tolerated at home (Steinberg, 1989).

The frequency with which children experienced symptoms and the pain of their parents without knowledge of the trauma that gave rise to them led researchers to explore not only the mechanism and effect of transmission but also the difference between unconscious and conscious communication (Lang, 1994). Communication between the generations varies from almost complete silence to rather open sharing with children of their harrowing experiences. Shoshan (1989) reports that in families marked by both silence and cases of incessant talk, children of survivors demonstrate repression and uncertainty as to what their parents had actually gone through. Okner and Flaherty (1988) suggest that excessive parental communication results in more guilt but less depression, demoralization, and anxiety. However, Trossman (cited in Bergmann & Jucovy, 1990) explains the depression of the children as a reaction to their parents' communications about their victimization.

Krell (1979) asserts that the Holocaust experience is inevitably transmitted to the child, and if experiences are not discussed openly, they are inevitably expressed as "veiled references" or "mysterious outbursts of grief." The parents' lack of communication may contribute to children's increased depression and other difficulties, and this could provoke fantasies about what the parents experienced, which may be even more frightening and pathogenic (Bergmann & Jucovy, 1990). Miller (1995) suggests that children unconsciously reenact their parents' fate, and the reenactments are even more intense when the children lack precise knowledge. From various bits of information gleaned, they create fantasies based on their own reality.

Survivor parents may also transmit emotional messages concerning the history and fate of relatives. According to Wardi (1992), children attempt to fill this emotional void and construct the continuation of the family history, creating a hidden connection with the relatives who perished in the Holocaust and providing the parents a way of discharging unresolved unconscious conflicts. Wardi also suggests that survivors may transmit the unconscious message to their children to "experience the Holocaust and solve it for us" (p. 46). Thus, by repeated simulations and fantasy reconstructions of their parents' experiences, the children try to understand the Holocaust and release the parents from their tortured past (Prince, 1985).

Klein and Kogan (cited in Shoshan, 1989) point out that survivor parents and their children share dreams and fantasies, thereby creating an illusion that parents and post-Holocaust children were together before the children's birth. Children have a need to discover, reenact, or live their parents' past (Bergmann & Jucovy, 1990; Prince, 1985). Many psychoanalytic authors (Steinberg, 1989; Bergmann, 1990a, 1990b) report that members of the second generation tend to project their Holocaust-related fantasies onto the current environment, just like their parents do. This leads to enactments in the lives of survivors' children that resemble their parents' experiences. This process is epitomized in the words of Barocas and Barocas (quoted in Bergmann & Jucovy, 1990) who noted that children of survivors seem to "share an anguished collective memory of the Holocaust in both their dreams and fantasies reflective of recurrent references to their parents' traumatic experiences. These children wake up at night with terrifying nightmares of the Nazi persecution, with dreams of barbed wire, gas chambers, firing squads, torture, mutilation, escaping from enemy forces and fears of extermination" (p. 331).

Herzog (1990) and Kestenberg (1989) describe survivors' children as living a simultaneous double existence—in their current world and in the parental Holocaust world. Kestenberg termed this transposition into the past an organization of the self in relation to time and space. It is a mechanism used by a person living in the present and in the past, and it is based on identification with one or both parents who are working through past traumatic experiences in today's reality. Transposition transcends identification as it serves to perpetuate the influence of major historical events through generations (Kestenberg, 1989). Children of survivors who descend into the time tunnel of their parents' past may play different roles—of the parent, various relatives, or the persecutors—but they have to struggle to integrate this fantasized past with the present and with fantasies arising from present day conflicts and their own past (Kestenberg, 1989, 1993).

Transposition may be found more frequently when a child was named for one who had perished at the hands of the Nazis. While the act of naming a newborn after a dead relative is a common Jewish custom, additional responsibility is placed on those children whose parents consider them to be "memorial candles" (Wardi, 1992; Jucovy, 1992). These children are perceived as symbols of everything the parents had lost in the course of their lives. They feel they have a mission to live in the past and to change it so that their parents' humiliation, disgrace, and guilt can be converted into victory over the oppressors, and the threat of genocide can be undone with a restitution of life and worth. The young people who are burdened in this way often feel destined to live two lives and fulfill goals fueled by the idea of who they and their lost sibling should or could have been in order to somehow heal their parents' pain. In this way, their own expectations may exceed the rigorous ones imposed by their parents.

A QUALITATIVE STUDY OF THE SECOND GENERATION

After reviewing studies on the children of survivors, Solkoff (1992) provides a critical evaluation of the methodologies, unwarranted interpretations, and generalizations of these studies. Most failed his criteria for good research. It may be unrealistic to expect a definitive understanding of intergenerational transmission in view of the interwoven strands of other variables beyond those which are Holocaust-related. The goal of the study underlying this chapter was more modest.

Its aim was to explore the phenomenology of the transmission of Holocaust-related trauma from survivors to their offspring and to elucidate the process of transmission by applying object relations theory.

This study was a qualitative analysis of six women's accounts using a method grounded in textual analysis of semistructured interviews. The six female subjects, aged between 32 and 49 years, were recruited from the Jewish community in Sydney, Australia, through a snowballing technique. The sample was not clinically derived, although two women had been in therapy. All were married and combined family responsibilities with a career. They were born after World War II and had at least one parent who had experienced the Nazi concentration camps. The study focused on women in order to isolate the dynamics, as previous research indicates gender differences in second-generation responses (Solkoff, 1992).

The method used was modified analytical induction (Gilgun, 1995) derived from the widely used Grounded Theory of Glaser and Strauss (Glaser & Strauss, 1967; Strauss & Corbin, 1990). Subjects were interviewed using an open-ended set of focus questions adapted from those used by Hass (1990). These questions were designed to explore the subjects' identity, with special attention to the potential influence of their parents' Holocaust experience and any conscious or unconscious themes. A sample of the questions used:

1. How do you believe your parents' experiences during the Holocaust affected the way they raised you as a child?
2. Has the Holocaust affected your outlook on life?
3. Do you ever have any daytime fantasies which relate to the Holocaust?

These allowed for in-depth exploration of the subjective experience of living as a child of Holocaust survivors. Interviews were conducted either in the subject's home or that of the researcher, according to the subject's preference. Interviews varied in length from 1 to 3 hr, and were audiotaped and transcribed verbatim. The analysis was conducted by breaking the individual interview texts into meaning units which were grouped together into themes and ultimately consolidated into four superordinate themes (Gilgun, 1995; Glaser & Strauss, 1967). The following superordinate themes were derived from the text: (a) heightened awareness of parents' survivor status, (b) parenting style, (c) overidentification with parents' experiences, and (d) transmission of fear and mistrust.

Heightened Awareness of Parents' Survivor Status

When asked what they knew of their parents' Holocaust experiences, subjects' responses ranged from having had parents who openly communicated their experiences to those whose parents completely avoided the subject. However, all subjects reported that they were aware of being the child of a survivor from a very early age:

> "Ever since I can remember I've known that she is a Holocaust survivor. … It just goes back to my earliest memories."

> "It was a fact. … I think we always sort of knew."

In some cases the topic was considered taboo, and it was sensed that to ask questions would cause parents pain:

> "I don't think I ever thought much about asking them questions. Maybe it was clear that this was an area not to be delved into."

Where there was communication, description was fragmentary and evolved slowly over time. Children were protected from being exposed to such pain, and details were reserved for their adulthood:

> "I have snippets of information only … 'cause they always protected us and said … you don't need to know this and you don't need to know that." "The underlying theme [was] … 'I will tell you some things but we won't tell you the real gruesome stuff.'"

All subjects felt their survivor parents had communicated (directly or indirectly) an enormous amount of suffering. While some referred to details of their deprivation, there were still topics that they never spoke about—such as personal torture or humiliations:

> "Say, if I was complaining about something, they'd say 'Well, what do you know about … I mean, you try standing in the snow for a week without your shoes, then you know what cold is!' … So then you know they spent a week in the snow without their shoes."

This theme demonstrates that transmission of the impact of parents' experience was unavoidable, whether overt or covert. All subjects felt a sharpened awareness of their parents' suffering and an acute consciousness of being the child of a survivor.

Parenting Style

A common theme was extreme overprotection in parenting style. Many sports were perceived as too risky and the world was portrayed as a dangerous place. The sense of being a precious result of their parents' survival was inherent in their understanding of this protectiveness; thus there were no temptations to rebel or expressions of resentment at this aspect of how they had been parented:

"Watching every step I took ... just too over-the-top. ... "

"You can't be sick. ... You don't just have a cold—you've got pneumonia!"

 "Like with a trip overseas ... when I come back ... never any 'Welcome home,' rather it's [said with a concerned voice] 'How are you?' It's always my existence ... her feeling of fear ... the paranoia."

"They were fearful, protective ... overly protective. ... To climb a tree, you'd fall out of it and break an arm. To ride a bike, you'd break a leg. To swim, you'd drown. ... We were raised ... to be overly cautious and careful. Careful with strangers, careful with people, careful with the physical world as well." "She always looked so agitated and worried when we had the sniffles. ... I rarely tell her [I'm sick] to this day."

The two subjects who did not experience overprotection describe quite the opposite—apathy and even neglect from their parents. They understood this as partly due to their immigrant status which required the parents to focus on providing for the family and establishing a new life. However, there was also a feeling that their parents were still working at repressing their past and succeeded only through shutting out emotional expression:

"Dad was basically absent. ... He didn't figure in our lives. ... He didn't have a parenting function ... he was completely preoccupied elsewhere."

"The emotional gap [was] a wall that no one ever chose or sought to break through, and I think that's because Mum and Dad couldn't bear pain anymore. Couldn't bear to confront conflict in the family. ... They couldn't ... didn't want to know about any problems ... to block off anything that might harm them or upset them ... like they've had enough pain."

Other themes were lack of boundaries and difficulty with separation. Survivors often became totally involved in their child's life, receiving vicarious satisfaction and enforcing a symbiotic relationship. Individuation was thwarted as parents may have unconsciously communicated that they could not endure another separation. Separations of any kind could elicit feelings associated with previous separations and loss of family members in the camps. The child, even in adulthood, still was anxious about reopening this wound and felt responsible for having to be there as a source of comfort and joy for their emotionally fragile parents:

> "She says … 'you're all I've got' … and as a child she was everything to me. … As I got older … I just wanted her to ease off. … I feel that everything's on my shoulders to make things as pleasant as I can for her. … She's just so … terribly needy." "[After I left] home to get married … my mother … cried for the first year of my marriage!"

> "The way I related to my mother was with extreme care, and [in] our relationship … in a lot of ways, I guess, I became the parent. As I grew older, I used to often feel my youth was the youth that she'd missed out on."

Overidentification With Parents' Experiences

A powerful theme that permeated many narratives was the expression of ways in which subjects felt closely connected to the Holocaust experience; there was a sense that they themselves had experienced the war. This virtual reexperiencing manifested itself in a multitude of ways, including vivid reliving of experiences in daytime fantasies. These phenomena are conceptualized under the superordinate theme of overidentification with their parents' experiences.

When asked whether they ever experienced dreams that had Holocaust content, most subjects reported difficulty in recalling any dreams at all. However, two subjects recounted nightmares:

> "I do have a recurring dream which I think is related to the Holocaust. It's … related to … being able to … get yourself out of a situation, where one way you choose is life and one way you choose is death, so it was saying the right things. So it's like at, at an interrogation or selection process, like … do you tell them that you've eaten or not eaten? Which is the right answer … ?"

> "There was a dream … wanting to get on a train to go away, on a flash beautiful train and I ended up on this dark old rattler being taken off to … something like Auschwitz."

Daytime fantasies were more commonly manifested and were described by five of the subjects. Questioning often unleashed detailed descriptions of vivid imagery, emotions, and perceptions associated with reliving of—and identification with—their parents' experiences:

> "If I get cold in the bathroom I remember stories of them standing in the snow without shoes on. ... I almost try and make myself feel the fear and the pain. ... In my own mind, I think how the hell must they have felt to be standing there ... with the cold feet thing. ... I will think I'm my mother ... and I think of all the details. I think who am I standing next to and why am I standing here and how am I feeling ... trying to think what she might have been thinking."

> "I have imagined myself being cramped up in those beds ... and how I would survive ... the cattle cars ... having to go to the toilet in front of people. How would I have coped with that?"

> "As a child, I used to think ... what would I do? Would I be as strong? Would I be as brave? I had very strong images of where they were. I can paint it ... to the stones and the blades of grass ... the smells ... as if I was there."

Another theme relating to overidentification is that of transposition (Kestenberg, 1990) whereby the survivor's child descends into the past and enacts the role of the parents, attempting to restore what they have lost. Thus, the children feel the loss as if they have experienced the trauma:

> "I feel like I've been through what my parents have been through. ... I almost feel like it passed from my parents to me."

> "Every story they've told me ... I worked through in my mind. ... It's like almost wanting to be involved ... somehow want to feel a bit of what they went through."

> "Trying to live through their experience ... because I feel like it's been passed on. ... It's a very strong, deep feeling of loss and pain."

> "She named me after her mother ... the loss ... I didn't feel that I was a replacement ... but ... I was going to somehow make up for my mother and what she went through. ... To lose a little boy [mother lost a son in camps] ... I sort of felt a loss myself."

> "I feel that it's one ... hers and mine is one story."

This process may result in the child's developing a sense of having to rescue and protect the parent from past and current pain. Thus, a number of subjects referred to the need to be very good children and overly compliant as there was always the thought of not wanting to hurt their parents any further than the pain they had already suffered:

"There was a lot of pressure on me to make him happy and do well."

"The way the interaction works is me still being very tentative around his vulnerability and thinking that he is going to crack"

"and I was the perfect child ... I did everything right."

"I think to block off anything that might harm them or upset them, like they've had enough pain."

"I didn't want to upset them. Always ... subjugating ... my own needs."

"With Dad, there's just a big void ... I am scared of him ... I'm scared of hurting him ... "

"If I did well at school it was all I lived for, to do well for them. ... I think that comes a lot from wanting to ... please them because of all the stuff they'd been through. ... I felt I just wanted to make them happy."

There were also examples of the transmission of some of the survivors' remaining wartime behaviors and idiosyncrasies. Subjects reported that although they mimic these behaviors partly consciously, there is a sense that they themselves have lived through the experience. These behaviors generally concerned the need to ensure future security. Messages such as "Be aware of the enemy," "Food must not be wasted," "One should be financially independent," and "Education is crucial as knowledge cannot be removed," help explain some of the following comments:

"I have to have more than enough ... and it's not for greed ... I like the feeling of having it ... in case I need it ... it's the security ... something terrible might happen. ... "

"In many ways, I try and shop for bread in a way that I'm not throwing out a lot."

Children of survivors tend to be empathic to their parents' suffering to a degree that leads to overidentification. Children feel a desire not only to get in touch with their parents' past pain but also to heal the wounds, fill voids left from past loss, and be hypervigilant so that they do not cause further distress.

Transmission of Fear and Mistrust

A significant theme among all subjects was the transmission of fear and mistrust. Survivor parents viewed the world (especially the Gentile world) as potentially hostile. As children, these lessons were learned well and were translated into wariness and suspicion. Being Jewish was felt as a potential cause for victimization and danger:

> "I'm a fairly suspicious person … kind of a paranoia. … It's like, don't believe what you hear or see. … I mean it's about trusting people. … I do think I have an exaggerated, but real, fear of anti-Semitism."

> "My parents always were saying, 'What's in your head they can never take away from you.'… I never knew who 'they' were but it was … always this scary person who might come and take my knowledge from me. … "

> "With individuals … especially at work … I am very wary … I'm a very cautious person."

> "We had to strive intellectually because that couldn't be stolen. … My brother and I had to be each other's best friend, because there weren't going to be any others. No one else to trust outside of your family. … The world was not a place to trust."

The level of observance of Jewish culture varied among the subjects, and some were from families that emphasized assimilation. Nevertheless, there was a clear message of wariness regarding every Gentile as a potential anti-Semite. All subjects admitted that despite having non-Jewish friends, their close friends were Jewish. In one instance, with the ongoing fear of renewed persecution, there were doubts about a non-Jew's loyalty in the event of another Holocaust:

> "You'd have to call it a lack of trust. … My parents … said … sooner or later, he'll turn around and call you a 'bloody Jew.'"

> "I'm much more comfortable with Jewish people … I'm not totally at ease [with others] … I always feel that there is some kind of anti-Semitism in people … with Jewish people they have gone through what I've gone through."

> "I sometimes look at people that I know who aren't Jewish and wonder … would you be protective towards me if something like that [the Holocaust] happened? Would you hide me?"

Most subjects feared the possibility of another Jewish Holocaust. Constant exposure to the survivor's perception of a malevolent non-Jewish world is etched into the minds of their offspring, leaving them with similar fears and insecurities. All Jews are aware of the persecution of Jews throughout the centuries. However, with children of survivors, it is a part of history that they live with and feel intensely. Thus, it becomes more than just words in a history text; it is a very possible reality.

> "Why should there not be another attempt? There have been so many attempts to get rid of the Jews ... why should there not be another Nazi idiot?"

> "I feel it could happen again. ... There's so much hate in the world ... and so much of it is directed against the Jews."

As Hass (1990) suggests, for many Jews, Israel is testimony to the endurance of their people and is often perceived as the safeguard averting another Holocaust. I, therefore, explored these subjects' feelings about Israel. These responses are conceptualized under the superordinate theme of fear and mistrust because most of the subjects saw Israel as providing them with protection against the enemy and a place to go if another explosion of anti-Semitism were to happen:

> "I see it [Israel] as a sign of victory for the Jews ... I see it as a haven for Jews. If there's ever a problem, there would be Israel to fight for us ... I just feel happy knowing that there's something there to protect the Jews."

> "It's a nice feeling to know that I really have a country to go to ... if the whole world turns on me."

The Odd One Out

Unlike the other subjects, Subject 5 in the study felt that her parents' survival of the camps had little impact on her. Her parents, who had each lost their previous spouse and children in the Holocaust, communicated very little about their experience, and she respected their decision to keep this part of their lives buried. She did not feel that it was a forbidden area, but she had no desire to delve into their past. Although she described her parents as extremely protective, she never felt restrained and describes a relationship that did not feel intrusive, enmeshed, absent, or preoccupied:

> "They tried very hard not to allow their past to influence the future."

> "I would find it very difficult to say how their lives were affected because I thought both of my parents were pretty normal in their behaviour, their behaviour to each other, their behaviour towards me."

Any daytime fantasies reflecting Holocaust imagery were attributed to reading material or movies. There was no expression of feeling vulnerable as a Jew or fear of renewed persecution. Although most of her close friends were Jewish, she clearly felt no mistrust or discomfort with friends who were Gentiles. Given her feelings of safety, there was no evidence of attachment to Israel or a feeling that it provided a haven in the event of another Holocaust:

> "I would never feel that [mistrust or fear] unless there was evidence to warrant that sort of thing. I don't ... think of people in that way."

Overall, she described very few ways in which the Holocaust impinged on her life; she even found the term *child of survivors* inappropriate as she felt her parents' experiences were separate from her identity:

> "I feel ... that they [her parents] probably did a very good job in terms of coping themselves with the difficulties that they must have had and then protecting me from feeling the effect of it."

However, she did acknowledge that on some level there had been a form of subtle transmission.

> "There was obviously something there, I can't quite put my finger on it, but it obviously made me aware that things were different."

DISCUSSION

Systematic analysis of the texts of open-ended interviews with children of Holocaust survivors has provided evidence of intergenerational transmission of the trauma of the concentration camps. To what extent can one assume that this transmission has occurred through unconscious processes? The second generation has had ample opportunity to learn about Nazi persecution from many conscious sources, but important aspects of this transmission appear to be more intimate, intrapsychic, and unconscious. Converging evidence from the interviews and from the published literature suggests that this is so.

The results of the data analysis of these interviewees are remarkably similar to those reported by other analytic writers and which include heightened awareness of parents' suffering despite reluctant and fragmentary verbal communication, a sense of having experienced the camp trauma themselves, vivid Holocaust-related nightmares or fantasies, quirky behaviors linked specifically to camp experiences, a deep sense of fear and mistrust of non-Jews, and enmeshment in parent–child relationships where the price of individuation is the risk of inflicting pain on a parent whose losses have already been unbearable. There is pervasive anxiety despite few objective dangers in their present lives.

Concepts from psychoanalytic thinking—in particular, the process of projective identification—are offered here in an attempt to account for the compelling quality of subjects' accounts of Holocaust-related imagery and affect, and the binding nature of parent–child relationships and their reversals. These processes represent (a) unconscious attempts by parents at self-healing and (b) reciprocal participation by children (despite the cost to themselves). These phenomena exist along a continuum, the more severe end of which might constitute a distinct pathological syndrome.

Communication from the survivors to their children is sometimes direct and at other times more subtle and coded. It is not uncommon for children to discover more about their parents' story as the children enter adulthood and the parents consider them better able to deal with the information. Additionally, the passing of time may have enabled the parent survivor to process and deal with painful material better (Hass, 1990). However, irrespective of communication style, transmission occurs in such a manner that the child attempts to process the parent's experience—both consciously and unconsciously.

The interviews elicited numerous instances of overidentification with parents' experience, such as Holocaust imagery in dreams and fantasies. These include the fear of being at the hands of Nazis and imagining what must be done in order to survive (e.g., hiding, denying one's Judaism). The most recurrent theme is placing themselves in a situation analogous to that of their parents. Graphic intrusive imagery, nightmares, and daytime fantasies may be conceptualized as not only overidentification but as a form of reenactment—a way of trying to resolve and undo their parents' pain. One may also interpret these phenomena as an attempt to make meaning of their parents' horrific past and to share their suffering. Sensations of mourning, angst, and fear become shared experiences.

The relationship between survivor parents and their offspring may be seen as symbiotic. When such blurring of boundaries occurs, the child's innate drive toward separation and individuation causes problems for both parent and child. The survivor parent may find any separation difficult as it reactivates losses experienced during the Holocaust, arousing fear and anxiety. Consequently, the struggle for individuation may result in the parent either clinging tenaciously or withdrawing emotional support. The child is fearful as to what this will do to the parent and, left with feelings of guilt, may remain enmeshed at the expense of autonomy. The wishes of the differentiated self may need to be repressed because they threaten the solidarity of the family which remains strong by being united against a hostile world (Freyberg, 1989). Children may then introject these fears of abandonment and feel that they cannot distance themselves from their parents without completely losing the object. Also, the symbiotic relationship should be considered in the context of mutual interaction; not only do parents cling to their children, but children also cling to their parents in the hope of receiving some parenting from them (B. Ebert, personal communication).

Overidentification is further evidenced by other behaviors. Mistrust of others and vulnerability in the Gentile world are described as more than feelings of being a minority group. There is a sense that the children have been traumatized themselves and cannot eliminate the state of hypervigilance that has been instilled in them. This is also seen in repetitions of survivors' behaviors and idiosyncrasies, which have no current adaptive value. The children's own sense of security (both physical and interpersonal) has been compromised. One may understand this as their attempt to process a trauma which, although alien to their own experience, has been internalized throughout their development and now forms an integral part of their psychological identity.

These experiences may be explained as evidence of transposition, the "tendency to go back in time and explore their parents' past" (Kestenberg, 1989, p. 78). Once they descend into the time tunnel, the children become more aware of their parents' suffering and loss, and feel a responsibility to heal their parents' wounds and ensure that their parents will suffer no further pain. In this way, they often take on a parental role and feel their own loss of a carefree childhood. The loss of a carefree childhood may have been further compounded by their migrant status, in which it is common for children to take on a role of responsibility for the family. The concept of transposition explains identification and the penetration of Holocaust imagery into fantasy and dream life within a more classical psychoanalytic framework. The process of transmission may be further understood within an object relations model which places more emphasis on the dual direction of communication between parent and child and incorporates a mutual unconscious dialogue to explain the transmission mechanism.

Shoshan (1989) suggests that long before verbal communication, the baby (child of the survivor) absorbs the sadness, excessive concern, or simply the parents' emotional absence. As the child develops, the dynamic has been set for the process of overidentification and closeness as a way of being with, loving, and protecting the parent. With very traumatized parents, children may receive little mirroring as infants and thus learn that in order to feel held (Winnicott, 1965), they must offer themselves as a source of joy to diminish their parents' fears and pain. Unconscious transmission of parents' fantasies adds to this process. The fantasies may be that the child is a replacement of a lost family member (especially a former child) or has a mission to restore family pride through achievements. If children introject these fantasies, one may presume that there is pressure on the children to return to the parents what they have lost. Thus the child lives a life governed by the aim of fulfilling the parents' wishes and protecting them from further emotional pain.

The best explanation for the transmission of parental trauma involves the process of projective identification. This process, originally proposed by Melanie Klein, is considered to be a primitive mechanism used by the baby to communicate to its mother by projecting unbearable terrors and anxieties into her. The mother needs to be able to process and hold these feelings for the baby and return them in a more palatable form. The reverse occurs with the children of Holocaust survivors—they become the containers for their parents' projections.

Survivor parents enter a process of self-healing and unconsciously use their children as a means of psychic recovery through a form of projective identification whereby the parent splits off the unwanted part of the self, which is then projected into the child. The child internalizes the projection and then starts to think, feel, and act in accordance with the projection (Ogden, 1991). Through the projection of this massive anxiety and pain, the parent diminishes unbearable feelings associated with the past. The children return the projected feelings in the form of attempts to compensate the parents' losses by being compliant, impeding their own separation, replacing lost objects, and living lives that attempt to make up for the parents' losses.

Parental projection and child introjection are suggested by the vivid ways in which subjects describe their parents' pain and loss, often as if they have experienced the concentration camps themselves. This has occurred despite parents' unwillingness to burden their children with such knowledge. Accounts of pressure for the child to process and return these feelings and to provide containment are supported by those of reverse parenting, overcompliance, enmeshment, and attempted restitution. Pervasive anxiety and mistrust of others suggest that parental trauma has left the second generation with a lasting legacy.

Despite the nonclinical nature of this sample, the findings are similar to those of past research using clinical samples or case studies (though outcomes were often more severe in those studies). The lack of major pathology in this sample may be due to these subjects' ability to participate in their parents' self-healing combined with the parents possessing sufficient ego strength to avoid burdening their children to an extreme degree. Consequently, the children may have managed to integrate the repercussions of living with the transmission of trauma in a form that proved to be comparatively adaptive.

An Explanation of the Odd One Out

While it is true that children of survivors should not be seen as a homogenous group and all themes are not common to all subjects, it is valuable to try to understand why Subject 5 differs so markedly.

She describes herself as fairly shy and reserved, and her parents as undemonstrative but supportive. She comments that her parents seem to have blocked out the Holocaust part of their lives. Perhaps in this family, repression and denial have been effective mechanisms in buffering transmission to the next generation. Nevertheless, there is a subtle indication of some unconscious transmission. The unconscious dialogue between parents and child may have enforced repression as the only way to tolerate intense emotion and taught her to keep her innermost fears and emotions highly defended and split off. Perhaps this has proved adaptive as she feels none of the anxieties or repercussions described by other subjects. This interpretation is supported by her description of having difficulty with opening up and being guarded with any emotional expression.

CONCLUSION

In this chapter, I have used inferences drawn from a qualitative study of six daughters of Holocaust survivors to propose a model of healing that may occur across generations. The subjects in this study are relatively strong women living productive lives despite the lingering shadows of the Holocaust. The phenomena of their experience may lie on a continuum, at one end of which is a process of self-healing and restitution that occurs between parent and child. The process of projective identification plays a central role in this healing, though at some cost to the child. The more severe end of this spectrum may constitute a more pathological and identifiable type of secondary traumatic stress. As the sample size was small and nonclinical, this model of interactive healing remains tentative. Further research, using a similar methodology but with clinical subjects and a comparison group, may help to substantiate and delineate this model.

REFERENCES

Barocas, H., & Barocas, C. (1973). Manifestations of concentration camp effects on the second generation. *American Journal of Psychiatry, 103*, 820–821.

Berger, L. (1988). The long-term psychological consequences of the Holocaust on the survivors and their offspring. In R. L. Braham (Ed.), *The psychological perspectives of the Holocaust and of its aftermath* (pp. 145–168). New York: Columbia University Press.

Bergmann, M. S. (1990a). Recurrent problems in the treatment of survivors and their children. In M. S. Bergmann & M. E. Jucovy (Eds.), *Generations of the Holocaust* (pp. 247–266). New York: Columbia University Press.

Bergmann, M. S. (1990b). Thoughts on superego pathology of survivors and their children. In M. S. Bergmann & M. E. Jucovy (Eds.), *Generations of the Holocaust* (pp. 287–309). New York: Columbia University Press.

Bergmann, M. S., & Jucovy, M. E. (Eds.). (1990). *Generations of the Holocaust*. New York: Columbia University Press.

Chodoff, P. (1963). Late effects of the concentration camp syndrome. *Archives of General Psychiatry, 8*, 323–333.

Epstein, H. (1979). *Children of the Holocaust: Conversations with sons and daughters of survivors.* New York: Penguin.

Freyberg, J. T. (1989). The emerging self in the survivor family. In P. Marcus & A. Rosenberg (Eds.), *Healing their wounds: Psychotherapy with Holocaust survivors and their families* (pp. 85–104). New York: Praeger.

Gilgun, J. F. (1995). We shared something special: The moral discourse of incest perpetrators. *Journal of Marriage and the Family, 57*, 265–281.

Glaser, B. G., & Strauss, A. L. (1967). *The discovery of grounded theory.* San Francisco: Aldine.

Hass, A. (1990). *In the shadow of the Holocaust: The second generation.* Ithaca, NY: Cornell University Press.

Herzog, J. (1990). World beyond metaphor: Thoughts on the transmission of trauma. In M. S. Bergmann & M. E. Jucovy (Eds.), *Generations of the Holocaust* (pp. 103–119). New York: Columbia University Press.

Jucovy, M. E. (1992). Psychoanalytic contributions to Holocaust studies. *International Journal of Psychoanalysis, 73*, 267–282.

Kaminer, H., & Lavie, P. (1994). Sleep and dreams in well-adjusted and less adjusted Holocaust survivors. In M. S. Stroebe, W. Stroebe, & R. O'Harrison (Eds.), *Handbook of Bereavement* (pp. 331–345). New York: Cambridge University Press.

Kestenberg, J. S. (1989). Transposition revisited: Clinical, therapeutic, and developmental considerations. In P. Marcus & A. Rosenberg (Eds.), *Healing their wounds: Psychotherapy with Holocaust survivors and their families* (pp. 67–82). New York: Praeger.

Kestenberg, J. S. (1990). Survivor-parents and their children. In M. S. Bergmann & M. E. Jucovy (Eds.), *Generations of the Holocaust* (pp. 83–102). New York: Columbia University Press.

Kestenberg, J. S. (1993). What a psychoanalyst learned from the Holocaust and genocide. *International Journal of Psychoanalysis, 74*, 1117–1129.

Krell, R. (1979). Holocaust families: The survivors and their children. *Comprehensive Psychiatry, 20*, 560–568.

Lang, M. (1994). Silence: Therapy with Holocaust survivors and their families. *Australian and New Zealand Journal of Family Therapy, 16*, 1–10.

Miller, A. (1995). *The drama of the gifted child* (2nd ed.). London: Virago.

Niederland, W. G. (1968). Clinical observations on the "survivor syndrome." *International Journal of Psychoanalysis, 49*, 313–315.

Ogden, T. H. (1991). *Projective identification and psychotherapeutic technique.* New York: Jason Aronson.

Okner, D. F., & Flaherty, J. (1988). Parental communication and psychological distress in children of Holocaust survivors: A comparison between the U.S. and Israel. *The International Journal of Social Psychiatry, 35*, 265–273.

Prince, R. M. (1985). Second generation effects of historical trauma. *Psychoanalytic Review, 72*, 9–29.

Shoshan, T. (1989). Mourning and longing from generation to generation. *American Journal of Psychotherapy, 43,* 193–207.

Solkoff, N. (1992). Children of survivors of the Nazi Holocaust: A critical review of the literature. *American Journal of Orthopsychiatry, 62,* 342–358.

Solkoff, N. (1992a). The Holocaust: Survivors and their children. In M. Basoglu (Ed.), *Torture and its consequences: Current treatment approaches* (pp. 136–148). London: Cambridge University Press.

Steinberg, A. (1989). Holocaust survivors and their children: A review of the clinical literature. In P. Marcus & A. Rosenberg (Eds.), *Healing their wounds: Psychotherapy with Holocaust survivors and their families* (pp. 23–48). New York: Praeger.

Strauss, A. L., & Corbin, J. (1990). *Basics of qualitative research: Grounded theory procedures and techniques.* Thousand Oaks, CA: Sage.

Wardi, D. (1992). *Memorial candles: Children of the Holocaust* (N. Goldblum, Trans.). London: Tavistock/Routledge.

Winnicott, D. W. (1965). *The maturational processes and the facilitating environment.* New York: International Universities Press.

Part II

RESEARCH

7

The Relationship Between Traumatic Stress and Marital Intimacy

VALERIE E. WHIFFEN AND LUIS E. OLIVER

In this chapter, we review the literature on the association between trauma and marital intimacy. Clinical wisdom holds that high quality relationships moderate the impact of trauma. Specifically, individuals with good relationships are thought to be comparatively resilient to trauma while those with poor relationships are at risk of experiencing such adverse consequences as emotional distress. For most adults, the relationship with one's spouse is the most significant of any social relationship. Thus, marital relationships should be a particularly potent resource for individuals coping with trauma. In the first section of this chapter, we assess the empirical evidence to support this hypothesis. In the second section, we introduce a parallel hypothesis: trauma has an impact on individuals' ability to develop and sustain good interpersonal relationships. We conclude with a section on possible mechanisms of action that may account for the apparent effects of trauma on marital relations. Throughout the chapter, we adopt a broad definition of traumatic stress. The *DSM-IV (Diagnostic and Statistical Manual of Mental Disorders, Fourth Edition)* definition of a traumatic event is generally regarded to be too narrow. We accept Carlson and Dalenberg's (2000) definition of a traumatic event as any event that is uncontrollable, extremely negative, and unpredictable or sudden.

DO MARITAL RELATIONS MODERATE THE IMPACT OF TRAUMA?

Clinicians generally believe that the quality of intimate relationships moderates the impact of trauma (Carlson & Dalenberg, 2000). For instance, Judith Herman (1992), in her widely influential book on the treatment of trauma survivors, *Trauma and Recovery*, asserted that a critical component of therapy with this population is the therapist's "bearing witness," that is, hearing empathically and validating the story of the trauma. Other clinicians who work extensively with trauma survivors also emphasize the importance of intimate, validating relationships in the recovery process. If intimate relationships are so strongly implicated in recovery, then it follows logically that adverse emotional responses to trauma, such as posttraumatic stress disorder (PTSD) and depression, may be avoided altogether by the presence of warm, supportive relationships. Who better to provide this warmth and compassion than one's spouse?

Methodological Considerations

This intuitively sensible proposal is, from an empirical point of view, surprisingly difficult to demonstrate. Ideally, a researcher would need to have a measure of the quality of marital relations before the trauma because, as we will show in the second section, there is ample evidence that the experience of trauma can have a negative impact on marital relations. Therefore, if the researcher evaluates the marriage after the trauma has occurred, it is difficult to disentangle cause and effect. This research requirement is virtually impossible to meet because, in most instances, researchers cannot predict that an individual will experience a traumatic event. One possible exception is with novice emergency workers and policemen who are highly likely to experience critical incidents in the course of their work. Researchers who are interested in the buffering effects of marital relations may find this an ideal population on which to test their hypotheses.

The remaining requirements for demonstrating moderation are methodological and statistical. How a researcher demonstrates moderation differs depending on the nature of the group sampled. If all of the individuals in the sample experienced traumatic stress, then the researcher only needs to show that better quality relationships are associated with better outcomes. However, if the sample included both individuals who experienced traumatic stress and those who did not, a different set of statistical analyses would be required. Baron and Kenny (1986) provided a relatively simple method for demonstrating moderation under these conditions. Conceptually, the researcher examines the association between the independent variable (traumatic stress: present versus absent) and the dependent variable (emotional distress) at different levels of the moderator (marital relations). Typically, high, medium, and low levels of the moderator are examined. Moderation is demonstrated if the association between traumatic stress and emotional distress differs as a function of high, medium, or low levels of marital relations. Thus, a researcher might predict that traumatic stress is associated with emotional distress more strongly if the marital relationship is of poor quality. Although this is the standard procedure for testing moderating effects that is widely used in the social support literature, few of the studies we reviewed formally tested for moderation.

The final requirement is methodological. Most of the research we reviewed was cross-sectional; that is, data were collected from participants at one point in time only. Thus, trauma, marital relations, and emotional distress were all measured at the same time. While cross-sectional studies are useful for pointing researchers in the direction of meaningful relationships, they are not conclusive because, conceptually, the IV (independent variable), DV (dependant variable), and moderator are confounded with one another. Ideally, the demonstration of moderation requires the collection of longitudinal data. Levels of traumatic stress and the moderator at Time 1 would be used to predict levels of emotional distress at Time 2. None of the studies we reviewed collected longitudinal data and tested for moderation. Therefore, we must conclude before we have even begun our review that, up to this point in time, no study can conclusively support the hypothesis that marital relations moderate the impact of traumatic stress.

Literature Review

Clinicians often write about the importance of marital relations in coping with trauma. For instance, Dyregrov (2001) published a paper based on his years of experience counseling families coping with trauma and loss. He argued that the family's level of functioning at the time of the loss is an important determinant of individual outcomes. One common source of difficulty is "asynchrony" in the reactions of family members to the trauma that can create misunderstanding and conflict. In particular, he discussed the typical asynchrony that arises between husbands and wives who tend to cope with trauma in radically different ways. Women's emotional reactions tend to be intense and long lasting and they tend to want to talk extensively about the trauma. In contrast, men use distraction and avoidance to cope and they tend to prefer solitary coping strategies. Couples who default to asynchronous coping strategies may become maritally distressed, or the emotional distress of one or both partners may be exacerbated. Similarly, Johnson and Williams-Keeler (1998) asserted that the marital relationship has the potential to be a "recovery environment" for individuals coping with the emotional aftermath of trauma. Spouses are in an ideal position to help trauma survivors regulate their negative emotions, and the survivor's experience of the partner as caring, responsive, and accessible provides a corrective emotional experience that contradicts the learning that took place during the trauma. Furthermore, we speculate that the spouse's provision of this corrective experience is especially potent when the trauma has been interpersonal. These observations are consistent with our own clinical experiences, which suggest that the quality of marital relationships influence the trajectory of therapy.

Clinical observations are supported by the results of a handful of qualitative studies. Cagnetta and Cicognani (1999) used the grounded theory method to analyze their interviews with 20 individuals who sustained serious, permanent injuries after motor vehicle accidents (MVAs). They reported that the stage immediately after the injury was characterized, in part, by patients being anxious about the security of their relationships with family members and about the continuity of these individuals' love for them. The patients tended to seclude themselves at home and to derive a great deal of relief and comfort from their relationships with significant others. Similarly, Valentine and Feinauer (1993) interviewed 22 women who had been sexually abused as children. Most of them felt that support from others in both childhood and adulthood had been important in helping them to overcome their abuse. In particular, many respondents felt that the support they experienced in their marriages had been pivotal to their recovery. Even trauma that does not have direct negative consequences for the individual shows similar effects. McCarroll, Ursano, Wright, and Fullerton (1993) interviewed several hundred individuals who handled human remains after major disasters. The authors reported that many workers wanted to tell their spouses about their experiences but felt that they were unwilling to listen. Those who perceived their spouses as sensitive and caring were more likely to talk about their experiences (see section "Why Does Trauma Have a Negative Impact on Marital Relations," p. 000) which helped them to make the transition "back to the real world" after returning from the disaster site. The major limitation of these studies is the lack of comparison groups. Without them, we do not know that marital relations are more important after trauma than they are normally.

The empirical support for this hypothesis is very limited. A recent meta-analysis concluded that there is support for the general notion that social support buffers the impact of trauma (Brewin, Andrews, & Valentine, 2000). The authors reviewed 11 studies that correlated lack of social support with PTSD symptoms among trauma survivors. Their analysis showed the average association between lack of support and PTSD symptoms to be .40, which was the largest effect size they obtained among the risk factors they evaluated. However, there was significant variation in the effect size from one sample to another. In particular, lack of social support was more strongly correlated with PTSD symptoms in military (.43) than civilian (.30) samples, which suggests that lack of social support is particularly detrimental to individuals who experience combat-related trauma.

We were able to locate only two empirical studies that assessed marital relations specifically and tested appropriately for moderating effects. Both studies were cross-sectional and both involved samples of women who were sexually victimized. The first was a study of 29 married or cohabiting women who were sexually assaulted in the month prior to data collection (Moss, Frank, & Anderson, 1990). Women's perceptions of the preassault quality of their relationships, as well as the amount of support provided by their partners since the assault, were determined from their responses to a structured interview. More than half of the women reported problematic relations since the assault, including temporary separations from their partners, physical and verbal abuse, and sexual problems. About a third of the women who reported that they did not have marital problems prior to the assault reported low levels of partner support postassault. Consistent with the moderating hypothesis, women with poor partner support reported higher levels of depression, anxiety, and fear and lower levels of self-esteem than did women with supportive partners. These effects were even more pronounced among women whom the researchers characterized as "let down"; these were the women without previous relationship problems who experienced poor partner support after the assault. The researchers speculated that an unexpected lack of support from the spouse is particularly demoralizing.

The second study examined marital relations in a community sample of 60 women, 22 of whom had a history of childhood sexual abuse (CSA). Whiffen, Judd, and Aube (1999) found that the relationship between CSA and depressive symptoms was moderated by marital intimacy and comfort with closeness. CSA survivors were better protected from depression when they perceived their relationships to be high in intimacy and when they preferred to be emotionally close to their partners. While these effects also were present among women without a CSA history, they were stronger among the survivors. It is important to emphasize that, in contrast to the Moss et al. study (1990), these women were not coping with the immediate emotional aftermath of trauma. Thus, intimate and supportive marriages appear to buffer both the immediate and the long-term effects of sexual victimization.

To summarize, the clinical wisdom that marital relationships are an important determinant of recovery from trauma is supported by three qualitative studies and by two empirical studies that used appropriate methods to analyze data for moderation. However, our conclusion must be seriously qualified because both empirical studies sampled very small numbers of women who had been sexually victimized. Therefore, we do not know whether or not these results would generalize to survivors of other forms of traumatic stress. It may be the case that good quality relations with husbands are particularly critical when the trauma being coped with is sexual victimization. While there is evidence from a qualitative study that marital relations help buffer the impact of MVAs involving serious injuries as well, this hypothesis, ideally, needs to be tested empirically with a variety of trauma populations. We also do not know if these results would generalize to male trauma survivors. Given that women and men have been found to cope differently with traumatic events, gender differences may exist in the moderating impact of intimate relationships. Thus, more research is needed to determine whether the above findings also are applicable to traumatized men. Finally, both studies were cross-sectional. Ideally, longitudinal research is needed to demonstrate that marital relations facilitate adaptation to the trauma or recovery from acute symptoms of emotional distress over time.

DOES TRAUMA HAVE A NEGATIVE IMPACT ON MARITAL RELATIONS?

In the following subsections, we review the evidence that trauma has an impact on marital relations. We review the research separately for traumas that occurred in childhood and adulthood, and for different types of trauma. This approach permits us to evaluate the possibilities that different types of trauma have different impacts on the relationship, and that trauma that occurred before the development of the relationship has a different impact than trauma that occurs during the relationship.

Childhood Trauma

Childhood sexual abuse. A history of sexual abuse during childhood has a clear, deleterious impact on adult interpersonal functioning. In a review of the interpersonal consequences of CSA for women, Rumstein-McKean and Hunsley (2001) concluded that CSA survivors experience greater interpersonal difficulties than do nonabused women. They feel more detached and isolated, and report difficulties becoming emotionally engaged with others. Specifically, CSA adversely affects the quality of marital relationships. Most research finds that CSA survivors, compared to nonabused controls, are more likely to avoid developing close adult relationships and to have never married. Although the data are inconsistent across studies, CSA survivors also tend to report lower levels of marital satisfaction and higher levels of marital disruption and divorce than do nonabused women.

Further exploration of this general finding suggests that women with a CSA history have specific difficulties forming secure adult attachment relationships with romantic partners. The studies reviewed by Rumstein-McKean & Hunsley (2001) generally found that CSA survivors report less security in their adult attachment relationships than do women who were not sexually abused. A study by Roche, Runtz, and Hunter (1999) found that, as a whole, women who had been sexually abused in childhood were less secure and more fearful–avoidant than were women who had not experienced CSA. Individuals who are fearful–avoidant in adult attachment relationships want to be close to romantic partners but they are afraid of being rejected by them, a dilemma that they resolve by maintaining emotional distance in their close relationships (Bartholomew & Horowitz, 1991). Within the abused group, women who had experienced intrafamilial sexual abuse were even less secure, more fearful, and less dismissing than those who had experienced extrafamilial abuse. Thus, incest appears to be particularly strongly associated with insecure adult attachment. The finding that incest survivors are both more fearful and less dismissing suggests that they are ambivalent about romantic relationships. Individuals who are dismissing discount the importance of close relationships. Thus, the combination of higher levels of fearfulness with lower levels of dismissing attachment suggests that romantic relationships are simultaneously important and the source of painful fears.

One of the most frequently researched and consistent findings in this literature is that sexual abuse in childhood is associated with sexual problems later in life (cf., review by Beitchman et al., 1992). Although the strength of this association varies widely across studies, CSA survivors in both community and clinical samples experience higher levels of sexual dissatisfaction and dysfunction than do nonabused women (Rumstein-McKean & Hunsley, 2001). Survivors report higher levels of bodily shame, sexual shame, fears, anxieties, and guilt about sexuality, confusion about sexual orientation, difficulties with sexual arousal and desire, and coital pain (Andrews, 1995; Barnes, 1995; Briere & Runtz, 1988; Gold, Milan, Mayall, & Johnson, 1994). Some studies found survivors to show higher levels of sexual distrust and conflicts with men

(Barnes, 1995), as well as multiple sexual partners and brief sexual relationships (Wyatt, Guthrie, & Notgrass, 1992). A recurrent finding is that CSA survivors are at risk for being sexually revictimized as adults (Beitchman et al., 1992; Briere & Runtz, 1988; Gold et al., 1994; Wyatt et al., 1992). The highest rates of sexual disturbance are found in cases involving penetration or father–daughter incest, which suggests that abuse severity contributes to greater problems in sexual relationships later in life (Beitchman et al., 1992).

CSA not only affects the survivor's ability to form and maintain positive, intimate relationships, but may also have an adverse impact on partners. Support for this hypothesis stems primarily from clinical observations. For instance, Oz (2001) argued that husbands of women being treated for CSA may experience feelings of rejection, loneliness, guilt, and inadequacy, and may perceive their wives as making unrelenting demands on them for support. She also speculated that CSA survivors often choose men who have trauma histories themselves and who may have their own difficulties with intimacy and sexuality. There is limited empirical evidence from clinical samples that romantic partners feel frustrated, isolated, and dissatisfied, and that they experience a variety of communication problems in their relationships (Rumstein-McKean & Hunsley, 2001).

It is important to emphasize that these studies did not include clinical comparison groups. Therefore, we do not know how much these results are due to an individual being treated specifically for CSA-related problems, rather than for other emotional problems that may be unrelated to CSA. Nelson and Wampler (2000) sampled couples that were requesting treatment at a marital and family therapy clinic, and classified couples into abuse groups based on the clients' self-reports about childhood physical and sexual abuse. They found that the partners of individuals with an abuse history who had no history themselves reported more emotional distress than did no-abuse couples, although they did not report less marital satisfaction or rate their relationships as less cohesive. The generalizability of these results is limited by the fact that all of the couples were experiencing marital problems; a clinical sample of clients being treated individually for CSA versus nonabuse emotional problems would better reflect the array of marital outcomes that are associated with CSA. However, the results do suggest that partners of abused individuals experience more emotional distress, which partly confirms clinical observations.

Finally, there is some evidence that the association between CSA and emotional distress is mediated by the negative impact of CSA on intimate relationships. That is, the deleterious impact of CSA on emotional functioning is due to the disruptive effects of CSA on the quality of survivors' intimate adult relationships. Roche et al. (1999) found that insecure attachment accounted statistically for the association between CSA and emotional distress in a sample of female undergraduates. Similarly, in a community sample of women and men, Whiffen, Thompson, and Aube (2000) found that interpersonal problems partially mediated the association between CSA and depressive symptoms for both sexes. Thus, there is evidence that CSA not only contributes to relationship difficulties, but that these difficulties, in turn, contribute to the emotional distress consistently associated with CSA.

To summarize, the impact of CSA on marital relations is negative. Women who are CSA survivors are more likely than nonabused women to avoid establishing intimate relationships, possibly because they tend to feel insecurely attached to romantic partners and to fear that their partners will reject them if they get too close. Even when they are able to establish intimate relationships, they experience attachment insecurity (Whiffen et al., 1999) and a variety of sexual problems ranging from guilt and shame about their sexuality to low sexual desire and pain with intercourse. These results are particularly pronounced among incest survivors who appear to differ along at least two dimensions from survivors of extrafamilial abuse. First and most obviously, incest involves interpersonal victimization by a family member. It makes sense that this fact alone may be sufficient to account for incest survivors' pervasive insecurity in subsequent intimate relationships. Second, incest tends to extend over a longer period of time and the abuse is more likely to involve intercourse (Beitchman et al., 1992). Abuse severity also may be implicated in the finding that incest survivors generally experience more difficulties in their marital relations than do survivors of extrafamilial abuse.

In closing, it is important to emphasize that the vast majority of this research was done with female CSA survivors. Therefore, we know nothing about the marital relations of male CSA survivors. One study that compared male and female survivors found that the men's interpersonal relationships were not characterized by the mistrust and disengagement that is pervasive among female survivors (Whiffen et al., 2000). In contrast, male survivors reported difficulties with feeling overly responsible and unassertive in their relationships. This study underscores the need for research with male CSA survivors, and cautions the clinician against generalizing from the research on women to their male clients.

Physical abuse and witnessing interparental violence. Very little research has examined the impact of childhood physical abuse on intimate relationships in adulthood. There is evidence that children who have been physically abused or neglected are more likely to be insecurely attached during childhood than are those who have not (Carlson, Cicchetti, Barnett, & Braunwald, 1989). Severely maltreated children develop a disorganized attachment style that has components of both approach and avoidance (cf., review by Cassidy & Mohr, 2001). While there is speculation that physically abused children may be more vulnerable to attachment difficulties in their romantic relationships later in life (Downey, Khouri, & Feldman, 1996), this hypothesis has not been tested directly.

There is evidence that childhood physical abuse increases the risk of being in a physically abusive marital relationship—both as a perpetrator and as a victim (cf., meta-analysis by Busch, Lundeberg, & Carlton, 2000). Witnessing interparental violence also is a risk factor for being in a physically abusive adult relationship (Busch et al., 2000). While it may be plausible to infer that physically abusive relationships are less intimate, we did not find any research that tested this hypothesis. The handful of studies that directly examined the effects of childhood physical abuse on adult intimacy produced conflicting results. Ducharme, Koverola, and Battle (1997) reported that male and female university students who were physically abused as children reported lower levels of intimacy in their relationships than did nonabused controls. However, this finding was not replicated in a study of female undergraduates (Davis, Petretic-Jackson, & Ting, 2001). Similarly, Belt and Abidin (1996) did not find an association between physical abuse and perceived marital support in a community sample of couples, once other childhood variables such as parental care were taken into account.

Multiple forms of childhood abuse. The research on childhood abuse is complicated by the fact that many children are multiply victimized. For instance, in one study of female undergraduate students, 18% of the sample reported a history of sexual abuse, 11% reported physical abuse, and 7% reported both forms of abuse (Davis et al., 2001). The existing evidence suggests that adults with histories of multiple forms of abuse are particularly at risk for interpersonal problems. For instance, Allen et al. (2001) compared a community sample of women with a clinical sample of female inpatients receiving treatment for trauma. The women in the latter group typically had a severe trauma history which included multiple forms of childhood trauma (e.g., sexual, physical and emotional abuse, and neglect). While the community sample was predominantly secure in their attachment classification on a number of measures, the trauma sample was chiefly fearful–avoidant and preoccupied. These styles will give rise to competing demands in relationships, with the fearful style creating a desire to avoid close relationships while the preoccupied style creates a desire to pursue and cling in close relationships. Similarly, Davis et al. (2001) found that multiply abused female undergraduate students reported a greater fear of intimacy than did individuals reporting either a single form of childhood abuse or no abuse.

Trauma in Adulthood

Sexual assault. In a review of the empirical literature on the psychological impact of sexual assault on women, Hanson (1990) reported that up to a quarter of women show ongoing interpersonal difficulties in the mild to moderate range for as long as several years after the assault. However, there appears to be surprisingly little controlled research specifically on the effects of sexual assault on marital intimacy. Some studies examined the impact of sexual assault on one form of intimacy—sexuality. Most women experience sexual disturbances in the weeks and months following a sexual assault. These problems can include reduced sexual desire and arousal, flashbacks during sex, physical discomfort, and phobic responses to specific sex acts associated with the assault (cf., reviews by Barnes, 1995; Hanson, 1990). Not surprisingly, sexual problems are more common among sexual assault victims than among victims of nonsexual crimes such as armed robbery (Hanson, 1990).

Sexual difficulties may be particularly problematic when the assaulted woman is involved in an ongoing intimate relationship. Holmstrom and Burgess (1979) interviewed 16 married or cohabiting women and 11 of their boyfriends or husbands within three months of the assault. Notably, the majority of couples did not discuss the assault openly; this finding is significant in light of empirical results indicating that the romantic partner's support is a crucial moderator of women's emotional distress after sexual assault (Moss et al., 1990). All of the couples interviewed experienced some problems when they tried to resume sexual relations. Some men believed that their partners had been sexually unfaithful or they felt physically repulsed by knowing that the women "had sex" with another man. Most of the men wanted to have sex soon after the rape as a test of the impact that the assault would have on their sexual relationships. However, it was common for the couples to delay intercourse for as long as several weeks after the assault.

Talking about the assault and expressing feelings is seen by victims to be very helpful immediately after the assault, and the majority of women list their boyfriends or husbands among the people that they have talked to (Frazier & Burnett, 1994). However, romantic partners are perceived to be the least supportive members of victims' social networks. The fact that their wife or girlfriend was assaulted sexually may be difficult emotionally for boyfriends and husbands in ways that interfere with their relationships. Earlier in this chapter, we described the results of a study by Moss et al. (1990) who assessed a small sample of married or cohabiting women shortly after they were sexually assaulted. More than half of the women reported problematic marital relations since the assault, including temporary separations and physical and verbal abuse by their partners. About a third of the women who reported that they did not have marital problems prior to the assault reported low levels of partner support postassault which suggests that it may be difficult for some men to cope with the immediate aftermath of their wives' and girlfriends' sexual assaults even in the context of a good relationship.

There also is evidence that relationship difficulties can persist long after the assault. Miller, Williams, and Bernstein (1982) assessed a sample of 43 couples in which the female partner had a history of sexual assault. To attract couples to the research, they offered free marital therapy and, as a result, we consider this an uncontrolled clinical study even though less than half of the couples accepted treatment. The results are interesting because they indicate that these couples exhibited many difficulties in empathy, commitment, emotional support, and communication, in addition to the sexual problems observed by other researchers. The researchers observed that both the assaulted women and their partners appeared to lack empathy for one another due to their emotional reactions to the assault. While women experienced intense fear and concerns about safety, their partners often experienced rage and they desired retribution; both emotional reactions appeared to attenuate the partners' sensitivity to one another. These researchers speculated that communication problems played a major role in the sexual problems of these couples, in that neither partner was able to communicate clearly about how to resume their sexual relationship. Clinically, the researchers noted that the couples were very difficult to treat—in part because of both partners' unwillingness to discuss the assault and in part because of the many symptoms of emotional distress experienced by the women.

To summarize, sexual assault has a clear impact on women's sexual functioning and can disrupt established intimate relationships. Men's anger toward the perpetrator may overwhelm their empathy and compassion for their partners, while women's pervasive and persistent fears and difficulties with sex also are likely to have a negative impact. Both clinical observation and empirical research suggest that the couple's ability to discuss the assault and to provide support to one another may be an important determinant of the extent to which the assault has a long-lasting impact on the relationship.

Exposure to combat. An early empirical study compared the marital relations of Vietnam veterans who experienced combat during their tours of duty to those who did not (Penk et al., 1981). All of the veterans were voluntarily receiving inpatient treatment for substance abuse. The combat veterans were best discriminated from the noncombat veterans by their reports of greater difficulty getting along with their spouses or mates, marital problems, and difficulties trusting others. Married combat veterans also reported higher levels of conflict in their families of procreation.

Researchers soon began to focus their efforts on veterans who developed symptoms of PTSD because they reasoned that PTSD is the mechanism that creates the marital problems. For instance, Carroll, Rueger, Foy, and Donahoe (1985) identified 21 vets with PTSD and 18 without PTSD among former combat veterans who were voluntarily receiving psychiatric services. When the researchers compared the two groups of veterans, they found no differences in the amount of affectionate behavior the men reported in their marriages. However, the vets with PTSD were less self-disclosing and emotionally expressive with their partners, they were more hostile and physically aggressive, and they were less satisfied with their marriages, describing more conflicted and less engaged marriages, in particular. Levels of hostility statistically discriminated the PTSD and non-PTSD veterans. High levels of hostility are likely to have a dramatic impact on marital relations, promoting both conflict and emotional disengagement. A study by Roberts and his colleagues (Roberts et al., 1982) compared PTSD veterans with both non-PTSD veterans and a noncombat clinical control group. The authors reported that the PTSD veterans reported more difficulties with intimacy and sociability than either of the control groups, which indicates that it is PTSD rather than combat which is associated with intimacy problems. Similarly, Caselli and Motta (1995) showed that combat exposure was a redundant predictor of marital dissatisfaction when PTSD symptoms were taken into account.

Such findings are not confined to veterans of the Vietnam War. One study assessed Israeli soldiers who experienced acute stress reactions during combat in the 1982 war with Lebanon (Solomon et al., 1992). A large proportion of these men went on to develop chronic PTSD. First, the researchers confirmed the results found with Vietnam veterans: Six years after the war, the wives of veterans who experienced stress reactions were less happily married than the wives of men who did not experience stress reactions. Next, the researchers tried to determine whether or not differences existed in these men's marital relations prior to the war. The researchers asked the wives a series of questions about their marriages at four points in time: at marriage, 1 year before the war, 1 year after the war, and in the previous year which was approximately 6 years after the end of the war. The women's responses were coded by two independent judges who rated the marriage at each time point along such dimensions as intimacy, conflict, and emotional expressiveness. The researchers compared the scores of 49 women whose husbands experienced stress reactions to 31 women whose husbands did not. The wives whose husbands experienced stress reactions reported marked reductions in marital satisfaction and cohesion immediately after the war. However, they reported many more significant differences before the war. They viewed their marriages as less intimate, less emotionally expressive, less cohesive, less satisfactory, more conflicted, and less integrated even before the war. These results must be interpreted with caution because the retrospective method may introduce a source of bias into the results: Having marital difficulties currently may color these women's perceptions of their entire married life. However, this research raises the possibility that preexisting interpersonal and emotional difficulties may contribute to both marital difficulties and the development of PTSD.

Gimbel and Booth (1994) tested this hypothesis in a large, representative sample of Vietnam veterans. They were interested in understanding why combat exposure in the 20th century is associated with increased rates of divorce. They compared the empirical support for two alternatives: First, the same factors that lead to adverse reactions to combat also interfere with marital stability, and second, marital stability is negatively affected by combat exposure. They assessed early emotional problems by asking veterans about anxiety, depression, and phobias prior to service, and early antisocial behavior by asking about misbehaving, fighting, truancy, and being suspended or expelled from school. They found that veterans who reported childhood emotional problems also were more likely to report combat-related PTSD symptoms. However, these symptoms did not subsequently predict marital breakdown. Similarly, veterans who reported childhood behavioral problems were more likely to engage in antisocial behavior after the war, such as physical violence and crime, which did predict marital breakdown. The researchers speculated that, in a combat situation, young men are rewarded for antisocial behavior, which encourages them to extend these behaviors into civilian life. While PTSD symptoms may have an adverse impact on the quality of marital relations, antisocial behavior may be intolerable and result in marital breakdown.

Few of the veterans of Vietnam were married prior to the war. Therefore, we can reasonably conclude that combat exposure has a variety of adverse consequences for subsequent marital relations. Combat veterans in general report more difficulties trusting others and greater conflict in their marriages. These effects are both more pervasive and more pronounced when the veteran develops PTSD. Veterans with PTSD report a range of marital difficulties, particularly with intimacy and the control of anger. In addition, combat exposure may promote the development of antisocial behaviors, such as the use of physical violence to resolve interpersonal problems, which ultimately lead to marital breakdown.

Death of a child. The death of a child is generally considered to be among the most stressful events an adult can experience, and parental grief following such a death has been found to be one of the most severe and enduring forms of bereavement. We include it in this chapter because the death of a child is uncontrollable, extremely negative, and unpredictable in the sense that parents expect to outlive their children. In a review of the literature on the impact of the death of a child on the marital relationship, Oliver (1999) found that up to a third of couples go through a significant disruption in marital functioning after a child's death. These couples experience increased marital dissatisfaction, friction and conflict, disengagement and withdrawal, and breakdowns in communication. Compared to nonbereaved couples, parents who have lost a child are also more likely to seriously consider separation or divorce. One of the most consistent findings is that the death of a child can have a pronounced negative impact on couples' sexual intimacy. Numerous studies have concluded that sexual intimacy and satisfaction decrease significantly following the child's death, even when other forms of intimacy do not.

However, many couples do not experience enduring disruptions to their relationships, and some relationships are actually strengthened as the couple grieves the loss together. Qualitative studies suggest that the quality of the marital relationship prior to the death may be an important factor in determining outcome because the death can amplify preexisting marital difficulties (Oliver, 1999). Thus, this literature provides evidence for both the mediating and moderating effects of marital relations. This trauma also is interesting because it is a shared trauma. Most traumatic stress occurs only to one partner in the relationship, which leaves the other person in the position of providing emotional support. The death of a child is traumatic for both partners and, as such, may present special challenges to the couple.

SUMMARY

There is a good deal of evidence that traumatic stress has an adverse impact on individuals' ability to develop and maintain positive marital relationships. Much of the research has focused on individuals with a history of childhood traumatic stress, and the evidence is clear: With few exceptions, the research shows that childhood sexual abuse and experiencing multiple forms of abuse have a negative impact on the levels of intimacy and attachment security in subsequent adult relationships. Because the research has not been done yet, the jury is still out on the impact on the capacity for adult intimacy of childhood physical abuse and witnessing violence between one's parents.

In terms of trauma that occurs in adulthood, similar difficulties with intimacy appear to result from combat exposure, particularly when the veteran goes on to develop PTSD. Veterans with PTSD report more difficulties with intimacy and the control of anger in their marriages than do veterans without PTSD. Anger likely has an impact on intimacy because anger creates emotional distance. The death of a child also is a traumatic stress that can create emotional distance between couples. Sexual assault, specifically, appears to have an impact on the capacity for sexual intimacy—a finding that makes good sense intuitively. Individuals who are not involved in romantic relationships at the time of the sexual assault may cope with their sexual disinterest or aversion by avoiding the development of new sexual relationships. However, problems with sexual intimacy are likely to be especially detrimental to the relationships of married and cohabiting couples. Sexual intimacy is an important part of marital relations and its absence may create more general intimacy deficits in these couples.

However, there is a need for studies that examine gender differences in samples where the same trauma was experienced. Studies of female trauma survivors typically involve the trauma of sexual assault, while males have been studied almost exclusively as survivors of combat exposure. Although we know that both traumas have an impact on marital intimacy, we do not know that the impact is identical for men and women.

WHY DOES TRAUMA HAVE A NEGATIVE IMPACT ON MARITAL RELATIONS?

The specific causal link between trauma and marital difficulties remains undetermined. In this last section, we discuss two plausible mechanisms.

PTSD as a confounding variable. The first possibility is that group differences between individuals with and without trauma histories may be due largely to those individuals who develop PTSD as a consequence of their exposure to traumatic stress. This would mean that not all trauma survivors develop marital problems but that these problems predominate among individuals with PTSD. Both central aspects of the PTSD syndrome—avoidance and hyperarousal—may have a negative impact on marital intimacy (Mills & Turnbull, 2001). The avoidance features of PTSD that could influence intimacy include diminished interest in activities, feelings of detachment from others, and restricted affect, while hyperarousal could have an impact through preoccupation with the trauma, irritability, and anger. Both avoidance and immersion in the trauma may leave spouses and romantic partners feeling alone and abandoned in their relationships (Johnson & Williams-Keeler, 1998), while an inability to regulate negative emotions may create or exacerbate marital conflict (Cassidy & Mohr, 2001; Johnson & Williams-Keeler, 1998).

This hypothesis is well-supported by the studies of combat veterans which show that veterans with PTSD show more pervasive and more profound disturbances in their marital relations than do veterans without PTSD. When combat exposure and PTSD symptoms are considered jointly in multiple regression equations, combat exposure is a redundant variable (Caselli & Motta, 1995). Recent research on other traumas also is consistent with this hypothesis. For instance, Regehr and Marziali (1999) assessed a sample of women sexually assaulted an average of 4½ years prior to the study. The researchers used measures of interpersonal difficulties to predict levels of PTSD and depressive symptoms. When all of the interpersonal measures were entered into a multiple regression equation, higher levels of PTSD symptoms were associated with mistrusting others, having difficulty expressing feelings, and feeling interpersonally exploited. In contrast, depressive symptoms were associated with egocentrism and feeling overly responsible in relationships. The interpersonal problems associated with PTSD symptoms are commonly reported to be among the sequelae of traumatic stress, while those associated with depressive symptoms are not.

These studies support our hypothesis that the negative impact of trauma on marital intimacy may be attributable to the subset of trauma survivors who develop PTSD. This hypothesis is well developed in Vietnam veteran literature where most research now focuses on veterans with PTSD rather than those with combat exposure. The possibility of a confound with PTSD needs to be considered in other trauma populations as well. For instance, it is possible that not all survivors of CSA inevitably encounter marital problems (see Whiffen et al., 1999, for an example) and that the general finding can be accounted for by those women who develop chronic PTSD. This hypothesis also raises an interesting conceptual problem. Does trauma independently have an impact on both marital intimacy and the risk for PTSD? Or does trauma increase the risk of PTSD which subsequently creates marital problems? The answer to this question has implications both for future research and for treatment.

The impact of childhood trauma on attachment security. Carlson and Dalenberg (2000) argued that peoples' response to traumatic stress is greatly influenced by their developmental level at the time of the trauma. Generally, children are thought to have more severe responses to traumatic stress than adults, and childhood trauma is thought to have a more pervasive impact on functioning. We believe that attachment theory provides a framework for understanding the differential impacts of childhood and adult trauma. Our review indicates that childhood trauma, especially sexual abuse, is associated with stable and organized disruptions to interpersonal functioning that are evident in adult attachment insecurity. Unfortunately, researchers interested in adult trauma have not assessed attachment security in their participants, so we do not know whether or not adult trauma also has a negative impact on the ability to form secure attachments. However, attachment is a pivotal developmental task during childhood. Developmental psychologists believe that a child's ability to form secure attachments sets the stage for later emotional and interpersonal functioning (Cassidy & Mohr, 2001). If a child's ability to form secure attachments is compromised by trauma, this difficulty is likely to persist into adulthood. While traumatic stress during adulthood could result in an inability to form secure attachments, theoretically it is much less likely to do so. Thus, childhood trauma may be more likely to impinge upon an individual's ability to form secure adult attachments than adult trauma, and attachment insecurity may be one way of understanding why childhood trauma survivors have difficulty in marital relationships.

From an attachment perspective, trauma both intensifies attachment needs for comfort and reassurance while shattering trust in the benevolence of others (Cassidy & Mohr, 2001; Johnson & Williams-Keeler, 1998). Paradoxically, traumatized individuals may seek out attachment figures while simultaneously fleeing them emotionally. We propose that attachment insecurity among survivors of childhood trauma is likely to take the form of ambivalence or disorganization where competing approach and avoidance behaviors are observed. For example, a disorganized individual may pursue her partner for closeness but reject him when he responds to her. These competing behaviors are extremely difficult for potential partners to understand and tolerate, and may be a significant factor in the perpetuation of attachment insecurities and dissatisfying relationships.

CONCLUSION

There is evidence to support the presence of both moderating and mediating links between traumatic stress and marital intimacy. Women who were sexually victimized are less distressed if they experience their romantic and marital relationships as close, intimate, and emotionally supportive, and these protective effects are apparent both in the immediate aftermath of the trauma and many years later. However, there also is good evidence that trauma, in the forms of childhood sexual abuse, sexual assault, the death of a child, and combat exposure, has a negative impact on sexual and emotional intimacy in marital relationships. Part of this impact may be attributable to PTSD symptoms of both avoidance and hyperarousal. In addition, traumatic stress during childhood may have a lasting impact on the ability to form secure adult attachment relationships. Clinicians argue that in order to recover from trauma, individuals need to reestablish trust. This can be accomplished through corrective adult relationships, but impaired intimacy in these same relationships will interfere with the healing process and maintain and perpetuate trauma symptoms. Thus, the solution—marital intimacy—may become part of the problem.

REFERENCES

Allen, J., Huntoon, J., Fultz, J., Stein, H., Fonagy, P., & Evans, R. (2001). A model for brief assessment of attachment and its application to women in inpatient treatment for trauma-related psychiatric disorders. *Journal of Personality Assessment, 76,* 421–447.

Andrews, B. (1995). Bodily shame as a mediator between abusive experiences and depression. *Journal of Abnormal Psychology, 104,* 277–285.

Barnes, M. F. (1995). Sex therapy in the couples context: Therapy issues of victims of sexual trauma. *American Journal of Family Therapy, 23,* 351–360.

Baron, R., & Kenny, D. (1986). The moderator-mediator variable distinction in social psychological research: Conceptual, strategic, and statistical considerations. *Journal of Personality and Social Psychology, 51,* 1173–1182.

Bartholomew, K., & Horowitz, L. (1991). Attachment styles among young adults: A test of a four-category model. *Journal of Personality and Social Psychology, 61,* 226–244.

Beitchman, J., Zucker, K., Hood, J., DaCosta, G., Akman, D., & Cassavia, E. (1992). A review of the long-term effects of child sexual abuse. *Child Abuse and Neglect, 16,* 101–118.

Belt, W., & Abidin, R. (1996). The relation of childhood abuse and early parenting experiences to current marital quality in a nonclinical sample. *Child Abuse and Neglect, 20,* 1019–1030.

Brewin, C. R., Andrews, B., & Valentine, J. D. (2000). Meta-analysis of risk factors for posttraumatic stress disorder in trauma-exposed adults. *Journal of Consulting and Clinical Psychology, 68,* 748–766.

Briere, J., & Runtz, M. (1988). Post sexual abuse trauma: Data and implications for clinical practice. *Journal of Interpersonal Violence, 2,* 367–379.

Busch, A., Lundeberg, K., & Carlton, R. (2000). The intergenerational transmission of spouse abuse: A meta-analysis. *Journal of Marriage and the Family, 62,* 640–654.

Cagnetta, E., & Cicognani, E. (1999). Surviving a serious traffic accident. *Journal of Health Psychology, 4,* 551–564.

Carlson, E., & Dalenberg, C. (2000). A conceptual framework for the impact of traumatic experiences. *Trauma, Violence, and Abuse, 1,* 4–28.

Carlson, V., Cicchetti, D., Barnett, D., & Braunwald, K. (1989). Disorganized/disoriented attachment relationships in maltreated infants. *Developmental Psychology, 25,* 525–531.

Carroll, E. M., Rueger, D. B., Foy, D. W., & Donahoe, C. P. (1985). Vietnam combat veterans with posttraumatic stress disorder: Analysis of marital and cohabitating adjustment. *Journal of Abnormal Psychology, 94,* 329–337.

Caselli, L. T., & Motta, R. W. (1995). The effect of PTSD and combat level on Vietnam veterans' perceptions of child behavior and marital adjustment. *Journal of Clinical Psychology, 51,* 4–12.

Cassidy, J., & Mohr, J. (2001). Unsolvable fear, trauma, and psychopathology: Theory, research, and clinical considerations related to disorganized attachment across the life span. *Clinical Psychology: Science and Practice, 8,* 275–298.

Davis, J., Petretic-Jackson, P., & Ting, L. (2001). Intimacy dysfunction and trauma symptomatology: Long term correlates of different types of child abuse. *Journal of Traumatic Stress, 14,* 63–79.

Downey, G., Khouri, H., & Feldman, S. (1996). Early interpersonal trauma and later adjustment: The mediational role of rejection sensitivity. In D. Cicchetti and S. Toth (Eds.), *Developmental perspectives on trauma: Theory, research, and intervention.* Rochester, NY: University of Rochester Press.

Ducharme, J., Koverola, C., & Battle, P. (1997). Intimacy development: The influence of abuse and gender. *Journal of Interpersonal Violence, 12,* 590–599.

Dyregrov, A. (2001). Early intervention—a family perspective. *Advances in Mind-Body Medicine, 17,* 160–196.

Frazier, P. A., & Burnett, J. W. (1994). Immediate coping strategies among rape victims. *Journal of Counseling and Development, 72,* 633–639.

Gimbel, C., & Booth, A. (1994). Why does military combat experience adversely affect marital relations? *Journal of Marriage and the Family, 56,* 691–703.

Gold, S., Milan, L., Mayall, A., & Johnson, A. (1994). A cross-validation study of the Trauma Symptom Checklist: The role of mediating variables. *Journal of Interpersonal Violence, 9,* 12–26.

Hanson, K. (1990). The psychological impact of sexual assault on women and children: A review. *Annals of Sex Research, 3,* 187–232.

Herman, J. L. (1992). *Trauma and recovery.* New York: Basic Books.

Holmstrom, L. L., & Burgess, A. W. (1979). Rape: The husband's and boyfriend's initial reactions. *The Family Coordinator, 28,* 321–330.

Johnson, S., & Williams-Keeler, L. (1998). Creating healing relationships for couples dealing with trauma: The use of emotionally focused marital therapy. *Journal of Marital and Family Therapy, 24,* 25–40.

McCarroll, J. E., Ursano, R. J., Wright, K. M., & Fullerton, C. S. (1993). Handling bodies after violent death: Strategies for coping. *American Journal of Orthopsychiatry, 63,* 209–214.

Miller, W. R., Williams, A. M., & Bernstein, M. H. (1982). The effects of rape on marital and sexual adjustment. *American Journal of Family Therapy, 10,* 51–58.

Mills, B., & Turnbull, G. (2001). After trauma: Why assessment of intimacy should be an integral part of medico-legal reports. *Sexual and Relationship Therapy, 16,* 299–308.

Moss, M., Frank, E., & Anderson, B. (1990). The effects of marital status and partner support on rape trauma. *American Journal of Orthopsychiatry, 60,* 379–391.

Nelson, B. S., & Wampler, K. S. (2000). Systemic effects of trauma in clinic couples: An exploratory study of secondary trauma resulting from childhood abuse. *Journal of Marital and Family Therapy, 26,* 171–184.

Oliver, L. (1999). Effects of a child's death on the marital relationship: A review. *Omega Journal of Death and Dying, 39,* 197–227.

Oz, S. (2001). When the wife was sexually abused as a child: marital relations before and during her therapy for abuse. *Sexual and Relationship Therapy, 16,* 287–298.

Penk, W. E., Robinowitz, R., Roberts, W. R., Patterson, E. T., Dolan, M. P., & Atkins, H. G. (1981). Adjustment differences among male substance abusers varying in degree of combat experience in Vietnam. *Journal of Consulting and Clinical Psychology, 49,* 426–437.

Regehr, C., & Marziali, E. (1999). Response to sexual assault: A relational perspective. *Journal of Nervous and Mental Disease, 187,* 618–623.

Roberts, W. R., Penk, W. E., Gearing, M. L., Robinowitz, R., Dolan, M. P., & Patterson, E. T. (1982). Interpersonal problems of Vietnam combat veterans with symptoms of posttraumatic stress disorder. *Journal of Abnormal Psychology, 91,* 444–450.

Roche, D., Runtz, M., & Hunter, M. (1999). Adult attachment: A mediator between child sexual abuse and later psychological adjustment. *Journal of Interpersonal Violence, 14,* 184–207.

Rumstein-McKean, O., & Hunsley, J. (2001). Interpersonal and family functioning of female survivors of childhood sexual abuse. *Clinical Psychology Review, 21,* 471–490.

Solomon, Z., Waysman, M., Belkin, R., Levy, G., Mikulincer, M., & Enoch, D. (1992). Marital relations and combat stress reaction: The wives' perspective. *Journal of Marriage and the Family, 54,* 316–326.

Valentine, L., & Feinhauer, L. (1993). Resilience factors associated with female survivors of childhood sexual abuse. *The American Journal of Family Therapy, 21,* 216–224.

Whiffen, V., Judd, M., & Aube, J. (1999). Intimate relationships moderate the association between childhood sexual abuse and depression. *Journal of Interpersonal Violence, 14,* 940–954.

Whiffen, V., Thompson, J., & Aube, J. (2000). Mediators of the link between childhood sexual abuse and adult depressive symptoms. *Journal of Interpersonal Violence, 15,* 1100–1120.

Wyatt, G., Guthrie, D., & Notgrass, C. (1992). Differential effects of women's child sexual abuse and subsequent sexual revictimization. *Journal of Consulting and Clinical Psychology, 60,* 167–173.

8

The Quality of Life Among Survivors' Loved Ones

MARIANNE AMIR AND RACHEL LEV-WIESEL

"You ask me what does it mean to be a Holocaust child survivor's wife? I'll answer you. It means to wake up during the night in panic because the man beside you screams or cries in his sleep, to wake him up, and to try calming him down. It means to protect my children from his sudden unexpected anger outbursts. To listen to his memories, to understand him, his behaviors, his moods ... to walk on your toes ... to give up your own needs, to understand that you actually have a very disturbed child-partner who will never recover [from] the trauma he experienced, to fail fulfilling his needs ... to be his mother, his sister, his wife, his companion, his therapist, his friend, yet often be treated by him as his worst enemy. ... I am not a child survivor myself. My family was not in Europe during the Second World War. ... Living with him for more than 40 years [has] had such an impact on me. ... You know that I have nightmares on the Holocaust ... as if I myself [were] a survivor. ... I pity him, yet I am angry [with] him ... I do not deserve his criticism, scolding ... undermining ... I do not deserve being humiliated by him. ... I understand what he has been going through. ... It does not get better over the years; it gets worse. ... Sometimes he shares with me his memories. ... It's so hard. ... He doesn't cry, I do! I wish I could tell him to stop sharing his memories with me ... but I can't do that. I am the only person in the world he has. ..."

N, aged 67, has been married for over 40 years to Y, aged 69, a Holocaust child survivor. The couple has two married daughters and five grandchildren; all live in the same city. According to N, there were times when she thought of leaving her husband, but her daughters' and her own feelings for him prevented her from doing it.

Living with partners who suffer from posttraumatic stress disorder (PTSD), depression, anxieties, anger, and hostility, and sharing their painful reminisces, identifying with them, and understanding their irrational behaviors is likely to create an emotional burden on the spouse. N has ambivalent feelings toward her husband. On one hand she empathizes with him, while on the other hand she feels humiliated and unappreciated by him. It seems she has been traumatized herself by the Holocaust through him.

This chapter deals with the quality of the lives of those persons who live with traumatized people. The term *quality of life* (QoL) is conceptualized here in the broad sense; it is as an overall evaluation of the person's life, including both positive and negative aspects. Quality of life research tries to define what a good life is and how well reality meets these standards (Veenhoven, 1997). We will present research showing various aspects of the lives of people who share their existence with trauma survivors. After a brief review of the literature, we will examine one study of the psychological state of individuals living with spouses who were children during the Holocaust and who are now close to retirement or already retired.

SECONDARY TRAUMATIZATION

Research has shown that caring for people who have experienced highly stressful, negative life events puts the caregivers (e.g., spouses, parents, and rescue teams) at risk for developing stress-related symptoms similar to those of the victims (Barnes, 1998; Figley, 1995; Stamm, 1995). This phenomenon, known as secondary traumatic stress (STS) or secondary traumatic stress disorder (STSD) (Figley, 1995) is characterized by symptoms nearly identical to those of PTSD. While the prevalence of PTSD varies with different types of trauma, war and the Holocaust are two events that consistently place the survivors at high risk for developing it (Brandis, 1996; Danieli, 1985; Mikulincer, Florian, & Solomon, 1995).

PTSD can result in long-term changes in the victim's personality and behavior. These changes may affect not only the victim but the family as well (e.g., Mikulincer et al., 1995). To date, most studies examining the way in which PTSD evokes STS in the victim's family have focused either on the wives of war veterans (Krantz & Moos, 1987; Williams & Williams, 1987) or on the wives of soldiers suffering from combat stress reaction (CSR) (Figley, 1986; Mikulincer et al., 1995). Overall, these studies have shown that the higher the levels of PTSD among the husbands, the higher the degree of STS in their wives (Coughlan & Parkin, 1987; Maloney, 1988; Solomon, 1989; Williams & Williams, 1985). Recently, Arzi, Solomon, and Dekel (2000) examined the effect of husbands' PTSD and postconcussion syndrome (PCS) on the wives and found that participants married to both PTSD and PCS husbands experienced higher levels of burden and distress in addition to more somatization symptoms, obsessive–compulsive problems, depression, anxiety, paranoid ideation, and psychoticism. They also reported more anger, suspicion, and blame toward their spouses than controls.

It is well established that PTSD is negatively correlated with QoL and with personal and social resources (e.g., Milo, 1999). A good example of the moderating effect of personal resources is the construct of potency, defined as the level of one's self-evaluation, self-control, and commitment to society, in addition to one's perception of the society as being a significant and orderly entity (Ben-Sira, 1985). In a study of the relationship between potency, PTSD, and QoL among child Holocaust survivors, it was found that the higher the level of potency, the lower the intensity of PTSD symptoms, and the better was QoL (Lev-Wiesel & Amir, 2001). Others (Zatzick et al., 1997) have found that male Vietnam veterans have impaired functioning and diminished QoL and this situation was uniquely attributable to PTSD.

MARITAL QUALITY

Marital quality can be considered as one of the important social resources. Examining the elements of marital relationships which distinguish distressed from nondistressed marriages represents a long tradition in the marriage and family literature (Abbey, Andrews, & Halman, 1995). The impact of the couple's relationship on both partners' psychological health has been demonstrated in a number of studies (Fisher, Terry, & Random, 1990; Lavee, McCubbin, & Olson, 1987). Billings and Moos (1984), for instance, found that family cohesiveness and couples intimacy predict psychological adjustment of all family members. Open communication between spouses is perceived by both clinicians and researchers to be an important coping strategy for couples struggling with certain traumas such as the death of a child. Such communication is thought to provide a means of airing concerns, fears, guilt, and anger (Broman, Riba, & Trahan, 1996). However, in some cases, less communication appears to be better. Studies of the marital satisfaction of spouses of severely ill partners have found that the less the spouses know about their partners' illnesses and treatment, the higher are their ratings of marital quality (Peyrot, McMurry, & Hedges, 1988).

Research in the trauma field has focused mostly on the beneficial aspects of supportive relationships, particularly the healing impact of marital relationships on spouses who have survived traumatic events (van der Kolk, Perry, & Herman, 1991; van der Kolk & McFarlane, 1996). Many adult survivors of childhood trauma find current intimate family relationships to be extremely important to their sense of well-being. The family often provides a sense of companionship and belonging, which not only provides practical and emotional support in daily life but can serve as an antidote to survivors' feelings of isolation, low self-esteem, depression, and guilt (Mason, 1990).

The marital relationship is considered by many investigators to be one of the most important elements of the recovery environment (van der Kolk et al., 1991; van der Kolk & McFarlane, 1996). Conger, Lorenz, Elder, Simon, and Ge (1993) suggest that the consequences of childhood trauma can be moderated by the adaptive mechanism of perceived spousal support. These investigators maintain that spousal support combined with the lingering effects of the trauma shape overall marital quality and the victim's sense of well-being.

Van der Kolk and McFarlane (1996) suggest that the ability to derive comfort from another human being predicts—even more powerfully than does the trauma history itself—whether or not symptoms improve and self-destructive behavior is regulated. These authors suggest that a supportive relationship can help survivors regulate their affective states and manage symptoms such as the disturbing nightmares, flashbacks, intrusive thoughts, and psychological reactivity characteristic of PTSD. The ability to turn to a spouse for support at the beginning of a flashback, for example, is likely to reduce later self-injurious behavior. A secure marital relationship can also help survivors to (a) modulate overwhelming negative affects such as shame and anger; (b) improve adjustment to the alarming, severe symptoms of a trauma response such as feelings of terror; and (c) curtail withdrawal and avoidance (Mikulincer et al., 1995).

Other researchers have proposed that supportive marital relationships can mitigate the effects of trauma by acting as a corrective emotional experience. The relationship with the spouse may become a source of comfort and security. A sense of emotional safety with a partner can promote the continued reprocessing and integration of the trauma, thereby enabling the survivor to become less immersed in the past (McCann & Pearlman, 1990).

While the marital relationship can be potentially supportive to trauma victims, research has shown that victims' marriages are often characterized by negative affect, especially fear evoked by feeling vulnerable to another person's distress. This fear tends to be intense and compelling, and is typified by hypervigilance and reactivity (Figley, 1986, 1995). The result is that emotional engagement, one of the central predictors of personal well-being, becomes tentative and feelings of alienation and isolation increase in both spouses (Pierce, 1995). Solomon (1989) highlights this alienation when discussing the marital relationships of combat veterans. She found that veterans' withdrawal and immersion in traumatic memories leave their partners feeling extremely lonely and susceptible to a variety of psychological and somatic complaints. Combat survivors' partners frequently feel humiliated and angry. The survivors themselves perceive this reaction in their partners as an inability to truly understand what they had gone through. Consequently, the same withdrawal that is so detrimental to an already distressed marriage is intensified still further in the survivor. This dynamic has been reported to characterize the marriages of other kinds of survivors (Matsakis, 1996; Mason, 1990). Withdrawal on the part of the survivor may be intensified when they feel shame at having been victimized. Pierce (1995) maintains that this feeling may lead the survivor to "hide" from people who have not gone through similar experiences, including their spouses.

Of course, the quality of the relationship can moderate the effects of the spouse's STS, just as it does with the survivor's PTSD. For example, a study of the wives of veterans suffering CSR as a result of the 1982 Lebanon War found that the higher the wives' ratings of marital intimacy were, the less were their negative emotions and the better their mental health status 6 years after the war (Mikulincer et al., 1995).

HOLOCAUST SURVIVORS AND MARRIAGE

While no exact information exists regarding the number of children who survived the Holocaust, approximately 50,000 children settled in Israel after World War II. The clinical literature indicates that the effects of Holocaust trauma were intensified in individuals who were children during the war (Gampel, 1992; Krell, 1993). These children lacked the security and stability ordinarily provided by adult caregivers (Adelman, 1995). Even in cases in which the children had adult support, the adults were unable to provide basic protection, a necessary condition for normal development. This appears to be true of both children who were hidden during the war and children who were sent to concentration camps.

Research indicates that despite the many years that have passed since World War II, high levels of PTSD persist among many Holocaust survivors (Yehuda, Schmeidler, Siever, Binder-Brynes, & Elkin, 1997). They are particularly vulnerable to stressors associated with the process of aging, such as the loss of work roles as the result of retirement, health problems, and the age-related losses of friends and relatives. As survivors become older, former coping strategies may no longer be effective, and bereavement and health problems may reactivate earlier terrors associated with the Holocaust.

Such processes in Holocaust victims add to the burdens already experienced by spouses who have assumed a caregiving role (Johnson & Williams-Keeler, 1998). In a study by Pennebaker, Barger, and Tiebout (1989), it was found that the divorce rate in marriages between two Holocaust survivors is only half that of marriages between survivors and American-born spouses. They suggested that this lower divorce rate may be an indication of the palpable admiration of each survivor for the strength, tenacity, and humanness of their partner in the face of ongoing suffering. In addition, Hass (1995) and Venaki, Nadler, and Gershoni (1985) found that in survivor–survivor marriages, both partners expressed a deep, common bond arising from a life-defining catastrophe.

Communication patterns between Holocaust victims and their spouses may also affect the degree to which the experience of trauma is transmitted to a spouse. The spouses of Holocaust survivors may be exposed vicariously to the deeply traumatic experiences of their partners. This exposure may cause them to develop similar stress-related behaviors and other symptoms of psychological distress, analogous to trauma therapists' STS.

In our study (Lev-Wiesel & Amir, 2001), we examined STS among a nonclinical sample of spouses (husbands and wives) of Holocaust survivors who were children during the war. We assessed (a) the frequency of PTSD among survivors and the frequency of STSD among their spouses, (b) the relationship between PTSD symptoms and psychological distress in the (adult) child survivors, (c) the relationship between STS symptoms and psychological distress in the nonsurvivor spouses, and (d) the effect of the degree to which survivors shared their traumatic memories with their spouses on the level of STS in the spouses. In addition, we assessed the effect of survivors' PTSD symptomatology and extent of memory sharing on marital quality as perceived by their spouses (we also inquired into gender differences).

THE LEV-WIESEL AND AMIR STUDY

The participants in this study (Lev-Wiesel & Amir, 2001) were 90 married couples (180 individuals). In each couple, one spouse was a Holocaust child survivor (born after 1926) and the other spouse was a nonsurvivor (born and raised outside of Europe during World War II). Couples were recruited from lists of members of two Hidden Child (Holocaust child survivors) organizations in Israel. Of the survivors, 55% were men and 45% were women (thus, 45% of spouses were men and 55% were women). The mean age of survivors was 65 years and that of spouses, 64.5.

Both survivors and their spouses completed the same anonymous questionnaires which were then paired. An attempt was made to standardize the procedure but, as expected, many of the survivors had difficulty discussing their past, and the interviewers reported that extra time had to be devoted to establishing rapport with some interviewees. Data were included in the analysis only when both partners agreed to complete the questionnaire.

Instrumentation

Instruments used in the study included (a) a PTSD inventory, (b) the SCL-90, (c) a questionnaire that explored whether the survivor had shared reminisces of war experiences with the spouse, and (d) the Enrich Scale for Marital Quality (Olson, Fournier, & Druckman, 1982). In completing the PTSD scale, the participants specifically related to their experiences "during the Holocaust," even if they had experienced additional traumatic events since that time. Spouses were instructed to think about the experience of their partner "during the Holocaust."

The SCL-90 (Derogatis, 1977) measures the severity of general psychiatric symptomatology and contains nine subscales: somatization, obsessive–compulsive problems, interpersonal sensitivity, depression, anxiety, hostility, phobic anxiety, paranoid ideation, and psychoticism. The Enrich Scale for Marital Quality (Olson et al., 1982) assesses potential problems and strengths of relationships, such as personality issues, communication, conflict resolution, financial management, leisure activities, sexual relationship, parenting and marital roles, and feelings and concerns about relationships with relatives, in-laws, and friends.

Statistical Analyses

The following analyses were conducted: (a) frequency of survivors and spouses suffering from full or partial PTSD or STSD; (b) Pearson correlations between measures of survivors' PTSD symptomatology, psychological distress, reminiscence sharing as reported by the survivor, and perceived marital quality, and the measures of spouses' STS symptomatology, psychological distress, and perceived marital quality; (c) a hierarchical regression analysis predicting spouses' marital quality; (d) a hierarchical regression analysis predicting spouses' STS symptoms; and (e) a multivariate analysis of variance (MANOVA) with survivors' level of PTSD (high–low) and spouses' gender as the independent variables, and spouses' STS symptoms, SCL-90, and marital quality as the dependent variables. In all the analyses, the variables of age, education and whether or not the person was currently working were controlled.

Frequency of PTSD and STSD

The frequency of PTSD for the survivors and STSD for the spouses was calculated, and it produced the following significant findings. More survivors than spouses suffered from *full* PTSD or STSD (16% and 10%, respectively), but no difference was found between the survivors and spouses with regard to *partial* PTSD/STSD (21% and 22%, respectively). Among the survivors, no gender differences were evident regarding full PTSD (10% males and 6% females). However, significantly more females than males had partial PTSD (7% males and 14% females). Among the spouses, no significant gender differences were found regarding full STSD. However, significantly more females than males had partial STSD (1% males and 21% females).

Trauma Symptoms, Psychological Distress, and Marital Quality

There were positive and significant correlations between survivors' and spouses' intrusion scores, and between survivors' arousal and spouses' intrusion scores. Moreover, the data reveal that, of the three symptoms of STS in the spouses, only intrusiveness correlated with most of the measures on the SCL-90. Several patterns were evident. First, the highest correlations present are related to anger–hostility in the survivor, which is also highly and negatively related to marital quality as perceived by the spouse. *The angry–hostile survivor will have an unhappy spouse who suffers from a wide range of psychiatric symptoms and from a relatively high level of STS scores.*

In addition, it can be seen that *paranoia in the survivor is related to relatively high levels of distress in the spouse.* The same is true, albeit to a slightly lesser degree, with regard to psychoticism and interpersonal sensitivity. Interestingly, only obsessive–compulsive problems in the spouse are consistently and significantly related to all the distress scores in the survivor, including PTSD symptoms. The only exception is the phobic anxiety score which is significantly related only to avoidance behavior in the survivor. Another pattern indicated in the data is that marital quality as perceived by the spouse is significantly related to several of the SCL-90 scores, but not to the PTSD scores of the survivor or to whether or not the survivor shared traumatic memories with the spouse. In other words, *marital quality was related to psychiatric symptomatology but not to PTSD scores or to whether the survivor had shared traumatic memories.*

To examine the issue of spouses' perceptions of marital quality in greater depth, we performed a forced-step hierarchical regression. In step one, we entered the demographic variables in which age was the only significant variable; that is, *greater age predicted better marital quality*. In the second step, we entered the PTSD diagnosis of the survivors (full, partial, or none) and sharing (partial or full). Neither contributed significantly to the explanation of the variance. In the third step, we entered the interaction between the PTSD diagnosis and sharing. This variable was significant, adding another 7% to the explanation of the variance. When the survivor evidenced no symptoms of PTSD, marital quality as perceived by the spouse was not affected by memory sharing. However, when the survivor had either full or partial PTSD, memory sharing significantly affected marital quality as perceived by the spouse: *Spouses who had heard all of the partner's traumatic stories in full reported the lowest marital quality*.

An additional hierarchical regression was performed with spouses' STS (total score) as the dependent variable. The spouses' STS was significantly explained by their level of education, in that *the higher the spouses' level of education, the lower their STS symptoms*. Furthermore, survivors' degree of PTSD contributed significantly to the explanation of the variance. *Spouses married to survivors with full or partial PTSD had significantly more STS symptoms*.

Spouses' STS and Gender

To examine the effects of gender on spouses' STS, a one-way analysis of variance was conducted comparing PTSD, psychological symptoms, and marital quality. Female spouses were found to have slightly lower mean levels of paranoia than male spouses. No gender differences were found on any of the other measures. This finding led us to inquire whether gender differences were related to the survivors' levels of PTSD. To examine the impact of both variables (gender and survivors' levels of PTSD) on spouses' STS, psychological distress, and perceptions of marital quality, we divided the spouses into four groups according to gender and their survivor partner's placement with respect to the median score on the PTSD Scale. The four groups were as follows: (a) female spouses whose partners suffer high levels of PTSD, (b) female spouses whose partners suffer low levels of PTSD, (c) male spouses whose partners suffer high levels of PTSD, and (d) male spouses whose partners suffer low levels of PTSD. A MANOVA was conducted among the four groups with spouse gender and their partner's level of PTSD as the independent variables, and spouses' STS scores, SCL-90 scores, and perceived marital quality as the dependent variables.

The MANOVA revealed a main effect for PTSD for the following variables: anger and hostility, anxiety, depression, interpersonal sensitivity, obsessive–compulsive behavior, and spouses' PTSD. A main effect for gender was found for the following variables: somatization, GSI scores, psychoticism, phobia, paranoia, and spouses' PTSD. In addition, the results revealed a significant interaction, in that *female spouses whose partners suffered from high levels of PTSD had higher levels of STS and psychological symptoms of distress than male spouses whose partners suffered from high levels of PTSD.* This effect was present for the following variables: depression, interpersonal sensitivity, obsessive–compulsive behavior, somatization, and marital quality. No interaction effect was found for spouses' PTSD.

DISCUSSION

The findings presented here indicated that about one third of the spouses, both wives and husbands, suffered either full or partial STSD. The results further showed that intrusion and arousal in the survivor were significantly associated with intrusion in the spouse, though this correlation was relatively low. On the other hand, it was found that distress in the survivor, particularly in the form of anger–hostility, paranoia, and interpersonal sensitivity, was highly correlated with a wide range of distress scores in the spouses.

Two variables were found to significantly explain STS among spouses—their partner's level of PTSD and their own level of education. Another finding was that female spouses displayed more evidence of psychological distress than male spouses, especially when their partner suffered high levels of PTSD. Finally, spouses whose partners suffered from full or partial PTSD and who shared their traumatic reminisces reported significantly lower marital quality than spouses whose partners did not suffer from PTSD, irrespective of whether the survivor had shared the story or not.

PTSD AS A FAMILY SYSTEM

Findings regarding the frequency of full and partial STSD among spouses clearly suggest that Holocaust-related distress is, in many cases, part of the family system. Despite the fact that they did not physically experience Holocaust trauma themselves, spouses of survivors suffer trauma-related symptoms such as intrusive thoughts, avoidance, and heightened arousal. In light of these results, the question that arises is this: By what mechanism does this secondary traumatization come about?

One answer may lie within the context of the couple-dyad in the family system—spouses of survivors may develop an ongoing sense of responsibility for their suffering partner. This may occur as a result of prolonged exposure to their partner's anguish as expressed in the partner's traumatic reminiscences, psychological symptoms of distress, and PTSD symptomatology. Figley (1995), when discussing STS with therapists and other caregivers, suggested that a lack of relief from the burden of responsibility for the sufferer, together with a sense of prolonged exposure, is likely to stimulate symptoms of PTSD, depression, and generalized anxiety in the caregiver.

EMPATHY

Miller, Stiff, and Ellis (1988) studied secondary traumatization in rescue teams and proposed that STS occurs as a result of one's empathic capacity, actions toward the sufferer, inability to obtain relief from these actions through depersonalization, and a sense of satisfaction derived from helping to relieve suffering. Extending this hypothesis to the processes occurring in a marital dyad, it is likely that spouses of Holocaust child survivors empathize with their partners' constant suffering and pain. To ease this pain, spouses may encourage their partners to share their traumatic memories with them. While sharing usually adds to couples' marital quality, this is not the case with Holocaust survivor couples. When horrifying, terrible memories are shared by the survivor and the spouse empathizes (and often identifies) with the feelings of the sufferer, the spouse may be swept up in the emotions of the survivor. As one survivor's wife said:

> "When I think about what he had to endure, how much he suffered, I forgive him for all his angry outbursts and inconsiderate behavior ... if I could only help him forget ... my heart breaks when I hear him cry at night during his nightmares. ..."

Figley (1995) suggested that empathy and emotional contagion account for the extent to which the caregiver makes an effort to reduce the pain of the sufferer. Survivors' spouses, especially women, seem to become a sort of perpetual container for their partners' distress (Feld, 1997). From an object relations perspective on couple interaction, which assumes that each partner grows through attachment to the other, it may be that survivors expect their spouses to provide them with a permanent containing environment (Feld, 1997). Metaphorically, survivors have a "black hole" in their interpersonal, intersubjective space. This space is dominated by an intensely compelling feeling of inner deadness (Eshel, 1997). Even if they succeed in detaching themselves from this feeling, they remain petrified within their interpersonal space because the threat of being drawn back again remains imminent. Consequently, survivors may find it difficult to form object relations characterized by closeness and intimate bonding (Eshel, 1997). Eventually, spouses' acceptance and identification with the difficult role of containing their partner is likely to influence their own psychological well-being (Rosenbaum & Garfield, 1996).

LIVING WITH AN ANGRY PARTNER

Interestingly, the results also suggested that the most difficult situation to live with is when the survivor displays angry–hostile behavior. One interpretation of this finding is that the angry survivor externalizes frustrations, making the spouse the target. Thus the spouse may be trapped between empathy, identification, and understanding the survivor's suffering and being constantly hurt and rejected. The results imply that the mechanism of transmission of STS may be more about the demands of living with a symptomatic spouse with anger, hostility, and paranoia than the result of empathic listening (and hearing of the horrors of the trauma from someone who is close enough to cause the listener to lower defensive assumptions of being safe and trauma happening only to others). It seems that it is not empathy that makes it difficult to live with a trauma survivor but the fact that the survivor might be a very difficult person. In the words of a survivor's wife:

> "I frequently feel so helpless, he gets so mad over small things, unimportant issues, makes such a fuss over stupid things … nothing I say calms him … sometimes, I feel he blames me for his parents' death, for what he had suffered … me and our grown up children learned to be so cautious when approaching him … not to make him upset. … I remember once I came back from shopping with my daughter, he was furious with no apparent reason. … After bursting out he shuts up, doesn't talk to me or to the children, doesn't pick up the phone, behaves as if we are air to him … it lasts days in which I try every way I possibly can to restore contact. … Secretly, I sometimes wish he was dead. …"

Another survivor's wife said:

> "My biggest problem is that I pity him. I think I am actually a battered wife, not physically but emotionally. … He becomes so bitter, sometimes detached, [like] I am invisible. … [He doesn't] care how it makes me feel. …

A male spouse of a survivor described:

> "I never know when and how to approach her ... how she will react. ... She tends to be so depressed ... anxious at times with no apparent reasons. ... It makes me furious and I am afraid one day I will be violent."

The results here suggest that the survivor's anger, hostility, and paranoia are more powerful factors than the trauma variables of intrusion, avoidance, and hyperarousal. *It is possible that the spouse of the survivor suffers more from living with a difficult person than living with a suffering person.* The guilt that both spouses and society at large feel towards Holocaust survivors may interfere with the freedom to admit that one is dealing with demanding people, often with immature personalities.

SHARING MEMORIES

Waysman, Mikulincer, Solomon, and Weisenberg (1993) suggested that wives who perceive their marital relationship as satisfying may be less affected by the "compassion trap" (i.e., giving up one's own needs in order to satisfy those of another) than wives who are dissatisfied. However, in our study, some spouses of survivors who reported having good marriages still evidenced psychological symptoms of distress. This was particularly true when the survivor has shared his or her traumatic memories with the spouse. Marital quality was negatively affected by memory sharing only when the survivor had PTSD. In general, these findings suggest that the survivor who has PTSD (i.e., the survivor who displays continual symptoms of distress) and who also talks about the traumatic experiences creates the least positive marital environment. In these cases, PTSD may lead to obsessive and repetitive talking about past trauma. Under these conditions, the survivor's spouse may be more likely to feel helpless in the role of a container. Survivors who do not have PTSD may be able to talk about their experiences less emotionally so that the marital relationship is not affected negatively.

GENDER DIFFERENCES

The findings regarding gender differences are consistent with a large body of scientific knowledge indicating that, in general, women suffer more mental disorders than men, particularly depression and anxiety (Kessler, 1995). According to our results, women suffer more psychological distress than men when they are married to a Holocaust child survivor. One explanation of this difference may be that women often perceive marriage as proof of their abilities and achievement in society. As such, marriage may be associated with these women's sense of self-esteem (Hyde, 1991). Therefore, the more the wife invests efforts in relationships at home (in the current study by acting as a container to her spouse's sufferings), the greater her success or failure in sustaining the well-being of each member of the family (Conger et al., 1998).

CONCLUSION

One implication of this study is that spouses who live with traumatized partners are themselves in need of support. Living intimately with a symptomatic person who has experienced atrocities can exert a profound influence on one's life. The findings of this study indicate that this influence may be felt through experiencing similar trauma-related symptoms or by becoming depressed and anxious. The question of who contains the container remains as yet unanswered.

The current findings suggest that living with a trauma survivor is indeed a difficult task. In contrast to previous studies, we have found that the spouses' secondary traumatic stress symptoms were related more to the survivor's hostility, anger, paranoia, and interpersonal sensitivity than to the survivor's having shared reminiscences with the spouse. Further studies will help clarify the process of transmission, but the results of this study lead us to reconsider the nature of secondary traumatic stress. Perhaps secondary traumatization within a marriage is less about a survivor's trauma being transmitted to, or vicariously experienced by, the spouse, and is more the result of living with and caring for a traumatized person who manifests difficult, nontrauma-related, interpersonal symptoms.

IN MEMORIAM

Professor Marianne Amir, born in Denmark, valued staff member of Ben-Gurion University's Behavioral Science and Social Work Departments, died of cancer on January 7, 2004 at the age of fifty-three. Professor Amir left behind a husband and two sons, as well as numerous friends, students, and admirers. Marianne Amir was a leading researcher, both in Israel and worldwide, in the fields of trauma, post-traumatic disorder and quality of life. She made a unique contribution to understanding the connection between trauma, psychological symptoms of distress, post-traumatic growth and quality of life among diverse population groups such as Holocaust survivors, former army soldiers, cancer and fibromyalgia patients, disabled invalids, and casualties of violence. As a researcher, she served as a member of the World Health Organization and won research grants from prestigious foundations. As a lecturer, her students admired her for her knowledge, her humor and the importance she placed on advancing the next generation of researchers. And as a person, Marianne Amir displayed courage and dedication at the end of her life by using her own personal experiences as the basis for a study on how society responds to, and copes with, terminally ill individuals and by documenting her own coping process so that her fellow lecturers might use it as a teaching aid.

REFERENCES

Abbey, A., Andrews, F. M., & Halman, L. J. (1995). Provision and receipt of social support and disregard: What is their impact on the marital life quality of infertile and fertile couples? *Journal of Personality and Social Psychology, 68,* 455–469.

Adelman, A. (1995). Traumatic memory and the intergenerational transmission of Holocaust narratives. *Psychoanalytic-Study-of-the-Child, 50,* 343–367.

Amir, M., Kaplan, Z., & Kotler, M. (1996). Type of trauma, severity of post traumatic stress disorder core symptoms and associated features. *Journal of General Psychology, 123,* 341–351.

Arzi, N. B., Solomon, Z., & Dekel, R. (2000). Secondary traumatization among wives of PTSD and post-concussion casualties: Distress, caregiver burden and psychological separation. *Brain-Injury, 14*(8), 725–736.

Barnes, M. F. (1998). Understanding the secondary traumatic stress of parents. In C. R. Figley (Ed.), *Burnout in families: The systemic costs of caring* (pp. 75–89). Boca Raton, FL: CRC.

Ben-Sira, Z. (1985). Potency: A stress buffering link in the coping-stress-disease relationship. *Social Science and Medicine, 21*(4), 397–406.

Billings, A. G., & Moos, R. H. (1984). Coping stress and social resources among adults with unipolar depression. *Journal of Personality and Social Psychology, 46,* 877–891.

Brandis, A. (1996). *Adult survivors of abuse.* Atlanta, GA: Psychological Associates.

Broman, M., Clifford, L., Riba, M. L., & Trahan, M. R. (1996). Traumatic events and marital well-being. *Journal of Marriage and the Family, 58,* 908–916.

Conger, R. D., Lorenz, F. O., Elder, G. H., Simon, R. L., & Ge, X. (1993). Husband and wife differences in response to undesirable life events. *Journal of Health and Social Behavior, 34,* 71–88.

Coughlan, K., & Parkin, C. (1987). Women partners of Vietnam veterans. *Journal of Psychosocial Nursing and Mental Health Services, 25,* 25–27.

Danieli, Y. (1985). The treatment and prevention of long-term effects and intergenerational transmission of victimization: A lesson from Holocaust survivors and their children. In C. R. Figley (Ed.), *Trauma and its wake: The study and treatment of post-traumatic stress disorder* (pp. 295–313). New York: Brunner/Mazel.

Derogatis, L. R. (1977). *The SCL-90-R manual 1: Scoring, administration, and procedures for the SCL-90.* Baltimore: Johns Hopkins University, School of Medicine.

Derogatis, L. R., & Clearly, P. A. (1977). Confirmation of the dimensional structure of the SCL-90: A study in construct validation. *Journal of Clinical Psychology, 33,* 981–989.

Derogatis, L. R., Rickels, K., & Rock, A. F. (1976). SCL-90 and the MMPI: A step in the validation of a new self-report scale. *British Journal of Psychiatry, 128,* 280–289.

Dutton, M. A., & Rubinstein, F. L. (1995). Working with people with PTSD: Research implications. In C. R. Figley (Ed.), *Compassion fatigue* (pp. 82–100). New York: Brunner/Mazel.

Dyregrove, A. (1989). Caring for helpers in disaster situations: Psychological debriefing. *Disaster Management, 2*, 25–30.

Eltus, Z. (1994). *The relationship between family of origin, patterns of communication, and quality of marriage.* Unpublished master's thesis: Haifa University, Israel.

Feld, B. G. (1997). An object relations perspective on couples group therapy. *International Journal of Group Psychotherapy, 47*, 315–332.

Figley, C. R. (1983). Catastrophes: An overview of family reactions. In C. R. Figley & H. I. McCubbin (Eds.), *Treating stress in families.* New York: Brunner/Mazel.

Figley, C. R. (1986). Traumatic stress: The role of family and social support system. In C. R. Figley (Ed.), *Trauma and its wake: Vol. II: Traumatic stress theory, research, and intervention* (pp. 39–54). New York: Brunner/Mazel.

Figley, C. R. (1993). Compassion stress and the family therapist. *Family Therapy News* (pp. 1–8).

Figley, C. R. (1995). Compassion fatigue as secondary traumatic stress disorder: An overview. In C. R. Figley (Ed.), *Compassion fatigue: Coping with secondary traumatic stress disorder in those who treat the traumatized* (pp. 1–21). New York: Brunner/Mazel.

Fisher, L., Terry, H. E., & Ransom, D. C. (1990). Advancing a family perspective in health research: Models and methods. *Family Process, 29*, 177–189.

Gampel, Y. (1992). I was a Shoah child. *British Journal of Psychotherapy, 8*, 390–400.

Hyde, J. S. (1991). *Half the human experience: The psychology of women.* Lexington, MA: D.C. Heath & Company.

Johnson, S. M., & Williams-Keeler, L. (1998). Creating healing relationships for couples dealing with trauma: The use of emotionally focused marital therapy. *Journal of Marital and Family Therapy, 24*, 25–40.

Kessler, R. C. (1994). The National Comorbidity Survey: Preliminary results and future directions. *International Journal of Methods in Psychiatric Research, 5*, 139–151.

Krantz, S. E., & Moos, R. H. (1987). Functioning and life context among spouses of remitted and non-remitted depressed patients. *Journal of Consulting and Clinical Psychology, 55*, 353–360.

Krell, R. (1990). Holocaust survivors: A clinical perspective. *Psychiatry Journal of University of Ottawa, 15*, 18–21.

Lavee, Y., McCubbin, H. I., & Olson, D. H. (1987). The effect of stressful life events and transitions on family functioning and well-being. *Journal of Marriage and the Family, 49*, 857–873.

Lev-Wiesel, R., & Amir, M. (2001). Secondary traumatic stress, psychological distress, sharing of traumatic reminisces, and marital quality among spouses of Holocaust child survivors. *Journal of Marital and Family Therapy, 27*, 433–444.

Lev-Wiesel, R., & Shamai, M. (1998). Living under the threat of relocation: Spouses' perception of the threat and coping resources. *Contemporary Family Therapy, 20*, 107–121.

Maloney, L. J. (1988). Post traumatic stresses of women partners of Vietnam veterans. *Smith College Studies in Social Work, 58*, 122–143.

Matsakis, A. (1996). *Vietnam wives: Facing the challenges of life with veterans suffering post-traumatic stress* (2nd Ed.). Baltimore, MD, US: The Sidran Press.

McCann, L. I., & Pearlman, L. A. (1990). Vicarious traumatization: A framework for understanding the psychological effects of working with victims. *Journal of traumatic Stress, 3*, 131–149.

Mikulincer, M., Florian, V., & Solomon, Z. (1995). Marital intimacy, family support, and secondary traumatization: A study of wives of veterans with combat stress reaction. *Anxiety, Stress, and Coping, 8*, 203–213.

Miller, K. I., Stiff, J. B., & Ellis, B. H. (1988). Communication and empathy as precursors to burnout among human service workers. *Communication Monographs, 55,* 250–265.

Milo, T. (1999). Posttraumatic stress disorder and functioning and quality of life outcomes in a nationally representative sample of Vietnam veterans: Comment. *American Journal of Psychiatry, 156,* 804–805.

Olson, D. H., Fournier, D. G., & Druckman, J. M. (1982). ENRICH. In D. Olson et al. (Eds.), *Family inventories* (pp. 46–68). St. Paul, MN: University of Minnesota, Family Social Science.

Pagel, M. D., Becker, J., & Coppel, D. B. (1985). Loss of control, self-blame, and depression: An investigation of spouse caregivers of Alzheimer's disease patients. *Journal of Abnormal Psychology, 94,* 169–82.

Pennebaker, J. W., Barger, S. D., & Tiebout, J. (1989). Disclosure of traumas and health among Holocaust survivors. *Psychosomatic-Medicine. 51*(5), 577–589.

Pierce, T. W. (1995). Skills training in stress management. In W. O'Donohue, & L. Krasner, (Eds)., *Handbook of psychological skills training: Clinical techniques and applications,* (pp. 306–319). Needham Heights, MA, US: Allyn & Bacon.

Rosenbaum, B., & Garfield, D. (1996). Containers, mentaspace and psychodynamics. *British Journal of Medical Psychology, 69,* 281–297.

Rosenheck, R., & Nathan, P. (1985). Secondary traumatization in the children of Vietnam veterans. *Hospital and Community Psychiatry, 36,* 538–539.

Rosenheck, R., & Thompson, J. (1986). Detoxication of Vietnam war trauma: A combined family-individual approach. *Family Process, 25,* 559–570.

Solomon, Z. (1989). A 3-year prospective study of post traumatic stress disorder in Israeli combat veterans. *Journal of Traumatic Stress, 2,* 59–73.

Stamm, B. H. (1995). *Secondary traumatic stress: Self care issues for clinicians, researchers, and educators.* Luthersville, MD: Sidran.

van der Kolk, B., Perry, C., & Herman, J. (1991). Childhood origins of self-destructive behavior. *American Journal of Psychiatry, 148,* 1665–1671.

van der Kolk, B. A., & McFarlane, A. C. (1996). The black hole of trauma. In B. van der Kolk, A. McFarlane, & L. Weisaeth (Eds.), *Traumatic stress* (pp. 3–19). New York: Guilford.

Veenhoven, R. (1997). Progress in understanding of happiness. *Revue-Quebecoise-de-Psychologie, 18,* 29–74.

Venaki, S. K., Nadler, A., & Gershoni, H. (1985). Sharing the Holocaust experience: Communication behaviors and their consequences in families of ex-partisans and ex-prisoners of concentration camps. *Family-process, 24*(2), 273–280.

Waysman, M., Mikulincer, M., Solomon, Z., & Weisenberg, M. (1993). Secondary traumatization among wives of posttraumatic combat veterans: Family typology. *Journal of Family Psychology, 7,* 104–118.

Williams, C. M., & Williams, T. (1987). Family therapy for Vietnam veterans. In T. Williams (Ed.), *Post-traumatic stress disorder of Vietnam veterans* (pp. 221–231). Cincinnati, OH: Disabled American Veterans.

Yehuda, R., Schmeidler, J., Siever, L. J., Binder-Brynes, K., & Elkin A. (1997). Individual differences in posttraumatic stress symptom profiles in Holocaust survivors in concentration camps or in hiding. *Journal of Traumatic Stress, 10,* 453–463.

Zatzick, D., Marmar, C. R., Weiss, D. S., Browner, W. S., Meltzer, T. J., Golding, J. M., Stewart, A., Schlenger, W. E., & Wells, K. B. (1997). *American Journal of Psychiatry, 154,* 1690–1695.

9

The Systemic Impact of Traumatized Children

BRIANA S. NELSON GOFF AND KAMI L. SCHWERDTFEGER

The child appeared to be about 18 months old, based on her size. In a small 20 × 25 ft playroom with approximately 25 children between the apparent ages of 18 months and 3 years, this small child stood out to me. She was extremely thin with dark hair and large eyes—too large. As I sat in the room with so many children seeking my attention, some using almost desperate methods, this child captured my attention because she almost avoided my attention. But her behavior caught my attention because of its bizarre nature. She covered her ears with her hands; in an attempt to engage her, I began to mirror her behavior. The instant I raised my hand up to my head, she flinched and withdrew. Eventually she returned, drawing close, but never too close—always at a safe distance. Gradually, this child inched closer to me and I allowed her to have control over her safety zone. Eventually, she moved close enough to touch me. On the second day, she continued her progression until she wrapped my arm around her, sat on my lap with her ears covered, and rocked back and forth. None of these behaviors alone stood out to me. What was most striking—what was most disturbing—was that this child whom I thought was 18 months was, in fact, almost 5 years old.

The above story is a true experience from the first author's work in a country profoundly affected by war and terror. This could have been any country, even the more affluent Western nations. After the trauma has passed, there still may be *No Place to Be a Child* (Garbarino, Kostelny, & Dubrow, 1991). Perhaps the most serious implications from traumatic events occur when the trauma is experienced by a child. Clinicians and researchers know the depth of destruction that occurs for child victims of traumatic events—destruction that affects their cognitive, emotional, behavioral, physical, social, and spiritual development. Whether among child victims or adult survivors of childhood victimization, the developmental impact of trauma is extensive and often permanently alters the trajectory of normal development (Pynoos, Steinberg, & Goenjian, 1996).

The impact of traumatic events on children has received much clinical and empirical attention. The literature spans a variety of traumatic events, including war (Apfel & Simon, 1996; Goldson, 1996; Green & Kocijan-Hercigonja, 1998), terrorist attacks (Dremen & Cohen, 1990; Schuster et al., 2001), community violence (Dulmus & Wodarski, 2000; Rozensky, Sloan, Schwarz, & Kowalski, 1993), childhood physical abuse (Duncan, Saunders, Kilpatrick, Hanson, & Resnick, 1996), childhood sexual abuse and incest (Courtois, 1988; McLeer, Deblinger, Atkins, Foa, & Ralphe, 1988; Trickett, Reiffman, Horowitz, & Putnam, 1997), domestic violence (Black & Newman, 2000; Kilpatrick & Williams, 1997; Osofsky, 1995; Osofsky & Fenichel, 2000), natural disasters (Aptekar & Boore, 1990; Bradburn, 1991; Miller & Kraus, 1994; Swenson et al., 1996), and traumatic accidents (Stallard, Velleman, & Baldwin, 1998). The symptoms, neurological effects, clinical treatments, and other factors related to posttraumatic stress are found in a variety of sources. However, there is limited literature on the systemic effects when a child has been traumatized.

Children do not develop in isolation; they develop within the context of human systems. As members of those systems, children both influence the systems and are influenced by them. Hence, it is important to develop a conceptualization of the systemic effects when a child is traumatized. The purpose of this chapter is to provide an overview of the systemic effects that occur when a child has been traumatized. The chapter begins with a general description of childhood trauma, followed by (a) the individual subsystem effects on the child and (b) the family system effects, including the parent–child subsystem, the sibling subsystem, and the extended family subsystem. While it certainly is necessary to recognize the significant negative effects of childhood trauma, it also is important to identify the resilience factors that protect many children from the long-term effects of trauma. The chapter addresses those resilience factors and concludes with implications for future research which address the systemic effects of traumatized children.

CHARACTERISTICS OF CHILDHOOD TRAUMA

In the past 20 years, we have seen increased recognition of the extreme impact traumatic events can have on adults and children. In the initial description of PTSD in the *Diagnostic and Statistical Manual of Mental Disorders*, Third Edition (*DSM-III*; American Psychiatric Association [APA], 1980), the criteria stated that "this disorder can occur at any age, including during childhood" (p. 237). The *DSM-III-R* (APA, 1987) provided age-specific features to clarify the differential effects of trauma in childhood and adulthood. The *DSM-IV* (APA, 1994) included a diagnostic features section that provided a more detailed description of potentially traumatic experiences, including those experienced specifically by children. The recent developments in the description of PTSD (*DSM-IV-TR*; APA, 2000) described specific age features and familial patterns of PTSD. Thus, recognition of both the individual impact on children and the systemic impact within the family context is increasing.

One of the factors frequently cited as a primary cause of PTSD and other complex disorders in adulthood is the experience of severe traumatic events during childhood (Bingham & Harmon, 1996; Pynoos et al., 1996). There are several factors that contribute to the negative effects of trauma on children. According to a review of prevalence data by Saigh, Yasik, Sack, and Koplewicz (1999), the current PTSD rates among children who have experienced traumatic events range from 0–95%, with the average and median rate at 37%. Our current knowledge of PTSD prevalence rates in children is limited because the majority of the studies are about children who have already been traumatized, rather than community studies that assess the prevalence of PTSD in the general population. It is important to note that most research has focused on the symptoms of PTSD in children (Pynoos et al., 1996). In fact, children who experience the most negative and intense effects of trauma (i.e., develop posttraumatic stress disorder) may be the minority of childhood survivors. Another minority are the trauma survivors who actually experience "posttraumatic growth" (Tedeschi, Park, & Calhoun, 1998), or who go on to excel beyond what might be expected, given their previous traumatic experiences.

The range of outcomes from trauma is raised here as a description of the various impacts of trauma on children. There are many outcomes from trauma, just as there are many types of traumatic events and many ways in which symptoms are exhibited. In fact, our knowledge of what trauma *does* cause (e.g., PTSD) may be more enhanced by understanding what trauma does *not* cause (i.e., when the effects are less damaging).

Much of the past research on traumatized children has focused on gaining an empirical understanding of the individual effects on those individuals who are most severely traumatized. In order to develop a broader understanding of the impact of childhood trauma, it is necessary to gain a perspective of what factors are instrumental in reducing or preventing long-term negative effects of trauma. The factors that have received empirical support related to childhood resiliency will be described later in this chapter.

Primary traumatic stress. Traumatic events that are experienced directly by children include, but are not limited to, violent personal assault, being kidnapped or taken hostage, terrorist attack, school and community violence, torture, war, natural or human disasters, severe accidents, and being diagnosed with a life-threatening illness (APA, 1994). Other events that are not identified in the *DSM-IV* (APA, 1994) as traumatic, but which may have traumatizing effects on children either because of the primary or secondary effects of the event, may include parental death or divorce (Burman & Allen-Meares, 1994; Dremen, 1991; Hendricks, Black, & Kaplan, 1993; Karkazis & Lazaneo, 2000), removal of the child from the home, which results in placement in foster or other institutional care (Kenrick, 2000), chronic medical conditions and invasive treatment procedures (Best, Streisand, Catania, & Kazak, 2001; Fukunishi, Tsuruta, Hirabayashi, & Asukai, 2001; Kazak, 1998; Stuber & Houskamp, 1996), and related events.

When potentially traumatizing events are experienced directly by children, a number of factors determine the extent of the repercussions from the trauma. Particularly for children, the extent of threat or danger involved in the traumatic experience (Bingham & Harmon, 1996; Keppel-Benson & Ollendick, 1993; Monahon, 1993; Pynoos et al., 1996), the severity or duration of the event (Pynoos et al., 1996; Saigh et al., 2000), the accumulation of events (Keppel-Benson & Ollendick, 1993; Waller, 2001), the pretrauma or contextual vulnerability (Monahon, 1993; Shalev, 1996), and the postevent responses from sources of guidance or support (Keppel-Benson & Ollendick, 1993; Monahon, 1993) all play a role in the immediate and long-term effects of trauma on primary victims.

Secondary traumatic stress. In addition to events that are directly experienced by children, other situations, like witnessing or hearing about traumatizing events experienced by others, have been acknowledged to have deleterious effects on children (APA, 1994). The indirect effects of trauma have been described most frequently in the literature as secondary traumatic stress (Figley, 1983). The concept of secondary traumatic stress contends that being in close contact with, and emotionally connected to, a traumatized person becomes a chronic stressor, and family members often experience symptoms of traumatization (Catherall, 1992; Figley, 1983, 1995; McCann & Pearlman, 1990; Solomon et al., 1992). In children, secondary traumatic stress was first described by Rosenheck and Nathan (1985); they identified the depression, guilt, and rage experienced by the child of a veteran as a response to the child's exposure to the parent's

PTSD symptoms. Steinberg has suggested that "there are two ways that children can develop secondary traumatic stress: either through witnessing their loved ones undergo traumatic experiences or merely by the knowledge that these significant others were traumatized, and perhaps living with the aftermath of the victim's nightmares, violence, anxiety, or other symptoms" (1998, p. 31). The problem with this secondary traumatization hypothesis is that there is limited empirical support for the theory.

TRAUMA IN THE FAMILY SYSTEM

The repercussions from trauma can be compared to a ripple in a pond in which a stone (i.e., trauma) is thrown. A similar picture describes what happens when the system surrounding the child becomes traumatized, as in the case of community violence, war, natural disasters, or other large-scale traumatic events. Figley (1995) identified these events as simultaneous traumas. Some traumatic events may not directly affect the context that surrounds the child; however, when the social world around the child is fractured by trauma, the child is directly affected.

Although the literature on secondary trauma provides a systemic focus and an understanding of the potential effects traumatic events may have within the traumatized person's system, a clear description of the systemic or interpersonal effects of traumatic stress is needed. In order to appreciate the systemic implications of child traumatization, we will review what is known about the individual impact of trauma on children and the systemic impact of trauma on family systems.

CHILDREN'S REACTIONS TO TRAUMA

Although the specific impact of traumatic events may vary among individuals, children's responses to trauma can be categorized into four general areas: cognitive, affective, behavioral, and severe symptom formation.

Cognitive

The cognitive effects of trauma represent some of the most widespread symptoms in children exposed to trauma. Of the PTSD symptom categories, cognitive alterations are most commonly represented in intrusion-reexperiencing symptoms. In children, cognitive changes involve recurrent and intrusive recollections (Cuffe et al., 1998; Green et al., 1991; Bradburn, 1991; Terr, 1991), learning problems or a decline in school performance (Rossman, 1998; Shannon, Lonigan, Finch, & Taylor, 1994), and cognitive distortions or lapses in memory (McLeer et al., 1988; Terr, 1981, 1990).

Green and colleagues (1991) found that the most frequent symptom reported by child trauma survivors ranging from 2 to 15 years of age involved intrusive mental states of psychological distress, which occurred when the child was exposed to situations or thoughts resembling the traumatic event. Common intrusion-reexperiencing symptoms reported in other studies of children include: vivid flashbacks (Cuffe et al., 1998; McLeer et al., 1988; Terr, 1991), intrusive images (Cuffe et al., 1998; Nader, Pynoos, Fairbanks, & Frederick, 1990; Yule & Williams, 1990), and recurring dreams and nightmares (Bradburn, 1991; Cuffe et al., 1998; Kinzie, Sack, Angell, Manson, & Rath, 1986; McLeer et al., 1988).

The cognitive changes affecting learning and school performance in children also are associated with intrusive mental states and recollections. Deterioration in scholastic performance and learning in children following a traumatic experience is commonly explained by limited attention span and difficulty in concentrating. Research has suggested that limited attention span and inability to concentrate may be due to certain cognitive symptoms such as intrusive thoughts, sounds, and images that many child victims of trauma experience (McLeer et al., 1988; Nader et al., 1990; Shannon et al., 1994). These cognitive effects also could be described as symptoms of hyperarousal.

Cognitive distortions often are reported as misperceptions, disturbances in thought, and lapses in time among children. In a study of 23 children involved in the Chowchilla school bus kidnapping, Terr (1981) reported such disturbances in cognitive functioning. Terr noted that some children misperceived their kidnapper, visually hallucinated during the experience, and developed a confused sense of time. Although less frequently reported in children, Yule and Williams (1990) reported that some children show memory lapses in the form of amnesia following a traumatic event.

Affective

Children exposed to trauma may also exhibit adverse emotional effects. These alterations in affect may be described best within the hyperarousal and constriction-avoidance categories of PTSD. Symptoms of psychic numbing (Terr, 1990, 1991), feelings of detachment (Kinzie et al., 1986), and constricted affect (Green et al., 1991) have been identified in the literature on children. Other affective responses may include anger, anxiety, fear, guilt, confusion, helplessness, distrust, loneliness, and depression (McLeer et al., 1988; Monahon, 1993; Nader et al., 1990; Terr, 1991).

In a study of children who had been involved in a school hostage situation, Vila, Porche, and Mouren-Simeoni (1999) discovered that 81% of the children were found to have PTSD symptoms associated with disturbances of emotion. These affective alterations were primarily manifested as separation and generalized anxiety.

Fear is another commonly noted emotional effect among children following a traumatic experience. Although fear is not unusual among children in general, the fears typically related to the shock and stress of trauma within the life of a child are unique. Through years of research and study involving childhood trauma victims, Terr (1990, 1991) offered that children experience two specific kinds of fear following a traumatizing event: trauma-related fears and "fear of the mundane." Trauma related fears are those specific fears that maintain characteristics particular to the traumatic event. For example, Bradburn (1991) noted that children interviewed following the 1989 San Francisco Bay area earthquake, expressed an unusual fear of bridges. Fear of the mundane may be expressed more generally in childhood trauma victims as fear of strangers, fear of the dark, or fear of being alone. Although general fear is not unique to traumatized children, it is the severity and the long-lasting nature of these fears that set them apart.

Symptoms of emotional numbing also may develop in children. Specific numbing effects may include a feeling of detachment and alienation from other people, a loss of interest in activities previously enjoyed, and a restricted range of affect (Keane, Weathers, & Foa, 2000; Terr, 1990, 1991). According to Terr (1990, 1991), although children may experience denial or numbing immediately following a trauma, emotional numbing is primarily associated with repeated, long-standing, or extremely severe traumas.

Finally, depressive symptoms frequently appear in children following traumatic experiences (Boney-McCoy & Finkelhor, 1996; Trickett et al., 1997). Kinzie et al. (1986) reported that adolescents exposed to massive trauma reported a number of depressive symptoms including resentfulness, guilt, self-pity, pessimism, and apathy.

Behavioral

Along with the emotional effects described previously, Vila et al. (1999) found that a high percentage of children exposed to trauma reported behavioral disturbances. As with the affective responses to trauma, the behavioral reactions may fall into the hyperarousal and avoidance categories of PTSD. The most frequently identified behavioral symptoms in traumatized children are hypervigilance (Green et al., 1991) and avoidance or withdrawal behaviors (Bradburn, 1991; Kinzie et al., 1986; McLeer

et al., 1988; Nader et al., 1990; Thabet & Vostanis, 2000). Behavioral indicators related to hypervigilance may include extreme fear or phobic reactions, exaggerated startle responses, reenactments or repetitive
posttraumatic play, and sleep disturbance (Kinzie et al., 1986; Monahon,
1993; Nader et al., 1990; Terr, 1990, 1991). Avoidance and withdrawal
behaviors may include avoidance of activities, individuals, and places that
serve as a reminder of the trauma, as well as a loss of interest in previously enjoyed activities or individuals (Terr, 1991). Bradburn (1991) found
that 55% of the children in his study reported actively avoiding situations
and places that reminded them of the traumatic event.

Severe Symptoms

As described previously, PTSD in children has been identified as one
of the outcomes associated with severe traumatic experiences. In addition, childhood disorders such as attention deficit and hyperactivity disorder (Wozniak et al., 1999), conduct disorders (Pelcovitz, Kaplan,
DeRosa, Mandel, & Salzinger, 2000), separation anxiety disorder (Pelcovitz et al., 2000), major depression and suicidality (Pelcovitz et al., 2000;
Terr, 1991; Whitbeck & Hoyt, 1999; Wozniak et al., 1999), high risk or self-
injury behaviors (Terr, 1991; Mahony & Campbell, 1998), substance abuse
(Pelcovitz et al., 2000), and other childhood disorders may result from
traumatic experiences.

Research has suggested that children are more likely to develop severe
symptoms with more serious traumatic events. Wozniak et al. (1999)
found a significant association between trauma and the development of
major depression and dysthymia in children. Boney-McCoy and
Finkelhor (1996) reported that among traumatically victimized children,
sexual abuse victims reported the highest level of PTSD and depression
symptomatology.

Although these severe symptoms and disorders may be easy to
identify and diagnose when manifested in childhood trauma victims, this
does not guarantee that severely affected children will receive the
appropriate treatment following a traumatic event. The critical,
immediate attention required by these serious problems may mask the
true source of the problems and leave the traumatic experiences
unrecognized and unresolved (Terr, 1991).

EFFECTS ACROSS DEVELOPMENTAL STAGES

For children, traumatic experiences occur within the context of growth
and development. Recent studies have found that the consequences and

effects of traumatic events do, in fact, vary according to the age and developmental level of the child involved (Johnson, 1998). Shannon et al. (1994) found significant differences in PTSD symptomatology between groups of older and younger children involved in their study. Similarly, Green and colleagues (1991) discovered that younger children exposed to a traumatic natural disaster reported fewer avoidance and withdrawal symptoms than older children. The authors reasoned that these observed differences, associated with age and developmental levels, were the result of varying levels of cognitive capability. According to Green et al. (1991), younger children lack the cognitive ability to organize and understand the traumatic event and, consequently, operate in a more disorganized state following the trauma. Older children with greater cognitive ability are able to understand and respond to the trauma in a more sophisticated manner and use more avoidance techniques.

The variance in the effects of trauma on children can be divided into three primary stages of age and development: early childhood (birth to 5 years), middle childhood (6 to 12 years), and adolescence (13 to 18 years). The following sections summarize the research that describes the various effects of trauma at these developmental stages.

Early childhood. The developmental limitations of early childhood often hinder infants and young children from assessing and communicating the specific effects of a traumatizing event. Terr (1988) reported that children typically only develop verbal memory of a traumatic event between 2½ to 3 years of age and, even then, most recollections are spotty and incomplete. Therefore, it is not surprising that the most common symptoms reported in younger victims of trauma fall under the category of behavioral effects rather than cognitive symptoms. In a study of preschool-age children exposed to trauma, Terr (1988) found that the most consistent and prevalent behavioral effects included posttraumatic play, personality changes, and trauma-specific fears. Saylor, Swenson, and Powell (1992) also noted that parents of preschool-age children exposed to a traumatic natural disaster reported several observable behavioral effects in their children represented by increased aggressive, antisocial, and hyperactive behaviors.

Other commonly reported effects specific to preschool-age children include withdrawal, reenactments involving traumatic themes (Johnson, 1998; Swenson et al., 1996), anxious attachment behaviors or separation fears (Erickson, Egeland, & Pianta, 1989; Swenson et al., 1996), regression to previous levels of developmental functioning (Mahony & Campbell, 1998; Swenson et al., 1996; Terr, 1991), disruptions in sleeping and toileting (Mahony & Campbell, 1998), startle responses or freezing behaviors (Swenson et al., 1996), repeated retelling of the traumatic event (Swenson et al., 1996), changes in behavior, mood, and personality (Terr,

1988), general or trauma-specific fears, and psychosomatic symptoms (Monahon, 1993; Terr, 1988).

Middle to late childhood. Effects specific to school-age children may include a decline in school performance or learning problems, restricted and depressed affect, anxious arousal or hypervigilance, fearfulness or fear of recurrence of the trauma, sleep disturbances, behavioral problems, regression to previous levels of developmental functioning, visual image and traumatic memory intrusion, problems relating to peers, more elaborate reenactments in their play, psychosomatic symptoms, and feelings of guilt (Johnson, 1998; Mahony & Campbell, 1998; Monahon, 1993; Thabet & Vostanis, 2000).

Lystad (1984) reported that although confusion and anxiety were apparent for children across all developmental stages, psychosomatic symptoms and depression did not emerge until middle childhood for traumatized children. Terr (1991) reported that trauma-related dreams and nightmares become more prevalent in school-aged children. Differences in the manifestation of traumatic effects in males and females also become more visible during middle childhood. Males tend to display more aggressive and disruptive behaviors and attitudes, whereas females begin to show less obvious symptoms and signs of trauma, for example, eating disorders and changes in relationships (Mahony & Campbell, 1998).

Adolescence. Effects specific to adolescent development include acting-out and risk-taking behaviors, self-criticism, efforts to avoid overwhelming feelings (e.g., substance abuse and sexual promiscuity), social withdrawal, thoughts of revenge, and action-oriented responses to trauma, anxiety, hostility, running away, delinquency, and flight into adulthood (Mahony & Campbell, 1998; Monahon, 1993; Osofsky, 1995; Sugar, 1999). Lystad (1984) indicated that aggressive behaviors emerged during adolescence in traumatized children. Yule and Williams (1990) found that adolescents exposed to trauma reported more avoidance symptoms than intrusion symptoms.

Research findings also have suggested that adolescents are more likely to exhibit severe symptom formation. Pelcovitz and colleagues (2000) reported that adolescents exposed to trauma had significantly higher rates of diagnosis for a number of disorders, including major depression, conduct disorders, and oppositional defiant disorders. In his review of research on adolescent maltreatment, Garbarino (1989) concluded that "adolescents at high risk for maltreatment are less socially competent and exhibit more developmental problems than their peers" (p. 701).

Child-focused research provides important information needed to understand childhood trauma on an individual level, but in order to truly understand the relationship between children and trauma, the impact of a child's traumatic experience upon the larger family system also must be assessed.

FAMILY SYSTEM EFFECTS

Child traumatization affects the family in different spheres of functioning and in different relational areas. It is helpful to view the impact of the child's trauma on the different subsystems of the overall family system.

Parent–Child Subsystem

Parents, siblings, grandparents, members of the extended family, and people in the child's social network often are the hidden victims of a child's trauma (Monahon, 1993). The range in responses of parents and family members is as diverse as the types of traumatic experiences and reactions of the individual survivors. Reactions similar to the primary survivor's trauma responses may be present, such as recurrent memories of the events, feelings of isolation, helplessness, guilt, and shattered beliefs (Monahon, 1993; Rinear, 1988). Parents may constantly search for ways to make sense of or explain the event, often in an attempt to reduce their sense of helplessness or lack of power.

The family may serve as a resource for increased support and coping or as an obstacle that blocks the traumatized child's adjustment and recovery (Compas & Epping, 1993). The term *trauma membrane* refers to the protective environment surrounding a trauma survivor (Lindy, 1985; Rozensky et al., 1993). The trauma membrane imposed by the family system of the traumatized child can provide the protection needed for the child, or it may block outside resources (e.g., mental health professionals and medical personnel) from entering the system to provide necessary services. These family systems may become "trauma-organized systems" (Banyard, Englund, & Rozelle, 2001; Bentovim, 1992), with interactions, cycles, and patterns related to the traumatic experience manifested on a systemic level.

Parental response to children's trauma. A primary component in the parent–child subsystem effects of trauma is parental reaction to the trauma (Fletcher, 1996). When parents were overwhelmed by their own traumatic experiences or were unable to provide effective emotional support to their children, their traumatized children experienced more negative effects, including greater stress and increased length of recovery (Willard, 1998). Steinberg (1998) identified one of the main systemic themes in the literature as the vulnerability of children to their parents' reactions. In her review of research on various traumatic events, she found that the reactions of parents or significant others may have a greater negative impact on children than the severity of the children's own trauma experiences or their direct exposure to these.

Barnes emphasized that "parents who must deal with the sudden traumatization of someone they love, who must cope with the physical, emotional, and behavioral changes that often follow trauma, and who must face their own uncertainty and personal vulnerability are clearly candidates for this secondary traumatization" (1998, p. 76). The secondary traumatic effects on parents and significant others may result from exposure to the symptoms of the primary victim of the event (Barnes, 1998; Figley, 1995). Thus, the impact on parents of traumatized children most often involves the traumatic nature of the primary victims' physical and emotional condition (Barnes, 1998). This pattern has also been seen in the parents of children diagnosed with a life-threatening illness (Kazak, 1998).

Some research has suggested that mothers whose children have reported being sexually abused have heightened stress and PTSD symptoms—particularly women who experienced their own sexual abuse during childhood (Timmons-Mitchell, Chandler-Holtz, & Semple, 1996). Newberger, Geremy, Waternaux, and Newberger (1993) found elevated emotional distress symptoms in mothers of CSA victims; however, a significant correlation between mothers' and children's symptoms was not found. Although the authors suggest caution in the interpretation of these results, it appears from this study that symptoms in the mothers may be more directly related to the trauma of the sexual abuse than to the specific trauma symptoms of the children. Lipton (1997) found that higher caretaker distress was positively related to child distress in a sample of sexually abused children. Compas and Epping (1993) indicated that "parental distress may impede the ability of parents to assist their children in coping with both major and minor levels of stress" (p. 22). Research on other traumatic events has found that parents of murder victims experienced symptoms characteristic of PTSD (Applebaum & Burns, 1991; Rinear, 1988). This research supports the premise that distress levels in parents may significantly affect the amount of distress experienced by traumatized children.

The family's current level of adaptation and the amount of disruption caused by the trauma are primary systemic factors that affect children (Cicchetti, Toth, & Lynch, 1997). When there are disparate reactions or coping styles in each of the parents of a traumatized child, a cycle of tension may occur in the couple relationship that has a negative impact on the child (Handford et al., 1986; Monahon, 1993). This may create a polarizing cycle that is difficult to break; it is similar to what is seen in couples in which one or both partners have been directly traumatized (Nelson, Wangsgaard, Yorgason, Kessler, & Carter-Vassol, 2002).

Some parents may be overwhelmed by a traumatic event (their own or their child's) and may minimize the effects, which may leave them immobilized and unable to effectively support the child (Marans,

Berkman, & Cohen, 1996). Minimization of the effects may occur in parents because of their own past traumatic experiences (e.g., "It wasn't as bad as what I experienced.") or because they feel inadequate to help the child cope with the effects of the trauma. Parents who are able to manage and regulate their reactions to traumatic events will be more likely to effectively support and protect their child (Monahon, 1993). Conversely, parents may overidentify with the child's trauma, either because of retraumatization from the parents' previous trauma experiences or because of the secondary trauma effects of wanting to care for and protect their child.

Impact of parental trauma on children. Steinberg (1998) identified two different avenues through which children can develop secondary traumatic stress as a result of parental trauma: (a) direct witnessing of a parent's trauma (e.g., domestic violence and sexual assault) or (b) direct experiencing of the posttraumatic reactions or symptoms in the parent (e.g., nightmares, flashbacks, and startle responses). Much of the literature on the children of trauma survivors has focused on the children of war survivors, primarily the Holocaust (Bar-On, 1996; Bergmann & Jucovy, 1982; Danieli, 1985; Kestenberg, 1982; Swenson & Klingman, 1993) and Vietnam veterans (Ancharoff, Munroe, & Fisher, 1998; Kulka et al., 1990; Parsons, Kehle, & Owen, 1990; Rosenheck, 1986; Rosenheck & Fontana, 1998; Rosenheck & Nathan, 1985). Another body of literature addresses the experiences of a more personal "war," the intergenerational transmission of sexual and physical abuse (Buchanan, 1996; McCloskey & Bailey, 2000).

Research by Dulmus and Wodarski (2000) found greater psychological distress in children whose parents had been directly victimized by community violence rather than those affected by war. The general conclusions that can be drawn from this literature suggest that depression, anxiety, psychosomatic problems, aggression, guilt, and related issues may be common in the offspring of trauma survivors (Felsen, 1998). An important conclusion by Kestenberg (1982) that could describe the generations of trauma survivors is that issues related to survival may be a common trait that is transmitted from parents to children. The fight to survive which was central to the survivors of trauma may become central in the development of their children.

An area that requires further study is the traumatic effects on children who are not direct victims of abuse or trauma but who witness abuse of a parent or sibling (Black & Newman, 2000; Kilpatrick & Williams, 1997; Monahon, 1993). Child witnesses of domestic violence or parental homicide may experience intrusive memories of the violence, helplessness, guilt, and PTSD (Kilpatrick & Williams, 1997; Monahon, 1993; Osofsky, 1995). Research indicates that a large number of children, especially young children, are exposed to domestic violence between their parents (Fantuzzo, Boruch, Beriama, Atkins, & Marcus, 1997). Many children who experience domestic violence without being the primary targets of the abuse experience negative effects related to a survivor syndrome, sometimes seen in other nondirect victims or survivors of traumatic events (Duran, Duran, Brave Heart, & Yellow Horse-Davis, 1998; Felsen, 1998).

Sibling Subsystem

Siblings of traumatized children may experience feelings of guilt, fear, anxiety, and (secondary) trauma symptoms similar to those of the traumatized child (Monahon, 1993). One area of primary trauma involves sibling abuse, which has been largely unaddressed in the literature (Wiehe, 1997). Two studies (Green, 1984; Rosenthal & Doherty, 1984) indicated that abusive siblings were themselves victims of abuse, often by their parents, highlighting both the intergenerational and intragenerational impact of trauma within families.

Secondary effects of trauma in siblings also occur. Applebaum and Burns (1991) found that children who had a sibling die unexpectedly (through accident or murder) were at risk of developing PTSD symptomatology. Freeman, Shaffer, and Smith (1996) described the impact of a child's murder on the siblings, which included unresolved grief and trauma reactions, continual reminders of the murder, fear of retaliation, and limited mental health services. An interesting result from this study was the concern expressed by children about the impact of the sibling's death on their parents. These studies suggested that the emotional unavailability or symptomatology of parents following a traumatic event is problematic for children, both primary and secondary victims (Applebaum & Burns, 1991; Freeman et al., 1996; Monahon, 1993). Because of the impact of the trauma on parents, secondary stress reactions in siblings may be overlooked or ignored (Applebaum & Burns, 1991).

Other Subsystems

As has been shown here, the focus on family trauma from a systemic lens is limited. Currently, literature is not available that reports the impact of child traumatization on the extended family system. Amick-McMullan, Kilpatrick, and Resnick (1991) identified PTSD symptoms in surviving family members of homicide victims. However, they included parents, children, spouses, siblings, grandparents, and grandchildren in the same group, and hence identifying differential effects between immediate family members (children, parents, siblings, spouses, and partners) and extended family members (grandparents and grandchildren) was not done.

Further research on the direct effects on the social interactions and relationships of traumatized children is necessary. The circle of impact should be expanded beyond the immediate family system because the symptoms present in a traumatized child can affect those with whom the child interacts at all system levels.

RESILIENCE TO CHILDHOOD TRAUMA

It is not unusual that one child will somehow emerge as more competent or successful than siblings who were exposed to the same negative environment. The resilient child is one who emerges as competent and confident when others are adversely affected by negative circumstances such as poverty, neglect, alcoholism, violence, and abuse (Tedeschi et al., 1998). Resilience refers to some underlying characteristic that allows certain individuals to succeed in spite of adversity (Waller, 2001). "Resilient children are those who have benefited from protective factors, show a pattern of successful adaptation, and are expected to continue to do well despite the presence of powerful risk factors" (Aldwin & Sutton, 1998, p. 49). The ability of resilient children to obtain successful outcomes involves an interplay between the child's basic traits and the environment (Waller, 2001). Certain personality traits or behaviors in children can elicit positive responses from the environment (e.g., positive performance by a child may initiate praise from a significant adult). In addition, certain environmental factors must create a positive crucible in order for the resilient child to find success. Resiliency factors are evident in two ways: (a) They help children recover from trauma more successfully, and (b) they provide protection to help children sustain competence under threat (Masten, Best, & Garmezy, 1990).

Research on resiliency factors in children can be described in the following four categories: (a) personality, (b) cognitive, (c) affective, and (d) behavioral. Personality factors that render children more resilient include having an agreeable temperament, an ability to feel empathy for others (including the perpetrator), and being extroverted and social (Aldwin & Sutton, 1998; Waller, 2001). Cognitive factors include children's ability to be creative and show initiative in getting their needs met, being insightful, and possessing a world view beyond the trauma (Tedeschi, 1999). Affective or emotional resilience involves the ability of children to manage their emotional reactions, to experience and express a broad range of emotions, and to maintain a sense of humor (Apfel & Simon, 1996; Waller, 2001). Behavioral characteristics include the ability of resilient children to be tenacious in their pursuit of goals, even when not encouraged or rewarded by others, to actively generate positive relationships with peers and adults, to be resourceful in dire situations, and to provide self-soothing when necessary (Apfel & Simon, 1996; Valentine & Feinauer, 1993).

FUTURE RESEARCH ON THE SYSTEMIC EFFECTS OF TRAUMATIZED CHILDREN

There is much work to be done empirically to investigate the impact of traumatized children. Further investigation needs to focus on the child and particularly on the interaction between the child and the broader system.

The Individual Child

Further research on the individual impact of trauma needs to focus on understanding the differential effects of various types of traumatic events and the longitudinal effects of trauma in children. Much of the current research focuses on adult survivors of childhood trauma and is retrospective in nature. There are few studies that track the long-term effects of trauma from childhood through adulthood and later life. Notable exceptions are the work by Nader et al. (1990), Terr (1991), Ventegodt (1999), and Wozniak et al. (1999). Nader et al. (1990) found continued symptoms of PTSD in children exposed to a school attack at the 14-month follow-up; however, the severity of symptoms had decreased for all participants. Similarly, Thabet and Vostanis (2000) found a reduction in PTSD symptoms at the 1-year follow-up in children traumatized by war.

It is also important to know more about the population of childhood trauma survivors who do not endure the most severe symptoms (e.g., PTSD). Research tends to focus on the minority who appear to suffer the most, but it may be helpful to understand what seems to be the majority—those who suffer some symptoms but do not qualify for the full PTSD diagnosis. This group also could include those more resilient individuals who are less negatively affected but do not rise above, or even "excel" from, the trauma. This less visible group requires further study, particularly since they may not be the population most likely to seek mental health services related to their previous trauma experiences.

The Broader System

It is necessary to gain a thorough empirical understanding of the broader systemic impact of trauma. This systemic focus is lacking in current literature. Research on the systemic effects of trauma can address the specific interpersonal dynamics that are affected when a child is traumatized, the posttrauma changes in the family structure and function, and the appearance of secondary and transgenerational traumatic stress in other family members. In addition, several specific issues are still poorly understood when families must contend with a traumatized child.

The child's developmental age. One area that requires more research is the impact of the child's developmental age at the time of the trauma, not only for understanding the effects of the trauma on the child but also for understanding the effects of the child's reaction on the rest of the family system. For example, in families with younger children who have not developed the cognitive capability to understand what has occurred, there may be increased stress placed on the family system, particularly the parents or caregivers who are struggling to understand and cope with increased fears, posttraumatic play, nightmares, or other symptoms in the child.

Extent of family resources. In family systems with limited resources, additional stress placed on the family system by the traumatized child is likely to compound problems already present in the family.[1] Increased blaming of the child, denial of negative repercussions from the trauma, general lack of support or concern for the child, and failure to access necessary services may become a primary mode of operating within the family and place members at risk of further traumatization.

Unrevealed trauma. For many traumatized children and families, their pain becomes a central focus in their functioning. Many traumatized children maintain in silence the "secret" of the trauma and their pain; they are then deprived of the support they need from their parents, siblings, and others. When parents and other members of the family system are not aware that the trauma occurred, trying to understand the symptoms or changes can be especially difficult and may affect the treatment significantly.

FAMILY THERAPY

We believe that family therapy still holds considerable undeveloped potential for helping families dealing with child trauma. Although often viewed as an adjunctive treatment for trauma (Riggs, 2000), family-focused treatment may be the most effective treatment when the victim is a child. It takes advantage of the most influential relationships in a

---

1. *Editor's note:* See chapter 2 for an in-depth discussion of the loss spirals that develop in families with limited resources.

child's life, both by supplementing the parents' direct efforts to provide external ego support to the child and by increasing the support and resources available to the entire family. Family therapy can also help reduce the barriers and limitations imposed by an impaired trauma membrane. Effective family therapy interventions and clinical approaches need to be developed and evaluated in order to provide the most beneficial treatment to child trauma survivors and their families.

CONCLUSION

This chapter provided a review of the current research on the traumatization of children. The child survivor experiences many cognitive, affective, behavioral, and psychological changes. In addition, the interpersonal or family system experiences extensive repercussions from trauma to a child member. Understanding trauma within the family system is important to gain a perspective of trauma beyond the individual or primary trauma victim.

When we consider the extent to which a traumatic event affects a child and the number of people with whom that child has contact throughout its life, we cannot help but conclude that a single traumatic event does not have a single victim. The repercussions from trauma ripple through many human systems, particularly when the trauma occurs to a child. Identifying and understanding those repercussions are a necessary next step in the overall treatment of traumatized children.

REFERENCES

Aldwin, C. M., & Sutton, K. J. (1998). A developmental perspective on posttraumatic growth. In R. G. Tedeschi, C. L. Park, & L. G. Calhoun (Eds.), *Posttraumatic growth: Positive changes in the aftermath of crisis* (pp. 43–63). Mahwah, NJ: Erlbaum.

American Psychiatric Association. (1980). *Diagnostic and statistical manual of mental disorders* (3rd ed.). Washington, DC: Author.

American Psychiatric Association. (1987). *Diagnostic and statistical manual of mental disorders* (3rd ed., rev.). Washington, DC: Author.

American Psychiatric Association. (1994). *Diagnostic and statistical manual of mental disorders* (4th ed.). Washington, DC: Author.

American Psychiatric Association. (2000). *Diagnostic and statistical manual of mental disorders* (4th ed., text rev.). Washington, DC: Author.

Amick-McMullan, A., Kilpatrick, D., & Resnick, H. (1991). Homicide as a risk factor for PTSD among surviving family members. *Behavior Modification, 15,* 545–559.

Ancharoff, M. R., Munroe, J. F., & Fisher, L. M. (1998). The legacy of combat trauma: Clinical implications of intergenerational transmission. In Y. Danieli (Ed.), *International handbook of multigenerational legacies of trauma* (pp. 257–276). New York: Plenum.

Apfel, R. J., & Simon, B. (1996). Introduction. In R. J. Apfel & B. Simon (Eds.), *Minefields in their hearts: The mental health of children in war and communal violence* (pp. 1–17). New Haven, CT: Yale University Press.

Applebaum, D. R., & Burns, G. L. (1991). Unexpected childhood death: Posttraumatic stress disorder in surviving siblings and parents. *Journal of Clinical Child Psychology, 20,* 114–120.

Aptekar, L., & Boore, J. A. (1990). The emotional effects of disaster on children: A review of the literature. *International Journal of Mental Health. 19,* 77–90.

Banyard, V. L., Englund, D. W., & Rozelle, D. (2001). Parenting the traumatized child: Attending to the needs of nonoffending caregivers of traumatized children. *Psychotherapy, 38,* 74–87.

Bar-On, D. (1996). Attempting to overcome the intergenerational transmission of trauma. In R. J. Apfel & B. Simon (Eds.), *Minefields in their hearts: The mental health of children in war and communal violence* (pp. 165–188). New Haven, CT: Yale University Press.

Barnes, M. F. (1998). Understanding the secondary traumatic stress of parents. In C. R. Figley (Ed.), *Burnout in families: The systemic costs of caring* (pp. 75–89). Boca Raton, FL: CRC.

Bentovim, A. (1992). *Trauma organised systems.* London: Karnac Books.

Bergmann, M. S., & Jucovy, M. E. (Eds.). (1982). *Generations of the Holocaust.* New York: Basic Books.

Best, M., Streisand, R., Catania, L., & Kazak, A. E. (2001). Parental distress during pediatric leukemia and posttraumatic stress symptoms (PTSS) after treatment ends. *Journal of Pediatric Psychology, 26,* 299–307.

Bingham, R. D., & Harmon, R. J. (1996). Traumatic stress in infancy and early childhood: Expression of distress and developmental issues. In C. R. Pfeffer (Ed.), *Severe stress and mental disturbance in children* (pp. 499–532). Washington, DC: American Psychiatric Press.

Black, D., & Newman, M. (2000). Children: Secondary victims of domestic violence. In A. Y. Shalev, R. Yehuda, & A. C. McFarlane (Eds.), *International handbook of human response to trauma* (pp. 129–138). New York: Plenum.

Boney-McCoy, S., & Finkelhor, D. (1996). Is youth victimization related to trauma symptoms and depression after controlling for prior symptoms and family relationships? A longitudinal, prospective study. *Journal of Consulting and Clinical Psychology, 64,* 1406–1416.

Bradburn, I. S. (1991). After the earth shook: Children's stress symptoms 6–8 months after a disaster. *Advances in Behaviour Research and Therapy, 13,* 173–179.

Buchanan, A. (1996). *Cycles of child maltreatment: Facts, fallacies, and interventions.* Chichester, U.K.: Wiley.

Burman, S., & Allen-Meares, P. (1994). Neglected victims of murder: Children's witness to parental homicide. *Social Work, 39,* 28–34.

Catherall, D. R. (1992). *Back from the brink: A family guide to overcoming traumatic stress.* New York: Bantam Books.

Cicchetti, D., Toth, S. L., & Lynch, M. (1997). Child maltreatment as an illustration of the effects of war on development. In D. Cicchetti & S. L. Toth (Eds.), *Rochester Symposium on Developmental Psychology: Vol. 8. Developmental perspectives on trauma: Theory, research, and intervention* (pp. 227–262). Rochester, NY: University of Rochester Press.

Compas, B. E., & Epping, J. E. (1993). Stress and coping in children and families: Implications for children coping with disaster. In C. E. Saylor (Ed.), *Children and disasters* (pp. 11–28). New York: Plenum.

Courtois, C. A. (1988). *Healing the incest wound.* New York: Norton.

Cuffe, S., Addy, C., Garrison, C., Waller, J., Jackson, K., McKeown, R., & Chilappagari, S. (1998). Prevalence of PTSD in a community sample of older adolescents. *Journal of the American Academy of Child and Adolescent Psychiatry, 37,* 147–154.

Danieli, Y. (1985). The treatment and prevention of long-term effects and intergenerational transmission of victimization: A lesson from Holocaust survivors and their children. In C. R. Figley (Ed.), *Trauma and its wake* (pp. 295–313). New York: Brunner/Mazel.

Dremen, S. (1991). Coping with the trauma of divorce. *Journal of Traumatic Stress, 4,* 113–121.

Dremen, S., & Cohen, E. (1990). Children of victims of terrorism revisited: Integrating individual and family treatment approaches. *American Journal of Orthopsychiatry, 60,* 204–209.

Dulmus, C., & Wodarski, J. (2000). Trauma-related symptomatology among children of parents victimized by urban community violence. *American Journal of Orthopsychiatry, 70,* 272–277.

Duncan, R. D., Saunders, B. E., Kilpatrick, D. E., Hanson, R. F., & Resnick, H. S. (1996). Childhood physical assault as a risk factor for PTSD, depression, and substance abuse: Findings from a national survey. *American Journal of Orthopsychiatry, 66,* 437–448.

Duran, E., Duran, B., Yellow Horse Brave Heart, M., Yellow Horse-Davis, S. (1998). Healing the American Indian soul wound. In Y. Danieli (Ed.), *International handbook of multigenerational legacies of trauma* (pp. 341–354). New York: Plenum.

Erickson, M. F., Egeland, B., & Pianta, R. (1989). The effects of maltreatment on the development of young children. In D. Cicchetti & V. Carlson (Eds.), *Child maltreatment: Theory and research on the causes and consequences of child abuse and neglect* (pp. 647–684). New York: Cambridge University Press.

Fantuzzo, J., Boruch, R., Beriama, A., Atkins, M., & Marcus, S. (1997). Domestic violence and children: Prevalence and risk in five major U.S. cities. *Journal of the American Academy of Child and Adolescent Psychiatry, 36,* 116–122.

Felsen, I. (1998). Transgenerational transmission of effects of the Holocaust: The North American research perspective. In Y. Danieli (Ed.), *International handbook of multigenerational legacies of trauma* (pp. 43–68). New York: Plenum.

Figley, C. R. (1983). Catastrophes: An overview of family reaction. In C. R. Figley & H. I. McCubbin (Eds.), *Stress and the family: Vol. 2. Coping with catastrophe* (pp. 3–20). New York: Brunner/Mazel.

Figley, C. R. (1989). *Helping traumatized families.* San Francisco: Jossey-Bass.

Figley, C. R. (1995). Compassion fatigue as secondary traumatic stress disorder. In C. R. Figley (Ed.), *Compassion fatigue: Coping with secondary traumatic stress disorder in those who treat the traumatized* (pp. 1–20). New York: Brunner/Mazel.

Fletcher, K. E. (1996). Childhood posttraumatic stress disorder. In E. J. Mash & R. A. Barkley (Eds.), *Child psychopathology.* New York: Guilford.

Freeman, L. N., Shaffer, D., & Smith, H. (1996). Neglected victims of homicide: The needs of young siblings of murder victims. *American Journal of Orthopsychiatry, 66,* 337–345.

Fukunishi, I., Tsuruta, T., Hirabayashi, N., & Asukai, N. (2001). Association of alexithymic characteristics and posttraumatic stress responses following medical treatment for children with refractory hematological diseases. *Psychological Reports, 89,* 527–534.

Garbarino, J. (1989). Troubled youth, troubled families: The dynamics of adolescent maltreatment. In D. Cicchetti & V. Carlson (Eds.), *Child maltreatment: Theory and research on the causes and consequences of child abuse and neglect* (pp. 685–706). New York: Cambridge University Press.

Garbarino, J., Kostelny, K., & Dubrow, N. (1991). *No place to be a child: Growing up in a war zone.* San Francisco: Jossey-Bass.

Goldson, E. (1996). The effect of war on children. *Child Abuse and Neglect, 20,* 809–819.

Green, A. H. (1984). Child abuse by siblings. *Child Abuse and Neglect, 8,* 311–317.

Green, A. H., & Kocijan-Hercigonja, D. (1998). Stress and coping in children traumatized by war. *Journal of the American Academy of Psychoanalysis, 26,* 585–597.

Green, B., Korol, M., Grace, M., Vary, M., Leonard, A., Gleser, G., & Smitson-Cohen, S. (1991). Children and disaster: Age, gender, and parental effects on PTSD symptoms. *Journal of the American Academy of Child and Adolescent Psychiatry, 30,* 945–951.

Handford, H. A., Mayes, S. D., Mattison, R. E., Humphrey, F. J., Bagnato, S., Bixler, E. O., & Kales, J. D. (1986). Child and parent reaction to the Three Mile Island nuclear accident. *Journal of the American Academy of Child Psychiatry, 25,* 346–356.

Hendriks, J. H., Black, D., & Kaplan, T. (1993). *When father kills mother: Guiding children through trauma and grief.* London: Routledge.

Herman, J. L. (1997). *Trauma and recovery* (2nd ed.). New York: Basic Books.

Johnson, K. (1998). *Trauma in the lives of children: Crisis and stress management techniques for teachers, counselors, and student service professionals* (2nd ed.). Alameda, CA: Hunter House.

Karkazis, J. L., & Lazaneo, S. L. (2000). Unyielding custody disputes: Tempering loss and courting disaster. In J. H. Harvey & E. D. Miller (Eds.), *Loss and trauma: General and close relationship perspectives* (pp. 375–384). Philadelphia: Brunner-Routledge.

Kazak, A. E. (1998). Posttraumatic distress in childhood cancer survivors and their parents. *Medical and Pediatric Oncology Supplement, 1,* 60–68.

Keane, T. M., Weathers, F. W., & Foa, E. B. (2000). Diagnosis and assessment. In E. B. Foa, T. M. Keane, & M. J. Friedman (Eds.), *Effective treatments for PTSD* (pp. 18–36). New York: Guilford.

Kenrick, J. (2000). "Be a kid": The traumatic impact of repeated separations on children who are fostered and adopted. *Journal of Child Psychotherapy, 26,* 393–412.

Keppel-Benson, J. M., & Ollendick, T. H. (1993). Posttraumatic stress disorder in children and adolescents. In C. E. Saylor (Ed.), *Children and disasters* (pp. 29–43). New York: Plenum.

Kestenberg, J. S. (1982). Survivor-parents and their children. In M. S. Bergmann & M. E. Jucovy (Eds.), *Generations of the Holocaust* (pp. 83–102). New York: Basic Books.

Kilpatrick, K. L., & Williams, L. M. (1997). Post-traumatic stress disorder in child witnesses to domestic violence. *American Journal of Orthopsychiatry, 67,* 639–644.

Kinzie, J., Sack, W., Angell, R., Manson, S., & Rath, B. (1986). The psychiatric effects of massive trauma on Cambodian children: I. The children. *Journal of the American Academy of Child Psychiatry, 25,* 370–376.

Kulka, R., Schlenger, W., Fairbank, J., Hough, R., Jordan, B., Marmar, C., & Weiss, D. (1990). *Trauma and the Vietnam war generation: Report of findings from the National Vietnam Veterans Readjustment Study.* Philadelphia: Brunner/Mazel.

Lindy, J. (1985). The trauma membrane and other clinical concepts derived from psychotherapeutic work with survivors of natural disasters. *Psychiatric Annals, 15,* 153–160.

Lipton, M. (1997). The effect of the primary caretaker's distress on the sexually abused child: A comparison of biological and foster parents. *Child and Adolescent Social Work Journal, 14,* 115–127.

Lystad, M. (1984). Children's responses to disaster: Family implications. *International Journal of Family Psychiatry, 5,* 41–60.

Mahony, D. L., & Campbell, J. M. (1998). Children witnessing domestic violence: A developmental approach. *Clinical Excellence for Nurse Practitioners, 2,* 362–369.

Marans, S., Berkman, M., & Cohen, D. (1996). Child development and adaptation to catastrophic circumstances. In R. J. Apfel & B. Simon (Eds.), *Minefields in their hearts: The mental health of children in war and communal violence* (pp. 104–127). New Haven, CT: Yale University Press.

Masten, A., Best, K., & Garmezy, N. (1990). Resilience and development: Contributions from the study of children who overcome adversity. *Development and Psychopathology, 2,* 425–444.

McCann, I. L., & Pearlman, L. A. (1990). Vicarious traumatization: A framework for understanding the psychological effects of working with victims. *Journal of Traumatic Stress, 3,* 131–149.

McCloskey, L. A., & Bailey, J. A. (2000). The intergenerational transmission of risk for child sexual abuse. *Journal of Interpersonal Violence, 15,* 1019–1035.

McLeer, S., Deblinger, E., Atkins, M., Foa, E., & Ralphe, D. (1988). Post-traumatic stress disorder in sexually abused children. *Journal of the American Academy of Child and Adolescent Psychiatry, 27,* 650–654.

Miller, T. W., & Kraus, R. F. (1994). Natural and environmental disasters: Psychological issues and clinical responses. *Integrative Psychiatry, 10,* 128–132.

Monahon, C. (1993). *Children and trauma: A guide for parents and professionals.* San Francisco: Jossey-Bass.

Nader, K., Pynoos, R., Fairbanks, L., & Frederick, C. (1990). Children's PTSD reactions one year after a sniper attack at their school. *American Journal of Psychiatry, 147,* 1526–1530.

Nelson, B. S., Wangsgaard, S., Yorgason, J., Higgins Kessler, M., & Carter-Vassol, E. L. (2002). Single and dual trauma couples: Relationship characteristics and dynamics. *American Journal of Orthopsychiatry 72,* 58–69.

Newberger, C., Geremy, I., Waternaux, C., & Newberger, E. (1993). Mothers of sexually abused children: Trauma and repair in longitudinal perspective. *American Journal of Orthopsychiatry, 63,* 92–102.

Osofsky, J. D. (1995). *Children who witness domestic violence: The invisible victims* (Social Policy Report, Vol. IX, No. 3). Ann Arbor, MI: Society for Research in Child Development.

Osofsky, J. D., & Fenichel, E. (Eds.). (2000). *Protecting young children in violent environments: Building staff and community strengths.* Washington, DC: Zero to Three: National Center for Infants, Toddlers, and Families.

Parsons, J., Kehle, T. J., & Owen, S. V. (1990). Incidence of behavior problems among children of Vietnam war veterans. *School Psychology International, 11,* 253–259.

Pelcovitz, D., Kaplan, S., DeRosa, R., Mandel, F., & Salzinger, S. (2000). Psychiatric disorders in adolescents exposed to domestic violence and physical abuse. *American Journal of Orthopsychiatry, 70,* 360–369.

Pynoos, R. S. Steinberg, A. M., & Goenjian, A. (1996). Traumatic stress in childhood and adolescence: Recent developments and current controversies. In B. A. van der Kolk, A. C. McFarlane, & L. Weisaeth (Eds.), *Traumatic stress: The effects of overwhelming experience on mind, body, and society* (pp. 331–358). New York: Guilford.

Riggs, D. S. (2000). Marital and family therapy. *Journal of Traumatic Stress, 13,* 584–585.

Rinear, E. E. (1988). Psychosocial aspects of parental response patterns to the death of a child by homicide. *Journal of Traumatic Stress, 1,* 305–322.

Rosenheck, R. (1986). Impact of posttraumatic stress disorder of World War II on the next generation. *Journal of Nervous and Mental Diseases, 174,* 319–327.

Rosenheck, R., & Fontana, A. (1998). Warrior fathers and warrior sons: Intergenerational aspects of trauma. In Y. Danieli (Ed.), *International handbook of multigenerational legacies of trauma* (pp. 225–242). New York: Plenum.

Rosenheck, R., & Nathan, P. (1985). Secondary traumatization in children of Vietnam veterans. *Hospital and Community Psychiatry, 36,* 538–539.

Rosenthal, P. A., & Doherty, M. B. (1984). Serious sibling abuse by preschool children. *Journal of the American Academy of Child Psychiatry, 23,* 186–190.

Rossman, B. B. R. (1998). Descartes's error and posttraumatic stress disorder: Cognition and emotion in children who are exposed to parental violence. In G. W. Holden, R. Geffner, & E. N. Jouriles (Eds.), *Children exposed to marital violence: Theory, research, and applied issues.* (pp. 223–256). Washington, DC: American Psychological Association.

Rozensky, R. H., Sloan, I. H., Schwarz, E. D., & Kowalski, J. M. (1993). Psychological response of children to shootings and hostage situations. In C. E. Saylor (Ed.), *Children and disasters* (pp. 123–136). New York: Plenum.

Saigh, P. A., Yasik, A. E., Sack, W. H., & Koplewicz, H. S. (1999). Child-adolescent posttraumatic stress disorder: Prevalence, risk factors, and comorbidity. In P. A. Saigh & J. D. Bremmer (Eds.), *Posttraumatic stress disorder: A comprehensive text* (pp. 18–43). Needham Heights, MA: Allyn & Bacon.

Saylor, C. F., Swenson, C. C., & Powell, P. (1992). Hurricane Hugo blows down the broccoli: Preschoolers' post-disaster play and adjustment. *Child Psychiatry and Human Development, 22,* 139–149.

Schuster, M. A., Stein, B. D., Jaycox, L. H., Collins, R. L., Marshall, G. N., Elliott, M. N., Zhou, A. J., Kanouse, D. E., Morrison, J. L., & Berry, S. H. (2001). A national survey of stress reactions after the September 11, 2001 terrorist attacks. *New England Journal of Medicine, 345,* 1507–1512.

Shalev, A. Y. (1996). Stress versus traumatic stress: From acute homeostatic reactions to chronic psychopathology. In B. A. van der Kolk, A. C. McFarlane, & L. Weisaeth (Eds.), *Traumatic stress: The effects of overwhelming experience on mind, body, and society* (pp. 77–101). New York: Guilford.

Shannon, M., Lonigan, C., Finch, A., & Taylor, C. (1994). Children exposed to disaster: I. Epidemiology of post-traumatic symptoms and symptom profiles. *Journal of the American Academy of Child and Adolescent Psychiatry, 33,* 80–93.

Solomon, Z., Waysman, M., Levy, G., Fried, B., Mikulincer, M., Benbenishty, R., Florian, V., & Bleich, A. (1992). From front line to home front: A study of secondary traumatization. *Family Process, 31,* 289–302.

Stallard, P., Velleman, R., & Baldwin, S. (1998). Prospective study of post-traumatic stress disorder in children involved in road traffic accidents. *British Medical Journal, 317,* 1619–1623.

Steinberg, A. (1998). Understanding the secondary traumatic stress of children. In C. R. Figley (Ed.), *Burnout in families: The systemic costs of caring* (pp. 29–46). Boca Raton, FL: CRC.

Stuber, M. L., & Houskamp, B. (1996). Stress and pediatric medical technology. In C. R. Pfeffer (Ed.), *Severe stress and mental disturbance in children* (pp. 249–275). Washington, DC: American Psychiatric Press.

Sugar, M. (1999). Severe physical trauma in adolescence. In M. Sugar (Ed.), *Trauma and adolescence* (pp. 183–201). Madison, WI: International Universities Press.

Swenson, C. C., & Klingman, A. (1993). Children and war. In C. E. Saylor (Ed.), *Children and disasters* (pp. 137–163). New York: Plenum.

Swenson, C. C., Saylor, C. F., Powell, M. P., Stokes, S. J., Foster, K. Y., & Belter, R. W. (1996). Impact of a natural disaster on preschool children: Adjustment 14 months after a hurricane. *American Journal of Orthopsychiatry, 66,* 122–130.

Tedeschi, R. G. (1999). Violence transformed: Posttraumatic growth in survivors and their societies. *Aggression and Violent Behavior, 4,* 319–341.

Tedeschi, R. G., Park, C. L., & Calhoun, L. G. (1998). Posttraumatic growth: Conceptual issues. In R. G. Tedeschi, C. L. Park, & L. G. Calhoun (Eds.), *Posttraumatic growth: Positive changes in the aftermath of crisis* (pp. 1–22). Mahwah, NJ: Erlbaum.

Terr, L. (1981). Psychic trauma in children: Observations following the Chowchilla schoolbus kidnapping. *American Journal of Psychiatry, 138,* 14–19.

Terr, L. (1988). What happens to early memories of trauma? A study of twenty children under age five at the time of documented traumatic events. *Journal of the American Academy of Child and Adolescent Psychiatry, 27,* 96–104.

Terr, L. (1990). *Too scared to cry.* New York: Basic Books.

Terr, L. (1991). Childhood traumas: An outline and overview. *American Journal of Psychiatry, 148,* 10–20.

Thabet, A. A., & Vostanis, P. (2000). Post traumatic stress disorder reactions in children of war: A longitudinal study. *Child Abuse and Neglect, 24,* 291–298.

Timmons-Mitchell, J., Chandler-Holtz, D., & Semple, W. E. (1996). Post-traumatic stress symptoms in mothers following children's reports of sexual abuse: An exploratory study. *American Journal of Orthopsychiatry, 66,* 463–467.

Trickett, P. K., Reiffman, A., Horowitz, L. A., & Putnam, F. W. (1997). Characteristics of sexual abuse trauma and the prediction of developmental outcomes. In D. Cicchetti & S. L. Toth (Eds.), *Rochester symposium on developmental psychology: Vol. 8. Developmental perspectives on trauma: Theory, research, and intervention* (pp. 289 314). Rochester, NY: University of Rochester Press.

Valentine, L., & Feinauer, L. L. (1993). Resilience factors affiliated with female survivors of childhood sexual abuse. *American Journal of Family Therapy, 21,* 216–224.

Ventegodt, S. (1999). A prospective study on quality of life and traumatic events in early life—a 30-year follow-up. *Child: Care, Health, and Development, 25,* 213–221.

Vila, G., Porche, L., & Mouren-Simeoni, M. (1999). An 18-month longitudinal study of posttraumatic disorders in children who were taken hostage in their school. *Psychosomatic Medicine, 61,* 746–754.

Waller, M. A. (2001). Resilience in ecosystemic context: Evaluation of the concept. *American Journal of Orthopsychiatry, 71,* 290–297.

Whitbeck, L., & Hoyt, D. (1999). *Nowhere to grow.* New York: Gruyter.

Wiehe, V. R. (1997). *Sibling abuse: Hidden physical, emotional, and sexual trauma* (2nd ed.). Thousand Oaks, CA: Sage.

Willard, S. E. (1998). The impact of the Oakland-Berkeley Hills firestorm on parent-child relationships (Doctoral dissertation, Pacific Graduate School of Psychology, 1997). *Dissertation Abstracts International, 59–04B,* 1872.

Wozniak, J., Crawford, M. H., Biederman, J., Faraone, S. V., Spencer, T. J., Taylor, A., & Blier, H. K. (1999). Antecedents and complications of trauma in boys with ADHD: Findings from a longitudinal study. *Journal of the American Academy of Child and Adolescent Psychiatry, 38,* 48–55.

Yule, W., & Williams, R. M. (1990). Post-traumatic stress reactions in children. *Journal of Traumatic Stress, 3,* 279–295.

10

Adult Attachment and Trauma

ROBERT T. MULLER, ERIN R. KRAFTCHECK, AND LISE A. McLEWIN

One of the most significant areas of risk studied in developmental psychopathology has been that of child maltreatment. Children who experience maltreatment exhibit difficulties in most developmental domains and in their ability to successfully resolve stage-salient developmental issues including attachment, self-development and autonomy, emotion regulation and development, behavioral regulation, and social development (Cicchetti, 1989; Cicchetti & Howes, 1991). Maltreated infants are at increased risk of having an insecure attachment (Cicchetti & Barnett, 1991; Crittenden & Ainsworth, 1989; McCrone, Egeland, Kalkoske, & Carlson, 1994) or an atypical attachment (Crittenden, 1988; Toth & Cicchetti, 1996) with their primary caregivers. Maltreatment appears to have a lasting impact on individuals, continuing through adolescence and adulthood. Formerly maltreated adults have difficulty with interpersonal adjustment, relationships, and substance abuse (Alexander & Anderson, 1997; Roche, Runtz, & Hunter, 1999). Personality disorders and psychiatric symptoms are also commonly reported (Alexander et al., 1998; Briere & Runtz, 1988; Muller, Sicoli, & Lemieux, 2000). Many of these psychiatric symptoms and maladaptive behaviors are being linked to both infant and adult attachment styles (Alexander & Anderson, 1997; Briere & Runtz, 1988).

ATTACHMENT AND INTERNAL WORKING MODELS

Theory and research on attachment were pioneered by John Bowlby. Bowlby's attachment theory was based on ethology and evolution theories; he emphasized the importance of child–caregiver interactions in the development of basic cognitive, behavioral, and affective systems (Bowlby, 1980). He conceived the attachment process as a behavioral system with the purpose of regulating *contact-maintaining* behaviors by infants with specific caregivers who provide physical or psychological safety or both (Bowlby, 1969; Berman & Sperling, 1994). He defined attachment as an emotional bond characterized by proximity-maintaining behavior with a specific person, especially under stressful circumstances. Bowlby (1988) maintained that the capacity to establish close, secure attachments to other people through affectional bonding is essential to adaptive development and functioning throughout life.

Research on Attachment

Ainsworth, Blehar, Waters, and Wall (1978) designed an experimental observation technique called "the Strange Situation" to examine the attachment bond between infants and caregivers. The Strange Situation involved the observation of infants' reactions to controlled separations from, and subsequent reunions with, their caregivers. Ainsworth was able to identify three specific categories of attachment. *Securely attached* infants trust their caregivers and a bond forms that ensures safety (Bowlby, 1980; Crittenden & Ainsworth, 1989). These children show signs of distress when separated from their parents, seek contact and comfort from the parents when reunited, and then are able to use their caregivers as secure bases from which to investigate their surroundings and return to play (Berman & Sperling, 1994). Another type of attachment category is the *insecure–avoidant* style. Insecure–avoidant children tend to feel that they are unloved and they also tend to lack self-defensive and help-seeking behaviors. This style is characterized by exhibiting distress signs during separation from the parent and rejection of, or inattention to, the parent upon reunion (Berman & Sperling, 1994). The third type of attachment category identified by Ainsworth (1973) was the *insecure–resistant* style. This category is characterized by high distress during separation from the caregiver and ambivalence—observed as a combination of approach and rejection directed toward the caregiver—upon reunion.

It should be noted that children characterized by these three attachment patterns have also shown specific behavioral differences outside the Strange Situation. Secure children have been observed to have better interactions with others, to feel comfortable exploring their environment, and to demonstrate resiliency in their emotions. The avoidant children are often considered to be more attention-seeking at school and anxious or fearful with caregivers at home. The resistant children are often reported to show clinging behaviors, fear of their surrounding environment, and emotional reactivity (Berman & Sperling, 1994).

Child attachment researchers describe a fourth attachment category to encompass many children who do not fall in the traditional classifications (Carlson, Cicchetti, Barnett, & Braunwald, 1989; Crittenden, 1985; Main & Solomon, 1986; Main & Weston, 1981). Crittenden (1985) referred to this fourth category as *avoidant–ambivalent*. It is considered to arise when the primary caregiver's behavior is consistently and severely distorted. Avoidant–ambivalent infants show a combination of high proximity-seeking, high avoidance, and high resistance, a combination of behaviors evidenced in traditional attachment styles. Other researchers have proposed a fifth category called the *disorganized–disoriented type* (Type D) (Main & Solomon, 1986), characterized by a lack of coping abilities for dealing with separations and a lack of coherent behavioral organization in the Strange Situation. Type D infants may show odd symptoms when they are with caregivers, such as dazing, freezing, apprehension, and interrupted movements. Unpredictability in the primary caregiver's behaviors and responses may be the crucial factor in the formation of the disorganized attachment style (Greenberg, Cicchetti, & Cummings, 1990; Main & Solomon, 1986).

Working Models of Self and Other

Bowlby (1969) considered the primary attachment bonds critical to personality and social development, operating through the creation of internal working models of the self and others. He posited that internal working models grow from repeated experiences with the primary caregiver through which children start to develop expectations about how future interactions will operate (Bretherton, 1990; Main, Kaplan, & Cassidy, 1985). A sense of security is derived from positive models of self and others. The positive working model of others represents a child's views of attachment figures as reliable for support and protection when required. Similarly, the positive working model of self represents a child's beliefs that he is loved and accepted by other people. If the mother provides consistent responses to the child's signals, the child will develop a representational model of her as sensitive and trustworthy. The child will also feel that he is worthy of attention and affection from his mother and is able to elicit her response when necessary. This security in relationships can generalize to other adults and people whom he discovers he can trust (Crittenden & Ainsworth, 1989). Early positive attachment experiences lead to positive self-worth and positive identity, while also facilitating the trust in others necessary for future interpersonal relationships and support (Gilbert, 1992).

An insecurely attached child who has not experienced predictable, sensitive care from primary caregivers may develop a model of others as being inconsistent or unpredictable. These experiences will then translate into a view of the self as unworthy of love and unable to gain positive attention, and there will be a sense of the relationship as unsatisfactory (Cicchetti, Toth, & Lynch, 1995). Children with insecure attachments have been found to have greater difficulty with peer relationships and tend to make more incorrect cognitive judgments of cues in the environment (Reider & Cicchetti, 1989; Sroufe, Carlson, Levy, & Egeland, 1999). Internalizing these views of self and other (whether negative or positive) contributes to an individual's future ability to cope with distress (Muller, Sicoli, & Lemieux, 2000). Individuals who develop a negative view of self present with low self-esteem, lack of self-respect, and a core belief that they are not worthy of love and support from others (Herman, 1992; Roberts, Gotlib, & Kassel, 1996). When the view of self is damaged, individuals lose their sense of agency and power to direct their lives in relationships, which often lead to their sense of trust in others being compromised (Herman, 1992).

Although working models tend to be complementary, a child may hold two simultaneous conflicting models of an attachment relationship, resulting from conflicting information (Bowlby, 1980; McCrone et al., 1994). For example, if children have experienced a parent as abusive, they may attempt to maintain the attachment relationship by maintaining a positive view of the parent, while viewing themselves as unworthy of their care and attention (McCrone et al., 1994). A child may also hold different models for different relationships; children may show different attachment patterns with each parent (Bretherton, 1995) or have a different relationship model for a peer (Lynch & Cicchetti, 1991; Toth & Cicchetti, 1996). Early working models of specific relationships are believed to contribute to the development of more generalized models of relationships (Bowlby, 1980; Crittenden & Ainsworth, 1989; Lynch & Cicchetti, 1991). Resulting attachment styles are expected to remain relatively stable across development, with change becoming increasingly difficult as development progresses (Ainsworth, 1973; Bowlby, 1980; Sroufe et al., 1999).

Attachment is not independent of subsequent experience, however, and shifts in working models may still occur (Cicchetti et al., 1995; Toth & Cicchetti, 1996). Consequently, the organization of working models becomes increasingly complex with experience (Collins & Read, 1994). Early working models of self and others are considered to affect the development of more global models of relationships throughout life

(Bowlby, 1980; Crittenden & Ainsworth, 1989). In addition, these internal working models either facilitate or limit acquisition of new information about the self and others (Main et al., 1985). As such, internal working models guide the individual's contact with others into adulthood. The consolidation of insecure attachment styles during development may lead to an inability to develop the capacity for integrated and stable representations of others (Diamond & Blatt, 1994). These negative working models are then expected to lead to maladaptive views of self and others throughout development.

Collins and Read (1994) have developed an organizational hierarchy of adult working models. The hierarchy is composed of a network of interconnected models, moving from general representations at the top of the hierarchy to more specific models at the bottom. The most general representations of the self, other people, and relationships reside at the top, followed by models corresponding to different classes of relationships (i.e., parent–child peers). The most specific models of particular relationships (i.e., mother, a particular friend) are at the bottom of the hierarchy. Development of the hierarchy of working models begins in childhood with a single relationship (normally with the primary caregiver). Consistent with Bowlby's (1980) contentions, individuals form more general models of the self and others over time, which then shape the construction of more specific models in subsequent relationships. Thus, in adulthood, a new model of a particular relationship will be constructed in part out of existing expectations, although the new relationship-specific models do provide opportunities to refine and update more general models. Bowlby (1980, 1982) asserted that although models will become more resistant to change over time, they are still active constructions that can be modified and reconstructed over the course of experience. Collins and Read (1994) acknowledge that any one relationship is not likely to cause extensive change to more general models, although given the complexity of working models, consistent cumulative experiences may result in greater alterations.

Developmental changes in attachment. A major developmental shift occurs in the nature of attachment relationships. Early in life, they are asymmetrical in nature, with the caregiver holding most of the power and responsibility (Krappmann, Schuster, & Youniss, 1998). With development, attachments become more symmetrical and reciprocal in nature (Hazan & Zeifman, 1999). In middle childhood, children become more integrated into the world of peers, and by adolescence, they tend to emphasize peer relationships over those with parents (Youniss & Haynie, 1992). Hazan and Zeifman (1999) investigated this shift with regard to attachment and found that between the ages of 8 and 14, peers come to be preferred over parents as sources of comfort and emotional support. A second study with adults revealed a peer orientation with regard to proximity-seeking and safe-haven behaviors. Further, they reported their main attachment figure as their romantic partner when in a relationship beyond 2 years. The romantic relationships met definitional criteria for attachment such as proximity-seeking, safe-haven behavior, and separation anxiety. Many attachment researchers acknowledge the shift in attachment figures with development, and base adult attachment measures on either current relationships alone or a combination of past and present relationship experiences.

Review of Adult Attachment Styles

Adult attachment patterns are presumed to follow from the representational models of self and others that develop during childhood and adolescence (Main et al., 1985). Several researchers have begun to examine various adult attachment styles (Bartholomew, 1990; Hazan & Shaver, 1987; Main et al., 1985; Rothbard & Shaver, 1994). Methods of assessing adult attachment have proliferated over recent years, utilizing both interview and self-report techniques. The most widely used interview technique was developed by Main and colleagues (see Hesse, 1999, for a review) to assess adults' current representations about their past experiences. The Adult Attachment Interview (AAI) bases its assessment on discussion with adults of their childhood relationships with their parents and the perceived effects of the experiences on their development as adults and as parents. Interviewers attend to both content and how individuals describe, evaluate, and reason about the experiences. A scoring system was developed resulting in attachment styles similar to the traditional childhood classifications.

Autonomous (secure) adults coherently present a balanced view of early relationships, and value attachment relationships and attachment-related experiences as influential in their development. Insecure attachments include dismissing (avoidant) and preoccupied (ambivalent) behaviors, marked by incoherence in interviews. Dismissing adults are uncomfortable with the discussion, deny any impact of early attachment relationships on development, have difficulty recalling specific events, and often idealize their experiences. Preoccupied adults show confusion or oscillation or both about their past experiences; their descriptions of relationships with parents are marked by active anger or passivity. An unresolved category may also be coded along with a major category for those reporting attachment related traumas of loss or abuse or both. These individuals are deemed insecure, often showing confusion and disorganization in their discussion of the topic. Research with the AAI has shown that the attachment classifications are predictive of the mother's attachment with her own child (Main & Goldwyn, 1984).

Several self-report measures of adult attachment have been developed (Crowell, Fraley, & Shaver, 1999). Hazan and Shaver (1987) noted the similarities between many behavioral and emotional dynamics character- istic of both adult romantic relationships and infant–mother relation- ships. They argued that the major attachment categories described by Ainsworth (1973) are conceptually similar to styles in love relationships. They developed a forced-choice questionnaire where adults selected one of three brief descriptions of current attachment relationships as most personally applicable. Hazan and Shaver (1987) administered their scale to 108 young adults and found similar proportions of each attachment style in adulthood as in childhood. Further, individuals endorsing differ- ent attachments had different kinds of love experiences. Their working models differed over the course of romantic love, the availability and trustworthiness of partners, and their own love worthiness. Since the forced-choice nature of the measure does not acknowledge variations within the three classifications, subsequent measures have attempted to correct this limitation (Crowell et al., 1999).

Bartholomew (1990) noted that one particular difference between the two models of adult attachment styles presented by Main et al. (1985) and Hazan and Shaver (1987) lies in the difference between each of their respective "avoidant" categories. Main et al. (1985) identified dismiss- ing–avoidant adults as dismissing their personal attachment require- ments and not acknowledging their own feelings of distress. In contrast, Hazan and Shaver (1987) view avoidant individuals as possessing high amounts of personal distress and as being worried about the possibility of becoming close to other people (Bartholomew, 1990; Muller et al., 2000). Because of these differences, Bartholomew contends that two unique types of avoidance are apparent. One is an attachment style based on wanting to hold on to self-sufficiency, a "dismissing" attachment style. The other is based on a fearful awareness that one may be rejected by others, a "fearful" attachment style (Bartholomew & Shaver, 1998).

To address this and other limitations of previous research, Bartholomew and Horowitz (1991) proposed a four-category model of attachment based on internal working models of the self and others. An individual may hold a "self" model as either positive (self as worthy of love) or negative (self as unworthy) and an "other" model as either positive (other as responsive and loving) or negative (other as unresponsive and not loving). Different combinations of the two poles of self and other models produce four attachment categories: secure (positive–positive), preoccupied (negative–positive), fearful (negative–negative), and dismissing (positive–negative). Figure 10.1 shows the four combinations of the two poles of self and other. Secure individuals view themselves and others as positive and worthy of love; they find relationships rewarding. Preoccupied individuals carry a sense of unworthiness; they strive for self-acceptance by gaining acceptance from valued others. Fearful individuals view themselves as unworthy and others as rejecting and untrustworthy. They tend to avoid close involvement with others in order to avoid rejection and hurt. Dismissing individuals carry a sense of worthiness, while viewing others as untrustworthy and rejecting. They also avoid others to escape disappointment, but appear to maintain a sense of independence and invulnerability.

The four-category model is unique in acknowledging two types of avoidant individuals. This distinction is made possible by considering both positive and negative poles of self and other working models. Dismissing individuals seem to cope with attachment needs by maintaining independence and denying any distress, which enables them to maintain a sense of self-worth. In contrast, fearful individuals desire close relationships, but avoid them for fear of loss or rejection (Bartholomew & Horowitz, 1991; Feeney, 1999). Three-category attachment models would include these two separate patterns under the same avoidant category, which would obscure the different underlying conceptions of self and other.

Another advantage to the use of a four-category model of attachment is that it allows for a closer conceptual fit with the theoretical framework of attachment security developed by Bowlby. The working models of self and other are conceptualized as distinct constructs, each having a

		View of Self	
		Positive Self	Negative Self
View of Other	Positive Other	*Secure* Self – Positive Other – Positive	*Preoccupied* Self – Negative Other – Positive
	Negative Other	*Dismissing* Self – Positive Other – Negative	*Fearful* Self – Negative Other – Negative

FIGURE 10.1. Attachment categories based on view of self and other. From "Attachment styles, coping strategies, and posttraumatic psychological distress: The impact of the Gulf War in Israel," by M. Mikulincer, V. Florian, and A. Weller, 1993, *Journal of Personality and Social Psychology, 64*, 817–826.

positive and negative pole. Bartholomew's model follows directly from this framework.

In fact, two measures reflecting the four-category model have been developed. The Relationship Questionnaire (RQ) (Bartholomew & Horowitz, 1991) and the Relationship Scales Questionnaire (RSQ) (Griffin & Bartholomew, 1994b) employ intensity ratings instead of forced-choice questions. The scales were first examined with interviews and self-report ratings, initially by using the RQ on 77 young adults (Bartholomew & Horowitz, 1991). The four attachment styles were found to be distinctive, with each style characterized by a different pattern of interpersonal problems. Self and friend reports were consistent across style. In a second study, significant correlations were found between family and peer attachment representations with 69 young adults (Bartholomew & Horowitz, 1991). The authors interpreted the findings as confirmation for the independent dimensions of self and other models. Griffin and Bartholomew (1994a) extended the previous work by examining the self and other dimensions with confirmatory factor analyses on the RSQ. They found strong support for the construct validity of the two-dimensional structure (self and other dimensions). They also examined other models of attachment, including Hazan and Shaver's model (1987), and found they measured constructs similar to the self and other models dimensions.

ATTACHMENT, MALTREATMENT, AND PSYCHOPATHOLOGY

Victims of abuse and maltreatment are at greater risk for developing various types of psychopathology, particularly if they fall into the insecure attachment category (Muller et al., 2000). Even among those at greatest risk, notable individual differences exist, with some showing the ability to overcome the effects of their misfortune (Egeland, Carlson, & Sroufe, 1993). These individuals are often referred to as "resilient" in the face of adversity. Resilience has been described as the capacity for positive adaptation despite high-risk experiences or circumstances such as prolonged or severe trauma (Masten, Best, & Garmezy, 1990). Higgins (1994) described such individuals as those who are able to negotiate significant challenges to development yet consistently "snap back" in order to complete the developmental task that confronts them as they grow. Existing research has highlighted several protective factors that are believed to promote resilience in maltreated individuals. Protective factors appear to buffer the effects of a high-risk environment and are related to positive or adaptive functioning in later development (Egeland, 1997). Protective factors include internal characteristics of the individual, such as intelligence, self-esteem, and positive social orientation (Cicchetti, Rogosch, Lynch, & Holt, 1993; Werner, 1993), as well as factors external to the individual, such as familial cohesion and social support (Higgins, 1994; Rutter, 1987). A secure attachment with a caregiver in childhood is considered a protective factor promoting resilience in maltreated individuals (Beeghly & Cicchetti, 1994; Masten et al., 1990).

Attachment Patterns in Maltreated Children

Research has found that maltreated children form attachments to their caregivers, but they are more likely to be insecure or atypical (Carlson et al., 1989; Crittenden, 1988; McCrone et al., 1994). Carlson et al. (1989) classified 82% of their maltreated sample as Type D, as opposed to 19% of their control sample. Lynch and Cicchetti (1991), studying school age children, found that 30% of their maltreated sample had confused patterns of relatedness to their mothers, compared with 15% of nonmaltreated children. These atypical attachment patterns are purported to develop in response to caregiver behavior that is frightening, distorted, or unpredictable. These children try to adapt to their experiences with their primary caregivers by developing unusual and distorted attachment responses (Crittenden, 1985; Main & Hesse, 1990). As maltreatment involves both frightening behavior and unpredictability, it is not surprising that maltreated children display atypical attachment patterns.

Having an insecure or atypical attachment pattern, in conjunction with experiencing trauma, places children at extreme risk for many developmental difficulties, including difficulties with peer relationships, problems with self-esteem and mood, and possibilities of atypical personality development (Crittenden & Ainsworth, 1989). Insecurely attached children who have experienced trauma often respond to frightening and challenging experiences with "desperate strategies" including frozen withdrawal, dependent and childlike behavior, and rages or aggressive behavior (Cassidy & Mohr, 2001; Solomon & George, 1999). All of these factors can contribute to difficulties in interpersonal relationships both in childhood and throughout life, which influence the internal working models of both self and others.

Researchers have also proposed that an insecure attachment may be modified in response to abuse to include victims and victimizers in the internal models of relationships (Cicchetti & Howes, 1991; Crittenden & Ainsworth, 1989; Dodge, Pettit, & Bates, 1994). Wekerle and Wolfe (1998) examined male and female adolescents' maltreatment and attachment histories as predictors of more recent victim–abuser experiences. They found that the interaction of a history of maltreatment and an insecure attachment was predictive of adolescents abusing their partners among both males and females. While only an insecure attachment was predictive for females becoming a victim, the interaction of a history of maltreatment and an insecure attachment was a strong predictor for males' victim status. The victim–victimizer models which may stem from maltreatment experiences may partially explain the intergenerational cycle of abuse (Kaufman & Zigler, 1989).

Maltreated insecurely attached children also have difficulty with self-development. In a study of the use of internal state language, the group most at risk for abnormal development of internal state language was composed of infants who were both maltreated and insecurely attached. Maltreated infants who were securely attached did not evidence the same difficulties (Beeghly & Cicchetti, 1994). The development of a self-condemning view of self in relation to other people has been found to have a damaging effect on both psychosocial and emotional development (Bowlby, 1980; Crittenden, 1997; Janoff-Bulman, 1992; McCann & Pearlman, 1990). McCrone et al. (1994) found that maltreated children seemed to attend selectively to negative aspects of relationships, suggesting that they were assimilating new information into existing negative relationship models.

Attachment Patterns in Adult Survivors of Trauma

Research with high-risk samples of formerly maltreated individuals indicates an increased incidence of insecure attachments within this population. Muller et al. (2000), using the Relationship Scales Questionnaire (Griffin & Bartholomew, 1994b) reported that 76% of their sample of 66 formerly maltreated adults endorsed an insecure attachment style, with 63% endorsing one of the avoidant types (dismissing or fearful). The combination of maltreatment and an insecure attachment style may place such individuals at increased risk for developing psychopathology. Similarly, Alexander et al. (1998) examined attachment and psychopathology among 92 adult incest survivors and found a high incidence of insecure attachment styles. Of the sample, 60% reported a fearful attachment pattern. This same subsample of fearfully attached individuals notably also scored higher on measures of distress, avoidance, self-injurious behaviors, and borderline personality disorder than secure or dismissing individuals. Of the sample, 21% reported a pre-occupied style and had higher scores on measures of dependent and borderline personality disorders than secure or dismissing individuals. Those who reported attachment patterns characterized by positive self models (secure and dismissing) scored lower on all psychopathology measures (Alexander et al., 1998). Roche, Runtz, and Hunter (1999) administered the Relationship Questionnaire to 307 women with a history of childhood sexual abuse. They found that attachment styles mediated the relationship between childhood sexual abuse and psychological adjustment, continuing to predict adjustment when the effects of abuse were controlled. Moreover, one's model of self appeared as the most important attachment dimension for predicting adjustment.

Researchers have begun to turn their attention to examining the relationship between types of insecure attachment patterns in adults and how these particular patterns are linked to the development of psychopathology. Recent research has indicated that both the anxious and avoidant subtypes are associated with psychiatric disorders in adults, including major depression, panic disorder, and PTSD (Mickelson, Kessler, & Shaver, 1997). Fonagy and colleagues (1996) found an association between insecure or unresolved attachment styles and the development of anxiety disorders and borderline personality disorders in adults who experienced trauma. These researchers based their work on Bartholomew's model of adult attachment, arguing that each of the insecure attachment styles has features that increase the risk for psychopathology in trauma survivors. Notable features in anxious and ambivalent adults include fear of abandonment and preoccupation with relationships. In avoidant adults these features include discomfort with intimacy, closeness, and interdependence (Mickelson et al., 1997).

The Impact of Negative View of Self

Some research has shown that the preoccupied and fearful attachment styles are particularly problematic among adult survivors of abuse (Alexander 1992; Mikulincer, Florian, & Weller, 1993; Muller et al., 2000). Preoccupied and fearful attachment subtypes are both characterized by an underlying negative model of self (Bartholomew, 1990; Muller & Lemieux, 2000), which appears to be especially damaging. Theorists note that individuals with a history of maltreatment are especially at risk for developing a negative self model (Briere, 1992, 1996; Cole & Putnam, 1992; Herman, 1992). This negative self view is characterized by a lack of self-respect and a lack of autonomy in relation to others.

Muller et al. (2000) found that a negative view of oneself was a better predictor of PTSD symptoms than either physical abuse or a negative model of others among adult survivors of maltreatment. Similarly, Alexander et al. (1998) reported that those who endorsed attachment patterns characterized by positive self models (secure and dismissing) scored lower on all psychopathology measures. A study of formerly abused women indicated that attachment style mediated the relationship between childhood sexual abuse and psychological adjustment, and continued to predict adjustment when the effects of abuse were controlled (Roche et al., 1999). One's model of self appeared as the most important attachment dimension for predicting adjustment. These findings indicate that the model of self requires further investigation regarding its role in contributing to adjustment or psychopathology among high-risk individuals.

Self-blame. Individuals who have a negative view of self are more apt to blame themselves for negative events in their lives (Janoff-Bulman, 1992; Muller et al., 2000). When maltreated children attribute responsibility for their abuse experiences to their own negative character traits in order to conceive the world as predictable and other people as benevolent, they are also developing negative self-perceptions. Herman (1992) contends that an abused child is likely to infer that his or her innate defectiveness is the cause of the abuse in order to preserve the attachment relationship with the abusing parent. When abuse is chronic, the tendency to self-blame is continually reinforced and not readily relinquished even after the abuse has stopped (Cole & Putnam, 1992). Instead, the inner sense of badness becomes a stable part of the child's personality structure. Establishing a negative view of self may lead to feelings of guilt and the idea that one lacks an ability to care for oneself. In adulthood, this negative, incohesive self may be characterized by a lack of self-respect, a lack of autonomy in relation to others, and a belief that the self is unworthy of love and support (Roberts et al., 1996). These negative feelings ultimately jeopardize adaptive psychological functioning and coping mechanisms (Foa, Steketee, & Rothbaum, 1989; Muller et al., 2000; Wolfe & McGee, 1994).

Dysfunctional beliefs. Researchers have found that those individuals who have a negative view of self have a greater number of dysfunctional beliefs (Roberts et al., 1996). These dysfunctional beliefs may lead people to see themselves as unworthy of love, affection, and fulfillment of their basic needs by others. Such individuals' belief in their ability to keep themselves safe from harm may also be impaired. They may get caught up in self-fulfilling prophecies and, as a result, may be unable to view themselves as responsible for any positive interpersonal experiences. These dysfunctional beliefs may be sustained by the negative view of self since these individuals have a tendency to continually blame themselves for negative life events and consistently make negative attributions when examining their experiences (Janoff-Bulman, 1992). Individuals with a history of abuse tend to feel a lack of human connection, which leads to the developing belief that the world is a dangerous place and that others are untrustworthy, often leading to problems with interpersonal relationships. This is another type of dysfunctional belief that results in these individuals not reaching out to others to try to improve their sense of self in relation to others (Roberts et al., 1996). Having more dysfunctional beliefs about the self and doubting one's ability to successfully interact with others may contribute to higher levels of psychological distress (Cummings & Cicchetti, 1990; Gotlib & Hammen, 1992; Muller et al., 2000).

Coping with stress. Negative self-perceptions resulting from earlier traumatic experiences are thought to interfere with a person's future ability to cope with stress, particularly if they have not developed adequate coping mechanisms (Alexander et al., 1998; Muller & Lemieux, 2000). Children who experience trauma form negative self-schemas; they do not believe they are competent in dealing with threats to their physical and emotional well-being (Cassidy & Mohr, 2001). Low self-efficacy may actually place these individuals at risk because they are less likely to assert themselves when faced with personal experiences of adversity, and they are less likely to develop effective coping strategies to help them face challenging developmental tasks. These individuals often do not believe that they are capable of changing their own negative experiences, and so they develop a negative view of self (Cassidy & Mohr, 2001).

There are many possible reasons why negative view of self may interfere with healthy development and one's ability to cope with stress. Crittenden (1997) proposed that children growing up in an abusive environment develop a style of interacting with others and their environment that leads them to be at greater risk for maladaptive functioning. He argues that in adulthood this style of interacting is based on the individuals' use of affect to guide their behaviors, rather than cognition. This is likely to be particularly true of those who have an attachment style characterized by a negative view of self. These individuals are prone to feel the "rawness" of their emotions, are less likely to use cognition in evaluating their experiences, and are thought to have difficulty with their affective response. This will affect their ability to reason through difficult experiences in a positive fashion; they often tend to view themselves as being unable to cope with adversity (Crittenden, 1997).

Cognitive processing. At the information processing level, traumatic experiences may lead children to develop parallel, simultaneous cognitive processes that are incompatible for responding to future threats in adulthood (Cassidy & Mohr, 2001). These simultaneous cognitive processes are thought to be similar to the approach–avoidance responses that insecure children display in the presence of a caregiver who is unpredictable or frightening (Main & Hesse, 1990). Such processes may arise in order to cope with the threat which occurs when a caregiver acts in a manner that is frightening to the child, particularly to a "disorganized" insecurely attached child. This frightening behavior by a beloved caregiver and protector conflicts with the safe and trusting feelings the child has learned to associate with that caregiver, and as a result, the child is forced to try to negotiate feelings of ambivalence toward the caregiver. Due to this ambivalence, disorganized individuals may not be able to cope effectively with difficult situations because they are faced with the activation of contradictory behavioral strategies that serve to abolish each other (Cassidy & Mohr, 2001). As a result, these individuals are expected to be less capable of using future life experiences to develop new and increasingly mature coping strategies. They also do not develop positive cognitive processes to challenge their negative view of self (Cassidy & Mohr, 2001). A negative self model may thus hamper adaptive cognitive functioning in dealing with future life stressors or traumatic experiences (Foa et al., 1989; Muller et al., 2001; Roberts et al., 1996; Wolfe & McGee, 1994).

Interpersonal relationships. A negative view of self can also adversely affect interpersonal functioning by hampering the ability to sustain satisfying relationships and secure attachments (Cole & Putnam, 1992). Previous research has found that when compared to those with positive self models, individuals with a negative view of self show lower levels of competent functioning in areas which encompass relating to and interacting with others (Bylsma, Cozzarelli, & Sumer, 1997). For this reason, it is thought that having a negative view of self may interfere with adaptive interpersonal functioning (Foa et al., 1989; Muller et al., 2001; Roberts et al., 1996).

The original parent–child attachment relationship may influence later levels of involvement in adult intimate relationships, which in turn could reinforce the already established working models of self and other (Alexander et al., 1998). It has been suggested that an early insecure attachment style decreases an individual's capability to both give and receive care, which are requirements in successful intimate and loving adult relationships (Berlin & Cassidy, 1999; Kobak & Hazan, 1991). Such individuals may have difficulty establishing appropriate boundaries with others, either appearing too clingy or too removed (Briere, 1996; Herman, 1992). In addition, fearfully avoidant and preoccupied adults are at greater risk of being involved in adult relationships which confirm their already negative views of self (Alexander et al., 1998; Carnelly, Pietromonaco, & Jaffe, 1994). In contrast, dismissing adults may overtly deny that they have interpersonal or psychological problems (Alexander et al., 1998; Kobak & Sceery, 1988). This research finding is consistent with the proposed notion that dismissing adults actually deny their negative affect as a way to avoid and protect against possible future rejection from attachment figures (Main, 1990).

Self and Other Models

Research has consistently shown that negative view of self has a greater association with psychopathology than negative view of other (Muller & Lemieux, 2000; Muller et al., 2000). Research on depression has found that the negative perception of self is a greater risk factor for development of depression than perception of others, and those individuals who have fearful or preoccupied attachment patterns are more likely to present with depression than those with either a secure or dismissing attachment style (Carnelly et al., 1994; Muller et al., 2000; Murphy & Bates, 1997).

It has been asserted that possessing a negative view of other may actually allow for more adaptive coping strategies to develop (Muller et al., 2000). This is thought to be true for individuals with the dismissing attachment style as they have a greater reliance on themselves and tend to dismiss the value of interpersonal relationships (Alexander, 1993). On the other hand, it may be argued that promotion of self-isolation over reliance on others is a maladaptive coping strategy because it interferes with the possibility of revising the internal working model of others. However, this coping strategy may serve to bolster the individual's perceived self-worth and so help protect against psychopathology development by facilitating the ability to cope with life stressors (Cicchetti & Rogosch, 1997; Muller et al., 2000). Those individuals who are able to hold onto a positive sense of self-efficacy and self-control, even if they hold a negative other model, appear to be more able to view the world as manageable and thus function adaptively (Herman, 1992).

CLINICAL AND EMPIRICAL STUDIES

Currently, research labs are only beginning to conduct empirical studies on the association between fearful and preoccupied attachment styles and various types of psychopathology. Existing studies demonstrate a link between fearful and preoccupied attachment styles and development of depression (Murphy & Bates, 1997), personality disorders (Alexander et al., 1998), and PTSD (Alexander et al., 1998; Mikulincer et al., 1993; Muller et al., 2000). These findings have led other researchers (Muller et al., 2001; Rondeau, Muller, Lemieux, & Diamond, 2002) to become interested in the impact of the underlying negative view of self for the preoccupied and fearful attachment styles.

Attachment Styles

Mikulincer et al. (1993) investigated the relationship between adult attachment styles and responses to the trauma of the Iraqi missile attack on Israel during the Gulf War among 142 Israeli students. They hypothesized that attachment working models are based on particular learned rules that determine or influence an individual's response to stress. Using Hazan and Shaver's (1987) attachment instruments to classify the attachment styles, they found that ambivalent adults showed higher levels of anxiety, depression, hostility, and somatization than secure adults. Avoidant adults showed higher levels of hostility and somatization than secure adults. Mikulincer et al. (1993) suggested that ambivalent individuals were hypervigilant to the missile attacks and responded with increased emotion-focused coping and higher levels of posttraumatic emotional distress, while avoidant individuals relied more on distancing from the trauma, thereby removing anxiety and depression from their emotional responses and displaying their distress through greater levels of somatization.

Alexander et al. (1998) used Bartholomew and Horowitz's (1991) family attachment interview to examine attachment styles in a sample of 92 women who reported specific abuse memories by a family member during childhood. They found that a history of incest is associated with a greater likelihood of insecure attachment, particularly the "fearful" style (9% of the sample was classified as secure, 60% was classified as fearful, 21% as preoccupied, and 11% as dismissing). These findings can be contrasted with the normative sample reported by Bartholomew and Horowitz (1991), where 57% of their sample was secure, 15% fearful, 10% preoccupied, and 18% dismissing. The high number of insecure (particularly fearful) attachment styles found in the incest survivor sample is consistent with previous literature on physically abused and neglected children (Carlson et al., 1989; Egeland & Sroufe, 1981). Insecure attachment was particularly associated with the presence of personality disorders in this sample. Fearful adults were more likely to have borderline, avoidant, and self-defeating traits than secure or dismissing adults. Preoccupied adults were more likely to have dependent, avoidant, self-defeating, and borderline traits than secure or dismissing adults.

View of Self

Alexander et al. (1998) interpreted their findings to mean that fearfully avoidant and preoccupied adults may be more likely to develop and establish interpersonal relationships which serve to confirm their existing negative view of self. Fearfully avoidant adults tended to be in committed relationships less frequently; thus their avoidance of interpersonal relationships may have interfered with the opportunity to challenge their attachment styles while involved with a supportive partner. Mikulincer et al. (1993) hypothesized that emotional responses to trauma (especially personal self-efficacy and sense of personal control), as well as global trust and optimism, may be contributing more to the different outcomes observed in response to trauma and distress than the global attachment styles. Individuals who have positive self-efficacy as well as high levels of trust and optimism appear to respond better to traumatic situations, suggesting better coping resources. Self-efficacy and sense of personal control are subsumed under the *view of self* construct, while feelings of global trust and optimism link to the *view of other* construct.

Muller et al. (2001) examined the relationship between the underlying attachment poles of view of self and other (using Bartholomew's measures) and various symptoms of general psychopathology among 66 adult survivors of child maltreatment. They found a significant relationship between psychopathology and view of self, while view of other was unrelated. They further broke down their sample based on predominant attachment categories (secure, preoccupied, dismissing, and fearful) and found that individuals with secure and dismissing attachment styles had the lowest mean levels of psychopathology. Both of these attachment styles are characterized by a positive view of self. Conversely, the two attachment categories characterized by a negative view of self, the preoccupied and the fearful styles, were associated with the highest mean levels of psychopathology, so that negative view of self did emerge as the strongest predictor of psychopathology (Muller et al., 2001). Research using this same sample found that symptoms of PTSD were higher for those individuals who had a fearful attachment style than for those with either a secure or dismissing attachment style. When examining the underlying attachment poles, negative view of self was the best predictor of PTSD symptoms, while negative view of other was not significantly related to PTSD symptoms (Muller et al., 2000). The results of these studies converge to illustrate that individuals with attachment styles characterized by an underlying negative self model are at increased risk for developing psychopathology symptoms (Alexander et al., 1998; Mikulincer et al., 1993; Muller et al., 2001).

Rondeau et al. (2002) examined the contribution of attachment and social support to adaptive functioning in a sample of 294 maltreated and 575 nonmaltreated university students. Attachment security and underlying dimensions of self and other were all significant predictors of functioning even when examined simultaneously with social support (a known protective factor). Attachment security acted in a protective fashion, with view of self emerging as the strongest factor when examined simultaneously with view of other and social support. The finding that view of self is the strongest predictor of functioning provides further support for the hypothesis that a positive self model is more important as a protective factor than a positive other model (Rondeau et al., 2002).

CLINICAL IMPLICATIONS OF EXISTING EMPIRICAL RESEARCH

The research on negative view of self and other emphasizes the need to address both attachment security and the specific aspect of the self in therapy, especially following childhood maltreatment. How one views oneself appears to be fundamental for adaptive functioning. Attachment theory provides one therapeutic approach to addressing the self in relation to others (Crittenden, 1997). The view that internal models act in concert with current relationships (Hazan & Shaver, 1987) implies that new attachment experiences can provide the opportunity for individuals to rework expectations about the self, others, and relationships (Bowlby, 1988; Jordan, Kaplan, Miller, Stiver, & Surrey, 1991; Roche et al., 1999). The hypothesis that attachment styles can change in response to psychotherapy has been supported theoretically and empirically (Bowlby, 1988; Crittenden, 1997; Fonagy et al., 1996; Kirkpatrick & Hazen, 1994). Crittenden (1997) suggests that the therapist can serve as a secure base from which clients can explore threatening aspects of their experiences while receiving support and protection. The therapist can facilitate the reorganization of internal representational models of the self and others, and associated interpersonal skills. Finally, clients can be taught to derive relatively accurate representations of reality instead of holding on to the distorted and rigid representations of the past. This engenders in the client a more flexible structure with which to organize and reorganize future behavior.

The self-trauma model (Briere, 1992, 1996) provides an approach to therapy that addresses difficulties in self-functioning stemming from traumatic experiences. Self-trauma theory proposes a relative failure of internal capacities to resolve overwhelming trauma. The internal capacities of concern include a sense of identity, appropriate boundaries between the self and others, and the ability to regulate affect when under stress. The goals of therapy are (a) to help the client build a positive source of identity, (b) to help the client develop the ability to monitor internal states and call upon inner resources in times of stress, (c) to help the client maintain internal coherence in interactions with others (appropriate boundaries), and (d) to help foster improved affect regulation. As with an attachment approach, a supportive therapeutic relationship is essential. The client needs to feel safe when exploring potentially distressing inner experiences by which they can gain self-awareness and self-development. The relationship should be one of respect with appropriate boundaries, allowing the client to gain exposure to the distressing experiences in manageable quantities. Cognitive restructuring also may be incorporated, whereby the client is taught to recognize and alter distorted views of past experiences, self, and others (Briere, 1992, 1996).

Altering View of Self

The self-trauma model is tailored especially for individuals who have a history of abuse. Like other treatments for abuse (Herman, 1992), the model emphasizes recognition of the trauma and the safety of the therapeutic relationship, an essential factor when dealing with a population that is not accustomed to feeling safe in a relationship. Recognition of the origins of their psychological difficulties plays a major role in altering abuse survivors' view of self; they no longer need to attribute the cause of the abuse to an inherent defect in the self. Once they realize they are not at fault, they can begin to rebuild their view of self.

The finding that self-perception predicts psychopathology has important implications for treatment. The results of the research by Muller and colleagues (e.g., 2000, 2001) suggest that therapeutic intervention can be particularly beneficial if it provides clients with a combined promotion of positive self-development and opportunity for social connectedness. Group therapy has been shown to be effective for adult survivors of trauma (Herman, 1992; Wright, Woo, Muller, Fernandes, & Kraftcheck, in press). Developing the sense of self is generally considered to require relationships with others (Jordan et al., 1991; Muller et al., 2000). By experiencing positive, supportive, and empowering relationships with others in conjoint forms of therapy—group as well as family and couple therapy—survivors may be able to embrace the trust and respect put forth in those relationships and transform their view of themselves as not worthy of love and respect. Overall, a positive self model is related to more independence, increased optimism and resourcefulness, better emotional health, and less frequent use of immature defense mechanisms (Diehl, Elnick, Bourbeau, & Labouvie-Vief, 1998; Rondeau et al., 2002).

FUTURE DIRECTIONS

A growing body of literature is establishing the importance of attachment in predicting risk for psychopathology among trauma survivors and other high-risk samples. Further studies may help inform the treatment process, particularly for individuals with a negative view of self. It would be useful to conduct research on the effect of a client's attachment style on the process and progress of therapy and to study the changes in attachment styles as an outcome of therapy. Individual therapy and conjoint forms of therapy may be examined and compared for their capacity to modify negative models of self and others.

Future research on attachment, trauma, and psychopathology should incorporate longitudinal designs, allowing researchers to follow individual attachment styles throughout development to determine how traumatic experiences at different points in life may affect attachment and coping responses. The cross-sectional nature of the existing literature makes it difficult to discern whether the individual's view of self is being influenced by the symptoms of psychopathology; longitudinal research would allow for a clearer ordering of causal effects, especially if attachment style could be assessed prior to exposure to traumatic events. It also would be valuable to look at the relationship between maltreatment, attachment, and view of self over time.

Existing research has relied mainly on one type of reporting of attachment and psychopathology. Future research on attachment, trauma, and psychopathology should try to incorporate the use of multiple informants. This would reduce potential memory biases in cases of adults reporting on childhood experiences, as well as compensate for distortions due to defensive operations such as denial, embellishment, and minimization. Since it is possible for individuals to have different attachments with different people in their lives, it would be interesting to see whether others involved in relationships with the participants classify the attachment styles into the same categories as the participants themselves.

Using more extreme samples of adults with greater clinical levels of psychopathology may improve our understanding of the association between negative view of self and psychopathology. Carnelley et al. (1994) found that the relationship between attachment and symptoms of psychopathology differed according to whether the subjects' symptoms were rated at clinical or subclinical levels. The pattern of results found in current studies may not be generalized for those with varying levels of psychopathology or with different levels of symptoms. It would be useful to incorporate specific measures of psychopathology rather than relying on general checklists of behaviors.

It may be that certain characteristics of individuals with an underlying negative view of self predispose them to emotional maladjustment and that those characteristics become more apparent when the individual is forced to try to cope with distress. It would be important to examine the association between the various attachment styles and personality characteristics that could be classified as stress-buffering resources, including hardiness, sense of coherence, attributional style, and optimism. Perhaps those individuals with a negative view of self lack coping resources for dealing with distress because they have not developed such emotional resources as trust, optimism, and self-control (Mikulincer et al., 1993).

Finally, it would be important to more fully investigate the dismissing style, particularly the tendency of dismissing individuals to deny distress and negative affect in order to avoid rejection from the attachment figure (Alexander et al., 1998; Main, 1990). Dismissing individuals, although they are not likely to acknowledge problems or seek help, are actually not problem-free (Dozier & Kobak, 1992; Kobak & Screery, 1998). These individuals may dismiss the importance of relationships and instead increase the value of their own self-reliance (Alexander, 1993). This type of coping strategy may be maladaptive because it promotes isolation and preempts the ability to challenge and revise working models of others.

REFERENCES

Ainsworth, M. D. S. (1973). The development of infant–mother attachment. In B. M. Caldwell & H. N. Ricciuti (Eds.), *Review of child development research* (pp. 1–94). Chicago, IL: University of Chicago Press.

Ainsworth, M. D. S., Blehar, M. C., Waters, E., & Wall, S. (1978). *Patterns of attachment: A psychological study of the strange situation.* Hillsdale, NJ: Erlbaum.

Alexander, P. C. (1992). Application of attachment theory to the study of sexual abuse. *Journal of Consulting and Clinical Psychology, 60,* 185–195.

Alexander, P. C. (1993). The differential effects of abuse characteristics and attachment in the prediction of long-term effects of sexual abuse. *Journal of Interpersonal Violence, 8,* 346–362.

Alexander, P. C., & Anderson, C. L. (1997). Incest, attachment, and developmental psychopathology. In D. Cicchetti & S. Toth (Eds.), *Rochester Symposium on Developmental Psychopathology: Developmental perspectives on trauma* (pp. 344–377). Rochester, NY: University of Rochester Press.

Alexander, P. C., Anderson, C. L., Brand, B., Schaeffer, C. M., Grelling, B. Z., & Kretz, L. (1998). Adult attachment and long-term effects in survivors of incest. *Child Abuse and Neglect, 22,* 45–61.

Bartholomew, K. (1990). Avoidance of intimacy: An attachment perspective. *Journal of Social and Personal Relationships, 7,* 147–178.

Bartholomew, K., & Horowitz, L. (1991). Attachment styles among young adults: A test of a four-category model. *Journal of Personality and Social Psychology, 61,* 226–244.

Bartholomew, K., & Shaver, P. R. (1998). Methods of assessing adult attachment: Do they converge? In J. A. Simpson & W. S. Rholes (Eds.), *Attachment theory and close relationships* (pp. 25–45). New York: Guilford.

Beeghly, M., & Cicchetti, D. (1994). Child maltreatment, attachment, and the self system: Emergence of an internal state lexicon in toddlers at high social risk. *Development and Psychopathology, 6,* 5–30.

Berlin, L. J., & Cassidy, J. (1999). Relations among relationships: Contributions from attachment theory. In J. Cassidy & P. R. Shaver (Eds.), *Handbook of attachment: Theory, research, and clinical applications* (pp. 688–712). New York: Guilford.

Berman, W. H., & Sperling, M. B. (1994). The structure and function of adult attachment. In M. B. Sperling & W. H. Berman (Eds.), *Attachment in adults: Clinical and developmental perspectives* (pp. 1–30). New York: Guilford.

Bowlby, J. (1969). *Attachment and loss: Vol. 1.* New York: Basic Books.

Bowlby, J. (1980). *Attachment and loss: Vol. 3. Loss, sadness, and depression.* New York: Basic Books.

Bowlby, J. (1982). *Attachment and loss: Vol. 1. Attachment.* London: Hogarth.

Bowlby, J. (1988). *A secure base: Clinical applications of attachment theory.* London: Routledge.

Bretherton, I. (1990). Open communication and internal working models: Their role in the development of attachment relationships. In R. A. Thompson (Ed.), *Nebraska Symposium on Motivation, 1988: Socioemotional development* (pp. 57–113). Lincoln: University of Nebraska Press.

Bretherton, I. (1995). Attachment theory and developmental psychopathology. In D. Cicchetti & S. Toth (Eds.), *Rochester symposium on developmental psychopathology: Vol. 6. Emotion, Cognition, and representation* (pp. 231–260). Rochester, NY: University of Rochester Press.

Briere, J. (1992). *Child abuse trauma: Theory and treatment of the lasting effects.* Newbury Park, CA: Sage.

Briere, J. (1996). The self-trauma model for treating adult survivors of severe child abuse. In J. Briere, L. Berliner, J. A. Bulkley, C. Jenny, & T. Reid (Eds.), *The APSAC handbook on child maltreatment* (pp. 140–157). Thousand Oaks, CA: Sage.

Briere, J., & Runtz, M. (1988). Symptomatology associated with childhood sexual victimization in a nonclinical adult sample. *Child Abuse and Neglect, 12,* 51–59.

Briere, J., & Runtz, L. Y. (1990). Differential adult symptomatology associated with three types of child abuse histories. *Child Abuse and Neglect, 14,* 357–364.

Bylsma, W H., Cozzarelli, C., & Sumer, N. (1997). Relation between adult attachment styles and global self-esteem. *Journal of Basic and Applied Social Psychology, 19,* 1–16.

Carlson, E. A. (1998). A prospective longitudinal study of attachment disorganization/disorientation. *Child Development, 69,* 1107–1128.

Carlson, V., Cicchetti, D., Barnett, D., & Braunwald, K. (1989). Disorganized/disoriented attachment relationships in maltreated infants. *Developmental Psychology, 25,* 525–531.

Carnelly, K. B., Pietromonaco, P. R., & Jaffe, K. (1994). Depression, working models of others, and relationship functioning. *Journal of Personality and Social Psychology, 66,* 127–140.

Cassidy, J., & Mohr, J. J. (2001). Unsolvable fear, trauma, and psychopathology: Theory, research and clinical considerations related to disorganized attachment across the life span. *Clinical Psychology, 8,* 275–307.

Cicchetti, D. (1989). How research on child maltreatment has informed the study of child development: Perspectives from developmental psychopathology. In D. Cicchetti & V. Carlson (Eds.), *Child maltreatment: Theory and research on the causes and consequences of child abuse and neglect* (pp. 377–421). Cambridge, MA: Cambridge University Press.

Cicchetti, D., & Barnett, D. (1991). Attachment organization in maltreated preschoolers. *Development and Psychopathology, 3,* 397–411.

Cicchetti, D., & Howes, P. W. (1991). Developmental psychopathology in the context of the family: Illustrations from the study of child maltreatment. *Canadian Journal of Behavioral Science, 23,* 257–281.

Cicchetti, D., Rogosch, F. A., Lynch, M., & Holt, K. D. (1993). Resilience in maltreated children: Processes leading to adaptive outcome. *Development and Psychopathology, 5,* 629–647.

Cicchetti, D. & Rogosch, F. A. (1997). The role of self-organization in the promotion of resilience in maltreated children. *Development and Psychopathology, 9,* 797–815.

Cicchetti, D., Toth, S. L., & Lynch, M. (1995). Bowlby's dream come full circle: The application of attachment theory to risk and psychopathology. *Advances in Clinical Child Psychology, 17,* 1–75.

Cole, P. M., & Putnam, F. W. (1992). Effect of incest on self and social functioning: A developmental psychopathology perspective. *Journal of Consulting and Clinical Psychology, 60,* 174–184.

Collins, N. L., & Read, S. J. (1994). Cognitive representations of attachment: The structure and function of working models. In K. Bartholomew & D. Perlman (Eds.), *Advances in personal relationships: Attachment processes in adulthood* (pp. 53–90). Bristol, PA: Jessica Kingsley.

Crittenden, P. M. (1985). Maltreated infants: Vulnerability and resilience. *Journal of Child Psychology and Psychiatry, 26,* 85–96.

Crittenden, P. M. (1988). Relationships at risk. In J. Belsky & T. Nezworski (Eds.), *Clinical implications of attachment theory* (pp. 136–174). Hillsdale, NJ: Erlbaum.

Crittenden, P. M. (1997). Truth, error, omission, distortion, and deception: The application of attachment theory to the assessment and treatment of psychological disorder. In S. M. C. Dollanger & L. F. DiLalla (Eds.), *Assessment and intervention: Issues across the life span* (pp. 35–76). Mahway, NJ: Erlbaum.

Crittenden, P. M., & Ainsworth, M. D. S. (1989). Child maltreatment and attachment theory. In D. Cicchetti & V. Carlson (Eds.), *Child maltreatment: Theory and research on the causes and consequences of child abuse and neglect* (pp. 432–463). Cambridge, MA: Cambridge University Press.

Crowell, J. A., Fraley, R. C., & Shaver, P. R. (1999). Measurement of individual differences in adolescent and adult attachment. In J. Cassidy & P. R. Shaver (Eds.), *Handbook of attachment: Theory, research, and clinical implications* (pp. 434–465). New York: Guilford.

Cummings, E. M., & Cicchetti, D. (1990). Toward a transactional model of relations between attachment and depression. In M. T. Greenberg, D. Cicchetti, & E. M. Cummings (Eds.), *Attachment in the preschool years: Theory, research, and intervention* (pp. 339–372). Chicago, IL: University of Chicago Press.

Diamond, D., & Blatt, S. J. (1994). Internal working models and the representational world in attachment and psychoanalytic theories. In M. B. Sperling & W. H. Berman (Eds.), *Attachment in Adults: Clinical and Developmental Perspectives* (pp. 72–97). New York: Guilford.

Diehl, M., Elnick, A. B., Bourbeau, L. S., & Labouvie-Vief, G. (1998). Adult attachment styles: Their relations to family context and personality. *Journal of Personality and Social Psychology, 74,* 1656–1669.

Dodge, K. A., Pettit, G. S., & Bates, J. E. (1994). Effects of physical maltreatment on the development of peer relations. *Development and Psychopathology, 6,* 43–55.

Dozier, M., & Kobak, R. R. (1992). Psychophysiology in attachment interviews: Converging evidence for deactivating strategies. *Child Development, 63,* 1473–1480.

Dozier, M., Stovall, K. C., & Albus, K. E. (1999). Attachment and psychopathology in adulthood. In J. Cassidy & P. R. Shaver (Eds.), *Handbook of attachment: Theory, research, and clinical applications* (pp. 497–519). New York: Guilford.

Egeland, B. (1997). Mediators of the effects of child maltreatment on developmental adaptation in adolescence. In D. Cicchetti & S. Toth (Eds.), *Rochester Symposium on Developmental Psychopathology: Developmental perspectives on trauma* (pp. 403–434). Rochester, NY: University of Rochester Press.

Egeland, B., Carlson, E., & Sroufe, L. A. (1993). Resilience as process. *Development and Psychopathology, 5,* 517–528.

Egeland, B. & Sroufe, L. A. (1981). Attachment and early maltreatment. *Child Development, 52*(1), 44–52.

Feeney, J. A. (1999). Adult romantic attachment and couple relationships. In J. Cassidy & P. R. Shaver (Eds.), *Handbook of attachment: Theory, research, and clinical applications* (pp. 355–377). New York: Guilford.

Foa, E. B., Steketee, G., & Rothbaum, B. O. (1989). Behavioural/cognitive conceptualizations of posttraumatic stress disorder. *Behaviour Therapy, 20,* 155–176.

Fonagy, P., Leigh, T., Steele, M., Steele, H., Kennedy, R., Mattoon, G., Target, M., & Gerber, A. (1996). The relation of attachment status, psychiatric classification, and response to psychotherapy. *Journal of Consulting and Clinical Psychology, 64,* 22–31.

Gilbert, P. (1992). *Depression: The evolution of powerlessness.* New York: Guilford.

Gotlib, I. H., & Hammen, C. L. (1992). *Psychological aspects of depression: Toward a cognitive interpersonal integration.* Chichester, U.K.: Wiley.

Greenberg, M. T., Cicchetti, D., & Cummings, E. M. (1990). *Attachment in the preschool years: Theory, research, and intervention.* Chicago: University of Chicago Press.

Griffin, D., & Bartholomew, K. (1994a). The metaphysics of measurement: The case of adult attachment. In K. Bartholomew & D. Perlman (Eds.), *Advances in personal relationships: Attachment processes in adulthood* (pp. 17–52). Bristol, PA: Jessica Kingsley.

Griffin, D., & Bartholomew, K. (1994b). Models of the self and other: Fundamental dimensions underlying measures of adult attachment. *Journal of Personality and Social Psychology, 67,* 430–445.

Hazan, C., & Shaver, P. (1987). Romantic love conceptualized as an attachment process. *Journal of Personality and Social Psychology, 52,* 511–524.

Hazan, C., & Zeifman, D. (1999). Pair bonds as attachments. In J. Cassidy & P. R. Shaver (Eds.), *Handbook of attachment: Theory, research, and clinical applications* (pp. 336–354). New York: Guilford.

Herman, J. L. (1992). *Trauma and recovery.* New York: Basic Books.

Hesse, E. (1999). The adult attachment interview: Historical and current perspectives. In J. Cassidy & P. R. Shaver (Eds.), *Handbook of attachment: Theory, research, and clinical applications* (pp. 395–433). New York: Guilford.

Higgins, G. O. (1994). *Resilient adults: Overcoming a cruel past.* San Francisco, CA: Jossey Bass.

Janoff-Bulman, R. (1992). Shattered assumptions: Towards a new psychology of trauma. Toronto: Free Press.

Jordan, J. V., Kaplan, A. G., Miller, J. B., Stiver, I. P., & Surrey, J. L. (1991). *Women's growth in connection: Writing from the Stone Center.* New York: Basic Books.

Kaufman, J., & Zigler, E. (1989). The intergenerational transmission of child abuse. In D. Cicchetti & V. Carlson (Eds.), *Child maltreatment: Theory and research on the causes and consequences of child abuse and neglect* (pp. 129–150). Cambridge, MA: Cambridge University Press.

Kirkpatrick, L. A., & Hazen, C. (1994). Attachment styles and close relationships: A four-year prospective study. *Personal Relationships, 1,* 123–142.

Kobak, R., & Hazan, C. (1991). Attachment in marriage: Effects of security and accuracy of working models. *Journal of Personality and Social Psychology, 60,* 861–869.

Kobak, R., & Sceery, A. (1988). Attachment in late adolescence: Working models, affect regulation, and representations of self and others. *Child Development, 59,* 396–399.

Krappmann, L., Schuster, B., & Youniss, J. (1998). Can mothers win? The transformation of mother–daughter relationships in late childhood. In M. Hofer, J. Youniss, & P. Noack (Eds.), *Advances in applied developmental psychology: Vol. 15. Verbal interaction and development in families with adolescents.* (pp. 11–29). Stanford, CT: Ablex.

Lynch, M., & Cicchetti, D. (1991). Patterns of relatedness in maltreated and nonmaltreated children: Connections among multiple representational models. *Development and Psychopathology, 3,* 207–226.

McCrone, E. R., Egeland, B., Kalkoske, M., & Carlson, E. A. (1994). Relations between early maltreatment and mental representations of relationships assessed with projective storytelling in middle childhood. *Development and Psychopathology, 6,* 99–120.

Main, M. (1990). Cross-cultural studies of attachment organization: Recent studies, changing methodologies, and the concept of conditional strategies. *Human Development, 33,* 48–61.

Main, M., & Goldwyn, R. (1984). Predicting rejection of her infant from mother's representation of her own experience: Implications for the abused–abusing intergenerational cycle. *Child Abuse and Neglect, 8,* 203–217.

Main, M., & Hesse, E. (1990). Parents' unresolved traumatic experiences are related to infant disorganized attachment status: Is frightened and/or frightening parental behavior the linking mechanism? In M. T. Greenberg, D. Cicchetti, & E. M. Cummings (Eds.), *Attachment in the preschool years: Theory, research, and intervention* (pp. 161–182). Chicago, IL: University of Chicago Press.

Main, M., Kaplan, N., & Cassidy, J. (1985). Security in infancy, childhood, and adulthood: A move to the level of representation. *Monographs of the Society for Research in Child Development, 50,* 66–106.

Main, M., & Solomon, J. (1986). Discovery of an insecure–disorganized/disoriented attachment pattern. In T. B. Brazelton & M. W. Yogman (Eds.), *Affective development in infancy* (pp. 95–124). New Jersey: Ablex.

Main, M., & Weston, D. R. (1981). The quality of the toddler's relationship to mother and to father: Related to conflict behavior and the readiness to establish new relationships. *Child Development, 52,* 932–940.

Masten, A. S., Best, K. M., & Garmezy, N. (1990). Resilience and development: Contributions from the study of children who overcome adversity. *Development and Psychopathology, 2,* 425–444.

Mickelson, K. D., Kessler, R. C., & Shaver, P. R. (1997). Adult attachment in a nationally representative sample. *Journal of Personality and Social Psychology, 73,* 1092–1106.

Mikulincer, M., Florian, V., & Weller, A. (1993). Attachment styles, coping strategies, and posttraumatic psychological distress: The impact of the Gulf War in Israel. *Journal of Personality and Social Psychology, 64,* 817–826.

Muller, R. T., & Lemieux, K. E. (2000). Social support, attachment, and psychopathology in high risk formerly maltreated adults. *Child Abuse and Neglect, 24,* 883–900.

Muller, R. T., Lemieux, K. E., & Sicoli, L. A. (2001). Attachment and psychopathology among formerly maltreated adults. *Journal of Family Violence, 16,* 151–169.

Muller, R. T., Sicoli, L. A., & Lemieux, K. E. (2000). Relationships between attachment style and posttraumatic stress symptomatology among adults who report the experience of childhood abuse. *Journal of Traumatic Stress, 13,* 321–332.

Murphy, B., & Bates, G. W. (1997). Adult attachment style and vulnerability to depression. *Personality and Individual Differences, 2,* 835–844.

Pearlman, E. M. (1990). Separation-individuation, self-concept, and object relations in fraternal twins, identical twins, and singletons. *Journal of Psychology, 124,* 619–628.

Reider, C., & Cicchetti, D. (1989). Organizational perspective on cognitive control functioning and cognitive–affective balance in maltreated children. *Developmental Psychology, 25,* 382–393.

Roberts, J. E., Gotlib, I. H., & Kassel, J. D. (1996). Adult attachment security and symptoms of depression: The mediating roles of dysfunctional attitudes and low self-esteem. *Journal of Personality and Social Psychology, 70,* 310–320.

Roche, D. N., Runtz, M. G., & Hunter, M. A. (1999). Adult attachment: A mediator between child sexual abuse and later psychological adjustment. *Journal of Interpersonal Violence, 14,* 184–207.

Rondeau, L. A., Muller, R. T., Lemieux, K. E., & Diamond, T. (2002, May). Attachment style and social support in the prediction of psychopathology among formerly maltreated young adults. Poster presented at the Annual Convention of the Canadian Psychological Association, Vancouver, BC, Canada.

Rothbard, J. C., & Shaver, P. R (1994). Continuity of attachment across the lifespan. In: M. B. Sperling & W. H. Berman (Eds.), *Attachment in adults: Clinical and developmental perspectives* (pp. 31–71). New York: Guilford.

Rutter, M. (1987). Psychosocial resilience and protective mechanisms. *American Journal of Orthopsychiatry, 57,* 316–331.

Solomon, J., & George, C. (1999). The place of disorganization in attachment theory: Linking classic observations with contemporary findings. In J. Solomon & C. George (Eds.), *Attachment disorganization* (pp. 3–32). New York: Guilford.

Sroufe, L. A., Carlson, E. A., Levy, A. K., & Egeland, B. (1999). Implications of attachment theory for developmental psychopathology. *Development and Psychopathology, 11*, 1–13.

Toth, S. L., & Cicchetti, D. (1996). Patterns of relatedness, depressive symptomatology, and perceived competence in maltreated children. *Journal of Consulting and Clinical Psychology, 64*, 32–41.

van der Kolk, B. A. (1996). The complexity of adaptation to trauma: Self-regulation, stimulus discrimination, and characterological development. In B. A. van der Kolk, A. C. McFarlane, & R. Weisaeth (Eds.), *Traumatic stress: The effects of overwhelming experience on mind, body, and society* (pp. 182–213). New York: Guilford.

Wekerle, C., & Wolfe, D. A. (1998). The role of child maltreatment and attachment style in adolescent relationship violence. *Development and Psychopathology, 10*, 571–586.

Werner, E. E. (1993). Risk, resilience, and recovery: Perspectives from the Kauai longitudinal study. *Development and Psychopathology, 5*, 503–515.

Wolfe, D. A., & McGee, R. (1994). Dimensions of child maltreatment and their relationship to adolescent adjustment. *Development and Psychopathology, 6*, 165–181.

Wright, D. C., Woo, W. L., Muller, R. T., Fernandes, C. B., & Kraftcheck, E. R. (in press). An investigation of trauma-centered inpatient treatment for adult survivors of abuse. *Child Abuse & Neglect*.

Youniss, J., & Haynie, D. L. (1992). Friendship in adolescence. *Journal of Developmental and Behavioral Pediatrics, 13*, 59–66.

11

Family Support in the Aftermath of Trauma

SUMMER SHERBURNE HAWKINS AND
SHARON L. MANNE

During times of stress and trauma, we turn to our loved ones for support. The situation is complicated; family members may be coping with their own reactions to the trauma even as they are required to provide support. Victims turn to those they trust most and family members usually respond even as they deal with their own reactions. Children and adolescents may turn to parents and siblings when faced with stressors (Manne & Miller, 1998; Rossman, Bingham, & Emde, 1997). Parents count on their partners when their child or adolescent is diagnosed with illness or dies (Barbarin, Hughes, & Chesler, 1985; Lehman, Lang, Wortman, & Sorenson, 1989) and turn to each other when one is faced with illness (Manne, 1998). A parent may depend on her children to provide support during divorce (Nestmann & Niepel, 1994). Elderly parents can also usually count on their grown children for practical as well as emotional support (Haley et al., 1996; Pillemer & Suitor, 1996). When viewed from this perspective, a study of the role of family support in the aftermath of trauma can provide a rich source of information on both social support and trauma.

DEFINITIONS OF FAMILY SUPPORT

Family support falls under the rubric of the social support construct, so we will begin with a brief overview of social support (for a comprehensive review of social support see Pierce, Sarason, Joseph, & Henderson, 1996). Barrera (1986) proposed defining the global construct of social support into three distinct components: (a) *perceived support*, (b) *social network and embeddedness*, and (c) *enacted support*.

Perceived support: Perceived social support is an individual's perception of the support that would be available should it be needed. Among the support constructs, perceived support has shown the strongest and most consistent associations with psychological adjustment to negative life events (Pierce et al., 1996). Most measures focus on global ratings of the availability and adequacy of support in which various functions of support such as the availability of information, tangible assistance, and emotional support are typically rated (Barrera, 1986).

Social network and embeddedness: Social network and embeddedness measures individuals' social integration into a group and their interconnectedness within that group. Measures of social network include network density (the extent of mutual linkages among individuals in the network), size, and type of support provided. It is proposed that one mechanism for support is belonging to a social network which allows an individual to achieve a sense of stability and recognition of self-worth (Cohen & Wills, 1985). As described in the social support literature, individuals who identify themselves with a greater number of roles are less likely to be affected by a stressor in one area or within one role because fewer areas are disrupted (Weiss, 1974).

Enacted support: Enacted support refers to actual support behaviors performed by members of the support network. Some researchers have delineated multiple dimensions of support, including categories of emotional support (turning to others for comfort), esteem support (bolstering of self-esteem by others), tangible aid (concrete instrumental assistance), and information support (advice or guidance) (Cutrona & Russell, 1990). The present chapter will focus solely on the four categories of support described by Barrera (1986); emotional support, esteem support, tangible aid, and information support will be considered part of enacted support. A proposed mechanism is that stressful events signal enacted support from the social network to supply resources to individuals during times of stress (Barrera, 1986).

INSTRUMENTS FOR MEASURING SUPPORT

Most instruments that generate a global measure of an individual's social support do not distinguish between support provided by family members from support given by other members of the person's social network. It is then unclear who provides the support, and we cannot make conclusions about family support. Table 11.1 provides an overview of self-report support measures that specify the provider of support.

TABLE 11.1
Self-Report Support Measures That Specify the
Provider of Support

Recipients of Support	Self-Report Measures	Used in Studies of	Citation
Adolescent and adult	Network of Relationships Inventory; Furman & Buhrmester, 1985	Caregivers of patients with Alzheimer's disease	Creasey et al., 1990
		Adolescent cancer patients	Manne & Miller, 1998
		Community violence	Kliewer et al., 1998
	Significant Others Scale; Power & Champion, 1991	Adult HIV patients	Nott, Vedhara, & Power, 1995
	Social Support Questionnaire; Sarason et al., 1983	Adult HIV patients	Swindells et al., 1999
	Social Support Questionnaire, Short Form—Revised; Sarason et al., 1987	Caregivers of patients with Alzheimer's Disease	Haley et al., 1996
	Sources of Help Questionnaire; Wan, Jaccard, & Ramey, 1996	Divorced mothers	Bretherton, Walsh, & Lependorf, 1996
	Cancer Support Inventory; Manne & Schnoll, 2001	Mothers of cancer patients	Manne et al., 2002
Child and adolescent	Social Support Scale for Children; Harter, 1985	Natural disasters	La Greca et al., 1996
		Pediatric rheumatic disease patients	Von Weiss et al., 2002
	Children's Inventory of Social Support; Wolchik et al., 1987	Children of divorced parents	Wolchik et al., 1989
	Parent Perception Inventory; Hazzard, Christensen, & Margolin, 1983	Violent families	McCloskey, Figueredo, & Koss, 1995
	Social Support Rating Scale; Cauce, 1986	Adolescent cancer patients	Kazak & Meadows, 1989

(Continues)

TABLE 11.1 (Continued)

Recipients of Support	Self-Report Measures	Used in Studies of	Citation
	Perceived Social Support Scale; Procidano & Heller, 1983	Bereaved Israeli adolescents	Bachar et al., 1997
Family	Family Environment Scale; Moos & Moos, 1986	Community violence	Kliewer et al., 2001
		Adult cancer patients	Bloom & Spiegel, 1984; Molassiotis, van den Akker, & Boughton, 1997
		Adolescent sickle cell disease patients	Burlew et al., 2000
		Siblings of pediatric rheumatic disease patients	Timko et al., 1992
	Family Adaptability and Cohesion Evaluation Scales—Version II; Olson, Portner, & Bell, 1982	Community violence	Kliewer et al., 2001
		Adolescent cancer patients	Kasak & Meadows, 1989
		Siblings of cancer patients	Cohen et al., 1994

Negative Aspects of Support. Researchers neglected the negative aspects of support until Rook's (1984) seminal findings showed that negative social outcomes were significantly related to lower well-being, while supportive social outcomes were unrelated to well-being. Wortman and Lehman (1985) categorized people's responses to victims of trauma into three unsupportive areas:

1. Contact with victims makes people feel vulnerable.
2. Many people feel uncertain about how to react to victims because of lack of experience with trauma.
3. People hold misconceptions about how one should react to traumas.

All three responses reduce the likelihood that supportive behavior will be perceived as effective.

Negative family support. The negative impact of inadequate levels of support has been found in studies of family support and includes increased depression and decreased quality of life in patients with HIV (Nott, Vedhara, & Power, 1995; Swindells et al., 1999) and symptoms predictive of posttraumatic stress disorder (PTSD) in children following a home fire (Greenberg & Keane, 2001). A longitudinal investigation of acute stress disorder and PTSD following road traffic accidents revealed that those who rated high on use of social control and on perceived negative social support (assessed via the Social Support Inventory, an author-created measure which appeared as a dissertation) at Time 1 had a much greater probability of developing PTSD at Time 2 (Holeva, Tarrier, & Wells, 2001).

Negative spousal behavior. Manne (1999) and Manne, Alfieri, Taylor, and Dougherty (1999) found that spousal criticism and avoidance were significantly related to increased psychological distress and negative mood and coping among cancer patients. Among women with rheumatoid arthritis, the attitude of the spouse affected patient adjustment indirectly by influencing the wife's adaptive or maladaptive coping (Manne & Zautra, 1989). These three studies utilized the Perceived Negative Spouse Behaviors Scale (created by Manne for the Manne & Zautra, 1989 study) because it specifically addresses how spouses responded in the previous month regarding exchanges involving medical treatment. Ingram, Jones, Fass, Neidig, and Song (1999) have created a similar measure of negative support called the Unsupportive Social Interactions Inventory to assess social relationships in people with HIV.

Few studies have investigated the role of children as providers of support to single parents. A qualitative study (Nestman & Niepel, 1994) suggests that parents are aware that children should not be providers of support, but report their children do provide some forms of support, including love, inspiration, and a reason to continue living. However, this study did not address children's perceptions of their function as members of their parents' support network.

MECHANISMS OF SOCIAL SUPPORT

Support from significant others is one of the most common ways people cope with trauma. Indeed, a meta-analysis of 77 studies of PTSD revealed that a lack of social support is a risk factor for adults developing PTSD during or after a trauma (Brewin, Andrews, & Valentine, 2000). There are several models that could account for the beneficial effects of social support on traumatic stress symptoms. Resiliency models, stress-buffering models, and coping models have each been used to explain how social support affects the impact of stress on individuals.

Resiliency models: The concept of resiliency has typically been applied to understand children's reactions to traumatic life experiences. Garmezy (1983) proposed that individuals possess *protective factors* described as attributes of persons and environments that attenuate risk of psychopathological responses. His review of child and adolescent literature revealed three factors related to characteristics of resilient children: (a) dispositional and constitutional characteristics, for example, temperament, high self-esteem, and autonomy; (b) supportive family environment; and (c) supportive individual or group support system that provides modeling in coping. In the child trauma literature, a supportive family environment has been identified as one of the three characteristics of resilient children (Garmezy, 1983).

The concept of resiliency has been applied to families in regard to coping with stress (see McCubbin & Patterson, 1983). The FACES-II (Family Adaptability and Cohesion Evaluation Scores) (Olson, Portner, & Bell, 1982) is composed of three constructs. *Family cohesiveness* emphasizes the importance of considering individuals to be both autonomous and part of a group; *family flexibility* is the ability to balance stability and adjustment; and *family communication* emphasizes communicating shared expectancies about cohesiveness and flexibility.[1] Finally, families develop meanings about stressors, their identity as a family, and their worldview. Resiliency is similar to the construct of perceived support in that both target characteristics and resources that can be utilized in times of stress. Family resiliency relates to assets in the family environment.

Stress-buffering models: Cohen and Wills (1985) propose that the positive relationship between social support and psychological well-being is linked to the benefits of stress-buffering effects of social support against the negative effects of trauma. Two proposed mechanisms illustrate how support could have a stress-buffering role in a stressful event. First, support after a stressor may reduce negative cognitive appraisal of the event and also the stress reaction. Second, support may facilitate a reappraisal of the event or reduce maladaptive responses to the stress reaction.

Social support and coping models: Thoits (1986) expanded the stress-buffering theory of social support by reclassifying support as coping assistance, defined as the "active participation of significant others in an individual's stress-management efforts" (p. 417). Social support assists an individual in coping with stressors. Supportive others can: (a) offer problem-solving or other adaptive coping suggestions that guide or assist the person in solving the problem, (b) assist the person in thinking differently about a situation by finding benefit or meaning in the situation, (c) reduce appraisals of threat or harm in a situation by proposing different ways of thinking about the event, and (d) reduce the use of maladaptive coping efforts such as avoidance and substance use. Thoits suggests that members of an individual's social support network facilitate coping and thereby influence adaptation to traumatic events. Manne and colleagues

---

1. *Editor's note:* See chapter 15 for a discussion of Olson's model.

(1999) and Holahan and Moos (1990) found results consistent with Thoits' conceptualization of social support as coping assistance in populations of cancer patients and college students, respectively.

DEVELOPMENTAL PROCESSES IN SOCIAL SUPPORT

The ability to effectively provide and accurately perceive social support and cultivate and maintain supportive relationships is probably an acquired emotional response learned from parents and other family members. A secure bonding experience, usually with the mother, provides the foundation for other secure social relationships in childhood (Bowlby, 1969). These early relationships begin the acquisition of support skills that allow children to foster supportive relationships into adulthood.

The family network is a unique environment for supportive exchanges between parent and child. The parent–child relationship is bidirectional despite assumptions that children do not influence parental behavior (Bell, 1968). Burleson and Kunkel (1996) discuss how children cultivate social support behaviors through interactions between parent and child. Children learn social support skills through parent modeling, praise, and parental attribution of an act to prosocial disposition within the child. Parents can also reinforce desired supportive behaviors through punishment, moral exhortation, instruction, and reasoning. Indirectly, parents influence child acquisition of social acts through talking about feelings and emotions, comforting acts and parental nurturance toward the child or sibling, and inductive discipline. Children learn to both provide and receive support through these mechanisms.

The lack of support can have detrimental effects on a child's perception of social support or response to trauma. Camras and colleagues (1990) found that children abused by their mothers are less able to recognize facially expressed emotions. These authors argue that not only does the abuse inhibit the development of support behaviors but also instructs the child to respond to distressed peers with hostility. This research demonstrates the malformation of support acts through negative modeling, inductive discipline, and lack of comforting acts and parental nurturance. Lack of satisfaction in family support has also been inversely related to posttraumatic stress symptoms in children after a traumatic event (Greenberg & Keane, 2001). Ultimately, positive or negative experiences will shape a child's schema of supportive relationships.

Children from middle to late childhood and adolescence continually develop the discriminatory skills to provide and receive social support from family members and peers (Burleson & Kunkel, 1996). Research on developmental changes in the parent–child relationship suggests that support from peers increases during adolescence, while support from parents remains stable (Cauce, Reid, Landesman, & Gonzales, 1990); however, in some cultures, parents are still considered the primary source of support into adolescence (DeRosier & Kupersmidt, 1991; Van Horn & Cunegatto-Marques, 2000).

TRAUMA EXPERIENCED BY THE ENTIRE FAMILY

Traumatic events can be divided into events directly experienced by the entire family unit (e.g., natural disasters and acts of terrorism) and events that happen to one or more of the family members that have an impact on the entire family (e.g., divorce, major illness, death, or accident). Some traumatic events experienced by family members need to be dealt with both individually and as a family unit. In this section, we will review the effects of war, terrorism, natural disasters, and community violence on the entire family.

War-related stressors. The incidence of armed conflict has increased dramatically over the past several decades (Gantzel & Schwinghammer, 1995). Unlike wars prior to the 1970s, recent conflicts have been within nations (e.g., Northern Ireland and Bosnia). Thus, the victims are increasingly unarmed civilians. Although precise figures on the numbers of children and families affected are not known, a vast number of victims are children. It has been estimated that in the past 10 years, over 10 million children have been traumatized by war around the world (United Nations, 2000). Even when civilian children and families flee and find refuge in another country, psychological problems are common. Research has attempted to quantify the psychological impact of war in terms of PTSD diagnoses and symptoms among civilians (Farhood et al., 1993; Michultka, Blanchard, & Kalous, 1998), soldiers and veterans (Solomon, 2001), and children (Barath, 2002; Klingman, 2002; Sack et al., 1994).

The effect of war-related stress on family members as well as the role of social support has received considerable attention; however, little is known about the role of family-specific support. A review of the social support literature for soldiers and veterans has revealed that studies focus on the impact of social support as a global construct on PTSD without specifying familial relationships (e.g., spouse support, sibling support).

Farhood and colleagues (1993) examined the impact of war-related stressors (e.g., acts of violence and migration) as seen in the psychological symptoms of mothers, fathers, and adolescents in a sample of families in Beirut. For mothers and fathers, a reduction in social network—defined as the inability to see relatives or friends—was significantly related to depression and marital problems. For adolescents, the reduction in the number of persons in the teen's social network was substantially related to depression and psychological symptoms. A global measure of social support (unknown measure) found it to be a protective factor against depression as well as psychological, physical, and marital problems for fathers. For mothers, social support only protected against marital problems. For adolescents, social support was a mediator for depression and interpersonal relations, described as problems that occurred in relationships (e.g., argumentativeness or isolating oneself).

A study of the psychological adjustment of children living in Sarajevo after the 1992–1995 war (Barath, 2002) revealed that children still experience many unhealthy life conditions and psychosocial stressors. An evaluation of predictors of maladjustment indicated that a lack of social support within a child's family is considered a risk factor for child health and development. Both studies about war reveal that family members endure considerable stressors, and support is an important factor in psychological well-being. Both studies are also cross-sectional, which limits the generalizability of the findings to other war-stricken populations.

Terrorism. Although terrorism has immediate effects on individuals directly exposed to the trauma and far-reaching effects worldwide (Gurwitch, Sitterle, Young, & Pfefferbaum, 2002), it is virtually unknown how familial social support affects the relationship between terrorism and the development of posttraumatic stress symptoms. We are only aware of studies that have investigated social support as a general construct without specifically delineating family member support. For example, a global measure of social support revealed that a low level of support 6 months prior to the September 11 terrorist attacks was a predictor of depression (Galea et al., 2002).

Community violence. Community violence is composed of physical or threatened harm that occurs in or around the home, school, or neighborhood; it can be witnessed, heard about, or experienced and can involve known or unknown perpetrators (Kupersmidt, Shahinfar, & Voegler-Lee, 2002). Community violence is often a chronic stressor that is generally concentrated in inner cities and can affect psychological, behavioral, cognitive, social, and academic functioning (Kupersmidt et al., 2002). Kliewer and colleagues (1998) investigated community violence exposure and psychological impact in children aged 8 to 12 years from Richmond, Virginia. Maternal support moderated the relationship between violence exposure and child adjustment (assessed via the NRI [Furman & Buhrmester, 1985]). Similarly, in adolescents ranging from age 12 to 18 years from Colombia, South America, support from the family mediated the relationship between violence exposure and adjustment (assessed via the FES [Moos & Moos, 1986], and the FACES-II [Olson et al., 1982]). The relationship was strongest for girls and younger adolescents (Kliewer, Murrelle, Mojia, Torres, & Angold 2001).

Natural disaster. Families around the world are affected by natural disasters, including earthquakes (Carr et al., 1997; Karanci, Alkan, Aksit, Sucuoglu, & Turkey 1999), hurricanes (La Greca & Prinstein, 2002; La Greca, Silverman, Vernberg, & Prinstein, 1996), and floods (Jacobs et al., 2002). Kaniasty and Norris (1993) provided evidence for a mediational model of social support (immediate and longer-term) after a devastating flood in Kentucky. Personal loss and community destruction were associated with declines in an elderly sample's perceptions of support. Non-kin support (via the Louisville Social Support Scale [Norris & Murrell, 1987]) mediated the impact of personal loss on depression after the flood. Deterioration in perceived kin support was only marginally linked to long-term elevations of depressive symptoms.

La Greca and colleagues (1996) assessed 3rd- to 5th-grade children 3, 7, and 10 months after Hurricane Andrew for the longitudinal prevalence of trauma symptomatology. Although PTSD symptoms decreased over time, 18% of children still reported symptoms in all three symptom clusters at 10 months posttrauma. Children reported moderate levels of support at 3 months—with greatest support from parents and close friends (via the Social Support Scale for Children [Harter, 1985]); however, lower levels of social support predicted higher PTSD symptoms.

TRAUMA EXPERIENCED BY MEMBERS OF THE FAMILY

Researchers have also focused on how a stressor to one family member affects the entire family unit. These studies do not examine a specific relationship dyad, but instead the support from the whole family. We will organize our review by discussing family support and adaptation to adult-onset illness, followed by a discussion of family support and adaptation to childhood-onset illness.

Family support and adult adjustment. A study of social support in adult cancer patients by Molassiotis and colleagues (1997) provides further evidence for the importance of family networks on quality of life. Global perceptions were that social support (assessed by the Norbeck Social Support Questionnaire [Norbeck, Lindsey, & Carrieri, 1981]) was significantly higher among post–bone marrow transplant patients compared to a control group of patients receiving chemotherapy. However, no differences were found in family support (assessed by the FES [Moos & Moos, 1986]) between the two groups. Specifically, family support was characterized as low family conflict, a high degree of cohesion, and a moderate degree of dependency. Family relationships in both groups were significantly associated with domestic adjustment, extended family adjustment, reduced psychological distress, and overall psychological adjustment. The authors suggest that family relationships may act as a protective factor against the impact of major stressors.

Bloom and Spiegel (1984) investigated how dimensions of social support, specifically, emotional support and social activity, affect psychological well-being in women with metastatic breast cancer. Emotional support provided by the family (assessed by the FES [Moos & Moos, 1986]) predicted patient outlook in life, and social activity predicted both patient outlook and social functioning. This provides support for the position that the impact of stressful events is reduced by the quality of emotional support from the family. Social activity also increases social interactions and the opportunity for supportive exchanges. Therefore, different aspects of social support provide different functions in mental well-being.

Alferi, Carver, Antoni, Weiss, and Duran (2001) focused on the impact of early stage breast cancer in low-income Hispanic women and the importance of perceived social support, including emotional and instrumental support (assessed by an author-created measure) from spouse and female family members, other family members, and friends. The division of family support was based on the cultural importance of female family support. Shifts in support occurred from pre- to postsurgery. Instrumental support increased from spouses and women in the family, while emotional support increased from women in the family and other family members over the same time period. Elevated distress presurgery predicted less instrumental support from female family members; postsurgery, it indicated an "erosion" of support. The authors concluded that social support provides an emotional benefit since instrumental support from spouse presurgery predicted less distress postsurgery even after controlling for initial distress level. The authors present an important methodological implication that cultural differences in social support, or any construct, may influence outcome.

Social support and HIV/AIDS research has focused on the impact of support in areas of quality of life and adjustment. HIV-infected patients who adjusted poorly to their condition compared to those who adjusted well, defined by the Brief Symptom Inventory (Derogatis & Spencer, 1982), reported significantly less global social support than the latter group (Grassi, Righi, Sighinolfi, Makoui, & Ghinelli, 1998).

Nott and colleagues (1995) investigated social support networks in HIV positive men for 6 months. In this study, 91 gay men (mean age 38 years) evaluated actual, ideal, and discrepancy levels of emotional and practical support from a partner, mother, father, closest sibling, important relative, best friend, and others (via the SOS [Power & Champion, 1991]). Highest levels of actual support were received from a partner and best friend, while the lowest levels were received from a father. The authors collapsed support into one variable in subsequent analyses. Higher levels of emotional and practical support correlated with increased emotional well-being. Higher levels of discrepancy between desired and received support predicted greater emotional distress, providing support for the optimal matching hypothesis (Cutrona & Russell, 1990).

Swindells and colleagues (1999) examined whether quality of life in patients with HIV was affected by availability, satisfaction, and sources of social support and coping. Predominantly male HIV-infected adult patients assessed tangible, information, and emotional support from family or partner (via the SSQ [Sarason, Levine, Basham, & Sarson, 1983]). Satisfaction with tangible, information, and emotional support, regardless of source, was related to better quality of life. Dissatisfaction with support at 6 months revealed a trend toward decreased quality of life. Higher levels of tangible, information, and emotional family support were related to significantly more problem-focused coping.

Family support and child adjustment. Over 10 million adults in the parenting ages 18 to 44 have a chronic health condition, yet few empirical studies have investigated how this affects child and adolescent development (Champion & Roberts, 2001). Few studies have focused on child and adolescent adjustment to parental chronic illness or major stressors despite evidence that parental stressors have negative psychological outcomes (see Champion & Roberts, 2001 for a review). Children who witnessed violent behaviors directed toward their mothers for approximately 6 years developed notably more posttraumatic symptoms compared to children exposed to minor stressors, but not more than children exposed to a dog attack (Rossman et al., 1997). Future studies of child and adolescent trauma victims require an emphasis on self-report measures of social support and adjustment. Although investigations have examined the impact of parental trauma on an adolescent's well-being, little is known about the role of social support during these times.

Since adolescents are more cognizant and emotionally mature than children, they not only can understand more about the stressor but can also be more realistic about the outcome. Research on adolescent adjustment to parental illness has been focused on adult cancer populations. Compas and colleagues (1994) have concentrated their investigations on the psychosocial impact of a parental cancer diagnosis on young adults, adolescent, and preadolescent children. Adolescent girls with an ill mother reported more anxiety and depression than any other combination of adolescent and patient gender (Compas et al., 1994; Grant & Compas, 1995; Welch, Wadsworth, & Compas, 1996); however, parents did not report that their children were distressed (Welch et al., 1996). Welch et al. (1996) found that adolescent girls reported a reduction in anxiety and depression over a 4-month period, yet it is virtually unknown how adolescents are adjusting at or beyond 6 months postdiagnosis. Although Compas and colleagues have established that children and adolescents are distressed by parental illness, social support networks in this population are virtually unknown.

Champion and Roberts (2001) suggest that parental illness can affect children's view of their family environment. They hypothesize that increased conflict and lower levels of family cohesion disrupt family member adjustment. Similarly, such factors could also affect enacted and perceived social support within the family unit. Future studies should incorporate the FES (Moos & Moos, 1986) and the FACES-II (Olson et al., 1982) to directly address these hypotheses.

Life-Threatening Illness in a Child

The advent of a serious illness in a child can have a substantially different impact on the family.

Family support and child adjustment. Few studies have evaluated the role of family support in how children or adolescents adjust to their own life-threatening illness. A great deal of information is assumed when researchers make conclusions based on studies utilizing parental perceptions of familial support. One of the few studies to employ self-reports of support was by Kazak and Meadows (1989) who investigated support networks of adolescent cancer survivors. In this study, familial relationships (via the FACES-II [Olson et al., 1982]) and social support from family, friends, and school/other adults (via the Social Support Rating Scale [Cauce, 1986]) was assessed at baseline and 6 months into the school year among 35 childhood cancer survivors (mean age 12 years) disease-free for at least 5 years. At Time 2, survivors reported they received significantly less emotional support and caring from their families, friends, teachers, and nonfamily adults, than at Time 1. The child's perceived family adaptability and age at diagnosis predicted satisfaction with emotional support.

Burlew and colleagues (2000) assessed factors that influenced adaptation of African American adolescents (14 to 19 years) with sickle cell disease. Lower self-reported state and trait anxiety was related to the use of social support as a coping strategy and the perception of a more supportive family environment (via the FES [Moos & Moos, 1986]). Lower self-reported depression scores were related to the use of social support as a coping strategy and better family relations.

Family support and parent adjustment. The diagnosis of a chronic illness in a child affects each parent and the marital relationship. Barbarin and colleagues (1985) interviewed married couples with a child cancer patient (age 4 to 21 years). Most parents reported that the quality of their marriage and the cohesion of their family had improved since the diagnosis. Spouses were also identified as the most important sources of social support. The wife's perception of support was related to her husband's involvement in the care of their child, while the husband's perception of support was related to the wife's availability in the home.

Manne and colleagues (2002) studied mothers of children (9 months to 20 years) undergoing bone marrow transplantation and found several predictors of PTSD, including exposure, distress, fear network, enacted support, and perceived negative behaviors. The *perceived negative behaviors* construct was indirectly predictive in that unsupportive responses by a partner and family, reported at transplantation, predicted PTSD symptom severity at 6 months posttransplant. Enacted support was reported by the Cancer Support Inventory (Manne & Schnoll, 2001) separately for both family and friends. However, *enacted social support* was not associated with PTSD symptoms. The authors note that although this finding is inconsistent with previous social support literature, the type of social support (perceived versus enacted) assessed is an important distinction.

Divorce

Divorce is a universally disruptive experience, always stressful and at times traumatic. Few studies have investigated familial support networks utilized by postdivorce families and, specifically, assessing child perceptions of support.

Family support and parent adjustment. Leslie and Grady (1985) found that recently divorced women reported that their support networks were composed of close relationships consisting primarily of kin and work friends who provided emotional and instrumental support. After 1 year, networks became more homogeneous and denser, and consisted of significantly more kin.

Bretherton and colleagues (1996) assessed 50 divorced mothers with preschool children for social support. These women reported (via the Sources of Help Questionnaire (Wan, Jaccard, & Ramey, in 1996) their parents as the most helpful in companionship and less so in tangible help, emotional support, or parenting advice. Close friends were rated the highest in providing emotional support. Relatives were turned to more than coworkers for tangible help, companionship, emotional support, or parenting advice. Finally, divorced mothers were least satisfied with their fathers' support and fathers were perceived as the least helpful to them in all areas. The women did rate fathers as "mildly" helpful in terms of tangible support and parenting advice.

Family support and child adjustment. Wolchik and colleagues (1989) investigated the social support networks and adjustment of 104 children (8 to 15 years) approximately 14 months after divorce. Children with high levels of stress and high parental support self-reported (via the Children's Inventory of Social Support [Wolchik, Sandler, & Braver, 1987]) fewer adjustment problems than children with low support. Support from siblings was not significantly associated with adjustment, measured from either the parent's or child's perspective.

There has been little research on the role of grandparents in child adjustment following divorce. However, intergenerational relationships can be an important source of support during family transitions or major stressors. Lussier, Deater-Deckard, Dunn, and Davies (2002) assessed child contact and closeness with grandparents in different family structures following divorce (assessed via an author-created measure). Less child contact was found for grandparents related to the child's nonresident parent. Children living with stepparents reported less contact with grandparents than those living with single parents. Therefore, the authors suggest that the difference is in whether the parent has re-partnered. Children from virtually all combinations of family structures reported similar rates of contact suggesting that grandparents are important factors in children's lives. Children from intact families reported feeling closer to their grandparents compared to children living with single mothers. The authors also found that, in general, closeness with grandparents was related to better adjustment in children following divorce, even after controlling for other risk factors; closeness of maternal grandparents was associated with better adjustment in biological mother–stepfather families. These data indicate that grandparents are important sources of support in children's lives, even after their parents' divorce. Future studies should include grandparents when evaluating child social support networks.

Family Violence

Physical or emotional violence within a family considerably affects the family unit, family relationships, and the psychological and physiological well-being of family members. Family violence includes physical abuse, sexual assault, or witnessing violence. Mothers' and children's reports about family violence have been found to be greatly correlated (McCloskey, Figueredo, & Koss, 1995). Although family violence is, unfortunately, prevalent worldwide, few studies have examined how support from family members affects individual or family outcome.

Family support and child and parent adjustment. McCloskey and colleagues (1995) examined whether close ties within the family (to the
mother or sibling) buffered children in violent homes. Interviews about
abuse at home, and support and closeness within the nuclear family were
conducted with 365 mothers and one child of each mother (6 to 12 years).
Because both mother and child assessments were included, there was a
more thorough understanding of the situation. Children rated parental
warmth and support via the Parent Perception Inventory (Hazzard,
Christensen, & Margolin, 1983). In contrast to a comparison group, 69.5%
of mothers reported being beaten. More children witnessed violence by
their fathers than experienced it, but most of the children in the total sample reported being slapped; more than a third were hit with an object at
least once. Violent families displayed less sibling and parental warmth
than a comparison group. When family support did occur, it failed to
buffer the children from adverse psychological effects.

Childhood Trauma

Child trauma has pervasive effects on the psychological well-being of
both the child and other family members. The difficulty with child
trauma and social support research is the lack of studies utilizing self-
report. Although there are concerns relating to the reliability of self-
reports (Cauce et al., 1990), researchers must be conservative when generalizing findings reported by parents. In addition, much research on
child trauma has focused on parental impact and adjustment rather than
child or sibling adjustment.

Family support and child adjustment. Children (4 to 9 years) exposed to a
single dog attack displayed significantly more posttraumatic stress
symptoms than children exposed to repeated parental violence and children with minor stressors (Rossman et al., 1997). Greater maternal support predicted fewer child internalizing and externalizing problems
(assessed via the Child Behavior Checklist [Achenbach & Edelbrock,
1983]). Mothers' posttraumatic stress symptoms predicted children's
stress symptoms. The authors propose that children may observe and
model maternal reactions to stress.

Von Weiss and colleagues (2002) assessed psychosocial adjustment in
pediatric rheumatic disease patients (ages 8 to 17 years) via self-report
measures of daily hassles, distress, social support (via the Social Support
Scale for Children [Harter, 1985]), and behavior problems. Greater parental support was related to lower levels of depression, state anxiety, trait
anxiety, and externalizing behavior problems. The authors found evidence for a main effects model of support indicating that support was

beneficial regardless of the level of self-reported stress. In pediatric rheumatic disease patients, parent and classmate support were the best predictors of adjustment as compared to other sources of support.

Family support and parent adjustment. The loss of a child is a devastating event affecting both the spousal relationship and the parents individually. Lehman and colleagues (1989) investigated the impact of sudden bereavement from death of a child on marital relationships. Spousal relationships were likely to either strengthen or end in divorce following a child's death. In response to a question about their individual relationship with their other children, 32% reported that their relationship had improved, while 13% reported that the relationship had weakened. Although parents use each other as sources of support, we are not aware of any additional studies focusing on the spousal relationship.

Trauma in Adolescence

Although adolescent and parental relationships are characterized by conflict, parents are significant providers of support to adolescents (Cauce et al., 1990). From a developmental perspective, a child's and adolescent's sense of parental support may be directly or indirectly influenced by parents' perception of the child and their behavior toward the child. Sarason, Pierce, Bannerman, and Sarason (1993) concluded that adolescents' current perceptions of availability of parent support are related to the way parents view them and are associated with the probability of a supportive behavior. Current adolescent and sibling trauma and social support literature has utilized self-report measures from multiple perspectives, thus creating a more thorough view of this multifaceted area of research.

Johnson and Kenkel (1991) assessed psychological adjustment and family support in female teenaged incest victims, a majority of whom were molested by a father figure. Greater perceived maternal support was a significant predictor of adolescent self-reported distress level at the time of disclosure of the abuse to her mother.

Manne and Miller (1998) examined social support networks, conflict, and adjustment among adolescents (12 to 20 years) diagnosed with cancer. In this study, enacted support from mother, father, sibling, and best friend (via the NRI [Furman & Buhrmester, 1985]) was assessed among 50 adolescents approximately 6 months after diagnosis. Compared to healthy adolescents, no differences were found with regard to family or peer support variables; however, adolescents with cancer reported much more conflict with their mothers and fathers. Social support did not predict psychological distress in adolescents with cancer, but conflict with mothers was a major predictor of distress even after controlling for physical impairment. This study illustrates how these adolescents report receiving similar amounts of social support compared to healthy teens. The authors suggest that maternal conflict may be due to the increased time an adolescent and mother spend together, combined with an adolescent's struggle with independence despite the need for assistance.

Death of Parent or Family Members

Children who lose a family member are not only losing a key component of their familial support network but are also faced with a significant source of stress. This literature base has focused mainly on the loss of a parent, but additional studies have investigated loss of siblings and extended family members. Parents reported that 73% of their children suffered negative effects of the death of a parent or sibling; specifically, 47% of parent responses were coded as "extremely negative effects" including depression, drug abuse, and suicide (Lehman et al., 1989). Adolescents have contributed most of the information in this field due to their cognitive development and emotional maturity.

Gray (1987) examined adolescent response to sudden versus expected parental death. Adolescents with low global social support (assessed by the Informal Social Support Scale; author-created measure from semistructured interview that include questions about perceived and enacted support) and poor relations with the healthy parent following parental death reported considerably higher levels of depression. The combination of sudden loss (less than 3 months) with poor prior relations was related to a marked increase in major depression.

Few studies have provided longitudinal adjustment of adolescents over the course of parental illness, and even less empirical research is available on adolescent's psychological adjustment to the loss of the parent. Siegel and colleagues (1992) found that preadolescent children and adolescents with a terminally ill parent self-reported significantly higher levels of depressive symptomatology and anxiety than community controls; however, by 7 to 12 months after parental death, no differences were found (Siegel, Karus, & Raveis, 1996).

Bachar and colleagues (1997) investigated social support networks, psychological well-being, and psychiatric symptoms among Israeli adolescents who lost relatives (parents, brothers, grandfathers, uncles, and cousins) nearly 10 years prior in war or road accidents, compared to healthy adolescents. War-bereaved adolescents did not differ in amount of social and family support compared to accident-bereaved adolescents and nonbereaved adolescents (assessed via the PSSS [Procidano & Heller,

1983]). War-bereaved adolescents reported significantly higher psychological well-being and lower psychiatric symptoms than accident-bereaved adolescents. The authors propose that the resiliency of war-bereaved adolescents may be due to the highly valued effect of death in battle, while road accidents are perceived to be a purposeless event.

Trauma to Sibling

Support provided by siblings has been documented throughout development. Studies have indicated that siblings provide a key source of support from childhood (Dunn & Munn, 1986) through adolescence (Tucker, McHale, & Crouter, 2001) and into adulthood (Avioli, 1989). Children as young as 2 years old are capable of sharing, helping, and comforting a distressed sibling (Dunn & Munn, 1986). Despite evidence from developmental psychology, the impact of sibling trauma on the healthy sibling has been virtually unknown. Studies of the impact of child or adolescent trauma on the family have generally focused on parental outcome variables and support as a global measure of the family (Bachanas et al., 2001; Kazak et al., 1998). Recent developments have focused on healthy sibling psychological outcome variables and utilization of supportive relationships in sibling trauma.

A sibling's role can be that of a mentor, as in the parent–child relationship, or that of a peer. Adolescent siblings more often assume reciprocal roles with regard to familial issues and complementary roles as peers in the areas of social life, schoolwork, and risky behavior Tucker, McHale, & Crouter, 2001). Tucker and colleagues (2001) conclude that adolescents remain important sources of support into late adolescence.

Chronic illness in a sibling is a persistent stressor for the healthy sibling (Drotar & Crawford, 1985; Gardner, 1998). The cognitive appraisals of young siblings of children with a chronic illness were categorized as negative thoughts relating either to self or others (Gardner, 1998).

Cohen, Friedrich, Jaworski, Copeland, and Pendergrass (1994) examined variables predicting adjustment for siblings (4 to 16 years) of pediatric cancer patients (8 months to 17 years). In this study, 129 parents (97% mothers) completed a measure of family adaptability and cohesion no more than 4 years postdiagnosis (FACES-II [Olson et al., 1982]). A highly cohesive family was related to better sibling adjustment.

Children with juvenile rheumatoid arthritis and healthy siblings at least 10 years old completed a family resources index measuring cohesion, expressiveness, and conflict among family members (via the FES [Moos & Moos, 1986]) (Timko, Stovel, Moos, & Miller, 1992). Moderate and severe patients engaged in fewer activities with their families, and perceived their families as having fewer resources than mild patients and siblings; however, no differences were found in family activities 1 year later.

Trauma in Early Adulthood

Trauma to a spouse has pervasive effects on the marital relationship and the psychological and physical well-being of the healthy parent. Cutrona (1996) has identified four mechanisms through which spousal support can contribute to marital quality: (a) Support can prevent emotional withdrawal and isolation. (b) The belief that one is part of a team may prevent isolation during bereavement and subsequent marital damage. (c) Spousal support can prevent the onset of clinically significant depression and prevent conflicts from escalating to destructive levels. (d) Emotional intimacy strengthens the marital bond and can protect against damaging coping behaviors. All these mechanisms can be applied to marriages placed under extreme stress. Men and women who encounter stress are more likely to receive spousal support if they are satisfied with the marital relationship (Cutrona & Suhr, 1994).

The diagnosis of a chronic illness in a spouse affects the family unit and the marital relationship; however, little research addresses the role of spousal support in patient or spouse outcome variables. An extensive review of cancer literature by Manne (1998) indicates that only a small group of patients and spouses are at risk for adjustment problems. For diseases that are highly curable, distress will lessen with time, but diseases with a poor prognosis are related to escalating levels of distress. Younger partners and females (patients and wives) are at higher risk for distress. Spouses tend to be utilized differently depending on gender of patient and phase of treatment. It is still unclear whether these factors are cancer-specific or can be generalized to other illnesses and stressors.

Losing a spouse has devastating effects on both the healthy spouse and family network. The spouse has lost a key component of his or her social support network and is faced with new stressors related to family, social, and work domains. Spouses who suddenly lost their partner reported feeling more tense, upset, and emotionally worn out when thinking about their current position as a parent (Lehman et al., 1989). More than half of the parents reported that the relationship with their remaining children had either improved or stayed the same. The experience of losing one's spouse can lead to increases in incidence of depression, mental illness, physical illness, mortality, and suicide related to bereavement (Stroebe & Stroebe, 1983). Specifically, men appear to suffer more than women in response to spousal death (Stroebe & Stroebe, 1983).

Trauma in Late Adulthood

Two major areas of research in caregiver literature are studies that explore the impact of social relationships on caregiver outcome and those that examine the effect of caregiving on social relationships (Pillemer & Suitor, 1996). Female caregivers of an elderly parent with at least mild memory difficulties report negative effects on mental health, physical health, and lifestyles (including not spending enough time with spouse and children) (Abel, 1989; Brody, Hoffman, Kleban, & Schoonover, 1989).

The area of support in older adulthood most researched is in caregivers of family members with Alzheimer's disease or a related dementia. When caregiving is provided to a parent who was once a source of support for the adult child, there is a loss of reciprocity of support for the caregiving child. This loss is particularly felt by children caring for parents with dementia. As the disease progresses, there are increases in upsetting behaviors such as incontinence, wandering, aggression, and loss of recognition of family members (Pillemer & Suitor, 1996). Pillemer and Suitor (1996) examined the social support network of married female caregivers of a parent with dementia. Friends provided the most emotional support followed by spouses and siblings; siblings provided the most instrumental support. Siblings of parent caregivers have been shown to be both sources of support and conflict (Brody et al., 1989; Suitor & Pillemer, 1993; Pillemer & Suitor, 1996).

Haley and colleagues (1996) found that female caregivers dominate the caregiver role in black and white families caring for adults with Alzheimer's disease. There were no differences in number of social supports, total satisfaction with social support, or total number of visits with relatives and friends (assessed via the SSQSR [Sarason, Sarason, Shearin, & Pierce, 1987). Black caregivers had lower appraisals of caregiving stressors (e.g., memory and behavioral problems) and lower levels of depression than white caregivers. The authors suggest that these differences may be due to cultural differences in values and beliefs, such as expecting to be a caregiver for a parent.

Creasey, Myers, Epperson, and Taylor (1990) investigated relationships in families with and without elderly parents with Alzheimer's disease. Assessment of family relationships (via the NRI [Furman & Buhrmester, 1985]) revealed that female adults (daughters and daughters-in-law) from the Alzheimer's group perceived a lack of support from the elderly parent and their own husbands when compared to the control group. Adult men (sons and sons-in-laws) in the Alzheimer's group also reported a perceived lack of support from the elderly parent compared to the control group. Reports of wife burden were correlated with negative interactions with both the husband and parent, while husband burden is specifically related to whether the patient is a parent and female. In contrast to the authors' hypothesis that the data would fit with a family systems approach, families with an Alzheimer's patient did not perceive disruptions among all relationships.

SUMMARY

Social support from family members can facilitate adjustment in children (La Greca et al., 1996; Wolchik, Ruehlman, Braver, & Sandler, 1989), adolescents (Burlew, Tefair, Colangelo, & Wright, 2000; Manne & Miller, 1998), adults (Bloom & Spiegel, 1984; Nott et al., 1995), and the elderly (Creasey et al., 1990; Haley et al., 1996) after exposure to traumas through a variety of mediums that affect the whole family unit or individual family members. Regardless of who experiences the trauma, the entire family network is affected. Although previous findings suggest that social support is generally beneficial, little is known about the impact of trauma on family functioning and subsequent family processes. Family functioning variables, for example, cohesion and adaptability, are potential moderators of the relationship between trauma and psychosocial outcome.

Research has shown the most effective type of support is one that matches the needs of the stressor. Cutrona and Russell (1990) outlined an optimal matching model of stress and social support where optimal adjustment is achieved when the support received is appropriately matched to stressor characteristics. Defining preference variables provides insight into the complex relationship of the matching between stressors and social support. Therefore, it is essential to understand how and what is considered supportive in order to construct effective interventions to empower families faced with trauma.

METHODOLOGICAL ISSUES

Although literature on the role of social support in trauma has grown considerably in the last 10 years, the focus on family support comprises a relatively small portion of this work. A review of the literature shows that family members are important components of support networks; however, more work is needed in the areas of methodology and measurement.

Acitelli (1996) emphasizes three methodological considerations for social support research of marital relationships; these points are also applicable to all areas of social support research. First, studies of support need to focus on relationship-specific social support instead of global measures. Second, both providers and recipients of support need to be included, especially when assessing reciprocity of support; if only one member of the dyad reports, then the investigation is really studying an individual's perception of reciprocity. Third, an emphasis on social support and outcome variables will provide more meaningful context to the impact of relationships. Each point will be elaborated upon within the context of the familial relationship.

Only a few social support measurements allow for the evaluation of support from different family members. Support measures need to be designed to assess relationship-specific social support in order to tease out types of support provided by specific family members in specific contexts. Some recent examples of these measures are the Partner Support Inventory for Cancer (Manne & Schnoll, 2001) and the Adolescent Diabetes-Specific Support From Family Members Measure (La Greca & Bearman, 2002).

A second issue regards how enacted support is evaluated. Enacted support typically captures support from the recipients' point of view rather than what the providers view as what they provide to the recipient. Studies should incorporate perspectives of both the recipient and the provider of support (Kessler, 1991). This approach to assessing support will contribute to a more thorough understanding of why some well-intended support is perceived negatively, as well as a greater understanding of so-called "invisible" support that is provided but not recognized by the recipient (Bolger, Zuckerman, & Kessler, 2000).

Another construct that might be incorporated into studies of family support in the aftermath of trauma is reciprocal support. Support in familial relationships is a dynamic process where there may be less clear boundaries between who gives and who receives support because of the communal nature of family relationships. Assessments taking into account the reciprocal nature of support would be particularly helpful in the family context and have been very rarely used in this research. For example, instead of assessing support from both the provider and the recipient perspective, researchers only assess perceptions of support from one person, as in spousal relationships and parent–child dyads. Antonucci and Jackson (1990) emphasize the importance of reciprocity in social support research as a means to facilitate understanding of support exchanges across the life span. This is especially pertinent to parent–child dyads. Most parental reports are completed by the mother, and none of the studies presently reviewed consisted of parent reports by the father. This missing component of family relationships is important to include in future research design.

Assessing child or adolescent social support by the family includes behavioral observation, parent reports, and self-reports. Although there are advantages and disadvantages to each method, self-report allows direct evaluation of a child's support network (Cauce et al., 1990). Future research on social support networks in children and adolescents should take into account measures from both members of the desired relationship, for example, both parent and adolescent views of social support.

Outcome measures should be included in evaluations of family relationships in times of trauma. Not only is it important to determine who is providing the support in response to traumatic events but also psychological and physical outcome for the support recipient. In studies targeting children and adolescents, self-report should be utilized, when possible, in order to create the most accurate picture of the impact of stressful event and support relationships.

Finally, nearly all studies reviewed are cross-sectional designs, which significantly limit the generalizability of findings. Longitudinal designs will allow a more thorough understanding of support in families regarding how families utilize support to adjust to trauma immediately and over time.

REFERENCES

Abel, E. K. (1989). The ambiguities of social support: Adult daughters caring for frail elderly parents. *Journal of Aging Studies, 3,* 211–230.

Achenbach, T. M., & Edelbrock, C. S. (1983). *Manual for the child behavior checklist and revised child behavioral profile.* Burlington, VT: University of Vermont Department of Psychiatry.

Acitelli, L. K. (1996). The neglected link between marital support and marital satisfaction. In G. R. Pierce, B. R. Sarason, & I. G. Sarason (Eds.), *Handbook of social support and the family* (pp. 83–103). New York: Plenum.

Alferi, S. M., Carver, C. S., Antoni, M. H., Weiss, S., & Duran, R. E. (2001). An exploratory study of social support, distress, and life disruption among low-income Hispanic women under treatment for early stage breast cancer. *Health Psychology, 20,* 41–46.

Antonucci, T. C., & Jackson, J. S. (1990). The role of reciprocity in social support. In B. R. Sarason, I. G. Sarason, & G. R. Pierce (Eds.), *Social support: An interactional view* (pp. 173–198). New York: Wiley.

Avioli, P. S. (1989). The social support functions of siblings in later life. *American Behavioral Scientist, 33,* 45–57.

Bachanas, P. J., Kullgren, K. A., Schwartz, K., McDaniel, J. S., Smith, J., & Nesheim, S. (2001). Psychological adjustment in caregivers of school-age children infected with HIV: Stress, coping, and family factors. *Journal of Pediatric Psychology, 26,* 331–342.

Bachar, E., Canetti, L., Bonne, O., Denour, A. K., & Shalev, A. Y. (1997). Psychological well-being and ratings of psychiatric symptoms in bereaved Israeli adolescents: Differential effects of war- versus accident-related bereavement. *The Journal of Nervous and Mental Disease, 185,* 402–406.

Barath, A. (2002). Psychological status of Sarajevo children after war: 1999–2000 survey. *Croatian Medical Journal, 43,* 213–220.

Barbarin, O. A., Hughes, D., & Chesler, M. A. (1985). Stress, coping, and marital functioning among parents of children with cancer. *Journal of Marriage and the Family, 47,* 473–480.

Barrera, M. (1981). Social support in the adjustment of pregnant adolescents: Assessment issues. In B. H. Gotlieb (Ed.), *Social networks and social support* (pp. 69–96). Beverly Hills, CA: Sage.

Barrera, M., Jr. (1986). Distinctions between social support concepts, measures, and models. *American Journal of Community Psychology, 14,* 413–445.

Bell, R. Q. (1968). A reinterpretation of the direction of effects in studies of socialization. *Psychological Review, 75,* 81–95.

Bloom, J. R., & Spiegel, D. (1984). The relationship of two dimensions of social support to the psychological well-being and social functioning of women with advanced breast cancer. *Social Science and Medicine, 19,* 831–837.

Bolger, N., Zuckerman, A., & Kessler, R. (2000). Invisible support and adjustment to stress. *Journal of Personality and Social Psychology, 79* (6), 953–961.

Bowlby, J. (1969). *Attachment and loss, Vol. 1: Attachment.* New York: Basic Books.

Bretherton, I., Walsh, R., & Lependorf, M. (1996). Social support in postdivorce families. In G. R. Pierce, B. R. Sarason, & I. G. Sarason (Eds.), *Handbook of social support and the family* (pp. 345–373). New York: Plenum.

Brewin, C. R., Andrews, B., & Valentine, J. D. (2000). Meta-analysis of risk factors for post-traumatic stress disorder in trauma-exposed adults. *Journal of Consulting and Clinical Psychology, 68,* 748–766.

Brody, E. M., Hoffman, C., Kleban, M., & Schoonover, C. B. (1989). Caregiving daughters and their local siblings: Perceptions, strains, and interactions. *Journal of Gerontology, 29,* 529–538.

Burleson, B. R., & Kunkel, A. W. (1996). The socialization of emotional support skills in childhood. In G. R. Pierce, B. R. Sarason, & I. G. Sarason (Eds.), *Handbook of social support and the family* (pp. 105–140). New York: Plenum.

Burlew, K., Tefair, J., Colangelo, L., & Wright, E. C. (2000). Factors that influence adolescent adjustment to sickle cell disease. *Journal of Pediatric Psychology, 25,* 287–299.

Camras, L. A., Ribordy, S., Hill, J., Martino, S., Sachs, V., Spaccarelli, S., & Stefani, R. (1990). Maternal facial behavior and the recognition and production of emotional expression by maltreated and nonmaltreated children. *Developmental Psychology, 26,* 304–312.

Carr, V. J., Lewin, T. J., Kenardy, J. A., Webster, R. A., Hazell, P. L., Carter, G. L., & Williamson, M. (1997). Psychosocial sequelae of the 1989 Newcastle earthquake: III. Role of vulnerability factors in post-disaster morbidity. *Psychological Medicine, 27,* 179–190.

Cauce, A. (1986). Social networks and social competence: Exploring the effects of early adolescent friendships. *American Journal of Community Psychology, 14* (6), 607–628.

Cauce, A. M., Reid, M., Landesman, S., & Gonzales, N. (1990). Social support in young children: Measurement, structure, and behavioral impact. In B. R. Sarason, I. G. Sarason, & G. R. Pierce (Eds.), *Social support: An interactional view* (pp. 64–94). New York: Wiley.

Champion, K. M., & Roberts, M. C. (2001). The psychological impact of a parent's chronic illness on the child. In C. E. Walker & M. C. Roberts (Eds.), *Handbook of clinical child psychology* (3rd ed., pp. 1057–1073). New York: Wiley.

Cohen, D. S., Friedrich, W. N., Jaworski, T. M., Copeland, D., & Pendergrass, T. (1994). Pediatric cancer: Predicting sibling adjustment. *Journal of Clinical Psychology, 50,* 303–319.

Cohen, S., & Wills, T. A. (1985). Stress, social support, and the buffering hypothesis. *Psychological Bulletin, 98,* 310–357.

Compas, B. E., Warsham, N. L., Epping-Jordan, J. E., Grant, K. E., Mireault, G., Howell, D. C., & Malcarne, V. L. (1994). When mom or dad has cancer: Markers of psychological distress in cancer patients, spouses, and children. *Health Psychology, 13,* 507–515.

Creasey, G. L., Myers, B. J., Epperson, M., & Taylor, J. (1990). Couples with an elderly parent with Alzheimer's disease: Perceptions of familial relationships. *Psychiatry, 53,* 44–51.

Crouter, A., Head, M., Bumpus, M., & McHale, S. (2001). Household chores: Under what conditions do mothers lean on daughters? *New Directions for Child and Adolescent Development, 94,* 23–41.

Cutrona, C. E. (1996). Social support as a determinant of marital quality. In G. R. Pierce, B. R. Sarason, & I. G. Sarason (Eds.), *Handbook of social support and the family* (pp. 173–194). New York: Plenum.

Cutrona, C. E., & Russell, D. W. (1990). Type of social support and specific stress: Toward a theory of optimal matching. In B. R. Sarason, I. G. Sarason, & G. R. Pierce (Eds.), *Social support: An interactional view* (pp. 319–366). New York: Wiley.

Cutrona, C. E., & Suhr, J. A. (1994). Social support communication in the context of marriage: An analysis of couples' supportive interactions. In B. R. Burleson, T. L. Albrecht, & I. G. Sarason (Eds.), *Communication of social support: Messages, interactions, relationships, and community* (pp. 113–135). Thousand Oaks, CA: Sage.

Derogatis, L. R., & Spencer, P. (1982). *The Brief Symptom Inventory (BSI) administration scoring and procedures manual-I.* Baltimore, MD: Johns Hopkins University School of Medicine.

DeRosier, M. E., & Kupersmidt, J. (1991). Costa Rican children's perceptions of their social networks. *Developmental Psychology, 27,* 656–662.

Drotar, D., & Crawford, P. (1985). Psychological adaptation of siblings of chronically ill children: Research and practice implications. *Journal of Developmental and Behavioral Pediatrics, 6,* 355–362.

Dunn, J., & Munn, P. (1986). Siblings and the development of prosocial behavior. *International Journal of Behavioral Development, 9,* 265–284.

Furman, W., & Buhrmester, D. (1985). Children's perceptions of the personal relationships in their social networks. *Developmental Psychology, 21,* 1016–1024.

Furman, L., Zurayk, H., Chaya, M., Saadeh, F., Meshefedjian, G., & Sidani, T. (1993). The impact of war on the physical and mental health of the family: The Lebanese experience. *Social Science and Medicine, 36,* 1555–1567.

Galea, S., Ahern, J., Resnick, H., Kilpatrick, D., Bucuvalas, M., Gold, J., & Vlahov, D. (2002). Psychological sequelae of the September 11 terrorist attacks in New York City. *The New England Journal of Medicine, 346,* 982–987.

Gantzel, K., & Schwinghammer, T. (1995). *Die Kriege nach dem Zweiten Weltkrieg, 1945 bis 1992: Daten und Tendenzen* [Wars since World War II, 1945 to 1992: Figures and trends]. Munster, Germany: Lit Verlag.

Gardner, E. (1998). Siblings of chronically ill children: Towards an understanding of process. *Clinical Child Psychology and Psychiatry, 3,* 213–227.

Garmezy, N. (1983). Stressors of childhood. In H. Garmezy & M. Rutter (Eds.), *Stress, coping, and development in children* (pp. 43–84). New York: McGraw-Hill.

Grant, K. E., & Compas, B. E. (1995). Stress and anxious-depressed symptoms among adolescents: Searching for mechanisms of risk. *Journal of Consulting and Clinical Psychology, 63,* 1015–1021.

Grassi, L, Righi, R., Sighinolfi, L., Makoui, S., & Ghinelli, F. (1998). Coping styles and psychosocial-related variables in HIV-infected patients. *Psychosomatics, 39,* 350–359.

Gray, R. E. (1987). Adolescent response to the death of a parent. *Journal of Youth and Adolescence, 16,* 511–525.

Greenberg, J. S., & Keane, A. (2001). Risk factors for chronic posttraumatic stress symptoms and behavior problems in children and adolescents following a home fire. *Child and Adolescent Social Work Journal, 18,* 205–221.

Gurwitch, R. H., Sitterle, K. A., Young, B. H., & Pfefferbaum, B. (2002). The aftermath of terrorism. In A. M. La Greca, W. K. Silverman, E. M. Vernberg, & M. C. Roberts (Eds.), *Helping children cope with disasters and terrorism.* Washington, DC: American Psychological Association.

Haley, W. E., Roth, D. L., Coleton, M. I., Ford, G. R., West, C. A. C., Collins, R. P., Isobe, T. L. (1996). Appraisal, coping, and social support as mediators of well-being in black and white family caregivers of patients with Alzheimer's disease. *Journal of Consulting and Clinical Psychology, 64,* 121–129.

Harter, S. (1985). *Manual for the social support scale for children.* Denver, CO: Author.

Hazzard, A., Christensen, A., & Margolin, G. (1983). Children's perceptions of parental behaviors. *Journal of Abnormal Child Psychology, 11,* 49–60.

Hobfoll, S. E., & Stephens, M. A. P. (1990). Social support during extreme stress: Consequences and Intervention. In B. R. Sarason, I. G. Sarason, & G. R. Pierce (Eds.), *Social support: An interactional view* (pp. 454–481). New York: Wiley.

Holeva, V., Tarrier, N., & Wells, A. (2001). Prevalence and predictors of acute stress disorder and PTSD following road traffic accidents: Thought control strategies and social support. *Behavior Therapy, 32,* 65–83.

Ingram, K. M., Jones, D. A., Fass, R. J., Neidig, J. L., & Song, Y. S. (1999). Social support and unsupportive social interactions: Their association with depression among people living with HIV. *AIDS Care, 11,* 313–329.

Jacobs, G. A., Boero, J. V., Quevillon, R. P., Todd-Bazemore, E., Elliott, T. L., & Reyes, G. (2002). Floods. In A. M. La Greca, W. K. Silverman, E. M. Vernberg, & M. C. Roberts (Eds.), *Helping children cope with disasters and terrorism* (pp. 157–174). Washington, DC: American Psychological Association.

Johnson, B. K., & Kenkel, M. B. (1991). Stress, coping, and adjustment in female adolescent incest victims. *Child Abuse and Neglect, 15,* 293–305.

Kaniasty, K., & Norris, F. H. (1993). A test of the social support deterioration model in the context of natural disaster. *Journal of Personality and Social Psychology, 64,* 395–406.

Karanci, N. A., Alkan, N., Aksit, B., Sucuoglu, H., & Turkey, I.(1999). Gender differences in psychological distress, coping, social support, and related variables following the 1995 Dinal (Turkey) earthquake. *North American Journal of Psychology, 1,* 189–204.

Kazak, A., & Meadows, A. T. (1989). Families of young adolescents who have survived cancer: Social-emotional adjustment, adaptability, and social support. *Journal of Pediatric Psychology, 14,* 175–192.

Kazak, A. E., Stuber, M. L., Barakat, L. P., Meeske, K., Guthrie, D., & Meadows, A. T. (1998). Predicting posttraumatic stress symptoms in mothers and fathers of survivors of childhood cancer. *Journal of the American Academy of Child and Adolescent Psychiatry, 37,* 823–831.

Kessler, R. C. (1991). Perceived support and adjustment to stress: methodological considerations. In H. O. F. Veiel & U. Baumann (Eds.), *The meaning and measurement of social support* (pp. 259–271). New York: Hemisphere.

Kliewer, W., Lepore, S. J., Oskin, D., & Johnson, P. D. (1998). The role of social and cognitive processes in children's adjustment to community violence. *Journal of Consulting and Clinical Psychology, 66,* 199–209.

Kliewer, W., Murrelle, L., Mojia, R., Torres de G. Y., & Angold, A. (2001). Exposure to violence against a family member and internalizing symptoms in Colombian adolescents: The protective effects of family support. *Journal of Consulting and Clinical Psychology, 69,* 971–982.

Klingman, A. (2002). Children under stress of war. In A. M. La Greca, W. K. Silverman, E. M. Vernberg, & M. C. Roberts (Eds.), *Helping children cope with disasters and terrorism* (pp. 359–380). Washington, DC: American Psychological Association.

Kupersmidt, J. B., Shahinfar, A., & Voegler-Lee, M. E. (2002). Children's exposure to community violence. In A. M. La Greca, W. K. Silverman, E. M. Vernberg, & M. C. Roberts (Eds.), *Helping children cope with disasters and terrorism* (pp. 381–401). Washington, DC: American Psychological Association.

La Greca, A., & Bearman, K. (2002). The diabetes social support questionnaire—family version: Evaluating adolescents' diabetes-specific support from family members. *Journal of Pediatric Psychology, 27(8),* 665–676.

La Greca, A., & Prinstein, M. J. (2002). Hurricanes and earthquakes. In A. M. La Greca, W. K. Silverman, E. M. Vernberg, & M. C. Roberts (Eds.), *Helping children cope with disasters and terrorism* (pp. 107–138). Washington, DC: American Psychological Association.

La Greca, A., Silverman, W. K., Vernberg, E. M., & Prinstein, M. J. (1996). Symptoms of posttraumatic stress in children after Hurricane Andrew: A prospective study. *Journal of Consulting and Clinical Psychology, 64,* 712–723.

Lazarus, R. S., & Folkman, S. (1984). *Stress, appraisal, and coping.* New York: Springer.

Lehman, D. R., Lang, E. L., Wortman, C. B., & Sorenson, S. B. (1989). Long-term effects of sudden bereavement: Marital and parent-child relationships and children's reactions. *Journal of Family Psychology, 2,* 344–367.

Leslie, L. A., & Grady, K. (1985). Changes in mother's social networks and social support following divorce. *Journal of Marriage and the Family, 47,* 663–673.

Lussier, G., Deater-Deckard, K., Dunn, J., & Davies, L. (2002). Support across two generations: Children's closeness to grandparents following parental divorce and remarriage. *Journal of Family Psychology, 16,* 363–376.

Manne, S. (1998). Cancer in the martial context: A review of the literature. *Cancer Investigation, 16,* 188–202.

Manne, S. L. (1999). Intrusive thoughts and psychological distress among cancer patients: The role of spouse avoidance and criticism. *Journal of Consulting and Clinical Psychology, 67,* 539–546.

Manne, S., Alfieri, T., Taylor, K., & Dougherty, J. (1999). Preferences for spousal support among individuals with cancer. *Journal of Applied Social Psychology, 29,* 722–749.

Manne, S., DuHamel, K., Nereo, N., Ostroff, J., Parsons, S., Martini, R., Williams, S., Mee, L., Sexson, S., Wu, L., Difede, J., & Redd, W. H. (2002). Predictors of PTSD in mothers of children undergoing bone marrow transplantation: The role of cognitive and social processes. *Journal of Pediatric Psychology, 27,* 607–617.

Manne, S., & Miller, D. (1998). Social support, social conflict, and adjustment among adolescents with cancer. *Journal of Pediatric Psychology, 23,* 121–130.

Manne, S. L., Pape, S. J., Taylor, K. L., & Dougherty, J. (1999). Spouse support, coping, and mood among individuals with cancer. *Annals of Behavioral Medicine, 21,* 111–121.

Manne, S., & Schnoll, R. (2001). Measuring supportive and unsupportive responses during cancer treatment: A factor analytic assessment of the partner responses to cancer inventory. *Journal of Behavioral Medicine, 24,* 297–321.

Manne, S. L., & Zautra, A. J. (1989). Spouse criticism and support: Their association with coping and psychological adjustment among women with rheumatoid arthritis. *Journal of Personality and Social Psychology, 56,* 608–617.

McCloskey, L. A., Figueredo, A. J., & Koss, M. P. (1995). The effects of systemic family violence on children's mental health. *Child Development, 66,* 1239–1261.

McCubbin, H. I., & Patterson, J. M. (1983). Family adaptation to crises. In H. I. McCubbin, A. E. Cauble, & J. M. Patterson (Eds.), *Family stress, coping, and social support* (pp. 26–47). Springfield, IL: Charles C Thomas.

McFarlane, A. C., & Yehuda, R. (1996). Resilience, vulnerability, and the course of posttraumatic reactions. In B. A. van der Kolk, A. C. McFarlane, & L. Weisaeth (Eds.), *Traumatic stress: The effects of overwhelming experience on mind, body, and society* (pp. 155–181). New York: Guilford.

Michultka, D., Blanchard, E. B., & Kalous, T. (1998). Responses to civilian war experiences: Predictors of psychological functioning and coping. *Journal of Traumatic Stress, 11,* 571–577.

Molassiotis, A., van den Akker, O. B., & Boughton, B. J. (1997). Perceived social support, family environment, and psychosocial recovery in bone marrow transplant long-term survivors. *Social Science and Medicine, 44,* 317–325.

Moos, R. H., & Moos, B. S. (1986). *Family environment scale manual.* Palo Alto, CA: Consulting Psychologists Press.

Nestmann, F., & Niepel, G. (1994). Social support in single-parent families: Children as sources of support. In F. Nestmann & K. Hurrelmann (Eds.), *Social networks and social support in children and adolescence* (pp. 323–345). New York: Walter de Gruyter.

Norbeck, J. S., Lindsey, A. M., & Carrieri, V. L. (1981). The development of an instrument to measure social support. *Nursing Research, 30,* 264–269.

Norris, F., & Murrell, S. (1987). Transitory impact of life-event stress on psychological symptoms in older adults. *Journal of Health and Social Behavior, 28,* 197–211.

Nott, K. H., Vedhara, K., & Power, M. J. (1995). The role of social support in HIV infection. *Psychological Medicine, 25,* 971–983.

Olson, D., Portner, J., & Bell, R. (1982). FACES II. In D. H. Olson, H. I. McCubbin, H. Barnes, A. Larsen, M. Muxen, & M. Wilson (Eds.), *Family inventories* (pp. 5–23). Minneapolis, MN: University of Minnesota Press.

Pierce, G. R., Sarason, B. R., Sarason, I. G., Joseph, H. J., & Henderson, C. A. (1996). Conceptualizing and assessing social support in the context of the family. In G. R. Pierce, B. R. Sarason, & I. G. Sarason (Eds.), *Handbook of social support and the family* (pp. 3–23). New York: Plenum.

Pillemer, K., & Suitor, J. (1996). Family stress and social support among caregivers to persons with Alzheimer's disease. In G. R. Pierce, B. R. Sarason, & I. G. Sarason (Eds.), *Handbook of social support and the family* (pp. 467–494). New York: Plenum.

Power, M. J., & Champion, L. A. (1991). The significant other scale. In D. Milne (Ed.), *Assessment: A mental health portfolio* (pp. 18–29). London: NFER-Nelson.

Procidano, M. E., & Heller, K. (1983). Measures of perceived social support from friends and from family: Three validation studies. *American Journal of Community Psychology, 11,* 1–24.

Rook, K. (1984). The negative side of social interactions: Impact on psychological well-being. *Journal of Personality and Social Psychology, 46,* 1097–1108.

Rossman, B. B. R., Bingham, R. D., & Emde, R. N. (1997). Symptomatology and adaptive functioning for children exposed to normative stressors, dog attack, and parental violence. *Journal of the American Academy of Child and Adolescent Psychiatry, 36,* 1089–1097.

Sack, W. H., McSharry, S., Clarke, G. N., Kinney, R., Seeley, J., & Lewinsohn, P. (1994). The Khmer adolescent project I: Epidemiologic findings in two generations of Cambodian refugees. *The Journal of Nervous and Mental Disease, 182,* 387–395.

Sarason, I. G., Levine, H. M., Basham, R. B., & Sarason, B. R. (1983). Assessing social support: The social support questionnaire. *Journal of Personality and Social Psychology, 44,* 127–183.

Sarason, B. R., Pierce, G. R., Bannerman, A., & Sarason, I. G. (1993). Investigating the antecedents of perceived social support: Parents' views of and behavior toward their children. *Journal of Personality and Social Psychology, 65,* 1071–1085.

Sarason, I. G., Sarason, B. R., Shearin, E. N., & Pierce, G. R. (1987). A brief measure of social support: Practical and theoretical implications. *Journal of Social and Personal Relationships, 4,* 497–510.

Siegel, K., Karus, D., & Raveis, V. H. (1996). Adjustment of children facing the death of a parent due to cancer. *Journal of the American Academy of Child & Adolescent Psychiatry, 35,* 442–450.

Siegel, K., Mesagno, F. P., Karus, D., Christ, G., Banks, K., & Moynihan, R. (1992). Psychosocial adjustment of children with a terminally ill parent. *Journal of the American Academy of Child and Adolescent Psychiatry, 31,* 327–333.

Solomon, Z. (2001). The impact of posttraumatic stress disorder in military situations. *Journal of Clinical Psychiatry, 62,* 11–15.

Stroebe, M. S., & Stroebe, W. (1983). Who suffers more? Sex differences in health risks of the widowed. *Psychological Bulletin, 93,* 279–301.

Suitor, J. J., & Pillemer, K. (1993). Support and interpersonal stress in the social networks of married daughters caring for parents with dementia. *Journal of Gerontology: Social Sciences, 48,* S1–S8.

Swindells, S., Mohr, J., Justis, J. C., Berman, S., Squier, C., Wagener, M. M., & Singh, N. (1999). Quality of life in patients with human immunodeficiency virus infection: Impact of social support, coping style, and hopelessness. *International Journal of STD and AIDS, 10,* 383–391.

Thoits, P. A. (1986). Social support as coping assistance. *Journal of Consulting and Clinical Psychology, 54,* 416–423.

Timko, C., Stovel, K., Moos, R. H., & Miller, J. J. (1992). Adaptation to juvenile rheumatoid disease: A controlled evaluation of functional disability with a one-year follow-up. *Health Psychology, 11,* 67–76.

Tucker, C. J. N., McHale, S., & Crouter, A. (2001). Conditions of sibling support in adolescence. *Journal of Family Psychology, 15(2),* 254–271.

United Nations. (2000). What the United Nations does for humanitarian assistance. Retrieved November 22, 2002 from http://www.un.org.Overbiew/brief4.html.

van Horn, K. R., & Cunegatto-Marques, J. (2000). Interpersonal relationships in Brazilian adolescents. *International Journal of Behavioral Development, 24,* 199–203.

von Weiss, R. T., Rapoff, M. A., Varni, J. W., Lindsley, C. B., Olson, N. Y., Madson, K. L., & Bernstein, B. H. (2002). Daily hassles and social support as predictors of adjustment in children with pediatric rheumatic disease. *Journal of Pediatric Psychology, 27,* 155–165.

Wan, C. K., Jaccard, J., & Ramey, S. (1996). Relationship between social support and life satisfaction as a function of family structure: An analysis of four types of support. *Journal of Marriage and the Family, 58,* 502–513.

Weiss, R. S. (1974). The provisions of social relationships. In Z. Rubin (Ed.), *Doing unto others* (pp. 17–26). Englewood Cliffs, NJ: Prentice-Hall.

Welch, A. S., Wadsworth, M. E., & Compas, B. E. (1996). Adjustment of children and adolescents to parental cancer. *Cancer, 77,* 1409–1418.

Wolchik, S. A., Ruehlman, L. S., Braver, S. L., & Sandler, I. N. (1989). Social support of children of divorce: Direct and stress buffering effects. *American Journal of Community Psychology, 17,* 485–501.

Wolchik, S. A., Sandler, I. N., & Braver, S. L. (1987). Social support: Its assessment and relation to children's adjustment. In N. Eisenberg (Ed.), *Contemporary topics in developmental psychology* (pp. 319–349). New York: Wiley.

Wortman, C. B., & Lehman, D. R. (1985). Reactions to victims of life crisis: Support attempts that fail. In I. G. Sarason & B. R. Sarason (Eds.), *Social Support: Theory, research, and applications* (pp. 463–489). Dordrecht, Netherlands: Martinus Nijhoff.

12

Research Assessing Couple and Family Therapies for Posttraumatic Stress Disorder

JAY LEBOW AND KATHLEEN NEWCOMB REKART

Couple and family therapies offer ways of responding to posttraumatic stress disorders (PTSD) that ecologically resonate with the problem in focus. Traumas do not just affect individuals; they also affect those who share the lives of the traumatized person, whether the trauma is recent or in the distant past. Often, the traumatic events themselves are shared by families. But there is precious little research assessing the outcomes of the numerous innovative couple and family approaches to the treatment of PTSD and no research at all assessing what matters in the process of these treatments.

What are we to make of this state of affairs? Should we take this to mean that couple and family approaches to treating PTSD sound interesting but fail to affect the problem? The answer to this question is almost certainly a resounding "no." A large body of work assessing the connection between PTSD and family points to the existence of powerful effects of PTSD on family members and equally powerful effects of family member's responses to PTSD. Clearly, families affect and are affected by PTSD. Furthermore, the much larger literature assessing the impact of couple and family therapy on other related disorders suggests the likelihood that research will show that couple and family therapies do have a significant impact on PTSD. Consistent with this expectation, the small number of existent studies assessing the effect of couple and family therapies on PTSD has found a positive impact of these treatments.

So what then explains the paucity of research assessing the effectiveness of couple and family therapies on PTSD? Although calling for some speculation, the answer to this question appears straightforward. PTSD typically has been thought of as an individual disorder, following the traditional psychiatric view of this disorder. Although there is a widespread recognition among clinicians and researchers regarding the impact of PTSD on families, the first generation of research on the treatment of PTSD has taken the simplest pathway, focusing exclusively on the individual with the disorder and building treatments for those individuals treated alone. The small number of researchers involved in this treatment research and the additional pragmatic complexity brought about by involving family members in treatment have added to the problem. Consequently, no major studies of couple and family therapies for PTSD have yet been conducted that are comparable to those that have been conducted on couple and family therapies for such problems as alcohol and substance abuse, major mental illness, or depression.

Given this background, we have extended this chapter beyond a mere review of the few studies assessing couple and family therapy for PTSD. We present the logical case for why it is likely that these treatments can be expected to have a positive effect on PTSD and on family members, based on the broader research that has probed the relationships between PTSD and family factors and the research assessing couple and family therapy. We will first review the research assessing the impact of PTSD on the family, then the research assessing the family's impact on PTSD and also some of the findings of research assessing the impact of couple and family therapy on other specific disorders. We will conclude with a summary of the small body of work assessing the impact of couple and family therapies on PTSD.

RESEARCH LINKING PTSD AND THE COUPLE/FAMILY

When one family member is suffering from any *DSM* Axis I disorder (e.g., substance abuse disorder, depression, or panic disorder), the whole family is likely to feel the effects. Of particular concern for clinicians and researchers is how such psychopathology affects and confers increased risk to others in the family system. In general, research suggests that if one member of a couple has a disorder, there is often increased tension and discord and decreased relationship satisfaction (Benazon, 2000; Collins, Maccoby, Steinberg, Hetherington, & Bornstein, 2000; Connell & Goodman, 2002). If a parent has a disorder, parenting abilities are often compromised, and when a child has a disorder, family life may become consumed by the child's difficulties (Benazon, 2000; Collins, Maccoby, Steinberg, Hetherington, & Bornstein, 2000; Connell & Goodman, 2002).

In many ways, PTSD affects the family much like any other disorder, yet in addition to dealing with a symptomatic family member, the family often must regroup in the wake of a trauma. Additionally, the *Diagnostic and Statistical Manual of Mental Disorders* (American Psychological Association, 1994) treats witnessing or learning about a tragic or life-threatening event that happened to a close friend or relative as tantamount to experiencing the event and qualifying for the diagnosis of PTSD. Thus, the line between the affected individual and the rest of the family can be much less distinct than with other disorders.

Impact of PTSD on the Couple/Family

The National Comorbidity Survey (Kessler, Sonnega, & Bromet, 1995) found a 7.8% lifetime prevalence of PTSD across all types of traumatic experiences. Moreover, the study reveals that the condition persists over many years for about one third of all PTSD cases, irrespective of treatment (Kessler et al., 1995). PTSD has been studied in a variety of populations (Brewin, Andrews, & Valentine, 2000). The largest group studied is composed of male combat veterans, while in civilian samples a major focus has been female assault victims (Nishith, Mechanic, & Resick, 2000). Some research indicates that family members of the person who directly experiences the trauma can themselves develop a PTSD. For example, mothers and fathers of childhood cancer survivors showed significantly higher levels of posttraumatic stress symptoms than comparison parents (Barakat et al., 1997; Kazak et al., 1997) Similar research indicates that PTSD may be among the most prevalent psychological comorbidities in families of children with spinal cord injury (Boyer, Knolls, Kafkalas, Tollen, & Swartz, 2000).

Figley (1988) has suggested four ways in which families are likely to be affected by trauma. *Simultaneous effects* refers to an event that happens to the whole family at the same time (i.e., a car accident, hurricane, or tornado). In this case, everyone who experiences the event faces a potential posttraumatic reaction. *Vicarious effects* describes the situation when an event happens to one family member who is out of contact with the rest of the family (i.e., at war or taken hostage). *Intrafamilial trauma* conveys the situation when one family member might have caused the trauma for another member (i.e., child abuse, incest, or domestic violence). And finally, *chiasmal effects* conveys what occurs when an event happens to one member but the subsequent stress affects the whole system.[1] Each of

---

1. *Editor's note*: Figley's earlier use of the term chiasmal effects has evolved into the more specific term secondary traumatic stress (STS) which he defines as "the experience of tension and distress directly related to the demands of living with and caring for someone who displays the symptoms of PTSD." He notes that STS can be "associated not only with the demands of a family member with PTSD but with a feeling of empathy for the traumatic experiences of the loved one" (Figley, 1998, p. 7).

these types of effects has implications for conceptualizing the ramifications of the disorder. It is conceivable that several of the effects might be operating within the same family. For example, if a mother and daughter were in a serious motor vehicle accident, the family might experience both simultaneous effects (i.e., mother and daughter) and chiasmal effects (son and father). While the kinds of family effects might depend on the traumatic event, the PTSD syndrome is a common denominator.

The symptoms of PTSD, as with the symptoms of other clinical disorders, can be very disruptive to family life. The three PTSD symptom clusters have implications for interpersonal relationships. Reexperiencing symptoms can affect the extent to which the affected individual can be a functioning member of the family. Reexperiencing symptoms underscores the fact that much of what the individual with PTSD is going through is a private, *internal* battle with the past. This can disrupt daily functioning, yet leave families without an understanding of the individual's behavior. This lack of understanding of the person's internal experience may create embarrassment, frustration, and alienation for the individuals and for their loved ones (Harkness & Zador, 2001; Johnson, 2002).

The emotional numbing and avoidance may cause the individual to appear cold or unfeeling toward family members. While to the individual this blunted affect is apparently uncontrollable, family and friends suffer the loss of the individual as an active participant in a mutually reinforcing and satisfying interpersonal relationship (see Harness & Zador, 2001; Johnson, 2002). In the absence of corrective information about why their loved one is behaving in such a cold manner, family members may make judgments and attributions that perpetuate family distress (Halford & Bouma, 1997; Johnson & Sims, 2000).

The hyperarousal symptoms have been related to arousal components of other anxiety disorders (Foa, Zinbarg, & Rothbaum, 1992), but they also include irritability, difficulty managing anger, sleep problems, and hypervigilance. Family members may have difficulty understanding the individual's anxiety and anger, and may bear the brunt of volatile tempers and angry outbursts. Additionally, volatile parental outbursts might both disrupt effective parenting and model aggression as a way of dealing with frustrations, contributing to child behavior problems (Connell & Goodman, 2002).

Thus, in insidious ways, PTSD may isolate sufferers from those who love them and create more problems for couples and families. It is not surprising that research suggests that PTSD is related to the intensity of marital discord (Johnson & Williams-Keeler, 1998), disrupted family functioning (Jordan et al., 1992; Solomon, Mikulincer, Freid, & Wosner, 1987), and child behavior problems (Jordan et al., 1992). For example, Jordan and colleagues (1992) examined interviews conducted in a nationally representative sample of 1,200 male Vietnam veterans and the spouses or partners of 376 of these veterans. Compared with families of male veterans without current PTSD, families of male veterans with current PTSD showed significantly more problems in marital and family adjustment, in parenting skills, and in violent behavior.

Spouses or partners may experience the burden of caring for the individual with PTSD (Beckham, Roodman, Barefoot, & Haney, 1996; Figley, 1998) and may develop psychiatric symptoms themselves (Jordan et al., 1992; Solomon, Gerrity, & Muff, 1992). For example, Verbosky and Ryan (1988) studied 23 female partners of Vietnam veterans receiving treatment for PTSD and discovered a significant relationship between PTSD symptoms and the female partner's poor self-esteem, limited coping skills, and ineffective overcompensation to deal with the problem. Additionally, the children of the veterans with PTSD appeared to be more at risk of developing behavior or psychiatric problems, or to be more likely to have behavioral problems than children of veterans without PTSD (Davidson, Smith, & Kudler, 1989; Jordan et al., 1992; Rosenheck & Nathan, 1985). There is considerable empirical evidence that families are affected by PTSD.

Family Impact on PTSD

Not all individuals exposed to a trauma develop PTSD. The social–cognitive processing theories of adaptation to traumatic life events (Horowitz, 1986; Janoff-Bulman, 1992; Pennebaker, 1989) suggest that traumatic life events challenge individuals' assumptions about themselves and their environment (e.g., their beliefs in a just world or personal vulnerability [Horowitz, 1986]), and having someone to talk to often helps individuals come to terms with, and move on from, traumatic experiences. Indeed, a meta-analysis of 85 data sets and 14 pretrauma and posttrauma risk factors revealed that a lack of social supports was one of three variables conveying the strongest risk of PTSD (Brewin, Andrews & Valentine, 2000). The effect size of social support on PTSD in this analysis was moderate (r = .40) in Cohen's (1988) terms suggesting a clear and important impact (far stronger than, for example, the effect size of smoking on developing cancer). Thus, social support, often defined as close confiding relationships with others, is a predictor of adjustment to trauma and of who develops the PTSD. Yet, characteristics of the family might influence whether or not the family is a valuable source of social support.

Figley (1998) suggests that family members are in a unique position to promote recovery of individuals from trauma. Helpful family members might be more apt to detect the presence of traumatic stress and to mobilize resources to deal with the stress, including getting the person professional help. Supportive family members can help the individual confront, revisit, and reinterpret the incident in a more adaptive manner (e.g., involving less negative self-judgment). A large body of research indicates that being able to count on others for social support helps individuals cope better with life stress and promotes psychological well-being (Cohen & Syme, 1985; Pierce, Sarason, & Sarason, 1996; Sarason, Sarason, & Gurung, 1997; Vaux, 1988a, 1988b). For example, Lavee, McCubbin, and Olson (1987) examined the effects of stressful life events on family relationships in a survey of 1,140 families and discovered that marital adjustment counteracted the effect of stressful experiences. Emotional support provided by spouses has been shown to be associated with better psychological adjustment when dealing with life-threatening illnesses like cancer (Manne & Glassman, 2000; Manne, Taylor, Dougherty, & Kemeny, 1997; Primomo, Yates, & Woods, 1990).

Protective factors identified in the research on children and adolescents exposed to violence include support from parents (Hill & Madhere, 1996; Kliewer, Lepore, Oskin, & Johnson, 1998), a high-quality parent–child relationship (Boney-McCoy & Finkelhor, 1996), and family cohesion (DuRant, Cadenhead, Pendergrast, Slavens, & Linder, 1994) are all important in adjustment. For example, data from the National Youth Victimization Prevention Study indicate that Victimization and poor parent-child relationships predicted PTSD symptoms, but that the latter appeared to be the more influential risk factor (Boney-McCoy & Finkelhor, 1996). Similarly, Kliewer and colleagues (1998) found that inner-city youths who had witnessed or experienced violence were less likely to report intrusive thoughts about the violence if they had high levels of support from their parents or felt they could talk to their parents about the violence they had experienced.

Yet, supporting a family member through a trauma may not be an easy task. In the wake of a traumatic event, family members may engage in (a) overtly unsupportive behaviors (e.g., excessive criticism of the individual), (b) intentionally helpful behaviors perceived as unsupportive (e.g., giving unsolicited advice), or (c) unintentionally unhelpful behaviors (e.g., avoiding the individual or conveying discomfort when he or she tries to talk about the traumatic experience) which may affect the availability of support (Dakof & Taylor, 1990; de Ruiter, de Haes, & Tempelaar, 1993; Manne & Glassman, 2000; Manne et al., 1997). The negative effects of these unsupportive behaviors have been found in individuals facing cancer (de Ruiter et al., 1993; Manne et al., 1997), coping with other serious illnesses (Manne & Zautra, 1989), and dealing with other stressful life events (Rook, 1984; Vinokur & Van Ryn, 1993).

Why are families unsupportive? One reason may be that individuals have difficulty managing their own responses to the trauma sequelae. Work by several researchers (Dunkel-Schetter, 1984; Wortman & Conway, 1985; Wortman & Dunkel-Schetter, 1987) with individuals coping with life-threatening illness suggests that family members may have negative emotional reactions which conflict with how they feel they should act around the individual (i.e., cheerful, optimistic); hence, they may (a) physically avoid the individual (b) avoid talking about the event with the individual or (c) minimize the severity of the individual's circumstances (see Dakoff & Taylor, 1990). Such responses may prevent the individual from being able to process the trauma openly with them. For example, the tendency toward minimization of the trauma has been demonstrated as extremely unhelpful in individuals diagnosed with cancer (Dakof & Taylor, 1990). It appears that the more family members can manage their own reactions to the trauma and understand what will be helpful, the more they will be able to provide the vital social support that can help ameliorate PTSD.

This brings the discussion full circle. The reactions of the traumatized individual and the other family members become connected in a circular process. The extent to which the family can support the individual is related to how well the family members manage their own reactions to the trauma, while specific features of the trauma and the affected member's symptom presentation affect the impact of the trauma on the family.

THE EFFECTIVENESS OF COUPLE AND FAMILY THERAPY

Research spanning 3 decades has documented the effectiveness of couple and family therapy. Numerous reviews (Alexander & Barton, 1995; Christensen & Heavey, 1999; Lebow & Gurman, 1995; Sandberg et al. 1997) and meta-analyses of the existent research (Stanton & Shadish, 1997) have shown couple and family therapy to have considerable effects. In the meta-analyses, the power of these effects is at least as strong as those for individual therapy. Couple and family therapies produce effect sizes in meta-analyses of about .65 in comparison with no treatment controls (Shadish & Baldwin, 2002). Typically, research shows two of three cases to have positive outcomes.

More specifically, couple and family therapies are the only therapies that have been shown to produce a significant impact on relational disorders. Numerous studies have shown couple therapy, in particular, to influence couple-relationship difficulties (Hahlweg & Markman, 1988; Johnson & Lebow, 2000). Indeed, a number of quite different conjoint couple therapies have been shown to be effective in reducing levels of marital distress (Sprenkle, 2002).

Conjoint Therapies for Individual Problems

These positive findings are also reflected in the research assessing the impact of couple and family therapy on specific Axis I disorders

(*DSM-IV*). Couple and family therapies have been found to be effective treatments for adult depression, anxiety, alcohol use disorder, substance use disorder, and major mental illness, and for child and adolescent conduct disorder, delinquency, substance use disorder, alcohol use disorder, anxiety, and depression (Sprenkle, 2002). Couple and family therapies appear to have quite extraordinary effects on several disorders, leading these therapies to emerge as treatments of choice for major mental illness, adolescent delinquency and substance abuse, and adult substance abuse, as well as in treating distressed couple relationships (Sprenkle, 2002; Gurman & Lebow, in press).

There now are numerous couple and family therapies that have sufficient research support to qualify as empirically supported therapies (ESTs). ESTs have been gaining increasing recognition among government, third-party payer, and care delivery systems as therapies that have been established as being effective in the treatment of specific disorders and difficulties. Couple and family therapies have emerged as ESTs for treating distressed marriages; for adolescent substance abuse and delinquency; for adult alcoholism, depression, and severe mental illness; for childhood conduct disorder, attention deficit disorder, anxiety, and depression; and for a number of problems involving physical health.

The inclusion of partners or spouses has become a very important aspect of the treatment of several disorders including depression, alcohol use disorder, substance use disorder, and anxiety (Sprenkle, 2002). Similarly, the involvement of family has a well-established effect in the treatment of virtually all child and adolescent disorders (Sprenkle, 2002). Research shows couple and family therapies to be especially helpful in those situations where the person who has the disorder does not recognize the difficulty or is reluctant to seek treatment, such as in substance abuse. In these situations, couple and family therapies can promote engagement and completion of treatment in many who would not otherwise engage in treatment (O'Farrell & Fals-Stewart 2002; O'Farrell & Fals-Stewart, 2000). Better engagement in treatment thereby becomes a route to greater levels of improvement.

The Advent of Integrative Approaches

It should be noted that the therapies involved in the great majority of research assessing the impact of couple and family therapy on specific disorders are of a particular kind. Although meta-analyses do not find differences between broad categorizations of couple and family therapy (as behavioral, structural, humanistic, etc.) in their effectiveness (Shadish & Baldwin, 2002), the great majority of studies that have been conducted assessing the impact of couple and family therapies involve integrative therapies (Lebow, 1997; Lebow, 1984). These therapies often include individual sessions with clients as well as sessions with the whole family. Confrontation in these therapies may be present but is rare, and paradoxical interventions are nowhere to be seen. Instead, what emerges is a kinder, gentler family therapy, grounded in the building of change over time rather than in single eventful moments. Most of the approaches which have acquired evidence for their effectiveness carefully nurture the building of alliances with family members. In marked contrast to the older vision of family therapies, most of these therapies freely mix individual, couple, family, and group session formats. In this context, family therapy becomes a systemic cabinet that includes many specific containers. The notion of seeing families all at once is replaced by the cobbling together of the most effective mix of session formats. Intervention strategies similarly combine structural, strategic, cognitive, behavioral, and systemic notions. What once was largely ideology has been replaced by a pragmatism centered on what works.

Limitations

Several caveats need to be added to this optimistic picture of the impact of couple and family therapy. The problems typically addressed with these therapies are quite difficult and it would be inappropriate to oversell the effects of these treatments. The small amount of research assessing the impact of couple and family therapy on relationships over long periods of follow-up indicates that the changes occurring may not be lasting when outcomes are considered over many years (Jacobson & Addis, 1993; Lebow & Gurman, 1995). It appears that such relationship difficulties are more appropriately thought of as often-recurring problems that require continued attention over time. Another limitation is that, while improvement can be expected in couple and family therapy, it is also quite difficult to move relationship difficulties in those receiving therapy to the levels in those who are not identified as troubled (Jacobson & Follette, 1985; Kazdin, 1999).

We should also note that many of the best known couple and family therapies have not been subject to research evaluation. There is almost no evidence for the effectiveness of a number of the most widely circulated couple and family therapies, including Bowen therapy, strategic therapy, narrative therapy, symbolic-experiential therapy, solution-focused therapy, Imago therapy, object relations therapy, psychodynamic therapies, intergenerational therapies, and a plethora of others that claim special effectiveness with specific groups of clients.[2] While this may have been a tolerable state of affairs in 1975, after 30 years of outcome research on couple and family therapies, it no longer remains acceptable. Finally, the large *Consumer Reports* study (Seligman, 1995) of psychotherapy indicates that for many, couple and family therapy may be a less acceptable form of therapy than individual therapy. A group of clients may not want to participate in couple or family therapy, or value it once in it, particularly in the absence of therapists with special training in these therapy formats.

RESEARCH ON THE IMPACT OF FAMILY AND COUPLE THERAPIES ON PTSD

While some early writing on family therapy for PTSD suggested that the family might be the desired context of treatment (Figley & Sprenkle, 1978; Stanton & Figley, 1978), there has been relatively little research focused on couple/family treatment of PTSD. However, the studies that have been conducted offer hope that this modality can be effective in ameliorating the effects of PTSD for both individuals and families.

As noted above, the distinction between individual treatments and couple/family treatments in the treatment of individual disorders is becoming increasingly blurry. In a review of couple and family therapies targeted at individual disorders, Baucom and colleagues (1998) classified these therapies into one of three broad types.

1. In the first type, couple or family therapy is used with the intent of assisting the treatment of an individual's disorder based on the principle that "the functioning of the couple or family contributes to the development or maintenance of individual symptoms" (Baucom, Shoham, Mueser, Daiuto, & Stickle, 1998).
2. In the second type, disorder-specific couple or family interventions "target the couple's or family's relationships, but only as they appear to directly influence either the disorder or its treatment" (Baucom et al. 1998, p.63).
3. In the third type, partner-assisted or family-assisted interventions (PFAIs) refer to interventions that involve the partner or family in a coaching role, assisting the identified patient in conducting therapy assignments outside the therapy session. In PFAIs, the couple or family relationships are "used to support the treatment plan, but these relationships are not a focus of the intervention" (Baucom et al., 1998, p. 63).

---

2. *Editor's note:* Many of these well-known approaches are presented in this volume. While we lack research support for their efficacy, there is still value in understanding the theoretical basis and application of these therapeutic models. It is hoped that this volume will spur further research in these areas.

Within this framework, existent research on couple/family treatments of PTSD has only included examples thus far of the first two kinds of intervention.

Emotionally Focused Therapy

In terms of ameliorating distress in the couple's relationship that might affect the development or maintenance of PTSD symptoms, pioneering research has been conducted utilizing Emotionally Focused Therapy (EFT; Greenberg & Johnson, 1988; Johnson & Greenberg, 1994, 1995). EFT is a short-term, structured approach aimed at repairing distressed relationships based on the rebuilding of attachment and the experiencing and processing of emotion. EFT helps partners examine and process their emotional responses to each other and change their interaction patterns to foster better interpersonal attachment and relationship functioning (Johnson & Williams-Keeler, 1998). EFT has a well-established record as a treatment for marital discord (Johnson & Lebow, 2000; Johnson, Hunsley, Greenberg, & Schindler, 1999; Baucom et al., 1998).

This approach has been successfully used in treating relationship distress that co-occurs with extreme stress due to chronic illness, sexual abuse, physical abuse, violent crime, natural disasters, and posttraumatic stress disorder (Johnson, 1989; Johnson & Williams-Keeler, 1998; Walker, Johnson, Manion, & Cloutier, 1996). For example, Walker, Johnson, Manion, and Cloutier (1996) conducted a randomized control trial assessing the efficacy of EFT in decreasing marital distress for 32 couples with chronically ill children. Couples were randomly assigned to EFT or to a wait-list control group. Results indicate that the 16 EFT couples demonstrated significant decreases in marital distress at posttreatment in comparison to the 16 control couples. These effects were statistically and clinically significant and were maintained at a 5-month follow-up. Improvements in marital functioning following EFT were also demonstrated (Walker et al., 1996).

Behavioral Family Therapy

In terms of couple or family interventions designed to improve the ways in which a couple or family interacts or addresses situations related to the individual's disorder, which might contribute to the maintenance or exacerbation of the disorder, at least one study has attempted to assess such family training in conjunction with individual treatment for PTSD. Behavioral family therapy (BFT; Falloon et al., 1985; Mueser & Glynn, 1995) adopts a skills-training approach in teaching families to best cope with individual disorders. BFT, although not widely researched for PTSD, has been found to reduce relapse rates and symtpoms in schizophrenia and other disorders (Falloon et al., 1982; Randolph, et al., 1994) in which the family's ability to manage the individual's symptoms appears to play a role in affecting the disorder.

With this rationale, Glynn and colleagues (1999) conducted the first randomized clinical trial of BFT in chronic combat-related PTSD. The treatment included (a) psychoeducation focusing on legitimizing the disorder; (b) problem-solving skills training, (c) anger-negative affect management instruction; and (d) a clear, well-articulated structure designed to support the adoption of modest expectations for change (Glynn et al., 1999). Results of this study indicate that BFT, when added to directed exposure to traumatic stimuli, did not produce additional symptom reduction beyond that offered by the exposure treatment, yet whether BFT alone might have been helpful was not tested (Glynn et al., 1999). Glynn and colleagues posit that the limited BFT effects may reflect an insufficient dosage to confront the profound difficulties faced by the families in their sample. They suggest that, in cases of more acute PTSD, in cases charactrized by high anxiety, and in cases where motivation to resume prior higher levels of functioning is strong, BFT might have a more powerful therapeutic role.

To sum up the general findings from the few studies researching couple and family therapies for PTSD, there is some indication that involving partners and families may help but there is very little research from which to draw. The study by Glynn et al. (1999) suggests that despite the strong indications that couple/family therapies have a natural fit with PTSD, we cannot simply assume that involving partners or family will contribute to positive outcomes beyond the impact of individual therapy for clients with PTSD. Much more research is needed to further elucidate the potential impact of couple/family therapy on PTSD. Of particular import may be treatments for PTSD designed to involve PFAIs that appear to be effective in other anxiety disorders. Research should also examine the effects of these treatments on partners and family as well as on the person with PTSD.

Impact on Other Anxiety Disorders

There is more research examining the impact of couple/family therapies on other anxiety disorders than there is on PTSD. The involvement of the partner or other family member in the treatment of agoraphobia has been evaluated as a means of improving treatment outcomes (see Baucom et al., 1998). In family-assisted treatment for agoraphobia, the family member helps to plan, carry out, and reinforce all exposure attempts

(Barlow & Waddell, 1985; Mathews, Teasdale, Munby, Johnston, & Shaw et al., 1977). Partner-assisted exposure therapy has been shown to be equivalent to comparison therapies (Baucom et al., 1998). Other studies indicate that viewing interpersonal relationships in an environmental context that may maintain phobic symptoms (Barlow & Waddell, 1985) and adding a communication skills training component (Arnow, Taylor, Agras, & Telch 1985) can improve on the effectiveness of exposure therapies (see Baucom et al., 1998).

The effect of involvement of the partner or other family member in the treatment of obsessive–compulsive disorder (OCD) has also been evaluated (see Baucom et al. 1998). A few studies suggest that including a family member in exposure treatment is no more or less effective in treating OCD, but helps in cases in which reinforcement by a significant other is likely to help the patient follow through with exposures to feared stimuli and compliance with treatment protocols (Emmelkamp, de Haan, & Hoogduin, 1990; Emmelkamp & de Lange, 1983; Mehta, 1990). There also is extensive evidence that family-based cognitive–behavioral therapies substantially affect anxiety disorders in children (Sprenkle, 2002).

CONCLUSION AND RECOMMENDATIONS

Couple and family therapies have an established track record of having considerable effects, both when viewed as a whole and in relation to a number of *DSM* Axis I disorders. Although there is little research directly assessing the impact of couple and family therapies on PTSD, the body of research on PTSD suggests that couple and family therapies are likely to have a unique and powerful role in the treatment of this disorder. It is clear that families are greatly affected by PTSD and to some extent share in the trauma. Family reactions to PTSD also have powerful effects on the person with the disorder. Research assessing the circular impact of PTSD and family factors strongly suggests the value of the development of couple and family therapies for PTSD and the likelihood that such treatments would positively affect both the individual with PTSD and the family system. Not surprisingly, several of the few available studies assessing couple and family therapies in relation to PTSD have found positive results.

Promising interventions. What kinds of intervention might be most promising, given what we know from the research on other disorders? Family psychoeducation about PTSD offers one obvious pathway. PTSD is a confusing disorder for family members. With other disorders that are confusing for family members, such as schizophrenia, bipolar disorder, and depression, an improved understanding about the disorder has proved very helpful (McFarlane, et al., 1995). Therapies that tap into emotion and the management of emotion also have proven very helpful in the context of work on marital distress and appear well suited to these difficulties (Johnson, 1996). So, too, do those therapies that accentuate the communication and acceptance of feeling states (Christensen & Jacobson, 2000). When individuals with PTSD are not able to see their own difficulty or seek treatment, the kinds of couple and family engagement procedures developed in the context of alcohol and substance use disorders also seem likely to be helpful (O'Farrell, 1996). It is important to note that it has been, primarily, engagement of spouses and family members in efforts to understand the problem, differentiate from it, and promote engagement in treatment that has been effective and not dramatic confrontation of the person with the disorder (O'Farrell & Fals-Stewart, 2002).

We should not take these limited findings to mean that couple and family therapies' impact on PTSD has been established. Determining the effectiveness of various couple and family therapies for PTSD awaits testing.

Future research. There are many crucial questions that need to be answered in future research involving couple and family treatments for PTSD. First, there are the questions concerned with establishing these treatments as effective. Can one or more family therapies be established to have a significant impact on PTSD? There also are questions about whether these approaches can produce unique outcomes. Do these therapies add unique benefits beyond individual therapy for PTSD? What is the impact of these therapies beyond their influence on the traumatized individual's impact on family members?

Additional questions center on treatment acceptability. How does client willingness to participate in these treatments compare with that in the individual-oriented approaches? Can the involvement of partners and family of those with PTSD help reluctant clients enter treatment and have successful outcomes? Still other questions center on the possible impacts of these treatments on others in the family beyond the individual with PTSD. Do couple and family approaches produce unique effects on couple and family relationships beyond the impact on the individual with PTSD (as they are in depression)?

Once treatments are established as effective, there remain questions concerning which components are most potent. What are the crucial components of interventions that drive the positive effects? What techniques and approaches with couples and families have the most impact? Then there are questions concerned with individual differences in response to treatments. Does the nature of the trauma make a difference in outcomes? Does it make a difference if the trauma has been shared by the family or not? Does the gender or culture of family members make a difference? All these questions remain to be examined.

Couple and family therapy show great promise as treatments for PTSD. We await the next few decades of research that will fill in our knowledge about the effects of these treatments on this set of difficulties.

SUMMARY

A large body of work assessing the connection between PTSD and family points to the existence of powerful effects from PTSD on family members and of the equally powerful effects of family members' responses to PTSD. The literature assessing the impact of couple and family therapy on other related disorders suggests the likelihood that when research is conducted assessing couple and family therapies for PTSD, the impact will be positive. The few existent studies that assess the effect of couple and family therapies on PTSD offer hope that systemic treatment modalities will prove effective in ameliorating the symptoms and effects of PTSD for the individual and for the family.

REFERENCES

Alexander, J. F., & Barton, C. (1995). Family therapy research. In R. H. Mikesell, D. D. Lusterman, & S.H. McDaniel (Eds.), *Integrating family therapy: Handbook of family psychology and systems theory* (pp. 199–215). Washington, DC: American Psychological Association.

American Psychological Association. (1994). *Diagnostic and statistical manual of mental disorders* (4th ed.). Washington, DC: Author.

Arnow, B. A., Taylor, C. B., Agras, W. S., & Telch, M.J. (1985). *Enhancing agoraphobia treatment outcome by changing couple communication patterns. Behavior Therapy, 14,* 339–348.

Barakat, L. P., Kazak, A. E., Meadows, A. T., Casey, R., Meeske, K., & Stuber, M. L. (1997). Families surviving childhood cancer: A comparison of posttraumatic stress symptoms with families of healthy children. *Journal of Pediatric Psychology, 22,* 843–859.

Barlow, D. H., & Waddell, M. T. (1985). Agoraphobia. In D. H. Barlow (Ed.), *Clinical handbook of psychological disorders: A step-by-step treatment manual* (pp. 1–68). New York: Guilford.

Baucom, D. H., Shoham, V., Mueser, K. T., Daiuto, A. D., & Stickle, T. R. (1998). Empirically supported couple and family interventions for marital distress and adult mental health problems. *Journal of Consulting and Clinical Psychology, 66,* 53–88.

Beckham, J. C., Roodman, A. A., Barefoot, J. C., & Haney, T. L. (1996). Interpersonal and self-reported hostility among combat veterans with and without posttraumatic stress disorder. *Journal of Traumatic Stress, 9,* 335–342.

Benazon, N. R. (2000). Predicting negative spousal attitudes toward depressed persons: A test of Coyne's Interpersonal Model. *Journal of Abnormal Psychology, 109*(3), 550–554.

Boney-McCoy, S., & Finkelhor, D. (1995). Psychosocial sequelae of violent victimization in a national youth sample. *Journal of Consulting and Clinical Psychology, 63,* 726–736.

Boney-McCoy, S., & Finkelhor, D. (1995). Is youth victimization related to trauma symptoms and depression after controlling for prior symptoms and family relationships? A longitudinal, prospective study. *Journal of Consulting and Clinical Psychology, 64,* 1406-1416.

Boyer, B. A., Knolls, M. L., Kafkalas, C. M., Tollen, L. G., & Swartz, M. (2000). Prevalence and relationships of posttraumatic stress in families experiencing pediatric spinal cord injury. *Rehabilitation Psychology, 45,* 339–355.

Brewin, C. R., Andrews, B., & Valentine, J. D. (2000). Meta-analysis of risk factors for post-traumatic stress disorder in trauma-exposed adults. *Journal of Consulting and Clinical Psychology, 68*, 748–766.

Christensen, A., & Heavey, C. L. (1999). Interventions for couples. *Annual Review of Psychology, 50*, 165–190.

Christensen, A., & Jacobson, N. S. (2000). *Reconcilable differences.* New York: Guilford.

Cohen, J. (1988). Statistical power analysis for the behavioral sciences (2nd ed.). Hillsdale, NJ: Erlbaum.

Cohen, S., & Syme, S. (1985). Issues in the study and application of social support. In S. Cohen & S. L. Syme (Eds.), *Social support and health* (pp. 3–22). San Diego, CA: Academic Press.

Collins, W., Maccoby, E. E., Steinberg, L., Hetherington, E., & Bornstein, M. H. (2000). Contemporary research on parenting: The case for nature and nurture. *American Psychologist, 55*, 218–232.

Connell, A. M., & Goodman, S. H. (2002). The association between psychopathology in fathers versus mothers and children's internalizing and externalizing behavior problems: A meta-analysis. *Psychological Bulletin, 128*, 746–773.

Dakof, G., & Taylor, S. E. (1990). Victims' perceptions of social support: What is helpful from whom? *Journal of Personality and Social Psychology, 58*(2), 80–89.

Davidson, J. R., Smith, R. D., & Kudler, H. S. (1989). Familial psychiatric illness in chronic posttraumatic stress disorder. *Comprehensive Psychiatry, 30*, 339–345.

de Ruiter, J. H., de Haes, J. C., & Tempelaar, R. (1993). Cancer patients and their network: The meaning of the social network and social interactions for quality of life. *Supportive Care in Cancer, 1*(3), 152–155.

Dunkel-Schetter, C. (1984). Social support and cancer: Findings based on patient interviews and their implications. *Journal of Social Issues, 40*(4), 77–98.

DuRant, R. H., Cadenhead, C., Pendergrast, R. A., Slavens, G., & Linder, C.W. (1994). Factors associated with the use of violence among urban Black adolescents. *American Journal of Public Health, 84*, 612–617.

Emmelkamp, P., de Haan, E., & Hoogduin, C. (1990). Marital adjustment and obsessive-compulsive disorder. *British Journal of Psychiatry, 156*, 55–60.

Emmelkamp, P., & de Lange, I. (1983). Spouse involvement in the treatment of obsessive-compulsive patients. *Behaviour Research and Therapy, 21*, 341–346.

Falloon, I. R., Boyd, J. L., McGill, C. W., Razani, J., Moss, H. B., & Gilderman, A. M. (1982). Family management in the prevention of exacerbations of schizophrenia: A controlled study. *New England Journal of Medicine, 306*, 1437–1440.

Falloon, I. R., McGill, C. W., Williamson, M., Razani, J., Moss, H. B., Gilderman, A. M. & Simpson, G. M. (1985). Family management in the prevention of morbidity of schizophrenia: Clinical outcome of a two-year longitudinal study. *Archives of General Psychiatry, 42*, 887–896.

Figley, C. R. (1988) Post-traumatic family therapy. In F. M. Ochberg (Ed.) Post-traumatic therapy and victims of violence (pp. 83-110). New York: Brunner/Mazel.

Figley, C. R. (1988). A five-phase treatment of post-traumatic stress disorder in families. *Journal of Traumatic Stress, 1*, 127–141.

Figley, C. R. (Ed.). (1998). *Burnout in families: The systemic costs of caring.* Boca Raton, FL: CRC Press.

Figley, C. R., & Sprenkle, D. H. (1978). Delayed stress response syndrome: Family therapy indications. *Journal of Marital and Family Therapy, 4*(3), 53–60.

Foa, E. B., Zinbarg, R., & Rothbaum, B. O. (1992). Uncontrollability and unpredictability in post-traumatic stress disorder: An animal model. *Psychological Bulletin, 112*, 218–238.

Glynn, S. M., Eth, S., Randolph, E. T., Foy, D. W., Urbaitis, M., Boxer, L., Paz, G.G., Leong, G. B., Firman, G., Salk, J. D., Katzman, J. W., & Crothers, J. (1999). A test of behavioral family therapy to augment exposure for combat-related posttraumatic stress disorder. *Journal of Consulting and Clinical Psychology, 67*, 243–251.

Greenberg, L. S., & Johnson, S. M. (1988). *Emotionally focused therapy for couples.* New York: Guilford.

Gurman, A. S. & Lebow, J. (in press) Couple and family therapy. In Sadock, H. & Sadock, R., *Comprehensive Textbook of Psychiatry VIII,* New York: Williams & Wilkins.

Hahlweg, K., & Markman, H. J. (1988). Effectiveness of behavioral marital therapy: Empirical status of behavioral techniques in preventing and alleviating marital distress. *Journal
of Consulting and Clinical Psychology, 56,* 440–447.

Halford, W., & Bouma, R. (1997). Individual psychopathology and marital distress. In W. K.
Halford & H. J. Markman (Eds.), *Clinical handbook of marriage and couples interventions*
(pp. 291–321). New York: John Wiley & Sons.

Harkness, L., & Zador, N. (2001). Treatment of PTSD in families and couples. In J. P. Wilson,
M. J. Friedman, & J. D. Lindy (Eds.), *Treating psychological trauma and PTSD* (pp.
335–353). New York: Guilford.

Hill, H. M., & Madhere, S. (1996). Exposure to community violence and African-American
children: A multidimensional model of risks and resources. *Journal of Community Psychology, 24,* 26–43.

Horowitz, M. J. (1986). Stress-response syndromes: A review of posttraumatic and adjustment disorders. *Hospital and Community Psychiatry, 37,* 241–249.

Jacobson, N. S., & Addis, M. E. (1993). Research on couples and couple therapy: What do we
know? Where are we going? *Journal of Consulting and Clinical Psychology, 61,* 85–93.

Jacobson, N. S., & Follette, W. C. (1985). Clinical significance of improvement resulting from
two behavioral marital therapy components. *Behavior Therapy, 16,* 249–262.

Janoff-Bulman, R. (1992). *Shattered assumptions: Towards a new psychology of trauma.*
New York: Free Press.

Johnson, S., & Lebow, J. (2000). The "coming of age" of couple therapy: A decade review.
Journal of Marital and Family Therapy, 26, 23–38.

Johnson, S., & Sims, A. (2000). Attachment theory: A map for couples therapy. In T. M. Levy
(Ed.), *Handbook of attachment interventions* (pp. 169–191). San Diego, CA: Academic Press.

Johnson, S. M. (1989). Integrating marital and individual therapy for incest survivors: A
case study. *Psychotherapy, 26,* 96–103.

Johnson, S. M. (1996). *The practice of emotionally focused marital therapy: Creating connection.*
Philadelphia: Brunner/Mazel.

Johnson, S. M. (2002). *Emotionally focused couple therapy with trauma survivors: Strengthening
attachment bonds.* New York: Guilford.

Johnson, S. M., & Greenberg, L. S. (1995). The emotionally focused approach to problems in
adult attachment. In N. S. Jacobson & A. S. Gurman (Eds.), *Clinical handbook of couple
therapy* (pp. 121–141). New York: Guilford.

Johnson, S. M., & Greenberg, L. S. (Eds.). (1994). *The heart of the matter: Perspectives on emotion in marital therapy.* New York: Brunner/Mazel.

Johnson, S. M., Hunsley, J., Greenberg, L., & Schindler, D. (1999). Emotionally focused couples therapy: Status and challenges. *Clinical Psychology—Science and Practice, 6,* 67–79.

Johnson, S. M., & Williams-Keeler, L. (1998). Creating healing relationships for couples dealing with trauma: The use of emotionally focused marital therapy. *Journal of Marital and
Family Therapy, 24,* 25–40.

Jordan, B., Marmar, C. R., Fairbank, J. A., Schlenger, W. E., Kulka, R.A., Hough, R.L. &
Weiss, D.A. (1992). Problems in families of male Vietnam veterans with posttraumatic
stress disorder. *Journal of Consulting and Clinical Psychology, 60,* 916–926.

Kazak, A. E., Barakat, L. P., Meeske, K., Christakis, D., Meadows, A. T., Penati, B., & Stuber,
M. L.(1997). Posttraumatic stress, family functioning, and social support in survivors of
childhood leukemia and their mothers and fathers. *Journal of Consulting and Clinical Psychology, 65,* 120–129.

Kazdin, A. E. (1999). The meanings and measurement of clinical significance. *Journal of Consulting and Clinical Psychology, 67*(3), June 1999, 52–92.

Kessler, R., Sonnega, A., & Bromet, E. (1995). Posttraumatic stress disorder in the national
comorbidity survey. *Archives of General Psychiatry, 52,* 1048–1060.

Kliewer, C., & Drake, S. (1998). Disability, eugenics, and the current ideology of segregation:
A modern moral tale. *Disability and Society, 13,* 95–111.

Kliewer, W., Lepore, S. J., Oskin, D., & Johnson, P. D. (1998). The role of social and cognitive
processes in children's adjustment to community violence. *Journal of Consulting and Clinical Psychology, 66,* 199-209.

Lavee, Y., McCubbin, H. I., & Olson, D. H. (1987). The effect of stressful life events and transitions on family functioning and well-being. *Journal of Marriage and the Family, 49,* 857–873.

Lebow, J. (1997). The integrative revolution in couple and family therapy. *Family Process, 36,* 1–17.

Lebow, J. L. (1984). On the value of integrating approaches to family therapy. *Journal of Marital and Family Therapy, 10,* 127–138.

Lebow, J. L., & Gurman, A. S. (1995). Research assessing couple and family therapy. *Annual Review of Psychology, 46,* 27–57.

Manne, S., & Glassman, M. (2000). Perceived control, coping efficacy, and avoidance coping as mediators between spousal unsupportive behaviors and psychological distress. *Health Psychology, 19*(2), 155–164.

Manne, S. L., Taylor, K. L., Dougherty, J., & Kemeny, N. (1997). Supportive and negative responses in the partner relationship: Their association with psychological adjustment among individuals with cancer. *Journal of Behavioral Medicine, 20*(2), 101–125.

Manne, S. L., & Zautra, A. J. (1989). Spouse criticism and support: Their association with coping and psychological adjustment among women with rheumatoid arthritis. *Journal of Personality and Social Psychology, 56,* 608–617.

Mathews, A. M., Teasdale, J., Munby, M., Johnston, D., & Shaw, P. (1977). A home-based treatment program for agoraphobia. *Behavior Therapy, 8,* 915–924.

McFarlane, W. R., Lukens, E., Link, B., Dushay, R., Deakins, S. A., Newmark, M., DSunne, E. J., Horen, B., & Toran, J. (1995). Multiple-family groups and psychoeducation in the treatment of schizophrenia. *Archives of General Psychiatry, 52,* 679–687.

Mehta, M. (1990). A comparative study of family-based and patient-based behavioral management in obsessive-compulsive disorder. *British Journal of Psychiatry, 157,* 133–135.

Mueser, K. T., & Glynn, S. M. (1995). *Behavioral family therapy for psychiatric disorders.* New York: Simon & Schuster.

Nishith, P., Mechanic, M. B., & Resick, P. A. (2000). Prior interpersonal trauma: The contribution to current PTSD symptoms in female rape victims. *Journal of Abnormal Psychology, 109,* 20–25.

O'Farrell, T. J. (1996). Marital and family therapy in the treatment of alcoholism. In *The Hatherleigh guides series: Vol. 7. The Hatherleigh guide to treating substance abuse Part 1* (pp. 101–127). New York: Hatherleigh.

O'Farrell, T. J., & Fals-Stewart, W. (2000). Behavioral couples therapy for alcoholism and drug abuse. *Behavior Therapist, 23*(3), 70.

O'Farrell, T. J., & Fals-Stewart (2002) Alcohol abuse. In D. Sprenkle (Ed.) Effectiveness research in marriage and family therapy (123-161). Washington, DC: American Association for Marriage and Family Therapy.

Pennebaker, J. W. (1989). Confesssion, inhibition, and disease. In L. Berkowitz (Ed.) *Advances in experimental social psychology: Vol. 22. Confession, inhibition, and disease* (pp. 211–244). Orlando, FL: Academic Press.

Pierce, G. R., Sarason, I. G., & Sarason, B. R. (1996). Coping and social support. In M. Zeidner & N. S. Endler (Eds.), *Handbook of coping: Theory, research, applications* (pp. 434–451). New York: Wiley.

Primomo, J., Yates, B. C., & Woods, N. F. (1990). Social support for women during chronic illness: The relationship among sources and types to adjustment. *Research in Nursing and Health, 13,* 153–161.

Randolph, E. T., Eth, S., Glynn, S. M., Paz, G. G., Leong, G. B., Shaner, A. L., Strachan, A., Van Vort, W., Escobar, J. L., & Liberman, R. P. (1994). Behavioural family management in schizophrenia: Outcome of a clinic-based intervention. *British Journal of Psychiatry, 164,* 501–506.

Rook, K. S. (1984). The negative side of social interaction: Impact on psychological well-being. *Journal of Personality and Social Psychology, 46,* 1097–1108.

Rosenheck, R., & Nathan, P. (1985). Secondary traumatization in children of Vietnam veterans. *Hospital and Community Psychiatry, 36,* 538–539.

Sandberg, J. G., Johnson, L. N., Dermer, S. B., Gfeller-Strouts, L. L., Seibold, J. M., Stringer-Seibold, T. A., Hutchings, J.B., Andrews, R.L., & Miller, R.B. (1997). Demonstrated efficacy of models of marriage and family therapy: An update of Gurman, Kniskern, and Pinsof's chart. *American Journal of Family Therapy, 25*(2), 121-137.

Sarason, B. R., Sarason, I. G., & Gurung, R. A. (1997). Close personal relationships and health outcomes: A key to the role of social support. In S. Duck (Ed.), *Handbook of personal relationships: Theory, research, and interventions* (2nd ed.) (pp. 547–573). New York: Wiley.

Seligman, M. E. P. (1995). The effectiveness of psychotherapy: The Consumer Reports study. *American Psychologist, 50*, 965-974.

Shadish, W. R. & Baldwin, S. A. (2002). Meta-analysis of MFT interventions. In D. Sprenkle (Ed.), *Effectiveness research in marriage and family therapy* (pp. 339–370). Washington DC: American Association for Marriage and Family Therapy.

Solomon, S. D., Gerrity, E. T., & Muff, A. M. (1992). Efficacy of treatments for posttraumatic stress disorder. An empirical review. *The Journal of the American Medical Association, 268*, 633–638.

Solomon, Z., Mikulincer, M., Freid, B., & Wosner, Y. (1987). Family characteristics and posttraumatic stress disorder: A follow-up of Israeli combat stress reaction casualties. *Family Process, 26*, 383–394.

Sprenkle, D. (2002) *Effectiveness research in marriage and family therapy.* Washington DC: American Association for Marriage and Family Therapy.

Stanton, M. D., & Figley, C. R. (1978). Treating the Vietnam veteran within the family system. In C. R. Figley (Ed.), *Stress disorders among Vietnam veterans: Theory, research, and treatment* (pp. 281–290). New York: Brunner/Mazel.

Stanton, M. D., & Shadish, W. R. (1997). Outcome, attrition, and family-couples treatment for drug abuse: A meta-analysis and review of the controlled, comparative studies. *Psychological Bulletin, 122*, September 1997, 170-191.

Vaux, A. (1988a). Social and emotional loneliness: The role of social and personal characteristics. *Personality and Social Psychology Bulletin, 14*, 722–734.

Vaux, A. (1988b). *Social support: Theory, research, and intervention.* New York: Praeger.

Verbosky, S. J., & Ryan, D. A. (1988). Female partners of Vietnam veterans: Stress by proximity. *Issues in Mental Health Nursing, 9*(1), 95–104.

Vinokur, A. D., & Van Ryn, M. (1993). Social support and undermining in close relationships: Their independent effects on the mental health of unemployed persons. *Journal of Personality and Social Psychology, 65*, 350–359.

Walker, J. G., Johnson, S., Manion, I., & Cloutier, P. (1996). Emotionally focused marital intervention for couples with chronically ill children. *Journal of Consulting and Clinical Psychology, 64*, 1029–1036.

Wortman, C. B., & Conway, T. L. (1985). The role of social support in adaptation and recovery from physical illness. In S. Cohen & S. L. Syme (Eds.), *Social support and health* (pp. 281–302). San Diego, CA: Academic Press.

Wortman, C. B., & Dunkel-Schetter, C. (1987). Conceptual and methodological issues in the study of social support. In A. Baum & J. E. Singer (Eds.), *Handbook of psychology and health: Vol. 5. Stress* (pp. 63–108). Hillsdale, NJ: Erlbaum.

Part III

PRACTICE

13

Assessment and Treatment of Trauma From a Bowen Family Systems Theory Perspective

STEVEN M. HARRIS AND GLADE L. TOPHAM

Writing on a Bowen Family Systems (BFS) approach to the assessment and treatment of traumatized families is a task that presents some interesting challenges. Little has been written in terms of problem-specific applications of Bowen theory, although some notable publications do exist (see Titelman, 1998). In his own writings, Murray Bowen expressed concern over the tendency for theory to become secondary to technique. He worried that, for some, a focus on technique could become more important than fidelity to theory. He also stressed that the most important component of successful therapy was the therapist's own understanding of the theory and the therapist's willingness to apply the theoretical concepts to self. For these reasons, Bowen devoted his attention primarily to theory and spent little time on specific applications.

BFS theory posits a general paradigm, or overarching theory, for understanding and treating human problems. Regardless of the nature of the traumatic event experienced by the family or current symptomatology with which the family presents to treatment, there is little variability in the approach to assessment and treatment in a BFS framework. Instead of the location or form of the symptom as a primary concern, more attention is placed on emotional process. For this reason there is little value within this approach for specialization according to presenting problems or symptoms (Friedman, 1991).

Bowen theory's contribution to the assessment and treatment of trauma is primarily to help the mental health professional understand how family emotional process influences one's experience of trauma. It emphasizes the core treatment issue as differentiation of self and, while acknowledging the impact of traumatic events, chooses not to make them the sole focus of treatment. A crisis-intervention stage of treatment focuses on immediate needs of stabilization and safety planning, but the longer-term goals often associated with psychotherapy are somewhat analogous to what Bowen referred to as a process of emotional differentiation.

NATURAL SYSTEMS ENCOMPASS ALL LIFE

BFS theory focuses on natural systems or systems embedded in nature, attempting to solidify a number of unifying principles that might explain a range of systemic phenomena discovered in cells, ant colonies, and human families. Bowen contended that these systemic processes could be as easily observed in human families as they could at a cellular (or any other) level found in nature (Kerr, 1981). With such a strong emphasis on nature, Bowen spoke clearly about humans' connection to other types of life forms, specifically:

> Bowen's assumption was that family relationship processes had been created from an evolutionary mold and their importance to the relationship between living things was probably well-established long before the emergence of the *homo sapiens*. (Kerr & Bowen, 1988, p. 10)

One of the key features that appears to distinguish humans from other species is the separation of functioning found in a human brain. Friedman (1991) notes that there is a crucial distinction between the human's neocortex and the limbic system of the brain. In humans there seems to exist an almost never-ending tension between evolution and reactivity (from the limbic system of the brain) and higher levels of operating (those which develop in the neocortex). The limbic system has as its main function all aspects related to survival. This system's primary functions include the origins of pain, pleasure, sexual feelings, anger, rage, fear, etc. Some have called this particular part of the brain the *emotional brain*. The neo-cortex, however, has primary responsibility for cognitive functioning and can override the impulses of the limbic system. Without intervention of the neo-cortex, actions will be based solely on emotional reactivity.

Two Life Forces

Bowen theory contends that two life forces continually influence all human interactions, a force toward autonomy and a force toward inclusion. Other names such as individuality and togetherness, individuation and community, or separation and connection also describe these forces. These terms have been used to describe maternal–infant bonding (Ainsworth, Blehar, Waters, & Wall, 1978; Bowlby, 1969, 1973), family life-cycle trends (Carter & McGoldrick, 1980), individual adult development (Kegan, 1982) and interfamilial processes (Roberto, 1991; Kerr & Bowen, 1988; Neil & Kniskern, 1982; Whitaker & Keith, 1981). Bowen suggested that these two life forces influence every living system. Kerr (1981) offers examples from cellular biology, entomology, and human behavior to illustrate that these forces seem to know no boundaries and seem to operate in a universal manner.

BFS theory is concerned with family emotional process and the variables that influence it. The degree to which an individual is influenced more by one force than the other (i.e., fusion or cutoff) has implications for how an individual experiences relationships. BFS theory suggests that these forces influence all behaviors within family systems and that an individual's mental and emotional health and a family's emotional climate depend on an individual's ability to negotiate these life forces via a process of differentiation.

ASSESSMENT

BFS theory identifies emotional process within a family as the primary mediator for all traumatic or stressful events, whether internal or external to the family and regardless of the severity of the trauma. Family emotional process is the primary influence in determining the impact of traumatic and stressful events on members of a family. Therefore, the primary focus of assessment is placed not on the nature of the traumatic event but on distinguishing and understanding family emotional process as it influences the family's experience of the trauma (Harris & Busby, 1997).

Five Central Concepts

The central concepts of BFS theory are differentiation, chronic anxiety, emotional triangles, nuclear family emotional systems, and multigenerational emotional process. These five concepts are interdependent—an understanding of one of the concepts is incomplete without understanding the other four and their interrelatedness (Friedman, 1991). A thorough family evaluation requires attention to all five concepts. The first two concepts, differentiation and chronic anxiety, are the keystones of BFS theory and are the primary focus of assessment and treatment. The other three concepts describe how a person's level of differentiation and chronic anxiety influence, or are influenced by, the emotional process of his or her family.

Differentiation The most basic of the five concepts is the concept of *differentiation*. An individual's level of differentiation is defined by his or her ability to distinguish between the feeling process and the intellectual process and to choose which will guide his or her behavior (Kerr & Bowen, 1988). Differentiation is the ability to make self-directed choices and to be aware of and act according to one's own values and goals, rather than reacting to the emotional climate of relationships or to conditions external to the individual. The lower the level of an individual's differentiation, the more likely the individual is to *fuse* into relationships and to depend on the relationship to provide him or her with a sense of identity and self-worth. Those with low levels of differentiation are tightly connected to, and highly reactive to, emotional process in relationships. They may take responsibility for others' emotional reactions and set aside individual feelings and wishes to preserve harmony in relational systems (Brown, 1999). Or they may take no responsibility for others' emotional reactions, put their autonomy ahead of relational concerns and fail to recognize that their choices are still restricted and they are still controlled by relationships (like the willful adolescent who is compelled to do the opposite of what he is told). In contrast, those with higher levels of differentiation are more self-directed and less reactive. Instead of being driven by automatic reactions, their responses will largely be objectively thought through and self-determined (Kerr & Bowen, 1988). Those with high levels of differentiation are able to maintain emotional contact with the system without having to attack others or defend themselves. These people have clear boundaries and take responsibility for their own emotional well-being instead of blaming others or circumstance for their problems (Friedman, 1991).

Assessment of an individual's level of differentiation is challenging because the level of differentiation that is manifest by an individual—*functional* differentiation—is not necessarily representative of an individual's core level of differentiation—*basic* differentiation. Functional differentiation changes according to relationship processes and is dependent upon many factors including level of stress, amount of social support, how the system adapts to reduce anxiety, and what role the individual plays in that process. As any or all of these factors change, the functional level also changes.

In contrast, basic differentiation is stable and relatively unchanging. Basic differentiation is influenced by the degree of emotional separation an individual achieves from his or her family of origin and is fairly well established by the time a child reaches adolescence (Kerr & Bowen, 1988). Positive change in one's basic level of differentiation requires focused and systematic effort. It is basic differentiation that is of most interest to BFS therapists because basic differentiation is an indication of an individual's adaptiveness to external conditions. Functional differentiation, on the other hand, is more reflective of the conditions in which the individual exists and is not necessarily an enduring characteristic of the individual. Positive changes in basic differentiation make the individual more adaptive to stress. Changes in functional differentiation (i.e., changes in conditions or circumstances) may reduce anxiety in the present but leave the individual just as vulnerable to later stress and trauma.

Kerr and Bowen (1988) suggest that basic differentiation can be assessed by "evaluating both a person's average level of functioning over a lifetime and the average level of functioning of those closely involved with him" (p. 100). They state that notable differences in level of functional differentiation among individuals in a relationship system suggest that members of the system may be "borrowing" self from others in the system; thus, averaging functional levels both across individuals in the system and across time helps to uncover basic levels of differentiation.

Chronic Anxiety In order to understand the impact of traumatic events on family systems it is important to distinguish between two very different forms of anxiety: acute anxiety and chronic anxiety. Acute anxiety occurs in response to stressors which are real and typically time-limited. These stressors can range from minor, frequently experienced stress to intense trauma. Chronic anxiety is generally an automatic (unmediated by the cerebral cortex) response to an imagined threat (e.g., the fear that openly discussing a family death will be destructive to family members) and is not time-limited. It is fear of what might be instead of what is (Kerr & Bowen, 1988).

A child tends to develop a level of chronic anxiety similar to the average level of chronic anxiety of the family in which he or she grew up. The amount of chronic anxiety that is developed, however, might differ among children depending on how involved the children are in the family emotional process. The more involved a particular child is in the emotional process of the family, the more dependent the child becomes on family relationships and the more anxiety he or she develops (Kerr & Bowen, 1988).

The concepts of chronic anxiety and differentiation are interdependent. The amount of chronic anxiety experienced is largely dependent upon level of differentiation—the lower an individual's level of differentiation, the higher the individual's average level of chronic anxiety over time. Individuals with a low level of differentiation depend upon others for validation and a sense of worth and well-being. This dependence causes the individual to be highly sensitive and vulnerable to emotional process in relationships. An individual with a low level of differentiation tends to absorb and amplify the stress and anxiety that is experienced within these relationships. The individual reacts not just to what is occurring in the relationship but to what he or she imagines or fears will occur. This emotional reactivity is the essence of chronic anxiety. For a person with a high level of chronic anxiety or emotional reactivity, a small breeze in the emotional climate may be experienced as a full-scale tornado.

Individuals with relatively high levels of differentiation take responsibility for their own well-being and act in self-directed ways. They tend to experience low levels of chronic anxiety and may achieve a relative calm even in the face of a mild storm in the relationship system. The higher one's level of differentiation, the less he or she will be affected by and drawn into emotional reactivity in relationships and the less chronic anxiety he or she will experience.

This pattern determines how reactive people are to environmental stress and trauma as well. The higher an individual's level of differentiation and the lower the level of chronic anxiety, the more adaptive and flexible a person will be to the acute anxiety experienced as a result of stressors. The ability to act according to the intellectual system (neocortex) instead of the emotional system (limbic system) allows self-directed choice even when levels of acute anxiety become high.

It is important to note that no one is perfectly differentiated or completely without chronic anxiety. Everyone, given a large enough amount of stress, will reach a point at which tolerance for anxiety will be exceeded. The intellectual and emotional systems become fused and the emotional system begins to dominate functioning (Kerr & Bowen, 1988). As the emotional system overrides thinking, the individual loses the ability to adapt to the stress or trauma. Instead of carefully seeking out a long-term solution, his or her behavior becomes increasingly automatic (it usually operates outside of conscious awareness) and becomes more focused on immediate relief of discomfort. This becomes problematic because efforts for immediate relief frequently lead to greater long-term difficulties and discomfort (Papero, 1990).

Many of these long-term problems are a function of how an individual's emotional reactivity affects and is affected by the family emotional system. As the family emotional process intensifies, the individual experiences a greater need for emotional closeness (as well as a reaction to emotional closeness) and tends to become more dependent on others' emotionality (Kerr, 1981). Depending on the intensity of fusion in the family, the increased emotional reactivity or chronic anxiety of one individual may reverberate throughout the system generating an increase in emotional reactivity and chronic anxiety in the other members of the family as well. The increase of chronic anxiety creates disequilibrium within the family emotional system, and family members react immediately (and often automatically) by beginning efforts to regain emotional stability. These efforts result in the development of new or more intense patterns of interaction within the family system. These patterns may temporarily reduce anxiety, but will likely make the family more vulnerable and less adaptive to future stressors.

According to BFS theory the only long-term solution to the effects of trauma is an increase in the basic level of differentiation of family members. The presence of social support, however, can offer a degree of protection to a family against the effects of stress and trauma. When an individual is able to maintain emotionally significant relationships with others, the relationships act as a buffer for the individual against anxiety. Ironically, it is the very people who need these relationships the most—those with a low level of differentiation and a high level of chronic anxiety—who generally lack emotionally supportive relationships. Individuals with low levels of differentiation are likely to be overly dependent on supportive relationships, and the relationships tend to become strained. Instead of support, these strained relationships may generate more anxiety (Kerr & Bowen, 1988).

In sum, level of differentiation and chronic anxiety are the primary factors in determining how family members will react or respond to trauma and what effect the trauma will have on immediate and long-term family functioning. The remaining three BFS theory concepts describe family emotional processes that influence or are influenced by level of differentiation and intensity of chronic anxiety.

Emotional Triangles Bowen suggested that regardless of where people fall on the continuum of differentiation, they are likely to experience a certain level of anxiety in any two-person relationship. As long as the relationship is calm, it remains relatively stable, but when anxiety enters the system (and Bowen suggests it invariably does), the relationship becomes unstable. Initially the members of the dyad will utilize mechanisms for managing anxiety and restoring equilibrium such as conflict, distance, and adapting to preserve harmony (Kerr & Bowen, 1988). Typically, one member of the dyad will exert more effort than the other and, as a result, will experience a greater amount of discomfort. When the discomfort reaches a certain level, this member may seek to resolve the tension by involving a third person. The result is a relationship triangle.

Varying levels of anxiety will change the emotional process and structure of triangles. When anxiety is low, family members' functioning may appear autonomous and triangles may be relatively inactive. Increasing anxiety, however, increases the activity of triangles just as increasing heat will accelerate the movement of molecules (Kerr, 1981). If the anxiety becomes intense or if the tension becomes fixated on one relationship in the triangle, a simple triangle may not effectively diffuse the anxiety and a member of the original dyad will likely bring a fourth person into the relationship (Papero, 1990). The addition of the fourth person expands the triangle to a system of interlocking triangles. As anxiety increases in the system, more people are added and the web of triangles expands and becomes more complex.

The structure of triangles and the pattern of the activity of triangles varies widely. The third member of the triangle might include any number of people: a friend to whom one of the partners complains about the relationship, a partner in an extramarital affair, or a child on whom a parent begins to focus. Although it is frequently a third person brought into a two-person relationship, the third point of the triangle could be anything that takes the focus and anxiety away from the relationship: intense dedication to career, devotion to a particular cause, intense involvement in a particular hobby or interest, or addictive and compulsive behavior. Alcohol, drugs, gambling, pornography, and excessive eating are all examples of behavior that might be used as an effort to reduce anxiety in relationships.

Triangles are not always harmful; they can be healing. An important assumption of BFS theory is that "tension in a two-person relationship will resolve itself automatically when contained within a three-person system, one of whom is emotionally detached" (Kerr & Bowen, 1988, p. 145). When one member of the three-person system is able to maintain emotional contact with the other two while remaining autonomous or emotionally separate, responsibility for the problem is placed back on the members of the original dyad. When these people are able to take responsibility for the problem and are motivated to work it out in their relationship, they begin to function more objectively and less emotionally. Since emotional contact with a well-differentiated third person helps a dyad become more differentiated, one reasonably well-differentiated family member can nudge the other members toward greater differentiation.

Nuclear Family Emotional System   The nuclear family emotional system is a concept used to describe the emotional process families engage in to absorb or manage anxiety. It is anxiety that drives nuclear family emotional process as mediated by the level of differentiation of the marital partners. Each partner comes to the marital relationship with a particular level of differentiation and developed patterns of emotional functioning. Both are products of the emotional functioning of previous generations. BFS theory suggests that individuals typically select a mate who has a similar level of differentiation to their own and whose emotional functioning is complementary to their own. A relationship is then created which has the potential to replicate relationship processes from the partners' original families. As the partners experience tension, either external or internal to the relationship, they begin to experience an increase in emotional reactivity and chronic anxiety. The partners respond by using any of four different mechanisms to preserve stability. The four mechanisms are: emotional distance, marital conflict, giving up self to preserve harmony, and focus on a child. Families may use a combination of all or any of these mechanisms at different times. If a family overuses any of the mechanisms, the anxiety can become focused on one person and can lead to that individual becoming chronically impaired (Kerr & Bowen, 1988).

Emotional Cutoff The concept of emotional cutoff identifies the process of partners insulating themselves from their own emotional reactivity to each other (Kerr, 1981). Emotional cutoff takes many different forms. It may take the form of spouses spending little time together because of long work hours, intense community involvement, or excessive involvement with extended family or friends. Spouses may make an extended effort to avoid being alone together by ensuring that others will be present when they are together (Papero, 1990). The distance may also take more subtle forms like avoidance of particular emotionally charged subjects, not speaking to each other for extended periods of time (Kerr, 1981), or keeping conversations on a superficial level. All are forms of insulating oneself emotionally.

   In the case of trauma, the emotion may be so intense and intolerable to family members that in addition to distancing themselves from other family members' emotional reactions, they may cut off from their own. This prevents family members from working through traumatic experiences. Energy becomes focused on avoiding the experience of the trauma rather than adapting to it. If, instead, family members can tolerate anxiety and learn to experience the tension, anxiety, discomfort, and pain of the trauma, they can learn to adapt and become stronger and more flexible and ultimately more differentiated.

Marital Conflict Although it seems less logical, marital conflict also functions to manage anxiety and provide stability in the marital relationship. In marital conflict, each spouse focuses his or her emotional reactivity on the other spouse, a process that provides a release of anxiety. This is different from some of the other mechanisms for diffusing anxiety in that no one individual is the target for anxiety. Each spouse is convinced that the other spouse is the problem and each spouse is generally unaware of the part he or she plays in the conflict. The partners are heavily focused on each other in their search for flaws and evidence of wrongdoing. It is not unusual for there to be periods of calm in the conflict and even periods of warm closeness. These periods, however, are fleeting. As tension builds, the relationship quickly becomes engulfed again in conflict (Papero, 1990). The content of the marital conflict is unimportant; it is not the issue that drives the conflict but each partner's reactivity to the other. In addition to the benefit of projecting reactivity onto the other spouse, marital conflict may provide spouses with a way to maintain emotional contact with each other (albeit negative) or, just the opposite, it may provide justification for spouses to maintain a certain distance from each other (Kerr & Bowen, 1988).

Giving up Self to Preserve Harmony The third mechanism used to manage anxiety is the process of one spouse giving up self to preserve harmony in the relationship. People with low levels of differentiation have unrealistic expectations. They expect either too much or too little from themselves and from others (Kerr, 1981). This is manifest in the dominant–submissive pattern that is common in marital relationships. Submissive spouses typically learn to take responsibility for maintaining harmony in their families of origin. As a result, it is natural for them to expect too much of themselves and to assume too much responsibility within the marital relationship. Similarly, dominant spouses likely learned their role in their families of origin and naturally assume too little responsibility. Both spouses tend to put pressure on the other to play their respective roles. This reciprocal relationship can be calming for both spouses (Kerr & Bowen, 1988) and typically remains a functional pattern as long as the process can manage the stress on the system. However, if anxiety becomes intense and sustained, the patterns of interaction become more and more exaggerated and progressively impair the functioning of one of the spouses. Typically, this is the one who made the most compromises to preserve harmony in the system (Kerr, 1981).

Focus on a Child The fourth mechanism used by families to manage anxiety is parental focus on a child, in which spouses seek to reduce tension in the marital relationship by moving the focus away from their relationship to a particular child. This focus may be either positive or negative. The positive focus may come in the form of excessive parental coddling of the child. The parent may view the child as fragile and in need of extra care or protection. Few, if any, rules may be set for the child and the parent may anxiously hover over the child to make sure his or her comfort is in no way threatened. Negative focus on a child, in contrast, may come in the form of a parent becoming preoccupied with a real or imagined weakness in a child. The parent may become consumed with pointing out and correcting this weakness.

Frequently, the characteristic or behavior of the child is imagined or is something the parent fears will happen in the future instead of something that is actually occurring. In the course of the parent–child interaction, however, the child often develops the imagined characteristic or weakness (Kerr, 1981). The child becomes highly sensitive to the emotions of the parent and learns to fill the expected role. As the pattern develops, the parent and child begin to function in an emotional complimentarity in which both the parent and the child expect and evoke certain responses from the other. Although both the parent and the child act to perpetuate this reciprocal interaction, it is important to remember that it is not the characteristic or weakness of the child that began the process but the emotional reactivity of the parent.

As tension in the marital relationship escalates, parent involvement becomes more focused and more pronounced with a particular child. In some families, the focus may shift over time from one child to another. This spreads parental anxiety out across children and has less of a destructive effect on one particular child. If parental attention becomes fixed exclusively on one child, the child tends to absorb parental emotionality. If the focus of parental anxiety on the child is prolonged, the child may fail to develop a level of differentiation equal to that of his or her parents. At the same time, his or her siblings may escape the negative effects of parental anxiety and may develop higher levels of basic differentiation than their parents (Kerr, 1981).

If spouses experience an intense, sustained level of anxiety, as in the case of a severe traumatic experience, more than one child may become the focus of prolonged parental attention and may experience the accompanying negative effects. A high level of differentiation in the spouses, however, may provide some protection for the children from the effects of the traumatic event. The functioning of the children may be less compromised if the parents use other methods for managing their anxiety (e.g., emotional distance or marital conflict).

In summary, when anxiety in the marital relationship exceeds tolerance levels, spouses will use all or any combination of the four mechanisms described above for managing anxiety. The mechanism or combination of mechanisms a family uses to diffuse or manage anxiety is, in large measure, dependent upon the patterns of emotional functioning of the spouses' families of origin. A well-differentiated family may function quite well for long periods of time without requiring the use of any of the four mechanisms to maintain stability. A severe traumatic event, however, can cause even fairly well differentiated families to become emotionally reactive and to activate anxiety-managing mechanisms in an effort to return the family to its regular state of emotional equilibrium. The nature of the traumatic event and the specific family members who were most directly affected may also have an influence on which mechanism is used.

For example, in the case of a child who was sexually abused by a nonfamily member, the child may be a natural focus of parental anxiety and emotionality. This may play itself out in the parents' anxious attempts to try to protect the child from the pain of the abuse or to help the child get over the abuse. As the child absorbs parental anxiety, his or her ability to adapt to the trauma is compromised. In a reactive state, the parents are unable to provide emotional support and are unable to be a calming influence for their child. Instead, the parents unwittingly increase the child's anxiety and, if the child remains the focus of parental attention long enough, the child's emotional functioning may be severely compromised. This can result in the child developing social, physical, or emotional dysfunction and the family becoming less adaptive to stress.

Multigenerational Emotional Process The previous discussion of nuclear family emotional systems described parental undifferentiation, paired with external stress, as setting the pattern for emotional functioning in the nuclear family. However, both the emotional functioning of parents and the patterns that become established in the nuclear family system can only be understood in the context of the emotional process in the generations that preceded them. Level of differentiation and the functioning position people occupy in the nuclear family system are largely products of many generations of emotional process.

The primary mechanism through which undifferentiation is transmitted across generations is referred to as "family projection process" (Kerr, 1981). This occurs when spouses divert tension and anxiety from their marital relationship to the relationship with a particular child. It is important to mention that parents don't cause their children to develop certain levels of differentiation; they are simply the connection between the child and a family process that spans generations (Kerr & Bowen, 1988). Depending on the functioning position of children in a family, they may develop levels of differentiation higher or lower than their parents. Because of this, there are branches of the family tree progressing through time toward greater differentiation and branches moving toward greater undifferentiation (Kerr, 1981).

This is a slow process that typically requires several generations before marked changes in levels of differentiation develop (Kerr & Bowen, 1988). The process can be slowed down or sped up, depending upon how anxiety is managed in each generation and depending upon life circumstance (Papero, 1990). The transmission of undifferentiation across generations can be slowed down if marital anxiety is absorbed through marital conflict or emotional distance. In contrast, if anxiety is managed for several successive generations through projection, the transmission of undifferentiation can be dramatically sped up. Life circumstances can either provide a calming influence and slow down this process or can add anxiety to the system and speed up the process.

Knowledge of all five of the concepts described above provides a solid theoretical foundation from which to assess the functioning and adaptiveness of individuals and family systems. We now move to a discussion of the process of family assessment.

Process of Assessment

Because family emotional process is so pronounced after traumatic events, it may be an opportune time to identify and help family members become aware of family emotional process. Conducting family evaluation after a traumatic event may, however, present some additional challenges: family members' levels of anxiety may be so high that it may be difficult for them to begin to view family process objectively. Helping family members view family process objectively is the primary purpose of evaluation in BFS therapy.

> "Therapy based on systems theory is guided by the assumption that it is not necessary for the therapist to diagnose the family's problem. If the therapist is reasonably successful at maintaining a systemic orientation, the family will begin to diagnose its own problems and to develop its own direction for change. It is important for the therapist to make his own assessment of the nature of the family's problem, but he does this primarily to maintain his bearings in the family and to plan productive areas of inquiry." (Kerr & Bowen, 1988, p. 293).

The therapist asks questions to know what questions to ask next in an effort to help family members create an objective picture of family functioning. The very process of asking systemic questions can help family members begin to think differently about the family and self in the family. Through this process family members begin to identify their roles in the family emotional process and how they can begin to function outside of the emotional pull of the system.

A thorough family evaluation includes a discussion of the presenting problem, an evaluation of the nuclear family history, and an evaluation of the partners' extended families. In all three areas of assessment the focus is placed on developing a clear understanding of family functioning, specifically family emotional process across generations. This is important because it is frequently the emotional reaction of the family and not the precipitating stress that exacerbates family problems. Kerr and Bowen (1988) state that, "The emotionally driven chain reactions that can be set in motion in a family relationship system in response to an event are often a much greater source of stress to a family than the event itself" (p. 319).

PRESENTING PROBLEM

In the case of trauma or loss, a discussion of the presenting problem includes an examination of the nature of the traumatic event, an assessment of family members' reaction to the trauma, and an exploration of the current symptoms experienced in the family. This discussion allows family members the chance to tell their story and also provides clues into the emotional functioning of the family.

In assessing the nature of the recently experienced traumatic event, the therapist seeks to understand the severity of the stressor. This includes an examination of the intensity and duration of the traumatic experience, whether the onset of the event was sudden, whether the event was or is prolonged (e.g., continuing threat or enduring stress), the number of concurrent stressful events, which family members were directly affected by the event, how the family members make sense of the experience, and the level of social support a family receives. The presence of an emotional support system is important because it helps a family stabilize emotional functioning and diffuse the tensions associated with loss. Understanding the nature of the stress or trauma and the resources available to the family helps the therapist put the emotional reactivity of the family in context. Treating family trauma or loss on the basis of its perceived severity and without regard to family emotional process would be misguided.

In addition to the nature of the traumatic event, the therapist is interested in how the family has reacted to the stress and what symptoms have developed. An exploration of symptomatology in the family can provide information about how the family reacts to stress and manages anxiety. The therapist is interested specifically in how and when the symptoms developed, which family member or relationships are symptomatic, and the effect of the symptoms on other family members. Exact dates of symptom development may help make a connection between the symptoms and the traumatic event. Symptoms are not examined to develop knowledge of how to treat the symptoms themselves, but to provide a picture of the family's emotional process and the mechanisms used to manage anxiety.

Knowledge about the nature of the traumatic event and how the family experiences it and adapts or reacts to the stress helps the therapist begin to develop a picture of the emotional functioning of the system. To develop a thorough understanding of the adaptiveness of a family, however, it is important to evaluate the entire history of the nuclear family and not just reaction to the recent trauma. To create this picture the therapist evaluates the history of the nuclear family from its beginning (the spouses' marriage) to the present.

NUCLEAR FAMILY HISTORY

An evaluation of the nuclear family history is focused on the patterns and intensity of family emotional process over time. Kerr and Bowen (1988) suggest that evaluation of the nuclear family history should include (a) the stress the family has experienced, (b) the level of chronic anxiety or reactivity in the system, and (c) the family's level of adaptiveness. These three areas may be evaluated simultaneously as the history of the family is reviewed.

Stress. Stress tends to activate emotional reactivity in families. Stress refers to the actual events that disturb the emotional equilibrium of a family; it does not refer to the family reaction to the events. An evaluation of stress in a family's history is a review of those nodal events that increased acute anxiety in the family. Some examples of these events are moves to a new area, job loss, divorce, death, and serious illness. A discussion of previous trauma and loss in the family is central to this evaluation. Level of stress is determined by evaluating the number of stressors, the time between stressors, and the severity of the stressors. A family chronology or timeline of major stress events can be a useful tool for the therapist in developing a picture of family stress across time (McGoldrick, 1991). The timeline should include dates of important stressors and any important family changes. It should include dates of births, deaths, divorces, marriages, moves, job changes, financial hardships, traumatic experiences, loss experiences, and development of physical or psychological symptoms and their duration.

Chronic anxiety. Kerr and Bowen (1988) outline the important elements in the evaluation of chronic anxiety as "... the number of symptoms in the family, the degree of functional impairment associated with those symptoms, the amount of distance and/or conflict in relationships, and the amount of anxiety and reactivity family members appear to have" (p. 320). All of these elements reflect the presence of chronic anxiety and, when examined together, create a picture of family reactivity. It is important to not only examine symptoms but to objectively examine the place of symptoms in family process. When focus is placed on the interactive nature of components of the emotional system, family members can begin to understand and view family functioning objectively (Kerr, 1981).

Questions are asked about family process and the functioning of individual family members throughout the family's history. This includes an evaluation of family members' physical health as well as their psychological and social functioning. In addition, educational and occupational histories are discussed. Particular attention is given to individual and family functioning around anxiety-generating events in the family history.

In these discussions, the therapist is interested in determining how family members manage anxiety, i.e., which mechanisms the family uses to establish and maintain emotional equilibrium. This is key to understanding the emotional functioning of the family because a family's reactivity may not be outwardly evident. A family with a high level of chronic anxiety may seem relatively calm and nonreactive depending on the way anxiety in the system is managed. For example, if one of the spouses gives up self to maintain harmony in the system, the family may go years before symptoms develop. When the symptoms do develop, however, they are likely to be intense. An understanding of the mechanisms the family uses to manage anxiety makes it easier for the therapist to identify family emotional reactivity.

Adaptiveness. The adaptiveness of a family (i.e., level of differentiation) can be assessed by making a connection between the level of stress and the amount of chronic anxiety in that family. Through an evaluation of the relationship between these two variables, the therapist can begin to understand if the reactivity of a family is primarily a result of an intense level of stress or if it is reflective of a low level of adaptiveness (Kerr, 1981). Kerr and Bowen (1988) describe the relationship between stress and emotional reactivity this way:

> "A high level of emotional reactivity in response to a low level of stress is consistent with a low level of adaptiveness. A low level of emotional reactivity in response to a high level of stress is consistent with a high level of adaptiveness." (p. 321)

Family members may be unaware of the connection between stressors and family emotional reactivity and the development of symptoms. The therapist, however, can help the family make this connection during the process of recording exact dates of stressors, symptom development, and changes in family functioning.

Learning about a family's adaptiveness across its history helps the therapist understand the prognosis of the family as the family deals with the recent traumatic experience. If family members have a high level of adaptiveness, it is likely that they will recover relatively quickly and that the traumatic event will not have a lasting negative impact on family functioning. In contrast, if the family has a low level of adaptiveness, a severe traumatic experience has the potential to cause increased emotional reactivity to reverberate throughout the system for many years and possibly across generations.

NATURE OF EXTENDED FAMILY SYSTEMS

The information gathered about spouses' extended families is similar to the information gathered about the nuclear family, only less detailed. Kerr and Bowen (1988) suggest it is important to assess both the *stability* and the *intactness* of the extended family. They define stability as "the average level of functioning of the members of an extended family" (p. 323) and intactness as the number of people alive and available to the nuclear family being evaluated. An evaluation of the history of spouses' extended families provides an objective picture of extended family emotional functioning across time.

This evaluation reveals a great deal about the differentiation of each spouse and the functional role he or she played in the family of origin's attempts to manage anxiety. As these patterns are discovered and discussed, each partner begins to develop an objective picture of his or her position and role in this process. This helps provide a clearer understanding of their current functioning in nuclear family emotional process and guides them in understanding necessary differentiating moves in the family of origin.

An evaluation of the stability and intactness of the extended families of the spouses is also important because it identifies whether the family is an emotional support and resource to the nuclear family in their efforts to adapt to stress or if, instead, the extended family is a source of tension. The more stable and intact the extended family, the more likely it will be an emotional support to the nuclear family. In evaluating the supportiveness of the extended family it is also important to evaluate the level of spouses' emotional cutoff from extended families because emotional cutoff isolates the nuclear family from potential sources of support.

> "The person who is less cut off has a more reliable emotional support system than the person who is more cut off. In times of stress, therefore, the more cutoff person is more vulnerable for developing symptoms or for trading for yet another relationship." (Kerr & Bowen, 1988, p. 325)

The result of the nuclear family's isolation from extended families is more intense emotional reactivity and more intense efforts to manage anxiety; both of these tend to decrease family adaptiveness and create long-term problems for families.

Assessing the quality of emotional contact between spouses and their extended families is critical but difficult to perform because people are often misleading about the level of closeness in their relationship to their extended families. Assessment of where the family has lived in reference to extended family and if family moves have taken the family closer to or further away from extended family may provide some clues into the degree of cutoff (Kerr, 1981).

TOOLS OF EVALUATION

Performing a thorough assessment in the three areas described above can produce an unwieldy amount of information that can be challenging to combine and understand, making the use of family diagrams or geno-grams an indispensable part of the evaluation process. It is a method for collecting and organizing information about the family in a way that creates a picture of the underlying emotional process in the family. It reflects "the ebb and flow of emotional process through the generations" (Kerr & Bowen, 1988, p. 306). The family diagram should include dates of births, deaths, separations, divorces, and marriages. It should include levels of education, occupation, cause of death for those who have died, and any health problems experienced for each member of the family. The diagram should also reflect the level of contact or connection between family members, their relationship to one another, and the family's methods for managing anxiety. (For more information on family diagrams and the symbols used to communicate the information, see Kerr & Bowen, 1988, or McGoldrick, Gerson, & Shellenberger, 1999). A time line or family chronology is also a useful tool in the process of evaluation (McGoldrick, 1991).

It is through the discussion and *mapping* of family emotional process that family members begin to develop an objective understanding of the process and their functioning position in it. Kerr and Bowen (1988) state, "Learning enough about the multigenerational emotional history of one's family to change the way one thinks about the family and about oneself probably contributes more to the effort to 'grow up' than anything else a person can do" (p. 309). When those affected by trauma obtain an objective knowledge of the pattern of their own and their family's emotional reactions to anxiety, they place themselves in a position to act differently—to change patterns of reaction. They are more able to restrain their automatic reactions to the trauma and tolerate the stress and anxiety of the experience. Instead of attempting to escape the anxiety and pain they are able to face it, adapt to it, and grow from it.

TREATMENT

Treatment models for individuals and families who have experienced trauma can be classified into two groups: crisis intervention for immediate symptom relief, and long-term treatment to help heal the lingering effects of trauma. Crisis intervention treatment primarily involves a supportive therapeutic stance, externalizing blame for the crisis event, and creating safety plans. It may also include forensic data collection and interviewing techniques for use in future legal proceedings. Long-term psychotherapy for the effects of trauma may include enacting and maintaining safety plans, deconstruction and reprocessing of the traumatic event, and possibly confrontation of the offender or offending entity. All of these have the goal of achieving an acceptable level of, or a return to, normal functioning for the individual or family.

In BFS therapy the focus is on differentiation of self. It is likely therefore, that only one member of the family system would become the client in this type of therapy, although a spouse may be peripherally involved. BFS therapists often refer to the family member with the most motivation to change as the one who provides the therapist a portal or point of entry into the entire family system. It may seem strange to think that the member of the system in treatment may not be the particular individual who was personally traumatized. However, all members of the system are emotionally connected, therefore a change in one member would affect a change in the entire system. As an example, consider the case of a young child who is sexually molested by someone outside the family. In BFS therapy the most appropriate client for treatment would rarely be the child. A more appropriate person for treatment (of the entire system) might be a motivated parent or adult caregiver who must have the skills to move from highly emotional states of reactivity to moments of clear thinking so that family resources and relationships can be managed wisely. To use a metaphor, the well-differentiated individual becomes the domino that does not fall despite the pressure of all the other dominoes pressing against it. This is the individual that does not give in to the emotional pressures of the system but retains a choice in how he or she handles situations associated with the traumatic event.

THERAPIST STANCE

Titelman (1987) suggests that "a central goal in learning Bowen family systems theory is to develop the ability to see the theory as it relates to self" (p. 3). He outlines three key components to therapist development: (a) The therapist must develop an understanding of the theory, (b) the therapist must see how his or her own family might be conceptualized through this theoretical lens, and (c) the therapist must have his or her clinical work supervised. Friedman (1991) suggests that it would be impossible for a therapist to help a client through the process of differentiation unless the therapist has had an experience of differentiation within his or her own family of origin. It is this personal process of becoming more emotionally differentiated in one's own family (presumably the most emotionally charged system for any individual) that helps the therapist empathize with the client during their efforts at differentiating. Interestingly enough, these same three components outline the process that any client must undertake in successful BFS therapy. They must learn the theory, begin a process of differentiation in their family of origin, and receive coaching or supervision from their therapist on the differentiation process.

BFS theory differs somewhat from other psychotherapy theories in that it calls for a major portion of the time at the beginning of therapy to be dedicated to teaching the client the theory. Clients must be familiar with concepts such as differentiation, reactivity, anxiety, triangulation, etc. Once clients know the theory and are equipped with language tools sufficient to describe the emotional process in their relationships, they are able to begin applying the concepts to their own families and other interpersonal relationships. A Bowen therapist will ask clients to strive to understand their own anxiety and their own reactivity. Once clients understand the relationship between anxiety and their own personal reactivity, they can begin to make more informed choices regarding their behavior in relationships, specifically in highly emotional situations. After this happens, the therapist's role shifts somewhat from theory educator to coach. In this stage the therapist listens to the client describe complex interactions and encourages the client to react differently, especially in highly emotional interactions. The client is then asked to notice how his or her different reaction has changed a specific interaction (and ultimately the relationship) with the other person.

At some point in the treatment the motivated client realizes that his or her own behavior is the only variable over which he or she has control. It is the individual who makes a choice to be reactive (move toward fusion or cutoff), to take the next drink of alcohol, buy something that is not needed, engage in risky sexual behavior, etc. These problematic behaviors (symptoms) then become the domain and responsibility of the client. The therapist cannot make the client stop doing anything. Any attempts to do so would represent a manifestation of the therapist's own anxiety. The client must realize that his or her behaviors are not serving him or her well and that these behaviors are influenced by his or her own feelings of emptiness or chronic anxiety. Bowen contended that this chronic anxiety never leaves us. He further suggested that when we respond differently to our chronic anxiety by not reacting to our feelings of emptiness, change occurs throughout the family system.

A brief example can illustrate this point. Consider the man who is feeling emotionally reactive to his employment situation. Perhaps he is angry at his boss. As he returns home from work his anxiety about his situation weighs heavily on him. He knows that if he goes to a bar, a couple of drinks will take the emotional edge off and he will not be as aware of his situation at work, at least for the time being. In fact, stopping at the bar in the past has helped with a number of particularly challenging days. Over time, and as the situation at work does not improve, this individual sets himself up to develop problems related to his drinking. From a Bowen perspective, this man uses alcohol in a reactive manner. He uses it to separate himself from his experience of the emotional climate at work. A different response to this anxiety might be to simply acknowledge the temptation to go to the bar for drinks and then not act on it. By not acting on the desire he begins to be more in touch with his feelings of anxiety and his own reactivity. Over time this man will more readily recognize his own anxiety and enhance his ability to sit with the anxiety, as opposed to reacting to it.

The presence and stance of the therapist is the single most important variable in BFS theory. Therapists must be well differentiated and know how they are tempted to be reactive. Often therapists' reactivity is related to being helpful. There is a bit of a paradox when Bowen therapists learn that they are most helpful when they don't try to help. The perceived need to take care of one's clients exemplifies an undifferentiated stance on the part of the therapist. The two life forces of togetherness and separateness weigh upon the therapist in relation to the client. Too much separateness from the client may be interpreted as distancing or rejecting. Too much closeness or over involvement would also be detrimental to the client. After all, it is the client that supposedly needs the skills to emotionally fend for him or herself. Therefore, Bowen advocated a neutral stance in the therapeutic relationship.

The ability to be a nonanxious presence helps to stabilize emotionally turbulent relationships. In couples therapy, for example, a Bowen therapist who sides with one client over the other has lost the ability to be neutral. This loss will likely result in the loss of one or both clients. Achieving neutrality is difficult; clients want someone to side with them. Clients often present with the desire to have the therapist change the other person in the dyad and thereby try to ally themselves with the therapist (Jacobsen & Christensen, 1996). In reaction to trauma, a client may want the therapist to join in on the family's outrage toward the perpetrator or pity for the direct victim(s). However, getting the therapist to be outraged or sorrowful for the family's trauma does little to help the family negotiate a path toward recovery, healing, and protection.

Bowen theory has been criticized for supposedly valuing an intellectual, as opposed to an emotional, response to relational problems. We contend, however, that the process of differentiation of self helps create a balance between excessive connection in relationships on one hand and excessive distancing on the other. Family crisis literature highlights the findings that disengaged families, when exposed to a traumatic event, become more disengaged (separate) while those that are enmeshed become even more clingy in response to crisis events (fusion).

> "Enhancing choice within relationships is the key concept and goal and not the valuing of separation over connection or viceversa. Enhancing choice allows a person to be self-directed in significant relationships instead of constantly reacting to one's anxiety and the anxiety of others. It is assumed that as a person differentiates, s/he is less susceptible to the chronic anxiety and reactivity in the family emotional system and can make strides toward greater mental health." (Harris, 1996, p. 44)

This type of intervention promotes clarity of choice and differentiation between thinking and feeling states associated with the trauma.

CONCLUSION

For treating families who have been exposed to trauma, Bowen theory presents a bit of a dilemma. The theory would not necessarily dictate the inclusion of an entire family, or even a particular individual exposed to the traumatic event, in a family therapy session. In all cases, true BFS therapy looks different from therapy conducted from a traditional psychotherapy perspective. We believe this may represent a stumbling block for clinicians to accept a BFS theoretical conceptualization of trauma and its treatment. Bowen theory calls for the clinician to be more true to the theory than to the client. This may sound heartless to those of us who were trained to treat our clients with unconditional positive regard. However, a BFS theorist would suggest that by having an allegiance primarily to the theory, the clinician serves the client best because each and every individual's life can be viewed from a BFS theoretical perspective and increasing differentiation is ultimately what benefits our clients the most. Equipped with a higher level of differentiation, clients have more choices with regard to how they will respond in the face of any current trauma, its aftershocks, and any future traumatic experiences to which the individual or the family are exposed.

REFERENCES

Ainsworth, M. D. S., Behar, M., Waters, E., & Wall, S. (1978). *Patterns of attachment.* Hillsdale, NJ: Erlbaum.

Bowen, M. (1978). *Family therapy in clinical practice.* New York: Jason Aronson.

Bowlby, J. (1969). *Attachment and loss: Vol 1. Attachment.* London: Hogarth.

Bowlby, J. (1973). *Attachment and loss: Vol 2. Separation.* London: Hogarth.

Brown, J. (1999). Bowen family systems theory and practice: Illustration and critique. *Australia and New Zealand Journal of Family Therapy, 20,* 94–103.

Carter, E., & McGoldrick, M. (Eds.). (1980). *The family life cycle: A framework for family therapy.* New York: Garner.

Friedman, E. H. (1991). Bowen theory and therapy. In A. S. Gurman & D. P. Kniskern (Eds.), *Handbook of family therapy* (Vol. 2, pp. 134–170). New York: Brunner/Mazel.

Harris, S. M. (1996). Bowen and symbolic experiential family therapy theories: Strange bedfellows or isomorphs of life? *Journal of Family Psychotherapy, 7,* 39–60.

Harris, S. M., & Busby, D. M. (1997). Pant-legs and pathology: The marriage of individual and family assessment. *Contemporary Family Therapy, 19,* 507–521.

Jacobson, N. S, & Christensen, A. (1996). *Acceptance and change in couple therapy: A therapist's guide to transforming relationships.* New York: Norton.

Kegan, R. (1982). *The evolving self: Problem and process in human development.* Cambridge, MA: Harvard University Press.

Kerr, M. E. (1981). Family systems theory and therapy. In A. S. Gurman & D. P. Kniskern (Eds.), *Handbook of family therapy* (Vol. 1., pp. 226–264). New York: Brunner/Mazel.

Kerr, M. E., & Bowen, M. (1988). *Family evaluation.* New York: Norton.

McGoldrick, M. (1991). Echoes from the past: Helping families mourn their losses. In F. Walsh & M. McGoldrick (Eds.), *Living beyond loss: Death in the family.* New York: Norton.

McGoldrick, M., Gerson, R., & Shellenberger, S. (1999). *Genograms: Assessment and Intervention.* New York: Norton.

Neil, J. R., & Kniskern, D. P. (1982). *From psyche to system: The evolving therapy of Carl Whitaker.* New York: Guilford.

Papero, D. V. (1990). *Bowen family systems theory.* Boston: Allyn & Bacon.

Roberto, L. G. (1991). Symbolic–experiential family therapy. In A. S. Gurman & D. P. Kniskern (Eds.), *Handbook of family therapy* (Vol. 2., pp. 444–476). New York: Brunner/Mazel.

Skowron, E. A., & Friedlander, M. L. (1998). The differentiation of self inventory: development and initial validation. *Journal of Counseling Psychology, 45,* 235–246.

Titelman, P. (1998). *Clinical applications of Bowen family systems theory.* New York: Hawthorn.

Titelman, P. (1987). The therapist's own family. In P. Titelman (Ed.), *The therapist's own family: Toward the differentiation of self.* New York: Jason Aronson.

Whitaker, C. A., & Keith, D V. (1981). Symbolic–experiential family therapy. In A. S. Gurman & D. P. Kinskern (Eds.), *Handbook of family therapy* (Vol. 1., pp. 187–225). New York: Brunner/Mazel.

14

A Strengths-Based Approach to Child and Family Assessment

JANE F. GILGUN

Within the last decade, the demands of managed health care and evidence-based approaches have put heavy pressure on the practice of psychotherapy. Not only are clinical practitioners enjoined to use best research evidence, but they must do their work in as short a time as possible to hold down costs. At the same time, they must demonstrate the effectiveness of their interventions, preferably with quantified outcomes (Gray, 2002; Sackett, Straus, Richardson, Rosenberg, & Haynes, 2000). Demands for efficiency, efficacy, cost containment, and best research evidence are part of the context in which contemporary clinical practice takes place.

Another recent development is the understanding of the importance of identifying and building upon client strengths in order to foster clients' capacities for dealing with their risks (Fraser, 1997; Saleebey, 2002; Smith & Carlson, 1997; van Eys & Dodge,1999). Solution-focused therapy, narrative therapy, and competency-based practices are examples of this trend. Many of these approaches are also brief treatments that focus on capacity building. Developmental psychopathology, a branch of developmental psychology that studies high risks groups in order to identify factors that lead to positive and negative outcomes, provides many useful concepts to therapists interested in identifying and building on client capacities (Gilgun, 1996b; Gilgun, Keskinen, Marti, and Rice, 1999; Gilgun, Klein, & Pranis, 2000; van Eys & Dodge, 1999).

The clinical assessment tools that I have developed over the past several years are designed to respond to the contemporary demands that clinicians experience. They are based on best research evidence and give equal consideration to client strengths and deficits. They guide clinicians to focus on aspects of client functioning that research and theory have identified as fundamental to emotional and psychological well-being. These instruments potentially can contribute to efficiency in assessment and treatment planning and thus reduce the time clients spend in treatment. In addition, the tools were developed for practice with children and families in which children have experienced trauma and other adversities and have developed behaviors that bring them to the attention of clinical practitioners. These behaviors include conduct disorders, self-harming behaviors, and inappropriate sexual behaviors resulting from sexual abuse. The assessment tools are short, easy to use, can be scored so as to give quantified outcomes, and are based on research evidence and clinical expertise.[1] The tools are:

- Clinical Assessment Package for Client Risks and Strengths (CAS-PARS), tested on children and their families where the children are ages 5 to 13
- 4-D, strengths-based tools for youth in out-of-home care, tested on youth ages 12 to 19 and their families
- Risk Assessment in Child Welfare, useful to public child welfare practice and untested

These tools were constructed according to the tenets of evidence-based practice, which has developed from evidence-based medicine (EBM). EBM is composed of three dimensions: best research evidence, clinical expertise, and patients' wants and preferences. Proponents of EBM state that practice has several components, including diagnosis, treatment, and outcome. Each of these phases of practice requires the application of best research evidence (Evidence-Based Medicine Working Group, 1992; Sackett et al., 2000; Straus & McAlister, 2000). These components of medical practice are similar to the practice of psychotherapy.

The CASPARS, the 4-D, and the child welfare tools are not only based on best research evidence but they incorporate the professional experiences of clinical psychologists and social workers. In addition, the CAS-PARS and the 4-D have been piloted so as to see how clients respond to the concepts that the instruments incorporate. They are designed to help in assessment and treatment planning, to monitor the course of treatment,

---

1. *Editor's note:* These tools and other strength-based instruments are available on the Web at *ssw.che.umn.edu/faculty/jgilgun.htm.*

and to provide outcome scores. Thus, the tools are consistent with major tenets of evidence-based practice.

Psychometric testing has been performed on the five tools that compose the CASPARS and the four tools that make up the 4-D. The strengths-based child welfare tools are untested. The coefficient alphas for the CASPARS and the 4-D are 0.9 and above. Nunnnaly (1978) stated that alphas of 0.9 are required for instruments that are meant to be used with individuals. These nine instruments have reached this high standard. In addition, the CASPARS instruments have high inter-rater reliabilities and good construct validity (Gilgun, 1999a).

The purpose of this chapter is to demonstrate the features of one set of strengths-based tools—the CASPARS—and, in doing this, to provide a model for the development of other strengths-based instruments that could be customized to a variety of settings, populations, and theoretical frameworks. Clinical practitioners could use some of the ideas in this chapter and develop their own instruments. If there are items in the instruments that might be useful, then clinicians are encouraged to use them, with attribution, and to add them to their own custom-fit tools. Taynor, Nelson, and Daugherty (1990) provide another account of how practitioners worked with a university-based researcher to develop and test family assessment and outcome measures.

The 4-D for youth in out-of-home care is an example of how the ideas of the CASPARS can be used in the construction of other instruments. The conceptual base of the 4-D is the Circle of Courage, an American Indian Medicine Wheel that incorporates contemporary theories of human development (Brendtro, Brokenleg, & van Brocken, 1990; Gilgun, in press). This is not the conceptual base of the CASPARS, although the CASPARS are based on some of the same theories as the Circle of Courage. In addition, the 4-D are structured similarly to the CASPARS in that they give equal consideration to client strengths and risks and provide two scores: a risk score and a strengths score. Like the CASPARS, the 4-D are intended to be useful for assessment, intervention planning, predicting outcome of interventions, and the evaluation of the effects of treatment.

THE CASPARS

The CASPARS instruments are based on research and theory from developmental psychopathology, in-depth case study interviews, and the practice experience of social work clinicians and clinical psychologists. The five instruments composing the CASPARS are (a) emotional expressiveness, (b) family relationships, (c) family's embeddedness in the community, (d) peer relationships, and (e) sexuality.

As clinical rating scales (scales that are to be filled out by practitioners and not by clients), the instruments are designed to fit and add to practice. The instruments tap into risks and strengths that reside in individuals, families, peer groups, and the community. The measurement of individual functioning alone would neglect the multiple ecologies with which individuals interact (Beck, 1997; van Eys & Dodge, 1999). The CASPARS were tested for practice in such settings as child mental health and child welfare, including foster care, in-home services, and residential treatment.

Sources of CASPARS Items

The CASPARS instruments are composed of concrete indicators of assets and risks. The items were developed through 11 years of in-depth case study research conducted with adults who had experienced a range of childhood and adolescent risks. In the course of conducting case studies, it became clear that a variety of pathways lead to multiple developmental outcomes, some of which were quite adaptive and others maladaptive (Gilgun, 2000, June).

The factors that consistently differentiated good and poor outcomes were grouped under the domains that the five instruments composing the CASPARS, listed above, represent (Gilgun, in press, 2002, 1999a, 1999b, 1996a, 1996b, 1992, 1991, 1990; Gilgun, Klein, & Pranis, 2000; Gilgun, Keskinen, Martin, & Rice, 1999). The identification and conceptualization of the domains and the development of items were facilitated by research and theory on developmental psychopathology (Masten & Wright, 1998; Mahoney & Bergman, 2002; van Eys & Dodge, 1999; Werner & Smith, 1992) and social work's ecological, strengths-based perspectives (Baker & Steiner, 1995; DeJong & Miller, 1996; Goldstein, 1990; Greene, Jensen, & Jones, 1996; Saleebey, 2002; Tracy, Whittaker, Pugh, Kapp, & Overstreet, 1994).

Other related research provided added direction for the development of the CASPARS instruments, such as research in child development that recognizes appropriate emotional expressiveness as linked to academic and social success and good mental health across the life span, from childhood to old age (Boyum & Parke, 1995; Cassidy & Asher, 1992; Halberstadt, Cassidy, Stifter, Parke, & Fox, 1995; Parke & Ladd, 1992; Parker & Asher, 1987; Roberts & Strayer, 1996).

Finally, the practice knowledge of social work clinicians and clinical psychologists with long-term experience with children who had experienced adversities and with their families contributed to the development of the instruments. These clinicians critiqued drafts of the instruments, suggested additions and deletions, and participated in the piloting.

Key Concepts

The CASPARS instruments, as well as the other strengths-based measures, are built around several key concepts, including risks, assets, emotional expressiveness, family relationships, family embeddedness in the community, and peer relationships.

Risks. A probabilistic concept, risks predict that a portion of an at-risk group will have an associated outcome, but they cannot predict that any one individual will have the outcome (Masten, 1994; Masten, Best, & Garmezy, 1991; Rutter, 1987). Examples of risks include family separations and losses, a history of childhood and adolescent maltreatment, unsafe neighborhoods, family isolation, structurally based disadvantage and discrimination, exposure to persons who model violent behaviors, inability to access internal states such as emotions and wants, and genetic risks predisposing individuals to particular types of physiological reactivity (Cicchetti, 1987; Rende & Plomin, 1993; Richters & Martinez, 1993; Werner & Smith, 1992).

Assets. Assets, too, can be considered probabilistic concepts and are factors associated with adaptive outcomes. They predict that a proportion of groups with assets will have good outcomes, but they are not deterministic on the individual level. Some persons with assets have unsatisfactory outcomes and behaviors because they are not able to use whatever assets they have to moderate risks, or because the risks overwhelm assets (Masten, 1994; Masten et al., 1991; Rutter, 1987). Assets include factors such as high IQ, physical attractiveness, verbal facility, caring parents, safe neighborhoods, adequate family income, and well-functioning schools (Cicchetti, 1987; Garmezy & Masten, 1994; Masten et al., 1991; Richters & Martinez, 1993; Rutter, 1987; Werner & Smith, 1992). Assets become protective factors when they can be shown to have facilitated the overcoming of risks (Gilgun, 1996a; Masten, 1994).

Emotional expressiveness. When at-risk individuals have opportunities to express their emotions in constructive ways—both positive and painful emotional experiences—they are at lowered risk for adverse outcomes (Erickson, Korfmacher, & Egeland, l992; Fraiberg, Adelson, & Shapiro, l975). Conversely, at-risk persons who distance themselves from their emotions and do not experience or express them are at high risk for developing adverse outcomes (Cicchetti, Rogosch, Lynch, & Holt, 1993; Garmezy & Masten, 1994; Gilgun, in press, 1999b, 1996a, 1996b, 1991, 1990; Masten, 1994; Rutter, 1987; Werner & Smith, 1992).

Emotional expressiveness is embedded in a web of positive human relationships within and outside families (Boyum & Parke, 1995; Gilgun, 1996b; Cassidy et al., 1995; Roberts & Strayer, 1996). Among the benefits of emotional expressiveness is its facilitation of the sorting through of conflicting thoughts, feelings, and values and a consequent cognitive restructuring that can include many new understandings. These include (a) the reduction of the sense of self as defective, (b) a renewed sense of the self as connected to other persons, and (c) an affirmation of positive goals and values.

Family relationships. Consistent with attachment research and research on risk, assets, and protective factors, emotional expressiveness probably develops from secure attachments to parents or parental figures or both during infancy, early childhood, and across the life span (Bowlby, 1973; Cicchetti, 1987; Egeland, Carlson, & Sroufe, 1993; Masten & Garmezy, 1985). Emotional expressiveness is associated with long-term positive relationships with others.

Individuals who have a capacity for emotional expressiveness grow up in circumstances that afford them some assets, such as parental figures who maintain harmonious relationships with each other, family members who show sensitivity to children's feelings and wants, and family members who recognize children's accomplishments. Positive adaptation is problematic if individuals experienced disharmony, insensitivity, and maltreatment within families of origin.

Family embeddedness in the community. Families who are positively connected to extended family members and to other persons in the wider community have access to material and emotional resources. Such access bodes well for the adequacy of family functioning (Gilgun, in press, 1999b, 1996b; Werner & Smith, 1992). Involvement in community activities, work that is meaningful, and the availability of safe playgrounds, libraries, and other community-based resources are some of the characteristics of families who are embedded in their communities. The converse is resource-poor communities and disconnection from persons and institutions that might offer emotional and material support.

Peer relationships. Positive family relationships and a capacity for emotional expressiveness also are correlated with positive relationships with peers (Boyum & Parke, 1995; Gilgun, 1996b; Cassidy et al., 1995; Roberts & Strayer, 1996). Assets related to peer groups are friendships that endure over time, friends who behave in pro-social ways and who do well in school, friends who express a range of emotions and who respect the feelings of others, and the capacity to feel part of a peer group. Persons with problematic outcomes have relationships with peers who feel alienated from school and most other persons, who perform antisocial acts, and who inhibit their own expression of painful and private feelings and denigrate those of others.

Sexuality. Individuals whose sexual development and behaviors are adequate have exposure to healthy sexual attitudes and appropriate information about sexuality whether in families of origin or elsewhere. They experience sexuality as a natural part of being human. If they had experienced sexual abuse, they had opportunities to cope with or overcome the effects of the abuse. Persons who exhibit problematic sexual behaviors rarely had such positive experiences. Risks for poor sexual functioning include a history of child sexual abuse, exposure to distorted and partial information about sexuality, exposure to sexual boundary violations, and lack of opportunity to discuss sexual maltreatment and to obtain accurate information about sexuality (Gil & Johnson, 1993; Gilgun, 1996a, 1996b; Friedrich et al., 1992; Salter, 1988). Children, adolescents, and adults who have a history of sexual abuse or a history of exposure to distorted, sexist attitudes toward sexuality and have not experienced moderators of such experiences are at risk to develop sexual issues of various sorts.

Piloting

The five CASPARS instruments were developed on the basis of the research and theory discussed in the preceding text.

Reliability and validity studies were conducted with a sample of 146 girls and boys and their biological and foster families. (See Gilgun, 1999a, for details on sampling, testing, reliability, and validity.) The children had a variety of therapeutic issues, neuropsychological conditions, and behavioral difficulties, as well as several types of maltreatment, including physical abuse (38%), psychological maltreatment (41%), sexual abuse (58%), and witnessing physical or sexual abuse or both (47%). More than half the sample had been in out-home care at least once in their lives. A large group had been in therapeutic foster homes and in individual, group, and family therapy. Professionals such as social workers, child care workers, therapeutic foster parents, and psychologists filled out the instruments on the children.

DESCRIPTION OF THE CASPARS

As clinical rating scales, the CASPARS are designed to guide practitioners to identify and work with strengths and deficits in children and families where the children have a range of adjustment issues. The overall goal of treatment is to increase strengths and reduce deficits. The number of items range from 13 to 20. Table 14.1 describes the instruments and their coefficient alphas and inter-rater reliabilities.

The CASPARS are strong psychometrically. Coefficient alphas, which are an index of reliability, ranged from .90 to .97, highly satisfactory for clinical instruments. Item-total correlations were high, suggesting a unity among the items. Construct validity with instruments thought to measure similar concepts ranged from .46 to .81, which are in the highly

TABLE 14.1
Coefficient Alphas and Inter-Rater Reliabilities for the
CASPARS Instruments

Scales	N of Items	Alpha	IRR
Emotional expressiveness	14	0.94	0.92
Family relationships	20	0.97	0.93
Family embeddedness	13	0.96	0.92
Peer relationships	16	0.90	0.93
Sexuality	13	0.90	0.95

Note: From CASPARS: New tools for assessing client risks and strengths, by J. F. Gilgun, 1999, *Families in Society, 80*, p. 450.

acceptable range. The instruments have good face validity, as four experienced clinicians contributed to their development.

Scoring. The instruments yield two scores: a risk score and an asset score. Two scores often puzzle clinicians who are accustomed to instruments that provide only one. Since the goal of treatment is to increase assets and decrease risks, both assets and risks need to be identified and their relative strengths assessed. Furthermore, conceptually, risks and assets are not the same. The CASPARS are designed with the assumption that individuals can have positive and negative aspects of a single broad attribute. As Erikson (1950/1963) demonstrated in his theory of psychosocial development, the notion of nuclear conflict posits that aspects of the same quality coexist within individuals, such as capacities for trust and mistrust. In addition, semantic differentials are composed of bipolar items, but these instruments provide one score.

For the CASPARS, each item has two sides, and each side contains a 3-point scale. Practitioners rate clients as high (3), medium (2), or low (1) on assets, or as high (3), medium (2), or low (1) on risks in the same item category. Practitioners choose the number that best represents the child's situation. A score of 3 on an asset, for example, means that the child has a strong and stable strength factor. A score of 3 on the risk side of the item means that the child has a strong and stable risk factor. A score of 0 means that practitioners have not yet investigated this aspect of client functioning and therefore cannot provide a rating. Scores are the sums of the numerical ratings of each column. Figure 14.1 shows some of the items that form the Emotional Expressiveness Scale.

The items are described in broad terms in order to tap into the kinds of knowledge that practitioners have of clients and their situations. Thus, scoring requires clinical judgment. Clinicians draw upon their multiple sources of knowledge about the children and their families, such as (a) direct contact, (b) contact with collaterals such as teachers, social workers, and medical practitioners, and (c) record reviews. After thinking about their knowledge of clients, clinicians then decide upon a score.

		not known/		
		not observed/		
high	low	absent	low	high

1. Child shows a range of feelings;   Child does not show a range of feelings;
   not only a few, such as happiness, anger,   but shows only a few, such as happiness, or
   sadness   anger or sadness

3	2	1	0	1	2	3

2. Child puts own feelings into words   Child does not put own feelings into words

3	2	1	0	1	2	3

3. Child's expression of feelings   Child's expression of feelings is not
   is appropriate to situations   appropriate to situations

3	2	1	0	1	2	3

4. Child's feelings and reactions   Child's feelings and reactions are not linked
   are linked to the events that precipitated them to the events that precipitated them

3	2	1	0	1	2	3

FIGURE 14.1. Sample items from the Emotional Expressiveness instrument.

It is true that there is a certain amount of subjectivity involved when scoring such broadly stated attributes. However, the evidence that clinicians bring to bear in making their judgments is based on several sources, as pointed out in the earlier discussion of evidence-based practice. These include what clients bring to the situations, knowledge of clients, clinical experience, personal experience, and research and theory. Biases may be present in making judgments, but good clinical practice dictates that clinicians purposefully seek information that contradicts, and thus can modify, their emerging thinking.

THE INSTRUMENTS AS A METHOD OF TRIAGE

With two scores, children can be classified according to their mix of assets and risks as shown in Figure 14.2. Children will fall into one of four groups, described in asset–risk terms. The ideal is to move children into a high asset–low risk classification. The two scores help clinicians and clients identify and work with both assets and risks. This classification can help with triage, aiding clinicians to make decisions about the appropriate types and duration of treatment. The following describes the four groups.

High–low children. Children who are high on assets and low on risks require, along with their families, some psychoeducation, supportive counseling, and limit-setting, but not intense, long-term interventions. These children and their families will be fairly "easy" to deal with in treatment and are likely to do well over the long term.

High–high children. Children and families high on assets and high on risks require intense and long-term intervention and psychoeducation to decrease risks and to maintain and increase assets. Sometimes families

	Low Risks	*High Risks*
High Assets	high-low	high-high
Low Assets	low-low	low-high

FIGURE 14.2. A classification by assets and risks. From "Clinical applications of the CASPARS instruments: Boys who act out sexually," by J. F. Gilgun, S. Keskinen, D. J. Marti, & K. Rice, 1999, *Families in Society, 80* p. 629.

are functioning fairly well but the social environment is full of risks. Conversely, families might be struggling with substantial issues but reside in a resource-rich community and have strong positive relationships with extended family, community groups, and work. Children from families that have difficult issues may have important supports outside the family. These children and their families will be challenging and interesting in clinical intervention settings, and they are likely to do well in treatment.

Low–low children. Children and families who are low on assets and low on risks require psychoeducation and long-term intervention to increase assets and to deal with risk factors. Interventions are needed to increase their links to supportive systems outside their families and to increase supportive interactions within their families. These children and families may be difficult to "reach" in clinical intervention and may appear to be uninterested and unmotivated for change. If they do well as a result of clinical intervention, that will probably mean that clinicians were able to "hook" them in such ways that their interest in themselves and in changing their situations are engaged.

Low–high children. Children and families who are classified as low on assets and high on risks require intensive, long-term interventions focused not only on strengthening connections and interactions among family members but also in developing supportive connections with individuals and social institutions outside their families. Psychoeducation can also be helpful. Some low–high children will not have the support of their biological families and may be in foster or residential care. Chemical abuse and dependency issues, chronic neglect, and severe disorganization often are found in families of low–high children.

The goal of treatment is to move children to the high assets–low risks category. At the end of treatment, the hope is that children enter environments that are high assets–low risks. If a high assets–low risk child goes into a low assets–high risks environment, then the effects of treatment are unlikely to last. If a high assets–high risks child goes into a high assets–low risks environment, the child is likely to do well.

The results of administering the CASPARS over the course of treatment can be graphed. Most clients begin treatment high in risks and low in assets, at least on the issues that brought them into treatment in the first place. As discussed, the goal of treatment is to reduce risks and increase assets. Figure 14.3 shows the graph of a successful course of treatment when clients began as low–high and ended as high–low. In those cases, the asset line intersects with the risks line.

Using graphs to assess the effects of treatment has many benefits. They are a visual representation of progress or lack of progress in treatment. Clients can see for themselves how they are responding to treatment. Such easy-to-interpret information can spark discussions and insights

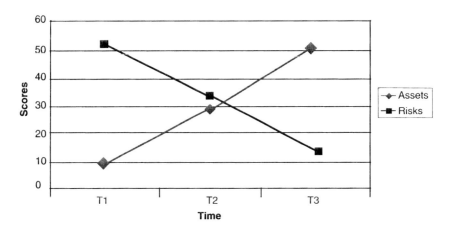

FIGURE 14.3. Hypothetical client classification change for low–high to high–low.

about what is working and not working in treatment in a variety of settings. That is, clinicians can talk to clients directly about their progress and can discuss the case in group and peer supervision. Finally, having scores and graphs documents the effectiveness of treatment. Such documentation is important to third-party funders and to the general public, as well as to clinicians, clients, and their agencies.

Summary

The design of the instruments has several advantages. First, assets are clearly spelled out. Practitioners are guided to give equal consideration to client assets and risks and thus are more likely to incorporate them into interventions. Given the overemphasis on risks in clinical practice (Berlin & Marsh 1993; Cowger, 1994; Saleebey, 2002; van Eys & Dodge, 1999), it is easy to overlook assets. Second, when assets and risks are both assessed, clients are much more likely to experience intervention as affirming and empowering. As Compton and Galaway (1999) asked their readers, "How would you feel if other people only paid attention to your deficits?"

DISCUSSION

The Clinical Assessment Package for Assessing Client Strengths and Risks (CASPARS) was developed for children who have a variety of adjustment issues related to long-term stress and trauma, such as sexually inappropriate behaviors, oppositional disorders, and anxiety disorders. They were constructed and tested for use in such settings as child and family mental health, family therapy, and child welfare, including foster care, in-home services, and residential treatment.

The CASPARS is composed of five instruments: family relationships, emotional expressiveness, peer relationships, sexuality, and family's embeddedness in the community. They assess for strengths and deficits within domains that influence child and family functioning and thus take social contexts into consideration. They identify the deficits to be decreased and the strengths to be increased through intervention.

Based on case study research, research and theory on risk and resilience, and consultations with social workers and psychologists, the CASPARS instruments were tested on a sample of 146 children and their families, where the children had a range of adversities and were at risk for poor outcomes. The CASPARS instruments have high reliabilities and validities. The instruments yield an asset score and a risk score. The items are written so they can account for changes over time. Thus they can be used for assessment, evaluation of the effects of intervention, and outcome.

As clinical rating scales, the instruments are filled out by practitioners and not by clients. Based on research, theory, and practice experience, the instruments can serve as a useful adjunct to treatment and help practitioners articulate how they see clients and how clients change over time. The two scores allow for a loose classification of children and families in terms of their relative risks and assets. Clients usually begin treatment as high on risks and low on assets and the goal of treatment is to reduce risks and increase assets.

The CASPARS instruments have a commonsense structure that guides clinicians to identify both strengths and risks. In addition, within the current climate, there is a great need to document the effects of practice. Instruments that are both grounded in clients' experiences and yet draw upon the insights that practitioners develop over time meet not only clinicians' demands for relevance but also third party funders' demands for documentation of the effects of treatment.

As Kwang and Cowger (1998) found, practitioners want to work with client strengths. Some view strengths as more important than risks, but they lack the tools that support their strengths-based perspectives. The structure of the CASPARS and the idea of giving equal consideration to assets and risks can be used to create other strengths-based instruments that are customized to other practice theories, settings, and populations.

Groups of practitioners can brainstorm items that might be useful for composing tools for their own settings and with their own clients. They can structure and score their instruments in ways similar to that of the CASPARS instruments and can pilot and modify their instruments until they are satisfied with them. Precedence for practitioner-developed, customized instruments are found in Taynor et al. (1990) and in discussions of individualized rating scales (Bloom, Fischer, & Orme, 1999). Examples of other instruments based on ideas similar to those that are foundational for the CASPARS include the 4-D, strengths-based instruments for youth in out-of-home care, and Risk Assessment in Child Welfare, discussed earlier.

CONCLUDING STATEMENTS

The current testing of the CASPARS instruments is preliminary. Testing with other samples and other raters will provide further information on reliability and validity. Future research would include exploring the properties of the CASPARS instruments with other populations of families and children, including comparisons of clinical with nonclinical samples.

The strategies used to develop the CASPARS respond to contemporary demands on clinical practice. In terms of evidence-based practice, they are built upon best research evidence, clinical expertise, and client situations. They direct attention to areas of client functioning that clinical and research knowledge identify as significant. Thus, they can decrease time needed for relevant assessments and increase the potential for brief treatment and cost containment. They provide scores that can be graphed both for estimates of progress in treatment and quantification of outcome. They also are strengths-based, another contemporary trend in clinical practice. Finally, they are short, easy to use, and, above all, useful to practice.

ACKNOWLEDGMENT

This research on which this chapter is based was funded by the Allina Foundation, Minnetonka, Minnesota, and the Minnesota Agricultural Experiment Station, St. Paul, Minnesota, Project No. 55-024. Previous funding was from the Institute for Child and Adolescent Sexual Health, Minneapolis, Minnesota.

REFERENCES

Baker, M. R., & Steiner, J. R. (1995). Solution-focused social work: Metamessages to students in Higher Education Opportunity Programs. *Social Work, 40,* 225–232.
Beck, B. M. (1997). Clients' right to effective treatment: Readers' responses. *Social Work, 42,* 620.
Berlin, S. B., & Marsh, J. C. (1993). *Informing practice decisions.* New York: Macmillan.

Bloom, M., Fischer, J., & Orme, J. G. (1999). *Evaluating practice: Guidelines for the accountable professional* (3rd ed.). Boston: Allyn & Bacon.

Bowlby, J. (1973). *Attachment and loss. Vol. II. Separation.* New York: Basic Books.

Boyum, L. A., & Parke, R. D. (1995). The role of family emotional expressiveness in the development of children's social competence. *Journal of Marriage and the Family, 57,* 593–608.

Brendtro, L. K., Brokenleg, M., & van Bockern, S. (1990). *Reclaiming youth at risk: Our hope for the future.* Bloomington, IN: National Educational Service.

Cassidy, J., & Asher, S. R. (1992). Loneliness and peer relations in young children. *Child Development, 63,* 350–365.

Cicchetti, D. (1987). Developmental psychopathology in infancy: Illustrations from the study of maltreated youngsters. *Journal of Consulting and Clinical Psychology, 55,* 837–845.

Cicchetti, D., Rogosch, F. A., Lynch, M., & Holt, K. D. (1993). Resilience in maltreated children: Processes leading to adaptive outcomes. *Development and Psychopathology, 5,* 629–647.

Compton, B. R., & Galaway, B. (1999). *Social work processes* (6th ed.). Pacific Grove, CA: Brooks/Cole.

Cowger, C. D. (1994). Assessing client strengths: Clinical assessment for client empowerment. *Social Work, 39,* 262–268.

DeJong, P., & Miller, S. D. (1996). How to interview for client strengths. *Social Work, 40,* 729–736.

DeVellis, R. F. (1991). *Scale development: Theory and applications.* Newbury Park, CA: Sage.

Egeland, B., Carlson, E., & Sroufe, L. A. (l993). Resilience as process. *Development and Psychopathology, 5,* 517–528.

Erikson, E. (1950/1963). *Childhood and society* (2nd ed.). New York: Norton.

Erickson, M. F., Korfmacher, J., & Egeland, B. (1992). Attachments past and present: Implications for therapeutic intervention with mother–infant dyads. *Development and Psychopathology, 4,* 495–507.

Evidence-Based Medicine Working Group (1992). Evidence-based medicine: A new approach to teaching the practice of medicine. *JAMA, (268),* 2420–2425.

Fraiberg, S., Adelson, E., & Shapiro, V. (1975). Ghosts in the nursery: A psychoanalytic approach to the problems of impaired mother–child relationships. *Journal of the American Association of Child Psychiatry, 14,* 387–421.

Fraser, M. W. (Ed.). (1997). *Risk and resilience in childhood.* Washington, DC: NASW.

Friedrich, W. N., Grambsch, P., Damon, L. Hewitt, S. K. Koverola, C., Lang, R. A., Wolfe, V., & Broughton, D. (1992). Child sexual behavior inventory: Normative and clinical comparisons. *Psychological Assessment, 4,* 303–311.

Garmezy, N., & Masten, A. S. (1994). Chronic adversities. In M. Rutter, E. Taylor, & L. Hersov (Eds.), *Child and adolescent psychiatry.* Oxford: Blackwell.

Gil, E., & Johnson, T. C. (1993). *Sexualized children.* Rockville, MD: Launch.

Gilgun, J. F. (1990). Factors mediating the effects of childhood maltreatment. In M. Hunter (Ed.), *The sexually abused male: Prevalence, impact, and treatment* (pp. 177–190). Lexington, MA: Lexington Books.

Gilgun, J. F. (1991). Resilience and the intergenerational transmission of child sexual abuse. In M. Q. Patton (Ed.), *Family sexual abuse: Frontline research and evaluation* (pp. 93–105). Newbury Park, CA: Sage.

Gilgun, J. F. (1992). Hypothesis generation in social work research. *Journal of Social Service Research, 15,* 113–135.

Gilgun, J. F. (1996a). Human development and adversity in ecological perspective: Part 1: A conceptual framework. *Families in Society, 77,* 395–402.

Gilgun, J. F. (1996b). Human development and adversity in ecological perspective, Part 2: Three patterns. *Families in Society, 77,* 459–576.

Gilgun, J. F. (1999a). CASPARS: New tools for assessing client risks and strengths. *Families in Society, 80,* 450–459. Tools available at http://ssw.che.umn.edu/faculty/jgilgun.htm.

Gilgun, J. F. (1999b). Mapping resilience as process among adults maltreated in childhood. In H. I. McCubbin, F. A. Thompson, A. I. Thompson, & J. A. Futrell (Eds.), *The dynamics of resilient families.* (pp. 41–70). Thousand Oaks, CA: Sage.

Gilgun, J. F. (2000, June). A comprehensive theory of interpersonal violence. Paper presented at Victimization of Children and Youth: An International Research Conference, Durham, NH, June 25–28.

Gilgun, J. F. (2002). Social work and the assessment of the potential for violence. In T. N. Tiong & Dodds, I. (Eds.), *Social work around the world II* (pp. 58–74). Berne, Switzerland: International Federation of Social Workers.

Gilgun, J F. (2002). Completing the Circle: American Indian Medicine Wheels and the promotion of resilience in children and youth in care. *Journal of Human Behavior and the Social Environment* 6(2), 65–84.

Gilgun, J. F., Keskinen, S., Marti, D. J. & Rice, K. (1999). Clinical applications of the CASPARS instruments: Boys who act out sexually. *Families in Society, 80,* 629–641.

Gilgun, J. F., Klein, C., & Pranis, K. (2000). The significance of resources in models of risk, *Journal of Interpersonal Violence, 14,* 627–646.

Goldstein, H. (1990). Strength or pathology: Ethical and rhetorical contrasts in approaches to practice. *Families in Society, 71,* 267–275.

Gray, S. H. (2002). Evidence-based psychotherapeutics: Presidential Address to the American Academy of Psychoanalysis. *Journal of the American Academy of Psychoanalysis, 30*(1), 3–16.

Greene, G. J., Jensen, C. & Jones, D. H. (1996). A constructivist perspective on clinical social work practice with ethnically diverse clients. *Social Work, 41,* 172–180.

Halberstadt, A. G., Cassidy, J., Stifter, C. A., Parke, R. D., & Fox, N. A. (1995). Self-expressiveness within the family context: Psychometric support for a new measure. *Psychological Assessment, 7,* 93–103.

Kwang, S., & Cowger, C. D. (1998). Utilizing strengths in assessment. *Families in Society, 79,* 25–31.

Mahoney, J. L., & Bergman, L. R. (2002). Conceptual and methodological considerations in developmental approach to the study of positive adaptation. *Applied Developmental Psychology, 23,* 195–217.

Masten, A. S. (1994). Resilience in individual development: Successful adaptation despite risk and adversity. In M. C. Wang & E. W. Gordon (Eds.), *Educational resilience in Inner-City America: Challenges and prospects* (pp. 3–23). Hillsdale, NJ: Erlbaum.

Masten, A. S., Best, K. M., & Garmezy, N. (1991). Resilience and development: Contributions from the study of children who overcome adversity. *Development and Psychopathology, 2,* 425–444.

Masten, A. S., & Garmezy, N. (1985). Risk, vulnerability, and protective factors in developmental psychopathology. In B. B. Lahey & Alan E. Kazdin (Eds.), *Advances in clinical child psychology (Vol. 8),* pp. 1–52. New York: Plenum.

Masten, A. S & Wright, M. O. (1998). Cumulative risk and protection models of child maltreatment (1998). *Journal of Aggression, Maltreatment and Trauma, 2*(1), 7–30.

Miller, L., Klein, R. G., Piacentini, J., Abikoff, H., Shah, M. R., Samoilov, A., & Guardino, M. (1995). The New York Teacher Rating Scale for Disruptive and Antisocial Behavior. *Journal of the American Academy of Child and Adolescent Psychiatry, 34,* 359–370.

Miller, S. D., Duncan, B. L., & Hubble, M. A. (1997). *Escape from Babel: Toward a unifying language for psychotherapy practice.* New York: Norton.

Nunnally, J. C. (1978). *Psychometric theory* (2nd ed.). New York: McGraw-Hill.

Parke, R. D., & Ladd, G. W. (1992). *Family–peer relationships: Modes of linkage.* Hillsdale, NJ: Erlbaum.

Parker, J. G., & Asher, S. R. (1987). Peer relations and later social adjustment: Are low accepted children at risk? *Psychological Bulletin, 102*, 357–359.

Rende, R., & Plomin, R. (1993). Families at risk for psychopathology: Who becomes affected and why? *Development and Psychopathology, 5*, 529–540.

Richters, J. E., & Martinez, P. E. (1993). Violent communities, family choices, and children's chances: An algorithm for improving the odds. *Development and Psychopathology, 5*, 609–627.

Roberts, W., & Strayer, J. (1996). Empathy, emotional expressiveness, and prosocial behavior. *Child Development, 67*, 449–470.

Rutter, M. (1987). Psychosocial resilience and protective mechanisms. *American Journal of Orthopsychiatry, 57*, 316–331.

Sackett, D. L., Straus, S. E., Richardson, W. S., Rosenberg, W., & Haynes, R. B. (2000). *Evidence-based medicine: How to practice and teach EBM* (2nd ed.). Edinburgh: Churchill Livingstone.

Saleebey, D. (1996). The strengths perspective in social work practice: Extensions and cautions. *Social Work, 41*, 241–336.

Saleebey, D. (Ed.). (2002). *The strengths perspective in social work practice* (3rd ed). New York: Longman.

Salter, A. C. (1988). *Treating child sex offenders and victims*. Newbury Park, CA: Sage.

Smith, C., & Carlson, B. E. (1997). Stress, coping and resilience in children and youth. *Social Service Review, 71*, 231–256.

Straus, S., & McAlister, F. A. (2000). Evidence-based medicine: A commentary on common criticisms. *CMAJ-JAMC, 163*(7), 837–841.

Taynor, J., Nelson, R. W., & Daugherty, W. K. (1990). The family intervention scale: Assessing treatment outcome. *Families in Society, 71*, 202–210.

Tracy, E. M., Whittaker, J. K., Pugh, A., Kapp, S. N., & Overstreet, E. J. (1994). Support networks of primary caregivers receiving family preservation services: An exploratory study. *Families in Society, 75*, 481–489.

Van Eys, P. P., & Dodge, K. A. (1999). Closing the gaps: Developmental psychopathology as a training model for clinical child psychology. *Journal of Clinical Child Psychology, 28*(4), 467–475.

Werner, E. E., & Smith, R. S. (1992). *Overcoming the odds: High risk children from birth to adulthood*. Ithaca, NY: Cornell University Press.

15

Multisystem Assessment of Stress and Health (MASH) Model

DAVID H. OLSON

Achieving a comprehensive assessment of the impact of stress and trauma on a family is a complicated task. Individuals and their families function on a variety of levels; individuals may fare better or worse than the couple or family relationships in which they participate. Also, they may function better in their work life than in their personal life, or vice versa. Stressors come from all areas of life and coping resources can also come from all areas of life. Consequently, what is needed is a comprehensive stress and coping model that includes all significant areas of a person's life. This chapter will describe a multisystem model of stress and coping that focuses on the four major areas of life (individual, work, couple, and family).

THE MASH MODEL

The multisystem assessment of stress and health (MASH) model is a biopsychosocial model that is multidimensional and is designed to bridge research, theory, and practice. The model builds on the circumplex of marital and family systems (Olson, Russell, & Sprenkle, 1989; Olson, 2000) which focuses on three major family system dimensions—cohesion, flexibility, and communication. The MASH model extends these to include the personal and work systems.

COPING AND STRESS PROFILES

The Coping and Stress Profile (CSP), built on the MASH model, is a comprehensive assessment tool which has been developed and validated. The CSP contains four profiles, one for each area of life: personal, work, couple, and family. Each profile contains six scales which assess (a) stress and the coping resources in (b) problem solving, (c) communication, (d) cohesion, (e) flexibility, and (f) satisfaction for each area of life. The CSP thus contains 24 scales with 6 scales for each of the four areas of life. All the CSP scales have high reliability, content validity, and construct validity. The CSP is designed for research, individual assessment and counseling, and programs for people in a variety of settings (work, couples, families, and religious groups).

Studies using the CSP in the United States (Stewart, 1988; Tasci, 1995), Germany (Schneewind, Weiss, & Olson, 1995), Norway (Piper, 1995), and Iran (Daneshpour, 1996) have demonstrated that the CSP scales are reliable and valid. It also demonstrates that the MASH model is useful in expanding our understanding of stress and coping and the interconnection of various aspects of life both in the United States and internationally.

The ultimate goal of the MASH model and the CSP is that they be used in a variety of work and counseling settings. The CSP is designed to help individuals and groups develop resources to more effectively manage stress. Stress can come from all aspects of life, and it is not necessary that coping resources come from the same area as that of the stress. Coping resources from one area of life can be effectively used to help a person manage stress from other areas of life. For example, a supportive spouse can help a partner in dealing better with a stress at work. The CSP is currently being used for counseling and in helping work groups become more effective and productive.

GLOBAL PERSPECTIVE ON FAMILY STRESS

The attack on the World Trade Center in New York City and the Pentagon in Washington, D.C., on September 11, 2001, demonstrated that stress can have a devastating impact on individuals, couples, families, and society. Ultimately, it is the family that is the major resource for helping people manage the stress in their life.

Family stress is something that families in all cultural groups have in common, though the cause of the stress and the ways of coping with the stress may differ greatly. Some observations about the commonalties about family stress across cultures will be briefly presented. However, it is also important to examine differences; an understanding of cultural differences can increase our appreciation of diversity and enhance our learning from these other cultures.

1. *All stress either begins, or ends up, in the family.* Whether the stressful issues come from outside the family system or are created inside the family system, most stressful issues end up affecting the family system at some point in time.
2. *Families from all cultures experience family stress.* While the specific causes of family stress and the specific types of issues that are most stressful may vary by culture, all families seem to experience and understand the concept of family stress.
3. *All families must find resources (internal or external or both) to help them manage the stress in their lives.* Families from various cultures may differ in the specific resources that they use to manage the stress in their family. However, family resources are often the first and most important way in which families manage their stressful life issues.
4. *Families first tend to use internal resources (inside the family system) before using external resources (outside the family system) to manage their family stress.* The definition of the family system used here is broad, and it includes both the nuclear and extended family systems. In many cultures, the extended family system plays a more significant role in managing family stress than the nuclear family system.
5. *Families from various cultures use a variety of different approaches or strategies to successfully manage their family stress.* While some work has been done to understand successful coping strategies in various cultures, there appears to be little work focused on identifying the range and variety of coping resources used by different cultural groups. This type of information could greatly enhance our understanding of stress and coping across cultures.
6. *All families have some internal strengths that they use for managing stress in their family system.* Many studies of various ethnic groups have assumed a deficit model of family functioning, often based on a Eurocentric model. Cross cultural studies of families have seldom sought to identify family strengths within a cultural group, but have tended to focus on the problems in families from different cultures. By building on a family strengths model, it is possible to more clearly identify useful coping strategies across cultures.

Multisystem Assessment of Stress and Health (MASH) Model

This chapter will provide an overview of a theoretical model that combines elements of previous family and individual stress research into an integrated MASH model. The MASH model has three major components: *stress, coping resources,* and *adaptation.* These major components are assessed at four system levels: *individual, couple, family,* and *work.* Measures of stress at each of the four levels focus on specific dynamic issues rather than life events. Coping resources focuses on the four generic relationship resources of *problem solving, communication, cohesion,* and *flexibility.* Adaptation focuses on physical health, psychological measures of adaptation, and satisfaction at each of the four system levels.

The goals of the MASH model are to build upon and extend the previous work on family stress and to develop a multidimensional and biopsychosocial model. Assessment scales built on the MASH model are included in a self-report questionnaire called the Coping and Stress Profile (CSP). The CSP is a self-report assessment of the stress, coping, and adaptational dimensions at four system levels. For research and clinical assessment, the CSP can provide a comprehensive and practical assessment for the family professional.

HISTORICAL REVIEW OF FAMILY STRESS MODELS

The ABCX model. Stress research in the social sciences has resulted in extensive investigations of either the family or the individual. Reuben Hill's (1958) pioneering work on family stress grew out of his study of war separation and reunion and was later modified to include a set of variables that have been the foundation for further work on family stress. Hill's theory had four components: A—the stressor event, which interacts with B—the family's crisis-meeting resources, which interacts with C—the definition the family makes of the event, producing X—the crisis. The resources (B) and family's definition of the event (C) come from within the family, while the event and the hardships associated with the event (A), come from outside the family.

The double ABCX model. Building initially on Hill's classic ABCX model, McCubbin and colleagues (McCubbin, Thompson, Thompson, & Fromer, 1998) developed the double ABCX model by adding post-crisis adaptation in families. In the double ABCX model, the C factor was expanded to include the family's perception of the original stressor and the pileup of stressor and strains (the A factor). In addition, the concept of coping was added to the model and it included both cognitive and behavioral strategies.

The SOC model. A sense of coherence was added to the double ABCX model based on Antonovsky's work (1994) that focused on the family's ability to know when to take charge and when to trust in the power of others. Antonovsky developed the Sense of Coherence (SOC) model that emphasizes the personal feeling of confidence which is composed of three dimensions: comprehensibility, manageability, and meaningfulness. *Comprehensibility* assumes that life is structured, predictable, and explicable. *Manageability* assumes a person has the resources to meet the current demands. *Meaningfulness* provides the context that the challenges are worthy of investment. Antonovsky (1994) reports extensive research validating the Sense of Coherence scale and model.

Boss' model. Boss (1999) has helped to expand the ABCX model to make it more systemic by adding several new concepts. Boss introduced the concept of *boundary ambiguity*, which focuses on whether a person is defined as being in or out of the family system. High boundary ambiguity occurs when there is physical presence and psychological absence or vice versa. A major premise is that families are most highly stressed when the losses are ambiguous.

Boss (2002) has also clarified the difference between coping as a family resource and coping as a process. Boss provides a variety of reasons why the concept of *managing* is more useful than *coping* for describing the process of dealing with stress. Describing the family as managing stress is more accurate than saying that the family is coping with stress. The family's coping resources are, therefore, considered strengths of the family members, but having these strengths does not mean that the family will use them.

Burr and Klein's systemic model. Burr and Klein (1994) provide a useful contribution to the field of family stress by providing a systemic model of family stress, that is in contrast to ABCX model which is considered more linear and deterministic. They focused on nine salient dimensions of family life (i.e., cohesion, marital satisfaction, communication, daily routines, contention, family development, leadership, family rituals, and emotional climate) and interviewed 46 families that experienced one of the following six stressors (bankruptcy, trouble teens, displaced homemaker, handicapped child, muscular dystropic child, or infertility). They assessed how the family's response to the stressor affected the family system functioning. Their descriptive analysis demonstrated the diversity of resources families use and the varied impact on family functioning over time.

Burr and Klein (1994) also provide an excellent summary evaluation of the coping strategies which past studies have found to be the most useful for families. They identified seven general strategies which contain a total of 20 more specific coping strategies. Their review demonstrated the salience of these coping strategies for a range of family stressors.

TABLE 15.1
Coping Resources by Burr and Klein and in Coping and Stress Profile (CSP)

General Resources	Specific Resources	Resources in CSP
Cognitive	Gain knowledge	Problem solving at four levels
Emotional	Express feelings Resolve negative feeling	Communication at four levels
Relationships	Increase cohesion Increase adaptability	Cohesion at four levels Flexibility at four levels
Individual	Develop autonomy Independence	Personal style scales

Note: The data in columns 1 and 2 are from Reexamining Family Stress (p. 133), by W. E. Burr and S. R. Klein, 1994, Thousand Oaks, CA: Sage.

Table 15.1 provides a summary of the coping strategies summarized by Burr and Klein (1994) and the major coping strategies integrated into the Coping and Stress Profile (CSP). This analysis clearly demonstrates the comprehensive nature of the CSP as it attempts to include a diverse variety of the most significant coping strategies.

COGNITIVE APPRAISAL MODEL OF STRESS AND COPING

Lazarus and Folkman (1984) have developed a theory of stress and coping based on individual, cognitive psychology. It is being included here because of the parallels it has to the double ABCX model and because of the unique contributions Lazarus has made to reconceptualizing stressor events and proposing a multilevel model of coping and adaptation.

Lazarus (1980) regards stress as a complex rubric, like emotion, motivation, or cognition rather than a simple variable. Influenced by neobehaviorist doctrines, Lazarus conceptualizes appraisal and coping as processes mediating between antecedent variables and outcomes, with appraisal processes and coping responses determining the long-term adaptational outcomes.

In the conceptual model of Lazarus and Folkman (1984), the person and environmental antecedent variables interact in such a way to produce a range of appraisals that regard the encounter as irrelevant, benign, or stressful (similar to Hill's C factor). If the encounter is appraised as stressful, the person engages various coping responses. In the process of appraisal, the variables of values and commitments the person has are integrated with environmental conditions that are faced, producing a variety of responses. Thus, appraisal affects the coping process, which in turn has an impact on the immediate outcome of the encounter and the long-term adaptational outcomes.

Lazarus and Folkman (1984) emphasize that no single variable accounts for stress in a multivariate, multiprocess system model. Stress occurs when the demands exceed the person's resources and the person perceives the demands as important. Lazarus and Folkman (1984) argue that research in stress, coping, and adaptation should be multilevel and interdisciplinary.

The central tenet of Hobfall's (1988) Conservation of Resources (COR) Theory is that individuals and systems strive to maximize resource gain and minimize resource loss.[1] Four types of resources are described: object resources (home), condition resources (good marriage), personal resources (self-esteem, mastery), and energy resources (money). Similarly, Boss (1999) maintains that resources are derived from all aspects of life: psychological, economic, sociological, and physical. Hobfall and Spielberger (1992) reviewed the research on family stress models and noted the importance of resources across all models.

MASH MODEL: A BIOPSYCHOSOCIAL APPROACH

The MASH model has three major components: stress, coping, and adaptation. Each of these components have four levels or systems of analysis: the individual, couple, family, and work systems. Each of the four systems contains stressors and strains, coping behaviors and coping resources, and adaptation. The coping resources and system types are mediating variables between stress and adaptation. The MASH model focuses on stress at four levels, coping resources at the four levels, and adaptation at the four levels. Each of the resources interact to produce a level of adaptation at the individual, couple, family, or work level.

The MASH model captures aspects of such a biopsychosocial model by providing a more integrative and eco-systemic approach to conceptualizing the recursive relationships between stress, coping, system variables, and adaptation at all four different system levels. The model can provide a *within-systems* analysis that would examine, for example, aspects of couple stress, the variety of couple coping behaviors and styles, and the degree of couple satisfaction (adaptation). This could be done separately for any of the four levels—individual, couple, family, or work levels. The model can also provide a *between-systems* analysis that would examine stress across the four levels, resources at all four levels

---

1. *Editor's note:* See chapter 2 for an in-depth description of Hobfall's conservation of resources model.

that might mediate the stress, and the final adaptation at one or all four levels (see Figure 15.1).

The need to include more than one system to the diagnosis and treatment of physical illness was raised by Dym (1987) utilizing cybernetic concepts. The clinical application of the biopsychosocial approach and its advantages were clearly presented by McDaniel, Campbell, and Seaburn (1989). A unified biopsychosocial field supersedes previous designations of illness as being merely physical or psychological. Illness can be located in the ongoing interaction of biochemical, psychological, and social experience. Dym argues that designating an illness as physical is an arbitrary punctuation of the larger field. Assuming a biopsychosocial model moves beyond such limitations and allows for diagnosis and treatment in a more holistic framework.

A cybernetic model presupposes both stable patterns and regular patterns of adjustment or change that are known as recursive cycles. Such recursive cycles can describe the relationship among various system levels: the biological, psychological, and interpersonal levels. These three system levels coevolve in continuous recursive cycles. This recursive cycle then becomes the basic level of analysis or diagnosis. Such an analysis would allow one to see that the processes in one level trigger processes in another level which are triggered by processes at yet another system level.

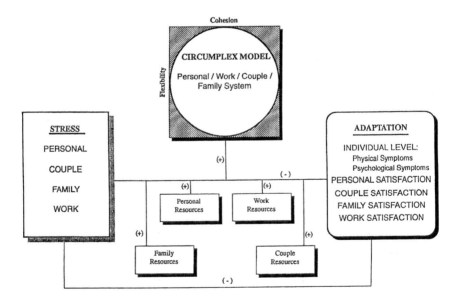

FIGURE 15.1. The multisystem assessment of stress and health (MASH) model.

Dym's proposed biopsychosocial model, Lazarus and Folkman's (1984) proposed interdisciplinary model for studying stress, and the MASH model are all attempts to move beyond previous linear models. All assume that multisystem cybernetic models will show heuristic value in future theory and research on the family and health behavior.

STRESS ASSESSMENT: SHIFT FROM LIFE EVENTS TO STRAINS

The MASH model includes the component of stress at the individual, couple, family, and work levels. Stress is defined as a state in which individuals are challenged by situations so that it overtakes the personal and collective (work, couple, family) resources and threatens the well-being of the person. Stress is conceptualized as life strains or daily hassles. Strains are used as issues for the assessment of stress at the personal, couple, family, and work levels. New stress scales have been developed for the four areas of life using strains rather than events.

Even though major life events have been the standard for assessing stress, research by Lazarus (1980) has shown that minor life strains, or daily hassles, are better predictors of subsequent psychological symptoms. Previously, the magnitude of life-event predictions of dysfunction in various retrospective and prospective studies has typically been low. Kanner et al. (1981) conducted a study of 100 middle-aged adults over nine months using measures that assessed daily hassles and uplifts, major life events, and psychological symptoms. Hassles were found to be better predictors of both concurrent and subsequent psychological symptoms than scores of major life events.

The use of *strains* to assess couple, family, and work stress was also a focus of Pearlin and Schooler (1978). These role strains related to social roles of people in their daily lives, as they go about fulfilling their personal, family, and occupational roles. Pearlin and his colleagues do not eschew the use of life events in their research, instead they examine how these events may give way to persistent role strains. Similar findings were also made with families by Lavee, McCubbin, and Olson (1986), which created a shift away from assessing events as a measure of stress to using strains.

COPING RESOURCES BASED ON THE CIRCUMPLEX MODEL

In their review of family stress theory and research, Hobfoll and Spielberger (1992) discovered certain variables were especially important in helping people manage stress: (a) flexibility or adaptability versus rigidity; (b) cohesion versus separateness; (c) communication versus privacy;

(d) boundary ambiguity versus boundary clarity; and (e) order and mastery versus chaos and helplessness.

The MASH model includes many of the variables identified by Hobfoll and Spielberger (1992) and it is primarily built upon the circumplex model of marital and family systems developed by Olson et al. (1989). The circumplex model has been widely used in couple and family research on both healthy and dysfunctional families (Olson, 2000). The model was formulated when Olson and his colleagues synthesized a number of family therapy and research concepts into three dimensions of *family cohesion, family flexibility,* and *family communication.* These three dimensions are hypothesized to function in a *linear manner* so that higher levels of cohesion and flexibility are seen as more functional for dealing with stress. Using the linear assessment model, it is hypothesized that systems which are higher in cohesion, flexibility, and communication will function more adequately and have higher levels of well-being than systems which are low (unbalanced) on these dimensions.

Previous research has primarily focused on the use of the circumplex model in assessing couple and family systems (Olson, 2000). The system dynamics in the MASH model include all four system levels: couple, family, personal, and work systems. The personal level is assessed through measures of a person's style in terms of closeness, flexibility, problem solving, and communication. How one communicates with others and the link between unexpressed emotions and adverse health outcomes have been well documented (McCubbin et al., 1998). The work system focuses on cohesion, flexibility, communication, and problem solving in the work setting.

In summary, a *linear* relationship is hypothesized to operate with cohesion, flexibility, communication, and problem solving at all four system levels and overall adaptation (satisfaction) as illustrated in Figure 15.2.

ADAPTATION: FROM PATHOGENIC TO SALUTOGENIC MODELS

In early stress research on the family (Hill, 1958), the outcome was the degree of crisis in the family system following a stressor event; that is, the degree to which the family system became disrupted and incapacitated and could not restore its stability. Such disruptions, however, are not always negative. Sometimes the family might even welcome the changes and see them as opportunities to restructure itself in a more positive manner.

Adaptation models. Lazarus and Folkman (1984) see adaptation on a continuum. In their interdisciplinary, multilevel model, they describe physical, psychological, and social health outcomes. These levels are related to three major long-term adaptational outcomes: (a) somatic

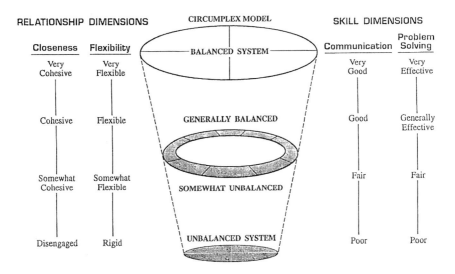

FIGURE 15.2. Linear assessment of coping resources.

health and the physiological changes generated by stressful encounters; (b) morale and the negative or positive affect a person may have both during and after stressful encounters; and (c) social functioning, or a range of effectiveness with which demands from stressful encounters are managed.

McCubbin et al. (1998) describe a continuum from *bonadaptation* to maladaptation to describe the postcrisis adjustment of the family. Bonadaptation is attained when the demand-capability balance between both the individual to family and the family to community is achieved. Family integrity is either maintained or strengthened, family independence is maintained, and family members can further grow and develop. Maladaptation, on the other hand, is characterized by unbalanced family functioning, deterioration in family integrity, decline in family independence, and deterioration in the personal health and well-being of the family unit.

The MASH model attempts to incorporate adaptation as a continuum by providing a measure of physical health and mental health at the individual level and separate measures of satisfaction at the individual, couple, family, and work system levels. By doing so, one can examine the presence or range of stress-related physical symptoms or both, as well as the extent of depression and anxiety that might exist at the physiological and psychological level within the individual. On the psychosocial level, the degree of personal, couple, family, or work satisfaction is also assessed.

Wellness models. The value of shifting from pathogenic models, which have psychopathology or illness as an outcome, to salutogenic models, which have wellness as an outcome, has been suggested by Antonovsky (1987). He argues that we cannot assume that stressors are intrinsically bad. While some stressors indeed might be, there are others that might be neutral and others that might even be salutary for the individual, as well as others that might have both negative and positive outcomes for the individual.

Lavee et al. (1986) found that family strains were associated with a more positive appraisal of the stressful situation. When marital adjustment was held constant, the sense of coherence (the general orientation that things will work out well) increased along with family strain. The experience of overcoming their difficulties may have a salutary effect on families by bolstering their sense of competence and confidence.

What is needed in stress research, according to Antonovsky, are more studies of families that do well and even prosper in the face of stress. Instead of studying the symptoms of disease, we might learn much by studying the symptoms of wellness. All of us are constantly being bombarded by stressors. If this is so, what needs to be asked is why do it some individuals (or families) respond better to stress than others?

Successful coping. The heart of Antonovsky's salutogenic model involves the study of successful coping or behavioral immunology. He argues that instead of studying what keeps people from getting sick, we might ask ourselves what facilitates a person becoming healthier. He suggests that coping variables need to be abstracted one step higher in order to find "generalized resistance resources" that will help researchers and scholars better understand how the individual copes successfully to reinforce health. By assessing social support and family system resources along with the individual resources, the multisystem MASH model attempts to lay the groundwork for such an approach.

COPING AND STRESS PROFILE (CSP): ASSESSMENT OF THE MASH MODEL

Constructs within the MASH model are measured by a number of self-report instruments included in the Coping and Stress Profile (Olson & Stewart, 1995), which is divided into four content area sections: *personal, couple, family,* and *work profiles.* Within each profile, the three dimensions of *stress, four coping resources,* and *satisfaction* are measured as illustrated in Table 15.2.

The 26 scales are based on previous research by the authors and other researchers. All of the CSP scales have rather good internal consistency reliability (alpha), averaging .80 with a range of .74 to .94 (see Table 15.3). A person would complete one or more of the relevant profiles. Each of the four profiles takes about 10 to 15 minutes to complete. Each profile

TABLE 15.2
Scales in the Coping and Stress Profile (CSP)

Dimensions	Personal	Work	Couple	Family
Stress	Personal stress Psychological distress Physical symptoms	Work stress	Couple stress	Family stress
Coping Resources	Problem solving style Communication style Closeness style Flexibility style	Work problem solving Work communication Work closeness Work flexibility	Couple problem solving Couple communication Couple closeness Couple flexibility	Family problem solving Family communication Family closeness Family flexibility Family satisfaction
Satisfaction	Personal satisfaction	Work satisfaction	Couple satisfaction Social desirability	Family satisfaction

assesses stress, coping resources, and satisfaction. The Coping and Stress Profile (CSP) is self-scoring and provides for easy interpretation of the person's scores on the various scales.

STRESS ASSESSMENT

The MASH model emphasizes persistent problems, role strains, and hassles of everyday life rather than categories of normative and nonnormative life events.

Personal, couple, and family stress. Three scales were developed by Olson and Stewart to provide a comprehensive array of strains rather than life events.

Work stress. The 35 items in this scale are used to assess the level of stress in the occupational realm are from an instrument developed by Fournier (1981) called PROFILES (Personal Reflections on Family Life and Employment). The instrument has four basic domains: (a) problems associated with work, (b) problems associated with the family, (c) impacts or effects associated with work, and (d) impacts associated with the family.

Physical health and emotional health. Adaptation at the personal level focuses in this scale on stress-related physical symptoms and a mental health index which includes a measure of psychological distress. It is assumed that individuals who are coping well with others will have fewer physical symptoms and lower levels of depression and anxiety, which are assessed by a measure of psychological distress.

TABLE 15.3
Coping and Stress Profile (CSP)—Scales and Reliabilities

Context	Source	Number of Items	Alpha Reliability
Individual Scales	Personal stress		
	Personal Stressors (Stewart & Olson, 1988)	32	.94
	Physical Symptoms (Stewart & Olson, 1988)	20	.83
	Psychological Distress (Viet & Ware, 1983)	10	.93
	Personal Coping Resources		
	Problem Solving Style (Stewart & Olson, 1988)	7	.83
	Closeness Style (Stewart & Olson, 1988)	10	.84
	Flexibility Style (Stewart & Olson, 1988)	10	.82
	Communication Style (Stewart & Olson, 1988)	10	.81
	Personal Outcomes		
	Personal Satisfaction (Veit & Ware, 1983)	14	.94
Couple Scales	Couple Stress		
	Couple Stress (Olson & Stewart, 1988)	12	.79
	Couple Coping Resources		
	Couple Problem Solving (Olson & Stewart, 1988)	10	.84
	Couple Cohesion (MACES) (Olson & Stewart, 1988)	8	.89
	Couple Flexibility (MACES) (Olson et al., 1985)	10	.78
	Couple Communication (Olson et al., 1986)	10	.85
	Couple Outcomes		
	Couple Satisfaction (Olson et al., 1986)	10	.89
Family Scales	Family Stress		
	Family Stress (Olson & Stewart, 1988)	9	.74
	Family Coping Resources		
	Family Problem Solving (Olson & Stewart, 1988)	11	.85
	Family Cohesion (FACES) (Olson et al., 1985)	8	.84
	Family Flexibility (FACES) (Olson et al., 1985)	9	.75
	Family Communication (Barnes & Olson, 1986)	10	.81
	Family Outcomes		
	Family Satisfaction (Olson & Wilson, 1985)	12	.89
Work Scales	Work Stress		
	Work Stress (Fournier, 1981)	35	.89

(continues)

TABLE 15.3
(Continued)

Work Coping Resources		
Work Problem Solving (Stewart & Olson, 1988)	6	.76
Work Cohesion (WACES) (Olson & Stewart, 1988)	5	.75
Work Flexibility (WACES) (Olson & Stewart, 1988)	6	.74
Work Communication (Olson & Stewart, 1988)	8	.84
Work Outcomes		
Work Satisfaction (Olson & Stewart, 1988)	14	.88

Measure of physical symptoms. A 20-item self-report measure developed by the authors that assesses the frequency of physical symptoms that have been shown to result from stress (Stewart & Olson, 1988). The 20-item scale does not cover the entire domain of psychosomatic symptoms, but it has good face validity based on reports of several physicians and constructs in the field of psychosomatic medicine. The second measure of individual adaptation is *Psychological Distress* from Viet and Ware (1983), a 10-item scale which focuses on anxiety and depression.

PERSONAL COPING RESOURCES

The following categories of personal strengths and styles comprise the personal coping resources.

Closeness style and flexibility style. How you connect with others is a significant resource for coping with stress. Closeness style and flexibility style measure what one prefers regarding closeness and flexibility in their relationships. A brief personality-type scale was developed for each dimension.

Communication style. Another important relationship resource is communication style, which focuses on how a person communicates with others. A 10-item self-report scale was developed by Olson and Stewart that assesses how often one expresses a variety of feelings. It also includes how often one empathizes with others, expresses frustration or disappointment, explains oneself clearly, remains in control of one's own feelings, and is appropriately assertive with others.

Problem-solving style. A problem-solving scale was developed by Olson and Stewart (1988) based on factors identified by Pearlin and Schooler (1978) and Lazarus and Folkman (1984) in their studies on coping. This is a short scale on positive problem solving which involves taking direct, positive steps to set goals, arrive at new or different solutions to problems, and remain empathic with others.

RELATIONSHIP COPING RESOURCES BASED ON CIRCUMPLEX MODEL

The system perspective, based on the circumplex model, is integrated into all four system levels and are considered as relationship coping resources. The three major dimensions from the circumplex model are *cohesion* (closeness), *flexibility,* and *communication. Problem solving* was added as the fourth relationship resource.

Couple coping resources. The four couple coping resources are *cohesion* (closeness), *flexibility, communication,* and *problem solving.* A couple scale called MACES III (Marital Adaptability and Cohesion Evaluation Scales) was developed by Olson, Portner, and Lavee (1985). This is a 20-item self-report instrument which assesses the level of *cohesion* (closeness) and *adaptability* (flexibility) within the couple system.

Couple communication is assessed by the 10-item self-report scale from the ENRICH Inventory (Olson, Fournier, & Druckman, 1989). It has an alpha reliability of .84 and test–retest reliability of .90. Items focus on the extent to which couples are able to share feelings with each other and feel understood.

Couple problem solving assesses the extent to which the couple cooperates in making decisions and finds effective ways to solve problems together. The 10-item assessment was developed by Olson and Stewart (1988) to tap into couple dynamics focused on problem solving; the scale had an alpha reliability of .84.

Family coping resources. Family resources parallel couple resources and for these there are two similar measures. FACES III (Family Adaptability and Cohesion Evaluation Scales) was revised for use in the CSP to assess *family closeness* and *family flexibility* (Olson et al., 1985). Family communication was measured using a 10-item self-report scale developed by Barnes and Olson (1986). High scores indicate that family members are able and willing to share feelings with each other and are able to feel good about their level of communication. *Family problem solving* (Olson & Stewart, 1988) assesses the family's coping behavior or coping style. Similar to the couple version, the family version of problem solving assesses decision making and cooperation in solving issues.

Work coping resources. As with the couple and family systems, there are four measures of coping resources. To assess the level of *cohesion* (closeness) and *adaptability* (flexibility) in the work group system, Work Adaptability and Cohesion Evaluation Scales (WACES) instrument was developed by Olson and Stewart (1988). There have been some attempts to apply insights gained from the family systems theory and therapy areas to work systems by White (1986). He utilized Olson's circumplex model and suggested that an enmeshed organizational family with low boundary permeability or a disengaged organizational family with high boundary permeability can be linked to increased stress and burnout in employees.

Another important resource is work communication (Olson & Stewart, 1988). This is an eight-item assessment that measures the effectiveness and clarity of interpersonal communication at work between coworkers, supervisors, and other levels of management. The fourth relationship coping behavior is work problem-solving. This is a six-item assessment developed by the authors that focuses on assertiveness, sense of humor, positive reframing, and brain storming skills (Olson & Stewart, 1988).

ADAPTATION ASSESSMENT

The following satisfaction measures are utilized in the four levels of personal, couple, family, and work.

Personal satisfaction. A 10-item Life Satisfaction Scale was developed by Viet and Ware (1983) that focuses on satisfaction and a meaningful life. Considerable research has demonstrated the empirical and clinical value of this domain, which is related to psychological satisfaction.

Couple satisfaction. This scale is a 10-item scale taken from the 125-item ENRICH Inventory by Olson, Fournier, and Druckman (1986). The *marital satisfaction* scale from ENRICH is a global measure of satisfaction in 10 areas of the couple's relationship. These areas are personality characteristics, role responsibilities, communication, resolution of conflict, financial concerns, management of leisure time, sexual relationship, parental responsibilities, relationships with family and friends, and religious orientation. High scores on the instrument are interpreted to mean compatibility with most aspects of the couple's marital relationship.

Family satisfaction. This domain is measured by a 10-item scale developed in part from the 14-item scale developed by Olson and Stewart (1988). The 14-item scale has items related to satisfaction, family cohesion, and family adaptability. The *family satisfaction* scale was developed with the idea that it is less important where the family is located on the circumplex model than how satisfied they feel about their present levels of cohesion and adaptability.

Work satisfaction. This is a 10-item scale developed by the authors for this study that assesses the degree of satisfaction gained from one's work and the degree to which one is enriched by that work as measured by Olson and Stewart (1988). It includes items that assess many of the same factors measured in the Work Stress Scale being used. These include satisfaction regarding work schedules, salary and benefits, job location, job characteristics, work atmosphere, work relationships, and work productivity. It was assumed that since these items assess most of the significant occupational issues conceptualized by Fournier (1981) in his

Work Stress Scale, the satisfaction scale should reflect similar dimensions.

STUDIES VALIDATING MASH MODEL AND CSP

In a study Stewart (1988) investigated 440 adults using the initial version of the Coping and Stress Profile (CSP) in order to test the utility of the MASH model. The study was designed to assess which resources at each of the four system levels were most characteristic of those who coped well with stress versus those who were under high levels of stress and high levels of physical or psychological symptoms or both. The 440 adults completed the CSP at a family medical practice clinic while attending a class on stress management, and were a sample of church members from a variety of denominations.

One hypothesis tested was that personal satisfaction would correlate negatively with physical symptoms and psychological distress. The findings clearly supported this hypothesis since the correlation of personal satisfaction with physical symptoms ($r = .36$) and with psychological distress ($r = .63$). As expected, physical symptoms and psychological distress were positively correlated ($r = .52$).

In order to identify what resources were used at each system level, four regression analyses were done separately for each level to predict satisfaction in that area of life. A multiple regression analysis was also done predicting overall satisfaction with life, using all the coping resources (four from each of the four areas of life). This overall measure of satisfaction was inversely related to the measure of physical symptoms and psychological distress.

The results of these five analyses demonstrated that the major resources that predicted satisfaction in one area of life were resources from that area of life. However, a study of total life stress shows that people tend to use resources from all four areas of life (Stewart, 1988).

The value of the MASH model and CSP is its ability to produce a truly comprehensive assessment. If theory or research only focused at one of the levels (i.e., individual, couple, family, or work), it would not give a realistic or comprehensive picture of all the resources that a person actually uses. Although these findings are intuitively obvious, this study clearly demonstrates the value of a multisystem model and assessment.

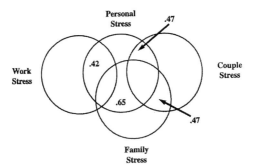

FIGURE 15.3. Connection between four stress areas.

GERMAN STUDY VALIDATES THE CSP

The CSP was translated into German by Schneewind and Weiss and Olson (1995) at the Institute for Psychology at the University of Munich. They used the CSP with 171 German adults and found that the mean scores and alpha reliabilities were very similar to the results from the U.S. The reliability of the CSP for the U.S. averaged .83 and it was .79 for the German sample.

An interesting finding from the German data was the intercorrelation of stress from the four areas of life. Figure 15.3 illustrates the significant correlations between personal stress and work stress (r = .42), between personal stress and couples stress (r = .47), between personal stress and family stress (r = .65), and between couple and family stress (r = .47). This data clearly demonstrates the value of the multisystem perspective and the interplay between the various areas of life. Similar findings were made when the various areas of satisfaction were compared. These illustrate not only the connection between the various areas of life, but also the importance of including all the areas in research, theory, and clinical practice since none of the areas alone are able to capture the comprehensive nature of stress, coping, or satisfaction.

CLINICAL USE OF THE CSP

For the professional counselor, the Coping and Stress Profile (CSP) offers a comprehensive assessment of stress, coping resources, and satisfaction in four areas of life. The CSP is designed as a starting point for clinical assessment and treatment planning. It also provides an assessment of the strengths a person has in terms of major coping resources. Figure 15.4 is an example of the CSP Profile Summary when all four of the profiles are completed and plotted onto the same form. In this example, stress

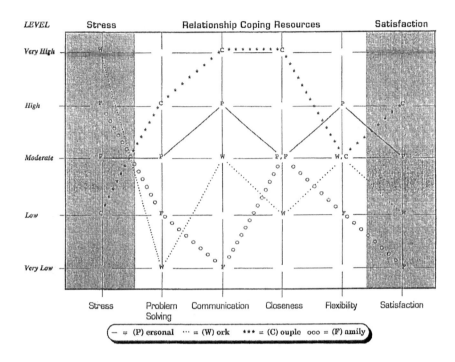

FIGURE 15.4. Coping and stress profile summary.

is highest in the work area and lowest in the couple relationship. The person also has the most coping resources in the couple relationship and much less at the work and family levels. Because of the lack of coping resources at the work and family level, it is not surprising that there is a low level of satisfaction at the work and family settings. Conversely, the high level of coping resources at the couple levels shows why couple satisfaction is high.

SUMMARY

The MASH model uses a biopsychosocial approach to understanding all the factors related to stress and coping rather than being fixated solely on symptoms and complaints. Stress is assessed in the four relevant areas of individuals' lives and coping is operationalized in terms of the interpersonal resources of problem solving, communication, cohesion, and flexibility. The CSP thus provides a more complete picture of the client's total life situation than assessments that focus only on one area of life. The value of the CSP is to identify stressful issues, coping resources, and levels of adaptation (satisfaction) in all four important aspects of an individual's life. Hopefully, this will facilitate a more meaningful dialogue between the professionals and the client, speed the process of diagnosis and treatment, and decrease the cost of professional care.

REFERENCES

Antonovsky, A. (1994). The structure and properties of the sense of coherence scale. In H. I. McCubbin, E. A. Thompson, A. I. Thompson, & J. E. Fromer (Eds.), *Sense of coherence and resiliency: Stress, coping, and health* (pp. 21–40). Madison, WI: University of Wisconsin.

Barnes, H., & Olson, D. H. (1986). *Parent-adolescent communication*. Minneapolis, MN: Life Innovations.

Boss, P. (1999). *Ambiguous loss: Learning to live with unresolved grief*. Cambridge, MA: Harvard University Press.

Boss, P. (2002). *Family stress management* (2nd ed.). Newbury Park, CA: Sage.

Burr, W. E., & Klein, S. R. (1994). *Reexamining family stress*. Thousand Oaks, CA: Sage.

Campbell, T. L. (1995). *The effectiveness of family interventions in the treatment of physical illness*. Unpublished manuscript, Department of Family Medicine, University of Rochester at Rochester, NY.

Daneshpour, M. (1996). *Stress and adaptation among Iranian families*. Unpublished doctoral dissertation, University of Minnesota, St. Paul.

Dym, B. (1987). The cybernetics of physical illness. *Family Process, 1*, 35–48.

Fournier, D. G. (1981). *PROFILES: Personal reflections on family life and employment stressors*. Stillwater, OK: Oklahoma State University.

Hill, R. (1958). Generic features of families under stress. *Social Casework, 39*, 139–150.

Hobfoll, S. E. (1988). *The ecology of stress*. Washington, DC: Hemisphere.

Hobfoll, S. E., & Spielberger, C. D. (1992). Family stress: Integrating theory and measurement. *Journal of Family Psychology, 6*(2), 99–112.

Kanner, A. D., Coyne, J. C., Schaefer, C., & Lazarus, R. S. (1981). Comparison of two modes of stress measurement: Daily hassles and uplifts versus major life events. *Journal of Behavioural Medicine, 4*, 1–39.

Lavee, Y., McCubbin, H. I., & Olson, D. H. (1986). The effect of stressful life events and transitions on family functioning and well-being. *Journal of Marriage and Family, 49*, 857–873.

Lazarus, R. S. (1980). The stress and coping paradigm. In D. Eisdorfer, D. Dohen, & A. Kleinman (Eds.), *Conceptual models for psychopathology* (pp. 173–209). New York: Spectrum.

Lazarus, R. S., & Folkman, S. (1984) *Stress, appraisal and coping*. New York: Springer.

McCubbin, H. I., Thompson, E. A., Thompson, A. I., & Fromer, J. E. (Eds.). (1998). *Stress, coping, and health in families: Sense of coherence and resiliency*. Thousand Oaks, CA: Sage.

McDaniel, S. H., Campbell, T., & Seaburn, D. (1989.) Somatic fixation in patients and physicians: A biopsychosocial approach. *Family Systems Medicine, 7*, 5–16.

McDaniel, S. H., Hepworth, J., & Doherty, W. J. (1992). *Medical family therapy*. New York: Basic Books.

Olson, D. H. (2000). Circumplex model of marital and family systems. *Journal of Family Therapy, 22* (2), 144–167.

Olson, D. H., Fournier, D. G., & Druckman, J. M. (1989). *PREPARE/ENRICH counselors manual*. Minneapolis, MN: Life Innovations.

Olson, D. H., Portner, J., & Lavee, Y. (1985). *FACES III—Family adaptability & cohesion evaluation scales*. Minneapolis, MN: Life Innovations.

Olson, D. H., Russell, C., & Sprenkle, D. H. (Eds.). (1989). *Circumplex model of marital and family system*. Newbury Park, CA: Sage.

Olson, D. H., & Stewart, K. L. (1987). *Scales in the Health and Stress Profile*. Minneapolis, MN: Life Innovations.

Olson, D. H., & Stewart, K. L. (1991. Family systems and health behaviors. In H. E. Schroeder (Ed.), *New directions in health: Psychological assessment* (pp. 27–64). New York: Hemisphere.

Olson, D. H., & Stewart, K. (1995). *Coping and Stress Profile (CSP)*. Minneapolis, MN: Life Innovations.

Parkerson, G. R., & Broadhead, W. E. (1995). Perceived family stress as a predictor of health related outcomes. *Archives of Family Medicine, 4*, 253–260.

Parkerson, G. R., Broadhead, E., & Tse, C. J. (1995). Perceived family stress as a predictor of health-related outcomes. *Archives of Family Medicine, 23*, 357–360.

Pearlin, L. I., & Schooler, C. (1978). The structure of coping. *Journal of Health and Social Behavior, 19*, 2–21.

Piper, J. (1995). *Work stress in Lutheran clergy women in the U.S. and Norway*. Unpublished doctoral dissertation, University of Minnesota, St. Paul.

Schneewind, K. A., Weiss, J., & Olson, D. H. (1995). *Coping and Stress Profile: A German and American comparison*. Unpublished manuscript, University of Munich at Germany and University of Minnesota at St. Paul, MN.

Stewart, K. L. (1988). *Stress and adaptation: A multisystem model of individual, couple, family, and work systems*. Unpublished doctoral dissertation, University of Minnesota, St. Paul.

Stewart, K. L., & Olson, D. H. (1988). *Scales in the Health and Stress Profile*. Minneapolis, MN: Life Innovations.

Tasci, D. L. (1995). *Family ghost in the corporate setting: Comparison of family of origin and work system using the Coping and Stress Profile*. Unpublished doctoral dissertation, University of Colorado, Gainesvilla.

Viet, C. T., & Ware, J. E. (1983). The structure of psychological distress and well-being in general populations. *Journal of Consulting and Clinical Psychology, 51*, 730–742.

White, W. (1986). *Incest in the organizational family: The ecology of burnout in closed systems*. Bloomington, IL: Lighthouse Training Institute.

16

The Contextual Treatment Model

STEVEN N. GOLD

Contextual therapy is a form of treatment specifically designed to meet the needs of clients with particularly extensive and intricate trauma histories. These individuals frequently present with the wide range of debilitating symptoms subsumed under the designation *complex posttraumatic stress disorder* (C-PTSD) (Herman, 1992a, 1992b), also known as *disorders of extreme stress* (DES) (Pelcovitz et al., 1997). Although over a decade has passed since the construct of C-PTSD was first introduced to the professional literature, and despite the existence of empirical evidence supporting its validity (Ford, 1999; Roth, Newman, Pelcovitz, van der Kolk, & Mandel, 1997; Zlotnick & Pearlstein, 1997), broad recognition of this syndrome has been slow, and C-PTSD has yet to be officially recognized via inclusion in the *DSM*.

The distinction between PTSD and C-PTSD remains blurred in the minds of many practitioners. Treatment for C-PTSD often consists of attempts to apply or extend therapeutic approaches originally developed to resolve PTSD (e.g., Herman, 1992a). The reasons for this trend are not difficult to identify. The very name "complex PTSD" implies that this syndrome, although more intricate in nature, is essentially a variation of PTSD. From its inception, the diagnosis of C-PTSD (Herman, 1992b), like PTSD (American Psychiatric Association, 1980), has been explicitly tied to the etiology of trauma. In contrast to other syndromes defined primarily on the basis of symptomatology, the presence of a trauma history is a requisite criterion for a diagnosis of either PTSD or C-PTSD.

THE CONCEPTUAL FRAMEWORK

Because the symptomatology of PTSD and C-PTSD are equated with traumatic origins, many clinicians consider it axiomatic that confronting and processing the content of the client's traumatic experiences is the cornerstone of therapeutic effectiveness with either of these diagnoses. However, clients who meet criteria for C-PTSD do not usually benefit from this type of intervention early in treatment; in fact, they are vulnerable to being overwhelmed by premature detailed confrontation of traumatic material (Academy of Traumatology, 2001; Barach, 1999; Courtois, 1999; van der Kolk, 1999; Ford & Kidd, 1998). Many authors have noted the importance of a protracted phase of establishing a sense of safety and security before proceeding to intensively trauma-focused intervention (e.g., Courtois, 1997; Phillips & Frederick, 1995; Herman, 1992a).

Survivors of Prolonged Child Abuse

Survivors of prolonged child abuse (PCA), the form of trauma most commonly associated in the literature with a diagnosis of C-PTSD or DES (e.g., Ford, 1999; Ford & Kidd, 1998; Roth et al., 1997; Herman, 1992a), comprised the primary population for which contextual therapy (CT) was originally developed. CT was devised in response to the observation that this population was distinct from clients with more circumscribed trauma histories in a number of important respects. Chief among these is the observation that trauma-focused forms of treatment, while frequently effective with other trauma populations, not only fail to produce the same positive outcomes but often lead to marked deterioration in functioning in PCA survivors.

Therapists who subscribe to a trauma-focused model of treatment often exhort clients to stick with the treatment by assuring them that sometimes it has to get worse before it gets better. Sadly, it is not unusual that after weeks or even months of trauma-focused treatment, there is no eventual improvement, only progressive decline (Gold & Brown, 1997). One of the most disturbing aspects in these cases is that the adverse impact of this type of intervention is often long-term. PCA survivors frequently leave this form of treatment with a markedly lower level of functioning than when they entered it. In addition, they often leave feeling that they have somehow failed, and they are more mistrustful of therapists and pessimistic about their prospects for recovery (Gold & Brown, 1997; Pearlman & Saakvitne, 1995).

The course of treatment for PCA survivors is often appreciably more erratic than that of those with less protracted trauma histories. It usually takes considerably longer—often many months—to establish a sufficiently stable therapeutic relationship to be able to productively concentrate on, and follow through with, specific interventions. A perplexing mixture of wariness of the therapist and simultaneously seeking out the therapist in response to an extensive series of crises often distracts PCA survivors from focusing effectively and consistently on working toward treatment goals. The varied spectrum of symptoms and difficulties presented by these clients often seems to spontaneously wax and wane, with apparent reduction in one problem immediately leading to exacerbation of another.

One of the most decisive observations that shaped the evolution of CT was identified when PCA survivors were allowed to guide exploration toward the elements in their history that were most salient to them, instead of being directed toward concentrating on their abuse experiences. What emerged was a picture entirely consistent with the overt instances of abuse they had experienced, but much broader in scope and implications. In contrast to survivors with less extensive trauma histories, PCA survivors described extremely chaotic and ineffective family and social environments (Harter, Alexander, & Neimeyer 1988; Long & Jackson, 1994; Williamson, Borduin, & Howe, 1991). Remarkably similar family patterns were described by PCA survivors, regardless of whether their abuse had been carried out by relatives or by individuals outside the family (Gold, Russa, Lucenko, & Vermont, 1998; Yama, Tovey, & Fogas, 1993; Ray, Jackson, & Townsley, 1991; Alexander & Lupfer, 1987). Clinical case assessment suggested that the inadequate family and social systems failed to provide these individuals with the resources required for adaptive daily living. This conjecture is supported by a number of studies indicating that family of origin environment contributes to the adult symptomatology of PCA survivors over and above the impact of abuse (e.g., Alexander, 1993; Fromuth, 1986; Harter et al., 1988; Melchert, 2000; Nash, Hulsey, Sexton, Harralson, & Lambert, 1993).

On the basis of this perspective, CT places primary emphasis on interventions designed to help survivors develop those capacities for effective adult functioning that were not adequately transmitted to them during their early development. Although the focus is not on their abuse experiences per se, CT acknowledges and examines the impact that abuse trauma has had on their adjustment and integrates that awareness into the larger focus on the acquisition of adaptive capacities.

The Family Context of Prolonged Child Abuse

When the therapist does not assume that incidents of abuse are the exclusive reason for the wide and varied range of difficulties the PCA survivor manifests, what emerges is a much fuller, more intricate, and clinically useful understanding of the client's background. Under these conditions, PCA survivors do not focus chiefly on explicit incidents of abuse. Instead, they describe growing up in circumstances in which emotional support—and guidance in practical matters—was at best inconsistently available and at worst almost entirely lacking.

Regardless of the socioeconomic status of the family of origin, one regularly hears accounts from this client population that challenge popular assumptions about the degree to which the fulfillment of basic emotional and practical needs is a universal given in the lives of children. These clients describe examples of concrete deprivation such as never having been taken to a doctor or dentist, never having had a birthday party, and going hungry because their parents limited their access to food. Due to the relative lack of guidance they received growing up, they may enter adulthood painfully unaware of how to execute basic tasks such as renting an apartment, brushing their teeth, or obtaining a bank account. As adults, they are at a loss as to how to even find out how to do many of these basic life tasks. On a more global level, these clients usually convey a picture of growing up never having felt secure or loved, frequently having been criticized or ignored, and having had little or inconsistent structure. Consequently, they often have extensive difficulties with broad and fundamental aspects of functioning such as establishing and navigating close relationships, recognizing and modulating feelings, and developing and maintaining a stable life structure.

The pervasive spectrum of deprivation these clients experienced during their formative years fall into three central categories:

1. *Attachment deficits.* The lack of reliable interpersonal connection, emotional support, and direction results in major gaps in the capacity to form secure and stable bonds with others.
2. *Inadequate social learning.* Due to the absence of sufficient guidance and direction, basic capacities required for effective adult functioning, ranging from concrete skills such as those involved in paying monthly bills to general abilities such as productively negotiating interpersonal conflicts, are weak or absent.
3. *Inappropriate modeling.* The family environments in which PCA survivors are reared not only fail to transmit adaptive living skills, but they frequently model maladaptive coping strategies. Examples of reactions to distress modeled by parental figures and other

familymembers include interpersonal violence, verbal denigration of self and others, substance abuse, and sexual acting out.

The effect of these three trends is that children reared in these circumstances are noticeably different from their peers in their interpersonal functioning. Due to their attachment difficulties and poor social skills, the very avenue that could provide remediation of these deficits—relationships with well-socialized peers—is not readily accessible to them. From an early age, a combination of influences and resulting difficulties make it extremely unlikely that other children, or even adults, will gravitate toward them or tolerate their behavior. Salient among these factors are an extremely negative self-concept (due to awareness of their inadequacies and the criticism with which they have often lived), mistrust of others (arising from a history of maltreatment), intense neediness (resulting from emotional deprivation), and inappropriate behavior (reflective of their poor social learning).

A repeating cycle is set in motion. Interpersonal deficits present an obstacle to connection with others, and the absence of intimate interpersonal contact perpetuates and widens the disparity between PCA survivors' level of social adjustment and that of their peers through childhood and adolescence into adulthood. Moreover, the recurring experience of ostracism by the outside world only seems to confirm their deeply held conviction of being unlovable, reprehensible, and inept.

Paired with a family system that often demands blind obedience (usually to capricious and constantly fluctuating rules) and provides little reliable affection, these self-perceptions and repeated experiences of rejection render these individuals particularly vulnerable to being manipulated, coerced, dominated, and abused—first in childhood and later in adulthood. Their unquestioning compliance and hunger for attention and approval are qualities that are instinctively noticed by those predatory individuals who gravitate toward others whom they can dominate and exploit. Consequently, rather than being universally shunned, individuals from this type of ineffective family environment are most likely to attract people who are controlling and malicious. Maltreatment and abuse, often at the hands of a number of people over time, further strengthen the certitude of PCA survivors that they are wretched and undeserving of compassion or acceptance, and that others are malevolent and untrustworthy. In addition, the traumatic impact of abuse compounds their already considerable distress and adjustment difficulties.

It has been proposed that traumatic events are destabilizing because they destroy core assumptions such as those about one's personal safety, the trustworthiness of others, and the predictability of the world (Janoff-Bulman, 1992; McCann & Pearlman, 1990; Horowitz, 1986). It would be difficult to argue, however, that this is the case for PCA survivors. When embedded in a familial and social context that fails to provide the resources needed to develop secure attachments and adequate social learning, explicit instances of abuse, far from disrupting their core beliefs, confirm their already considerable conviction that danger and chaos are constants. In this respect, explicit incidents of abuse merely comprise particular threads that are intertwined and entirely consistent with the larger fabric of their lives.

In addition to having a profound impact on their cognitive schema, the consistency between the interpersonal context in which PCA survivors develop and the discrete episodes of explicit abuse to which they are subjected has decisive practical implications. It is often the very lack of sufficient supervision and concern for the welfare of these children that makes it possible for them to be abused repeatedly over extensive periods of time. It is striking how often PCA survivors in therapy report that a parent was told about the abuse or actually witnessed them being assaulted but took no action to stop it (e.g., Gottlieb, Pardoll, Gold, & Schlessinger, 2001; Everill & Waller, 1995; Gold, Swingle, & Garcia-Larrieu, 1995). In fact, instead of reproaching the adult perpetrator and taking decisive action to prevent the abuse from continuing, the shocked parent frequently reprimands the child victim rather than the perpetrator. The sense of abandonment and experience of vilification for their own victimization painfully underscores the PCA survivor's perceptions of being doomed to perpetual isolation, helplessness, and misery.

The clinical picture that emerges from these observations is appreciably more multifaceted and convoluted than the common formulation that abuse trauma disrupts functioning in the form of PTSD, and that repeated trauma leads to progressively more extensive symptomatology in the guise of complex PTSD. Instead of suggesting a direct line of causation leading from abuse trauma in childhood to problems in adjustment in adulthood, the contextual perspective proposes the existence of a more complex and interacting constellation of sources of the broad range of disabling difficulties manifested by clients with a PCA history.

The key practical clinical implication of this conceptual framework is that many of the difficulties presented by these clients are attributable to their lack of access to resources needed for the adequate development of secure interpersonal attachment and social learning. To the extent that these clients' problems result from never having developed certain capacities (rather than to the disruption of functioning due to the impact of trauma), the confrontation and processing of traumatic material cannot be expected to resolve their problems. Trauma-focused intervention can restore abilities that have been subverted by trauma. However, no amount of trauma work will instill capacities that were lacking before trauma was encountered. In fact, in the absence of these fundamental adaptive capacities, the extreme stress imposed by interventions that entail direct confrontation with explicitly traumatic material is likely to result in exacerbation, rather than resolution, of symptomatology.

THE TREATMENT APPROACH

The conceptual model that informs CT attempts to address the varied and intricately interwoven factors that culminate in the broad range of debilitating symptoms commonly manifested by those meeting diagnostic criteria for complex PTSD. The CT treatment philosophy emphasizes the need to respond to the complexity of these clients' histories and symptom patterns with a plan of intervention that provides as much structure and simplicity as possible. This principle is invaluable to clients because it fosters an interpersonal environment that is markedly different from the unpredictable and chaotic interactions they have experienced previously. It is also essential in helping the therapist to maintain a sense of clarity, organization, and direction to a course of treatment that is often threatened by potential crises, disruptions, and digressions.

To assist the therapist in maintaining the utmost clarity and consistency, the numerous elements of the CT intervention process are conceptually divided into three primary aspects: the interpersonal component, the conceptual component, and the practical component.

The Interpersonal Component

One of the greatest challenges in conducting effective therapy with PCA survivors is their lack of familiarity with the type of collaborative interpersonal relationship that is indispensable to effective therapy. Both during their formative years and subsequently, most of these clients have encountered a preponderance of interpersonal experiences that have been characterized by overt contempt, domination, rejection, indifference, conflict, chaos, and unpredictability. This type of interpersonal history culminates in several consequences that create severe limitations in these clients' capacity to form a productive therapeutic relationship at the outset of treatment.

Distrust. Extensive disappointing past experiences with others leave them with little reason to believe that anyone will be positively disposed toward them. Instead, they are left with a deep conviction that rejection and eventual abandonment by others is inevitable. In conjunction with the expectation that those who do seem to take an interest in them will eventually maltreat and exploit them, these factors foster a deep-seated mistrust of others. Clinicians are not exempt from this perception. Even when PCA survivor clients are willing to believe that their therapist is benevolent and acts out of good intentions, they usually are certain that their own unworthiness and reprehensibility ensures that sooner or later the therapist will give up on them in disgust.

Dependency. Often simultaneously present alongside this abiding mistrust is excruciatingly painful longing stemming from unmet dependency needs. For many PCA survivors the experience of not having been loved by their own parents is even more profound and disturbing than the distress associated with explicit incidents of abuse. The lack of a secure sense of attachment with those who were responsible for providing care breeds both a profound sense of isolation from others and a contempt for themselves for being so unlovable. The resulting desperate desire for attention, validation, and affection often leads these clients to intensely cling to others, usually leading others to feel overwhelmed and to respond by pulling away. A recurring cycle of intensely latching onto others and being rebuffed only serves to reinforce survivors' core self-perception that they are despicable and incapable of being loved.

The unique situation of receiving the undivided attention of the therapist in session is so dramatically at odds with the PCA survivor's previous interpersonal encounters that it sometimes activates her or his unmet dependency needs in a particularly intense manner. This can lead to preoccupation with the therapist, having difficulty tolerating separation from the therapist, and a desperate desire to establish contact with the therapist between sessions. Although far from universal among PCA survivors, in the most extreme cases these factors result in a series of crisis situations (e.g., suicidal threats, episodes of self-mutilation, relapses into addictive behavior patterns) that provide the client with the opportunity to interact with the therapist between appointments. In the vast majority of cases the client is entirely unaware of, or at best only dimly cognizant of, this motivation. It is primarily the painful and destabilizing desperate need for contact with the therapist, rather than calculated manipulation, that fuels these crises. However, when these crises are successful in securing the attention of the therapist, they escalate in frequency and intensity rather than subsiding. Although interaction with the therapist may be temporarily experienced as soothing, it ultimately only serves to reinforce clients' conviction of their need for the therapist, exacerbating the sense of urgency for further contact.

The treatment situation can quickly become chaotic and unproductive if the therapist is too available to respond to these crisis situations. A way to avoid this is to provide resources for the client to contact in case a crisis occurs, such as crisis hot lines or hospital emergency rooms, at the outset of treatment. When crises do not create the opportunity to contact the therapist, they are drastically less likely to occur.

It is likely that those PCA survivor clients whose guardedness outweighs their dependent longing suffer in silence, not acting on or letting their therapist know of their feelings of neediness. The suppressed dependency longings of some PCA survivors may only be visible in the termination phase of treatment when overt expressions of intense attachment to the therapist and difficulty modulating the accompanying feelings finally emerge. Whether communicated overtly or not, however, these experiences can interfere with treatment progress.

The therapy relationship. The larger issue is that the gaps in social learning, unmet dependency needs, and mistrust of others prevalent among this population require therapists to be more attentive to fostering a productive therapeutic relationship than they might be with other clinical populations. Sensing the extreme deprivation these clients have experienced, it is not at all unusual for practitioners to be tempted to make exceptions, bend the usual treatment structure, and in general extend themselves in ways that they would not for other clients. Acting on these impulses, however, only confuses PCA survivors by raising their hopes that the therapist will be endlessly available and responsive. Many of these clients grew up in families that failed to model appropriate respect for interpersonal boundaries, and the survivors' privacy and personal limits were regularly violated. As a result, often they will not recognize when the clinician becomes over-involved and intrusive. Thus, a greater onus is placed on the therapist to monitor her or his behavior in this regard. It is imperative that the structure of the treatment situation be clearly defined at the outset, closely monitored, and carefully maintained.

While the particulars of this structure should be open to discussion and negotiation, the guiding principle behind them is to limit contact outside of sessions while providing clear parameters to maximize the likelihood that interactions during sessions are focused and productive. Since many PCA survivors are dissociative and only experientially present to a limited degree during the early phases of treatment, the therapist needs to make a special effort to stay focused and attentive during session to promote interpersonal contact. In this respect, the treatment structure is designed to maximize the quality of interaction during session by restricting the quantity of interaction between sessions.

Purposeful attention to, and maintenance of, the therapeutic relationship is crucial to the effectiveness of treatment for PCA survivors. The therapeutic alliance is simultaneously a means and an end. As a means, it allows clients to learn how to align with the therapist to work toward resolving their problems and improving their functioning. As an end, it is a forum for learning skills for forming and sustaining interpersonal relationships, skills that were not adequately transmitted to them in their formative years.

The conceptual component. Awareness of global influences on the functioning of PCA survivors can help clinicians understand many otherwise mystifying behaviors commonly observed in this population and help guide treatment in a productive direction. For example, consider the impact on the therapeutic alliance. These clients often grew up in families that did not model widely accepted cultural norms about interpersonal behavior, such as respect for boundaries. Thus, client behavior that appears intrusive or entitled may actually reflect ignorance of social norms. Recognition of this possible gap in social learning can help the therapist avoid viewing the client as being simply disrespectful or demanding. It is often sufficient to tactfully inform them about commonly accepted standards of behavior rather than assume that they "know better" but intentionally act otherwise.

Skills deficits. The general principle which is being alluded to here is that a contextual perspective alerts us to the possibility that many of the difficulties manifested by PCA survivors are skills deficits (i.e., the knowledge or skills required to carry out the behavior are not present) rather than performance deficits (i.e., behavioral capacities that are present but which for some reason are not being accessed). By virtue of their legacy of having grown up in an ineffective family system, PCA survivors often have gaps in knowledge and skills so fundamental that they are commonly assumed to be universal.

In the realm of conceptual skills, this principle manifests in pervasive deficits in the capacity for logical reasoning and critical thinking. In the families of origin of these clients, decisions were often capricious, rules were inconsistent and unpredictable, obvious but unpleasant facts were denied, and thoughts and feelings that others in the family found disturbing were invalidated. In short, logic and critical thinking were poorly or inconsistently modeled, and conclusions by the survivor that were disturbing to others in the family, regardless of how sound they were, were subject to derision and negation.

Limitations of therapist as expert. The usual impact of these circumstances is that PCA survivors frequently doubt their own perceptions, feelings, and reasoning capacities. They often enter therapy all too eager for the therapist to set them straight about the way things really are or were, including what the client actually has felt or experienced. This desire for the therapist to define the client's experience might seem easy to avoid but it is complicated by the client's genuine need for education about so many aspects of life. Educative efforts can be a useful strategy for imparting social norms and other aspects of social learning that were not transmitted to them during their early development. Clients cannot be expected to figure out for themselves concrete information that they have never been taught. This is particularly the case with social conventions, which are often derived from accidents of history and tradition rather than from logical deduction. As Harry Stack Sullivan (1953) once quipped, "the culture itself is based on no single great general principle that can be grasped even by a genius, but is based instead on many contradictory principles" (p. 191). However, educating clients can be an extremely detrimental tactic when it lapses into explaining clients to themselves.

Just as many clinicians' first inclination might be to respond to survivors' deprivation by extending themselves more than they normally would, they may be more inclined to provide these clients with information or clarification that has been previously denied. In many areas, such as explaining common social conventions or imparting concrete information about practical matters, this indeed can be helpful. However, to take this approach in order to help clients understand *themselves* would be an unfortunate mistake. Although these clients do not trust their own perceptions and conclusions, they are also are at a loss for criteria on which to base the decision regarding whom else to believe. Moreover, responding in this way can subtly confirm the belief of so many survivors that they are incapable of assessing their own subjective experience as a basis for coming to reliable conclusions on their own.

The client as expert. It is critical here to make the distinction between content and process. Only clients can be the experts regarding the content of their experience—the facts, memories, thoughts, and feelings that constitute the data from which they build a conceptual understanding of their circumstances and how they have shaped their current functioning. Thus, it is essential that PCA survivors themselves be the ones to formulate a conceptualization that makes sense of their lives and their difficulties. The therapist's legitimate role is to help structure the process through which survivor clients arrive at these conclusions. In the conceptual realm, the therapist supplies the skills that comprise the method of coming to sound conclusions.

In terms of therapeutic technique, this means employing nondirective interviewing strategies, such as active listening or Socratic questioning, that help the client follow a systematic and logical thread to examine the evidence available to them. The challenge to the therapist is to avoid allowing her or his preconceptions, biases, or hypotheses to unduly shape the conclusions reached. This can be particularly difficult for therapists who are in the habit of offering extensive interpretations of the material presented by clients.

The benefits of exercising this type of discipline are several. When the client is allowed to take the primary role in directing exploration, the deductions produced are more likely to be valid, because only the client is privy to the data on which they are based. There is also a greater probability that these conclusions will be congruent with the immediacy of the client's subjective experience. This means that the client is more likely to put credence in the outcome, not to second-guess her or his conclusions, and to better integrate the new viewpoint into her or his network of cognitive schema.

When the clinician's attention is focused on guiding the process rather than the content of exploration, the clinician intrinsically conveys how to exercise logical reasoning, critical judgment, and decision-making skills. In effect, therapist and client, while engaging in the process of exploration, are jointly "walking through" these processes together. The therapist intentionally focuses on not jumping to conclusions or unduly shaping the outcome of exploration. Therapists invite clients to attend to the evidence relevant to the issue at hand, encourage generation of alternative ways of thinking about the issue, and facilitate the critical examination of each of these possibilities. This approach is largely similar to the technique referred to by Meichenbaum (as cited in Hoyt, 1996) as "Colombo-like style" interviewing.

The Practical Component

The practical component of CT centers on helping clients acquire the adaptive and coping skills that they never adequately mastered. A central tenet of CT is that these skills are lacking or incomplete because they were not adequately modeled or otherwise transmitted to these clients by their families of origin. It is the practical component of CT that is most closely associated with specific, structured modes of intervention. However, there is an important reason why this component is presented here last. The CT treatment model is grounded in conceptualization, not technique.

The interventions employed in the practical component of treatment may vary widely from one client to the next. This is because the specific deficits in knowledge, skills, and functioning will obviously differ in many ways from one PCA survivor client to another on the basis of the particular warps that characterized their family of origin environment and the resulting gaps in their social learning history. However, there are general realms of functioning that tend to be problematic for most of these clients. Each of these domains corresponds to a broad treatment goal.

On one hand, these treatment goals are not addressed in a lock-step order; CT is an individualized, rather than a manualized, form of treatment. The interpersonal, conceptual, and practical components of treatment are interwoven and unfold simultaneously. Even within the practical component, it is likely that aspects of more than one treatment goal will be worked on in the same session. However, these goals are still best addressed in a logical sequence. To emphasize this point, they are referred to as prioritized treatment goals.

Goal 1: Reduce distress. The top priority in the practical component of CT is helping PCA clients reduce their usually considerable level of emotional distress. The most salient forms of distress in the clinical picture (e.g., anxiety, depression, rage, loneliness, and confusion) may differ appreciably from one client to another. However, the common element is that most of the time these clients are experiencing a level of misery that seriously interferes with their capacity to attend to and effectively carry out basic tasks of daily living. Consequently, until they learn to moderate their level of distress, little else in the way of improving practical functioning is likely to be accomplished. This is why this goal carries the highest priority.

From the perspective of the emphasis on skills acquisition that is central to CT, this treatment goal would consist of assisting the client to develop the capacity for self-soothing and managing distress. The primary objective is not to reduce distress per se, and especially not for the therapist to intervene to help the client feel more secure. Instead, the aim is for the client to learn how to do this for herself or himself. Otherwise, the value and generalizability of what is accomplished is severely limited, and the client's dependency on the therapist is only exacerbated.

Goal 2: Reduce dissociation. To the degree that some headway has been made in helping the client learn how to modulate distress, interventions can begin to address another difficulty characteristic of this population—dissociative symptomatology. While dissociative symptoms can appear varied in their manifestations (e.g., amnesia, depersonalization, and identity fragmentation), what they have in common, and what the term dissociation essentially connotes, is an underlying experiential *disconnection.* Dissociative symptoms can include disconnection from the sensory and perceptual immediacy of the here and now, from one's own subjective feelings and experience, or from a sense of experiential contact with other people. In this respect, dissociation interferes with the capacity to remain focused on one's present surroundings, thereby interfering with attention, concentration, memory, a sense of continuity, and effective information processing. Dissociative experiences generally appear to be triggered by high levels of distress. Thus, some progress in the mastery of distress reduction strategies is required before clients can reasonably be expected to learn how to modulate their ability to maintain focal attention on the here and now.

The origins of dissociative symptoms have traditionally been attributed almost exclusively to the disruptive impact of traumatic experiences (e.g., Ross, 1997; Kluft, 1996; Cardeña, 1994; van der Hart, Steele, Boon, & Brown, 1993). However, contextual and related theories (Gold, 2000; Alexander, 1992; Barach, 1991) and a growing body of empirical evidence (Liotti, 1999; Anderson & Alexander, 1996) suggest that insecure attachment and other aspects of disturbed family of origin environments may be major contributors to pathological dissociation. This is why CT stresses the relevance of the interpersonal component of treatment to helping the client learn to modulate dissociation. The experiential connection that emerges from the development of a solid therapeutic relationship contributes substantially to the client's developing capacity to remain grounded in and focused on the here and now.

Goal 3: Improve cognitive processing. Once substantial gains have been made in the capacities to modulate distress and maintain concentration, the client is better equipped to stay sufficiently focused to engage in cognitive processing. It is at this point, therefore, that it is beneficial to introduce more extensive cognitive interventions. These interventions, already discussed in relation to the conceptual component of CT, serve two primary functions. One is to help the client learn to challenge and dispel distortions and misunderstandings generated by the capricious and unpredictable experiences encountered in their families of origin and in subsequent relationships characterized by maltreatment and overt abuse. The other function is for clients to master the general abilities of exercising logical reasoning and critical thinking.

Goal 4: Eliminate maladaptive coping. A certain level of attainment in maintaining a stable sense of security, sustained focusing ability, and logical reasoning allows for work on the next priority, breaking maladaptive coping strategies. Most PCA survivors engage in a number of addictive and compulsive behaviors such as substance abuse, bingeing and purging, self-mutilation, compulsive spending or gambling, and sexual compulsions. The contextual conceptual framework proposes that in the absence of having learned more adaptive coping mechanisms, these addictive and compulsive patterns developed as a haphazard effort at reducing and distracting oneself from acute distress. Building on gains made in the prioritized treatment goals, CT employs a form of functional behavioral analysis to help clients (a) examine their compulsive and addictive patterns, (b) recognize the circumstances that trigger these patterns, and (c) appreciate how ineffective these behaviors are in managing distress. The understanding gleaned from this analysis helps clients develop the motivation and strategies for relinquishing these behaviors. (For a fuller discussion of this method of intervention, see Gold, 2000, and Gold and Seifer, 2002).

Goal 5: Process traumatic memories. The final item in the hierarchy of prioritized treatment goals in CT is the direct confrontation and processing of abusive incidents and other explicitly traumatic experiences. CT is based on two fundamental principles that are easily misconstrued as incompatible. On one hand, CT represents a significant departure from trauma-focused models of treatment. It posits that many of the adjustment difficulties manifested by PCA survivors are attributable to having grown up in ineffective family and social environments that failed to provide them with the adaptive capacities essential for adequate functioning. This perspective emphasizes that treatment which is primarily focused on the abuse experiences of these clients is not only unlikely to be effective but runs a high risk of fostering decompensation. In the absence of the ability to satisfactorily manage the stressors of routine daily living, the extraordinary stressor of confrontation with traumatic material can easily overwhelm PCA survivors, leading to rapid and extensive deterioration in functioning rather than therapeutic gains. Consequently, the major focus of CT is on fostering the establishment of adaptive capacities that were either disrupted by trauma or insufficiently developed in the first place.

On the other hand, CT does not assert that family environment is the sole cause of survivors' problems or deny that trauma plays a considerable role in the genesis of many of the difficulties experienced by PCA survivors. Trauma is seen as both a factor that greatly compounds the deficits resulting from growing up in an ineffective family of origin environment and a cause of symptomatology in its own right. CT cautions against the dangers of making trauma the cornerstone of treatment for PCA survivors, but it acknowledges the very substantial adverse impact of abuse trauma on the long-term functioning of these clients and the need to address traumatic material as one component of a broader treatment framework.

Depending upon the level of functioning and inclinations of the particular client, the issue of abuse may be addressed relatively early in the course of treatment. For example, concerns such as how abuse experiences have contributed to the client's psychological difficulties, shaped her or his beliefs about self and others, adversely affected interpersonal relationships, and interacted with other factors such as family of origin environment, may be discussed as early as the initial therapy session. However, the opening phases of CT trauma-related work primarily center on cognitive interventions directed at helping the client to develop a conceptual framework for understanding the impact incidents of abuse have had on her or him and for disputing the distorted beliefs that have been fostered by these experiences. What are likely to be destabilizing and therefore discouraged early in treatment are exposure-based interventions aimed at deconditioning PTSD symptoms through review of the explicit content of incidents of abuse. Although the goal of reducing reactivity to traumatic cues is pursued from the beginning of treatment, the methods of accomplishing this in the initial phases of treatment do not rely on remembering or confronting traumatic events. Instead, the client is taught to reduce reactivity through the mastery and regular practice of strategies for reducing and modulating distress.

In many cases, extensive processing of instances of explicit abuse is not even necessary in CT. By the time significant progress has been made toward the other prioritized treatment goals, there is little substantial post-traumatic symptomatology to address. If the client feels it would be helpful to process traumatic material in a systematic fashion at this point in treatment, there is no reason to discourage or avoid it. In effect, once appreciable gains have been established in the prioritized treatment goals, the PCA survivor will have attained a measure of functional parity with survivors of more circumscribed forms of trauma, and will be able to deal with the confrontation and processing of traumatic material without undue likelihood of destabilization.

FUTURE DIRECTIONS

In the final analysis, the value of a particular therapeutic approach lies in its effectiveness. As a first step in evaluating the effectiveness of CT, selected cases, accompanied by pre- and posttreatment standardized test scores, have been studied and the results suggest promising outcomes for CT (Sigmund, 2002; Gold et al., 2001; Gold & Elhai, 1999). However, CT is relatively new and more rigorous empirical assessments need to be conducted in order to adequately assess its clinical effectiveness.

Until recently, CT was considered solely in terms of the population for which it was conceived—survivors of prolonged child abuse. However, feedback from practitioners in settings such as VA centers and battered women's shelters indicates that this treatment approach may be applicable to survivors of other forms of trauma. This possibility raises some important theoretical issues. Among those who meet criteria for complex PTSD, perhaps it is not only PCA survivors whose difficulties are attributable to the combined effects of discrete traumatic incidents and having grown up in an ineffective family environment rather than to overt trauma alone.

A wide range of clinical theories and approaches has influenced the conceptual perspective that underlies CT, including person-centered, cognitive behavioral, feminist, and psychodynamic models. The conceptualization of the central problem as a skills deficit rather than a performance deficit is very similar to Linehan's (1993) Dialectical Behavior Therapy, developed primarily for group work with self-injuring clients. The central emphasis in CT on the impact of family and social context on PCA survivors also reflects the influence of systemic theory. A crucial implication of the CT model, therefore, pertains to how to work toward the imposing goals of reducing the prevalence of child maltreatment and increasing the safety and well-being of children. A contextual analysis suggests that accomplishing these ends rests to a large extent on fostering a society that is genuinely invested in providing families with the resources and parenting skills required to adequately prepare children for adaptive and productive functioning in adulthood. Ultimately, this is the challenge raised by a contextual understanding of ongoing child abuse.

REFERENCES

Academy of Traumatology. (2001). *Standards of traumatology practice.* Retrieved from http://www.greencross.org/academy.html

Alexander, P. C. (1992). Application of attachment theory to the study of sexual abuse. *Journal of Consulting and Clinical Psychology, 60,* 185–195.

Alexander, P. C. (1993). The differential effects of abuse characteristics and attachment in the prediction of long-term effects of sexual abuse. *Journal of Interpersonal Violence, 8,* 346–362.

Alexander, P. C., & Lupfer, S. L. (1987). Family characteristics and long-term consequences associated with sexual abuse. *Archives of Sexual Behavior, 16,* 235–245.

American Psychiatric Association. (1980). *Diagnostic and statistical manual of mental disorders (DSM-III).* Washington, DC: Author.

Anderson, C. L., & Alexander, P. C. (1996). The relationship between attachment and dissociation in adult survivors of incest. *Psychiatry: Interpersonal and Biological Processes, 59,* 240–254.

Barach, P. M. (1991). Multiple personality disorder as an attachment disorder. *Dissociation, 4,* 117–123.

Barach, P. M. (1999, November). *A threshold-of-vulnerability model for dissociation: Etiological and treatment considerations.* Plenary paper presented at the 16th International Fall Conference of the International Society for the Study of Dissociation, Miami, FL.

Cardeña, E. (1994). The domain of dissociation. In S. J. Lynn & J. W. Rhue (Eds.), *Dissociation: Clinical and theoretical perspectives* (pp. 15–31). New York: Guilford.

Courtois, C. A. (1997). Healing the incest wound: A treatment update with attention to recovered-memory issues. *American Journal of Psychotherapy, 51,* 464–496.

Courtois, C. A. (1999, November). *The scientifically-based treatment of memories of trauma.* Plenary paper presented at the 16th International Fall Conference of the International Society for the Study of Dissociation, Miami, FL.

Everill, J., & Waller, G. (1995). Disclosure of sexual abuse and psychological adjustment in female undergraduates. *Child Abuse and Neglect, 19,* 93–100.

Ford, J. D. (1999). Disorders of extreme stress following war-zone military trauma: Associated features of posttraumatic stress disorder or comorbid but distinct syndromes? *Journal of Consulting and Clinical Psychology, 67,* 3–12.

Ford, J. D., & Kidd, P. (1998). Early childhood trauma and disorders of extreme stress as predictors of treatment outcome with chronic posttraumatic stress disorder. *Journal of Traumatic Stress, 11,* 743–761.

Fromuth, M. E. (1986). The relationship of childhood sexual abuse with later psychological and sexual adjustment in a sample of college women. *Child Abuse and Neglect, 10,* 5–15.

Gold, S. N. (2000). *Not trauma alone: Therapy for child abuse survivors in family and social context.* Philadelphia: Brunner-Routledge.

Gold, S. N., & Brown, L. S. (1997). Therapeutic responses to delayed recall: Beyond recovered memory. *Psychotherapy, 34,* 182–191.

Gold, S. N., & Elhai, J. D. (1999, November). *Skills-based treatment of dissociation: Case presentation, outcome, and follow-up.* Paper presented at the 16th Annual Conference of the International Society for Dissociation, Miami, FL.

Gold, S. N., Elhai, J. D., Rea, B. D., Weiss, D., Masino, T., Morris, S. L., & Mcininch, J. (2001). Contextual treatment of dissociative identity disorder: Three case studies. *Journal of Trauma and Dissociation, 2*, 5–36.

Gold, S. N., Russo, S. A., Lucenko, B. A., & Vermont, P. (November, 1998). *Sexual abuse survivors' family environments: Intra- and extra-group comparisons.* Poster session presented at the International Society of Traumatic Stress Studies Annual Meeting, Washington, DC.

Gold, S. N., & Seifer, R. E. (2002). Dissociation and sexual addiction/compulsivity: A contextual approach to conceptualization and treatment. *Journal of Trauma and Dissociation, 3*(4), 59–82.

Gold, S. N., Swingle, J. M., & Garcia-Larrieu, M. (1995, July). *Childhood disclosure of sexual abuse and female adult survivors' symptomatology.* Paper presented at the 4th International Family Violence Research Conference, Durham, NC.

Gottlieb, C. D., Pardoll, M., Gold, S. N., & Schlessinger, K. M. (2001, December). *Disclosure of sexual abuse during childhood and adult symptomatology.* Poster session presented at the 17th Annual Meeting of the International Society for Traumatic Stress Studies, New Orleans, LA.

Harter, S., Alexander, P. C., & Neimeyer, R. A. (1988). Long-term effects of incestuous abuse in college women: Social adjustment, social cognition, and family characteristics. *Journal of Consulting and Clinical Psychology, 56*, 5–8.

Herman, J. L. (1992a). *Trauma and recovery: The aftermath of violence—from domestic abuse to political terror.* New York: Basic Books.

Herman, J. L. (1992b). Complex PTSD: A syndrome in survivors of prolonged and repeated trauma. *Journal of Traumatic Stress, 5*, 377–391.

Horowitz, M. J. (1986). *Stress response syndromes* (2nd ed.). Northvale, NJ: Jason Aronson.

Hoyt, M. F. (1996). Cognitive–behavioral treatment of posttraumatic stress disorder from a narrative constructivist perspective: A conversation with Donald Meichenbaum. In M. F. Hoyt (Ed.), *Constructive therapies: Vol. 2.* (pp. 124–147). New York: Guilford.

Janoff-Bulman, R. (1992). *Shattered assumptions: Towards a new psychology of trauma.* New York: Free Press.

Kluft, R. P. (1996). Multiple personality disorder: A legacy of trauma. In C. R. Pfeffer (Ed). Severe stress and mental disturbance in children (pp. 411–448). Washington, DC: American Psychiatric Press.

Linehan, M. M. (1993). *Cognitive–behavioral treatment of borderline personality disorder.* New York: Guilford.

Liotti, G. (1996). Understanding the dissociative processes: The contribution of attachment theory. *Psychoanalytic Inquiry, 19*, 757–783.

Long, P. J., & Jackson, J. L. (1994). Childhood sexual abuse: An examination of family functioning. *Journal of Interpersonal Violence, 9*, 270–277.

McCann, L., & Pearlman, L. A. (1990). *Psychological trauma and the adult survivor: Theory, treatment, and transformation.* New York: Brunner/Mazel.

Melchert, T. P. (2000). Clarifying the effects of parental substance abuse, child sexual abuse, and parental caregiving on adult adjustment. *Professional Psychology, 31*, 64–69.

Nash, M. R., Hulsey, T. L., Sexton, M. C., Harralson, T. L., & Lambert, W. (1993). Long-term sequelae of childhood sexual abuse: Perceived family environment, psychopathology, and dissociation. *Journal of Consulting and Clinical Psychology, 61*, 276–283.

Pearlman, L. A., & Saakvitne, K. (1995). *Trauma and the therapist.* New York: Norton.

Pelcovitz, D., van der Kolk, B., Roth, S., Mandel, F., Kaplan, S., & Resick, P. (1997). Development of a criteria set and a structured interview for disorders of extreme stress (SIDES). *Journal of Traumatic Stress, 10*, 3–16.

Phillips, M., & Frederick, C. (1995). *Healing the divided self: Clinical and Ericksonian hypnotherapy for post-traumatic and dissociative conditions.* New York: Norton.

Ray, K. C., Jackson, J. L., & Townsley, R. M. (1991). Family environments of victims of intrafamilial and extrafamilial child sexual abuse. *Journal of Family Violence, 6,* 365–374.

Ross, C. A. (1997). *Dissociative identity disorder: Diagnosis, clinical features, and treatment of multiple personality* (2nd ed.). New York: Wiley.

Roth, S., Newman, E., Pelcovitz, D., van der Kolk, B., & Mandel, F. S. (1997). Complex PTSD in victims exposed to sexual and physical abuse: Results from the DSM-IV field trial for posttraumatic stress disorder. *Journal of Traumatic Stress, 10,* 539–555.

Sigmund, H. (2002, November). Case illustration of contextual theory to treat complex PTSD. In S. N. Gold (Chair), *Contextual therapy for complex PTSD: Theory, research, and case study.* Symposium conducted at the 18th Annual Meeting of the International Society for Traumatic Stress Studies, Baltimore, MD.

Sullivan, H. S. (1953). *The interpersonal theory of psychiatry.* New York: Norton.

van der Hart, O., Steele, K., Boon, S., & Brown, P. (1993). The treatment of traumatic memories: Synthesis, realization, and integration. *Dissociation, 6,* 162–180.

van der Kolk, B. A. (1999, November). Trust in the treatment of PTSD, complex PTSD, and dissociative disorders: A debate. With S. Bloom (Chair), L. Tinnin, O. van der Hart, & J. Shay. Symposium conducted at the 15th Annual Meeting of the International Society for Traumatic Stress Studies, Miami, FL.

Williamson, J. M., Borduin, C. M., & Howe, B. A. (1991). The ecology of adolescent maltreatment: A multilevel examination of adolescent physical abuse, sexual abuse, and neglect. *Journal of Consulting and Clinical Psychology, 59,* 449–457.

Yama, M. F., Tovey, S. L., & Fogas, B. S. (1993). Childhood family environment and sexual abuse as predictors of anxiety and depression in adult women. *American Journal of Orthopsychiatry, 63,* 136–141.

Zlotnick, C., & Pearlstein, T. (1997). Validation of the structured interview for disorders of extreme stress. *Comprehensive Psychiatry, 38,* 243–247.

17

The Ecological Approach to Incestuous Families

JAMES W. MADDOCK AND NOEL R. LARSON

Professionals working with family sexual abuse can have very different assumptions about the nature of the problem and the proper approach to intervention. Substantial disagreement exists regarding the degree to which abuse and violence reflects *family* dysfunction rather than only *individual* psychopathology, as well as the extent to which certain attitudes or behaviors characterize family members other than a perpetrator or a victim (Finkelhor, 1988; Friedrich, 1990; Trepper & Barrett, 1986, 1989).

Some view the goal of intervention into incest as separating family members and enhancing their individuation (Selby & Livingston, 1999), while others advocate keeping family members together and improving interaction (Friedrich, 1990; Maddock & Larson, 1995; Trepper & Barrett, 1989). Some believe that adult victims of child abuse need support and connection with their families of origin (Courtois, 1988, 1995; Gil, 1988); others argue that these families are toxic and should be cut off from contact (Butler, 1985; Forward, 1989). Some consider most child sex abusers incurable (Corwin, 2002; Cohn & Daro, 1987), while others contend that therapeutic treatment in the context of family support can overcome antisocial behavior and permit the perpetrator to become a safe and useful citizen (Maddock & Larson, 1995; Marshall, 1993; Trepper & Barrett, 1989). Unfortunately, comprehensive data on which to base solid conclusions regarding these complex issues are still sparse (Patton, 1991).

These differences can impair coordination in the identification of sexual abuse and subsequent intervention by various professionals. A tension between concern for victims and concern for families is reflected in the child protection system. On the one hand, societal regard for the sanctity of the family and its right to privacy may inhibit investigations that could lead to removing an endangered child from a household. On the other hand, accusations of child abuse followed by severe family disruption, foster care, and lengthy court battles have led some parents to form organizations that claim abuse of parents exists in a system created to protect their children (Wakefield & Underwager, 1988; Wexler, 1990). Bias in either direction cannot guarantee protection, and social service workers are all too familiar with tragic cases when the system fails. Failure to recognize and acknowledge theoretical and personal biases about child sexual abuse can interfere with effective treatment and can harm rather than help clients.

THE INDIVIDUAL APPROACH

Even the professionals involved in incest treatment sometimes polarize into opposing camps. The victim advocacy approach grew out of the child advocacy and feminist (particularly anti-rape) movements of the 1970s (Berrick & Gilbert, 1991). The approach is popular among a variety of therapists, particularly those who are trained primarily in psychodynamic psychology and work mostly with individual clients who are victims of sexual abuse. In its purest form, victim advocacy assumes a pathological individual in a neutral context traumatizing an innocent and less powerful individual. Therefore, the task of helpers is to protect the victim(s) by removing the perpetrating individual from that context, mobilizing the monitoring skills of the nonoffending spouse, and teaching victims to better protect themselves (Fish & Faynik, 1989).

THE FAMILY SYSTEM APPROACH

The family systems approach is rooted in the origins of family therapy in the 1950s, but spread most rapidly through the mental health professions in the 1980s (Thomas & Wilcox, 1987). This approach assumes interdependence of family members' functioning so that behavioral problems such as incest "represent the cumulative interaction of all members of a system over one or more generations" (Friedrich, 1990, p. 168). The family systems approach assumes a set of pathological relationships to which *all* family members contribute in some measure. Therefore, the therapeutic task is to restructure the family in an effort to change their ways of relating (Ribordy, 1990).

BRIDGING THE DIFFERENCES

In our view, each of these approaches has some distinct advantages and disadvantages. Overall, however, neither is sufficient in itself. The two approaches reflect incompatible assumptions that prevent easy integration. A lack of theoretical integration has left the practice of incest treatment without a solid foundation for ensuring that *both* individuals and families in which children are sexually abused receive effective treatment whose positive outcomes can be documented. Many therapists using pure family systems principles have been ill-equipped to deal with the complex intrapsychic processes of traumatized victims and characterological perpetrators, and many victim advocate therapists have naively taken the recollections of self-identified incest victims at face value, implementing well-intended interventions that devastate the lives of families in ways that could have been avoided by a more balanced approach. Neither approach has been adequate to handle the complex power and control distortions that lie at the heart of child sexual abuse. Even the well-developed contemporary literature on trauma treatment is insufficient as a basis for comprehensive therapy with incest family members.

As an alternative to these approaches, we recommend an *ecological approach* that recognizes the extreme complexity of incestuous behavior as a family phenomenon as well as the intricacies of individual developmental responses to stress and trauma (Maddock & Larson, 1995). To be ecological is not to ignore societal contributors to violence or the ugly realities of bad behavior by individuals. Neither does it disregard the importance of moral responsibility and social accountability. Rather, ecology considers the importance of *all* of the complex influences on human behavior, meaning, and feelings, and ecological efforts are intended to increase the likelihood that interventions will effectively contribute something positive to *all* parties involved in the transaction. To be ecological is to be necessarily morally responsible for the survival and well-being of all parts of an ecosystem. An ecological examination of family sexual abuse pays careful attention to all of the factors in both foreground and background, and carries an attitude of personal ethical concern for everyone involved, even perpetrators.

THE ECOLOGICAL PERSPECTIVE

The ecological paradigm is characterized by its prominent emphasis on the interaction *between* systems rather than on the properties and processes of any one system. The core concept of *ecosystem* is the relationship between a system and its environment; a system's boundary separates the system from other systems and also connects the system to its environment (Bubolz & Sontag, 1993; Naess, 1989).

To fully comprehend ecological principles requires dialectical thinking. Like ecology, dialectics has many different meanings and applications. Within an ecological framework, dialectics refers to the relationships between various systems that, together, produce an ecosystem. At the heart of an ecological approach to therapy is the recognition that, in order to be dealt with effectively, any given system—such as an individual person or a family—must be recognized as *both* a subsystem *and* an ecosystem, that is, its ecology must be understood (Maddock, 1993; Odum, 1983). From the ecological perspective, a family can be defined as the *primary transformational unit in human experience*, regardless of its size or formal structure or the nature of the ties between its members. A family is the basic context in which human beings are transformed into persons—participants in complex social systems who retain autonomous identities as individuals; conversely, the family transforms elements of the social and material environment into meaningful components of experience for its members. A family can be thought of as a *process*, a way of relating humans to their near and distant environments via both concrete (behavioral) and abstract (symbolic) transactions (Chubb, 1990; Maddock, 1993).

Perhaps most importantly, viewing the family from an ecological perspective highlights the fact that families function in extremely diverse ways. Those families identified as having a specific problem such as sexual abuse cannot be characterized in a general way; there is no single type of incest family. Like all families, incest families have both healthy and unhealthy characteristics.

Ecological Intervention Into Family Sexual Abuse

Problems in assessment and diagnosis have plagued the field of family therapy from its earliest days. One major issue is whether a family can be labeled pathological or whether the term should be reserved for use only with an individual, who can then be said to be suffering from a mental disorder characterized by a psychiatric diagnosis (Denton, 1990; Glenn, 1984). Are incest *families* dysfunctional—perhaps incestogenic (Kutchinsky, 1994)—or are they merely unfortunate in having a dysfunctional *member*?

The dilemma is further complicated by the fact that intervention into child sexual abuse juxtaposes three different social institutions—the legal system, the mental health care system, and the social service system—with their various assumptions, methods of inquiry, terminologies, and even differing goals for intervention. Within this complicated context, the therapist is challenged to find ways to implement the crucial steps in an assessment process: making a connection with each family member, understanding each member's version of the problem, becoming familiar with each member's model of the world, and understanding the context within which the family has evolved a situation that requires treatment for one or more members. Assessing all of these factors determines what therapeutic steps can aid both the various family members and the family as a unit.

Our therapeutic work is premised on the assumption that family sexual abuse arises out of complicated combinations of mutually influencing variables, ranging from neuropsychological characteristics of individuals to relational interaction patterns of parents and children to contextual factors, such as spouses' gender role expectations or families' socioeconomic levels. Therefore, intervention and treatment need to address all of these complex, interrelated issues. The goal is to help family members work toward positive expressions of sexuality as well as to avoid sexual abuse. Too often, negative issues occupy full attention, and the articulation of positive objectives for sexual expression is avoided because of the anticipated complications of value conflicts. The overall goal of treatment should be more comprehensive than preventing a recurrence of abuse; it should be directed at helping family members grow as autonomous individuals and as an interconnected system that does not require distorted elements of structural enmeshment, emotional fusion, and ambivalence about intimacy.

Choosing a role. The therapist's decision about what role to take in the complex ecology of intervention is not as straightforward as it initially may appear, and herein lies one of the biggest traps in working with incest families. Friedrich (1990) aptly observes that the presence of a therapist is rarely viewed by an incestuous family as a positive opportunity for growth and change, at least initially. Most often, family members are in treatment because they are required or coerced rather than because they are voluntarily seeking to restructure the family system. Even apparent enthusiasm for therapy often masks a subtle form of resistance that can be thought of as pseudocompliance.

The relationship between the therapist and the family most likely reflects the same sort of ambivalence that distinguishes the relations between the family members themselves (McCarthy & Byrne, 1988). Even though the family may be working effectively on important issues, the connection between the therapist and individual members is seldom secure until well into the treatment process (Friedrich, 1990; Trepper & Barrett, 1989; Gil, 1996). Therefore, the therapist must be content with little or nothing in the form of direct feedback and must endure considerable ambiguity regarding the impact of treatment on family members.

Being a family therapist in a sexual abuse case largely precludes acting in other capacities with the family—particularly taking the role of formal evaluator. Most of the complaints or suits against therapists working with incest families have been based, at least in part, upon the clinician having a primary role in the formal (legal) evaluation of one or more family members, as well as in treatment. This dilemma is particularly acute in the early stages of intervention, when formal evaluations concentrate on ascertaining whether sexual abuse has actually occurred and what measures need to be taken to assure that it does not continue. The results of such evaluations often become part of a court record that will influence the criminal conviction and sentencing of the perpetrator as well as family members' living arrangements. When therapists' initial evaluations play a major role in determining these matters, it is not surprising that their subsequent efforts to help may be met with resistance. Such duality of roles can create insurmountable obstacles to effective family therapy, and we strongly recommend against it.

Selecting a client unit. The selection of a client system for treatment (one or more family members) poses a significant dilemma for the therapist: What constitutes the client unit that should survive as a result of intervention? In our view, the hallmark of a systemic and ecological approach is a focus on the *family* as the primary survival unit. That is, sessions with the family are considered the principal mode of treatment, and individual or group therapy with victims, perpetrators, and others are adjunctive. Many of the agencies that claim to have family therapy programs for incest seldom or never work with family members together (Hollin & Howells, 1991), at least until the reunification stage which occurs rather late in treatment—often a year or more after disclosure!

Family therapy has the potential to be the most crucial subsystem in the ecology of intervention into incest because it can create a powerfully influential environment for all family members simultaneously. Working collaboratively with family members to creatively restructure patterns of relating creates new contexts for both meaning and behavior—a key element in trauma resolution (Friedrich, 1990, 2002). Working with the entire family improves coordination of family goals as well as more practical treatment objectives. Organized appropriately and synchronized with other elements of treatment, family sessions can make use of existing family resources and family transactional patterns to facilitate positive restructuring with far-reaching positive consequences.

THE ECOLOGICAL TREATMENT APPROACH

Many therapy models that characterize themselves as ecological do little more than remind professionals of the importance of considering social class, ethnicity, and/or cultural influences on the occurrence of family sexual abuse. These are not enough; in our view, the treatment process itself should be conducted ecologically. The fundamental task of the therapist intervening into an incest family is *ecological balancing*—the process of transforming systemic relationships (Maddock & Larson, 1995).

Ecological Balancing

The ultimate goal of ecological therapy is transformative growth, not fixing or curing. The relationships between systems in an ecosystem require continuous balancing in order to assure the survival of both the systems themselves and their ecosystem (Bateson, 1972). In complex systems such as families, transformative processes can take many different forms; practically speaking, specific events and outcomes are unpredictable. Within families, these transformations are directed at creating dynamic balances that simultaneously (a) maintain the autonomous identities of individual members, (b) allow members to relate to one another in mutually helpful and meaningful ways, (c) preserve the family as a functional system, and (d) contribute to the integrity of the larger community and physical environment (Maddock, 1993; Maddock & Larson, 1995). In our view, all four of these criteria (see Figure 17.1) serve as objectives that guide intervention into family sexual abuse. Unfortunately, much incest treatment ignores one or several of these factors; often, the family system is sacrificed in the process. Treatment programs often will completely limit any form of contact—letters, phone calls, visits—between perpetrators and victims until they near the end of incarceration or treatment or both. This delay, frequently lasting two or more years, can contribute to more developmental disruption for the victims and greater alienation between family members, sometimes producing additional trauma in the form of reactive attachment disorder.

Assessment and Beginning Therapy

Particularly in its earliest stages, incest family treatment can be considered a form of crisis intervention. Using this rationale to offer help to all family members can provide a solid platform for building alliances and collaborating with the family as a unit to begin making important changes in their interactions as a system (cf., Pinsof & Catherall, 1986). The revealing of incest to uninvolved family members or others outside the family is most often what has precipitated the family crisis. Rather than intervention into crisis, often intervention *is* the crisis. The challenge of intervention into incest is to manage things well from the outset. The therapist must find a position from which both helpfulness and traction for change can be generated when these are likely to seem antithetical to some or all family members. Family members (including the perpetrator)

Maintain the autonomous identities of individual family members

Allow members to relate to one another in mutually helpful and meaningful ways

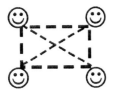

Preserve the family as a functional system

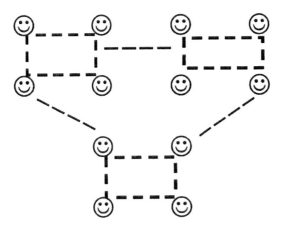

Contribute to the integrity of the larger community and physical environment

FIGURE 17.1. Transformative balances in ecological therapy.

must feel understood and respected by those who intervene before they can begin to cooperate in the process of ending the abuse by rebalancing some of their transactional patterns with each other and with their surrounding community.

Overall, the ecological approach to clinical assessment is characterized by an informality and fluidity that must be balanced with appropriate professional responsibility and personal integrity. Our goal is a comprehensive understanding of the individual family members as they interrelate to form a family unit that, in turn, interacts with a contemporary social community and a historical tradition (family-of-origin and cultural influences). This makes each assessment unique in terms of how interviews are scheduled and structured, as well as what clinical instruments are used. Clinical assessment is a prolonged process, intermingling with therapeutic efforts from the first moment of contact with family members. Even when asking questions designed to serve our treatment planning, we are simultaneously attempting to make things better for family members. The first stage of therapy, during which assessment is a primary focus, is given the very appropriate but not very scientific label of "juggling things into place" (for a more complete discussion, see Maddock & Larson, 1995).

Identifying the Problem

A key component of early intervention is to transform the statements of family members regarding the situation into an ecological problem. Recognizing that truth always comes in versions, the therapist absorbs the individual perceptions of the situation and then links them into a comprehensive description—the ecological problem. The construction of an ecological problem allows (a) the family to recognize problems and patterns as interconnected, (b) the therapist and family together to frame these interconnected problems in a *solvable* fashion (Haley, 1976) with opportunities for growth (Schnarch, 1991), and (c) the family members to view the therapist as facilitating changes that can lead to positive results for them, as individuals and as a family.

Unfortunately, this strength-based approach is often overlooked in incest treatment (Gelinas, 1986). Too often, a therapist will accept the problem that is defined by outsiders in the legal or social service systems. This can cause power and control struggles with the therapist over the definition of the *real* problem. Instead, we begin by basically accepting the problem as defined by the family members (even if these definitions are very discrepant among the members), and then we work with the family to define a general dilemma upon which all members basically can agree. Some examples: "Members of this family seem to be unhappy with each other, and there's a lot of confusion over what's been happening, who knows what, and whom to believe; so help is needed in getting things sorted out" or even "So you're here primarily because the court requires it so that the kids can move back home, and you would rather be left alone. Well, someone has to work with you because the court requires it. So I guess we're stuck in this together, and we need to find a

way to make the best of it." Within this broad structure of opportunity
for change, the therapist can become a resource for the family.

Doing Incest Family Therapy Ecologically

From an ecological perspective, therapy is an ongoing process of ecological balancing. Conceptually, this consists of using the big picture
issues of the overall family system to work with the concrete small details
of each family member's experience as part of that (eco)system. Balancing is considered both a property of the family as an ecosystem and a
series of moves made by the therapist in relation to that complex system.
Balancing is a collaborative process between therapist and family members that transforms the system by utilizing its actual and potential
resources for growth.

Pacing and leading. Formulating this process requires the use of several
additional concepts. Most prominent are the notions of *pacing* and *leading*.[1] Pacing refers to matching a client's current experience in some specific way via a verbal or nonverbal behavior on the part of the therapist.
Examples of pacing include:

- Matching a client's voice tone or body posture (head-nodding or
  hand gestures)
- Reflecting back a thought or emotion, as to perpetrator: "Am I understanding correctly that you continue to believe that she somehow
  imagined the abuse?"
- Utilizing a metaphor that has proven to be meaningful to one or
  more family members, as with children: "So when Dad gets home
  from work each evening, others—including Mom—feel as if they
  have to pass inspection with him just like he did with his drill
  instructor when he was in basic training in the Marines."

Leading refers to adding something new to a client's current experience in some specific way via a verbal or nonverbal behavior on the part
of the therapist. Some examples of leading:

- Open-ended questioning (to child victim): "Have you given any
  thought to why your mother would doubt your version of the story
  when you told her that your stepfather was molesting you?"

---

1. These are terms we have borrowed from the literature on hypnotherapy and
Neurolinguistic Programming, both of whose focus is primarily methodological
rather than theoretical.

- Interpretive commentary (to adult perpetrator): "You say you're angry at your wife, but your description of how you talk to her sounds to me more like rage—and that's almost always about anxiety."
- Extended metaphor or narrative story with an embedded solution to a client's dilemma (deShazer, 1994; Friedman, 1993; White and Epston, 1990).

Contrary to ordinary logic—and the behavior of most therapists—clients respond more readily with change when the therapist uses more pacing and less leading. Introductory hypnosis workshops teach students to make pacing statements and then insert a lead, followed by more pacing. When clients do not follow a lead, even more pacing—not more leading—is usually required. One of the most common pitfalls of therapy with incest families is the tendency of the therapist to get too far ahead of the clients by using too much leading and insufficient pacing. The challenge is one of *balancing* pacing and leading. The most elegant and effective interventions consist of well-timed and well-structured paces within which are embedded relevant leads—all of which must fit the client (eco)system in order to facilitate change and growth. To be fitting, therapy with incestuous families should focus on several relevant characteristics of the family system and its individual members: boundaries, the meaning and function of the incest, and power/control dynamics that result in prepetrator-victim interaction patterns.

Boundaries

Boundary issues (Figure 17.2) clearly are important in therapy with incest families (Alexander, 1985; Friedrich, 1990; Trepper & Barrett, 1986, 1989). However, the degree of dysfunction in each of four boundary areas will vary among families and even between members of the same family.

Family–society boundary. Most incest family members (including many victims) attempt to protect their sexual secret by using existing barriers between the family system and its social environment. An implicit rule has evolved that important emotional needs are to be met exclusively within the family system. Others to whom family members might turn for sharing and intimacy are regarded as hostile intruders who in some way threaten the survival of the family unit. This closed family system limits opportunities for growth and renewal, producing a scarcity of resources while fostering excessive dependence, enmeshment, and limitations on differentiation among family members (Bowen, 1978).

Intergenerational boundary. Dependency problems, developmental delays, and enmeshment produced by the emotional isolation of incest

Abusive Family Structure

Non-Abusive Family Structure

FIGURE 17.2.

family members promote the blurring of boundaries between adult and child generations (Alexander, 1985; Friedrich, 1990). Family members are pressed into service to meet each other's needs regardless of age or developmental stage. Children in incest families frequently perform developmental tasks appropriate to adults, while their parents abdicate certain important responsibilities and compete with the children for limited emotional resources, producing a widely recognized marker of family dysfunction—parentified children (Stiver, 1990).

Interpersonal boundaries. A family's interpersonal boundaries delineate individuals as subsystems within the family ecosystem. Incest families often are characterized by substantial boundary diffusion between members, inhibiting their capacity for differentiation. In order to be supported and nurtured in a system characterized by enmeshment and scarce resources, members must yield their autonomy (Maddock & Larson, 1995; Trepper & Barrett, 1989). Poorly boundaried interaction produces emotional fusion—relationship patterns in which each member believes that his or her survival is dependent upon the psychological and emotional status of the other members (Bowen, 1978). Members who threaten the system through autonomous behavior may become the targets of scapegoating and escalating abuse. These factors trigger a variety of dysfunctional reactions, including narcissistic attachments, pervasive fears of abandonment, increased shame, and a variety of double-bind type interaction patterns among family members.

Intrapsychic boundaries. Intrapsychic boundaries reflect the subsystems, or parts, of personality structure, whose significance is in their relationship to each other and to the overall organization of personality. In the psychologically healthy individual, various psychic structures are integrated in such a way as to support autonomy and to permit functioning of the personality in a coherent, coordinated way (Slipp, 1984). When psychopathology occurs, the intrapsychic ecology is structured in a maladaptive way that does not fit well with the structure of the environment, resulting in distortions of meaning and behavior. Defense mechanisms evolve to minimize the cognitive dissonance and emotional pain created by the familial abuse. Typically these fall somewhere along an arousal/dissociation continuum—ranging from hyper-vigilance (debilitating forms of anxiety) at one extreme to alexithymia—the inability to consciously recognize certain sensory experiences and/or emotions—on the other (Perry, Pollard, Blakley, Baker, & Vigilante, 1995; van der Kolk, McFarlane, & Weisaeth, 1996). Denial is common in abusing families of all kinds (Hoke, Sykes, & Winn, 1989). It enables family members to engage in distorted thought patterns that, in turn, lead to intricate rationalizations of symptomatic and problematic behaviors by both victims and perpetrators. Defense mechanisms impair feedback processes within the family and distort members' perceptions of reality (Trepper & Barrett, 1989).

Respecting and Repairing Boundaries

Due to the protective nature of denial, family members typically are thrown into crisis when the incest secret is revealed to the outside world or comes to light within the family. Emotional regression is common at this time, and accounts of the incestuous behavior may change as resistance is mobilized in an effort to ensure individual and collective survival. The family system's outside boundaries usually rigidify even more when incestuous families come into contact with outside social or legal systems in an attempt to maintain stability and keep the family intact. However, boundaries within the family may become even more inappropriate or chaotic. Few therapy objectives are as critical as boundary repair for relapse prevention and long-term treatment success.

Unfortunately, boundary problems often are aggravated by the very processes of reporting and intervention. Foremost are the investigative interviews during which children may experience feelings of disloyalty when they are asked to reveal family secrets. Though sometimes necessary for legal prosecution, convincing children to sit in judgment of a perpetrating parent or older sibling represents a clear instance of role reversal. It may even be structurally parallel to the seductive processes by which the victim and others in the family were first persuaded to keep the incest secret. No matter how much support is provided, the child incest victim is asked to be, in some sense, bigger than his or her parents by taking direct responsibility for stopping the abuse. There is a fine but crucial line to be drawn between helping the victim in the family use appropriate assertiveness to avert further abuse and making him or her responsible for relapse prevention.

As treatment progresses, further boundary violations may occur. The children may be asked to choose where they want to live, whether they wish to be visited by either parent, or when they are ready to return home from foster care. While a child's feelings and desires certainly should be seriously considered in such matters, we firmly believe that *adults* should make these decisions and that they should convey their responsibility for such decisions clearly to children. Another structural problem occurs when foster parents are invested with official authority over the children's biological parents rather than only over the children. If foster parents have direct authority to decide how often the children see one or both parents, the circumstances surrounding the contact, how long visits will last, and other issues, then the biological parents are being treated as children and intergenerational boundary confusion is prolonged. Here, too, we believe that such decisions should be made, when possible, by one or both parents or, when necessary, by an appropriate outside authority such as a protection worker. Unfortunately, probation and parole officers are often charged with making these decisions, usually with little or no knowledge of the family's interpersonal dynamics or life situation.

Exploring trust and loyalty issues in the incestuous family often is an excellent way to address the boundary diffusion and lack of individual differentiation. Some family members may explicitly voice their mistrust of the therapist. The therapist can respond by observing, quite accurately, that the lack of trust is understandable under the circumstances and is evidence of a willingness to take care of themselves in the face of intrusion by outsiders—a sign of family loyalty. This observation can become, in turn, the basis for dealing with trust and betrayal within the family or for exploring differences in meaning and behavior around loyalty among various family members. More subtle forms of resistance sometimes can be addressed by following up on the positive connotation of loyalty with observations about differences and conflicts between individual family members. Framing these issues, particularly in relation to the therapist, can produce creative triangulation within the family that is useful in restructuring boundaries. For example, the therapist might highlight differences between family members by commenting to someone: "You apparently agree with my observation on how your family avoids conflict, but that seems to contradict what your sister said earlier about how sick and tired she is of family members picking at each other all the time."

MEANINGS AND FUNCTIONS OF SEXUAL ABUSE

While most abusive family systems share the structural characteristics outlined above, the specific functions of symptoms vary from one family to another. The ecological therapist gives considerable effort to assessing the meanings and functions of the sexual abuse within a particular family system. In the broadest ecological sense, abusive behaviors of perpetrators are premised upon the need to reduce anxiety and to cope with life in the family and the broader social ecosystem—survival patterns learned in their families-of-origin and triggered by precipitating factors in their current lives (Barrett & Schwartz, 1993; Trepper & Barrett, 1989; Vasington, 1989). While incest does not serve the same specific functions in every family in which it occurs, it is somehow meaningful within its context. Planning for effective treatment requires that the therapist accurately assess the systemic function of the incest as quickly as possible. A general hypothesis regarding sexual meaning and the function of the incestuous contact should not be based upon the responses of one family member. Rather, the therapist should look for patterns in the combined responses of family members, and then attempt to confirm or disconfirm a hypothesis in ongoing work with the family. While each family is unique, we believe that incest can be understood as serving one of four broad functions in the interpersonal transactions of involved family members.

Affection-based incest. A significant amount of incestuous behavior appears to serve as a misguided means of expressing affection between the perpetrator and one or more family members of a different generation. Contrary to the stereotype, the incest perpetrator's motivation is seldom based solely upon not having enough sexual contact with his wife, although chronic sexual dissatisfaction typically plagues the marriages of incest perpetrators. Some incest fathers engage in a quasi-courtship process with their daughters or stepdaughters in a mistaken attempt to show affection and feel emotionally close. This objective increases the likelihood that the abuse will continue on a longer-term basis and that sexual intercourse will eventually take place as a result of the perpetrator's efforts to consummate the relationship between them as lovers.

Erotic-based incest. The incestuous behavior in what we have come to call a pansexual family often involves both parents and most or all of the children; the sexual contact may be a kind of game. The family's primary bond appears to be its projections of eroticism into everyday life—into language (especially humor), physical appearance, family rituals, and recreation. Family photograph albums or home movies may include sexual depictions; some families even make child pornography for home use or commercial sale. In erotic-based incest, the sexual contact may or may not include sexual intercourse, since much of the focus is on teasing and titillation that does not require consummation to have meaning and reinforcement value.

Aggression-based incest. Aggression-based incest families use sexualized anger to deal with their frustration and disappointment over various aspects of their lives. The perpetrator may interact angrily—even violently—with the victim, who may be only a scapegoat for the perpetrator's masked hostility toward another person. Father–daughter incestuous contact may occur in connection with the perpetrator's wish to punish his wife for her lack of attention or erotic interest. Or an adolescent male may sexually exploit a younger sister in retaliation for what he perceives as rejection by his father, whom he believes shows intense favoritism toward the girls in the family while physically abusing the boys. This pattern helps to maintain the family rule that direct confrontation and negotiation between conflicting members cannot occur.

Rage-based incest. The final functional category of incestuous behavior is rooted in conspicuous individual psychopathology. Here, the perpetrator acts out his existential rage with one or more family members. Rather than conscious, focused anger, the behavior is a primitive expression of the shame–rage cycle arising out of longstanding frustration. Typically, the perpetrator's rage is rooted in his own long history as a victim of abuse, violence, or developmental crisis, producing an internal psychic structure characterized by continuous vigilance against threats to survival. Sometimes, the abuse is impulsively explosive; other times, it is meticulously planned, carried out in a cold and calculating manner, and accompanied by earnest rationalizations. In either case, the sexual abuse and accompanying violence may be life threatening.

Distinguishing between subjective distortions of reality and more objective accounts of experience among incest family members can be a substantial challenge. In their strategies for survival in a climate of abuse, both victims and perpetrators create fluid realities. Frequently, this underlying fluidity is revealed in their responses to inquiries in the course of assessment. The message is: "Whatever I need to believe to get through this is what is real." Such reconstruction of reality can serve to protect others as well as themselves. Victims sometimes block memory of certain details of abusive episodes, both to ease their own pain and to protect other family members from being hurt. Similarly, perpetrators may construct elaborate rationalizations for their abusive behavior, both to avoid detection and to minimize difficulty for the child victim.

THE PERPETRATOR–VICTIM INTERACTION PATTERN

In addition to appraising boundaries and meanings in incestuous families, assessing power and control distortions is crucial to the therapist's understanding of both individual and family dynamics. Most incest literature focuses on issues between clearly identified perpetrators and their victims, often labeling other family members in terms of their lack of involvement, for example, the "non-offending spouse." We believe that there are *no* uninvolved family members—which is not to say that everyone is somehow morally responsible for the abusive behavior. The therapist should recognize that the stances taken by particular family members within the complex ecology of the incestuous family may extend beyond those of formally designated perpetrators or victims.

Power and Control

Both power and control are necessary and legitimate components of human experience, particularly in the context of close, ongoing relationships. Power can be defined as the capacity to influence, and control the capacity to limit, shape, or channel influence. Power and control can be considered two sides of the same coin, meaningful because they are different but related. Readers who find that reading this chapter changes the way they work with incest families are experiencing the *power* of this approach to influence them; conversely, readers who have already decided that a systemic approach to incest treatment is naïve or useless are *controlling* the impact of the chapter by limiting the effect it can have on their work. An incest perpetrator who is violent or threatens harm is using his physical prowess to *overpower* those he victimizes; the dissociative responses of many incest victims represents a complementary form of *control* that reflects an attempt to limit or block the impact of the abuse.

Deprivation–desperation. Excessive control in a human system leads to deprivation, that is, to limits on self-expression and/or meeting of personal needs. Situations characterized by control lacking sufficient power for balance are likely to create patterns of deprivation or desperation or both—loss of influence or access to resources for influence that, in turn produce feelings of anxiety, hopelessness, even despair. A preoccupation with control can be one significant result of being victimized, particularly if accompanied by posttraumatic stress responses. Numerous abuse victims develop psychic defenses to guard against further intrusion into the self. However, without sufficient self-efficacy (power), these defenses themselves become self-defeating. The victim's attempt to consolidate all behavior around control produces an identity character-ized by feelings of isolation accompanied by a sense of extreme vulnera-bility and reliance on others to provide safety. This victim stance is distinguished by what it can prevent rather than by what it can create.

Exploitation–violation. When power dominates a relationship system, the stage is set for exploitation. In more extreme cases, one party may overpower another, violating boundaries in ways that can produce phys-ical and psychological damage. Situations characterized by power with-out an appropriate balance of control often lead to patterns of exploitation and violation—the capacity and willingness to use coercion or force to achieve one individual's (or group's) goals at the expense of another. Some children who grow up in sexually abusive families develop a power-oriented, exploitive behavior pattern in response to their own victimization. Instead of attempting compensatory overcon-trol, they give up *self*-control and begin to bully and even abuse others; that is, they begin to be perpetrators. Though this response is most often found among abused males, it occurs among females as well, including those who continue to be victimized in their families.

The Relational Pattern

Because power–control is a single dialectical construct reflecting sys-temic dynamics, the distortions of deprivation and desperation and exploitation and violation are understood as the underlying structure of a complex and dangerous scenario—the perpetrator–victim interaction pattern. This term refers to negative transactional processes that often become self-perpetuating in the context of ongoing close relationships. Individuals are victimized when they are in control of something that is desired by other individuals who are willing and able to overpower the victims to obtain what they want. Insofar as the perpetrators fail to obtain what they desire from others, they are likely to escalate their use of power and to have less and less self-control. Similarly, insofar as vic-tims are underpowered and forced to give up what they control, they are likely to try harder to regain control, thereby triggering further efforts to overpower them. The longer it continues, the more skewed the perpetrator–victim interaction pattern becomes. Thus, the perpetra-tor–victim interaction pattern both originates in, and comes to character-ize, a particular form of recurring relational behavior—making it the best answer to the question of just what, specifically, is transmitted in the intergenerational transmission of violence and abuse (Alexander, Moore, & Alexander, 1991).

Individuals who eventually seek therapy are likely to demonstrate evidence of the neurologically based victim–perpetrator template and to **manifest perpetrator-victim interaction patterns,** particularly in the context of close relationships. Why do children reveal and then recant sexual abuse in order to return home? The answer is that they are trying to survive—and their coping and adaptation is rooted in the perpetrator–victim interaction patterns that have become so familiar to them (Maddock & Larson, 1995; Terr, 1990). Taking this seriously is one of the primary components of the ecological paradigm: Systems can and will behave on the basis of how they are structured, regardless of the conscious wishes of a client or the noble intentions of a therapist.

The Intrapsychic Template

Recent neurobiological research has clearly documented the impact of traumatic experiences on brain structure and biochemistry (Perry et al., 1995). Virtually all clients who present with victimization issues, as well as those who have been labeled perpetrators, actually have internalized the entire victim–perpetrator template. Therefore, they are capable of behaving *both* as victims and as perpetrators at various points in treatment. A sizeable number of sexual abuse victims engage in antisocial behavior, including legal infractions such as writing bad checks or minor shoplifting. A much smaller number survive by adopting a more significant perpetrator stance, including physical or sexual abuse of children and other major criminal behaviors. When working with victims, therefore, perpetrator issues will also need to be addressed. This does not make victims morally responsible for what happened to them; however, their distorted perceptions, ideas, and behavior patterns need to be acknowledged and dealt with in treatment as part of the system that they and a partner or other family members have co-created.

Similarly, every perpetrator has a victim part that needs to be recognized and addressed in treatment. In our experience, it is extremely rare to encounter a formally designated perpetrator who is not also demonstrably a victim of some form of abuse, early trauma, or extreme neglect. This is not simply a matter of having a difficult childhood or coming from a dysfunctional family. Rather, perpetrators of violence or abuse, almost without exception, have evolved an identity based on defending themselves against noteworthy adversity. Perpetration itself usually is a form of trauma response. Thus, an individual trapped in the abuse cycle may now be able to play the role of *either* victim *or* perpetrator. Therein lies a potential trap for those who wish to intervene into the perpetrator–victim interaction sequence without sufficient awareness of the ambivalence felt by all participants in the system regarding being rescued.

Resistance and Change

Both perpetrators and victims demonstrate resistance to therapy, even though victims initially may seem more cooperative. At certain times, any member of an incestuous family may deny feelings, motivations, intentions, or even the reality of objectively observed behaviors. The opposite also occurs; one or more members may obsessively rework every detail of a given event or ruminate endlessly about a particular issue. Of course, either of these patterns can disrupt intervention efforts. Assessing family members' forms of resistance—including pseudo-cooperation—can be extremely important in formulating treatment strategies, particularly in deciding whether direct or indirect approaches will be most helpful.

Many professionals in the sexual abuse field seem to believe that perpetrators' defenses are rigid and impervious, while victims are underdefended and vulnerable. In our experience, *both* perpetrators and victims are able to mobilize defenses against therapeutic intervention. While perpetrators' defensiveness is usually recognizable, victims' defenses may be masked by the appearance of pervasive vulnerability designed to elicit rescue behaviors from others. Both patterns reflect a brittle rigidity, making it challenging to devise therapeutic interventions that are not experienced as threatening. Metaphorically speaking, the defenses of victims reflect a porcelain-like brittleness, while those of perpetrators may be thought of as tough coconut shells, hiding a fluid interior.

The use of positive connotation—pointing to the functional or adaptive aspects of even negative interactions and defense mechanisms—is one excellent way to creatively meet family members' active or passive resistance to intervention. Another is to utilize inherent paradoxes that emerge within the family during treatment (Selvini-Palazzoli, Boscolo, Cecchin, & Prata, 1978). Utilizing these paradoxes, the therapist works to link together the behaviors of family members. In this way, family members experience themselves struggling together with the paradoxes of life.

Eliciting the emotions, thoughts, and self-disclosures of individual family members in relation to each other turns up the heat on the family system, providing an opportunity for members to take more differentiated stances while interacting with each other, both in the therapy office and at home (reflecting again the argument against separating incest family members from each other on a long-term basis). In our ecological approach, inherent paradoxes are elicited and elaborated carefully via the use of balanced pacing and leading questions and statements.

Finally, we are convinced that marital therapy is a necessity for successful incest treatment, even if the partners decide to divorce as a result of exploring the relationship. Work on the marriage should be spread across the course of treatment, highlighting various issues as they become relevant and complementing family sessions as well as any individual or group treatment of family members. In addition to dealing in depth with barriers to emotional intimacy and satisfying sexual expression, husband and wife are likely to require help in becoming a more effective parental coalition to fulfill their childrearing responsibilities. Repairing and strengthening the marital system, in the final analysis, may prove to be the best possible protection against recidivism and a contributor to better sexual health in the eventual marriages of the children.

THE STANCE OF THE ECOLOGICAL THERAPIST

Skillful ecological therapy works very effectively with strong emotions and utilizes the personality of the therapist in particularly powerful ways. Because ecology is inherently relational, ecological therapy strongly depends on developing collaborative alliances with each client. At the same time, ecological therapy reflects a paradox that is particularly significant when working with issues of abuse and violence: The therapist does not confront clients (even perpetrators) about their behavior, thoughts, or feelings; rather, the therapist raises the heat in the client system in ways that promote self-confrontation on the part of each client and thus set the stage for growth (Schnarch, 1991). This approach is dramatically different from most therapy done with victims and perpetrators of sexual abuse (Maddock, Larson, & Schnarch, 2000).

A therapist's theoretical orientation and individual style naturally influence his or her approach to treating family sexual abuse and forming a therapeutic alliance with the family system. Family members whose behavior is socially unacceptable—and perhaps personally offensive to the therapist—present a considerable challenge to collaborative alliances. The common admonition to find something to like about a client may not be enough. Two approaches can be helpful in making a therapeutic connection with each member of an incestuous family. First is the recognition that the perpetrator–victim interaction pattern underlying the family system signals that *each* individual is struggling with victimization issues that threaten his or her survival. This can assist the therapist in developing empathy for all family members, including the perpetrator. The second aid to connecting is the notion of rising to a challenge. Devising a successful strategy can create a bond between persons engaged in a common endeavor. Many perpetrators appreciate a well-played strategy; a surprising number admire a therapist who can see through them or outwit them elegantly. Paradoxically, this can be helpful in establishing rapport.

What is required for effective ecological balancing is that therapists at all times maintain a differentiated stance vis a vis the client (eco)system (Bowen, 1978). This means that therapists must manage their own anxieties while evoking and working with the collective anxieties of the family members. That is, the therapist must maintain autonomy while remaining closely connected to the client family system and *all* of its members, including the perpetrator, when working with abusive families. This is no easy task; however, it is crucial for the success of treatment.

THE SOCIAL ECOLOGY OF INCEST TREATMENT

The social ecology has a significant impact upon the process of intervention into family sexual abuse. First, it determines to a significant degree whether any intervention will take place at all. In this respect, the climate of public opinion is currently divided between those who consider incest to be part of an epidemic of violence against women and children that must be stopped and those who believe that concern with child sexual abuse is highly exaggerated as a result of feminist political zeal and false memory problem: (cf. Csurtois, 1999; Dineen, 1996; Gardner, 1996).

Second, the social context has an impact upon each specific intervention into family sexual abuse via the personal characteristics and actions of social service and legal personnel and organizations involved in the case. There is considerable opportunity for mishaps involving lack of coordination and replication of perpetrator–victim interaction dynamics among agencies and individuals. Amidst this complex ecology, the family therapist is challenged to maintain a close alliance with each family member and a clear set of objectives relevant to the good of the family system.

To improve the sociolegal process of handling family sexual abuse, we offer the following suggestions:

- At the broadest level, a framework for understanding family sexuality and for distinguishing healthy from unhealthy patterns of family sexual interaction should be included in sexuality education courses and in all other efforts at child sexual abuse prevention.
- Scientific research, clinical work, and public policy should all distinguish more carefully between descriptive, explanatory, and evaluative accounts of incestuous behavior.
- In the course of intervention, a balance should be struck between the welfare of the individual victim and that of the family system.

- The functions of evaluation (particularly when related to legal action) and therapy should be strictly separated.
- Standard protocols for interviewing children about sexual abuse should always be used in incest assessment (for example, videotapes that reduce the number of times a child must recount incidents of abuse and which can serve in lieu of court testimony).
- Long-term separation of family members should not be an automatic outcome of documented incestuous abuse.
- In the majority of incest cases, legal proceedings should be handled in the context of family courts rather than criminal courts.

CONCLUSION

We have argued throughout this chapter that the family system should be the centerpiece of incest treatment efforts. Despite its dysfunctional aspects, the incestuous family should be viewed as a potential therapeutic resource—the primary ecosystem within which transformations among members' relationships will take place—rather than simply as an impediment to outside efforts at social control. Ideally, treatment should be coordinated by someone who is designated the *family's* therapist.

Nothing can replace the dedication and sensitivity that must lie at the heart of the therapeutic endeavor when incestuous families enter treatment. The therapist who can see the ecological wisdom in every family's unique structure, who has faith in the positive possibilities for change, and who is willing to persist in establishing and maintaining a relationship of trust with clients whose previous life experiences have left them anxious and untrusting will be able to envision positive outcomes despite frequent obstacles and occasional setbacks. Faith in the possibilities of clients' lives, trust in the therapist's own sense of personal and professional identity, and commitment to struggle, practice, and persevere in the face of ambiguity can provide some assurance against recidivism and open up positive possibilities for *all* members of an incestuous family.

REFERENCES

Alexander, P. (1985). A systems theory conceptualization of incest. *Family Process, 24,* 79–88.

Alexander, P., Moore, S., & Alexander, E. (1991). What is transmitted in the intergenerational transmission of violence? *Journal of Marriage and the Family, 53,* 657–668.

Barrett, M. J., & Schwartz, R. (1993). The *systemic treatment of child sexual abuse, Part 2: Working with the perpetrator.* Paper presented at the 16th Annual Family Therapy Network Symposium, Washington, DC.

Bateson, G. (1972). *Steps to an ecology of mind.* New York: Ballantine.

Berrick, J. D., & Gilbert, N. (1991). *With the best of intentions: The child sexual abuse prevention movement.* New York: Guilford.

Bowen, M. (1978). *Family therapy in clinical practice.* New York: Jason Aronson.

Briere, J. (2002). Treating adult survivors of severe childhood abuse and neglect: Further development of an integrative model. In J. Myers, L. Berliner, C. Hendrix, T. Reid, & C. Jenny (Eds.), *The APSAC handbook on child maltreatment* (2nd ed., pp. 1–26). Newbury Park, CA: Sage.

Bubolz, M. & Sontag, M. (1993). Human ecology theory. In P. Boss, W. Doherty, R. LaRossa, W. Schumm & S. Steinmetz (Eds.), Sourcebook of family theories and methods: A contextual approach (pp. 419–448). New York: Plenum.

Butler, S. (1985). *Conspiracy of silence: The trauma of incest.* San Francisco: Volcano Press.

Chubb, H. (1990). Looking at systems as process. *Family Process, 29,* 169–175.

Cohn, A., & Daro, D. (1987). Is treatment too late? What ten years of evaluation research tells us. *Child Abuse and Neglect, 11,* 433–442.

Corwin, D. (2002). An interview with Roland Summit. In J. Conte (Ed.), *Critical issues in child sexual abuse* (pp. 1–27). Newbury Park, CA: Sage.

Courtois, C. (1988). *Healing the incest wound: Adult survivors in therapy.* New York: Norton.

Courtois, C. (1995). Assessment and diagnosis. In C. Classen (Ed.), *Treating females molested in childhood* (pp. 1–34). San Francisco: Jossey-Bass.

Courtois, C. (1999). Recollections of sexual abuse: Treatment principles and guidelines. New York: Norton.

Denton, W. (1990). A family systems analysis of DSM-III-R. *Journal of Marital and Family Therapy, 16,* 113–125.

deShazer, S. (1994). *Words were originally magic.* New York: Norton.

Dineen, T. (1996). Manufacturing Victims: What the psychology industry is doing to people. Westmount, Quebec: Robert Davies.

Finkelhor, D. (1988). The trauma of child sexual abuse: Two models. In G. Wyatt & G. Powell (Eds.), *Lasting effects of child sexual abuse* (pp. 61–84). Newbury Park, CA: Sage.

Fish, V., & Faynick, C. (1989). Treatment of incest families with the father temporarily removed: A structural approach. *Journal of Strategic and Systemic Therapies, 8,* 53–63.

Forward, S. (1989). *Toxic parents: Overcoming their hurtful legacy and reclaiming your life.* New York: Bantam.

Friedman, S. (Ed.). (1993). *The new language of change: Constructive collaboration in psychotherapy.* New York: Guilford.

Friedrich, W. (1990). *Psychotherapy with sexually abused children and their families.* New York: Norton.

Friedrich, W. (2002). *Psychological assessment of sexual abused children and their families.* Newbury Park, CA: Sage.

Gardner, R. (1996). Psychotherapy with sex abuse victims: True, false and hysterical. Cresskill, NJ: Creative Therapeutics.

Gelinas, D. (1986). Unexpected resources in treating incest families. In M. A. Karpel (Ed.), *Family resources: The hidden partner in family therapy* (pp. 327–358). New York: Guilford.

Gil, E. (1988). *Systemic treatment of families who abuse.* San Francisco: Jossey-Bass.

Gil, E. (1996). *Treating abuse adolescents.* New York: Guilford.

Glenn, M. (1984). *On diagnosis: A systemic approach.* New York: Brunner/Mazel.

Haley, J. (1976). *Problem-solving therapy.* San Francisco: Jossey-Bass.

Hoke, S., Sykes, C., & Winn, M. (1989). Systemic/strategic interventions targeting denial in the incestuous family. *Journal of Strategic and Systemic Therapies, 8,* 44–51.

Hollin, C. R., & Howells, K. (Eds.). (1991). *Clinical approaches to sex offenders and their victims.* New York: Wiley.

Kutchinsky, B. (1994). Child sexual abuse: Prevalence, phenomenology, intervention, and prevention: An overview. *Nordisk Sexologi, 12,* 51–61.

Langevin, R. (Ed.). (1991). *Sex offenders and their victims.* Oakville, Ontario, Canada: Juniper Press.

Maddock, J. (1993). Ecological dialectics: An approach to family theory construction. *Family Science Review, 6*(3, 4), 137–161.

Maddock, J., & Larson, N. (1995). *Incestuous Families: An ecological approach to understanding and treatment.* New York: Norton.

Maddock, J., Larson, N., & Schnarch, D. (2000). *Beyond victimhood: Toward a new paradigm for psychotherapy.* Paper presented at the 23rd Annual Family Therapy Network Symposium, Washington, DC.

McCarthy, I., & Byrne, N. (1988). Mistaken love: Conversations on the problem of incest in an Irish context. *Family Process, 27,* 181–198.

Naess, A. (1989). *Ecology, community, and lifestyle: Outlines of an ecosphere* (D. Rothenberg, Trans.). Cambridge, U.K.: Cambridge University Press.

Ney, P. (1988). Transgenerational child abuse. *Child Psychiatry and Human Development, 18,* 151–168.

Odum, H. (1983). *Systems ecology: An introduction.* New York: Wiley.

Patton, M. (Ed.). (1991). *Family sexual abuse: Frontline research and evaluation.* Newbury Park, CA: Sage.

Perry, B., Pollard, R., Blakley, T., Baker, W., & Vigilante, D. (1995). Childhood trauma, the neurobiology of adaptation, and "use-dependent" development of the brain: How "states" become "traits." *Infant Mental Health Journal, 16,* 271–289.

Pinsof, W., & Catherall, D. (1986). The integrative psychotherapy alliance: Family, couple, and individual therapy scales. *Journal of Marital and Family Therapy, 12,* 137–151.

Ribordy, S. (1990). Treating intrafamilial child sexual abuse from a systemic perspective. *Journal of Psychotherapy and the Family, 6,* 71–88.

Roundy, L., & Horton, A. (1990). Professional and treatment issues for clinicians who intervene with incest perpetrators. In A. Horton, B. Johnson, L. Roundy, & D. Williams (Eds.), *The incest perpetrator: A family member no one wants to treat* (pp. 164–190). Newbury Park, CA: Sage.

Schnarch, D. (1991). *Constructing the sexual crucible: An integration of sexual and marital therapy.* New York: Norton.

Selby, T., & Livingston, M. (1999). Family reunification decisions in parent–child molest cases. Paper presented at the 18th Annual Research and Treatment Conference of the Association for the Treatment of Sexual Abusers, Orlando, FL.

Selvini-Palazzoli, M., Boscolo, L., Cecchin, G., & Prata, G. (1978). *Paradox and counter-paradox: A new model in the therapy of the family in schizophrenic transaction.* New York: Jason Aronson.

Slipp, S. (1984). *Object relations: A dynamic bridge between individual and family treatment.* New York: Jason Aronson.

Stiver, I. (1990). *Dysfunctional families and wounded relationships—Part I: Work in progress.* Wellesley, MA: Stone Center Working Papers Series.

Terr, L. (1990). *Too scared to cry.* New York: Basic Books.

Thomas, D., & Wilcox, J. (1987). The rise of family theory: A historical and critical analysis. In M. Sussman & S. Steinmetz (Eds.), *Handbook of marriage and the family* (pp. 81–102). New York: Plenum.

Trepper, T., & Barrett, M. J. (Eds.). (1986). *Treating incest: A multiple systems perspective.* New York: Haworth.

Trepper, T. S., & Barrett, M. J. (1989). *Systemic treatment of incest: A therapeutic handbook.* New York: Brunner/Mazel.

van der Kolk, B., McFarlane, K., & Weisaeth, L. (1996). *Traumatic stress: The effects of overwhelming experience on mind, body, and society.* New York: Guilford.

Vasington, M. (1989). Sexual offenders as victims: Implications for treatment and the therapeutic relationship. In S. Sgroi (Ed.), *Vulnerable populations: Sexual abuse treatment for children, adult survivors, offenders, and persons with mental retardation* (pp. 329–350). Lexington, KY: Lexington Books.

Wakefield, H., & Underwager, R. (1988). *The real world of child interrogations.* Springfield, IL: Charles C Thomas.

Wexler, R. (1990). *Wounded innocents: The real victims of the war against child abuse.* New York: Guilford.

White, M., & Epston, D. (1990). Narrative means to therapeutic ends. New York: Norton.

18

When a Family Deals With Loss: Adaptational Challenges, Risk, and Resilience

FROMA WALSH AND MONICA McGOLDRICK

Loss can have a shattering impact on the family. It can reverberate in depression, substance abuse, rage, violent or self-destructive behavior, and anxiety about further loss, and it can fuel relationship conflict and cut-off. Yet resilience research reveals that the worst of times can also bring out the best in families with the potential for healing and growth out of tragedy (Walsh, 1998). This chapter presents a systemic framework for family assessment and intervention with loss, identifying major family adaptational challenges. We discuss crucial variables that can complicate loss and heighten the risk for immediate or long-term dysfunction. The impact of loss is considered in a sociocultural context and in relation to the multigenerational family life cycle. Key family processes that facilitate recovery and resilience are described to inform therapeutic approaches to loss.

SOCIOHISTORICAL PERSPECTIVE

Coming to terms with death and loss is the most difficult challenge a family must confront. From a family systems perspective, loss can be viewed in terms of transactional processes involving the deceased member with all survivors in a shared life cycle that acknowledges both the finality of death and the continuity of life. Throughout history, mourning beliefs and practices have facilitated both the integration of death and the transformations of survivors in moving forward with life. Different cultures and religious traditions, in varied ways, mark the passage and offer assistance to the community of survivors (McGoldrick et al., 2004; Parkes, Laungani, & Young, 1997; Walsh, 1999b; 2004). Although there is considerable diversity in individual, family, and cultural modes of dealing with death and loss, family processes are crucial in mediating healthy or dysfunctional adaptation to loss (Walsh & McGoldrick, 2004).

Contrary to the nostalgic myth of the traditional family as intact, stable, and secure (Walsh, 2003b), families over the ages have had to cope with the precariousness of life and disruptions wrought by death. Death struck young and old alike, with high rates of mortality for infants, children, and women in childbirth, a pattern that is still prevalent in impoverished communities worldwide. With life expectancy under 50 years, parental death often disrupted family units, shifting members into varied and complex kinship networks (Aries, 1982).

Until the advent of hospital and institutional care removed death from everyday life, people died at home, in the midst of family members, including children. Modern technological societies came to deny death and to distance from the full range of grief processes, losing traditional cultural supports to assist families in integrating death with ongoing life (Becker, 1973; Mitford, 1978). Geographical distance or emotional estrangement often separates members of families at times of death and dying. Increasingly, medical advances confront families with unprecedented and anguishing decisions at life's end.

The past decade—marked by the AIDS epidemic, the aging of the baby boom generation, terrorist attacks, and the war in Iraq—has brought heightened attention to death and loss. Amid the social, economic, and global upheavals of recent decades, families are dealing with multiple losses, transitions, and uncertainties. The stability and security of increasing numbers of families have been disrupted through dislocations such as divorce, job loss, and migration (Walsh, 2003b). This chapter focuses on loss through death, yet the family challenges and processes described have broad application to other experiences involving loss, recovery, and resilience. In helping families to deal with their losses, we can facilitate transformation and growth, strengthening their relationships and resources to meet future life challenges (Walsh, 1998).

LOSS IN SYSTEMIC PERSPECTIVE

A systemic approach attends to the impact of death and loss on the family as a functional unit, with immediate and long-term reverberations for every member and all other relationships. Recovery involves family processes that assist individual members in coming to terms with loss and moving forward with life, as well as rebounding as a family unit. The extensive literature on bereavement has focused primarily on individual grief reactions in the loss of a significant dyadic relationship (Bowlby, 1961; Kubler-Ross, 1969; Worden, 2002). A systemic perspective is required to appreciate the chain of influences that ripples throughout the family relationship network with any significant loss, affecting partners, parents, children, siblings, and extended family (Reilly, 1978). Legacies of loss find expression in continuing patterns of interaction and mutual influence among the survivors and across the generations. The pain of loss touches survivors' relationships with others who may never even have known the person who died.

Epidemiological studies have found that the death of a family member increases vulnerability to premature illness and death for surviving family members, especially for widowers and for parents who have lost a child (Huygen, van den Hoogen, van Eijk, & Smits, 1989). In view of the profound connections among family members, it is not surprising that loss by death is considered more stressful than any other life change (Holmes & Rahe, 1967).

Family systems theory introduced a new paradigm for understanding family relationships, yet the field of family therapy was slow to approach the subject of loss, reflecting the cultural aversion to facing and talking about death. As Murray Bowen (2004) noted: "Chief among all taboo subjects is death. A high percentage of people die alone, locked into their own thoughts, which they cannot communicate to others" (p. 43). Bowen saw at least two constraints: (a) intrapsychic processes that involve some denial of death; and (b) blocked communication, intended to protect family members and others from upset.

Bowen advanced our understanding of the loss experience as profoundly influenced by and, in turn, influencing family processes. He described the disruptive impact of death or threatened loss on a family's functional equilibrium. In his view, the intensity of the emotional reaction is governed by the level of emotional integration in the family at the time of the loss and by the functional significance of the lost member. Emotional shockwaves may ripple throughout the family system immediately or long after a traumatic loss. Beyond the usual grief reactions of individuals close to the one who died, they operate on an underground network of emotional interdependence of family members. As Bowen observed, symptoms may appear in a child or other family member, or conflict may erupt between members, without the family connecting such reactions to the loss event. There may even be a vigorous denial at the suggestion of a possible connection. Bowen maintained that awareness of such shock-waves is essential for therapy, so that the sequence of events is treated as relevant. Therefore, therapists need to assess the total family configuration, the functioning position of the deceased member, and the family's overall level of adaptation, in order to understand the meaning and context of presenting symptoms and to help the family in a healing process.

Norman Paul found that grief at the loss of a loved one or an important family member, when unrecognized and unattended, may precipitate strong and harmful reactions in other relationships, ranging from marital distancing and dissolution to precipitous replacement, extramarital affairs, and even sexual abuse (Paul & Grosser, 1965). Paul cautioned that a clinician's own aversion to death and grief may hamper the ability to inquire about loss issues, to notice patterns, and to treat a systemic problem correctly as grief related. Narrow therapeutic focus on observable here-and-now interactional patterns or on secondary problems can blind clinicians to the relevance of past or threatened losses. Paul advocated an active therapeutic approach that confronts hidden losses, fosters awareness of their relational connections, and encourages mutual empathy in conjoint couple and family therapy.

Loss is a powerful nodal event that shakes the foundation of family life and leaves no member unaffected. More than a discrete event, it involves processes over time, from the threat and approach of death through its immediate aftermath and on into long-term implications. Distress is not only due to grief but is also a consequence of changes in the realignment of the family emotional field (Kuhn, 1981). Loss modifies family structure, often requiring major reorganization of the family system. Perhaps most important, the meaning of a particular loss event and responses to it are shaped by the family belief system, which in turn, is modified by loss experiences (Reiss & Oliveri, 1980).

A death in the family involves multiple losses: a loss of the person, a loss of roles and relationships, the loss of the intact family unit, and the loss of hopes and dreams for all that might have been. In order to understand the significance of loss processes, we must attend to (a) the past, as well as the present and future, and (b) the factual circumstances of a death as well as the meanings for a particular family in its social context and developmental passage.

FAMILY ADAPTATION TO LOSS

A family life-cycle framework takes into account the reciprocal influences of several generations as they move forward over time and as they approach and respond to loss (McGoldrick & Walsh, 1999). Death poses shared adaptational challenges, requiring both immediate and long-term family reorganization and changes in a family's definitions of its identity and purpose. Beavers and colleagues (Beavers & Hampson, 1990) found that the ability to accept loss is at the heart of all processes in healthy family systems. In contrast, very dysfunctional families showed the most maladaptive patterns in dealing with inevitable losses—clinging together in fantasy and denial to blur reality, insisting on timelessness and the perpetuation of never-broken bonds.

Adaptation does not mean resolution, in the sense of achieving some complete, once and for all "getting over it." Nor does resilience mean simply bouncing back, cutting off from the emotional experience or quickly putting the loss behind you and moving on. Rather, resilience involves active coping, struggling well, and forging strengths to meet the many challenges that unfold over time (Walsh, 1996). Mourning and adaptation have no fixed timetable or sequence, and significant, traumatic losses may never be fully resolved. Coming to terms with loss involves finding ways to make meaning of the loss experience, put it in perspective, and integrate the experience into the fabric of family life (Neimeyer, 2001). The multiple meanings of any death are transformed throughout the life cycle, as they are integrated into individual and family identity along with subsequent life experiences, including other losses.

Research on loss has found wide diversity in individual coping styles and in the timing and intensity of normal grief responses (Wortman & Silver, 1989). Children's reactions to death depend on their stage of cognitive and emotional development, on the way adults deal with them concerning matters around the death, and on the degree of caretaking they have lost. Our research and clinical experience suggest that that there are crucial family adaptational challenges which, if unattended, leave family members vulnerable to dysfunction and heighten the risk of family dissolution. Parallel to the individual bereavement tasks identified by Worden (2002), there are four major family tasks which tend to promote immediate and long-term adaptation for family members and to strengthen the family as a functional unit. The first two involve shared acknowledgment of the reality of death (and shared experience of the loss). The second task is a reorganization of the family system and reinvestment in other relationships and life pursuits.

(1) Shared acknowledgment of the reality of death and (2) shared experience of the loss. All family members, in their own ways, must confront the reality of a death in the family. With the shock of a sudden death, this process may start abruptly. In the case of life-threatening condition (Rolland, 1994), it may begin tentatively, with hopes for recovery alongside fears of *possible* loss, then, to greater *probability*, and finally, the *certainty* of

impending loss as in the terminal phase of an illness. Bowen (2004) underscored the importance of direct contact with a dying loved one, urging visits and ways to include children. Well-intentioned attempts to protect children or vulnerable members from potential upset can isolate them from the shared experience and can impede their grief process. They may become upset more by the anxiety of survivors and their own fantasies.

Acknowledgment of the loss is facilitated by clear information and open communication about the facts and circumstances of the death. Inability to accept the reality of death can lead individuals to avoid contact with family members or become angry with others who are moving forward in the grief process. Longstanding sibling conflicts and cutoffs often can be traced back to the bedside of a dying parent.

Funeral rituals (Imber-Black, 2004) serve a vital function in providing direct confrontation with the reality of death and the opportunity to pay respects, share grief, and receive comfort in the supportive network of the community. Active participation by family members, including children, is encouraged. Activities such as giving eulogies, telling stories both poignant and humorous, offering musical or artistic expression, and displaying photographs and mementos can make participation meaningful for all family members. Sharing the experience of loss, in whatever ways a family can, facilitates adaptation.

Family communication is also crucial over the course of the loss process. While keeping in mind that individuals, families, and cultures vary in the degree to which open expression of feelings is valued, research on well-functioning families indicates that clear, direct communication facilitates family adaptation and strengthens the family as a supportive network for its members (Walsh, 1998, 2003a). A climate of trust, empathic response, and tolerance for diverse reactions is essential. The mourning process also involves sharing attempts to put the loss into some meaningful perspective that fits coherently with a family's life experience and belief system. This requires dealing with the ongoing negative implications of the loss, including the loss of dreams for the future that will never be.

Families are likely to experience a range of feelings depending on the unique meaning of the relationship and its loss for each member as well as the implications of the death for the family unit. Strong emotions may surface at different times, including complicated and mixed feelings of anger, disappointment, helplessness, relief, guilt, and abandonment, all of which are present to some extent in most family relationships. In the dominant American culture, expression of intense emotions tends to generate discomfort and distancing in others. The loss of control experienced in sharing overwhelming feelings can frighten other family members, leading them to block all communication around the loss experience to protect one another and themselves.

When we take into account the multiple, fluctuating, and often conflicting responses of members in a family system, we can appreciate the diversity and complexity of any family mourning process. Tolerance is needed for varied responses within families and for the likelihood that members may have different individual coping styles, be out of phase with one other, and have unique experiences in the meaning of a lost relationship. Mourning may be blocked by roles and responsibilities, as in single parenthood, with children and well-intentioned relatives colluding to keep the sole parent strong and functioning (Fulmer, 1983).

When communication is blocked, the unspeakable may go underground to surface in other relationships or in symptomatic behavior. If a family is unable to tolerate certain feelings, a member who directly expresses the unacceptable may be scapegoated or extruded. Unbearable feelings may be delegated and expressed in a fragmented fashion by various family members (Reilly, 1978). One member may carry all the anger for the family while another is in touch only with sadness, or one may show relief while another is numb. The shock and pain of a traumatic loss can splinter family cohesion, leaving members isolated and unsupported in their grief.

In one case, a mother sought help for her daughter's school problems. Inquiry to understand the question of "why now?" explored recent events in the family. The therapist learned that the oldest son had been caught in the cross fire of a gang-related shooting. The shot that killed him had also shattered the family unit. The father withdrew, drinking heavily to ease his pain. The next eldest son carried the family rage into the streets, seeking revenge for the senseless killing. Two other middle sons showed no reaction, keeping out of the way. The mother, alone in her grief, turned her attention to her daughter's school problems.

Family therapy provided a context for shared grief-work, building resilience in the family by repairing the fragmentation, opening communication, and promoting a more cohesive network for mutual support and healing. It was important to involve the "well" siblings, who had been holding in their own pain so as not to further burden their parents. On follow-up, the daughter's school problems and father's drinking had subsided. The experience of pulling together to deal with their loss had strengthened the family unit, increasing their coping capacity with other problems, as well.

(3) Reorganization of the family system and (4) reinvestment in other relationships and life pursuits. The death of a family member disrupts the family equilibrium and established patterns of interaction. The process of recovery involves a realignment of relationships and redistribution of role functions needed to compensate for the loss, buffer transitional

stresses, and carry on with family life. As in the following case, children can be harmed more by their family's inability to provide structure, stability, and protective caregiving than by the loss itself. The sibling bond can be a critical lifeline through such times.

> Marie, age 50, sought help for depression after the sudden death of her brother, who had been her mainstay in life since her mother's death when she was seven years old. She vividly recalled the night of the death, when relatives came and left her mother's bedroom. She put on her best dress, and sat in her room, holding her brother's hand, waiting to be called to say their goodbyes. No one came for them, nor were they taken to the funeral. In the upheaval, she and her brother were separated, sent to stay with various relatives, uncertain if or when they would be returned home to their father. After their return weeks later, her father, overwhelmed in his grief, frequently came into her bed at night for comfort and sexual contact. Eventually his remarriage brought stability and ended her secret ordeal. Feeling sorry for her father, she felt she had to take her mother's place to relieve his obvious suffering, thereby sacrificing her own needs. This self-sacrifice became a pattern in her life, enduring an abusive marriage for many years.

Promoting cohesion and flexible reorganization in the family system is crucial to restabilization and resilience. For children's optimal recovery, surviving family members need to rally and coordinate efforts to provide nurturance, security, and guidance through the upheaval. They should make every effort to clarify what will happen to them, to keep siblings together, and to ensure that generational boundaries are firm so that children are not inappropriately used to meet a grieving parent's emotional needs.

The turmoil experienced in the immediate aftermath of a loss leads some families to hold on rigidly to old patterns that are no longer functional to minimize the sense of loss and disruption in family life. Other families may make precipitous moves into new homes or relationships, taking flight or seeking immediate replacement for their losses. Further dislocations heighten the risk of dysfunction, and replacement relationships are complicated by the unmourned losses. It is important to help families pace their reorganization and reinvestment.

The process of mourning is quite variable, often lasting much longer than people expect. Each new season, holiday, and anniversary is likely to re-evoke the loss. Over-idealization of the deceased, a sense of disloyalty, or the catastrophic fear of another loss may block the formation of other attachments and commitments. Family members may refuse to accept a new member who is seen as replacing the deceased when the loss has not been integrated.

Family therapy with loss requires the same ingenuity and flexibility that families need to respond to various members and subsystems as their issues come to the fore. As changes occur in one part of a system, changes for others are generated. A widow's decision to remarry may spark upset reactions by former in-laws or children who will need to adapt. Decisions to meet with an individual, couple, or family unit at various points are guided by a systemic view of the loss process over time.

VARIABLES INFLUENCING FAMILY ADAPTATION TO LOSS

We can identify a number of variables in the loss situation and in the family processes and social context that influence the traumatic impact of a death (Walsh & McGoldrick, 2004). It is important for clinicians to be aware of patterns that can complicate family adaptation and heighten risk of dysfunction (Rando, 1991). In order to work preventively at the time of a loss, or to understand and repair long-term consequences, these variables should always be carefully evaluated and addressed in any intervention plan.

The Loss Situation

Sudden or lingering death. Sudden death or death following protracted deterioration are especially stressful for families and require different coping processes. When a person dies unexpectedly, family members lack time to anticipate and prepare for the loss, to deal with unfinished business, or in many cases even to say their good-byes. Like a bolt out of the blue, a sense of normalcy and predictability is shattered: Death can take a loved one at any time, in any place. Clinicians need to explore and help family members with painful regrets and guilt over what they wish they had done differently or how they might have prevented the death.

When the dying process has been prolonged, family caregiving and financial resources can become depleted, with needs of other members put on hold (Rolland, 1994; Rosen, 1998). Relief of family strain is likely to be guilt-laden. Moreover, families are increasingly faced with anguishing end-of life dilemmas, such as whether, and how long, to maintain life support efforts. Families can be torn apart by opposing positions of members or coalitions. Clinicians can help family members to prepare and discuss living wills and power of attorney, to share feelings and differences openly about such complicated dilemmas, and to come to terms with decisions taken.

Ambiguous loss. Ambiguity surrounding a loss interferes with adaptation, often producing conflict and depression (Boss, 1999). A family member may be physically absent but psychologically present, such as a soldier missing in action in wartime or a child who disappears without a trace. The uncertainty about whether a missing loved one is dead or alive can be agonizing. Family members may be consumed by desperate searches and attempts to gain information to confirm the fate of their loved one. Conflict may ensue as some give up hope while others refuse to do so. After a disaster, search efforts are very important for families to recover a body to bury or to retrieve some remains; otherwise, mourning is usually delayed.

In other situations of ambiguous loss, a family member may be physically present but psychologically dead, perhaps unable to recognize loved ones, as in the mental deterioration of Alzheimer's disease (Boss, 1999). It is important to help family members to deal with the progressive loss of mental functioning and important aspects of their relationship without extruding the person as if he or she were already dead.

Violent death. The impact of violent death can be devastating, especially for loved ones who witnessed it or narrowly escaped it themselves, as in a plane crash, a mutilating fatal accident, or a murder. Lethal firearms have contributed to an alarming increase in homicides and accidental shootings in the U.S., particularly of children by other youths. Murders are committed more often by relatives or acquaintances than by strangers. Clinicians should be especially vigilant in cases of couple or family violence and should take threats of harm quite seriously, especially when an abused spouse attempts to leave the relationship or, after separation, moves on into a new one.

The senseless loss of innocent lives is especially hard to bear, especially when a result of deliberate acts or negligence. An entire community can be traumatized by persistent violence and ever-present threatened loss, as experienced by children and families in blighted inner-city neighborhoods, where life is much like that of a war zone (Garbarino, 1992). Casualties in war are always personal tragedies for families. The taking and loss of lives in war may haunt survivors and their family relationships for years—and generations—to come (Figley, 1998; Figley, McBride, & Mazza, 1997).

War and terrorism have a broad impact beyond those immediately affected, now intensified by instantaneous televised broadcast worldwide. Studies of the aftermath of 9/11 have found that posttraumatic stress symptoms nationwide increased exponentially with the amount of television viewing (Silver, Holman, McIntosh, Poulin, & Gil-Rivas, 2002). Repeated broadcasts of scenes of bombing, death, and destruction are most distressing, especially for children. With the heightened risk of renewed terrorism and threatened loss, families and communities cannot simply return to normal life, but must construct a new sense of normality, vulnerability, and interdependence. Resilience, commonly described as bouncing back, can more aptly be thought of as bouncing forward to meet new challenges and uncertainties in a changed and less secure world (Walsh, 2002b).

Systemic resilience-oriented approaches are being developed to help families and communities pull together in the wake of a major disaster. For example, resilience-based multifamily groups were designed for Bosnian and Kosovar refugee families in Chicago in the wake of the genocidal atrocities and losses they had suffered. This program led to a collaborative project in Kosovo for resilience-based training of mental health workers to foster the recovery of families and communities throughout the war-torn region (Rolland & Weine, 2000; Walsh, 2002a). Similarly, Landau's LINC Model builds family and community resources for recovery from catastrophic loss, as does Saul's program in lower Manhattan neighborhoods directly affected by the attacks of 9/11 (Landau & Saul, 2004).

Recovery from traumatic loss is blocked by a passive, helpless, victim stance, whereas resilience is forged through active, collaborative coping efforts. Although denial or distraction may be necessary for psychological survival in the midst of traumatic experiences, if maintained over time dissociation can have dysfunctional consequences, constrict intimate relationships, and risk emotional fallout for other family members. Individual and family healing and resilience are fostered through remembrance and stories honoring the courage, perseverance, and mutual support shown by family members who suffered or were lost.

Suicide. Suicides are among the most difficult deaths for families to come to terms with (Cain, 1972; Dunne & Dunne-Maxim, 2004; Shneidman, 2001). The rise in adolescent suicide requires attention to peer drug cultures and larger social forces, as well as family influences. Clinicians should also be alert to family patterns, such as threatened abandonment or sexual abuse that may pose heightened risk of suicide. Current life-threatening family situations can trigger catastrophic fears of loss or self-destructive behavior.

When a suicide has occurred, clinicians need to help family members with anger and guilt that can pervade their relationships, particularly when they are blamed, or blame themselves, for the death (Dunne & Dunne-Maxim, 2004). The social stigma of suicide can contribute to family shame and cover-up. Such secrecy distorts family communication and can isolate a family from social support, generating its own destructive legacy (Imber-Black, 1995). Clinicians should routinely note family histories of suicide or other traumatic loss that may predict future suicide risk, particularly on significant dates such as an anniversary, birthday, or holiday. Although a therapist or loved ones cannot always prevent a suicide, the risk can be lowered by exploring covert linkages to trauma events, mobilizing family support, and helping members to integrate painful experiences, rekindle hope from despair, and envision a meaningful future beyond their losses.

Family Process Variables in Loss, Recovery, and Resilience

The general level of family functioning and the state of family relation-ships prior to and following the loss should be carefully evaluated, including the extended family and social network. Consistent with lead-ing research on family functioning and resilience (Walsh, 1998, 2003a), we observe that shared belief systems, family organization patterns, and communication processes are crucial mediating variables in adaptation to loss. Particular attention should be given to the following variables.

Family Belief Systems

Making meaning. A family's shared belief system significantly influ-ences adaptation to loss (Nadeau, 1998). Beliefs about death and the meanings surrounding a particular loss are rooted in multigenerational family legacies, in ethnic and religious beliefs, and in the dominant societal values and practices (Walsh, 2004). Clinicians need to appreciate the power of belief systems in healing the pain of loss as well as the destructive impact of blame, shame, and guilt surrounding a death (Rolland, 1994). In attempts to make meaning of a death, family members grapple with causal explanations: How could this have happened? Why me/us? Whose fault is it? Could it have been prevented? Such concerns are especially strong in situations of traumatic death where the cause is uncertain and questions of responsibility or negligence arise. Commonly, family members each hold a secret belief that they could have—or should have—done something to prevent a death. It is important to help families share such concerns, gather information in unclear situations, and come to terms with the extent of their accountability or limits of their control.

Mastering the possible. Western values of mastery and control can hinder acceptance of a death. Family members may despair that, despite their best efforts, optimism, or medical care, they cannot conquer death or bring back a loved one. Studies find that resilience involves mastery of the possible: engaging fully with loved ones in the dying and mourning processes, alleviating suffering, making the most of precious time, and healing relational wounds.

Transcendence and spirituality. In the aftermath of loss, meaningful memorial rituals, as noted above, foster healing bonds and the transfor-mation of relationships with the deceased from a living presence to an ongoing spiritual connection. Death ends a life, but not a relationship, which is sustained through memories, stories, and deeds. In traumatic loss, some survivors become blocked from healing, and may perpetuate suffering through self-destructive behavior or revenge and harm toward others. Studies of resilience find that healing is fostered by efforts to tap into the best aspects of the deceased person and the relationship. As one mother stated after a reckless driver took the life of her daughter, "My daughter wouldn't want me to become consumed by grief or rage; she would want me to honor her life by taking up some meaningful pursuit in her memory." Personal suffering may be transcended in sparks of creative expression, as in poetry or music, or in community social action to spare other families a similar tragic loss, as in Mothers Against Drunk Drivers (MADD).

Spiritual beliefs and practices can be wellsprings for resilience with life-threatening illness and loss (Wright, 1999). Research has found evidence of the positive physiological effects of deep faith, prayer, and congregational support (e.g., Dossey, 1993; Gilbert, 1992; Walsh, 1999b; 2004). In some cases, religious beliefs can be sources of distress (Domino & Miller, 1992). One mother in an interfaith marriage believed that the stillbirth of her second child was God's punishment for not having baptized her first child. It is important for clinicians not to exclude the spiritual dimension of the experience of death, dying, and loss from their assessment and therapeutic work and to consult with, or refer to, pastoral counselors as appropriate (Walsh, 1999).

Family Organization

Flexibility of the family system. Family organization—its system of rules, roles, and boundaries—needs to be flexible, yet clearly structured, for reorganization after loss. At one extreme, a chaotic, disorganized family will have difficulty maintaining the authoritative leadership, stability, and continuity necessary to manage transitional upheaval. At the other extreme, an overly rigid family may resist modifying set patterns to make necessary accommodations to loss.

Prior role and functioning in the family system. The more important a person was in family life and the more central this person's role was in family functioning, the greater the loss. The death of a parent with small children is generally far more devastating than the loss of an elderly grandparent who has become more peripheral to family functioning. The loss of a leader or caregiver will be sorely felt, whereas the death of a quarrelsome troublemaker may bring a sigh of relief. The death of an only child, the only son or daughter, or the last of a generation leaves a particular void. Families risk dysfunction if they avoid the pain of loss by denying its significance or seek instant replacement. At the other extreme, a family can become immobilized if the lost member is deemed so essential that surviving members are unable to reallocate role functions or form new attachments.

Family connectedness. Adaptation to loss is facilitated when family connectedness or cohesion enables mutual support and yet is balanced by tolerance and respect for individual differences in response to loss. Extreme family patterns of enmeshment or disengagement pose complications. At a fused extreme, any differences may be viewed as disloyal and threatening and lead members to submerge or distort feelings. Members may seek an undifferentiated replacement for the loss and have difficulty with subsequent separations, clinging to each other at normal developmental transitions, such as launching. At the other extreme, disengaged families are likely to avoid the pain of loss with distancing and emotional cutoffs. When families are fragmented, members are left to fend for themselves, isolated in their grief.

Conflicted or estranged relationships at the time of death. Family relationships are bound to have occasional conflict, mixed feelings, or shifting alliances. The mourning process is likely to be more complicated if conflict has been intense and persistent, if ambivalence is strong, or if relationships have been cut off altogether. When death is anticipated, as in life-threatening illnesses, clinicians should make every effort to help family members to reconnect and to repair strained relationships before the opportunity is lost. Often this requires overcoming members' reluctance to stir up painful emotions or to dredge up old conflicts. They may fear that confrontations could increase vulnerability and the risk of death. Family therapists need to be sensitive to these concerns and interrupt destructive interactional spirals, helping family members to share feelings constructively with the aim of healing pained relationships, forging new connections, and building mutual support. A conjoint family life review (Walsh, 1999a) can help members to share different perspectives, to clarify misunderstandings, to place hurts and disappointments in the context of life challenges, to recover caring aspects of relationships, and to update and renew relationships that have been frozen in past conflict.

Availability of extended family, social, and economic resources. The family loss experience is buffered by the availability of supportive kin and friendship networks. Such resources are especially important to draw upon in widowhood (Lopata, 1996; Parkes & Weiss, 1983). The lack of community for many contemporary families makes loss more difficult to bear. Family recovery is impaired by the draining of finances by costly, protracted medical care or by the loss of economic resources in the death of a breadwinner. When long-standing conflicts, cutoffs, or social stigma have left families disengaged and isolated, clinicians working with loss can be helpful by mobilizing a potentially supportive network and facilitation a healing reconciliation (Gutstein, 1991).

Communication

Clear, open communication versus secrecy. When a family confronts a loss, open communication facilitates processes of emotional recovery and reorganization, as described above. When certain feelings, thoughts, or memories are prohibited by family loyalties, social taboos, or myths, communication around the loss experience can be distorted and contribute to symptomatic behavior (Imber-Black, 1995). It is important for clinicians to foster a family climate of mutual trust, empathic response, and tolerance for a wide and often fluctuating range of responses to loss.

Sociocultural Influences in Recovery From Loss

Sociopolitical and historical context of loss. The experience of families who suffer war-related deaths is heavily influenced by social attitudes about the war involvement. The impact of the loss can be assuaged by a common sense of patriotism and heroism for a noble cause and victory. However, highly charged, conflicting positions about a war can complicate family adaptation. Bitter legacies of unresolved political, ethnic, and religious conflict can be passed down from generation to generation.

Cancer and AIDS have become the epidemics of our times, each generating tremendous anxiety and stigma (Sontag, 1988). The social stigma surrounding HIV–AIDS has contributed to secrecy and estrangement, impairing family and social support, as well as critical health care. The epidemic of AIDS in the gay community—and, increasingly, for men, women, and children in poor communities—is all the more devastating because of the multiple losses and anticipated losses of partners, parents, children, and other loved ones in relationship networks (Landau-Stanton, 1993; Walker, 1992).

More generally, societal heterosexist attitudes complicate all losses in gay and lesbian relationships (Laird, 2003). The death of a partner may be grieved in isolation when the relationship has been kept secret or has been disapproved of by the family or community. Lacking the legal standing of marriage, death benefits may be denied and the survivor who has coparented the biological child of his or her partner may find that relationship jeopardized (Werner-Linn & MORO, 2004).

Gender-based constraints. Although gender roles and relationships have been changing in recent decades, expectations for men and women in dealing with loss are still influenced strongly by gender-based socialization and role constraints (Stroebe, Stroebe, & Schut, 2001). With a death in the family, mothers are particularly vulnerable to blame and guilt because of expectations that they bear primary responsibility for the well-being of their husbands, children, and elders. Women have been socialized to assume the major role in handling the social and emotional tasks of bereavement, from the expression of grief to caregiving for the terminally ill and surviving family members, including their husband's extended family. Now that most women are combining job and family responsibilities, they are increasingly overburdened in times of loss.

Men, who have been socialized traditionally to manage instrumental tasks, tend to take charge of funeral, burial, financial, and property arrangements. They are more likely to become emotionally constrained and withdrawn around times of loss. Cultural sanctions against revealing vulnerability or dependency block emotional expressiveness and ability to seek and give comfort. These constraints undoubtedly contribute to high rates of serious illness and suicide for men following the death of a spouse (Lopata, 1996).

The different responses of men and women to loss can increase marital strain, even for couples with previously stable relationships. In one study of parents' reactions to sudden infant death syndrome (SIDS), fathers reported anger, fear, and a loss of control, wanting to keep their grieving private, whereas mothers responded more openly with sorrow and depression (DeFrain, Taylor, & Ernst, 1991). Men are more likely to withdraw, to take refuge in their work, or turn to alcohol or an affair. They may be uncomfortable with their wives' expressions of grief, not knowing how to respond and fearful of loss of control of their own feelings (culturally framed as breaking down and falling apart). Grieving individuals may perceive their partners' emotional unavailability as abandonment when they need comfort most, thereby experiencing a double loss. When both are expressive and involved in the family bereavement process, the quality of the relationship improves markedly.

These findings have important implications for loss interventions. Individual approaches appear to have limited impact on recovery when couple relationship dynamics are not addressed as well. Most commonly, it is women who seek treatment—or are sent by their husbands—for depression or other symptoms of distress concerning loss, while their husbands appear to be functioning well and see no need for help for themselves. Interventions need to be aimed at decreasing the gender-based polarization so that both men and women can more fully share in the range of human experiences in bereavement. Moreover, encouraging mutual empathy and support in couple and family sessions builds relational resilience to withstand and rebound from loss together (Walsh, 1998).

TIMING OF LOSS IN THE FAMILY LIFE CYCLE

The meaning and impact of a death vary depending on the developmental challenges the family is negotiating (Shapiro, 1994). In family assessment, a genogram and timeline are particularly useful in tracking sequences and concurrence of significant events and symptoms over time in the multigenerational family field (McGoldrick, Gerson, & Shellenberger, 1998). The particular timing of a loss may place a family at higher risk for dysfunction (McGoldrick & Walsh, 1999). Such factors include (1) untimely loss, (2) concurrence with other loss, major stresses, or life cycle transitions, and (3) history of traumatic loss and unresolved mourning. In each situation, the nature of the death, the function of the person in the family, and the state of relationships will interact. Whatever our therapeutic approach with loss, a developmental perspective can facilitate adaptation in ways that strengthen the whole family in future life passage.

Untimely losses. Deaths that are untimely in terms of chronological or social expectations, such as the death of a child, early parent loss, or early widowhood, tend to be most difficult for families. Such losses may be experienced as unjust, ending a life—or a relationship—before its prime and robbing hopes and dreams for a future that can never be. Untimely loss is complicated by the lack of social norms, models, or guidelines for adaptation. Prolonged mourning, often lasting many years, is common. Survivor guilt for spouses, siblings, or parents often blocks life pursuits or satisfaction.

The death of a child, reversing the natural generational order, is perhaps the most painful loss for a family (Rando, 1986). A sense of injustice can lead family members to profound questioning of the meaning of life or religious faith. As one father shouted: "I'm angry at God—how could a loving God take an innocent child who never had a chance at life?" Parental marriages are at heightened risk for discord and divorce. However, couples that are able to support each other through the ordeal may forge stronger bonds than before, underscoring the value of couple counseling in child loss (Hare-Mustin, 1979). Losses during pregnancy and perinatal deaths tend to be hidden and minimized (DeFrain, 1991; Werner-Lin & Moro, 2004).

With the death of a child, it is crucial not to neglect the impact on siblings, who may suffer prolonged effects (Cain, Fast, & Erickson, 1964). Normal sibling rivalry may contribute to intense survivor guilt, blocking developmental strivings. Siblings may also experience a secondary loss if parents are preoccupied with caretaking or grieving. In some cases, parents may turn to a sibling or quickly have another child as a replacement. The tendency to idealize the deceased child can burden surviving siblings who can never live up to fantasized expectations.

After Jimmy, age 13, attempted suicide, a family assessment revealed that he was born shortly before the drowning death of an older brother at the age of thirteen. He grew up attempting to take the place of the brother he had never known in order to relieve his parents' sadness, wearing his clothes and combing his hair to resemble photos of his brother. The father, who could not recall the date or events surrounding the death, wished to remember his first son as if he were still alive. The timing of the suicide attempt occurred as Jimmy reached the age of his brother's death and was concerned, at puberty, that he was changing from the way he was supposed to look. He felt that the only solution was to join his brother in heaven. Family therapy focused on the family's delayed grief process, enabling Jimmy to relinquish his surrogate position and supporting his own unique attributes and development.

Children who lose a parent may suffer profound consequences (Furman, 1974; Worden, 1996), including long-term vulnerability to illness, depression, and substance abuse. They may have difficulty forming other intimate attachments and may carry catastrophic fears of separation and abandonment. A child's recovery depends largely on (a) the emotional and functional state of the surviving parent, (b) sibling bonds, and (c) ongoing support of the extended family.

Early widowhood can be a shocking and isolating experience without emotional preparation or essential social supports (Parkes & Weiss, 1982). Other young couples and peers commonly distance to avoid facing their own vulnerability. As with the death of a child, well-intentioned relatives and friends may urge immediate replacement, without time to grieve the loss (Glick, Parkes, & Weiss, 1975).

Concurrence with other loss or stressful events. The pile-up of loss with other major stress events—including multiple losses, disruptive changes, or other developmental milestones—may overload a family. We pay particular attention to the concurrence of death with the birth of a child, since the processes of mourning and parenting an infant pose incompatible demands. Moreover, the child born at the time of a significant loss may assume a special replacement function that can complicate later separations and can spark high achievement or dysfunction. Similarly, a precipitous marriage in the wake of loss is likely to interfere with bereavement and with investment in the new relationship in its own right. When stressful events pile up, support by partners, kin, and social networks is crucial for coping and resilience.

Past traumatic loss and unresolved mourning. Past trauma and loss experiences heighten vulnerability to subsequent losses. They can intersect with current life cycle passage in many ways, often expressed in problems with attachment–commitment, separation, or self-destructive behavior, as in substance abuse (Coleman & Stanton, 1978). Whenever such issues are presented in therapy, it is important to explore past traumatic losses and their legacy. When couple relationships break down, losses that occurred at the start of the relationship and those coinciding with problem onset may be relevant. A wife's lack of sexual interest may go back to a child's drowning and her husband's lack of support at that time. We also note significant losses in the family around the birth of the symptom bearer and with attempts at separation, as in young adulthood, when unresolved loss issues may surface with disruption of the family equilibrium.

We pay special attention to intergenerational anniversary patterns when the occurrence of symptoms is found to coincide with death or loss in past generations at the same point in the life cycle. Some individuals make abrupt relationship changes or start new fitness regimens while others may behave self-destructively. In one case, couple conflict ensued when the husband adamantly opposed his wife's desire to have a second child. It was crucial to know that his mother had died in childbirth with his younger sister in order to understand his catastrophic fears.

Unresolved family patterns or scenarios may be replicated when a child reaches the same age or stage as a parent at the time of death or traumatic loss. It is crucial to assess a risk of destructive behavior at such times, which is most likely when such linkages are covert and disconnected in more dysfunctional families. In one chilling case, a 15-year-old boy stabbed a man in a dissociative episode, which the family ignored. After a third such stabbing event and psychiatric hospitalization, a family assessment revealed that the father, at the age of 15, had witnessed the brutal stabbing death of his own father.

An appreciation of the power of covert family scripts and family legacies is important to an understanding of the transmission of such patterns in loss (Byng-Hall, 2004). Anniversary reactions are most likely to occur when there has been a physical and emotional cut off from the past and when family rules, often unspoken, prohibit open communication about past traumatic events. In our clinical work, interventions are aimed to open up covert patterns to help family members come to terms with the past and differentiate present situations so that history need not repeat itself. Resilience studies have found that most individuals who were abused in childhood by their parents do not abuse their own children; they are able to heal and learn from that searing experience and go on to become loving parents (Kaufman & Zigler, 1987).

When loss is intertwined with past trauma, therapists can help families by reappraising family history, replacing deterministic assumptions of causality with a co-evolutionary perspective. Like the social context, the temporal context involves a matrix of meanings in which all behavior is embedded. Although a family cannot change its past, present and future changes occur in relation to that past. Systemic change in resilience involves a transformation of that relationship, yielding healing and growth.

CONCLUSION

Resilience research finds that individual, family, and larger social influences are intertwined in risk and resilience in the face of crisis and that the family can play a valuable protective role (Rutter, 1987). Thus, adaptation to loss is not simply a matter of individual bereavement; it is also a product of family mourning processes. Of all human experiences, death poses the most painful and far-reaching challenges for families. In this chapter, we have presented a systemic framework for clinical assessment and intervention with loss, examining the reverberations of a death for all family members, their relationships, and the family as a functional unit. An understanding of major adaptational challenges in loss and key family processes in recovery and resilience can guide intervention and prevention efforts. An awareness of crucial variables in the nature of the loss, in the family and social context, and in the timing of loss in the family life cycle alerts clinicians to issues that require careful attention in any systemic assessment and intervention approach.

Given the diversity of family forms, values, and life courses, we must be careful not to confuse common patterns in family bereavement with normative standards, nor assume that atypical responses are pathological. Resilience studies find many varied pathways in recovery from crisis events (Walsh, 1996). Helping family members to deal with a loss requires an understanding of their particular cultural and spiritual beliefs and practices. While it is generally better to foster openness about death, it is also important to respect family members' pain and their timing in dealing with loss. Where family processes have become blocked or distorted, members can be helped to support one another in their recovery journey, thereby strengthening the family as well as individuals in distress (Becvar, 2001). Although therapy may not be able to prevent death or bring back a loved one, we can help families to struggle well to master their adaptational challenges, reduce risks for dysfunction, and forge stronger bonds for healing and resilience.

REFERENCES

Aries, P. (1982). *The hour of our death* (H. Weaver, Trans.). New York: Vintage.
Beavers, W. R., & Hampson, R. B. (1990). *Successful families: Assessment and intervention*. New York: Norton.
Becker, E. (1973). *The denial of death*. New York: Free Press.
Becvar, D. (2001). *In the presence of grief*. New York: Guilford.
Boss, P. (1999). *Ambiguous loss*. Cambridge, MA: Harvard University Press.
Bowen, M. (2004). Family reaction to death. In: F. Walsh & M. McGoldrick (Eds.), *Living beyond loss: Death in the family* (pp. 47–60). New York: Norton.
Bowlby, J. (1961). Process of mourning. *International Journal of Psychoanalysis, 42*, 317–340.

Byng-Hall, J. (2004). Family scripts and loss. In F. Walsh & M. McGoldrick (Eds.), *Living beyond loss: Death in the family* (2nd ed.)(pp. 85–98). New York: Norton.

Cain, A. (Ed.). (1972). *Survivors of suicide*. Springfield, IL: Charles C Thomas.

Cain, A., & Cain, B. (1964). On replacing a child. *Journal of the American Academy of Child Psychiatry, 3,* 443–456.

Cain, A., Fast, I., & Erickson, M. (1964). Children's disturbed reactions to the death of a sibling. *American Journal of Orthopsychiatry, 34,* 741–752.

Coleman, S. B., & Stanton, D. M. (1978). The role of death in the addict family. *Journal of Marriage and Family Counseling, 4,* 79–91.

DeFrain, J. (1991). Learning about grief from normal families: SIDS, stillbirth, and miscarriage. *Journal of Marital and Family Therapy, 17,* 215–232.

Domino, G., & Miller, K. (1992). Religiosity and attitudes toward suicide. *Omega, 25,* 271–282.

Dossey, L. (1993). *Healing words: The power of prayer and the practice of medicine*. New York: Harper.

Dunne, E. & Dunne-Maxim, K. (2004). Working with families in the aftermath of suicide. In F. Walsh & M. McGoldrick (Eds.), *Living beyond loss* (2nd ed.)(pp. 272–284). New York: Norton.

Figley, C. R. (1998). *The traumatology of grieving*. Philadelphia: Brunner/Mazel.

Figley, C. R., McBride, B., & Mazza, N. (Eds.). (1997). *Death and trauma*. London: Taylor & Francis.

Fulmer, R. (1983). A structural approach to unresolved mourning in single parent family systems. *Journal of Marital and Family Therapy, 9*(3), 259–270.

Furman, E. (1974). *A child's parent dies: Studies in childhood bereavement*. New Haven, CT: Yale University Press.

Garbarino, J. (1992). *Children in danger: Coping with the consequences of community violence*. San Francisco: Jossey-Bass.

Gilbert, K. (1992). Religion as a resource for bereaved parents. *Journal of Religion and Health.*

Glick, I. O., Parkes, C. M., & Weiss, R. (1975). *The first year of bereavement*. New York: Basic Books.

Hare-Mustin, R. (1979). Family therapy following the death of a child. *Journal of Marital and Family Therapy, 5,* 51–60.

Holmes, T., & Rahe, R. H. (1967). The social adjustment rating scale. *Journal of Psychosomatic Research, 11,* 213–218.

Huygen, F. J. A., van den Hoogen, H. J. M., van Eijk, J. T. M., & Smits, A. J. A. (1989). Death and dying: A longitudinal study of their medical impact on the family. *Family Systems Medicine, 7,* 374–384.

Imber-Black, E. (2004). Rituals and the healing process. In F. Walsh & M. McGoldrick (Eds.), *Living beyond loss: Death in the family* (2nd ed.) (pp. 340–357). New York: Norton.

Imber-Black, E. (1995). *Secrets in families and family therapy*. New York: Norton.

Kaufman, J., & Zigler, E. (1987). Do abused children become abusive parents? *American Journal of Orthopsychiatry, 57,* 186–192.

Kubler-Ross, E. (1969). *On death and dying*. New York: Macmillan.

Kuhn, J. (1981). Realignment of emotional forces following loss. *The Family, 5,* 19–24.

Laird, J. (2003). Lesbian and gay families. In F. Walsh (Ed.), *Normal family processes: Growing diversity and complexity* (3rd ed., pp. 176–209). New York: Guilford.

Landau, J., & Saul, J. (2004). Facilitating family and community resilience in response to major disaster. In F. Walsh & M. McGoldrick (Eds.), *Living beyond loss* (2nd ed.) (pp. 285–309). New York: Norton.

Landau-Stanton, J. (1993). *AIDS, health, and mental health: A primary sourcebook*. New York: Brunner/Mazel.

Legg, C., & Sherick, I. (1976). The replacement child: A developmental tragedy. *Child psychiatry and human development, 7,* 113–126.

Lopata, H. (1996). *Current Widowhood: Myths and Realities.* Thousand Oaks, CA: Sage.

McGoldrick, M., Almeida, R., Hines, P., Garcia-Preto, N., Rosen, E., & Lee, E. (1991). Mourning in different cultures. In F. Walsh & M. McGoldrick (Eds.), *Living beyond loss: Death in the family* (pp. 172–206). New York: Norton.

McGoldrick, M., Gerson, R., & Shellenberger, S. (1998). *Genograms: Assessment and intervention* (2nd ed.). New York: Norton.

McGoldrick, M., & Walsh, F. (1999). Death and the family life cycle. In B. Carter & M. McGoldrick (Eds.) *The expanded family life cycle: Individual, family, and social perspectives.* Needham Heights, MA: Allyn & Bacon.

Mitford, J. (1978). *The American way of death.* New York: Touchstone.

Neimeyer, R. A. (Ed.). (2001). *Meaning reconstruction and the experience of loss.* Washington, DC: American Psychological Association Press.

Nadeau, J. W. (1998). *Families making sense of grief.* Thousand Oaks, CA: Sage.

Parkes, C. M., Laungani, P., & Young, B. (1997). *Death and bereavement across cultures.* New York: Routledge.

Parkes, C. M., & Weiss, R. S. (1983) *Recovery from bereavement.* New York: Basic Books.

Paul, N., & Grosser, G. (1965). Operational mourning and its role in conjoint family therapy. *Community Mental Health Journal, 1,* 339–345.

Paul, N., & Paul, B. B. (1982). Death and changes in sexual behavior. In F. Walsh (Ed.), *Normal Family Processes* (1st ed.). New York: Guilford.

Rando, T. (1986). *Parental loss of a child.* Champaign, IL: Research Press.

Rando, T. (1991). *Treatment of complicated mourning.* Champaign, IL: Research Press.

Reilly, D. (1978). Death propensity, dying, and bereavement: A family system's perspective. *Family Therapy, 5,* 35–55.

Reiss, D., & Oliveri, M. (1980). Family paradigm and family coping: A proposal for linking the family's intrinsic adaptive capacities to its responses to stress. *Family Relations, 29,* 431–444.

Rolland, J. (1994). *Families, illness, and disability: An integrative treatment model.* New York: Basic Books.

Rolland, J., & Weine, S. (2000). Kosovar Family Professional Educational Collaborative. *AFTA Newsletter, 79,* 34–35. Washington, DC: American Family Therapy Academy.

Rosen, E. (1998). *Families facing death: Family dynamics of terminal illness* (Rev. ed.). Lexington, MA: Lexington Books.

Rutter, M. (1987). Psychosocial resilience and protective mechanisms. *American Journal of Orthopsychiatry, 57,* 316–331.

Shapiro, E. (1994). *Grief as a family process.* New York: Guilford.

Shneidman, E. S. (2001). *Comprehending suicide.* Washington, DC: American Psychological Association Press.

Silver, R. C., Holman, E. A., McIntosh, D. N., Poulin, M., & Gil-Rivas, V. (2002). National longitudinal study of psychological responses to September 11. *Journal of the American Medical Association, 288* (10), 1235–1244.

Sontag, S. (1988). *AIDS and its metaphors.* New York: Farrar, Straus, & Giroux.

Stroebe, M., Stroebe, W., & Schut, H. (2001). Gender differences in adjustment to bereavement: An empirical and theoretical review. *Review of General Psychology, 5*(6), 62–83.

Walker, G. (1992). Family therapy in the context of AIDS. In T. Akamatsu, M. Parris Stephens, S. Hobfoll, & J. Crowther (Eds.) *Family health psychology.* Washington, DC: Hemisphere.

Walsh, F. (1996). The concept of family resilience: Crisis & challenge. *Family Process, 35,* 216–231.

Walsh, F. (1998). *Strengthening family resilience.* New York: Guilford.

Walsh, F. (1999a). Families in later life: Challenges and opportunities. In B. Carter and M. McGoldrick (Eds.), *The Expanded family life cycle* (3rd ed., pp. 307–326). Needham Heights, MA: Allyn & Bacon.

Walsh, F. (Ed.) (1999b). *Spiritual resources in family therapy.* New York: Guilford.

Walsh, F. (2002a). A family resilience framework: Innovative practice applications. *Family Relations, 51*(2), 130–137.

Walsh, F. (2002b). Bouncing forward: Resilience in the aftermath of September 11. *Family Process, 40*(1), 34–36.

Walsh, F. (2003a). Family resilience: A framework for clinical practice. *Family Process, 42*(1), 1–18.

Walsh, F. (Ed.) (2003b). *Normal family processes: Growing diversity and complexity* (3rd ed.). New York: Guilford.

Walsh, F. (2004). Spirituality, death, and loss. In F. Walsh & M. McGoldrick (Eds.), *Living beyond loss* (2nd ed.) (pp. 182–212). New York: Norton.

Walsh, F., & McGoldrick, M. (Eds.). (2004). *Living beyond loss: Death in the family* (2nd ed.). New York: Norton.

Werner-Lin, A., & Moro, T. (2004). Unacknowledged and stigmatiazed losses. In F. Walsh & M. McGoldrick (Eds.), *Living beyond loss* (2nd ed.) (pp. 247–271). New York: Norton.

Worden, J. W. (1996). *Children and grief.* New York: Guilford.

Worden, J. W. (2002). *Grief counseling and grief therapy: A practitioner's handbook* (2nd ed.). New York: Springer.

Wortman, C., & Silver, R. (1989). The myths of coping with loss. *Journal of Consulting and Clinical Psychology, 57,* 349–357.

Wright, L. (1999). Spirituality, suffering, and beliefs: The soul of healing with families. In F. Walsh (Ed.), *Spiritual resources in family therapy* (pp. 61–75). New York: Guilford.

19

Family Crisis Intervention

CHRYS J. HARRIS

Many of the family-trauma references cited in this chapter are over 10 years old. Very little has been reported in the trauma literature since the late 1980s regarding *systemic crisis intervention* for the emotional consequences of a family's exposure to a traumatic event. There is a fairly legitimate reason for this distinct omission of recent basic trauma journalism in the last decade—the emotional response to a traumatic event is usually considered individualized and very idiosyncratic (French & Harris, 1998) and the data regarding crisis intervention (prior to therapy) for the emotional response to traumatic events provides ambiguous results at best. Regardless of these facts, therapists who treat families from a systemic model for the emotional consequences of exposure to traumatic events recognize that individual and familial therapy is important but frequently not enough . . . there is a need for systemic crisis intervention.

Similar to individuals, families can go into crisis following the exposure of one or more family members to a traumatic event. Figley (1989a) suggests that families have unique ways in which they systemically produce stress, are exposed to stress, cope with stress, and master their stress responses as well as the stressor event itself. Further, they have "a remarkable 'feel' for the normative behavior of fellow family members" (Figley, 1989b, p. 12). Since normative behavior is described as behavior that is both expected and predictable (McCubbin & Figley, 1983), the family system will likely be the first to detect any nonnormative (unexpected and unpredictable behavior, e.g., emotional traumatic behavior) experienced by one or more family members (Figley & McCubbin, 1983).

In his decisive work on helping traumatized families, Figley (1989b) identifies four separate ways a family system can be emotionally traumatized:

1. Simultaneous effects, in which a catastrophic event occurs to the entire family system
2. Vicarious effects, in which family members learn that another member experienced a traumatic event
3. Chiasmal effects (Kishur, 1984), in which the entire family system is affected by the traumatized member's story
4. Intrafamily trauma, in which family members cause the trauma for other family members, as in the case of abuse

A number of authors (e.g., Figley, 1989a, 1989b; Nichols, 1989) suggest the use of family therapy to intervene with families in an emotional crisis state. Nichols (1989) defines family therapy as a concentration on individuals in their primary context—the family—and as being concerned with modifying the family system. He argues that a family system approach is useful because a crisis state in a family is more than the response or pathology of individual family members; it is also indicative of difficulties within the family system.

EMOTIONAL TRAUMA AND FAMILY SYSTEMS THEORY

General systems theory has been around since the late 1940s and early 1950s. It was originally used in science and mathematics by von Bertalanffy (1968). In his efforts to define organization in general with systems, von Bertalanffy adopted an organismic principle that animals live together as organized entities and must be considered as organized entities by science. The organismic principle established the foundation needed to identify the family as a system and to perceive the family and its members in a social context. Drawing from this work of von Bertalanffy, Harris (in press) constructed the Traumatized Family System Archetype (TFS Archetype) that will help discern how systemic crisis intervention theoretically can be useful. According to Harris, a traumatized family system possesses certain qualities:

- A unified organization of family members where one (or more) is traumatized
- The traumatized family system is different from the sum of its traumatized family members
- Any trauma experienced by one family member affects the rest of the family system

The traumatized family systems theory is concerned with

- Identifying the family code—the functional and structural rules of the pre- and posttrauma family system
- Identifying the attributes of the pre- and posttrauma family system which include
  family system methods of information processing
  family system methods of adaptation to changed circumstances
  family system methods of self-organization
  family system methods of self-maintenance
  family system methods of self-regulation through communication

Nichols (1989) suggests that family emotional trauma must be considered in systemic terms, not as the result of individual neurosis. Figley (1989a, p. 39) concurred when he wrote, "It is not necessary that anyone in the family have a diagnosable case of PTSD to qualify as a 'traumatized family.'"

McCubbin and McCubbin (1989) propose that some families do very well in adapting to stressful situations while others adapt poorly. They recommend families adapt to stressful situations in two phases: *adjustment* and *adaptation*. In the family adjustment phase, families tend to assess the stressor event in terms of its severity and assess their ability to master the stressor event through their vulnerability, their flexibility, their appraisal of the stressor event, and their problem-solving skills. Basically, these are the methods of information processing from the TFS Archetype as well as the beginnings of systemic recognition of pre- and posttrauma family attributes. Families tend to begin the assessment on an individual family member level. Each family member tries to come to terms with his or her own idiosyncratic appraisal of the stressor event (French & Harris, 1998). This process can begin as early as during the actual stressor event or, in cases of delayed stress, individual appraisal of the stressor event can begin as late as many years following the event. Family members may or may not resolve the stressor event to their individual liking; however, as the family prepares to confront the stressor event systemically, the individual family members gradually come together to address the stressor event as a group. The family members are likely to argue about their individual beliefs but not really understand what each other believes.

After the assessment, families move to systemically confronting the stressor event (McCubbin & McCubbin, 1989). The adaptation phase requires families to manage all the stress they are experiencing (the immediate stressor event plus any other stressors the family has been experiencing), bringing their family system into balance by applying strengths, capabilities, resources, and their unique attributes. It is the unique qualities of systems theory that allow families to assess (consciously or unconsciously) and confront stressor events.

For a family to accomplish the adjustment and adaptation phases, it must be systemically moderately healthy and functional (Nichols, 1989). The following are minimal basic prerequisites to ensure moderate systemic health and functionality:

1. The family is committed to getting well—as a systemic unit.
2. The family has a systemic acceptance of the traumatic event—that it happened to the whole family; that no family member is being overtly blamed.
3. The family agrees that *all* family members will participate and communicate in therapy.
4. There is an absence of family violence and substance abuse.

Without these minimal basic prerequisites for moderate systemic health and functionality, it is doubtful that a family can be successful in family therapy for emotional trauma.

The TFS Archetype suggests that family systems tend to promote functional and structural rules that originate from family rituals, traditions, myths, customs, culture, heritage, conventions, and ceremonies. These rules establish a number of family characteristics such as parental dominance, sibling dominance, family member tolerance of a number of problems, family affection, abusiveness, cohesiveness, flexibility, and many other details the family system might require to maintain itself. These systemic attributes are the crux of how one system actually differs from another. Assessing these attributes can help a family therapist detect how a system processes information, adapts to change, organizes itself, maintains itself, and communicates to regulate itself. When these TFS Archetype attributes are identified and disclosed to family members during crisis intervention, the system can be remarkably receptive to self-awareness and modification, which can lead to an eventual alleviation of any family traumatization.

PREVENTING EMOTIONAL TRAUMA

Research on the prevention of systemic emotional trauma is nonexistent, and the research on the prevention of individual emotional trauma is insufficient. The most prominent scrutiny of the prevention of individual emotional trauma has been focused on critical incident stress debriefing (CISD) and critical incident stress management (CISM), both being group crisis intervention techniques (Harris, 1995). In the past decade, CISD and CISM have been used to help individual victims reduce their risk of developing traumatic stress disorder from a number of prominent traumatic events, including the raid on the Branch Davidian compound in Waco, the bombing of the Alfred P. Murrah Federal Building in Oklahoma City, and both of the attacks on the World Trade Center in New York City.

Despite a number of outcome studies on the utility of CISD or CISM in preventing the onset of emotional trauma, conclusions are uncertain—sometimes CISD and CISM appear to work, sometimes not. The usefulness of individual or group therapy to prevent the onset of a traumatic stress disorder has not been confirmed either. This chapter offers a technique for preventing systemic emotional trauma in families. There are no outcome studies to confirm the efficacy of this model either, but there are informal case studies and anecdotal data available.

THE FAMILY CRISIS INTERVENTION MODEL

Families frequently move into a crisis mode of functioning as a result of traumatic exposure to one or more family members. Many of these families seek counseling or therapy for their systemic distress. Harris (1991) described a model for providing crisis intervention with such families and to help them reestablish stability. Harris' (1991) systemic model is based on crisis intervention principles identified by Slaikeu (1984) with individuals and includes five steps: (a) making psychological contact, (b) exploring the dimensions of the family problem, (c) examining possible solutions, (d) assisting in taking concrete action, and (e) follow-up.

The present family crisis intervention model attempts to revamp Harris' (1991) systemic crisis intervention model and bring it into the 21st century. A note of caution is offered to the reader. The assessment and treatment of the residuals of psychotrauma is a very specialized field. There are specific standards of assessment and treatment, and the mental health provider treating the family must be competently trained to treat the emotional residuals of a stressor event and to take on these clients, whether they are seen as individuals or as a family.

Stage 1—Making Therapeutic Contact

This stage has been modified from the original model (Harris, 1991). First, the use of the heading *therapeutic contact* instead of psychological contact reflects the importance of the family therapist as a crisis interventionist for emotionally traumatized family systems and a facilitator of family recovery from psychotrauma. Second, the term *understood* has been removed from the original model. Harris and Linder (1996) suggest it is rarely possible for family members to truly understand another family member's viewpoint. However, they point out, family members can come to *know* another family member's viewpoint, accepting it regardless of whether or not there is understanding. The concept of knowing will become significant later in the model when the family healing theory is discussed.

In Stage 1, the family members are encouraged to tell their individual stories. Figley (1989a) proposes that it is not enough to simply have family members relate their idiosyncratic viewpoints; they must also tell their trauma-related personal stories. All family members are given time to tell their individual story. This includes even the small children. The telling of one's story allows each family member to feel heard, to feel a part of the family, and, hopefully, to feel unfettered from what could be the burden of traumatic memory. If all the stories cannot be told during the session, the family is to have sessions at home—homework—where they continue telling their stories until each family member has enlightened the rest of the family.

Earlier, the concept of individual family appraisal of the stressor event was discussed. During Stage 1, all family members have an opportunity to either complete their individual appraisal of the stressor event or, if incomplete, present their idiosyncratic appraisal to the family. Each family member is encouraged to relate personal feelings, beliefs, thoughts, concerns, and needs.

The family therapist's role in Stage 1 is to primarily provide an open atmosphere where family members can be heard, accepted, and supported. The family therapist listens to facts, watches for unspoken feelings, corrects irrational thought, and, where necessary, tries to calm intense situations. Secondarily, the family therapist tries to identify the TFS Archetype family attributes that are disturbing and potentially in need of changing. Finally, the family therapist helps the family learn to listen to each other, watch each other, and support each other. All of this is accomplished in the session or during homework sessions.

It is also during Stage 1 that the goals of the rest of the crisis intervention are identified. The major goal of family trauma therapy is to restore the family system to some level of balance (homeostasis) and comfort. It is inconceivable to this author that the family that has been traumatized can be returned to a pretrauma state of equilibrium, so the purpose of family crisis intervention is to find a posttrauma state of equilibrium.

Stage 2—Exploring the Dimensions of the Problem

The TFS Archetype presumes that some or all of the pretrauma family code (the functional and structural rules that make up family rituals, traditions, myths, customs, culture, heritage, conventions, and ceremonies) was problematic and that is why the family is having trouble adapting posttrauma. As a result, one of the major goals of Stage 2 is for the family to simply identify pretrauma barriers within the systemic rituals, traditions, myths, customs, culture, heritage, conventions, and ceremonies. Going into the family code too deeply, however, may constitute shifting from crisis intervention to therapy. This is best done in session and not given as homework because the family may tend to go too deep without the family therapist's supervision and guidance.

The family's objective is to allow each family member to communicate the particulars of his or her idiosyncratic view of the traumatic event. Additionally, it is a family requisite to allow each member to communicate the particulars of his or her idiosyncratic view of the family and how the family system was before, during, and following the traumatic event. Here the family has to learn to accept that family communication is also comprised of individual experience. This is where systems theory and individual theory can become entwined and potentially confusing.

French and Harris (1998) present the opinion that it is one's idiosyncratic belief about one's self and the world in which one lives that dictates how one will cope with a traumatic experience. Janoff-Bulman (1992, p. 5) proposed that we humans have a conceptual system that "developed over time, [and] provides us with expectations about the world and ourselves." It is through this idiosyncratic conceptual system that we pass every personal experience so we can judge its impact on our lives. As a result, there is no systemic diagnosis for emotional trauma, only individual diagnosis.

In the TFS Archetype, the whole system is not simply a summation of the individual parts; it is different and has heuristic value in and of itself. The concept of a change in one part of the system affecting the rest of the system is paramount in present-day family systems theory (Nichols & Everett, 1986). Many family system therapeutic models subscribe to the belief that it is not the Freudian intrapsychic conflicts of the individual that is the focus of therapy but the lack of balance and comfort within the family system that is the preeminent treatment emphasis. The same is true for systemic crisis intervention. The family must have insight into individual family members before the family, as a system, can gain balance and comfort.

Stage 2 has three family therapist-oriented objectives:

1. To recognize, sort, and focus on the family-defined goals that should be dealt with immediately (putting off less demanding goals until later)
2. To create a positive recuperative climate by promoting favorable family communication
3. To enlist family social support skills

Social support skills, as defined by Figley (1987), include tangible aid (money, shelter, clothes, food, etc.), emotional aid (love, respect, caring, etc.), companionship, advice, and encouragement. Figley (1987) goes on to suggest that improving the social support skills of a family is the hallmark of any crisis intervention. He reports a number of studies that show that families are highly satisfied with the systemic effects of social support as a functional component of their therapy.

Systems therapists feel that individual intervention is important but is frequently not enough because families appear so dramatically affected by an individual family member's emotional response to trauma or the whole family system's response to a traumatic event, or both. This usually creates dysfunction within the family system and requires intervention or treatment that is oriented to more than an individual family member.

Stage 3—Examine Possible Solutions

The TFS Archetype identifies pre- and posttrauma attributes of the family system, which include the methods the family uses to process information (adapt to change, self-organization, self-maintenance, and self-regulate through communication). These attributes will be needed to process and solve the problems (barriers) identified in Stage 2.

As Stage 3 begins, the family members have told their stories and related their idiosyncratic view of the stressor event. They have discussed the family dynamics prior to, during, and following the stressor event. The family has hopefully assembled a great deal of information regarding how each family member thinks and feels; they are ready to look at potential systemic solutions for their difficulties. The family has to ask questions regarding what is making them out of balance and uncomfortable, and they have to look to what they will require to put themselves more in balance and comfort—the posttrauma state of being.

Homework during this stage is usually just having the family make lists of barriers without going into possible solutions. The discussion of solutions should not be done until the family has been trained to solve problems. The techniques of problem solving are too lengthy to go into here; however, it may be useful to identify the major problem-solving steps that are the most useful in crisis intervention. The four basic steps are:

1. The problem is owned by the presenter and stated in such a way as to indicate that the presenter, indeed, owns the problem. This is usually accomplished using "I" statements (e.g., I have a problem with …).

2. Problems are never presented to the family unless they are presented concurrently with potential solutions.
3. Families then debate and negotiate solutions, not problems.
4. Rules are put into place to prevent the family members from imposing barriers to problem solving.

The fundamentals of problem solving in crisis intervention focus on strengthening the family's skills to move beyond the obstacles that both allow problems to persist and prohibit solving the systemic predicaments the problems create.

In family crisis intervention, it has been discovered that the quickest intervention that helps a family reach balance and comfort is to fully know the stressor event. Harris (1995) suggested that the way an individual gains mastery over the emotional residue of a traumatic experience is to both assimilate (take internally) and accommodate (make it fit with one's view of self and life) the knowledge of the traumatic event. Figley (1984) proposed five victim questions that, when answered with little or no emotional response, indicate that one has assimilated and accommodated the traumatic event. We can adapt these victim questions systemically to help a family assimilate and accommodate to the traumatic event:

- What happened?
- Why did it happen?
- Why did we act as we did during and immediately following the traumatic event?
- Why have we acted as we have since the traumatic event?
- What are we going to do if it happens again?

With these questions, the family therapist is urging the family to review the traumatic event, explore the traumatic event, and reach a consensus of knowing what happened to them as a result of the traumatic event. They can accomplish this task by exploring the TFS Archetype systemic methods of information processing from a pre- and posttrauma point of view.

By exploring the last question, the family can look at how they will prepare for future traumatic events. As the family haggles through these five victim questions, they begin to move through their victimization into survivorship. The family therapist can help them learn that they are exchanging their family outcome of immobility and inaction (victim identity) for one of mobility and action, in spite of the traumatic event (survivor identity). However, as families negotiate through their perceptions of what is systemically wrong, it is the rare family that can come together for a common conviction of how to adjust.

Figley (1989a) developed a useful concept to bring the family together for a common assumption to align themselves—the family healing theory. The family healing theory is the creation of the family's systemic perspective regarding the traumatic event. It is derived out of their trauma stories, their individual beliefs and insights, their newly acquired systemic beliefs and insights, and their attempts to clarify, correct, and interpret.

Earlier it was noted that the concept of knowing has become more important than the concept of understanding (Harris & Linder, 1996) in this crisis intervention model. The family healing theory can exist because each family member does not have to understand the theory; they just have to know it. They have the power to suspend their individual beliefs, opting instead to take up the family healing theory as a systemic belief. The family healing theory is truly a compromise because it rarely makes everyone happy. Nevertheless, it provides a common and constant foundation for systemic methods of dealing with the trauma. Like a Phoenix being reborn in a flame, the family system can be reborn through the family healing theory.

Stage 4—Assist in Taking Concrete Action

When the family has reached a systemic identity of survivorship through the development of the family healing theory, it is ready to take concrete action to bring itself into balance and comfort. This stage truly relies on the skills and techniques of the family therapist. Harris (1991) identified some of the necessary therapeutic skills as a sense of timing, curiosity, creativity, and the use of self.

Families differ in the way they accomplish goals and tasks. They do things at different speeds and in different manners. It is usually incumbent on the family therapist to learn the family system and work from within its model of the world (Harris, 1995). The only way to ensure that change persists is to provide change that is consistent with the family system's convictions.

Since there are numerous systemic techniques and family therapeutic models, the crisis intervention model does not advocate a single approach by which the family therapist should assist the family in taking concrete action or try to change the family. It is prudent, however, to look at potential intervention problems. In their significant work regarding change, Fisch, Weakland, and Segal (1982) suggest that family therapists consider the following cautions regarding interventions:

Do not rush the interventions; let the stages take their course. The family therapist needs to recognize that the family which is seeking systemic crisis intervention for the consequences of a traumatic event must go at a pace that is agreeable to it. The stages herein described are designed to set a pace that the family can work within while giving the family therapist some leeway to move it forward.

Recognize there are dangers in improvement. Many of us have learned that behaviors that persist—whether positive or negative—are usually being reinforced in some manner. So it follows that to change a persistent behavior risks losing the sought-after reinforcement. As such, there is commonly a cost to remedial change—systemic or otherwise—and that cost often takes the form of lost reinforcement. There are those who will do anything to continue to receive the reinforcement, whether unconsciously (predictable, naturally occurring therapeutic resistance) or consciously (purposeful therapeutic sabotage).

Do not attempt to force something that can only occur spontaneously. Families can be differentiated according to their abilities to handle normative and nonnormative transitions, especially in regard to their differing degrees of shielding the system from stress (McCubbin & McCubbin, 1989). This suggests that some families will require very little crisis intervention while others will require a great deal. It is important to allow the family latitude to spontaneously repair issues that it is confronting during a crisis intervention. This is why homework is often very important.

Do not use postponement as a technique to master the fear of the traumatic event or traumatic issues. It is common for individuals and family systems to put off confronting fearful material. The family therapist should help the individual or family system confront the fear, albeit sometimes very slowly, when it arises, but confront it nonetheless.

Do not attempt to reach accord through opposition. This admonition is probably the most important of this group. It recognizes the interrelationship that a family has and how one member may try to manage another through opposition (typically a parent managing a child). Family members must feel that their contentions regarding the family and the traumatic event will not be endangered or rejected by the other family members, that they will be accepted as legitimate representations of the individual's view.

Do not confirm suspicions by allowing others to defend themselves. In Shakespeare's *Hamlet* (III, ii, 239), Queen Gertrude tells Prince Hamlet, "The lady doth protest too much, methinks." This protestation just served to heighten the beliefs and concerns about the lady's behaviors. When a family member is accused by another, the defense usually only manages to confirm the suspicion. The family therapist is urged to censure defensive conduct, opting instead for the view that differing perceptions can coexist. Harris and Linder (1996) have shown that individual family members can have diametrically opposed beliefs at the same time, and that a family can abide by this reality once they are trained to do so.

Attempt to reach compliance through volunteerism. Family members have to want to help one another. They have to want to reach compromise or positive sacrifice for the good of the family system. The idea of volunteering to do so is a good way to gain cooperation and teamwork in systemic problem solving. Compromise is not something we do very well in our culture.

When families try to compromise, they are negating all of their personal family member choices and are opting for a choice outside the system, one that will usually please no one. For example, when a family tries to decide where to eat, each family member chooses a restaurant. They debate the pros and cons and, finding they cannot choose from the suggested eateries, a compromise restaurant is chosen, one that no one really wants to frequent. The result of the compromise is that no one is happy and the dining is usually not enjoyable. Instead of compromise, a better approach is to *sacrifice*. We will opt to eat at a suggested restaurant—one recommend by another family member—so we can attend our choice of eateries at another time. At first glance, this appears to be a compromise; however, after looking deeper, we can see that it is indeed a sacrifice.

Positive sacrifice can be a unique state. Often we believe that when we sacrifice, we are granting concessions to our belief system. This may be true at times, but it does not have to be; positive sacrifice can occur without discounting one's beliefs. Positive sacrifices can be made by first stating your belief and then consciously choosing to place your beliefs aside and allowing the other's beliefs to take precedent. For example, a child seeks to go to camp and the parents must decide whether to approve or disapprove. Mother is worried and suggests their child has never spent a night away from home before; she wants to disapprove. Father is excited and reports he did the same camp when he was a child; he wants to approve. This discussion has no room for true compromise—the child will go to camp or not. One way this can work through positive sacrifice is for the father to explain his confidence in his belief, acknowledge the mother's concern, and then opt to allow the mother's concerns to take precedence—the child does not go to camp. The other way this issue can be resolved through positive sacrifice is for the mother to explain her confidence in her belief, then acknowledge the father's consideration and opt to allow the father's alternative to take precedence—the child goes to camp. In both cases, each parent detailed his or her beliefs (not changing, granting concessions, etc.) and chose to let their spouse's option take precedent.

Since there are probably other difficulties with interventions, the family therapist needs to be very careful with the assignment of homework.

Stage 5—Follow-up

Family therapy is a good resource for families in trouble. Rarely does a family therapist completely terminate a therapeutic relationship with a family. Usually, the immediate problem is terminated (following successful treatment) and the family is encouraged to return when they need future help with another difficulty. In family crisis intervention, the same is true, but with a twist.

Family crisis intervention can require a great deal of homework. The family therapist is advising the family to do much of the requirements in the first four stages at home. They report their discoveries in the intervention sessions and the family therapist tweaks the system from all the components of the TFS Archetype (family functional and structural rules, family attributes, family methods of information processing).

When family crisis intervention is not successful, the most common explanation is that one or more family members were so traumatized that it was impossible for them to reach a level where they could work successfully with the family; the traumatized family members were simply incapable of facing any additional stress. Such a case often requires the family therapist to refer the individual family members to a specialist who is qualified to treat the consequences of psychotraumatic stress. Once the affected family members have worked through the emotional residuals of the traumatic event and are ready to rejoin the family, family crisis intervention can resume.

The second most common explanation for the failure of family crisis intervention is that the technique is comparatively brief and not always effective enough to provide the desired systemic relief. In these cases, the family therapist may choose to move into a more sustained therapeutic relationship with the family, immediately terminating crisis intervention.

In any event, the family therapist assures the family that he or she is a resource and can be called upon as needed for follow-up (from the crisis intervention) or therapy. Also, most family therapists are aware of a number of useful resources in the community (e.g., other therapists, other counselors, physicians, psychiatrists, community agencies, etc.) that families can be referred to for added assistance.

CONCLUSIONS

"Trauma does not occur in a vacuum, and often a number of family members may be similarly traumatized ..." (Turnbull & McFarlane, 1996, p. 483). Following this statement, the major focus of this chapter has been on crisis intervention from a systemic perspective for the traumatized family. However, it should be noted that the family is not the only system within which we may function. When treating traumatized individuals or families, it is important to not ignore other larger systems that may be potentially traumatized (extended family, workplace, church group, social group, school class, etc.). Such unawareness can prove to be extremely unfavorable to the outcome of trauma crisis intervention because of the effects these other systems may be having on the presenting family.

Finally, the author wishes to remind the reader that this family crisis intervention model has not been subjected to rigorous research. Much of what has been written in this chapter is based on his unpublished, informal case studies. Case studies such as these are defined by Moon and Trepper (1996, p. 393) as "clinical action research that is undertaken by clinicians who wish to … disseminate their clinical innovations to a wider audience through publication." By definition, this research is not quantitative and cannot meet strict positivistic assumptions for hypothesis testing. However, informal case studies are extremely flexible and allow for hypothesis generation which is part of the sum and substance of this section.

REFERENCES

Figley, C. R. (1984). Treating post-traumatic stress disorder: The algorithmic approach. *Newsletter of American Academy of Psychiatry and Law, 9,* 25–26.
Figley, C. R. (1987). Post-traumatic family therapy. In F. Ochberg (Ed.), *Post-traumatic therapy* (pp. 83–109). New York: Brunner/Mazel.
Figley, C. R. (1989a). *Treating stress in families.* New York: Brunner/Mazel.
Figley, C. R. (1989b). *Helping traumatized families.* San Francisco: Jossey-Bass.
Figley, C. R., & McCubbin, H. I. (1983). *Stress and the family, Volume II: Coping with catastrophe.* New York: Brunner/Mazel.
Fisch, J., Weakland, J. H., & Segal, L. (1982). *The tactics of change: Doing brief therapy.* San Francisco: Jossey-Bass.
French, G. D., & Harris, C. J. (1998). *Traumatic incident reduction (TIR).* Boca Raton, FL: CRC.
Harris, C. J. (2002). Traumatic stress in family systems. In M. B. Williams and J.F. Sommer, Jr., (Eds.), *Simple and complex post-traumatic stress disorder: Strategies for comphrehensive treatmnet in clinical practice* (pp. 261–275). Binghamton, NY: Haworth.
Harris, C. J. (1991). A family crisis-intervention model for the treatment of post-traumatic stress reaction. *Journal of Traumatic Stress, 4,* 195–207.
Harris, C. J. (1995). Sensory-based therapy for crisis counselors. In C. R. Figley (Ed.), *Compassion fatigue: Coping with secondary traumatic stress disorder in those who treat the traumatized* (pp. 101–114). New York: Brunner/Mazel.
Harris, C. J., & Linder, J. G. (1996). Communications and self care: Foundational issues of communication. In B. H. Stamm (Ed.), *Secondary traumatic stress: Self care issues for clinicians, researchers and educators* (pp. 95–104). Lutherville, MD: Sidran.
Janoff-Bulmam, R. (1992). *Shattered assumptions.* New York: Free Press.
Kishur, G. R. (1984). *Chiasmal effects of traumatic stressor events: The emotional costs of support.* Masters thesis, Purdue University, West Lafayette, IN.
McCubbin, H. I., & Figley, C. R. (1983). *Stress and the family, Volume I: Coping with normative transitions.* New York: Brunner/Mazel.

McCubbin, M. A., & McCubbin, H. I. (1989). Theoretical orientations to family stress and coping. In C. R. Figley (Ed.), *Treating stress in families* (pp. 3–43). New York: Brunner/Mazel.

Moon, S. M., & Trepper, T. S. (1996). Case study research. In D. H. Sprenkle & S. M. Moon (Eds.), *Research methods in family therapy* (pp. 393–410). New York: Guilford.

Nichols, W. C. (1989). A family systems approach. In C. R. Figley (Ed.), *Treating stress in families* (pp. 67–96). New York: Brunner/Mazel.

Nichols, W. C., & Everett, C. A. (1986). *Systemic family therapy: An integrative approach.* New York: Guilford.

Slaikeu, K. A. (1984). *Crisis intervention: A handbook for practice and research.* Boston: Allyn & Bacon.

Turnbull, G. J., & McFarlane A. C. (1996). Acute treatments. In B. van der Kolk, A. McFarlane, & L. Weisaeth (Eds.), *Traumatic stress* (pp. 480–490). New York: Guilford.

von Bertalanffy, L. (1968). *General systems theory.* New York: Braziller.

20

Enhancing Resilience Through Multiple Family Groups

KAREN CALLAN STOIBER, REBECCA J. RIBAR, AND GREGORY A. WAAS

Families and children are facing new and diverse threats to their mental health and psychosocial well-being. High rates of divorce, single parenthood, community and domestic violence, and mental health problems have altered the social context of family functioning in the 21st century. The burden of such issues on children and families is significant and has likely lowered quality of life for many families (America's Children, 2002; Department of Health and Human Services [DHHS], 2000). Multiple family groups aimed at enhancing resilience and coping capacities emerge as a viable intervention structure for helping families with children.

The purposes of this chapter are to (a) overview indicators of stress and trauma that can be addressed through multiple family groups, (b) review general guidelines for conducting intervention groups involving multiple families, and (c) highlight special considerations for conducting multiple family groups to increase the family's resilience to stress and trauma. We also discuss meaningful ways of structuring groups for enhancing parenting and parent–child relationships, promoting positive outcomes for children, and improving home–school collaboration.

INDICATORS SUPPORTING THE NEED FOR MULTIPLE FAMILY GROUPS

Stress from a variety of sources shape the conditions surrounding children and families. Prevalence estimates indicate 10% to 22% (Burns et al., 1995; Costello et al., 1996; Roberts, Attkisson, & Rosenblatt, 1998) of children and adolescents in the U.S. experience considerable emotional and behavioral problems that affect the development of academic and social competencies. Yet, in any given year, approximately only one in five of such children receive needed specialty services (Burns et al., 1995). The recent report of children's mental health by the U.S. Surgeon General indicated serious concerns about the lack of appropriate diagnosis and treatment in responding to children's emotional and behavioral difficulties (DHHS, 2000).

Approximately 16% of children (over 11 million) live in families having incomes below the federal poverty threshold (America's Children, 2002). In 2000, 28% of all family households were single-parent (U.S. Bureau of the Census, 2000). Economic destitution is a grave problem for many single-parent homes; as recent reports indicate, more than a quarter of single parent families live below the federal poverty level (U.S. Bureau of the Census, 2000). Most community and domestic violence takes place in neighborhoods that are poor, socially isolated, and located in inner cities.

Perhaps one of the most compelling reasons for multiple family groups is that the unmet mental health needs of children and families remain as high as levels reported two decades ago (DHHS, 2000). The overwhelming mental health and health care needs of children, adolescents, and families present a strong argument for multiple family group interventions either provided in schools or coordinated through home–school collaboration. Group and family-focused intervention services are not only efficient but offer an essential and unique structure for prevention and intervention (Stoiber & Kratochwill, 1998; Stoiber & Waas, 2004).

ECOLOGICAL RISK AND RESILIENCY MODEL

Recent studies have documented the greater likelihood of children raised in high-risk family environments to be predisposed to serious social, developmental, and academic problems (Jones, Forehand, Brody, & Armistead, 2002; Murry & Brody, 1999). In particular, risk factors such as limited social and economic support and community violence, when fused with poverty and reduced parenting capacity, can have a marked negative impact on the development of children and family functioning.

Poverty emerges as one of the primary sources, and perhaps the most significant contributor, of distress on family functioning. The devastating role of poverty on family functioning has been delineated in work that has attempted to disentangle the impact of poverty and single parenting on child developmental outcomes. Recent analyses (Murry, Bynum, Brody, Willert, & Stephens, 2001; Kleist, 1999) suggest that financial strain influences youths' adaptive development indirectly through maternal psychological functioning and parenting quality. The educational attainment of single mothers was associated with better economic conditions, which in turn foster parental involvement and supportive, cognitively stimulating parenting practices. Such positive parenting practices were associated with greater cognitive skills and lower levels of behavioral problems in youths. Conversely, financial strain in single mothers was associated with depressive symptoms, less maternal self-confidence, and poor parenting quality (i.e., punitive, aggravated, unsupervised, and nonstimulating caregiving). These conditions in turn predicted heightened levels of youth social–behavioral difficulties, risk-taking, and academic problems. It appears that poverty and associated family processes, rather than family structure, are vital factors for understanding child risk and outcomes associated with single parenting.

Social support has been hypothesized to be a salient protective factor that diffuses the stress associated with economic hardship on maternal psychological functioning, thus facilitating adaptive child development. A series of studies have been conducted to assess the relationship between social support, maternal depression, stress, and children's behavioral problems among low-income, African-American single mothers and their children (see, for example, McGroder, 2000). Greater financial strain and instrumental support (e.g., monetary and child care assistance), in conjunction with lower levels of emotional support and paternal involvement, predicted elevated levels of maternal depression and stress. Such maternal difficulties were positively associated with increased physical punishment and child challenging behavior (Jones & Unger, 2000; Stoiber & Houghton, 1994). These results suggest that social support may intensify and lessen the effect of financial strain on maternal functioning, and by extension, child outcomes. As the challenges confronting parents who experience economic, psychological, and social stresses are numerous, several researchers recommend a comprehensive, competency-based approach to intervention (Fournier & Perry, 1998; Kesner & McKenry, 2001; Stoiber & Waas, 2004).

Children of a particular subgroup of lone caregiving—those born to adolescent, single mothers—are considered especially at risk for developing more social–emotional and coping problems than other youth (Spruijt, DeGoede, & Vandervalk, 2001; Stoiber & Anderson, 1996). Although not all children of adolescent mothers display problems in development, several researchers have reported less competent coping behaviors (i.e., poorer self-regulation, greater irritability, negative or sad affect, and poorer social engagement and adapting to situations) for children of adolescent mothers. In particular, children of adolescent mothers display poorer coping capacities when the adolescent mothers reported a heightened degree of distress (Stoiber & Anderson, 1996; Stoiber & Houghton, 1994). Stoiber's findings also provide support for maternal characteristics as mediating positive coping skills in young children and thus serving as potential protective factors. In particular, adolescent mothers who have positive and realistic expectations about their children and who demonstrate responsive parenting behaviors (e.g., positive verbal interactions, behavioral involvement, and monitoring) appear to have children who fare better in their coping than children of other adolescent mothers.

During the adolescent years, parental monitoring emerges as a key protective factor in predicting adolescent difficulties across family structure. Research has suggested that single mothers' lack of active monitoring presents notable risks (Friedman, Terras, & Glassman, 2000; Noack, Krettek, & Walper, 2001). For example, adolescents living in single-mother homes, particularly adolescent males, were found to be three times more likely to not complete high school compared to adolescents in two-biological-parent families, despite similar levels of school achievement (Cookston, 1999). Among adolescents in single-mother homes, school dropout appears to be more related to support and coping difficulties than to cognitive deficiencies. Both male and female adolescents living in single-parent homes engage in higher levels of risk-taking behaviors and conflictual exchanges, assume more independence, and are less likely to be supervised and monitored by an adult compared with children in two-biological-parent homes.

Rather than regarding children and families surrounded by stressful circumstances as uniformly at risk for dysfunctional patterns and negative outcomes, the ecological risk and resiliency model stresses individual differences in coping and adjustment (Jones & Unger, 2000; McGroder, 2000; Stoiber, Anderson, & Schowalter, 1998; Stoiber & Good, 1998). A sociocultural, ecological approach illuminates contextual processes associated with parental psychological functioning and child coping. Various dispositional characteristics and situational factors can influence whether parents and their children surmount or succumb to adversities (Murry et al., 2001; Stoiber & Houghton, 1994). Moreover, the resilience model avoids "pathologizing" caregivers who experience at-risk characteristics (e.g., poverty, single parenthood, community violence) and facilitates an examination of competencies that foster positive family functioning and adjustment.

MULTIPLE FAMILY GROUPS: CHARACTERISTICS AND CONSIDERATIONS

Multiple family group approaches were developed as clinically efficient and cost-effective approaches to respond to similar crises experienced by families due to lack of therapists to provide individual or family therapy (Carlson, 1998). O'Shea and Phelps (1985) provide an early description of multiple family group therapy:

> A deliberate, planful, psychosocial intervention with two or more families present in the same room with a trained therapist for all or most of the sessions. Each participating family should have two or more members that represent at least two generations in the family and are present for all or most of the sessions. Sessions should have an explicit focus on problems or concerns shared by all families in attendance. These focal problems should pertain directly or indirectly to cross-generational family interaction. Sessions should implicitly emphasize patterns in interfamilial interaction, as well as utilize actual or potential alliances among members of different families based on similarities of age, focal problem, or family role. (p. 573)

The essential distinguishing feature of multiple family groups is that several families with children meet together simultaneously, with group intervention processes facilitated by a group facilitator. Beyond this defining feature, there exists considerable variation in therapeutic goals, processes, and procedures incorporated within the broad category of multiple family groups. Terms used in reference to this intervention approach include the *multiple family group* (MFG), *multiple family group therapy* (MFGT), *multiple family therapy* (MFT), and *multiple family discussion group* (MFDG) (Carlson, 1998). In general, MFGT and MFT are varieties of family approaches that place a greater emphasis on therapy or therapeutic modalities. MFG and MFDG are variations of groups that involve supportive and psychoeducational features rather than direct clinical or therapeutic work. For the purposes of this chapter, the term MFG will be used because professional work with families experiencing high-risk conditions and multiproblems is conceptualized better as intervention based on a systems–ecological perspective rather than as therapy (Minuchin, 1995).

Similar to other forms of therapeutic or intervention work, MFG approaches require ongoing planning, monitoring, and evaluating of the therapeutic or preventative process. The primary goal of multiple family groups is to provide prevention and intervention services to families with children that share similar problems or issues. The intent of MFG is to enhance and support healthy family interactions and improved coping capacities. In addition, some forms of MFG may focus on promoting healthy family–school interactions, resolve current concerns or conflicts, and serve the welfare of the child within the family context (Christenson, 2002).

Multiple family groups are especially useful for addressing the needs of multicrisis families. Often conventional family therapy may not be available or relevant for poor, multiproblem families with children. Although direct therapeutic intervention with individual family members or an individual family unit may occur in conjunction with multiple family group approaches, assistance to multiproblem families frequently needs to be multifaceted. That is, for families experiencing multiple crises and stresses, individual approaches are often ineffective if the family's basic needs have not been met or if the family finds the therapy stigmatizing (Minuchin, 1995).

The general structure for multiple family groups is to improve or alter affective, cognitive, and behavioral functioning of families with children through group-focused prevention and intervention activities. Multiple family groups having a prevention purpose seek to support the productive functioning of children and families and thus reduce the incidence of psychological or social–behavioral problems or both in children and parents. Prevention-oriented multiple family groups utilize resistance-oriented activities and approaches prior to the development of serious concerns, risk-taking behaviors, or other behavioral problems (Stoiber & Kratochwill, 1998). An example of an MFG having a prevention focus is a group designed to support adolescent parent or single-parent families (Stoiber et al., 1998). Intervention-oriented MFG approaches focus on families for which a problem has already been detected. Hence, participants of MFGs with an intervention focus usually share a similar mental health issue, crisis, psychological problem, or behavioral disorder, such as depression, child abuse, a chronic illness, or the loss of a significant person (Stoiber & Kratochwill, 1998).

Group participant considerations. Prior to initiating an MFG, the clinician or interventionist should consider the following question: "What reasons and evidence exist to support conducting a multiple group intervention rather than an individual-based intervention?" This question should help delineate initial decision-making about the purpose and advantages of an MFG. A response to this question also requires a thoughtful analysis of the family group participants including type and severity of the problem, capacity to work in a group, and the family's social and emotional stability. Inherent within MFG approaches is interactive dialogue and activities among and across families, including receiving feedback from other group members.

Similar to conducting individualized interventions, MFG approaches should incorporate adequate family assessment procedures that are used for developing intervention goals and plans (Elliott, Witt, Kratochwill, & Stoiber, 2002; Stoiber & Waas, 2004). By using procedures that link assessment to intervention, the interventionist is able to evaluate important considerations and conceptualize intervention plans based on several relevant indicators about family functioning, including the severity of the presenting concern, source of stress, family needs for support and education, focus of the intervention (e.g., all family members, selected family members, mother–child dyad), and available family resources.[1] Individuals who demonstrate severe needs or severe psychosocial problems are not considered good candidates for an MFG. Attention needs to be given both to parent and child functioning. Parent or adult family members should have the capacity to function within the context of the group as a contributing group participant (e.g., listen to others, wait to voice needs, cope in a group) and to contribute to the group's goal of producing positive coping and functioning in families.

Children who exhibit particular problems that can interfere with group participation and processing, such as Attention Deficit Hyperactivity Disorder (ADHD) or severe antisocial or aggressive characteristics, may not be well matched to MFG intervention. Semrud-Clikeman (1995) aptly noted that children with severe impulsive tendencies, language deficits, withdrawal, autistic characteristics, or thought disorders may be poor candidates for many group interventions. Moreover, those families or individuals experiencing heightened crises or losses may require individualized attention, at least initially, which is not typically feasible in MFGs. The family must demonstrate the capacity to adapt to the social demands and expectations of the group structure. Additionally, some MFG approaches incorporate individual sessions with family units or family members to individualize the intervention and feedback (e.g., Baker, Landen, & Kashima, 1991). Thus, additional sessions with individual families, follow-up home visits, or other individual contact with a professional increase the options for helping families experiencing heightened levels of stress or difficulties.

Confidentiality. One further consideration in determining group participants for MFG is confidentiality. Although confidentiality issues pertain to all forms of therapeutic intervention, they emerge as a particular concern when conducting MFGs with multiproblem families having limited coping capacities. Adult family members who have a history with protective services and other social service agencies may fear being honest with the facilitator and other group members during group activities and discussion. Guidelines should be established at the onset of the MFG about the need to contain revealed information or aspects regarding parent–child interactions within the group and to

---

1. *Editor's note:* See chapters 14 and 15 for Jane Gilgun's and David Olson's family assessment tools which are particularly suited for determining where and how best to intervene.

not share sensitive information with nongroup members. Establishing clear rules about the confidentiality of group interactions can help prevent inappropriate sharing of information with nongroup members and promote an atmosphere of openness, personal safety, and honesty within the group.

Group size. Significant variability exists in the literature regarding the number of families and children included in multiple family groups. Some MFG approaches focus primarily on the adult family members with the goal of developing competencies in the parent. Groups of 8 to 12 parents are typically viewed as an optimal number when group sessions incorporate discussion, stress management, and skill demonstration. However, larger groups (12 to 18 participants) may provide greater opportunity for positive modeling and increase the likelihood that each member of the group will identify with a fellow member (with whom newly learned stress management skills can be shared). But larger groups also have a number of risks associated with them. The facilitator will find it more difficult to provide individual attention to each parent–child dyad or family unit and to plan activities that are therapeutically relevant and engaging to all families in the group, while it will be easier for some children to be "off-task," disruptive, or passive.

In general, MFG approaches that focus on family units contain fewer numbers of adult participants so that appropriate attention can be given to child issues and parent–child interactional components. One procedure for minimizing the disadvantages associated with larger groups is to recruit a co-therapist or assistant to help plan and implement group activities. The use of a co-facilitator also holds considerable advantage because therapeutic tasks can be split and thus more easily monitored (e.g., one facilitator is responsible for implementing the MFG intervention activities while the other has responsibility for monitoring affective and coping responses of group participants).

Group facilitator considerations. Consideration needs to be given to orientation, skills, and knowledge base of the group facilitator. Group intervention work involves a planned process of psychosocial interaction between the group facilitator and the family group participants. Although some groups focus primarily on adult family members because their functioning very directly affects child functioning, the parent–child relationship and family functioning remain a primary focus. The intent of MFG approaches is competence enhancement of both adult and child participants. As such, the skills required of group facilitators are diverse and involve making positive connections with adult family members and their children. Research has suggested that conducting MFGs is a highly complex task which involves building rapport with each participant, facilitating family interaction and cross-family interaction, developing group cohesion, and responding to individual member needs as indicated. As stated cogently by Dombalis and Erchul (1987, p. 488), "Assessing and influencing a single family system requires a great deal of finesse and skill; managing several families at once demands even more."

The group facilitator must adapt the MFG to the developmental levels of the child group members and phases of family life. Group facilitators need to have well-developed competencies in the areas of coping skill development, empathy, listening, collaboration, confronting, conflict resolution, and negotiating. Facilitation of intervention groups involves various multitasking capacities. As noted by Stoiber and Kratochwill (1998, p. 5),

> Although similar competencies are needed for individual counseling and therapy, knowledge and skill in their use is more complex when one needs continually to focus and re-focus attention on affective, emotional, and behavioral indicators across several individuals. The group facilitator should monitor the development and progress of each group participant, which frames what and how questions are asked and processed, guides observations, and informs when and how to proceed. An ongoing, conscious effort to attend to all group participants is extremely demanding work. Similar to other areas of mental health competence, group facilitation develops with deliberate reflective practice, explicit skill refinement, continuous monitoring, and careful supervision.

Group facilitators of MFGs must continually evaluate their own competence in dealing with and responding to the complex nature of family intervention so that they do not go beyond their professional skill and knowledge base. Although MFG can be a powerful form of intervention for families experiencing similar stresses and challenging life circumstances, it can produce unintended and adverse effects if facilitators enter into the process with naïve notions about the dynamics and mechanisms involved in conducting groups (Arnold & Hughes, 1999; Stoiber & Waas, 2004).

Group structure and development. An extensive body of literature exists on the stages of development for group intervention and in conducting MFGs (e.g., Carlson, 1998; Corey, 2000; Yalom, 1995). Although a detailed review of this literature is beyond the purview of this chapter, it is important for group facilitators to be aware of the typical stages a group goes through during the MFG process. Corey (2000), for example, has identified four general stages of group development. In Stage 1, group members define rules and goals and expectations, begin the process of establishing trust and identity with the group, and establish norms of behavior. For MFGs aimed at promoting coping capabilities, this stage may involve such tasks as assembling families and setting the schedule for group meetings, establishing rules for the group, and completing activities designed to encourage group cohesiveness and trust among group members.

During Stage 2, group participants confront and work through feelings of resistance and anxiety. For an MFG, several issues typically emerge in this stage, including fears of stigmatization, doubts and anxiety about trust and confidentiality, and the realization that change requires considerable effort on the part of family members.

During Stage 3, the MFG moves into a period of cohesiveness and productivity. This stage often represents the work phase of the MFG when groups focus on specific objectives that match participants' needs and provide a structure for therapy sessions (e.g., coping skill management and anger control, coping with a chronic illness or loss). Structured exercises such as role plays and nurturing activities may be used to help alter patterns of interaction within families and to foster peer help and support across families. In this stage, extra care should be taken to ensure the active involvement of all group members in each MFG session. For example, the group facilitator often assigns roles to all members of the group during activities (e.g., while two members are role-playing, two others are serving as judges and providing feedback).

Finally, in Stage 4, participants review the gains they have made during the group session and prepare for termination and possible aftercare. Particular attention may be given to helping families establish social support networks with each other. In addition, participants often review the use of self-management and coping approaches to respond to various potential and future stressors.

Intervention Goals of Multiple Family Groups

A broad range of intervention goals for MFG approaches has been delineated in the literature (Carlson, 1998; Clark, Paulson, & Seidl, 1998). Common goals of MFG include (a) better family functioning, (b) greater mutual liking and respect among family members, (c) increased capacity to enjoy day-to-day living, (d) sharing of attitudes and concerns about parenting, (e) recognizing and developing ways of coping with family conflict and difficulties, (f) reducing risk for maltreatment and neglect by focusing on the parents' needs and in increasing their sense of effectiveness, (g) providing peer support and reducing social isolation, (h) improving parent interactions and communication with their children, (i) eliminating or reducing negative thought patterns or dispositions about parenting and the parent–child relationship, and (j) increasing capacity to develop satisfying relationships within the family and with friends. Obviously, particular family needs and issues will determine which goals are selected and form the basis for intervention plans and individual session goals.

The types of goals that are selected and addressed as well as the format of the MFG also will determine the number and length of intervention sessions. Sessions generally extend for 1 hr to 2 hr in length and vary from weekly to monthly in frequency. Education-oriented MFG approaches tend to be more structured in form and short-term in duration (generally consisting of 6 to 8 sessions). MFG approaches aimed at altering parenting practices, improving family interactions, and enhancing problem-solving strategies for dealing with stressful life events may require more frequent and extensive sessions (10 to 20 sessions occurring on a weekly basis). An empirical study of MFGs by Cassanso (1989) suggested that more than 10 sessions might be optimal for extending the work phase and enhancing social support networks among families.

Multiple Family Group Features and Elements

The particular characteristics of any particular MFG will be influenced by a number of factors: orientation of the group facilitator, length of intervention, age of group members, motivation level, and problem severity of the participants, environmental constraints, etc. In addition, the primary focus of the MFG will require attention to specific considerations. In the following section, we discuss four approaches to multiple family groups: (1) multiple family groups for enhancing parenting based on a stress and coping framework, (2) multiple family groups for enhancing child functioning, (3) school-based multiple family groups, and (4) family–school collaboration.

Multiple family groups based on a stress and coping framework. We find the use of a systems or ecological model of stress and coping to be most productive for conceptualizing the group interventions for families experiencing crises or multiproblems. MFG approaches based on a stress-and-coping model focus on improving the family's capacity to handle the particular stressors or challenging circumstances in its members' lives. In this regard, the MFG enhances the adaptive capacities and competencies of the families as opposed to providing therapy to adult or child participants. In general, MFG approaches view families as demonstrating nonproductive or maladaptive functioning because of being overwhelmed by pressing demands and limited resources.

Most MFGs based on stress and coping models incorporate multicomponents including (1) self-monitoring procedures for evaluating and responding appropriately to stressful events, (2) muscle relaxation techniques for activating positive coping, and (3) systematic cognitive restructuring of negative thoughts and triggers. Despite the inherent benefits of stress-reduction-oriented MFGs, family stress can interact with the effectiveness of the intervention group; professionals need to be aware of the manner in which parent stress levels can influence the outcomes attained through group interventions. For some families, the demands of the MFG may simply increase family stress by creating additional constraints on already limited family resources (Fine, 1995).

There are several group approaches aimed at enhancing skills or competencies in parents sharing common characteristics or stressors. For instance, Stoiber et al. (1998) describe a therapeutic group approach for parenting teens. Topics such as feeding, health, bonding, nurturing, and discipline are included in this multiple family approach in which the parents and their infants or young children are involved. Strategies for enhancing parenting skills in this type of MFG include role-playing, discussion of parenting practices, and opportunities to practice skills.

Families at risk for child maltreatment (e.g., substance abuse, parental history of abuse, etc.) can also benefit from MFG approaches, especially when an explicit focus is given to the parent–child relationship. Generally, five to seven families can be served within a relationship-focused MFG (Clark et al., 1998). A separate group involving parent participants and one for children can be conducted simultaneously with different facilitators leading each group. These separate parent groups and child groups are then followed by a combined group wherein parent–child dyads function together within the MFG. Typically, fostering healthy parent–child interactions is the focus of the multiple dyadic group; however, the needs of the parent, child, and entire family can be considered within this MFG structure. Clark et al. suggest that children involved in these groups are generally young, ranging from approximately 3 to 24 months of age.

Promoting resilience in children. Stoiber and Waas (2004) discuss several important characteristics of group interventions aimed at promoting resilience. For instance, interactive techniques and comprehensive competency-based strategies should be employed to facilitate as much involvement from families as possible. Children in these groups can benefit from instruction of positive decision-making skills, motivation, and social competence. Also, children who are identified to be at risk should be targeted before serious problems occur. It is generally most effective to target a cluster of risk-taking behaviors rather than focusing on one very specific problem behavior (such as drug use, gang involvement, or violence). Interventions of this type should include realistic expectations for youth participants and be sensitive to developmental, cultural, and ethnic characteristics of the participants.

Topics typically covered in programs that aim to facilitate the development of resilience include goal setting, values clarification, communication, conflict resolution, social support, and problem solving (Stoiber & Waas, 2004). It is also important to stress the development of a positive relationship with at least one adult role model, such as an adult mentor from the community, if the parent is unavailable to participate in the MFG. The incorporation of such community resources can provide long-term benefits and ongoing social support to youth who are prone to at-risk behaviors.

School-based multiple family groups. Schools are viewed as key sites for MFGs for at least three reasons. First, the literature on the mental health needs of school-age children is replete with examples documenting the effect of family functioning on the child's school-related performance, including physical, academic, social, and behavioral functioning (e.g., Christenson, 2002; Jones & Unger, 2000; Stoiber & Good, 1998). A second reason centers on accessibility and acceptability issues. Both children and parents are more likely to engage in MFG services provided in schools as compared to community-based or clinic-based mental health services because schools connote a less stigmatizing environment. Third, groups are a natural context within which children function in the school. Schools are considered to be in a strategic position for conducting group prevention and intervention because groups involving family members can be formed naturally and utilized readily.

Several researchers (Carlson, 1998; Dombalis & Erchul, 1987) have discussed MFG approaches conducted within the school setting. Such approaches typically focus on the development of networks with the community to support and help families. Within this model, referrals for MFG are typically generated at the school level, with the group facilitated by various cross-disciplinary school staff (e.g., school psychologist, social worker, counselor). It should be noted that if a student has been determined to have a disability and the child's individual educational plan stipulates a need for family intervention, the school is then responsible for covering the cost of the treatment.

Advocates of MFG approaches conducted within, or coordinated by, the schools view student problems from a systems framework, and conceptualize coping difficulties and other problems as a culmination of many factors that may influence the child, rather than as individual shortcomings. To adequately assess the many forces affecting a child's life, several researchers suggest ongoing communication with the many individuals involved with the family to improve the child's response to the MFG. These individuals may include extended family, neighbors, friends, churches, and school and government employees. Stoiber and Waas (2004) also suggest that collaboration such as joint intervention planning and implementation between group facilitators, families, and school personnel can lead to improved outcomes for children. Such collaboration should facilitate the generalization of coping skills learned in the MFG to multiple settings.

One of the key advantages of conducting school-based MFGs is that they provide an opportunity to develop goals and objectives for positive change which maximize ecological validity. By conducting MFGs in the school milieu where many of the child's difficulties are manifested, the group facilitator can consult closely with teachers and observe the student's coping skills in critical settings (e.g., classroom, lunch, playground). Information collected through these procedures can then be used to carefully match the MFG objectives and activities with the child's needs (Elliott et al., 2002; Stoiber & Kratochwill, 2002). However, children and families might be concerned about possible stigmatizing effects of participating in an MFG. In this regard, school staff should make a concerted effort at "normalizing" participation in the group intervention. Facilitators may want to develop an acceptable name for the group or encourage families to construct a name that feels comfortable to them (e.g., The Family Friendship Group or The Moms–Pops–Tots Group) as a way to ameliorate possible stigmatizing effects.

In general, effective school-based prevention and intervention programs incorporate three important components (Greenberg, Domitrovich, & Bumbarger, 1999; Zins, Elias, Greenberg, & Weissberg, 2000). Effective programs (a) develop cognitive and behavioral skills in both the parent and child which are protective, (b) help families become better attuned to emotional regulation and potential stressors, and (c) improve social functioning and relationships of children with parents and peers. Those interventions found to be most efficacious integrate systems of mental health into systems of education and childcare. Effective approaches also assist in attaining resources at the individual (e.g., additional parent or child therapy or both, educational and job training), the family (e.g., parent–child interaction interventions, paternal involvement), and the community (e.g., affordable child and health care) level. Successful provision of these comprehensive services requires collaboration among psychologists, social workers, and community organizers.

Home–school collaboration for enhancing family resilience. The purpose of home–school collaboration is the enhancement of children's competence in four areas: academic, social, behavioral, and emotional (Christenson, 2002). According to Christenson, it is imperative for schools to create relationships with families so that success in all of these critical areas of functioning can be realized.

Various researchers have defined the process of collaboration in different ways. Esler, Godber, and Christenson (2002) refer to home–school collaboration as working relationships between families and schools to facilitate children's learning. Minke (2000) more broadly defines the concept as diverse individuals with various areas of expertise working as equal partners. Esler et al. stress the importance of collaborative relationships between schools and families because the influences of the two forces on children's lives are very difficult to separate. They further state that this process can only be successful if a family feels respected, empowered, and consulted. Minke echoes this sentiment and voices concern over the tendency for family involvement to be school-directed as opposed to family-focused.

As a testament to the importance of home–school collaboration, national standards for family involvement programs have been developed (Esler et al., 2002). First, communication between home and school should be regular, two-way, and meaningful. Next, parents' capacity to cope with the demands of parenting should be promoted and supported, and parents should play a role in student learning. Also, schools should be inviting environments where parents feel welcome and comfortable in requesting support or assistance from school staff. The standards call for parents as full partners in decision-making. Finally, community resources should be utilized to strengthen collaborative efforts between schools and families and to promote positive outcomes for children.

The standards provide some general guidelines, but they do not specifically provide any strategies for accomplishing the goal of improved home–school collaboration. Esler et al. (2002) describe a model that is based on attitudes, relationships, and actions. Key components include family-centered practices such as family orientation, positive attitudes, sensitivity, and friendliness. The development of trust is another important step in the process and can be accomplished through acceptance of families as they are, sharing of information and resources, and a focus on parents' concerns, needs, and goals. Further suggestions for school personnel for the development of a trusting relationship include keeping one's word, discussing issues openly, and being prepared for meetings involving family members. An additional component of the model is acknowledging parents as equal partners and experts on their children. Cultural diversity must also be respected, which can be accomplished by creating an environment that allows for the expression of many different cultures. Another important component is the development of personal connections through frequent calls home, face-to-face conversations, and relationships on a first-name basis. Finally, an overall welcoming climate is important for successful home–school collaboration. Family resource centers and open house events are some ideas for creating a family-friendly school environment.

Minke (2000) presents an alternative model of collaboration that is untested but shares some of the characteristics of the model presented above. The framework discussed by Minke is known as the CORE (connection, optimism, respect, empowerment) model. The first *connection* component consists of the development of trusting relationships, shared goals and a common vision, and the constructive use of conflict in the form of positive problem solving. The *optimism* component is crucial because of the difficult nature of the process of collaboration. Here school and family participants are encouraged to focus on systems rather than individual problems, link behaviors to the context, and assume those involved are doing their best. The *respect* component refers to the acknowledgment of others' expertise and the acceptance of unchangeable situations. In the *empowerment* component, participants are viewed as change agents, each with their own strengths, competencies, and growth potential.

Minke (2000) offers some additional strategies for successful collaboration. First, she suggests school personnel act as an effective role models by demonstrating systemic thinking, effective listening and communication skills, and solution-focused problem solving. Also, opportunities for the development of relationships should be created, which can be achieved through family–school teams and family-oriented social events. Collaborators also need to find and utilize resources pertinent to specific cases. Additional strategies include prioritizing collaboration and being judicious in collaborative decision making. Specifically, problems and existing resources should be examined within a systems approach, and efforts should focus on small changes that can affect the system. Finally, Minke stresses the need for patience in the collaborative process, as it could possibly take 3 to 5 years to reach a level of true collaboration.

Any discussion of home–school collaboration must consider the notion of social or cultural capital. According to Christenson (2002), many parents do not have a positive history of school experiences, or they may be unfamiliar with the practices and policies that guide education. This leaves them in a difficult position of trying to guide their children through the educational system. Most parents genuinely care about their children and want to assist them; however, issues of social and cultural capital may make parent involvement in school-related activities very difficult.

CONCLUSIONS AND IMPLICATIONS FOR THE PRACTICE OF MULTIPLE FAMILY GROUPS

Although evaluation research on group prevention and intervention generally supports the effectiveness of group approaches, the evidence base endorsing MFGs is not unequivocal, and continual focused research and program evaluation are needed. Nonetheless, as the challenges confronting multiproblem, poor, and distressed families are numerous, several researchers recommend a comprehensive, competency-based approach to intervention (Fournier & Perry, 1998; Kesner & McKenry, 2001; Stoiber et al., 1998). Thus, rather than focusing on remediating family deficits, the intent of MFG approaches is to enhance the coping and psychological resource management of families facing stressors and crises. Specifically, it is important for facilitators of MFGs to be cognizant of the effects of limited adult resources within multiproblem and stressful households, and thus, to provide families with the help and support needed to promote resiliency and adaptive outcomes. Approaching multiproblem families within an ecological–normative stress and coping framework also facilitates moving the focus of prevention and intervention from altering a deviant family structure to enhancing coping ability, optimizing parenting resources, and clarifying critical family roles and responsibilities regarding the child.

A competency-based approach does not preclude the need to be cognizant of the stresses surrounding families in crisis, including economic strain, childcare and health insurance issues, depression, and other life-transition circumstances. Therefore, facilitators of MFGs must be aware and must attempt to address these multiple issues. In addition, group facilitators should implement evidence-based practices (Stoiber & Kratochwill, 2000; Stoiber, 2002; Stoiber & Waas, 2004) by drawing upon prevention and intervention approaches that have been shown to reduce depression, aggressive and violent tendencies, and stress-related trauma. The most vital role for facilitators of MFGs is the promotion of healthy relationships and functioning—both for children and families.

REFERENCES

America's Children. (2002). Available from Web site, http://www.childstats.gov.

Arnold, M. E., & Hughes, J. N. (1999). First do no harm: Adverse effects of grouping deviant youth for skills training. *Journal of School Psychology, 37,* 99–115.

Baker, B. L., Landen, S. J., & Kashima, K. J. (1991). Effects of parent training on families of children with mental retardation: Increased burden or generalized benefit? *American Journal on Mental Retardation, 96,* 127–136.

Burns, B. J., Costello, E. J., Angold, A., Tweed, D., Stangl, D., Farmer, E. M. Z., & Erkanli, A. (1995). DataWatch: Children's mental health service use across service sectors. *Health Affair, 14,* 147–159.

Carlson, C. (1998). Multiple family group therapy. In K. C. Stoiber & T. R. Kratochwill (Eds.), *Handbook of group intervention for children and families* (pp. 268–279). Boston: Allyn & Bacon.

Cassanso, D. R. (1989). Research on patterns of interaction: II. *Social Work with Groups, 12,* 15–39.

Centers for Disease Control and Prevention. (2000). Available from Web site, http://cdc.gov.

Christenson, S. L. (2002). *Families, educators, and the family-school partnership: Issues and opportunities for promoting children's learning competence.* Paper presented at the 2002 Invitational Conference: The Future of School Psychology, Indianapolis, IN.

Clark, R., Paulson, A., & Seidl, M. E. (1998). Relationship-focused group intervention for at-risk families with infants and young children. In K. C. Stoiber & T. R. Kratochwill (Eds.), *Handbook of group intervention for children and families* (pp. 401–423). Boston: Allyn & Bacon.

Cookston, J. T. (1999). Parental supervision and family structure: Effects on adolescent problem behaviors. *Journal of Divorce and Remarriage, 32,* 107–122.

Corey, G. (2000). *Theory and practice of group counseling* (5th ed.). Pacific Grove, CA: Brooks/ Cole.

Costello, E. J., Angold, A., Burns, B. J., Erkanli, A., Stangl, D. K., & Tweed, D. L. (1996). The Great Smokey Mountains study of youth: Functional impairment and serious emotional disturbance. *Archives of General Psychiatry, 53,* 1137–1143.

Department of Health and Human Services. (2000). *Report of the Surgeon General's conference on children's mental health: A national action agenda.* Available from Web site, http:// www.surgeongeneral.gov/topics/cmh/childreport.htm.

Dombalis, A. O., & Erchul, W. P. (1987). Multiple family group therapy: A review of its applicability to the practice of school psychology. *School Psychology Review, 16,* 487–497.

Elliott, S. N., Witt, J. C., Kratochwill, T. R., & Stoiber, K. C. (2002). Selecting and evaluating classroom interventions. In M. Shinn, H. M. Walker, & G. Stoner (Eds.), *Interventions for academic and behavioral problems II* (pp. 243–294). Washington, DC: National Association of School Psychologists.

Esler, A. N., Godber, Y., & Christenson, S. L. (2002). Best practices in supporting home-school collaboration. In A. Thomas & J. Grimes (Eds.), *Best practices in school psychology IV* (pp. 389–412). Bethesda, MD: National Association of School Psychologists.

Fine, M. J. (1995). Family-school intervention. In R. H. Mikesell, D. D. Lusterman, & S. H. McDaniel (Eds.), *Integrating family therapy* (pp. 481–495). Washington, DC: American Psychological Association.

Fournier, C. J., & Perry, J. D. (1998). The report of the U.S. commission on child and family welfare: Implications for psychologists working with children and families. *Children's Services: Social Policy, Research, and Practice, 2,* 45–56.

Friedman, A. S., Terras, A., & Glassman, K. (2000). Family structure versus family relationships for predicting to substance use/abuse and illegal behavior. *Journal of Child and Adolescent Substance Abuse, 10,* 1–16.

Greenberg, M. T., Domitrovich, D., & Bumbarger, B. (1999). *Preventing mental disorder in school-aged children: A review of the effectiveness of prevention programs.* Report submitted to The Center for Mental Health Services (SAMHSA), Prevention Research Center, Pennsylvania State University. Available from Web site, http://www.prevention.psu.edu.

Jones, C. W., & Unger, D. G. (2000). Diverse adaptations of single parent, low-income families with young children: Implications for community-based prevention and intervention. *Journal of Prevention and Intervention in the Community, 20,* 5–23.

Jones, D. J., Forehand, R., Brody, G. H., & Armistead, L. (2002). Psychosocial adjustment of African American children in single-mother families: A test of three risk models. *Journal of Marriage and Family, 64,* 105–116.

Kesner, J. E., & McKenry, P. C. (2001). Single parenthood and social competence in children of color. *Families in Society: The Journal of Contemporary Human Services, 82,* 136–144.

Kleist, D. M. (1999). Single-parent families: A difference that makes a difference? *The Family Journal: Counseling and Therapy for Couples and Families, 7,* 373–378.

McGroder, S. M. (2000). Parenting among low-income, African American single mothers with preschool-age children: Patterns, predictors, and developmental correlates. *Child Development, 71,* 752–771.

Minke, K. M. (2000). Preventing school problems and promoting school success through family-school-community collaboration. In K. M. Minke & G. G. Bear (Eds.), *Preventing school problems—promoting school success: Strategies and programs that work* (pp. 377–420). Bethesda, MD: NASP Publications.

Minuchin, P. (1995). Children and family therapy: Mainstream approaches and the special case of multicrisis poor. In R. H. Mikesell, D. D. Lusterman, & S. H. McDaniel (Eds.), *Integrating family therapy* (pp. 113–124). Washington, DC: American Psychological Association.

Murry, V. M., & Brody, G. H. (1999). Self-regulation and self-worth of Black children reared in economically stressed, rural, single mother-headed families: The contribution of risk and protective factors. *Journal of Family Issues, 20,* 458–484.

Murry, V. M., Bynum, M. S., Brody, G. H., Willert, A., & Stephens, D. (2001). African American single mothers and children in context: A review of studies on risk and resilience. *Clinical Child and Family Psychology Review, 4,* 133–155.

Noack, P., Krettek, C., & Walper, S. (2001). Peer relations of adolescents from nuclear and separated families. *Journal of Adolescence, 24,* 535–548.

O'Shea, M. D., & Phelps, R. (1985). Multiple family therapy: Current status and critical appraisal. *Family Process, 25,* 555–582.

Roberts, R. E., Attkisson, C. C., & Rosenblatt, A. (1998). Prevalence of psychopathology among children and adolescents. *American Journal of Psychiatry, 155,* 715–725.

Semrud-Clikeman, M. (1995). *Child and adolescent therapy.* New York: Allyn & Bacon.

Spruijt, E., DeGoede, M., & Vandervalk, I. (2001). The well-being of youngsters coming from six different family types. *Patient Education and Counseling, 45,* 285–294.

Stoiber, K. C. (2002). Revisiting efforts on constructing a knowledge base of evidence-based intervention within school psychology. *School Psychology Quarterly, 17,* 533–546.

Stoiber, K. C., & Anderson, A. J. (1996). Behavioral assessment of coping strategies in young children at risk, developmentally delayed, and typically developing. *Early Education and Development, 7,* 25–42.

Stoiber, K. C., Anderson, A. J., & Schowalter, D. S. (1998). Group prevention and intervention with pregnant and parenting adolescents. In K. C. Stoiber & T. R. Kratochwill (Eds.), *Handbook of group intervention for children and families* (pp. 280–306). Boston: Allyn & Bacon.

Stoiber, K. C., & Good, B. (1998). Risk and resiliency factors linked to problem behaviors in culturally-diverse, urban adolescents. *School Psychology Review, 27,* 380–397.

Stoiber, K. C., & Houghton, T. G. (1994). Adolescent mothers' cognitions and behaviors as at-risk indicators. *School Psychology Quarterly, 9,* 295–316.

Stoiber, K. C., & Kratochwill, T. R. (Eds.) (1998). *Handbook of group intervention for children and families.* Boston: Allyn & Bacon.

Stoiber, K. C., & Kratochwill, T. R. (2000). Empirically supported interventions and school psychology: Rationale and methodological issues—Part I. *School Psychology Quarterly, 15,* 75–105.

Stoiber, K. C., & Kratochwill, T. R. (2002). Evidence-based interventions within school psychology: Conceptual foundations of the procedural and coding manual of Division 16 and the Society for the Study of School Psychology Task Force. *School Psychology Quarterly, 17,* 341–389.

Stoiber, K.C., & Waas, G. A. (2004). Group and psychoeducational approaches. In R.T. Brown (Ed.). *Handbook of pediatric psychology in school settings* (pp. 555–578). Mahwah, NJ: Erlbaum.

Stoiber, K. C., & Waas, G. A. (2002b). A contextual and methodological perspective on evidence-based intervention practices in school psychology in the United States. *Educational and Child Psychology, 19*(3), 7–21.

U.S. Bureau of the Census (2000). *Current population survey.* Available from http://www.census.gov.

Yalom, I. D. (1995). *The theory and practice of group psychotherapy* (4th ed.). New York: Basic Books.

Zins, J. E., Elias, M. J., Greenberg, M. T., & Weissberg, R. P. (2000). Promoting social and emotional competence in children. In K. M. Minke & G. C. Bear (Eds.), *Preventing school problems—promoting school success* (pp. 71–99). Washington, DC: National Association of School Psychologists.

21

Psychoeducational Treatment of Stressed and Traumatized Couples

CLAIRE RABIN AND ZEV APEL

Many factors determine how families cope with high levels of stress and trauma. Even the most catastrophic traumas are influenced by mediating factors that interact with the severity of the stress to determine the degree of damage and future coping. Having information and knowledge about stressful and traumatic situations is one such factor that can mediate the manner in which people process and understand difficult and potentially overwhelming situations. Equally important to positive coping is the degree of social support received before, during, and after stressful or traumatic events.

McCubbin and Figley (1983) note that families generally operate on an assumption of a predictable normal cycle, anticipating and accepting a sequence of events that will occur throughout the life course. When life brings sudden, unexpected, and even catastrophic events that impinge on the normative stress that families regularly undergo, families cannot rely on past experiences or the guidance of others; they are left to fend for themselves. In these situations, human contact is a primary antidote to both the direct experience of catastrophic events and the longer term adjustment to traumatic memories. Most of the literature on stress and trauma emphasizes the importance of support from family, friends, and helpers as crucial in cushioning and ameliorating the effects of extremely difficult life situations. Family members are more able to serve as resources for one another when they are themselves supported through stressful or traumatic events. Families who do not receive support may find that a previously warm atmosphere can be eroded by increasing conflict, bitterness, and alienation.

There are two major modes of helping people navigate and ameliorate the potential harmful effects of stress and trauma. The first involves cognitively processing stressful and traumatic events in a manner that makes them understandable, meaningful, and more predictable. Information, knowledge, and cognitive coping skills are all crucial in the treatment of stress and trauma. Patterson and Garwick (1998) have reviewed the literature on how families develop a sense of coherence and shared meaning in the light of serious stress. They note that almost all theories of family adaptability to stress include a cognitive aspect to coping well. Elements of this cognitive aspect of coping include the degree to which families develop and maintain a sense of mastery, a belief that the family can learn and gain control, the degree of openness to new information, a belief in their solidarity as a unit, and their overall sense of optimism, security, and meaningfulness.

The second mode of help comes through connections and bonds with others. Strengthening family and social support, and deepening connection to others—especially others who more readily recognize and understand the family's experience because they are experiencing similar stress—are the central goals in the treatment of stress and trauma. Clearly, cognitive and social support factors are highly interrelated. A family that develops a strong sense of coherence and solidarity is more likely to view stress in an optimistic and health promoting manner.

Psychoeducational methods are designed to meet these two treatment goals and therefore constitute a major resource in helping families deal with stress and trauma. Psychoeducational groups constitute a form of helping that is based on (a) creating cognitive change through education and (b) increasing social support through connections with people in similar situations. Psychoeducational groups give targeted populations knowledge and skills while fostering group solidarity, mutual help, and discussion as a form of social support.

While various types of psychoeducational methods differ significantly, they all contain certain philosophical and practical aspects in common. Psychoeducational groups, regardless of format, theoretical underpinning, or population targeted, are based on structured sessions that utilize standardized educational modules provided in a time-limited format. These modules are taught in groups using a variety of educational methods, including lectures, videotapes, group exercises, readings, discussions, and skill training. From the start, participants are provided with a syllabus which specifies the topics that will be covered and the learning goals for the experience.

Psychoeducational groups for families have appeared under different names over the years. In addition to the concept of psychoeducational programs (Leveat, 1986), they have been termed "family life education" (Groves & Groves, 1947), "marriage enrichment" (Mace & Mace, 1975), "relationship enhancement" (Guerney, 1977), "skill or competence training" (L'Abate, 1990), and "preventive approaches" (Berger & Hannah, 1999). Although Berger and Hannah make a distinction between preventive and therapeutic methods, such a distinction is not supported by research. Studies suggest that a sizable proportion of prevention participants are, in fact, distressed (DeMaria, 1998; Zimpher, 1988). Moreover, considerable change is effected within these types of groups, making the distinction between preventive and remedial methods difficult to maintain.

In the case of psychoeducational methods with populations at risk due to stress or trauma, the distinction between therapy and prevention breaks down entirely. Structured psychoeducational programs have been found to be particularly effective as a preliminary stage to individual treatment and thus serve a distinct function in the overall continuum of care. Psychoeducational methods are best conceptualized as a form of treatment that can either stand alone or be combined with other forms.

PSYCHOEDUCATIONAL METHODS FOR FAMILIES AND COUPLES

Family and couple psychoeducational groups have gained increasing support and interest in the last 20 years and especially in the area of trauma in the last 10 years. In this chapter we will review some of the literature on family and couples groups, which are usually classified under the heading of family and marriage enrichment or preventive approaches for families. What all these groups have in common is a structured format which includes (a) a time-limited predetermined course of study for the group, (b) a topic for each session, (c) use of lecture material combined with experiential exercises, (d) role play and demonstration of skills, and (e) use of educational teaching tools such as audio/video and handouts. This does not mean that these groups do not deal with people's emotions or problems. Group discussion and sharing is a crucial element in all these groups. However, group leaders and facilitators are trained to stay focused on the topic, to universalize individual concerns, and to bring the group discussion back to the predesignated topic. Strong bonds are often forged between group members as their mutual concerns become evident.

While the focus of psychoeducational work with families and couples is on teaching, an overall goal of all preventive work is strengthening and utilizing the family's inner existing resources. Thus, an emphasis on fostering family and couple strength and pride is a common factor in all the psychoeducational groups. For example, Lachariete and Daigneaut (1997) showed the effectiveness of an enrichment group for families with preschoolers. Their program showed increased parental perception of competence, a fairer division of household and child caring responsibilities between the mother and her main support figure, and a reduced degree of parental stress, especially around child difficulties. Even programs which target families with special needs, such as families of the mentally ill, emphasize the importance of identifying family strengths (Zipple & Spaniol, 1987). Alessi (1987) notes that the task of a parent group leader is to encourage the group to help members feel better about themselves as parents and people.

There are many different theoretical orientations for conducting family and marital enrichment groups. While the majority of programs focus on parents or couples, some programs include entire families and invite parents together with their children (Sawin, 1986). Some programs stress religious values and spirituality (McWhirter, 1989), while others focus on dual career issues (Avis, 1986) or normative crises such as letting children go off to college (Catron & Catron, 1989). Other populations targeted for psychoeducational groups include teenage fathers in preparation for parenthood (Kiselica, 1994), parents of children with intellectual disabilities (Schultz, 1993), and aging parents of adults with developmental disabilities (Smith, 1996).

Berger and Hannah (1999) review the major approaches that have contributed to the marriage enrichment field. These include programs based on Alfred Adler's work (Carlson & Dinkmeyer, 1999), on object relations theory (Hendrix & Hunt, 1999), on communication skill training (Miller & Sherrard, 1999), on the work of Virginia Satir and family systems theories (Gordon & Durana, 1999), and a program based on empirical studies of couples interactions (Gottman & Gottman, 1999). There is a wide diversity among these programs in regard to the number and duration of sessions, ranging from a single weekend to a 4-month course of study. From programs that demand professional degrees to programs that utilize lay couples as mentors, there is considerable variation in training and professional accreditation required of group leaders. Different programs stress different content material, depending on their theoretical orientation. However, all programs focus on some form of communication training and attempt to strengthen couple commitment and intimacy through creating shared values, increasing knowledge about marriage, and providing social support for married partners.

Many studies have evaluated the short-term benefits of these programs and consistently found them to increase (a) family and couple sense of well-being, (b) satisfaction with relationships, (c) cohesiveness, and (d) trust (Hickmon, Protinsky, & Singh, 1997). A meta-analysis of 85 programs which varied in content, format, duration, orientation, subject characteristics, outcome measures, and length of follow-up found these programs to be beneficial and to be providing at least some long-term gain (Giblin, 1986). However, some recent studies found that couples may experience more distress after psychoeducational programs, leading researchers to caution practitioners to evaluate their programs carefully and design them specifically for targeted populations and problems (Kelly & Fincham, 1999).

Psychoeducational Approaches for High-Level Stress and Trauma

While psychoeducational methods had their start in the prevention of distress among nonclinical populations, their use has expanded to populations undergoing severe stress and trauma. Most of these programs are not intended to replace individual, couple, or family counseling. Instead, they serve as an adjunctive form of treatment, assisting stressed and traumatized couples and families to make sense of their situation and obtain social support. Psychoeducational programs also help people who might not ordinarily make contact with professionals to do so under the auspices of a universal and normative educational experience.

Most programs offer an overview of general knowledge about the problem area to increase cognitive understanding of the particular stressors to be expected and the types of coping skills that are available. Each session allows participants to discuss their own personal experience related to the topic discussed and fosters mutual problem solving so that participants can experience their own expertise and the experience of helping others. Sessions generally consist of skill training and practice of cognitive and behavioral strategies used in coping with stress, often including homework assignments to help extend the new behaviors into everyday life.

Abuse has received considerable attention in the development of psychoeducational groups. Some abuse-related populations reached with this method include foster parents of sexually abused children (Barth, Yeaton, & Winterfelt, 1994), parents who have abused their children (Berry & Cash, 1998), children and adolescents living in violent communities (Jones & Clark-Selder, 1996), child sexual abuse survivors (Sweig, 2000), and nonabused children receiving sexual abuse prevention skills (Hazzard, 1993).

Addiction is another area that has sparked the development of creative psychoeducational groups. These groups include relapse prevention for compulsive crack cocaine smokers and other drug use (Wallace, 1989; la Salvia, 1993; Knight, 1994) and groups for family members who are exposed to the drug user (Dore, Nelson-Zlupko, & Kaufman, 1999).

Psychoeducational groups for mental illness have been found to be a useful adjunct to medication, family therapy, and traditional forms of group work. Thus patients with schizophrenia (Asher & Krause, 1991), depressed students (Burak-Maholik, 1993), patients with bipolar disorders (Miklowitz & Hooley, 1998), and troubled children (Brendtro & Van-Bockern, 1994) all have been offered the opportunity to take part in psychoeducational groups.

Psychoeducational work is especially empowering for people who suffer from some form of social stigma such as mental illness. Giving information about the disease and the problem area offers the chance to separate the person from the problem. The person is treated not as a schizophrenic but as someone who has to cope with the stresses associated with the disease and for whom knowledge and skills can be learned not just from the professional but also from others who are coping with similar situations. Psychoeducational groups have been found extremely useful for empowering families who are dealing with highly stressful and stigmatizing situations. Families dealing with AIDS (Pomeroy, 1995), unemployment and downsizing (Foley & Smith, 1999), bereaved children (Vickio & Clark, 1998), and immigration (Thomas, 1992) are all potentially traumatized populations that share a similar need for education and support.

PSYCHOEDUCATIONAL PROGRAMS FOR PRISONERS AND THEIR SPOUSES

Incarceration is frequently traumatic and has been viewed as a potential focus of psychoeducational methods. Adolescents preparing for sex offender treatment (Perry, Dimnik, Ohm, & Wilks, 2000), men arrested for patronizing prostitutes (Sawyer, Rosser, & Schroeder, 1998), and inmates suffering from anxiety, depression, and trauma (Pomeroy, Kiam, & Green, 2000) have all been offered the psychoeducational approach. As noted earlier, different programs stress different issues based on their theoretical orientation. For example, one program for sex offenders in prison focused on self-esteem as a concept to be learned about and understood (Stump, Beamish, & Shellenberger, 1999), while another program for the same population focused on teaching about the laws and norms in mainstream American culture and the consequences for choosing behaviors outside the norms (Sloan & Schafer, April 2001).

The idea of using psychoeducational approaches for offenders or prisoners is a relatively new one; however, there is literature on social work, especially group work, in prisons. Zimpfer (1992) found that group work with imprisoned criminals aims at preparing them for their return to normal life when they are released, as well as adjusting to life in prison, gaining insight, and developing self-control. Group work allows prisoners the opportunity to learn about their emotions and beliefs, and how their conduct is influenced by their emotions and beliefs.

Although families are highly affected by the incarceration of family members, there are no reports in the literature of psychoeducational groups with the families of prisoners. Families are cut off from the incarcerated member and suffer from the effects of separation, stigma, reallocation of roles at home, additional stress, and anger at the imprisoned member. There has been one report of a psychoeducational approach for families of U.S. Navy personnel who were gone for long periods of time (Blaisure & Arnold-Mann, 1992) but no report of a program for inmates and their partners.

We will describe the use of a psychoeducational program for prisoners and their partners in Israel. The program was based originally on the Practical Application of Intimate Relationship Skills (PAIRS) program (Gordon & Frandsen, 1993), which is a well-established program for marriage enrichment established by Lori Gordon. It was brought to Israel by Lori Gordon and has been taught for 10 years at Bar Ilan University by Dr. Zev Apel. As a requirement for fulfilling the course to become a PAIRS leaders, students have to do field placement for one year. Many chose to carry out PAIRS in the prison system with male inmates. In 10 years, hundreds of prisoners and their wives have undergone PAIRS training.

EDUCATION, TREATMENT, AND REHABILITATION OF PRISONERS—THE ISRAELI SITUATION

"Anyone can be rehabilitated." This assertion was made by Hoffman (1990, Israeli Prison Rehabilitation Authority), relating the stories of 22 discharged prisoners who chose rehabilitation. Hence, it is our duty to open the gates, to open our hearts, for those seeking rehabilitation. Next to the penitentiaries and social deterrence institutions in Israel, there are certain social institutions that are supposed to rehabilitate the felons. Society is ambivalent about them; there is a desire to punish those who strayed, yet "the desire to rehabilitate the 'criminal' and make him follow the norms of the society they live in explicitly exists in most modern societies" (Wozner & Golan, 1994, p. 7).

The social need for the rehabilitation of outlaws has been expressed through legal amendments and the development and expansion of social services in the corrective field (Freiberg & Hovav, 1994). When social work started developing in prisons, it set two main goals: guarding the prisoners and keeping them under humane conditions, and changing deviant norms while encouraging the prisoners to change their deviant conduct during their prison term (Yelin, 1991). Regulation 47 of Prisons Regulations from the Israeli Prisons Act of 1978 states that: "Every prison shall organize and provide a study program, unless the commissioner ordered differently. The prisoners shall be given with the possible alleviations to expand their knowledge in their spare time. Special attention shall be paid to literacy classes for illiterate prisoners."

Educational activities in the prisons are part of the formal and informal education given there. Informal education includes theoretical studies, creative workshops, parent and children activities, parental guidance classes, playrooms, and educational and therapy workshops such as psychodrama, art therapy, and sports. As a rule, social work that deals with corrective activities focuses on changing irregular or deviant activities, preventing their recurrence, correcting their damages, helping the perpetrators manage distress situations, and leveling the psychosocial adjustment of the target population to the norms of social conduct.

Many researchers attribute considerable importance to the reincorporation of the prisoner into his family as a central element in the successful rehabilitation of the father (Hoffman, 1994). There is a clear relationship between the state of the prisoner's family and the chances of his rehabilitation being successful.

The Triangle Program is founded on the premise that bolstering the contacts between prisoners and their wives and children will improve the chances of their returning to their families and successfully rejoining society (Hoffman, 1985, 1986). The program combines tutors for the prisoners' children, groups for the prisoners' wives, and groups for the incarcerated fathers as a way of facilitating the development of more normative approaches to dealing with crises. The program helps improve family relations by aiding both the prisoner and the family—providing support for the mothers in shouldering their heavy load, while the prisoners' fatherly sentiments are facilitated through their positive involvement with their families while still in prison.

WHY PAIRS IN PRISON?

The PAIRS program for the enrichment of marriage was developed by Gordon and Frandsen (1993). It is based on developing five main skills:

communication, conflict management, self-understanding, sexuality and sensuality, and negotiations and agreements.

The PAIRS program has two main goals: (1) partners learning to take care of themselves and their spouses so that spouses can identify, recognize, and even enjoy the differences between them, instead of seeing them as threats or attacks, and (2) learning to enjoy the partner and maintain the relationship as an ongoing source of shared pleasure. These goals are attained through a process that combines lectures and group discussion in which an idea is presented along with practical exercises for skill enhancement. The works of many different family and couple therapists are featured in the PAIRS program, including Virginia Satir's concept of family laws, her focus on communication styles in stressful situations, and her recommendations regarding daily temperature reading; George Bach's anger ceremonies and concept of the fair right to make a change; Sherrod Miller's struggle styles; Murray Bowen's emphasis on family of origin and family mapping; Ivan Boszormenyi-Nagy and Geraldine Spark's (1973) concept of invisible loyalties; and Daniel Casriel's approach to bonding, emotional levels of maturity, emotional expression, and the logic of emotion (Ladd, 1989).

The intervention program includes 10 3-hr weekly meetings that are spread over three months. The instructors have been trained in group guidance for the enrichment of marriage, based on the PAIRS method, at Bar-Ilan University, Israel. The cognitive component focuses on altering behaviors through perception and thought changes (Klingman & Eisen, 1990). The theory covers several approaches, particularly Ellis's (1974) Rational Emotive Therapy and Michenbaum's Cognitive Behavior Modification (Klingman & Eisen, 1990). The assumptions at the basis of these approaches are: (a) people develop behavioral and emotional patterns through cognitive processes, (b) cognitive processes affect the creation of various emotions, and (3) identifying thinking patterns helps adaptive learning.

EXPERIENCES USING PAIRS IN ISRAELI PRISONS

Prisoners are at high risk for stress and trauma due to prolonged separation from their families and support networks, difficult living conditions in prison, physical threats, and prolonged removal from their daily routines. Their families, especially their wives, are suddenly burdened with financially supporting the family and having to take on all household and child care tasks. Family members deal with loneliness, stigmatization, and emotions such as anger and shame. Marital partners have to keep connected through telephone and brief weekly visits, which cause a high level of strain on the relationship. These couples are at risk for divorce as well as emotional and functional breakdown in either partner. Each program offered to the prisons was carried out in the prison system by a pair of students (male and female) who taught 12 classes to the men, 3 of which were with wives present. When the wives attended, they were already trained in some of the communication skills and were therefore able to practice with their husbands.

The following are notes from an interview of Rami Tsani, one of a team of two group leaders working weekly with a group of 20 prisoners and their wives over a period of 3 months. Due to lack of space, only the first few sessions can be described here to give a flavor of the way these men reacted to the PAIRS program.

> The first thing I was aware of upon entering the prison for the first time was the feeling of fear about the situation. I felt fear at suddenly being inside with all those locked doors and bars. I have done a lot of groups, but this was different, especially after going through all the security checks, having to wait at each stage for an okay to continue further inside. ... It is hard to think how to talk with prisoners about being open about their feelings when we are in such a closed restricted atmosphere. I did three such groups that year, but others from my class didn't want to go into the prison and work with prisoners about marriage; they were scared.
>
> The prison service offers all kinds of educational experiences, and when we arrived, there was already a long list of prisoners who wanted to enter our group, so we had to interview and decide whom to take since we couldn't have more than 20. The prisoners were told that this was a group about communication and intimacy with their partners, so we took only married men. They were concerned about trust from the initial interview, questions such as who would get the information that they brought up in the group, will this information be used against me? We assured them of confidentiality and talked with them from the start that only if they were willing for their partners to come for three meetings out of the 12, could they attend.
>
> We chose people of all ages, but not below 20 or above 60. We were told by the prison social worker that men doing time because of violence in the family would not be accepted in the group because they are rejected by the other prisoners and have especially low status. However, we insisted that the group be open to them and eventually they fit in fine, especially since many of the other prisoners talked about violence at home as well.
>
> During the first meeting, the men were closed and withdrawn. We asked not to know what their crimes were so as not to stereotype them. We talked about our goal of strengthening couple ties. We asked them to introduce themselves by telling one thing about themselves and one thing that their wives might have said about them. It was far easier for them to talk about themselves ("Society ruined me"; "I never had a chance since the day I was born") than to think of something their wives might have said. There were many negative opinions about women, such as "You can't trust them" or "You have to control them, always be one step ahead." One man said, "I

am very critical" and another said, "I know how to be responsible, but I am also negligent, my life is complicated, and she would say that I am complicated and that this ruined her life."

In the discussion following this introductory exercise, they began to tell us about their problems of communicating with their wives. What most bothered the men was that the wives were busy and not always available for talking when the husband called. They felt brushed off, and they felt that the wives had more power over the communication and over them. If it made them angry and they exploded in rage, their wives wouldn't talk with them.

Toward the end of the first session we asked for feedback and some of the men said it was the first time they have been asked to "get inside her shoes" and think how she must feel—it made them think. Others came back the next week saying that they had thought about it all week and had even asked their wives in phone conversations how they would have described them.

In the next session, we worked on a group contract related to confidentiality and the purpose of the sessions. They wanted reliability and a promise not to share any information with people in the prison system. They also said that they needed to feel more in control. They experienced a great deal of anxiety about what was happening at home (Were the wives being faithful? Were they considering divorce? Were they managing fine without them?). They wanted to improve their communication with their wives. However, they were also very clear that other people were to blame for their being in prison—society, their parents, their wives, or their wives' families. They found it difficult to empathize with any difficulty their wives were experiencing. They said that the pressures and stresses they were undergoing were worse than anything their families experienced.

During the second meeting, we taught about division of tasks at home, how roles are delegated, and what was their own role at home. This was preparation for family-of-origin work, and it opened up discussion about the families they came from. They shared their roles in their families of origin, as well as stories and experiences from their childhood.

During the third meeting, we taught Satir's defensive communication styles (the computer, the blamer, the placater, the irrelevant) and linked these to styles they had seen in their parents' marriages. We demonstrated the styles and had them do an exercise that gave each man a chance to experience each style. The blamer was, by far, the most familiar style for them. While at first they did the exercise in a monotonous way, they really went into it and started yelling and screaming in the blamer mode. Afterwards they talked about how they had never realized how hard it was to be blamed. Many of them talked about suddenly seeing how hard it might be for their wives to be blamed by them. They connected the styles to people they knew, especially people from their families of origins that had been mentioned in the previous session.

We gave them a hypothetical case in which they had to imagine what they would feel and do if their wife sold the family car and was cheated and lost money. How would they respond when they got home and heard the story from their wives? Although a few of them were critical in their reactions, many moved to a more supportive position, having been influenced by the previous exercise. Each was asked what their reaction would be, and we heard statements like "Too bad this happened, but I know that you are upset" but also some critical responses, such as "When I finish with them (the people who cheated the wife), I will take care of you." We handed out a list of supportive behaviors and how to move from a "you" position to an "I" position. They were absolutely amazed by this list. Although their natural response might have been "How could you have done this?," they role-played the supportive behaviors well, although rather mechanically, and felt good with it.

What was unique for me as a student was the intensity of their reactions. When we had learned all these skills in the university it was more sterile. In the prison, the men were very emotional, filled with anger and conflict and also amazed when they saw a different way to do things. It really upset them to realize how they had been behaving to their wives.

During the fourth meeting, we introduced them to the family of origin genogram by way of a guided imagery exercise. This exercise was a portrayal of their own birth as a child, but it was changed to describe being born to adoring and loving parents who received them with open arms and love. They got into the atmosphere and quieted down as we dimmed the lights and asked them to close their eyes. After the meditation, which takes about seven minutes, they reflected on their individual experiences. Most said it was the first time they ever considered whether they were wanted, how their parents acted towards them as infants and whether they got any warmth as babies. There were many different responses, from some who noted that their own experience was very different than the meditation (i.e., "Oh, another child") to those who experienced peace and happiness during the meditation.

These men talked about enjoying an experience they never had, and I was surprised how little embarrassment they displayed, how sensitive they were willing to be. One of the prisoners cried and my co-leader went over to sit with him. When she got up to leave, someone else went over and put an arm around him, in a kind of macho way. There were several expressions of physical closeness during this session. Their reactions included feeling that they could love their wives more now, love themselves, and feel more peaceful and quiet.

By the next session that was supposed to include the wives, group solidarity was well established. They always did the homework we gave them and were always waiting for us for about a quarter of an hour before we arrived. Although there were many problems for them in getting their wives to attend (babysitting, traveling, financial problems in taking time off from work), all the wives arrived. It was the first time the women had come into the prison and we had to get special permission for that. No other prisoners were allowed near the wives. The men were very excited about the visit, were allowed to walk in the inner court with their wives and held their hands.

We first met alone with the women for one hour. We used this time to talk about their feelings about having their husbands in prison and also shared the material we had taught their husbands. They mostly knew what their husbands had experienced in the group meetings as the husbands had already shared their reactions. But they had many complaints to air about being wives of prisoners: the economic pressures, dealing with their neighbors' gossip, and the feeling of having to cope alone with everything. They said that they were being punished although it was their husbands who had committed the crimes. Moreover, they experienced intense loneliness and were overwhelmed with responsibility and the expectation that they should support their husbands even though no one was supporting them. They said that they needed the program themselves, as they need more support to be able to give to their partners.

The meeting itself was amazing. The women had dressed up for the event and had brought a lot of food with them. Many had prepared for days for this, even bringing a tablecloth. There was a holiday atmosphere. We taught about the importance of sharing thoughts and feelings and used an exercise called the "daily temperature reading" to practice. In this exercise the participants give each other new information, ask questions, give compliments and criticism, ask for change and share their hopes, wishes and dreams. They were instructed in phone use of the exercise and role-played telephone conversations. At the end of the exercise, couples were close and holding hands, but when they were asked to say something good about their partner, most of them could not do it out loud. They asked to do this privately.

Although there was a holiday atmosphere they seemed to take the work we did together very seriously. Someone said it was the first time he felt that his wife really listened to him. They all mentioned how important it was to improve the quality of their telephone conversations, how important to stop and think before getting angry. With the phone conversation, there is always the possibility that one partner will get angry and disconnect, and this issue was a major focus of their discussion. We asked that they set up fixed times for conversations, as we discovered that the men often called when their wives were occupied with children. This idea was a new one for many of them and seemed to be very helpful to them. Many scheduled half an hour to talk after the children went to bed. While up to now they had free access to the phone, they suddenly became aware that the quality of their conversations determined the continuity and quality of their relationships.

In future sessions we taught them how to effectively handle conflict through fair fighting and a dialogue guide that deepens emotional expression. In addition, we spent several sessions working on their genograms, which informed them about patterns of behavior that had carried over from generation to generation. We also later practiced these skills in two more sessions with the wives. After all sessions, the men were given a summary of the teaching of the session, as well as practice homework to do in telephone conversations with their wives.

After 12 sessions feedback was very good. Each person talked about taking new things back into his life. Two topics that were mentioned the most were the importance of listening and physical contact. There was a sense that the group had gone a long way in overcoming their sense of isolation from their partners. They mentioned being able to relate with less anger and more self-awareness. One man discussed how afraid he had been before the group that his wife would leave him. He now was secure that, after 24 years of marriage, she would wait for him. Another said that he had moved beyond feeling traumatized in prison, feeling detached and embarrassed, to feeling that he was using the time well in learning important material that would help when he got back. Wives mentioned real changes in their relationship. One said we were doing "holy work." Most wives said that their partners were now more patient and under-standing about the burden they carried at home.

I have to say that running psychoeducational groups in prisons has changed me in many ways. I have gotten over my stereotypes of people in prison, realized they are like anyone else, that anyone can get in this situation. I have been changed by being exposed to stories of incredible hardship, drug use, and neglect in childhood, loss of freedom, being closed in. It was often good to know that at the end of the day I could leave. There was some degree of identifying with them and understanding what it is like to have to fight for everything. I understand now a bit of what it is like, only a bit. I love the humanness of these people, the moment that they gave us their trust, when they were no longer afraid to talk about everything, we felt so close.

ONGOING RESEARCH ON PAIRS FOR COUPLES AFFECTED BY INCARCERATION

In one study in Israeli prisons (Nehushtai, 1999), 14 prisoners were selected to attend a marriage enrichment workshop. The participants were about to end their term and were concerned about their coming reunions with their spouses. The workshop was intended to prepare them for their reunion, prior to returning to normal life. The study, which used the method of action examination through observations and interviews, found that the workshop helped the prisoners return to married life. The participants noted the usefulness of the tools for effective communication with their spouses.

A study presently being conducted by Bar-Ilan University is looking at the impact of the PAIRS program on prisoners in Israel. The study is examining (a) the level of differentiation of self, (b) differentiation of the family of origin, (c) anxiety levels, and (d) adjustment to marriage. The researchers assume that the intervention would lead to the following changes:

1. Differentiation of self would be clearly higher than before the intervention.

2. Differentiation of family of origin would be clearly higher than before the intervention.
3. Level of anxiety after the intervention would be clearly lower than before it.
4. Adjustment to marriage after the intervention would be clearly better than before it.

Findings from this study will help shed light on the effects of using the PAIRS program with prisoners and their partners.

CONCLUSIONS

Psychoeducational groups offer an innovative and effective adjunct to the treatment of a diverse range of traumatized populations. Psychoeducational methods offer a potentially effective method for creating social support, increasing sense of competence and normality, and improving cognitive coping with traumatic situations. These types of groups can be especially important as a source of positive reinforcement, support and caring in those situations in which the family's own resources are severely taxed. Psychoeducational groups can bolster families' positive coping and sense of mastery over potentially disabling situations.

Recently, psychoeducational groups have been offered in the rehabilitation of prisoners and their families in the Israeli prison system. These groups have demonstrated that the tools for improving communication and increasing self-awareness and intimacy, developed in the United States, can be useful in other countries with a range of stressful situations. These packages are clearly described and easily replicated and can be offered in a wide range of situations and populations, making cross-cultural research possible.

From our own clinical experience, it appears that families are helped and strengthened even when the program is directed at only one partner. We do not know yet whether the participation of the spouses in these groups is actually crucial or not. But we believe that strengthening the couples' bond through psychoeducational programs can result in a sense of mastery in a situation that often leads to chaos and family breakdown. Future research will be aimed at whether such programs reduce recidivism and whether marital relationships are indeed strengthened.

This chapter has proposed that psychoeducational group work be developed for other populations undergoing trauma. Hopefully our own enthusiasm for this method, strengthened by our students and the participants' enthusiasm, will encourage others to try out new and creative ways to use these methods.

REFERENCES

Alessi, J. (1987). Encouraging parents—encouraging leaders: The key to successful parent study groups. *Individual Psychology: Journal of Adlerian Theory, Research, and Practice, 4/3(2)*, 195–201.

Asher, S., & Krause, A. (1991). *Psychoeducational groups for patients with schizophrenia.* Gaithersburg, MD: Aspen Publishers.

Avis, J. (1986). "Working together": An enrichment approach for dual-career couples. *Journal of Psychotherapy and the Family, 2(1)*, 29–45.

Barth, R., Yeaton, J., & Winterfelt, N. (1994). Psychoeducational groups with foster parents of sexually abused children. *Child and Adolescent Social Work Journal, 11*, 405–424.

Berger, R., & Hannah, M. (Eds.). (1999). *Preventive approaches to couples therapy.* New York: Brunner/Mazel.

Berry, M., & Cash, S. (1998). Creating community through psychoeducational groups in family preservation work. *Families in Society, 79(1)*, 15–24.

Blaisure, K., & Arnold-Mann, J. (1992). Return and reunion: A psychoeducational program aboard U.S. Navy ships. *Family Relations, 41*, 178–185.

Brendtro, L., & Van-Bockern, S. (1994). Courage for the discouraged: A psychoeducational approach to troubled and troubling children. *Focus on Exceptional Children, 26(8)*, 1–14.

Burak-Maholik, S. (1993). Psychoeducational strategies for depressed students. *Journal of Emotional and Behavioral Problems, 2(2)*, 45–47.

Carlson, J., & Dinkmeyer, D. (1999). TIME for a better marriage. In R. Berger & M. Hannah (Eds.), *Preventive approaches to couples therapy* (pp. 149–168). New York: Brunner/Mazel.

Catron, D., & Catron, S. (1989). Helping parents let go: A program for the parents of college freshman. *Journal of College Student Development, 30*, 463–464.

Conrad, J. P. (1973). Corrections and simple justice. *Journal of Criminal Law and Criminology, 64*, 208–217.

Crowe, F. (1997). Quantifying conflict resolution styles among prison inmates. *Journal of Offender Rehabilitation, 25 (3/4)*, 131–146.

Davidson, W. S., Gottschalk, R., Gensheimer, I., & Mayer, J. (1984). *Interventions with juvenile delinquents: A meta-analysis of treatment efficacy.* Washington, DC: National Institute of Justice and Delinquency.

DeMaria, R. (1998). *A national survey of married couples who participate in marriage enrichment.* Ann Arbor, MI: UMI Dissertation Services, No. 983–3080.

Dore, M., Nelson-Zlupko, L., & Kaufman, E. (1999). "Friends in need": Designing and implementing a psychoeducational group for school children from drug-involved families. *Social Work, 44*, 179–190.

Elliot, W., & Walters, G. (1997). Conducting psychoeducational interventions with drug abusing clients: The lifestyle model. *Journal of Drug Education, 27*, 307–319.

Foley, P., & Smith, J. (1999). A model psychoeducational group for survivors of organizational downsizing. *Journal for Specialists in Group Work, 24*, 354–368.

Feriberg, R., & Hovav, N. (1994). Specialization in social work in the area of corrections. In Y. Wozner, M. Golan, & M. Hovav (Eds.), *Delinquency in social work: Theory and interventions* (Hebrew, pp. 57–84). Tel Aviv: Ramot.

Giblin, P. (1986). Research and assessment in marriage and family enrichment: A meta-analysis study. *Journal of Psychotherapy and the Family, 2*, 79–86.

Gordon, L., & Durana, C. (1999). The P.A.I.R.S. program. In R. Berger & M. Hannah (Eds.), *Preventive approaches to couples therapy* (pp. 217–236). New York: Brunner/Mazel.

Gordon, L., & Frandsen, J. (1993). *Passage to intimacy.* New York: Simon & Schuster.

Gottman, J., & Gottman, J. (1999). The marriage survival kit: A research based marital therapy. In R. Berger & M. Hannah (Eds.), *Preventive approaches to couples therapy* (pp. 304–330). New York: Brunner/Mazel.

Groves, E., & Groves, G. (1947). *The contemporary American family.* Chicago: Lippincott.

Guerney, B. (1977). *Relationship enhancement: Skill training programs for therapy, problem prevention and enrichment.* San Francisco: Jossey-Bass.

Hazzard, A. (1993). Psychoeducational groups to teach children sexual abuse prevention skills. *Journal of Child and Adolescent Group Therapy, 3,* 13–23.

Hendrix, H., & Hunt, H. (1999). Imago relationship therapy: Creating a conscious marriage or relationship. In R. Berger & M. Hannah (Eds.), *Preventive approaches to couples therapy* (pp. 169–195). New York: Brunner/Mazel.

Hickmon, W., Protinsky, H., & Singh, K. (1997). Increasing marital intimacy: Lessons from marital enrichment. *Contemporary Family Therapy: An International Journal, 19,* 581–589.

Hoffman, A. (1985). The social worker and the prisoner's family. *Work, Welfare, and National Insurance Journal* (Hebrew), July, 179–180.

Hoffman, A. (1986). Development of treatment tools for the children of prisoners. *Welfare and National Insurance Journal* (Hebrew). *August,* 5–15.

Hoffman, A. (1990). *Is there a chance to rehabilitate the prisoner?* (Hebrew). Jerusalem: The Rehabitation Authority of Israel.

Hoffman, A. (1994). The "Triangle Program": Big brothers for the children of prisoners. In Y. Wozner & M. Golan (Eds.), *Delinquency in social work: Theory and interventions* (In Hebrew, pp. 303–317). Tel Aviv: Ramot.

Izzo, R. L., & Ross, R. R. (1990). Meta-analysis of rehabilitation programs for juvenile delinquents: A brief report. *Criminal Justice and Behavior, 17,* 134–142.

Jones, F., & Clark-Selder, F. (1996). Psychoeducational groups to promote effective coping in school-age children living in violent communities. *Issues in Mental Health Nursing, 17,* 559–572.

Kelly, A., & Fincham, F. (1999). Preventing marital distress: What does research offer? In R. Berger & M. Hannah (Eds.), *Preventive approaches to couples therapy* (pp. 361–390). New York: Brunner/Mazel.

Kiselica, M. (1994). Preparing teenage fathers for parenthood: A group psychoeducational approach. *Journal for Specialists in Group Work, 9(2),* 83–94.

Klingman, A., & Eisen, R. (1990). *Counseling psychology: Principles, approaches, and intervention methods* (Hebrew). Tel Aviv: Ramot.

Knight, K. (1994). Knowledge mapping: A psychoeducational tool in drug abuse relapse prevention training. *Journal-of-Offender-Rehabilitation, 20(3–4),* 87–205.

L'Abate, L. (1990). *Building family competence: Primacy and secondary prevention strategies.* Beverly Hills, CA: Sage.

Lachariete, C., & Daigneault, M. (1997). The Harmony program: Evaluation of the impact of a family enrichment program on mothers having young children. *Revue-Canadienne-de-Psycho-Education, 26(1),* 25–38.

Ladd, A. (1989). *P.A.I.R.S.: A psychoeducational approach to marital intervention.* Unpublished masters thesis, Catholic University of America, Washington, DC.

La-Salvia, T. (1993). Enhancing addiction treatment through psychoeducational groups. *Journal of Substance Abuse Treatment, 10,* 439–444.

Leveat, R. (Ed.). (1986). *Psychoeducational approaches to family therapy and counseling.* New York: Springer-Verlag.

Mace, D., & Mace, V. (1975). Marriage enrichment—Wave of the future? *The Family Coordinator, 24,* 171–173.

McCubbin, H., & Figley, C. (1983). *Stress and the family: Vol. I Coping with normative transitions.* New York: Brunner/Mazel.

McWhirter, J. (1989). Religion and the practice of counseling psychology. *Counseling Psychologist, 17,* 613–616.

Miklowitz, D., & Hooley, J. (1998). Developing family psychoeducational treatments for patients with bipolar and other severe psychiatric disorders: A pathway from basic research to clinical trials. *Journal of Marital and Family Therapy, 24,* 419–435.

Miller, S., & Sherrard, P. (1999). Couple communication: A system for equipping partners to talk, listen and resolve conflicts effectively. In R. Berger & M. Hannah (Eds.), *Preventive approaches to couples therapy* (pp. 125–148). New York: Brunner/Mazel.

Nehushtai, I. (1999). *Back to marital life: A workshop of marriage enrichment for prisoners upon release*. Unpublished master's thesis, Derby University, Derby, U.K.

Patterson, J., & Garwick, A. (1998). Theoretical linkages: Family meanings and sense of coherence. In H. McCubbin, E. Thompson, A. Thompson, & J. Fromer (Eds.), *Stress, coping, and health in families: Sense of coherence and resiliency* (pp. 71–91). Thousand Oaks, CA: Sage.

Perry, G., Dimnik, S., Ohm, P., & Wilks, B. (2000). Psychoeducational groups for adolescent sex offenders. In L. Vandecreek & T. Jackson (Eds.), *Innovations in clinical practice: A source book* (pp. 311–322). Sarasota, FL: Professional Resource.

Pomeroy, E. (1995). Effectiveness of a psychoeducational and task-centered group intervention for family members of people with AIDS. *Social Work Research, 19(4),* 142–152.

Pomeroy, E., Kiam, R., & Green, D. (2000). Reducing depression, anxiety, and trauma of male inmates: An HIV/AIDS psychoeducational group intervention. *Social Work Research, 24(3),* 156–166.

Sawin, M. (1986). The family cluster approach to family enrichment. *Journal of Psychotherapy and the Family, 2,* 47–57.

Sawyer, S., Rosser, B., & Schroeder, A. (1998). A brief psychoeducational program for men who patronize prostitutes. *Journal of Offender Rehabilitation, 26,* 111–125.

Schultz, C. (1993). Psychoeducational support for parents of children with intellectual disability: An outcome study. *International Journal of Disability, Development and Education, 40,* 205–216.

Senior, P. (1991). Group work in the probation service: Care or control in the 1990s. *Group Work, 4,* 284–295.

Sloan, M., & Schafer, M. (2001, April). *An offender typology based upon psychoeducational needs: A collaborative climate for success.* Paper presented at the annual meeting of the American Educational Research Association, Seattle, WA.

Smith, G. (1996). Psychoeducational support groups for aging parents: Developmental and preliminary outcomes. *Mental Retardation, 34(3),* 172–181.

Stump, E., Beamish, P., & Shellenberger, R. (1999). Self-concept changes in sex offenders following prison psychoeducational treatment. *Journal of Offender Rehabilitation, 29,* 101–111.

Sweig, T. (2000). Women healing women: Time-limited, psychoeducational group therapy for childhood sexual abuse survivors. *Art Therapy: Journal of the American Art Therapy Association, 17,* 255–264.

Thomas, T. (1992). Psychoeducational adjustment of English-speaking Caribbean and Central American immigrant children in the United States. *School Psychology Review, 21,* 566–576.

Vickio, C., & Clark, C. (1998), Growing through grief: A psychoeducational workshop series for bereaved students. *Journal of College Student Development, 39,* 621–623.

Wallace, B. (1989). Relapse prevention in psychoeducational groups for compulsive crack cocaine smokers. *Journal of Substance Abuse Treatment, 6,* 229–239.

Wozner, Y., & Golan, M. (1994). Constellation of variables that impact on rehabilitation in modern society. In Y. Wozner & M. Golan (Eds.), *Delinquency in social work: Theory and interventions* (Hebrew, pp. 57–84). Tel Aviv, Israel: Ramot.

Yealin, N. (1991). The place of social work in Israeli prisons. In *Windows to Prisons* (In Hebrew, pp. 1–9). Jerusalem: Israeli Prison System Publications.

Zimpher, D. (1988). Reviews and developments: marriage enrichment programs, a review. *Journal of Specialists in Groupwork, 13,* 44–53.

Zimpfer, D. G. (1992). Group work with adult offenders: An overview. *The Journal for Specialists in Group Work, 17,* 54–61.

Zipple, A., & Spaniol, L. (1987). Current educational and supportive models of family intervention. In A. Hatfield & H. Lefley (Eds.), *Families of the mentally ill: Coping and adaptation* (pp. 261–277). New York: Guilford.

22

Object Relations Couple Therapy With Trauma Survivors

DENNIS MIEHLS AND KATHRYN BASHAM

This chapter will illustrate the use of object relations theory as one component of a synthetic model of couple assessment and practice with survivors of trauma (Basham & Miehls, in press). Many survivors experience intrapsychic and interpersonal difficulties in their intimate partnerships that necessitate clinical interventions. The literature documents that these individuals often experience relationship and sexual difficulties in the partnership (Balcolm, 1996; Maltz, 1998; Nadelson & Polonsky, 1991; Pistorello & Follette, 1998; Riggs, Byrne, Weathers, & Litz, 1998; Solomon, 1988). The difficulty trauma survivors often have in regulating and modulating affect (Shapiro & Applegate, 2000; van der Kolk, Pelcovitz, Roth, Mandel, McFarlane, & Herman, 1996) can exacerbate difficulties in affect regulation for one or both partners in an intimate partnership.

Many authors (Davis, 1991; Gil, 1992; Heiman, 1986; Karpel, 1995) have suggested that a psychoeducational approach geared toward the understanding and adaptation to symptoms of trauma is advisable when working with couples. Balcolm notes that many of the initial efforts in couple therapy are geared toward "helping the partner understand and adapt to the trauma survivor's changing symptoms and needs over the course of treatment" (1996, p. 433). Models geared toward psycho-education tend to assume that intellectual understanding of the signs, symptoms, and manifestations of complex posttraumatic stress disorder (PTSD) (Herman, 1992) will help the couple systems to manage interpersonal difficulties. Using a purely psychoeducational approach with these couples is seldom sufficient. Use of such an approach presumes that partners of traumatized individuals will have the ego strengths to appreciate the survivor partner's experience. This is unlikely if the other partner's interpersonal style is to be aggressive or further traumatizing to the survivor partner (Jehu, 1988), or does not respect limits or boundaries in the partnership (Talmadge & Wallace, 1991). It is not uncommon in clinical settings that both partners in a given couple have experienced trauma and will have difficulty with limits and boundaries (Balcolm, 1996; Basham & Miehls, 1998b). More important, the idea of the survivor as the pathologized identified patient is embedded in an approach that presumes a joining of the nontraumatized partner with the therapist to help the survivor. This model of intervention poses a risk of further blaming of the survivor or victim (Follette, 1991; Miehls, 1997; Reid, Wampler, & Taylor, 1996; Verbosky & Ryan, 1988).

The model presented here utilizes an object relations approach to assessment and intervention, and offers a rationale for using phase-oriented work with couples in which one or both partners are trauma survivors. A clinical example will be used to highlight the specificity of work at each phase of treatment. In some instances, it is clinically indicated to utilize object relations theory to promote insight in the couple system, but some couples cannot tolerate this level of insight work and may require interventions that are ego supportive. In either case, object relations theory informs the clinical interventions at different phases of treatment, whether it is used to promote insight or interventions that are ego supportive. We will begin with a brief summary of key concepts of object relations theory.

OBJECT RELATIONS THEORY

A basic tenet of object relations theory is that individuals form an internalized world that characterizes one's sense of self and other. This internalized world is populated by self and object mental representations that typify one's early experiences with primary caretakers (Bowlby, 1969; Fairbairn, 1963). An object relational world forms a template that is comprised of conscious and unconscious aspects, and influences one's perception of oneself, others, and relationships. Mahler, Pine, and Bergman (1975) describe how one's internal world develops sequentially in their model of separation–individuation. A number of developmental progressions in one's relationship with primary caretakers propel an individual in the development of *object constancy*. The child starts in a symbiotic-like relationship with the caretaker and gradually differentiates and develops a sense of self that is separate from the caregiver. If object constancy is achieved, the child is able to hold complex (ambivalent) feelings toward the caretaker even when there is frustration. Anna Freud (1968) noted that object constancy means that one can maintain an attachment even if the other is unsatisfying.

Object relations theory predicts that individuals will develop the capacity for satisfying partnerships if they have achieved object constancy (Bader & Pearson, 1988; Sharpe, 2000). Scharff and Savege Scharff (1991) point out that there is a dynamic interplay between one's intrapersonal world and one's interpersonal relationships. Object relations theorists contend that one consciously or unconsciously hopes that one's partner will provide a relationship opportunity for a corrective experience that will ameliorate earlier developmental frustrations (Lachkar, 1992; Sharpe, 2000; Solomon, 1989). Lachkar (1992) emphasizes that the internal worlds of both partners determines the satisfaction or dissatisfaction in the interpersonal dynamic. Object relations theory underscores the dialectic in couple relationships—each individual's intrapsychic world affects the couple relationship dynamic while the couple relationship dynamic affects the intrapsychic worlds of the partners.

Object relations theory notes that each individual in a couple will often use *projective identification* to attempt to maintain balance in his or her own intrapsychic world. Siegel (1991) describes the attempts of individuals in intimate partnerships to shape each other through projective identification mechanisms. Disavowed internal conflicts are often projected onto one's partner, followed by an attempt to engage the partner in the externalized conflict of oneself. In fact, projective identification is only complete when the partner has enacted some part of the conflict. Couples often collude in projective identification enactments so that neither individual is really conscious of his or her own internalized conflict (Willi, 1982).

BIOPSYCHOSOCIAL ASSESSMENT AND TREATMENT MODEL

Couples with trauma histories present for treatment with a wide range of presenting concerns or symptoms. Regardless of the specific presenting issues, it is imperative that the clinician completes a thorough biopsychosocial assessment of the couple system before treatment decisions are made. As these couples often present with a sense of urgency, many clinicians respond in kind, and precipitously attempt to work with complex trauma and intrapsychic issues. In an effort to help the clients relieve affective distress, some practitioners cut short the assessment process and begin to intervene in a manner that paradoxically further heightens the anxiety of both partners. For example, if a clinician prematurely attempts to do insight-oriented work or promotes the retrieval or uncovering of traumatic memories, many couples will become further embroiled in hostile and destructive interpersonal cycles. Couple systems in which one or both partners are trauma survivors generally require an initial phase of treatment that is geared toward stabilization, the establishment of safety, and the reinforcement of the strengths and resiliencies that will prepare them for more difficult work ahead.

The proposed model of synthetic couple therapy parallels many contemporary individual and group therapy stage models with trauma survivors (Courtois, 1988; Herman, 1992; Miller, 1994; Pearlman & Saakvitne, 1995). Early stages of treatment are generally conceptualized as preparatory work for the eventual working through of past traumatic events. We propose a phase-oriented model in which key concepts and themes may be revisited at different points in the therapeutic process. Though our model does presume different types of interventions during different phases of treatment, we do not hold to the idea that development only occurs in a linear manner. Rather, interconnected themes can be interwoven during different phases of treatment.

Biopsychosocial Assessment

Using a variety of theory models allows a comprehensive assessment, but for purposes of this chapter, we will focus on a thorough assessment of the couple's object relational history. We will briefly discuss other relevant aspects of assessment in a synthetic, phase-oriented approach to place the object relations assessment in the context of a culturally sensitive, relationally focused approach. At the outset, a central reciprocal question arises: In what ways do the aftereffects of trauma influence individual capacities for a partnership and in what ways do these aftereffects influence the relationship itself?

We look in three broad areas (institutional–sociocultural, interactional, and individual–intrapsychic) when completing biopsychosocial assessments of couple systems. Our starting place of assessment centers on presenting concerns and acute symptomatology. We presume each couple system will have unique resiliency and vulnerability, and we look for specific ways to determine the nature of the early stabilization work. Our assessment process moves with a fluidity of crisis management from the initial symptoms, which is geared toward the establishment and development of safety.

Institutional–sociocultural assessment. We are conscious of societal and political messages concerning trauma that may have influenced the couple and the clinician. The clinician's stance on trauma may be affected by attitudes of the agency in which the work is being conducted. Are trauma survivors viewed as difficult clients? Is there administrative support to do couple therapy with individuals who are trauma survivors? In addition to being aware of specific countertransference responses to trauma survivors (Chu, 1988; Francis, 1997), is the clinician aware of the potential for vicarious traumatization (Pearlman & Saakvitne, 1995)? What is the extent of support available to the couple? Does the couple therapist need to take on a coordinating role with other professionals who are involved with the couple? Relevant diversity themes need to be assessed as these factors also have an impact on the incidence and aftereffects of trauma. We explore themes related to race, ethnicity, religion, gender, sexual orientation, age, disability, and socioeconomic status for the couple (Allen, 1998).

Interactional assessment. The interactional or interpersonal assessment draws from intergenerational and narrative theory bases. Issues of power and control, sexuality, communication, and boundaries (Miller, 1994) are all assessed. A central feature is the assessment of the victim–victimizer–bystander dynamic (Herman, 1992) that is characteristic of many trauma survivors. In couple systems, partners often oscillate among the different dimensions of the internalized dynamic that set the stage for polarizations in thought, affect, and behaviors. The capacity to tolerate ambivalence and disappointment in relationships influences the extent of the polarizations in these interactional dynamics.

Individual–intrapsychic assessment. Lastly, we assess the individual–intrapsychic strengths and vulnerabilities of members of the dyad. Here, we assess the impact of Complex PTSD symptomatology. The mnemonic device, F-E-A-R-S, proposed by Herman (1990) is a useful tool to assess the most salient features of Complex PTSD. Briefly, we assess for the presence of *fears* (nightmares, flashbacks, and intrusive thoughts), *ego fragmentation* (dissociation or identity distortion), *affective changes–addictions–antisocial behavior, reenactment* and *suicidality–somatization* (insomnia, hypervigilance, numbness vs. hyperarousal, startle response, and bodily complaints).

Object Relations Assessment

There are three main avenues to an object relations assessment of the couple system: (a) the couple's interactional patterns, (b) each partner's early developmental history, and (c) the manner in which each partner positions himself or herself with the clinician.

Object constancy. The clinician needs to determine whether each individual has achieved a reasonable level of object constancy. Several questions must be considered. Do the individuals possess the capacity for whole object relations or do they use each other as part-objects in an attempt to have needs met? If using each other as part-objects, how does this affect the couple's sexual relationship? Is there any evidence of sadistic aggression in the sexual relationship? Is there evidence that these individuals can maintain complex and ambivalent images of the other even when their own needs are being frustrated? Is there a tendency for either individual to position the partner as the all-bad, frustrating, withholding object during times of conflict?

Developmental Themes

Bader & Pearson (1988) and Sharpe (2000) have elucidated how a couple system replicates the separation–individuation phases of individual object relations development. The authors find it useful to consider thematic areas related to developmental achievements, but they do not believe that couples follow stages in a discrete manner. However, in order to understand the presence of consistent developmental themes, the authors listen for material that is reflective of *symbiotic, practicing, or rapprochement* issues.

Symbiotic issues. Does the couple tend to be threatened if either individual shows different thoughts or feelings? Is there an injunction between the partners to stay merged in a symbiotic-like relationship? If symbiotic, the couple will likely present as either merged or, more commonly, as having hostile–dependent features. What evidence is there that any self-differentiation work has been accomplished? What is the primary level of anxiety within the couple system? Is it largely abandonment anxiety or is there a more regressive pull toward annihilation anxiety when the couple system is threatened? What is the response of one partner when the other partner attempts to develop some emotional distance? In summary, does either partner tolerate any difference in the other in terms of thoughts, feelings, or behavior?

Practicing issues. Practicing themes are related to issues of exploration and pursuit of individual interests. Here, however, themes are more likely to reflect an unbridled enthusiasm for pursuit of activities; concern for the partner's wishes or thoughts are essentially not considered. Practicing related themes tend to be more narcissistic in nature; there is often a remarkable lack of empathy in the couple system. For example, is there any ability to empathize, even cognitively, with the partner's trauma story or is the response more narcissistic (Lansky, 1982; Miehls, 1993; Solomon, 1989)? Often motivated by narcissistic envy, one partner may become very agitated if he or she perceives the other partner as having more success. Narcissistic rage is likely to be directed toward the partner who is perceived as standing in the way of one's individual pursuits and ambitions.

Rapprochement issues. The couple with rapprochement issues will present with a great deal of ambivalence. For example, a couple may have severe oscillations between closeness and distance, perhaps a tendency for one partner to move closer only to feel frightened and pull away. Is there an increased anxiety when one partner pushes for more emotional closeness? Rather than annihilation anxiety, here the anxiety will reflect concerns about loss of love or approval from the partner. Is there any capacity to maintain autonomy while still being connected in the relationship? Is there any capacity to share angry feelings in the system without symbolically destroying the partner (Benjamin, 1992; Miehls, 1999; Winnicott, 1971)?

Projective Identification

The nature of and processes of projective identification are central for all couples. The assessment challenge is to explore how the couple utilizes projective identification. What evidence is there of the couple's use of projective identification mechanisms in their interactions? Is the disavowal of a partner's conflicts operating on a conscious, preconscious, or unconscious level? Is the other partner conflicted about similar dynamic issues and colluding in the projection process? Can the site of various dynamic conflictual issues be determined? How are the dynamic themes similar or dissimilar for these individuals?

Understanding a couple's projective identification process is aided by careful examination of the therapist's personal experience in the presence of the couple. Are you, as therapist, also enjoined to take in the projections of one or both partners? Are you aware of what is motivating you to feel and/or behave in certain ways with this particular couple? Compared to how you usually work with couples, are you falling outside of your usual frame, or are you falling into a countertransference trap (Chu, 1998)? If so, is this particular response related to the projective identification enactments with this couple?

Partners who are trauma survivors will often use projective identification mechanisms to alleviate their own unwanted, overly stimulating, conflicted object relations dynamics.

Phase-Oriented Treatment Model

We propose three phases of couple therapy that are guided by the biopsychosocial assessment of participants.

Phase I: Stabilization and safety. This work often utilizes cognitive–behavioral interventions that are characterized as ego supportive work. Affect regulation is usually an important element of the stabilization of the couple.

Phase II: Reflection of trauma narrative. The goal of this phase is to create the setting for the exploration of meaning of earlier trauma histories. Intergenerational patterns of victim–victimizer–bystander (Herman, 1992) dynamics need to be exposed and altered. At times, clarification of projective identification patterns may be indicated. There also may be uncovering of traumatic memories. However, it is important to recognize that these treatment interventions are indicated only when each partner has the object relational capacities and ego strengths to tolerate the affect associated with memory retrieval. It is important to assess congruence with cultural beliefs about the efficacy of retrieval of traumatic memories before this task is pursued.

Phase III: Consolidation of new perspectives. Improved attitudes and behaviors are reflected in a number of domains. The participants develop increased empathy toward each other's trauma history. Each partner shows an enhanced ability to enact practices of self-care. There will often be a further shift in parenting styles, an enhanced sexual relationship, and a relationship style that is based upon reciprocity. There may be an improvement in the relationships with each partner's family of origin. Partners often report an enhanced spirituality and a broader definition of self. Self-definition tends to move beyond a survivorship identity. As there will have been relief from multiple internalized oppressions, many couple systems experience a shift in their social consciousness.

Clinical Illustration

Scott and Dianne had been referred for couple therapy by Dianne's individual therapist. Dianne had recently contacted her individual therapist and had resumed a therapy that she characterized as "on and off" for a couple of years. Dianne was three months pregnant with the couple's first child and she was becoming increasingly anxious that the couple "fix" all of their problems before their child was born. Briefly, Scott was a 32-year-old white male who works as an accounts manager for a small sporting goods company. Dianne was a 29-year-old white woman who works as a legal secretary. The couple had only been married for 6 months; they had lived together for 4 years before deciding to marry.

They decided to marry as they had consciously decided to have a child. The couple had met at a 12-step program 6 years earlier. Each had been alcoholic and had just started their recovery toward sobriety; each had remained sober to date. Scott was previously married to his high school sweetheart. His former wife left him after a brief marriage of 14 months. Scott reluctantly admitted that he had a tendency toward violence and that his former wife told him she would leave unless he stopped drinking. Dianne has not been married before; she had one former long-term relationship, which she ended when her partner was discovered in an extra-relationship affair.

Developmental histories. Scott disclosed a traumatic childhood. His alcoholic father regularly verbally abused Scott and his three younger sisters. Scott repeatedly observed his father's physical abuse toward his mother. Scott's mother often disciplined him with severe beatings, saying that she wanted to ensure that he would not be as bad as his father. Scott's sisters were spared the physical abuse of the mother. This perceived outrage propelled Scott to be abusive toward his sisters, which only exacerbated his mother's frequent beatings. He became a drug and alcohol user in his early teens and dropped out of high school. He lived with his girlfriend's parents for 2 years, and he and his former wife were married at a young age. His work history was poor; however, he did not have any trouble with the law. After his beginning sobriety, he completed his high school equivalency and attended a community college program to train for his current position. His father was deceased and he had limited contact with his mother and sisters.

Both of Dianne's parents were also alcoholics. She initially described her father as a passive man who continuously drank when he was not working. Dianne described her mother as being very controlling and domineering, often ridiculing her husband. Mother would chastise him for his drinking and his inadequacy as a wage earner. At times, she was verbally assaultive to Dianne and her sister. Father seldom responded to the mother's accusations; rather, he would become more withdrawn and sullen. Dianne's mother would often leave the home for nights; it was not uncommon for her to be away for the bulk of weekends. Dianne presumes that her mother had numerous sexual affairs. She described her father as being obsessed with sex; she noted that he would often bring pornographic material into the family home.

Dianne credits her older sister for attempting to protect her from some of the family pathology, but it was a common occurrence for her and her sister to have to take care of their father. Often, he would fall asleep in the living area of the house and they would get him to his bed. Dianne does not remember that her father ever had direct sexual contact with her; however, as a child, she often heard him masturbating. It was only as an adult that she understood the meaning of the father's noises; as a child, she worried that he was perhaps physically sick and in need of some help, but her sister discouraged Dianne from trying to help him. Dianne left home to attend college, and during that time of her life, she became a heavy alcohol user. However, she did start some therapy while in college and managed to finish an undergraduate degree. Her parents are now separated and she has limited contact with each parent. Her mother is now sober and often calls Dianne with unsolicited advice. While Dianne recognizes that her mother is still intrusive, she keeps hoping that she will finally respond to Dianne's longings to be parented.

Assessment. Neither of these individuals has achieved a sense of object constancy. In fact, the couple relationship is largely symbiotic. They have features of hostile dependence and each has a great fear of abandonment. At times of conflict, each regresses to annihilation anxiety. At times, when Scott attempts to make some efforts toward differentiation (e.g., by attending a different 12-step meeting than Dianne), Dianne becomes anxious and tries to pull Scott back into the relationship. This heightens his frustration and he perceives Dianne as being a "controlling bitch"; she unconsciously views him as her mother who went off and abandoned the family. Other aspects of mutual collusive patterns will be illustrated in the following clinical material.

Interventions. Considering the developmental assessment and the saliency of the presenting issues—anger management, relapse prevention, and parenting concerns—the initial sessions were focused on Phase I stabilization work with this couple. Essentially, the therapist worked in a cognitive–behavioral, problem-solving approach to the couple issues. The therapist also actively monitored the couple's ability to contain affect, and did ego-supportive work around affect tolerance and containment. The couple reported that they wanted to find ways of solving problems and resolving conflicts. They had slipped into patterns of verbal assaults with each other, though they denied any physical altercations. Scott did acknowledge his impulsivity and his tendency to feel rage during the couple's arguments. Dianne acknowledged that she was frightened that they would not know how to provide a stable environment for their child.

The therapist offered an explanation of what they might expect in couple therapy and set some ground rules for the time spent outside of sessions. These included the honoring of time-outs during arguments, the use of journaling about their angry feelings, the injunction to bring especially explosive material to the sessions for problem-solving, and some basic communication techniques. In order to decrease frustration, the coordination of household responsibilities and money management issues were discussed and they were helped to problem-solve about how they could be more effective in their budgeting. Using a psychoeducational model, the therapist talked with the couple about how their trauma histories understandably would cause worry about their own parenting style.

They agreed to focus on parenting issues in later sessions. The therapist also talked about the necessity for each of them to feel more emotionally stable and strong before the therapy would address past hurts and frustrations in the relationship.

In the sixth session, the couple reported that they had had a difficult week. They had argued extensively and felt estranged from each other. Dianne had come home early from work as she was feeling some flu-like symptoms. Scott had also stayed home with the flu and had spent a morning geared toward recuperation. Dianne walked in on Scott as he was masturbating and this sent the couple into a protracted argument. Dianne accused Scott of being perverted and wondered why a married man had to do such a thing. Scott retaliated by saying that he might not do such a thing if she wasn't so disinterested in their sexual relationship. He accused her of being controlling and manipulative in every area of their life, including their sexual relationship. Dianne further told Scott that she thought he was hooked on pornography. He retaliated by saying that she also, in the past, had shown interest in watching pornographic videos.

The reader will see the clear links of this interaction with each of the individuals' family-of-origin material. Essentially, Dianne's conscious and unconscious memories of her father's sexual behavior were being stirred up. Scott's view of his mother as controlling and hostile was being activated. While it would eventually be useful for the couple to identify and work through projective identification patterns, it is contraindicated for the clinician to attempt to do insight-oriented work with couples who are working on Phase I stabilization aspects of the treatment.

The therapist interrupted the escalation of angry exchanges in the session by pointing out to the couple that it appeared as if their interaction was becoming more destructive. The therapist reminded them of the need to slow down the interactions in order to do some damage control. Each partner seemed to appreciate the therapist's acceptance of responsibility for ensuring safety. Each partner positively responded to attempts to provide safety in the here-and-now interaction. Essentially, the therapist was providing external ego support so that the couple could become more reality-focused and more able to regulate their affect. By shifting the content to a cognitive level, the therapist linked content to presenting issues rather than pushing for insight about projective identification patterns or family-of-origin patterns.

The therapist inquired about how their attitudes about their sexuality had shifted since Dianne's pregnancy. The therapist wondered if the couple had preconceived ideas about the impact of sexual activity on a developing fetus. Dianne, while embarrassed, said that she did fear that somehow their baby would be hurt if the couple had intercourse. She rationally knew this was not so, but she also wondered what it would be like for their baby to *hear* the couple making love to each other. Though the therapist recognized the connection to her childhood memories of overhearing her father when he masturbated during his drunken stupors, he refrained from addressing it. The work of Phase I is to stabilize, educate, and use cognition to help to lessen hostility and victim–victimizer exchanges. Insight work is not yet indicated in these interactions.

The therapist normalized Dianne's response by suggesting that other pregnant women have shared her fears. Scott added that he had wondered if Dianne had been worried about damaging their baby but he had not known how to approach her about this subject area. He went on to say that he was missing the sexual relationship with Dianne but that he didn't want to force himself upon her. The therapist reinforced his ability to empathize with Dianne and empathized with his wish to have sexual contact with his partner. The therapist explored what it meant to them if one or both partners occasionally masturbated. Dianne replied that after their argument, she had coincidentally seen an article about this in a popular magazine. The article, she said, had reported that it is common for men to masturbate at times, even when in a relationship. The therapist congratulated her on seeking out this information and again reassured her that Scott's masturbation was not necessarily a sign that he was distancing himself from her. The therapist checked with Scott about his comfort with discussing the masturbation and, while he expressed some discomfort, he thought it might be useful to discuss it with Dianne. He reassured her that his masturbatory activity did not change how he felt about her. Dianne wondered if men were more apt to use masturbation as part of their sexual practices. The therapist indicated that there was potentially a gender difference in this area and that other couples have expressed similar patterns.

Shifting to a psychoeducational approach, the therapist talked with the couple about the idea that any behavior could become problematic if it was addictive or repetitive. Scott heard the implicit question and responded that he was not hooked on masturbation but that he occasionally did masturbate as it helped him to stay calm. They discussed the social construction of sexuality with heterosexual couples and the fact that many couples feel inadequate if they are not living up to the publicized, romanticized, and idealized image of the perfect, mutually orgasmic sexually satisfied heterosexual couple.

When the therapist was satisfied that the couple seemed to be staying in their cognitive worlds, he inquired if they would like to talk about their own sexual relationship. The therapist's intention was to ascertain the couple's ability to problem-solve about the here-and-now aspects of the relationship; it was still premature to push for insight about the dynamics potentially involved with sexuality. At a later point in treatment, it may be indicated to utilize the object relational assessment of the couple's sexual relationship more directly. Is the fear about hurting the fetus related to sadistic aggression? Is the wish for sexual connection linked to merger fantasies? Will a new baby be perceived as a major threat to the couple's symbiotic ties?

During Phase I interventions, the work stays focused on the cognitive–behavioral level. The couple agreed to talk about the patterns of their sexual relationship. They revealed that Dianne was the initiator of the couple's sexual activity. Scott felt flattered by this and he did not mind that Dianne took charge of this aspect of the relationship. Of course, when angry and agitated, he would accuse Dianne of being a control freak. In this exchange, the couple was encouraged to separate out ideas of affection and sexuality. They readily agreed that each enjoyed the affection and cuddling that they shared. Dianne said that she missed the intimacy of the sexuality but found herself to be too tired to initiate sex. She attributed this to her pregnancy and her full-time job demands. She said that she wished Scott would sometimes initiate the sexual relationship. He wondered if they should plan a time when they could be intimate so that they would not be so tired. The therapist acknowledged that this plan would contribute to reduced spontaneity and asked Dianne what it would be like for her to have Scott initiate a plan about their intimacy. She thought it would be okay but she once again wondered if the baby would be hurt in any way. The therapist again normalized her concern and suggested that if she was not in any physical discomfort, and if her physician had not specifically instructed her to avoid intercourse, there was no physical danger to her or the baby. They discussed how that may change at the later stages of pregnancy.

The therapist asked if they knew other couples who were pregnant. The intention was to encourage the couple to broaden their support systems and to increase their knowledge about the normative processes of pregnancy. The discussion included whether they were going to take any prenatal classes together or if they were doing any reading about changes during pregnancy. They acknowledged that they did know two other couples who were pregnant and that it would be useful for them to expand their support system. Scott disclosed that Dianne hoped that her mother would be supportive but that Dianne becomes agitated when she talks to her mother. Dianne agreed but said that she does need some support; she added that she would love to talk to her sister more but it was expensive to talk long-distance. Scott admitted that he had chastised Dianne about running up phone bills but that he now could see the benefit of Dianne's positive contact with her sister. They talked about what would be reasonable in terms of phone contacts. The therapist explored the possibility of getting the sister to share some of the cost of the long-distance bills. Dianne said that she did not want to be a burden;

the therapist suggested the sister might like to know how she could be more supportive.

The remainder of the session revisited some of the earlier agreements including the couple's daily schedule, self-care activities, their use of 12-step meetings and their sponsors, the benefits of time-outs, journaling, and the value of postponing discussion of affectively laden arguments to their next session. The therapist reinforced the idea that support systems were valuable resources for them. The session ended with a brief review of the plan in which Scott would take some responsibility for arranging some time for the couple's intimacy.

In summary, the object relations assessment informs Phase I work with Scott and Dianne. The developmental histories and the recognition of projective identification patterns can be used to guide the cognitive, behavioral, and psychoeducational interventions in this phase of the work, and the Phase I work may be revisited throughout the course of the treatment.

CRITERIA FOR PHASE II WORK

Let us now illustrate how this material would have been utilized in a different way had the couple been functioning at a higher level of object relational development. With consistent and ongoing progress in Phase I work, some couples stop treatment after stabilization has occurred, while others continue to work toward greater insight and clarification of projective identification processes. In order to responsibly engage in this work, couples need to have sound problem-solving tools and a cognitive understanding of issues that promotes beginning empathic exchanges. It is important they they have learned ways to effectively manage affect; in addition, the clinician needs to explicitly assess the couple's capacity to alter victim–victimizer stances (hostile dependent interactions) with each other. Phase I work may have assisted the couple to differentiate somewhat from each other. In terms of object constancy, each partner should be able to have some ability to tolerate ambivalence in the relationship. Full attainment of object constancy is unrealistic in a brief treatment model. It is often useful for the couple to reassure each other of the long-term nature of the commitment. It is equally important that the couple agree that each will not threaten abandonment (separation) when the relationship runs into difficult moments. If in recovery, the individuals need to be firmly in control of their sobriety. The clinician needs to monitor the couple's ability in any session to do insight or family-of-origin work. At times, it may be necessary to resume Phase I interventions that are based upon ego-supportive measures and cognitive–behavioral interventions.

PHASE II INTERVENTIONS

Phase II work centers on the unraveling of the projective identification patterns of the couple. The ability of the couple to offer some reparative functions to each other's object relational world often enhances the interpersonal relationship. Increased satisfaction and intimacy are possible when the object relations patterns are altered as a result of insights about intergenerational and family of origin patterns. In addition, the opportunity to work through aspects of hostility and rage is a developmental achievement that many couples can tolerate in Phase II work. Consequently, there is a deepening of the work with resulting reinforcement of ego strengths that allows each to better tolerate intimacy and regulate affect.

In this work, it is important to have each partner explore the meaning of his or her traumatic backgrounds. In this process, the clinician often fluidly moves back and forth between the individuals, creating an opportunity for each partner to story and restory his or her trauma history. Elaborating this historical work in the context of couples therapy offers an immediate context for the partners to become more empathically attuned to each other, and as mutual empathy increases, the process of unraveling the projective identification patterns can be initiated. The complex work of owning one's projections and working through those conflicts in a more adaptive manner can begin. The ability to use each other as objects who can offer corrective emotional experiences is complicated; however, when partners can begin to see each other in more expansive ways, the tendency to distort is diminished. If this work becomes too threatening for either partner, the therapist can reinstitute Phase I ego-supportive interventions.

It would be important for each of these partners to have an opportunity to discuss some aspects of their trauma history. But the discussion of the trauma history will be counterproductive if it is being used to further hurt or victimize the partner. If either individual is unable to move away from the stance of "See, I told you that you were further victimizing me like my parent," then exploring the meaning of the traumas is contraindicated. It is often difficult for partners to separate out their own behavior in the interpersonal exchange; this is improved by a structure in which one partner speaks of his or her history coupled with a frequent checking in with the other partner. We would have Dianne talk about her childhood memories of her father's drunken stupors and hearing his masturbatory activities. While we would encourage her telling some of her story, we would be checking in with Scott in terms of what he heard and to ensure that he was not taking in the message that he was being positioned like Dianne's father. It would be important to have Dianne describe her coping strategies, her resilience, and her adaptation to the events. In doing so, we would encourage her to own her current strengths and adaptation in dealing with her feelings of loss and betrayal. The Phase I work of the cognitive discussion of masturbatory activities could be revisited. We could then explore the rationale for her need to be the initiator of the couple's sexual activities. It is possible that Dianne may have new memories of abuse or trauma during this phase of the work. Again, assuming the ego strengths of the individuals and the strength of the therapeutic alliance, some opportunity to explore new memories may be indicated. The presence of the partner during these explorations again provides an opportunity to enhance intimacy and connection, and discussing strategies that promote empathy and healing is often a very rewarding process for partners.

Scott's work in the above exchange would center on his experience of Dianne as controlling and manipulative. He would need to understand that this perception is likely to be distorted as a result of his interactions with his controlling mother and perhaps sisters. He would need to examine his sexist, misogynistic attitudes. He would also need to examine his identification with his abusive father and his own explosive temper, thereby preparing himself for his own retelling of some of his trauma history. Dianne would need to witness Scott's insight work without feeling defensive or blaming herself. She would need to open up her empathic pathways so as to see the hurt, frightened little boy aspect of Scott. If other traumatic memories emerged for Scott, Dianne would have the opportunity to be a trusted intimate partner who could witness Scott's further growth toward resilience.

CONCLUDING COMMENTS

This vignette offers a glimpse of the range of approaches to addressing object relations issues as they are manifested in the projective identification patterns of the couple. Note that the therapist did not even acknowledge Scott's accusation that Dianne also enjoyed the use of pornography in their sexual relationship. To acknowledge such a statement would likely exacerbate the couple's hostility and victim–victimizer exchanges during the Phase I work. However, in Phase II, the couple will be ready to begin to work with this kind of projective identification pattern. A working through of such projective identification pattern may enhance the partners' object relations capacities in the relationship. This sort of work requires a long-term commitment to therapy.

Miehls (1997) has previously noted how survivors of childhood trauma can be positioned as identified patients in couple systems; it is not uncommon for trauma survivors to carry the burden of a psychological conflict that is experienced by both partners. The unraveling of projective identification is more challenging when both partners have been trauma survivors. Each partner would need to eventually understand his or her own conflicts around control, sexuality, and the unconscious wish to use the partner as a part-object in the sexual relationship. Dianne would need to recognize the impact of her parents' sexual behavior. It is likely that she felt some envy toward her mother's ability to escape the family home. Even though she consciously was aware that her mother had numerous affairs, Dianne may have identified with aspects of her mother's sexual acting-out behavior. Scott also may have identified with the sexist attitudes of his father. He would need to own his wish to retaliate against women. In addition, each would need to fully examine his or her fears of abandonment and how each has colluded with the other to play out issues of closeness and distance.

Phase III work in this treatment model would help the couple further consolidate new identities. Aspects of self-definition would assist Scott and Dianne to move beyond survivorship identity. Revisiting some Phase I parenting themes will reassure the couple that they can break the intergenerational pattern of violence and abuse. The ability of each to truly be empathic to the other will be consolidated. It is quite likely that the couple will experience further adaptation and pleasure in their sexual relationship.

This example shows the relevance of having a thorough object relations assessment history for each partner in the dyad. Although altering projective identification patterns is contraindicated in the beginning stages of couple treatment with trauma survivors, the patterns are addressed in a psychoeducational mode of intervention. At different points in treatment, when the couple is able to hold the tension inherent in the process of changing earlier developmental issues, movement toward further growth and resilience can be a satisfying endeavor for the couple.

REFERENCES

Allen, I. A. (1998). PTSD among African Americans. In A. J. Marsalla, M. J. Friedman, E. T. Gerrity, & R. M. Scurfield (Eds.), *Ethnocultural aspects of posttraumatic stress disorder: Issues, research, and clinical implications* (pp. 209–238). Washington, DC: American Psychological Association.

Bader, E., & Pearson, P. (1988). *In quest of the mythical mate: A developmental approach to diagnosis and treatment in couples therapy.* New York: Brunner/Mazel.

Balcolm, D. (1996). The interpersonal dynamics and treatment of dual trauma couples. *Journal of Marital and Family Therapy, 22,* 431–442.

Basham, K., & Miehls, D. (1998b). Integration of object relations theory and trauma theory in couples therapy with survivors of childhood trauma, Part II: Clinical illustrations. *Journal of Analytic Social Work, 5(3),* 65–78.

Basham, K., & Miehls, D. (in press). *Transforming the legacy: Couple therapy and survivors of childhood trauma.* New York: Columbia University Press.

Benjamin, J. (1992). Recognition and destruction: An outline of intersubjectivity. In N. Skolnick & S. Warshaw (Eds.), *Relational perspectives in psychoanalysis* (pp. 43–60). Hillsdale, NJ: Analytic Press.

Bowlby, J. (1969). *Attachment and loss: Vol. 1. Attachment.* New York: Basic Books.

Chu, J. (1988). Ten traps for therapists in the treatment of trauma survivors. *Dissociation: Progress in the Dissociative Disorders, 1,* 24–32.

Courtois, C. (1988). *Healing the incest wound: Adult survivors in therapy.* New York: Norton.

Davis, L. (1991). *Allies in healing.* New York: Harper Perennial.

Fairbairn, W. R. D. (1963). Synopsis of an object-relations theory of the personality. *International Journal of Psychoanalysis, 44,* 224–225.

Follette, V. M. (1991). Marital therapy for sexual abuse survivors. In J. Briere (Ed.), *Treating victims of child sexual abuse.* San Francisco: Jossey-Bass.

Francis, C. (1997). Countertransference with abusive couples. In M. Solomon & J. Siegel (Eds.), *Countertransference in couples therapy* (pp. 218–237). New York: Norton.

Freud, A. (1968). Remarks in panel discussion. *International Journal of Psychoanalysis, 49,* 506–507.

Gil, E. (1992). *Outgrowing the pain together: A book for spouses and partners of adults abused as children.* New York: Bantam.

Heiman, J. (1986). Treating sexually distressed marital relationships. In N. Jacobson & A. Gurman (Eds.), *Clinical handbook of marital therapy.* New York: Guilford.

Herman, J. (1990). *Trauma and developmental theory.* Workshop conducted at Cape Cod Symposia, Cape Cod, MA.

Herman, J. (1992). *Trauma and recovery.* New York: Basic Books.

Jehu, D. (1988). *Beyond sexual abuse: Therapy with women who were childhood victims.* New York: Wiley.

Karpel, M. A. (1995). The role of the client's partner in the treatment of multiple personality disorder. In L. Cohen, J. Berzoff, & M. Elin (Eds.), *Dissociative identity disorder: Theoretical and treatment controversies* (pp. 509–541). Northvale, NJ: Jason Aronson.

Lackhar, J. (1992). *The narcissistic/borderline couple.* New York: Brunner/Mazel.

Lansky, M. R. (1982). Mask of the narcissistically vulnerable marriage. *International Journal of Family Psychiatry, 3,* 439–449.

Mahler, M., Pine, F., & Bergman, A. (1975). *The psychological birth of the human infant: Symbiosis and individuation.* New York: Basic Books.

Maltz, W. (1998). Identifying and treating the sexual repercussions of incest: A couples therapy approach. *Journal of Sex and Marital Therapy, 14,* 142–170.

Miehls, D. (1993). Conjoint treatment with narcissistic couples: Strategies to increase empathic interaction. *Smith College Studies in Social Work, 64,* 3–17.

Miehls, D. (1997). Projective identification in sexual abuse survivors and their partners: Couple treatment implications. *Journal of Analytic Social Work, 4(2),* 5–22.

Miehls, D. (1999). Couple therapy: An integration of object relations and intersubjective theory. *Smith College Studies in Social Work, 69,* 335–355.

Miller, D. (1994). *Women who hurt themselves.* New York: Basic Books.

Nadelson, C., & Polonsky, D. (1991). Childhood sexual abuse: The invisible ghost in couple therapy. *Psychiatric Annals, 21(8),* 479–484.

Pearlman, L., & Saakvitne, K. (1995). *Trauma and the therapist: Countertransference and vicarious traumatization in psychotherapy with incest survivors.* New York: Norton.

Pistorello, J., & Follette, V. (1998). Childhood sexual abuse and couples' relationships: Female survivors' reports in therapy groups. *Journal of Marital and Family Therapy, 24,* 473–485.

Reid, K., Wampler, R., & Taylor, D. (1996). The "alienated" partner: Responses to traditional therapies for adult sex abuse survivors. *Journal of Marital and Family Therapy, 22,* 443–453.

Riggs, D., Byrne, C., Weathers, F., & Litz, B. (1998). The quality of the intimate relationships of male Vietnam veterans: Problems associated with posttraumatic stress disorder. *Journal of Traumatic Stress, 11,* 87–101.

Scharff, D., & Savege Scharff, J. (1991). *Object relations couple therapy.* Northvale, NJ: Jason Aronson.

Shapiro, J., & Applegate, J. (2000). Cognitive neuroscience, neurobiology and affect regulation: Implications for clinical social work. *Clinical Social Work Journal, 28,* 9–21.

Sharpe, S. (2000). *The ways we love: A developmental approach to treating couples.* New York: Guilford.

Siegel, J. (1991). Analysis of projective identification: An object–relations approach to marital treatment. *Clinical Social Work Journal, 19,* 71–81.

Solomon, M. (1989). *Narcissism and intimacy: Love and marriage in an age of confusion.* New York: Norton.

Solomon, Z. (1988). The effect of combat-related posttraumatic stress disorder on the family. *Psychiatry, 5,* 323–329.

Talmadge, L., & Wallace, S. (1991). Reclaiming sexuality in female incest survivors. *Journal of Sex and Marital Therapy, 17,* 163–181.

van der Kolk, B., Pelcovitz, D., Roth, S., Mandel, F., McFarlane, A., & Herman, J. (1996). Dissociation, affect dysregulation and somatization: the complex nature of adaptation to trauma. *American Journal of Psychiatry, 153,* 83–93.

Verbosky, S. J., & Ryan, D. A. (1988). Female partners of Vietnam veterans: Stress by proximity. *Issues in Mental Health Nursing, 9,* 95–104.

Willi, J. (1982). *Couples in collusion.* New York: Jason Aronson.

Winnicott, D. W. (1971). The use of an object and relating through identifications. In D. W. Winnicott (Ed.), *Playing and reality* (pp. 86–94). London: Tavistock.

23

Facing the Dragon Together: Emotionally Focused Couples Therapy With Trauma Survivors

SUSAN M. JOHNSON

The word *trauma* comes from the Latin word for wound. There is ample evidence that such wounds are not anywhere near as uncommon as the DSM suggests (Root, 1992; Waites, 1993), and will be particularly well represented in those clients who seek psychotherapy. It should not be surprising then that therapists note that a significant proportion of the distressed partners who come to a couple therapist for help are suffering not just from marital distress and the depression that often accompanies such distress but also from posttraumatic stress disorder (PTSD) (Whisman, 1999).

In old stories the image of fighting a dragon was used to symbolize the experience of helplessness and terror that is the essence of PTSD. In a fight with a dragon, we have a special need to know that we can count on those we love to stand beside us. At times of stress and vulnerability, attachment needs become particularly powerful and compelling (Bowlby 1969). Traumatic experience can initiate or exacerbate marital distress if a spouse is perceived as not responding in a caring manner and supporting the wounded partner in dealing with his or her distress. Couples therapy can then be a crucial part of treatment; a better spousal relationship can support healing while relationship distress can often undermine it. The couple therapist will also encounter a number of clients who suffer from complex PTSD (Chu, 1998: Herman, 1993; Moeller, Bachmann, & Moeller, 1993). Most of these clients have been traumatized by the very people they loved and relied on, by former spouses, by parents and relatives, or by older siblings, they have learned to associate fear and suffering with closeness and dependency. Their trauma has been a "violation of human connection" (Herman, 1992); the same kind of connection that the couple therapist is attempting to help them shape and improve. For these clients, the dragon is often standing right behind their partner; the whole relationship occurs in the dragon's shadow, and couples therapy is an opportunity to create a new corrective emotional experience of safe connection that can strike at the very heart of the wounds inflicted by past trauma.

The concept that a new experience of safe connection offers an antidote to wounds inflicted in past traumatic relationships is not new; however, this kind of connection has mostly been viewed as being provided by a therapist in individual therapy. Couples therapy can shape such a connection and so play a crucial role in the treatment of trauma, especially in cases of complex PTSD (Johnson, 2002; Johnson & Makinen, 2003); Gurman (2001) notes that it is also becoming clear that for change to endure it should occur in, and be supported by, the natural environment, and a client's primary relationships are a key part of such an environment.

AN INTERPERSONAL PERSPECTIVE ON TRAUMA

Trauma is usually formulated in individual terms as symptoms of reexperiencing, numbing and avoidance, and hyperarousal. There are now indications that the avoidance and numbing, the most interpersonally oriented of these symptoms, may be the most central and also the most difficult to treat of all the after-effects of trauma (Foa & Rothbaum, 1998; Riggs, Byrne, Weathers, & Litz, 1998). These specific symptoms do not fully capture the complex picture of the effects of trauma. Survivors have general problems with affect regulation; they often find toxic solutions to their stress, such as self-mutilation, that perpetuate shame and avoidance; they often develop a problematic relationship with their own body, which reverberates with traumatic memories and so seems out of control and contaminated; they have low self-efficacy and an impaired ability to set workable goals and, as an inevitable corollary to the above, survivors have problematic relationships with others colored by mistrust and a sense of isolation and estrangement (Johnson, 2002).

Everyday relationship behaviors, such as confiding or making love, are going to be colored and distorted by these kinds of problems.

If we place these problems in the social context in which survivors live, we can conceptualize traumatic stress disorder as a trap (Shalev, 1993), an absorbing state of unregulated negative emotion and a corresponding way of engaging the world and other people (Johnson, 2002, p. 21). In this state everything leads into, and nothing leads out of, helplessness and terror. For example, many ways of coping with trauma cues tend to exacerbate alienation from others. The inner experience of traumatic isolation is reinforced by interactional responses that make secure connections with others difficult to achieve. A lack of secure connection with others appears to preclude dealing with the dragons of trauma with a sense of efficacy. The new social context of couples therapy can change attachment patterns by fostering emotional experiences that are inconsistent with existing models of attachment (Epstein, Prezer, & Fleming, 1987).

If a survivor, who usually rises and cuts herself when the dragon comes for her in the middle of the night, instead can seek to be held by a responsive spouse, she may wake up to a new world the next morning. It is not trauma history that predicts the effects of trauma but whether one can seek comfort in the arms of another (van der Kolk, 1996). Both feminist and social constructivist perspectives encourage us to place the symptoms of trauma in an interpersonal context (Neimeyer, 1993; Jordan, Kaplan, Miller, Stiver, & Surrey, 1991). Attachment theory offers a comprehensive way to understand survivors in their interpersonal context and how that context can be a source of healing or a source of ongoing dysfunction. As McFarlane and van der Kolk (1996, p. 24) note, "emotional attachment is probably the primary protection against feelings of helplessness and meaninglessness."

ATTACHMENT AND TRAUMA

Attachment theory is a systemic theory that bridges self and system (Johnson & Best, in press) and offers couples therapists a theory of adult love and a way to understand how a sense of felt security with others enables us to cope with dragons and darkness. A premise of attachment theory is that the need for a secure connection with a few significant others is one of the main motivators of human behavior from the cradle to the grave. This approach has recently generated a large theoretical and research literature on adult love (Cassidy & Shaver, 1999; Simpson & Rholes, 1998). It is the perspective that informs Emotionally Focused Couples Therapy (EFT [Johnson, 1996]), now one of the best validated and most effective couples therapies (Johnson, Hunsley, Greenberg, & Schindler, 1999).

Attachment theory views bonds between lovers, parents and children, and other family members as physiological regulators. Contact with those we love and depend upon "tranquillizes the nervous system" (Schore, 1994). The safe haven of secure attachment, characterized by emotional accessibility and responsiveness, promotes resilience in the face of uncertainty, exploration of the environment, active learning, and adaptation. Those who are securely attached can optimally regulate their emotions in the face of stress, openly ask for their needs for comfort and reassurance to be met, and take in and use such comfort to calm themselves. They can then integrate their experience and flexibly deal with their environment. Secure attachment is associated with better affect regulation, increased capacity to process information, and openness to new evidence and more than one perspective (Mikulincer, 1997), as well as the ability to communicate with others effectively (Johnson & Whiffen, 1999). For example, securely attached adults, who believe that others will be there when they are needed, are more empathic and more self-disclosing in close relationships. Securely attached Israelis were better able to deal with Scud missile attacks (Mikulincer, Florian, & Weller, 1993) and were found to have a more positive, coherent, and elaborated sense of self (Mikulincer, 1995).

Attachment responses seem to be organized along two dimensions: anxiety and avoidance (Fraley & Waller, 1998). When the connection with an irreplaceable other is threatened but not yet severed, attachment behaviors become heightened and intense, as anxious clinging, pursuit, and even aggressive attempts to obtain a response from the loved one escalate. A second strategy for dealing with the lack of safe emotional engagement, especially when hope for responsiveness has been lost, is to suppress attachment needs, focus on tasks, and limit or avoid distressing attempts at emotional engagement with attachment figures. These two strategies, *anxious clinging* and *detached avoidance,* can develop into habitual styles of engagement with intimate others and require different interventions from the couples therapist (Johnson & Whiffen, 1999). A third fearful strategy that combines anxious clinging with avoidance is often found in survivors of trauma, particularly survivors of childhood sexual abuse (CSA) (Shaver & Clarke, 1994; Roche, Runtz, & Hunter, 1999). These survivors tend to have the most negative self-concepts and are found to be worse off on every measure of mental health. They tend to blame themselves for their traumatic experiences, and this self-blame has been found to mediate adult adjustment in CSA survivors (Coffey, Leitenberg, Henning, & Turner, 1996). This combination of anxious clinging and avoidance stems from a situation in which the attachment figure is both the source of fear and the solution to fear; it tends to create chaos in close relationships and to disorient the spouse as well as the survivor.

For survivors of interpersonal trauma, a basic level of secure attachment is desperately needed but difficult to obtain, and often crucial both to everyday functioning and to the ability to heal past wounds. Couples therapy offers an arena where survivors and their partners, who often suffer from secondary PTSD (Waysman, Mikulincer, Solomon, & Weisenberg, 1993; Nelson & Wampler, 2000), can address absorbing inner states of chaos and distress and learn to manage them together. They can also find ways to engage each other that create a sanctuary in which healing can occur.

COUPLES THERAPY FOR TRAUMATIZED COUPLES

Interventions in the multidimensional problems faced by trauma couples ideally should be based on a clearly formulated model that has been tested. Two models of couples therapy fit these criteria—cognitive behavioral and emotionally focused approaches—and both have been applied to couples dealing with trauma (Follette, 1994; Johnson & Williams-Keeler, 1998; Johnson, 2002, 2004). EFT seems particularly suited to addressing the needs of traumatized couples because: (a) it actively works with emotion, and PTSD is essentially a problem of affect regulation and integration; (b) EFT focuses on attachment and the building of secure bonds; (c) EFT is a humanistic approach that is explicitly collaborative and respectful of clients, and such an orientation is essential with trauma survivors; and (d) EFT appears to achieve better and more stable outcomes in general than the behavioral approaches (Johnson et al., 1999). EFT is also consonant with research on marital distress that stresses the importance of emotional engagement, soothing interactions, and the ability to exit from specific negative cycles such as critical pursuit followed by defensive withdrawal (Gottman, 1994).

The EFT Model

The EFT therapist considers both self and system and how they define each other. The therapist focuses on (a) how partners construct their experience (using an experiential approach reminiscent of Rogers, 1951) and (b) how partners then construct patterns of interaction (using a structural approach reflecting the work of Minuchin & Fishman, 1981). A snapshot of an EFT therapist might show the therapist (a) helping a client unfold a poignant moment (where, for example, she could not accept her partner's offer of love and support), (b) helping this client piece together this experience in a new way or expanding marginalized aspects of this experience, and then (c) using this new formulation of experience as the basis for a new kind of interaction with the other partner. So a client might begin by simply turning away and refusing to look at her spouse or by making a cynical remark about how anyone who trusts is pathetic. The therapist helps her to come to a place where she can turn and tell her partner about how afraid she is that if he comes close he will see her. He might then feel the disgust she feels for herself. The therapist will then work with the partner, who is hopefully pulled toward his spouse, by this latter disclosure, to respond in a caring, reassuring way. The tasks of EFT are always to expand and further process key emotional experiences and to structure interactions that contain negative responses, moving the relationship toward a more secure bond.

The three stages of EFT (applied to trauma couples) are similar to the steps in the change process with individual trauma (McCann and Pearlman, 1990). They are (a) the de-escalation of negative cycles and stabilization, (b) the creation of new interactions that restructure the relationship into a more secure bond that supports a positive sense of self and where partners can stand together against the dragon of trauma, and (c) consolidation and integration, where partners can actively problem-solve and integrate the changes made in therapy into their everyday lives.

Special considerations apply when initiating therapy with trauma couples (Johnson, 2002). Briefly, they include:

1. The need to liaise with any individual therapist who is working with the survivor to ascertain the stage of treatment and how couple and individual therapy can best potentiate each other. Survivors are often referred to couples therapy by individual therapists.
2. Issues of possible violence must be carefully assessed since one of the aftereffects of trauma is a loss of affect regulation and a tendency to rage and aggression.
3. The question of how survivors deal with encounters with the dragon must be directly addressed. Is there a tendency to self-harm such as cutting or suicide attempts? If so, the therapist has to create specific safety nets (sequences of agreed-on coping behaviors) to contain these behaviors.
4. An educational aspect of the nature of trauma has to be added to the traditional EFT model. Spouses of survivors often know only the barest of facts about the survivor's abuse or trauma. Survivors may not feel entitled to care and comfort and often present their history in a very diluted and sanitized manner. Spouses often know very little about the effects of trauma and may take many traumatic

stress responses as personal slights. Overall, the therapist helps the couple recognize the specific moments when the dragon rears his head in their relationship and controls the dance between them.

5. The goals of therapy and the length of the therapy process must be tailored to the needs of each couple. In research studies, EFT is conducted in 10 to 12 sessions. When working with survivors, the pace is slower and temporary relapses are expected, so treatment may take up to 30 sessions or more. The goals of therapy must also be sculpted to fit the couple. For example, CSA survivor will probably always desire a more controlled form of sexuality than a partner who has never been so traumatized. If partners can be open about these kinds of issues, they still can deal with them in a way that promotes satisfaction and intimacy.

6. Last, the alliance with the therapist and the therapist's ability to create a safe haven in the therapy session, the foundation on which EFT interventions stand, is even more crucial with survivors and their partners. It is important to expect rifts in this alliance and so to monitor and actively mend them. The therapist must be genuine and transparent and remain open to learning from every couple in every session. This is crucial in trauma cases, where the therapist is acting as a relationship process consultant but may never have faced a dragon personally, let alone tried to dance around one with a partner.

EFT Interventions

The focus of intervention and the specific interventions used may vary depending on the couple's stage in the change process. In Stage 1, the focus is on the de-escalation of negative cycles of interaction and accessing underlying attachment-oriented affect. The therapist will repeatedly reflect the process of interactions and frame negative cycles as the enemy that keeps both partners off balance and on guard. The therapist will use evocative questions, reflection, and interpretation to expand reactive emotions to include the more vulnerable affect that underlies them. The therapist will encourage the couple to share these core emotional responses in enactments, which usually involve various forms of fear of loss, abandonment or rejection, and grief and hurt. The therapist also reframes key responses in terms of attachment needs and fears and the aftereffects of trauma. At the end of Stage 1, the partners are kinder and more generous with each other and can view the negative cycle and traumatic stress as their mutual enemy (rather than labeling each other in this way), but the attachment between partners is still insecure.

In Stage 2, the focus is on restructuring interactions toward more secure attachment. The therapist works toward reengaging withdrawn partners and helping critical blaming partners to *soften* (ask for attachment needs to be met from a position of vulnerability). When both partners are accessible and responsive, bonding interactions reassure partners and define the relationship as a safe haven and a secure base, paving the way for the final stage of therapy. The therapist can structure new patterns of interaction, encouraging the couple to create a coherent narrative of how their relationship became distressed and how they then repaired it. The couple can also then problem-solve around how to prevent the incursions of traumatic stress into their relationship.

Emotional responses. The EFT therapist privileges emotional responses and views them as organizing interactions between the couple as music organizes a dance. When working with survivors, there are times when the therapist helps to contain chaotic and overwhelming emotional responses (see Johnson & Williams-Keeler, 1998) and to deconstruct negative responses such as shame. Often, the spouse is able to respond to a survivor in a more loving and compassionate way than the survivor can initially allow or accept. This compassion begins to act as an antidote to negative emotions like shame and validates the worth of the wounded partner.

Emotion is seen as a high-level information processing system that communicates to an individual and to others what that individual's needs and motives are. Emotion plays a central role in the creation of meaning; as Sartre commented, emotion can transform the world in an instant. It is also a body experience that organizes action. Negative emotion is (a) reframed in the context of cycles of distress, traumatic stress, and attachment, and (b) restructured, often by including marginalized elements. New emotional responses, such as fear of hurt and longing for comfort and reassurance, are used to structure new positive interactions between spouses.

How does the therapist know which emotion to focus on? The therapist focuses on the most present poignant emotions that arise in the therapy process, the nonverbal gesture or the hot image, or the emotion that is most salient in terms of attachment needs and fears. The therapist also focuses on the emotion that seems to organize problem interactions or has the potential to organize positive ones. For example, the therapist might highlight the look of sadness and compassion on a husband's face when his partner says that she interrogates him out of fear, not out of contempt. Fear is addressed extensively in EFT, primarily because fear tends to become an absorbing state that overrides other cues and constricts and constrains both information processing and interactional responses. Attachment longing, or its mirror opposite, the pain of isolation and fear of loss, is also used to prime new behaviors such as risk-taking and asking for caring responses. Emotion is designed to rapidly reorganize behavior in the interests of survival and the fulfillment of basic needs. Attachment longing and fears play a part in the establishment of negative cycles, but they can also be part of the way out of such cycles.

The core interventions in EFT used to reprocess emotional experience are as follows (Johnson & Denton, 2002):

Tracking and reflecting emotional experience

Example: "Could you help me to understand? I think you're saying that you 'stay on the surface' as you put it because this feeling of hopelessness comes up when you think of talking about how lonely you feel. And now there is another piece to this that makes you want to throw up your hands like you just did. This is that if you talk about your needs, you are afraid that you will not only feel more alone but you will also be told how demanding and impossible you are. Am I getting it?"
Main functions: Focusing the therapy process; building and maintaining the alliance; clarifying emotional responses underlying interactional positions.

Validation

Example: "You feel so alarmed right now that you can't even focus. When we're that afraid, we can't even concentrate, is that it? And you had to learn to stay vague and kind of numb. It was the only way to grasp a little safety. It was a way of saving your life, wasn't it?"
Main functions: Legitimizing responses and supporting clients to continue to explore how they construct their experience and their interactions; building the alliance.

Evocative responding: Expanding by open questions the stimulus, bodily response, associated desires, and meanings or action tendency implicit in an emotional response.

Examples: "What's happening right now, as you say that?" "What's that like for you?" "So when this occurs, some part of you just wants to run, run and hide?"
Main functions: Expanding elements of experience to facilitate the reorganization of that experience; formulating unclear elements of experience and encouraging exploration and engagement.

Heightening: Using repetition, images, metaphors, or enactments

Examples: "Could you say that again, directly to her, 'I can't let you in.'" "It seems like this is so difficult for you, like stepping off into space, so

terrifying." "Can you turn to him and tell him, 'It's too hard to ask you to hold me and help me feel safe.'"
Main functions: Highlighting key experiences that organize responses to the partner and new formulations of experience that will reorganize the interaction.

Empathic conjecture or interpretation

Example: "You turned your head, it is almost as if you were turning away from this feeling ... like you don't want to touch it ... to own it. It feels wrong, unacceptable almost, is that right? You don't want to know this ... to feel this way?"
Main functions: Clarifying and formulating new meanings, especially regarding interactional positions and definitions of self.

It is important when working with emotions to (a) repeat interventions since difficult emotions take longer to process, (b) be congruent with the affect (for example, to speak of sadness in a soft voice), and (c) to use simple language and simple images. The best images of all are the ones generated by the clients themselves.

Core interventions to restructure interactions in EFT are as follows:

Tracking, reflecting, and replaying interactions

Example: "So what just happened here? It seemed like you took a big risk and put your weapon down and asked for his comfort. Is that okay? But Bill, you were on guard, waiting for the slam, so you stayed cool and stepped behind your wall, yes?"
Main functions: Slows down and clarifies steps in the interactional dance; replays key interactional sequences.

Reframing in the context of the cycle, trauma, and attachment processes

Example: "You freeze because you feel like you're right on the edge of stepping into all that helplessness, yes?" "You freeze because she matters so much to you, not because you don't care."
Main functions: Shifts the meaning of specific responses and fosters more positive perceptions of the partner.

Restructuring and shaping interactions: Enacting present positions, enacting new behaviors based upon new emotional responses, and choreographing specific change events.

Examples: "Can you tell him, 'I promised myself never to be open and so easy to hurt again. You don't get to devastate me again'". "Can you tell him directly, 'I am so afraid, I have to hold you at a distance just to breathe ...

can't let you close ... feel like I have no skin ... so raw'?" "Can you ask him, 'Please'? Can you ask him for what you need?"
Main functions: Clarifies and expands negative interaction patterns, creates new kinds of dialogue and new interactional steps and positions, leading to positive cycles of accessibility and responsiveness.

New Developments in EFT

Two new developments in EFT are relevant to working with traumatized couples. First, process research has shown that positive outcomes, deeper emotional experiencing, and more affiliative responses are produced by a change event called a *softening*; i.e., where a previously blaming spouse is able to risk asking for attachment needs to be met from a position of vulnerability (Johnson & Greenberg, 1988). The steps that constitute this event have been mapped out, as have the specific therapist interventions that foster a specific change event. The EFT therapist uses evocative responding, reframing in terms of attachment, and heightening before choreographing an enactment where one spouse confides in the other. Therapists who were successful in helping couples complete these events also gave partners a picture of what a secure attachment response might look like, while at the same time validating how hard this was to do. The therapist might say, "So you could never, never turn and ask for reassurance, to just turn and say how afraid you are and how much you long for his soothing. You could never do that." This intervention seemed to offer partners an image of an alternative response, while encouraging them to acknowledge blocks to this response. This kind of intervention might be especially appropriate for traumatized couples who may never have experienced any kind of safe attachment and who need to begin by acknowledging how almost impossible it is to risk this kind of interaction.

The second recent development in EFT is the outlining of a form of relationship trauma that shatters the assumptions of secure attachment and becomes particularly salient when partners are asked to risk new levels of emotional engagement with their spouse in therapy. These past events, which are usually abandonments at moments of intense need (such as during a miscarriage or after a medical diagnosis), arise in the manner of a vivid flashback and block engagement in change events where partners reengage or soften. Such traumatic events appear to disproportionately influence the quality of the attachment in a relationship, defining it as insecure (Johnson, Makinen, & Millikin, 2001). It is not the event itself that appears to create an impasse but its attachment significance and the fact that past attempts to repair this relationship wound have confirmed the injuring spouse's unresponsiveness. If the therapist does not actively address these injuries, the couple does not complete the Stage 2 change events and are less likely to recover from distress at the end of therapy. The steps in the resolution of these relationship traumas appear to be as follows:

1. With the therapist's help, the injured spouse stays in touch with the injury and begins to articulate its impact and its attachment significance. New emotions frequently emerge at this point. Anger evolves into clear expressions of hurt, helplessness, fear, and shame. The connection of the injury to present negative cycles in the relationship becomes clear. For example, a spouse says, "I promised myself, never again. I won't let myself need him again, so he can just wipe out my hurt like that—like I was nothing to him."

2. The partner begins to hear and understand the significance of the injurious event and to understand it in attachment terms—as a reflection of his or her importance to the injured spouse, rather than as a reflection of his or her personal inadequacies or insensitivity. This partner then acknowledges the injured partner's pain and suffering and elaborates on how the event evolved for him or her.

3. The injured partner then tentatively moves toward a more integrated and complete articulation of the injury and expresses grief at the loss involved in it and fear concerning the specific loss of the attachment bond. This partner allows the other to witness his or her vulnerability.

4. The other spouse becomes more emotionally engaged and acknowledges responsibility for his or her part in the attachment injury and expresses empathy, regret, and remorse.

5. The injured spouse then risks asking for the comfort and caring from the partner which were unavailable at the time of the injurious event.

6. The spouse responds in a caring manner that acts as an antidote to the traumatic experience of the attachment injury. The partners are then able to construct together a new narrative of the event. This narrative is ordered and includes, for the injured spouse, a clear and acceptable sense of how the other came to respond in such a distressing manner during the event.

Once the attachment injury is resolved, the therapist can more effectively foster the growth of trust, softening events and the beginning of positive cycles of bonding and connection. The literature on trauma and attachment contributed immensely to our understanding of these events, and the mapping of such events and their resolution have allowed us to work more successfully with trauma survivors.

Case Illustration: "So Many Traumas I Can't Count Them"

Jane and Trevor were in their early thirties and had been married for 7 years. Both partners were in individual therapy. Trevor was being treated for depression and panic attacks. He referred to himself as "the rock" and viewed his problems as "out of character." Emotions were very much held in check in his family of origin and he did not understand how talking about them could ever be helpful. He related the problems in the relationship to the following series of events. First, Jane lost a baby; then she had surgery for medical problems arising from the loss. Shortly after, she was raped by a colleague when she was working late in the evening. The rape induced hemorrhaging and toxic shock, and she was rushed to a hospital where she remained in a coma for 4 months. She had a very difficult and slow convalescence and was now on a disability pension. Trevor stayed beside her all through her coma but then became enmeshed in the police investigation where he concluded that she had not been raped. When Jane awoke from her coma, he told her that he believed she had engaged in illicit sex. A few months after that, Jane's closest living relative, her aunt, committed suicide. Jane began to express suicidal feelings; she experienced Trevor as distant and she felt connected to no one.

A few months later, this couple walked into my office and told me the above story in a calm, reasonable monotone. They described small conflicts about his being late for supper and seemed to exhibit a careful withdraw–withdraw style of interaction. She described PTSD symptoms of nightmares, intrusive images and thoughts, numbing and avoidance, and hypervigilance concerning safety issues, as well as problems with chronic pain and somatic complaints. Trevor appeared to be suffering from secondary PTSD and I hypothesized that his skepticism about the rape might also constitute an attachment injury for his wife. For partners who had walked through this kind of nightmare, they appeared to be laid back and unemotional.

The pattern of mutual carefulness and distance soon changed to pursuit and attachment protest by Jane and appeasement and emotional distancing on the part of Trevor. Contact with the individual therapists revealed that Trevor's therapist felt that couples therapy was the treatment of choice while Jane's therapist viewed himself as mainly supporting Jane to adapt to her present life. He had placed Jane on medication for chronic pain and anxiety. The trauma trap this couple were caught in was that Jane's sense of traumatic helplessness and terror seemed to be constantly confirmed by her partner's distance and doubts about her fidelity, while her anxiety and threats to hurt herself cued Trevor to shut down more and so exacerbate her sense of isolation. Neither had a safe haven where they could deal with their loss, hurt, and fear. Their habitual ways of engaging each other in attachment interactions seemed to fit the *anxious preoccupied* (Jane) and the *avoidant dismissing* (Trevor) patterns. With support and validation, Jane talked of how she felt she had lost her identity. Before the events, she had been independent and strong; now she was disabled. Trevor shared some of the insights he had gained in his individual therapy; he related his panic to the pressure of work demands and his increasing fears that his wife would come to harm and he did not know how to take care of her properly. He did not confide in her because he saw her as overwhelmed already and his emotions "didn't make sense" anyway.

In the individual sessions for each partner that are part of the assessment phase in EFT, Jane confided that even before the trauma of the rape, she experienced Trevor as cold and suspicious regarding her fidelity. When her cousin died, Trevor stayed distant and so she viewed her threats to hurt herself as part of a desperate attempt to pull him closer. She wept at the memory of his accusations of infidelity after she awoke from her coma. At this point, however, she experienced him as trying to trust her and trying to be supportive. She now felt safe enough with him that they could make love without her experiencing flashbacks. The flashbacks she did experience were of her time in the hospital. Trevor talked of feeling controlled and how he had sat by his wife's bedside for months, only to be assailed by doubts and finally anger about her possible sexual betrayal of him.

In the fifth session we discussed the issue of the rape and the part it played in their carefulness with each other. They each had carefully avoided talking about the rape and other difficult topics, which left each of them feeling alone until Jane blew up over seemingly minor issues. Jane shared her despair that she could not prove that she had been faithful and pleaded with Trevor to understand that at the time of the rape she was still in postoperative pain and not sexually active. He explained that he had stopped sharing his doubts since it only hurt her. I encouraged him to talk about his fears and how they had been exacerbated by the police investigation. He acknowledged that his anxiety over possible betrayal had always been part of the relationship for him since he had always seen himself as the less able and attractive partner.

Trevor was able to own his fears and express deep regret that he had accused her. Jane expressed the pain of abandonment that this had brought up in her. The next few sessions then went on to deal with his sense of injury at her threats of suicide and how it had overwhelmed him and inhibited him in interactions with her. She was able to respond and empathize with his feelings and reassure him that she would not hurt herself. The relationship was becoming safer; both partners were able to share the skeletons in the closet that blocked their emotional engagement and their sadness about that. They were able to see the cycle of mutual withdrawal and pursue–criticize distance that prevented them from being close. Trevor talked about his panic attacks and related them to Jane's suicide threats and how his fear and anger ambushed him after he felt that he had successfully tuned out all these emotions. Both were able to talk about how they wanted to learn to open up, to listen, and to comfort each other in the face of their loss and fear. They were able to speak of the suicide of Jane's aunt and help each other grieve this loss. With many clients, attachment injuries come to the fore when they are asked to risk emotional engagement in change events in therapy. In this couple these injuries had to be addressed in the de-escalation phase to foster the creation of basic safety in the relationship and in sessions.

The task of the second phase of therapy was to foster secure bonding interactions that would create a healing environment. We began to work with Trevor's reluctance to express his emotions. He said, "I just tell her the surface and it is a bit lonely." He visited his fidelity fears again on a deeper level, and admitted that he had doubted that the baby she lost was his. He feared he would find out that "She doesn't love me and I don't matter to her. I don't know how to love her. I am so ordinary … never felt good enough for her." Jane responded supportively.

Jane had become more open in our sessions, but she now began to have flashbacks and nightmares that she was being held hostage by the rapist and could not reach Trevor. She found it very hard to share this with Trevor, fearing that she would be more of a burden if she came to him seeking comfort. Trevor responded that he wanted her to come to him and he wanted to learn how to comfort her. She then expressed the shame, so common in trauma survivors, that she felt "dirty" even talking about this and would "contaminate and hurt" him if she confided. He told her that he felt he was able to be responsive to her now. She shook her head and then brought up a recent incident, and I could see the dragon of trauma come between them.

Jane (very, very quietly): "If he's in the office—I know I can reach him—but he goes out and he forgets to turn his cell phone on. Like Wednesday when he played golf and I couldn't reach him. I asked him, and I have asked him and asked him. [Begins to cry very quietly.] If I can't reach him when I feel this way. He won't be there!!!"

Trevor (to the therapist): "Well, I do carry the phone with me most of the time, you know, but if I am out of the office it is hard to respond sometimes. This feels a bit unfair; it's a lot of pressure. I don't understand why you are so upset." (The therapist reflects and validates this.)

Therapist (turning to Jane): "It's scary for you to think of depending on Trevor, to think of reaching and not being able to get him to respond? That would feel just awful? [She nods and weeps.] Jane, recently you were telling Trevor some of the details of the rape—things that are very, very hard to talk about—things that you hadn't really told him before. [She nods.] I remember you mentioning that you kept passing out—and that was completely terrifying for you; you were bleeding and your body was going away on you. You were totally helpless …"

Jane: "Yes, I remember." (Weeps.)

Therapist (soft voice and speaking slowly): "You also said that you still have dreams of this, of drifting in and out of consciousness and of seeing the phone … just out of reach. You tried to reach for it each time you came to, but your body wouldn't respond, you couldn't reach it. And you were thinking, if I could call Trev, if I could just call him and he would come and help me—yes?" (She nods vigorously.)

Jane: "I couldn't reach it. I couldn't get to it. I couldn't get to Trevor."
Therapist: "Right … and you were dying. So now when you can't reach him, that panic comes up and takes you over. Yes … is that right? You are alone, helpless and held hostage all over again?"

Jane (looking down, very quietly): "He doesn't have the phone on. I can't get to him. [Looks at therapist.] I've told him, I feel so alone. I feel abandoned. [Changes her voice, looks away.] So sometimes I get mad instead and won't talk to him when he comes home. [Turns to Trevor.] You blame me and you find it inconvenient. You won't even turn the phone on for me. It's too scary to come to you, to try, so I get mad."

Trevor (quietly, sadly): "You get so mad, you even threaten to commit suicide. I get paralyzed."

Therapist: "You want to be there to hold and comfort Jane [he nods] but sometimes all the emotion and the fear get too much and you have blocked and shut down?" (He nods.)

Jane: "I have threatened suicide in the past … I have. Why not? I give up sometimes. It's such a struggle. I can't get through to you … and I feel even more alone."

Therapist: "So for you, in that moment, when you need to reach for Trevor and know he is there for you—in that moment, it is life and death, isn't it, Jane? He was your lifeline, every time you grabbed onto consciousness, you tried to reach for the phone … for Trevor. And it still feels like that? [She nods vigorously.] He was the only link to safety—the only way out of that terror, that helplessness …"

Jane: "Now when I call and realize that his phone isn't on, my body goes into overdrive. My face gets red hot; my temples pound; I am on alert."

Therapist: "Panic comes for you. You are alone … and so vulnerable. It is unbearable. So in the past the only escape route you could find was to think of suicide, ending the panic. Can you tell him?"

Jane: "Yes. [She looks up, dries her eyes and turns to Trevor.] But … how can I help you understand that? I don't want to restrict you … have you feel controlled."

Trevor: "I didn't understand; I didn't understand this. I don't want you to feel so panicked. I want you to reach for me. I will have my phone on always."

Therapist: "So Trevor, if I am hearing you right, you want Jane to know that you are there to hold and protect her. Yes? [He nods and reaches out his hand to Jane.] You are distressed at her helplessness, her terror. You want her to reach for you … to know she can reach for you, that you can stand against this together." (He agrees.)

Therapist (to Jane): "Can you tell him? 'I have to know I can reach you and you will respond. When this panic comes for me, I have to know you are there. You are my safety.' Can you tell him?"

Jane (in a cool voice): "He wants me to calm down and spend more time with his parents."

Therapist (refocusing the dialogue): "Can you tell him how scary it is to ask for his comfort, his caring, to put yourself in his hands?"

Jane (to Trevor, weeping): "In the hospital, I was a shell. I had lost me and then I had lost you. I still think about this when I want to ask you … when I can't get hold of you. Do I know you will be there another time? Do I risk it? Can you handle it?"

Trevor: "I want you to. I am learning." (She smiles at him.)

Therapist: "What do you need right now, Jane? Can you ask him?"

Jane (to Trevor): "Can you hold me very tight? Can I count on you?" (He stands up and pulls her into his arms.)

This is an example of a *softening* event in EFT where a vulnerable spouse asks for comfort and connection in a way that pulls the other spouse toward him or her. In a traumatized couple, the therapist has to prepare for these events more carefully, approach them more slowly and repeat the process more times than with a nontraumatized couple. This event occurred after 14 sessions. The therapist expected relapses, after which the couple would need to repeat this process, with the therapist supporting Jane's taking the risk to ask for comfort and Trevor's sharing his own fears. At the time of writing this chapter, this couple have completed therapy and are doing well. Trevor is now able to tell Jane when his fears and doubts arise and she is more able to turn to him when the dragon of trauma comes for her.

CONCLUSION

Attending to attachment and affect and the shaping of interactions that characterize secure attachment brings a focus to the sessions and provides a map of the overall process of change and a guide to specific moment-by-moment intervention. As Allen states (2001, p. xxii), "Attachment theory provides a unified framework for organizing our understanding of trauma, it's developmental impact and its treatment." Couples therapy that focuses on the creation of more secure attachment has a definitive contribution to make to the treatment of trauma. The process of emotionally focused couples therapy with couples such as Jane and Trevor reminds me of the lines from the famous hymn, "Abide with me, still falls the eventide. Darkness is falling—still with me abide."

REFERENCES

Alexander, P. C. (1993). Application of attachment theory to the study of sexual abuse. *Journal of Consulting and Clinical Psychology, 60,* 185–195.
Allen, J. G. (2001). *Traumatic relationships and serious mental disorders.* New York: Wiley.
Bowlby, J. (1969). *Attachment and loss: Vol 1. Attachment.* New York: Basic Books.
Cassidy, J., & Shaver, P. (Eds.). (1999). *The handbook of attachment: Theory, research, and clinical applications.* New York: Guilford.
Chu, J. A. (1998). *Rebuilding shattered lives: The responsible treatment of complex post-traumatic and dissociative disorders.* New York: Wiley.
Coffey, P., Leitenberg, H., Henning, K., & Turner, T. (1996). Mediators of the long term impact of child sexual abuse: Perceived stigma, betrayal, powerlessness and self-blame. *Child Abuse and Neglect, 20,* 447–455.
Epstein, N., Prezer, J., & Fleming, B. (1987). The role of cognitive appraisal in self-reports of marital communication. *Behavior Therapy, 18,* 51–69.
Foa, E. B., & Rothbaum, B. O. (1998). *Treating the trauma of rape: Cognitive-behavioral therapy for PTSD.* New York: Guilford.
Follette, V. (1994). Survivors of child abuse: Treatment using a contextual analysis. In S. C. Hayes, N. S. Jacobson, V. Follette, & M. J. Dougher (Eds.), *Accceptance and change: Content and context in psychotherapy* (pp. 255–272). Reno, NV: Context Press.
Fraley, R. C., & Waller, N. G. (1998). Adult attachment patterns: A test of the typological model. In J. A. Simpson & W. S. Rholes (Eds.), *Attachment theory and close relationships* (pp. 77–114). New York: Guilford.
Gottman, J. (1994). *What predicts divorce?* Hillsdale, NJ: Erlbaum.
Gurman, A. S. (2001). Brief therapy and family and couple therapy: An essential redundancy. *Clinical Psychology: Science and Practice, 8,* 51–65.
Herman, J. L. (1992). *Trauma and recovery.* New York: Basic Books.

Herman, J. L. (1993). Complex PTSD: A syndrome in survivors of prolonged and repeated trauma. *Journal of Traumatic Stress, 5,* 377–391.

Johnson, S., & Whiffen, V. (1999). Made to measure : Adapting emotionally focused couples therapy to couples attachment styles. In M. Whisman & D. Snyder (Eds.), *Special Edition of Clinical Psychology: Science and Practice, Affective and developmental considerations in couples therapy, 6,* 366–381.

Johnson, S. M. (1996). *The practice of emotionally focused marital therapy: Creating connection.* New York: Brunner/Mazel.

Johnson, S. M. (2002). *Emotionally focused couples therapy for trauma survivors: Strengthening attachment bonds.* New York: Guilford.

Johnson, S. M. (2004). An antidote to posttraumatic stress disorder: The creation of secure attachment. In L. Atkinson & S. Goldberg (Eds.), *Attachment issues in psychopathology & intervention* (pp. 207–228). Mahwah, NJ: Erlbaum.

Johnson, S. M., & Best, M. (2003). A systemic approach to restructing adult attachment: The EFT model of couples therapy. In P. Erdman & T. Caffery (Eds.), *Attachment and family systems: Conceptual, emprirical, and therapeutic relatedness* (pp. 165–189). New York: Brunner-Routledge.

Johnson, S. M., & Denton, W. (2002). Emotionally focused couples therapy: Creating connection. In A. S. Gurman (Ed.), *Clinical handbook of couple therapy,* (3rd ed.) (pp. 221–250). New York: Guilford.

Johnson, S. M., & Greenberg, L. (1988). Relating process to outcome in marital therapy. *Journal of Marital and Family Therapy, 14,* 175–183.

Johnson, S. M., Hunsley, J., Greenberg, L., & Schlindler, D. (1999). Emotionally focused couples therapy: Status and challenges. *Clinical Psychology: Science and Practice, 6,* 67–79.

Johnson, S. M., & Makinen, J. (2003). Creating a safe haven and a secure base: Couples therapy—A vital element in the treatment of post-traumatic stress disorder. In D. Snyder & M. Whisman (Eds.), *Treating difficult couples: Managing emotional, behavioral, and health problems in couples therapy.* New York: Guilford.

Johnson, S. M., Makinen, J., & Millikin, J. (2001). Attachment injuries in couple relationships: A new perspective on impasses in couples therapy. *Journal of Marital and Family Therapy. 27,* 145–155.

Johnson, S. M., & Williams-Keeler, L. (1998). Creating healing relationships for couples dealing with trauma: The use of emotionally focused therapy. *Journal of Marital and Family Therapy, 24,* 25–40.

Jordan, J., Kaplan, A., Miller, J., Stiver, I., & Surrey, J. (1991) *Women's growth in connection: Writings from the Stone Center.* New York: Guilford.

McCann, I. L., & Pearlman, L. A. (1990). *Psychological trauma and the adult survivor.* New York: Brunner/Mazel.

McFarlane, A. C., & van der Kolk, B. A. (1996). Trauma and its challenge to society. In B. A. van der Kolk, A. C. McFarlane, & L. Weisaeth (Eds.), *Traumatic Stress* (pp. 24–45). New York: Guilford.

Mikulincer, M. (1995). Attachment style and the mental representation of the self. *Journal of Personality and Social Psychology, 69,* 1203–1215.

Mikulincer, M. (1997). Adult attachment style and information processing: Individual differences in curiosity and cognitive closure. *Journal of Personality and Social Psychology, 72,* 1217–1230.

Mikulincer, M., Florian, V., & Weller, A. (1993). Attachment styles, coping strategies, and post-traumatic psychological distress. *Journal of Personality and Social Psychology, 64,* 817–826.

Minuchin, S., & Fishman, H. C. (1981). *Family therapy techniques.* Cambridge, MA: Harvard University Press.

Moeller, T., Bachmann, G., & Moeller, J. (1993). The combined effects of physical, sexual and emotional abuse during childhood: Long term health consequences for women. *Child Abuse and Neglect, 17,* 623–640.

Neimeyer, R. A. (1993). An appraisal of constructivist psychotherapies. *Journal of Consulting and Clinical Psychology, 61,* 221–234.

Nelson, B. S., & Wampler, K. S. (2000). Systemic effects of trauma in clinic couples: An exploratory study of secondary trauma resulting from childhood abuse. *Journal of Marital and Family Therapy, 26,* 171–183.

Roche, D., Runtz, M., & Hunter, M. (1999). Adult attachment: A mediator between child abuse and later psychological adjustment. *Journal of Interpersonal Violence, 14,* 184–207.

Riggs, D., Byrne, C., Weathers, F., & Litz, B. (1998) The quality of intimate relationships of male Vietnam veterans: Problems associated with posttraumatic stress disorder. *Journal of Traumatic Stress, 11,* 87–101.

Rogers, C. (1951). *Client centered therapy.* Boston: Houghton-Mifflin.

Schore, A. N. (1994). *Affect regulation and the organization of self.* Hillsdale, NJ: Erlbaum.

Shalev, A. Y. (1993). Stress versus traumatic stress: From acute homeostatic reactions to chronic psychopathology. In B. A. van der Kolk, A. C. McFarlane, & L Weisaeth (Eds.), *Traumatic Stress* (pp 77–101). New York: Guilford.

Shaver, P. R., & Clark, C. L. (1994). The psychodynamics of adult romantic attachment. In J. Masling & R. Bornstein (Eds.), *Empirical perspectives on object relations theory* (pp. 105–156). Washington, DC: American Psychological Association.

Simpson, J. A., & Rholes, W. S. (1998). *Attachment theory and close relationships.* New York: Guilford.

van der Kolk, B. A. (1996). The complexity of adaptation to trauma. In B. A. van der Kolk, A. C. McFarlane, & L. Weisaeth (Eds.), *Traumatic Stress* (pp. 182–213). New York: Guilford.

Waites, E. A. (1993). *Trauma and survival: Post-traumatic and dissociative disorders in women.* New York: WW Norton.

Waysman, M., Mikulincer, M., Solomon, Z., & Weisenberg, M. (1993). Secondary traumatization among wives of post traumatic combat veterans: A family typology. *Journal of Family Psychology, 7,* 104–119.

Whisman, M. A. (1999). Marital dissatisfaction and psychiatric disorders: Results from the National Comorbidity Survey. *Journal of Abnormal Psychology, 108,* 701–706.

24

Critical Interaction Therapy With Couples

DAVID READ JOHNSON

Immersed as we are in a multitude of relationships—past, present, and future, real and imagined, solacing and malignant—how is it possible for two people to sustain a loving bond in the midst of such cacophony? Couples presenting for treatment are often beset by the competing pulls of relatives, children, memories of dead parents, and imagined affairs. Too often the grip of inertia, income, or fear serves as the glue that keeps people together, with love relegated to infrequent encounters. The recursive nature of human interaction produces an ever-narrowing pattern of behavior within the relationship as each person accommodates to the ever-more predictable moves of the other. What cannot be mutually accommodated becomes distilled into an exquisitely refined conflict that periodically escalates in predictable, even scripted, form and ends in the tears, the slammed door, the separate beds, or the night drive, followed by the silence or politeness or the occasional apology at the next morning's ceasefire.

Couples therapy can help identify and sometimes sort out these forces that weaken the relationship. In the case where one or both members of the couple have experienced psychological trauma, couples work can be especially rewarding, since unlike many influences which are known to the couple, trauma has a way of remaining hidden, denied, and unattended to. The revelation of its profound influence on the couples' conflicts can liberate new resources to deal with their troubles, as well as produce a powerful basis for intimacy between them. Nothing separates like trauma, for trauma is a nothingness that eats away at experience; it is a strange attractor that draws individuals inward away from the increasing chaos of their everyday life. Worse in its intangibility than an affair, the trauma is a shadowy third in the couples' milieu; it continues to haunt their every action despite their collusive attempts to unname it, undo it, and unlive it.

This chapter will present a model of treatment for couples in which one or both partners have experienced a traumatic event either before or during their relationship, and either known or unknown to the other member of the couple. This model, critical interaction therapy, was initially developed with Vietnam veterans and their spouses (Johnson, Feldman, & Lubin, 1995) but has since been adapted in work with all forms of trauma.

TRIANGULATION WITH A SHADOW

The central concept of this model is that the couple has established a triangulated relationship with a person associated with the traumatic event, even if that person is unknown to one member of the couple. Triangulation is generally understood as a familial relationship pattern in which a couple manages its conflicts through a third party (usually one of their children) who may appear to be more attached to one member of the couple but actually serves to communicate with the other member (Bowen, 1978). The triangulated member is required for the successful maintenance of the couple's relationship, often interfering with their personal development and individuation. In cases of severe conflict, the triangulated member may develop symptoms and become an identified patient who is brought in for counseling. It is important to note that all three members collude with each other to maintain the triangulation. Most family dynamics are structured by these overlapping triangulations across generations (Roberto, 1992).

We have found that when one or both members of the couple have been traumatized, the couple develops a triangulated relationship with the shadow presence of a person associated with the traumatic event. While it is understandable that the traumatized person remains vulnerable to the influence of the traumatic event and may remain attached to the memory of the people involved in the event, that still does not explain how these shadows become entangled in the couple's relationship.

In the midst of a traumatic event, the individual is beset by horrendous fear; the person's very survival is at stake. It is this intensity of the trauma experience that allows for such deep insertion of the traumatic situation into the person's self schemas and memory. Other individuals associated with the event, especially the perpetrator, are inserted into the survivor's psychic core, albeit in disguised or distorted form. Sensory clues—the closeness, sweat, eyes, smell, and weight—associated with the enemy soldier in hand-to-hand combat, the rapist in the dark of night, the hands of the batterer around one's neck, and the sound of the child run over by the automobile all form images inside the victim in the most intimate way. Even the most passionate sex with one's spouse cannot come close to the intensity of traumatic experience. In terms of intimacy, marriage pales before trauma. Thus, the victims maintain a powerful relationship to the events and people associated with their trauma, and these may be present in their minds on a daily basis.

SHATTERING THE INTERPERSONAL BRIDGE

The interpersonal bridge refers to the assumption that we are in contact with each other, that there is a mode of communication between us, and that we both have agreed to this (Kaufman, 1980). What makes two individuals a couple is an illusory agreement that they are together. It is a specific element of the general social contract. That such an interpersonal contract is assumptive or illusory is revealed by trauma which shatters this bridge, throwing the persons into terror and a nothingness from which they will take a long time to return. Janoff-Bulman (1992) notes our "assumptive world ... developed over time, that provides us with expectations about the world and ourselves ... that reflect and guide our interactions in the world and generally enable us to function effectively" (p. 5). She defines trauma as the shattering of these assumptions. It is exactly this experience of losing one's world that leads the victim to grab onto elements of the traumatic situation so tightly.

Interestingly, Kaufman (1980) has noted that, in addition to trauma, one other more common condition breaks the interpersonal bridge—shame. "The interpersonal bridge is built upon certain expectations which we have come to accept and to depend upon. ... Shame is likely whenever our most basic expectations of a significant other are suddenly exposed as wrong. To have someone valued unexpectedly betray our trust opens the self inside of us and exposes it to view. The anger evidenced is but a mask covering the ruptured self" (Kaufman, 1980, p. 15). The experience of shame separates individuals, isolating them under their own scrutiny; that is why one feels all alone under a spotlight; one averts one's eyes from the other (Lewis, 1992; Wurmser, 1981). "One feels ashamed for *being exposed*, exposed as one who has acted in a way that reflects poorly upon oneself, by treachery, by bedwetting, by being a tattle tale, by having failed in school or life—in short, of failing someone else's expectations or failing the demands of performance by one's own conscience, standing under the glare of one's own mind's eye. To disappear into nothing is the punishment for such failure" (Wurmser, 1987, p. 67).

Many observers have commented on the frequency of shaming attacks between couples. Shaming attacks have been associated with domestic violence (Lansky, 1987), the natural cycle of intimacy–distance within couples (Nathanson, 1987), and unavoidable individual differences between partners (Lewis, 1992). Nearly all couples express their inability to accommodate to each other in the development of repetitive conflicts, where shame is frequently encountered.

DEVELOPMENT OF THE CRITICAL INTERACTION

The model posits that during the course of the couple's interactions, when a core conflict arises, a shaming situation breaks the interpersonal bridge between the couple. For the traumatized member, this break becomes a powerful reminder of the disconnection and shame experienced during the trauma, capable of shifting the attention internally from the spouse to the traumatic event. What produces the link that creates the critical interaction is the similarity of the breaking of the interpersonal bridge in the present with the shattering of the assumptive world during the traumatic event.

An example of this process appears in an article written by Lansky (1987) on shame and domestic violence. Lansky, of course, was not writing from a critical interaction perspective.

Mario: Because Anna seems to have a talent for pushing buttons that make me go. Nobody's been able to get to those buttons before because I always protected them very well. With Anna I'm much more open in that area. I'm much more emotional with her than I ever would get with anybody else. … I know what can set me off. Unfortunately she does too.

Anna: I don't realize it.

Therapist: Well, if you can tell me then she'll have a chance to listen.

Mario: Okay Anna and I, you know, had an affair before my marriage was ended.

Anna: You were separated and divorcing.

Mario: (Silent; becomes flushed.)

Therapist: What happened just now?

Mario: She aggravated me because she stepped in.

Therapist: You look furious at her. Do you feel that way?

Mario: Yes I do. She stepped in. She stepped all over what I was trying to say. She's broken a train of thought.

Therapist: Is that typical of what goes on between the two of you?

Mario: Yes, very much so.

[The therapist asks more about this interaction, and then asks Mario if this has been a problem in the past. Mario immediately speaks about his father, a Marine drill sergeant, who had humiliated him severely as a child.]

Mario: He'd come in in the middle of the afternoon and say, "Well, we're going down to the Post." I'd say, "Well, let me change clothes." He'd say, "No, no, that's what you're wearing, wear it, go on." He made me feel like an idiot. ... I got so that in school I'd take a piece of paper out of a notebook, and if it had a speck of dirt on it I'd throw it away because it wasn't neat enough, and that's ridiculous. ... (pp. 343–344)

Here we see the repetitive conflict, the shaming comment, the emotional withdrawal (picked up by the therapist), and certain evidence that he was thinking about his past emotional neglect and possible physical abuse. (Mario's comments about being "stepped all over" and "broken train" suggest a possible link to abuse by the father in Mario's childhood.)

Ironically, even though a horrible situation and the shame of being victimized are revived, there is also a revived attachment to the people associated with the trauma. Since the present is experienced as harsh and demanding (the critical spouse, the anger, and the relational cutoff), the past actually appears less demanding; it is filled with the now-familiar spirits and the well-known chronology. It may even have a solacing effect. The survivor reaches out to them, just as he or she reached out during that disorienting fall into nothingness so long ago.

Over time, the traumatized member of the couple increasingly associates the repetitive relational conflicts with the trauma, and his or her behavior is subtly shaped by these associations. Because of their solacing function, these associations provide short-term value; they help the couple to get through the conflict with withdrawal rather than violence. However, the long-term effect is that the couple fails to resolve the conflict. The other effect of the repetitive nature of this process is that the nontraumatized member of the couple is subtly influenced to match the behavior evoked by the traumatic schema with ever-greater precision. Thus, the repetitive conflict increasingly takes on aspects of the trauma.

This repetitive conflict, infiltrated with the traumatic residue, is the *critical interaction*. The critical interaction is thus an attempt by the couple, however dysfunctional, to bring together and integrate the family reality with a disturbing historical event. Like many symptoms, it is a compromise formation, a story encapsulating a double entendre. It is an attempt both to symbolize the traumatic experience within the couple's interaction and to avoid awareness of the trauma. Unfortunately, this lack of recognition does not allow for a working through or mourning of the past. The present remains conflictual while the past increasingly takes on a solacing quality. The other member of the couple unknowingly becomes shaped by the traumatic material and develops a relationship with the shadow in the service of managing the conflict with the spouse. The result is that the memory remains unmourned and unacknowledged, the partners each feel misunderstood, shamed, and enraged, and effective communication ends since neither person can listen without reacting defensively.

The critical interaction sequence follows these steps:

1. Core conflict with spouse
2. Shaming attack by one or both
3. Turning attention away from spouse onto memory
4. Withdrawal by victimized member
5. Either (a) withdrawal by spouse (in disgust or victory) and communication ends, or (b) withdrawal challenged by spouse (in anger), leading to rage and violence, and then communication ends
6. Further consolidation of each person's inner narrative as shaped by the interaction
7. Eventual repetition of conflict

When the traumatized partner[1] withdraws, the shaming spouse often also withdraws, though with a mixture of disgust and victory, and leaves the partner to stew in the shame. However, sometimes the argument touches off a different response in the nontraumatized spouse. If they sense the breaking of the interpersonal bridge and the inner attachment of their partner to something else, the nontraumatized spouse may try to reestablish the connection, usually by not allowing the withdrawal to

---

1. The traumatized partner is the one whose trauma is activated in the particular interaction. Since both partners may be trauma survivors, the role of traumatized partner and spouse may change from interaction to interaction. Indeed, in some interactions involving two trauma survivors, it is possible for each partner to play both roles; that is, both experiencing the activation of their own trauma schemata and behaving in such a fashion (e.g., shaming) as to stimulate the partner's trauma schemata.

continue. "Speak to me!" and "Don't ignore me!" usually will be followed by a physical withdrawal by the traumatized partner into another room. If the spouse follows and moves too close, the withdrawing member, unable to maintain the avoidant stance, explodes in rage and a violent interaction is the usual result. In either case, effective communication ends, a period of distance ensues, followed by a resumption of normal interaction, and the eventual return of the core conflict in another guise, precipitated by another glitch in the flow of daily life.

UNDERSTANDING SECONDARY TRAUMATIZATION

This model provides a basis for understanding the mechanism of *secondary traumatization*, in which members of a victim's family develop stress reactions and may even have thoughts that contain traumatic material that was never verbalized to them (Harkness, 1993; Herndon & Law, 1986; Jurich, 1983; Kishur & Figley, 1987). This phenomenon has been adequately described in several trauma populations, but its mechanism of action has not been detailed (Figley, 1989). It is proposed that this process involves triangulation with a shadow; that is, the family members' behaviors have been subtly shaped by the inner attachment of the victim to the traumatic schemas. In the midst of shame-evoking family conflicts, relational elements of the trauma are covertly communicated to the family members. The demands of the critical interaction result in progressive approximations of the traumatic scenario, eventually evoking behaviors and imagery in the family members that parallel those experienced during the trauma. This process is sometimes so powerful that later, during treatment, when the spouse does hear about the relevant traumatic event, a paradoxical feeling of familiarity, or déjà vu, is evoked, as though they had already been there. In a way, they had.

TREATMENT MODEL

The purpose of the critical interaction approach is (a) to bring to light the underlying traumatic memories of the traumatized partner, (b) to allow the spouse to engage in the role of witness to the traumatized partner's mourning, (c) to help the traumatized partner differentiate the past from the present, (d) to engage the spouse in the role of caretaker, and (e) to help the couple problem-solve and practice better communication. The treatment of the triangulated relationship involves opening the barricade between the spouse and the lost love objects. The aim is to establish a mutually held representation of their situation that integrates past and present. The basic principles include the balanced attention to the spouse's needs for support, utilization of physical comforting during the sharing of the traumatic material, and education of the couple about the dysfunctional process.

This method was devised to circumvent the need to meet individually with the victimized member of the couple to prepare them to reveal their traumatic experience, as suggested by previous writers (Rosenheck & Thomson, 1986; Williams & Williams, 1985). This method is not designed merely to reveal and allow the traumatized partner to process the trauma but to disentangle the couple from the covert traumatic schema.

Indication. Critical interaction work is indicated when the therapist senses that recurrent conflicts between the couple are being influenced by prior traumatic experiences. The method is appropriate whether or not the spouse has been told of the victimized partner's trauma, and whether or not the couple experienced the same traumatic event.

Timing. Theoretically, working with critical interaction can take place during any session within the treatment sequence. Usually, several sessions are required to make initial assessments, develop treatment goals, and collect enough background information, particularly about prior traumatic events. The method can be easily integrated into any family therapy approach being used by the clinician.

Contraindications. Generally, critical interaction therapy is appropriate when the couple is motivated to remain together. If separating or divorcing, or when there is a serious affair, the spouse may use the opportunity (in listening to the trauma story) to disrupt the relationship further through humiliating or denigrating comments. The therapist should be relatively confident that the spouse will be responsive to the victimized partner before proceeding.

Procedures. The critical interaction therapy process adheres to a specific sequence of interventions that occur in nine steps: (1) free discussion, (2) emergence of the critical interaction, (3) identifying the traumatic memory, (4) establishing the physical connection, (5) reporting the traumatic story, (6) linking trauma with current conflict, (7) checking in with spouse, (8) reviewing the critical interaction sequence, and (9) offering directives.

Critical Interaction Therapy Procedures

Step 1: Free discussion. The emergence of the critical interaction occurs during an interaction between the couple. Depending upon the approach used by a particular clinician, this can be at various points during the session. Nevertheless, we begin our sessions by asking each partner in turn to describe his or her perceptions of the various issues, weekly events, or progress being made, and then asking both partners to talk together about these issues. It is usually during this interaction that their conflicts emerge and eventually move back toward core conflicts. It is therefore important not to intervene early when they may be presenting more workable, surface conflicts so that the more enduring, underlying critical interaction will arise.

Step 2: Emergence of the critical interaction. When the critical interaction occurs, a perceived shaming attack will be followed by a withdrawal by the other partner from the interaction, signaled by an eye shift, pause, or postural shift. The conflict will usually reflect an oft-repeated disagreement in the relationship, yet be accompanied by a relatively high level of tension. The therapist must notice the withdrawal of the partner, which may be quite subtle.

Step 3: Identifying the traumatic memory. The therapist interrupts the dialogue between the partners, inquires about the traumatic memory, and often elicits it from the traumatized partner. The therapist may feel uncomfortable with interrupting, making what may appear to be a nonsequitur comment or distracting the couple from the immediate issue by saying, "What are you thinking about now?" or "Are you thinking about the rape now?" However, overcoming this discomfort is essential. We have been consistently amazed at how often the client will answer in the affirmative and begin saying more about it as if no shift in the conversation had taken place. The therapist should then ask a few questions about the memory to establish the basic setting and events, before proceeding to the next step. This will also allow the assessment of the spouse's initial reaction to hearing about the trauma.

Step 4: Establishing a physical connection. The spouse is asked to physically comfort the traumatized partner by holding both hands of the partners and looking into the partner's eyes. Holding only one hand is usually not sufficient enough of a connection, and hugging prevents eye contact. If the couple hugs initially, allow it, and then ask them to separate in order to hold hands. The use of a physical connection is an essential element of this process. We have found that spouses who do not physically touch the traumatized partner by holding hands often maintain an emotionally distanced, shut-off stance that the traumatized partner mirrors and responds to by becoming more vague in his or her reporting of the trauma. We have been impressed by the lack of physical intimacy and ability to provide physical comfort among these couples—a consequence of years of defensive withdrawal and fear of emotional expression. For some couples, holding hands may be extremely awkward (reflecting their alienation), but it is best to persevere through any resistance and work with them until a level of comfort is achieved. Nonverbal connection between couples appears to facilitate a rapid transfer of emotional states and provides a concrete demonstration of support to the traumatized partner. The result is often a burst of emotion and grieving from the traumatized partner who then clings to the spouse, who responds less defensively and with more caring.

Step 5: Reporting the traumatic memory. The traumatized partner is asked to tell his or her story to the spouse in detail, allowing them to grieve together. Sometimes the story just comes out on its own, with little need for direction from the therapist. Often, encouraging and inquiring comments from the therapist allow a fuller reporting of the events and feelings that occurred to the victimized partner. If the spouse attempts to derail the telling by stating they have already heard it, tell the spouse that he or she may not have heard all of it and direct the spouse to try listening again. This step may be brief or long; the criterion for moving on is when the therapist has enough information to make the link between the traumatized partner's trauma experience and the couple's repetitive conflict.

Step 6: Linking the trauma with the current conflict. Once the story has been told, the therapist allows the couple to let go of their hands or to embrace each other if they wish. The therapist then points out to the couple how the memory is connected to the original repetitive conflict in their relationship. This is done briefly and in just enough detail to clearly communicate to them how past and present have overlapped. Generally, the couple is not asked to respond, and there should not be a long discussion at this point.

Step 7: Checking in with the spouse. The traumatized partner is asked to check in with and comfort the spouse, demonstrating his or her own capacity for solacing. This is usually done with the resumption of holding hands and the statement, "Now I want you to check in with your wife (or husband), and ask her what she felt when you spoke about your experience." Without ensuring a balance of support in the relationship, the therapist may reinforce the dysfunctional role pattern of victim–caretaker which may already characterize their present relationship. The therapist should spend some time helping the traumatized partner inquire about how the spouse felt while listening to the partner, helping the spouse voice his or her own pain and needs, and encouraging the traumatized partner to express concern for the spouse. Often, traumatized partners will feel embarrassed and worried that they have overwhelmed, frightened, or disgusted their spouses. If the spouse does not immediately reassure the partner, he or she can be encouraged to do so. Spouses often exclaim, "I had no idea" or "I didn't realize how upsetting this still was for you."

Step 8: Reviewing the critical interaction sequence. Following the conclusion of the interaction, the therapist reviews the entire sequence and identifies the behaviors of each partner. The couple is again allowed to let go of their hands, while the therapist educates them about how their recurrent conflict triggers the link to the trauma and how that prevents effective problem-solving around the issue. The therapist underscores that the traumatic experience does not serve as an excuse for the trauma-tized partner's behavior; it is simply the reason the conflict cannot be resolved. The therapist determines the amount of time required and the style of presentation based on the couple's dynamics, the treatment goals, and other factors specific to the situation.

Step 9: Offering directives. In the final step in the sequence, the therapist gives directives to the couple—prescribing time for further retellings of the story and directives for interrupting the flow of future critical interac-tions and arguments. It is usually helpful for the traumatic story to be retold several more times; this helps the couple externalize it and desen-sitizes them to its previous secrecy. Avoidance is to be expected; there-fore, setting a specific (but limited) time during the week for further retelling is usually necessary. It is helpful to instruct the couple as to how to derail future critical interactions. This protective process includes (a) knowing what the critical interaction is so that it can be labeled when it arises, and (b) knowing what to do if it progresses to the withdrawal point; that is, the spouses can be directed to ask if the clients are thinking about their trauma and to listen to them. (One couple rapidly detoxified their frequent arguments by playfully shouting, "Oh, no, it's that thing again!" and giggling together.) We have found the sequence of steps listed above to be reliably effective. The following are three case examples using critical interaction therapy.

CASE EXAMPLES

Childhood Sexual Abuse

Susan and Michael were in their thirties with two small children. He was a workaholic manager in a large company, and a very affectionate man. She was from an enmeshed and conflictual Italian family that was in constant turmoil. The referral for couples treatment occurred after Susan found a videotape in their machine that showed a female neighbor undressing in her bedroom, filmed from outside the house. The film was obviously made on someone's home video camera. When confronted, Michael admitted to having taped it but denied having an affair.

The initial couples therapy sessions addressed this incident, their over-all relationship, and difficulties they were having with Susan's extended family. They demonstrated a repetitive conflict in which Susan criticized his working too much and his seeking recognition within his company, and then coming home and wanting to be admired. Michael would take offense at this and declare how hard he was working for his family, espe-cially for his demanding wife who wanted many material possessions and beautiful clothing which he "couldn't care about." During the course of these sessions, Michael revealed that something had happened in his childhood that bore on the videotape incident, and he had told Susan about it. Susan reported that he had told her that he had been "played with" by three older boys in his extended family. The therapist asked if she knew any more about it, and she said no. Michael said he did not want to go into it any more, and Susan sarcastically commented that she did not want to hear some "lame excuse" for his bad behavior, though "he'd better deal with it in his own therapy."

During the fourth session, the critical interaction was explored:

Michael: I feel under a lot of pressure at work, where they want me there all the time, and at home with you and the kids. [Step 1: Free discussion]

Susan: But you have said the same thing for years.

Michael: And you make the same critical remarks, like last weekend when you again mentioned that you wish we could afford better things.

Susan: I don't want to be seen in rags.

Michael: You're not in rags, besides I don't care about those things.

Susan: [Sarcastically] Oh well, it doesn't seem to stop you from prancing around in front of the girls at the office! [Shaming attack]

Michael: [Shifts his eyes downward, is silent.] [Step 2: Emergence of the critical interaction] [Pause]

Susan: Not that I don't appreciate how hard you are working, but …

Therapist: Michael, what are you thinking about now?

Michael: Nothing important.

Therapist: Are you thinking about the incident in your childhood?

Michael: [Pause] Yeah.

Therapist: Susan, Michael has been drawn toward the abuse he suffered as a child, and if it is okay with you, I'd like you to listen to him tell you about it in more detail. [Step 3: Identifying the traumatic memory]

Susan: I guess so.

Therapist: Can you reach over and hold his hands—yes, both of them. I just want you to listen to him and watch him as he talks about it. [Step 4: Establishing physical connection]

Susan: All right.

Therapist: Michael, I want you to describe to Susan what it is that you are seeing in your mind right now. Go ahead. [Step 5: Reporting the trauma story]

Michael: [With great difficulty, and increasing sadness] I am dancing. I am 7 years old, and my older two brothers and their two friends, maybe they were 14 or 15, were sitting on an old sofa in our basement. They are egging me on … [he pulls his hands away from Susan].

Therapist: Susan, don't let him let go of you. Continue, Michael.

Michael: [Bursting into tears] I am naked. They're making fun of my genitals. They are laughing at me.

Therapist: What are they doing?

Michael: Two of them are masturbating. Later, one of them sat on me, and … [heaving sigh] came all over my behind. The others applauded. I feel so disgusted! [He now grabs Susan's hands very tightly, and Susan is now tearful].

Therapist: Michael, you are doing fine. You haven't told Susan the details of this sad story. Now is the time to tell her, as much as you can.

Michael: Sometimes they punched me or spanked me, but most of the time I had to do a show for them … [very upset] and sometimes I did …

Susan: What did you do, honey? You can tell me.

Michael: I'd play with my penis, I'd do disgusting things. I just didn't want to get beat again.

Susan: That was awful.

Therapist: What else should Susan know?

Michael: One time they left me there and they took my clothes and locked the basement door, so I had to go outside and around the house to get in, only they locked the front door, too, so I had to ring the doorbell and beg them to let me in. I was on the porch, naked. I felt so frightened and humiliated!

Susan: They were sick.

Michael: They were my brothers. [Breaks down] I didn't know what to do … [Susan moves over to hug him and he cries into her shoulder for a few minutes].

Therapist: Michael, that took courage to share, for the events you describe were truly horrible, and I am sure that these memories have been a constant burden on you. Susan, perhaps you can see how Michael turned toward this memory when you made the comment about his "prancing around at work," and the two of you got into your typical argument about the importance of clothing. [Step 6: Linking trauma with current conflict]

Susan: Yes, I see that.

Therapist: Michael, I'd like you to hold Susan's hands now, and ask her how she felt in hearing your story. Check in with her. [Step 7: Checking-in with spouse]

Michael: Are you okay?

Susan: Yes, I am, honey.

Michael: You're not disgusted by me? I didn't want to tell you because I know how upset you'll be.

Susan: I am not disgusted by you. I feel so sad for you that you have had to deal with this. I had no idea it was this bad.

Michael: You probably think I'm just trying to make excuses for the video-taping.

Susan: You know how upsetting that was. But now I understand what was going on. Maybe now you can get some help for this. Maybe now we can get some help.

Michael: I love you, you know.

Susan: I love you too. [He moves over to embrace her.]

Michael: I can't believe you were able to listen to all that.

Therapist: Well, she did, Michael. And I agree with her that now it is possible to begin to work on this. So let me review what has happened here. Michael's memories of his childhood experiences weigh him down all the time. He has been trying to forget them and suppress them, and recently they have reemerged in his need to videotape. But Susan, by leaving the tape in the recorder, he unconsciously wanted you to know. You have known about his trauma through his behavior, without knowing why. Now you know why. Each time the two of you get into one of your old arguments, it tends to kick off these memories for Michael. The arguments are about the value of clothes, about being admired and prancing around, about making demands, about being locked out of the house, all themes that parallel Michael's abuse from so long ago. This is the way trauma tries to be heard. Of course, this does not excuse Michael's behavior, and he needs to deal with it in his own therapy. Any questions? [Step 8: Reviewing the critical interaction sequence]

Susan: I feel better that I know more about what happened. Those kids were cruel.

Therapist: They were. Now this week, I'd like the two of you to try something. When you have one of your arguments, and of course you still will, I'd like you to try something different, just this week. Susan, when you see Michael withdraw into himself just like he did here, I'd like you to stop and go into another room, to give the two of you a breather, for maybe 10 minutes. After that, you are free to resume the argument. How about that? [Step 9: Offering directives]

Susan: I guess I can try to do that.

Therapist: Susan, it is critical that the two of you practice this, so it is essential that you have one of your arguments. Is that a promise?

Susan: A promise.

Therapist: And Michael, I'd like you to do something. Once this week, when the two of you are alone, I want you to spend 15 minutes, no more, in telling Susan the story again, and I want you to answer any of Susan's questions about it. Just once. Okay?

Michael: It can't be worse than it was today.

Therapist: Great. See you next week.

Discussion. Susan's knowledge about Michael's childhood trauma was insufficient for her to fully understand the magnitude of its effect on his current behavior. Such minimization is common around trauma, as are the avoidance and displacement evident in Michael's coping strategies.

The dynamics of his voyeurism and her needs for attention interacted to form repetitive conflicts that served to alienate them from each other. As their connection became more conflictual, each resorted to separate strategies even more, which in turn intensified the conflict and led to Michael's acting-out (and call for help) with the videotape. The critical interaction work allowed Michael to communicate the trauma to Susan, revealed her continued commitment to him, and thus facilitated a healing process that moved toward forgiveness and collaboration. The couples therapy transformed the trauma from a covert shadow within Michael to a common challenge shared by both of them; the triangulated relationship loosened.

Physical Assault of a Couple

In the following case, both members of the couple experienced the same traumatic incident in which a burglar entered their apartment bedroom at night and proceeded to attack them with a knife, stabbing Bob nearly to death in his bed and striking Ramona in the face. At one point during the 10 min attack, Ramona had run into the apartment hallway to escape, the door closed and locked behind her. She sat for several minutes against this door, hearing her husband struggling with the perpetrator.

Eight years later, they came for couples treatment, each having been in separate trauma-based treatments. They came to work out some current conflicts. When asked about their trauma, they both acknowledged it and said they had been working on it in their therapies, and because they had gone through it together, it was not an issue between them. The couple's view that the shared trauma was not an issue in their current relationship was unlikely to be accurate. Though they did share the same traumatic event on one level, each of them was deeply alone in the midst of it, and each must have had an entirely unique experience of those 10 horrible minutes. It is best to assume that each had his or her own separate trauma.

In the critical interaction work with this couple, each one was given an opportunity to tell his or her story to the other, which at first they resisted because they "already know it." What emerged, of course, were two deeply distinct stories, each story communicating the terror of being alone. Ramona had felt enraged that the door had locked behind her and thought that the perpetrator had locked it. She felt she had abandoned her husband to die and was overwhelmed with a feeling of helplessness. Bob, on the other hand, felt he was keeping the attacker from her, but he did not know whether she had escaped unharmed or was lying in the next room dying. He purposefully did not cry out, though he was being stabbed numerous times, because he was afraid that she would return and the attacker would kill her.

Their current conflict that had brought them into therapy was her complaint that he was emotionally unavailable and uninterested in talking to her about his new job. She felt "locked out" of his inner world. He was angered by her recent brief hospitalizations in which she had a combination of depressive and somatic symptoms. He derisively termed these as "her pitiful calls for help," and felt she simply was being hysterical. Neither one had made the connections between these conflicts and his or her traumatic experiences. As they descended into their critical interaction, the feelings of being "locked out" and "calling for help" drew each one back into the past, preventing the possibility of any rational attempt at solving the current conflict.

Despite years of good trauma-based individual treatment, Bob and Ramona were surprised at how their current interactions had been infused by their specific experiences of that terrifying night. Over the course of the couples therapy, numerous conflicts were identified as being triggered by her helplessness over being locked out of his thoughts and his fears that calling for help would bring disaster. Both reactions, it turned out, were motivated by love of each other, and as they rediscovered this, their relationship improved significantly.

Combat Trauma

Roger and Sylvia had a unique arrangement. They had both divorced their previous spouses in order to be with each other. Sylvia had become pregnant with their child prior to the finalization of their divorces. She allowed her former husband to stay in her house until the day she went into the hospital to deliver the baby. Roger had moved into his mother's apartment, supposedly on a temporary basis. After the baby was born, Sylvia did not want Roger to move into the house immediately, and later revealed that she was allowing her former husband to visit the house during the day to walk the dog since he "loved it so much." She was worried about his mental fragility and felt guilty because she had initiated the divorce. Roger responded compliantly, though he was anxious to move in. This situation continued for many months. As could be expected, they began to argue about this arrangement and it quickly became an ongoing, repetitive conflict. Sylvia felt she was not yet ready for a more intimate commitment; Roger accused her of not loving him, which she denied. When she would go out to visit friends, she did allow him to babysit their daughter alone. Roger's friends and family told him she was crazy and just using him for financial support, and that he needed to move on. He agreed with their assessment but was unable to move on. Both had been seeing individual therapists for several years. Eventually, they agreed to come to couples treatment to work on their impasse.

During the critical interaction work, Roger was able to make the connection between his inability to move on and a prior trauma from his Vietnam war experience. His unit had been based near a village for some months. As the medic, Roger had been in charge of distributing food and other supplies to the children, and he had become quite fond of them. One day, his unit was attacked by a large enemy force. They were required to retreat and call in an air strike. The enemy advanced into the nearby village and held the villagers hostage. As Roger's unit watched from a distant hilltop, the airstrike came and destroyed the entire village, presumably killing some or all of the children. Roger was ordered not to return, and his unit was pulled back from the region. He never knew if any of the children survived.

Each time Roger and Sylvia got into an argument about moving in or breaking up, Roger was faced with the issue of leaving his daughter behind and having the other husband "move back in," thus repeating his traumatic experience. They now understood why he had become so immobilized. On the basis of this work, Roger decided he would wait for Sylvia to decide to commit to the relationship, "since now no one is ordering me to pull back; well, my mother is, but now I don't have to comply like I did in Nam." When Sylvia saw that Roger was willing to wait for her, she came to understand how important it was for Roger to move in and reconstitute a family. This reduced her mistrust, and she committed herself to work toward having him move in, and she no longer allowed her former husband to visit the house.

CONCLUSION

Critical interaction therapy is a method that can be used to facilitate the untangling of traumatic schemas from current conflicts in couples' relationships. As a technique, it can be readily integrated within ongoing couples therapy when the need arises. The method is based on a conceptual proposition that traumatized couples have established a triangulated relationship with people associated with the trauma, and that this link is outside their awareness. Over time, the traumatic schema becomes a formula that is recursively applied to their interactions, progressively altering the interactions to reflect aspects of the trauma. The collusive and covert nature of the critical interaction prevents successful problem-solving, interferes with standard treatment interventions, and maintains the repetitive cycle.

The method is based on concepts of trauma theory related to secondary traumatization and is not merely the application of an existing family therapy approach to traumatized clients. Though it includes elements of psychoeducational, experiential, and strategic family therapy, critical interaction therapy specifically targets distortions and impasses in the couple's relationship that are due to prior traumatic events. As more experience with this method is gained, we hope that further insights and modifications will be incorporated.

ACKNOWLEDGMENTS

The author expresses his appreciation to Susan Feldman, M.S.W., whose clinical work originated the critical interaction approach, and to Hadar Lubin, M.D., the other member of the family research team at the National Center for PTSD, Veterans Affairs Medical Center, West Haven, Connecticut.

REFERENCES

Bowen, M. (1978). *Family therapy in clinical practice.* New York: Jason Aronson.

Figley, C. (1989). *Helping traumatized families.* San Francisco: Jossey-Bass.

Harkness, L. (1993). Transgenerational transmission of war-related trauma. In J. P. Wilson & B. Raphael (Eds.), *The international handbook of traumatic stress syndromes* (pp. 635–644). New York: Plenum.

Herndon, A., & Law, J. (1986). Post-traumatic stress and the family: A multimethod approach to counseling. In C. Figley (Ed.), *Trauma and its wake,* Vol. 2 (pp. 264–279). New York: Brunner/Mazel.

Janoff-Bulman, R. (1992). *Shattered assumptions: Towards a new psychology of trauma.* New York: Free Press.

Johnson, D., Feldman, S., & Lubin, H. (1995). Critical Interaction Therapy: Couples therapy in combat-related posttraumatic stress disorder. *Family Process, 34,* 401–412.

Jurich, A. (1983). The Saigon of the family's mind: Family therapy with families of Vietnam veterans. *Journal of Marital and Family Therapy, 9,* 355–363.

Kaufman, G. (1980). *Shame: The power of caring.* Cambridge, MA: Schenkman.

Kishur, G., & Figley, C. (1987). *The relationship between psychiatric symptoms of crime victims and their supporters: Evidence of the chiasmal effects of co-victimization.* Unpublished manuscript, Purdue University, West Lafayette, Indiana.

Lansky, M. (1987). Shame and domestic violence. In D. L. Nathanson (Ed.), *The many faces of shame* (pp. 335–362). New York: Guilford.

Lewis, M. (1992). *Shame: The exposed self.* New York: Free Press.

Nathanson, D. L. (Ed.) (1987). *The many faces of shame.* New York: Guilford.

Roberto, L. G. (1992). *Transgenerational family therapies.* New York: Guilford.

Rosenheck, R., & Thomson, J. (1986). Detoxification of Vietnam war trauma: A combined family-individual approach. *Family Process, 25,* 559–569.

Williams, C. M., & Williams, T. (1985). Family therapy for Vietnam veterans. In S. Sonnenberg, A. Blank, & J. Talbot (Eds.), *The trauma of war: Stress and recovery in Vietnam veterans* (pp. 193–210). Washington, DC: American Psychiatric Press.

Wurmser, L. (1981). *The mask of shame.* Baltimore, MD: Johns Hopkins University Press.
Wurmser, L. (1987). Shame: The veiled companion of narcissism. In D. L. Nathanson (Ed.), *The many faces of shame* (pp. 64–92). New York: Guilford.

25

Acceptance and Commitment Therapy for Sexual Abuse Survivor Couples

MANDRA L. RASMUSSEN HALL AND
VICTORIA M. FOLLETTE

Researchers in the area of traumatic stress have produced an extensive literature examining the impact of sexual trauma on adult intrapersonal functioning. Though not all women with a history of sexual trauma experience problems later in life (Rind, Bauserman, & Tromovitch, 1998), studies indicate that adults who have histories of child sexual abuse and adolescent or adult sexual assault report a wide range of individual problems more often than adults without such histories. These problems, usually described as long-term correlates of sexual trauma, include posttraumatic stress disorder (PTSD) symptomatology, depression, anxiety, substance abuse, self-injury, dissociation, eating disorders, and physical health complaints (for reviews, see Browne & Finkelhor, 1986; Polusny & Follette, 1995).

Fewer studies have systematically investigated the long-term interpersonal correlates of sexual trauma (DiLillo, 2001), but relationship distress has been identified in the clinical and empirical literature as a significant problem among many survivors of sexual trauma (e.g., Briere, 1992; Davis & Petretic-Jackson, 2000; DiLillo, 2001; Polusny & Follette, 1995). Researchers have suggested that a history of child sexual abuse

(CSA) can have a significant negative effect on adult couple functioning (e.g., Briere, 1992; Briere & Runtz, 1991; Johnson, 1989). Couples in which one partner is a survivor of CSA commonly report problems in social and relationship adjustment, emotional expressiveness and intimacy, physical violence and revictimization, and sexual dysfunction (Compton & Follette, 1998; for reviews, see Davis & Petretic-Jackson, 2000; DiLillo, 2001).

Despite these findings, the couple treatment literature suggests that couples in which one partner is a survivor of sexual trauma may not benefit from traditional behavioral couple therapy (Epstein & Baucom, 1988; Jacobson & Margolin, 1979; Stuart, 1980), a well-established, empirically supported approach to couples treatment (Hahlweg & Markman, 1988). Some researchers have argued that traditional behavioral couple therapy may be limited in its emphasis on current relationship functioning as opposed to a more contextual understanding of the couple (Jacobson & Holtzworth-Munroe, 1986) that includes a balance between acceptance and change (Jacobson & Christensen, 1996). This chapter will describe the theory and rationale for a contextual behavioral conceptualization of treatment for trauma in the context of the couple and will provide a thorough overview of an acceptance-based behavioral treatment approach to couple therapy for sexual abuse survivors.[1]

TREATMENT THEORY, RATIONALE, AND OVERVIEW

A theoretical framework is essential in the development and effective delivery of any treatment. Theory offers a foundation from which to build, refine, and empirically evaluate treatment, as well as organize, clarify, and understand complex relationships between phenomena. In addition, theory guides the way in which treatment is delivered when confronted with a novel problem or situation (Hayes, Strosahl, & Wilson, 1999). Given the range of problems observed in survivor couples, a coherent theoretical conceptualization of interactions between partners is crucial in order to (a) understand the development and maintenance of problematic behavior patterns and (b) effectively intervene to change those patterns. Without such a theoretical framework, a set of therapeutic techniques may be applied to a broad array of problems with few guiding principles, potentially leading to diluted treatment outcomes.

---

1. The term *survivor couple* will be used to refer to couples in which one partner reports a history of CSA. The treatment principles and examples in this chapter can be applied to same-sex as well as heterosexual couples.

A Contextual Behavioral Perspective

A contextual behavioral approach is one useful way to understand the problems experienced by couples in which one partner is a survivor of sexual abuse. This perspective fosters the examination of individuals and couples in the context of both historical and environmental factors in order to understand how clinically relevant behaviors develop, function, and are maintained. For example, a couple may identify one partner's alcohol use as a problem which they wish to address in treatment. During assessment, the partner reports that she experiences anxiety, guilt, and flashbacks about her abuse whenever her husband shows affection toward her, and that she drinks in order to be able to have sex with her husband. Further assessment reveals that the partner's husband displays less affection and interest in sex for two or three days after sexual intercourse, while the partner reports a decrease in flashbacks and unpleasant emotion.

From a contextual behavioral perspective, the therapist can understand the partner's drinking behavior both historically and environmentally. Current sexual advances may serve as a trigger for the survivor partner's flashbacks and subsequent feelings of fear and guilt. Her drinking may have developed as a short-term strategy for escaping these unpleasant memories and feelings and for tolerating sexual intimacy. In addition, participating in sexual intimacy with her husband temporarily reduces her husband's sexual advances and displays of affection, thereby reducing the frequency of her flashbacks, fear, and guilt. In other words, the partner's drinking behavior has become negatively reinforced over time by both the temporary reduction of pressure for sexual intimacy in the relationship and the alleviation of painful memories and feelings related to her abuse history.

This conceptualization of the partner's drinking behavior provides the therapist with a more informed understanding of how the problem functions currently and historically, allowing the therapist to intervene more precisely than if the behavior were treated as an individual problem outside the context of the relationship. Hayes, Wilson, Gifford, Follette, and Strosahl (1996) have suggested that functional classification of psychopathology is superior to a more traditional syndromal approach because it increases identification of underlying change processes and strengthens treatment utility. Understanding topographically different collections of symptoms as behaviors that have functional similarity may yield powerful implications for treatment by providing clinicians with clear targets for change (Hayes et al., 1996). This approach allows for the treatment of specified behaviors in context (e.g., hypervigilance; attempts to avoid specific thoughts, feelings, or activities; detachment from others) rather than the amelioration of collections of symptoms (e.g., posttraumatic stress disorder).

Experiential Avoidance, Trauma, and the Couple

The theory of experiential avoidance has been described as one such functional diagnostic dimension that may organize the topographies of several different forms of psychopathology, including substance abuse, anxiety disorders, obsessive–compulsive disorder, and posttraumatic stress disorder (Hayes et al., 1996). Hayes et al. (1996) suggest that the different characteristic behaviors of these disorders may actually function similarly to eliminate or reduce the frequency of unpleasant private experiences. For example, obsessive–compulsive disorder is defined by repeated behavioral efforts to alleviate or escape distressing obsessive thoughts; agoraphobia involves overt efforts to avoid symptoms of panic, and posttraumatic stress disorder includes attempts to avoid both private and external trauma cues.

Hayes et al. (1996) describe experiential avoidance as "the phenomenon that occurs when a person is unwilling to remain in contact with particular private experiences (e.g., bodily sensations, emotions, thoughts, and memories, behavioral predispositions) and takes steps to alter the form or frequency of these events and the contexts that occasion them" (p. 1154). In its more extreme forms, experiential avoidance is the unhealthy effort to escape, avoid, or control thoughts, emotions, memories, and other private experiences.

Experiential avoidance is one way of functionally conceptualizing the broad range of individual problems and relationship difficulties associated with a history of interpersonal victimization (Hayes et al., 1996; Polusny & Follette, 1995). Polusny and Follette (1995) have hypothesized that women with a history of interpersonal trauma may seek to avoid or escape negative private events such as distressing thoughts and feelings about their trauma histories by engaging in such behaviors as dissociation, substance abuse, and self-injury. While these behaviors may provide survivors of CSA with short-term relief from negative internal events, such behaviors may eventually lead to many of the other long-term correlates of interpersonal trauma discussed in the literature, particularly relationship distress. CSA survivors often report relationship dissatisfaction (e.g., Briere, 1988; Russell, 1986), difficulties trusting others (Briere, 1992; Herman, 1992), sexual dysfunction (e.g., Briere, 1992; Polusny & Follette, 1995), and revictimization (e.g., Herman, 1992; Polusny & Follette, 1995).

For survivors of CSA, the context of the relationship may serve as a cue or stimulus for unpleasant private events (e.g., memories, feelings, physical sensations) leading to subsequent efforts to escape those events. These escape efforts are then reinforced by the temporary relief of those unpleasant internal experiences, yet they also produce significant costs to the relationship. For example, a display of affection by the survivor's partner may trigger memories of the abuse and intense feelings of shame or fear. She may then dissociate, thereby eliminating these memories and feelings in the short-term yet distancing herself from her partner in the long-term (Follette & Pistorello, 1995). Because sexual abuse most often occurs in the context of an intimate relationship, interpersonal intimacy may have become associated with invalidation, emotional or physical pain or both, and intrusion. As an adult, interpersonal closeness may then elicit feelings of anxiety, memories of the abuse, and flashbacks, hindering survivors' willingness to trust others and decreasing relationship satisfaction and sexual interest (Pistorello & Follette, 1998). For these reasons, the context of the couple relationship provides a powerful setting in which to address survivors' avoidance of interpersonal closeness and to assist both partners with communication and sexual issues (Follette & Pistorello, 1995).

Treating Individual Issues in the Context of the Couple

Individual and group therapies are common treatment approaches for many of the problems reported by survivors of CSA, but couple therapy may be an effective treatment strategy for addressing both individual issues and problems in interpersonal functioning in survivor couples. Couple therapy has been used successfully to treat both intra- and interpersonal problems for a wide range of individual difficulties (Jacobson, Holtzworth-Munroe, & Schmaling, 1989). A reciprocal relationship has been found between intrapersonal distress and couple functioning when one partner has been diagnosed with individual psychopathology. Couples with a diagnosed partner tend to focus on the diagnosed partner's individual problems while avoiding shared issues in the relationship (Beach, Sandeen, & O'Leary, 1990). In addition, when one partner is depressed, relationship dynamics appears to be a significant factor in the development, maintenance, and treatment of individual distress (e.g., Jacobson, Dobson, Fruzzetti, Schmaling, & Salusky, 1991).

Although empirical investigation of relationship problems and treatment needs in survivor couples is in its infancy, some preliminary findings lend further support for a couple therapy approach to treatment for CSA survivors, particularly when relationship problems are primary. Treatment outcome studies examining group therapy for CSA survivors found that married survivors had smaller treatment gains (Follette, Alexander, & Follette, 1991) and were more likely to drop out of treatment (Fisher, Wine, & Ley, 1993) than unmarried survivors. These studies also found that marital satisfaction was correlated with adjustment at pretreatment (Follette et al., 1991) and that reports of domestic violence and partner objection to therapy were associated with attrition (Fisher et al., 1993). In another study, survivors of CSA reported that involvement of their partners in treatment was critical in addressing relationship problems, sustaining their partners' support, and educating their partners about CSA (Reid, Taylor, & Wampler, 1995). More recently, Saxe and Johnson (1999) found that time-limited group treatment for adult survivors of CSA was less effective in alleviating interpersonal difficulties than in reducing intrapersonal symptomatology.

Traditional behavioral couple therapy seems a logical choice for treating survivor couples, given its well-established reputation as an empirically supported treatment for relationship distress. However, studies show that traditional behavioral couple therapy is less effective for couples who report more severe levels of relationship distress (Baucom & Hoffman, 1986), emotional disengagement and conflict avoidance (Gottman & Krokoff, 1989; Hahlweg, Schindler, Revenstorf, & Brengelmann, 1984), and more traditional and rigid gender roles (Jacobson, Follette, & Pagel, 1986). Survivor couples may be among these treatment nonresponders.

Integrative Couple Therapy (ICT; Jacobson & Christensen, 1996) was developed to address some of the limitations proposed by researchers as explanations for traditional behavioral couple therapy ineffectiveness with these couples. ICT expands the treatment emphasis of traditional behavioral couple therapy to include an understanding of the couple in a broader context with the inclusion of acceptance interventions as a supplement to change-focused treatment strategies. ICT bears a number of similarities to Acceptance and Commitment Therapy (ACT; Hayes et al., 1999) in its emphasis on a behavior analytic conceptualization of problems. In both approaches, assessment and treatment of problematic behaviors are based on a foundation that emphasizes acceptance and change. While a thorough discussion of the distinctions between ACT and ICT is beyond the scope of this chapter, in general, ACT differs from ICT in its use of Relational Frame Theory (Hayes, Barnes-Holmes, & Roche, 2001) as its underlying theoretical framework. ICT was developed specifically for the treatment of relationship distress, while ACT was originally developed as an individual intervention. However, the functional contextual assessment of problematic behaviors is of central importance in ACT, allowing for the coherent application of ACT to relationship problems. The remainder of the chapter describes ACT as it has been adapted for use with distressed survivor couples.

Overview of Acceptance and Commitment Therapy

ACT is a contextual behavioral intervention designed to treat experiential avoidance and foster commitment to behavior change in individuals experiencing a wide range of problems. The principles of

ACT are easily applied to survivor couples in addressing both individual and relationship treatment targets. ACT is founded on the premise that avoidance of private experience plays a significant role in many forms of psychopathology. While the avoidance of private experience is not a new concept and has been identified by clinicians from a number of theoretical perspectives, Hayes and colleagues explain experiential avoidance within a unique behavioral framework (see Hayes et al., 1999 and Hayes et al., 2001).

Avoidance in couples. In part, ACT is based on the idea that human beings take steps to avoid situations or feelings that give rise to unpleasant thoughts, memories, or physical sensations, or engage in efforts to escape such painful private experiences at the time they occur. Although some avoidance of private experience may be necessary for healthy functioning and may in fact serve as effective coping (e.g., taking a walk to distract from work-related stress), routine avoidance of unpleasant private stimuli may result in psychological distress when the avoidance gets in the way of effective living.

The process of experiential avoidance in survivor couples can be seen in the case of an individual who has difficulty engaging intimately with her husband and experiences a variety of aversive private events including feelings of shame, memories of sexual abuse, thoughts associated with feeling shame such as "I'm dirty and worthless," and thoughts related to her memories such as "I can't handle these memories." She may then dissociate, which, in the short-term, distracts her from the abuse memories and reduces the intensity of the shame (experiential avoidance) but in the long-term reduces intimacy with her husband.

Similarly, an individual who has difficulty trusting her partner may experience a set of aversive private events when her partner returns home late from work and she has feelings of fear, memories of betrayal by her perpetrator, thoughts associated with feeling fear such as "He's planning to leave me," and thoughts related to her memories of betrayal and distrust such as "He's just like [perpetrator]." She may then angrily accuse her partner of intending to leave her, lying to her, or not loving her, temporarily escaping or distracting herself from feelings of fear and memories of abuse and betrayal, while engaging in behaviors that function to distance her from her partner. If her partner responds by reassuring her of his commitment or coming home on time the following day, this may only further serve to reinforce her expression of anger in place of the more accurate labeling and expression of fear. In both examples, excessive experiential avoidance by these survivors will likely become a significant barrier to functioning effectively in their lives, especially in their intimate relationships.

Principles of change. ACT treats experiential avoidance by emphasizing experiential acceptance, values clarification, and commitment to behavior change. These goals are achieved through several different types of therapeutic strategies, including metaphors and experiential exercises in session, as well as outside homework assignments. In its most basic form, acceptance involves the experience of difficult thoughts and emotions without attempts to control or eliminate their presence. For survivors of CSA, this might include experiencing abuse memories and associated thoughts and feelings without engaging in efforts to escape them. For partners of survivors, this might involve experiencing feelings of helplessness or fear in response to their partners' histories without engaging in behavior that distances them from their partners. Acceptance of history, self, and others are additional forms of experiential acceptance that are key treatment targets for survivor couples.

Intervening. Commitment to behavior change in accordance with specified values involves challenging the link between aversive private experience and overt behavior rather than the content of the aversive private experience itself. Clients are taught to make behavioral choices on the basis of what will produce valued life changes, rather than on the basis of what emotions or thoughts they may be experiencing. For example, rather than challenging the content of the thought, "I can't handle these memories" by searching for evidence contrary to that thought, the ACT therapist would challenge the client's behavioral response to the thought. The therapist would encourage the client, who usually dissociates in response to the thought, "I can't handle these memories," to observe her private experiences while remaining fully engaged in a given activity with her partner. In other words, the client is pushed to experience directly that she can participate in exchanges with her partner while remembering the abuse, while having thoughts like "I can't handle these memories," and while feeling painful emotions like shame and fear. Over time, clients are shown through direct experience that urges to escape painful thoughts and feelings need not drive their behavior.

A critical component of ACT is assisting clients in identifying and clarifying core values and goals, as well as recognizing barriers to achieving those goals, in several life domains. ACT takes the perspective that treatment success requires a great deal more than symptom reduction. When clients participate in defining their own valued life directions, treatment gains are maintained. In other words, "values can motivate behavior even in the face of tremendous personal adversity" and compared to control or avoidance of private experience, "chosen values provide a far more stable compass reading" (Hayes et al., 1999, p. 204). This strong emphasis on client-defined values and goals is a crucial treatment component in ACT for survivor couples. Not only is it important for partners to clarify their own values, but it is also critical that both partners share in the identification of their values as a couple.

ACT AND THE TREATMENT OF SURVIVOR COUPLES

Assessment

A functional analysis of both relationship and individual factors is crucial to the successful treatment of survivor couples using ACT. In a functional analysis, the context in which behaviors occur is examined in order to understand the relationship between events prior to and immediately following the behavior of interest (Compton and Follette, 1998). This type of assessment allows the therapist to better understand how problem behaviors develop, function, and are maintained. Close attention is paid to categories of behavior that may appear topographically different but serve a similar function either individually or in the relationship.

The major area of interest with survivor couples is (a) whether or not individual partner behaviors serve an avoidance function and (b) how those same behaviors function within the context of the couple. Levels of closeness and emotional expression between partners can be greatly affected by avoidance patterns in the relationship. For example, a couple identifies one partner's bad temper and the other partner's constant nagging as one of their reasons for seeking treatment. During assessment, the therapist discovers an interesting transaction between partners. When one partner raises his voice in response to a request from his wife, she withdraws. The longer she remains quiet in session, the less her husband engages in verbally aggressive behavior. The therapist hypothesizes that the husband's verbal aggression functions to reduce behavior in his wife that he finds unpleasant (nagging), while the wife's withdrawal functions to reduce behavior in her husband that she finds aversive (temper). Over time, this creates decreased intimacy and emotional expression in the relationship, described by the couple as "acting like strangers" and "feeling hostile and resentful" toward each other.

In addition to more overt behaviors, assessment of experiential avoidance with respect to specific private events is also important. Therapists examine how both partners deal with unpleasant thoughts, feelings, or memories and how effectively those strategies are working for them. It is important to recognize that while the CSA survivor's history plays a role in the couple's current relationship functioning, both partners bring to the table a variety of historical variables that may be sources of individual avoidance and that subsequently contribute to their interactions with each other. In the couple described above, each partner's overt behavior (temper and nagging) functions to change the behavior of the other. However, their behavior may also simultaneously function to avoid their own private responses to each other. For example, the husband may experience shame or guilt when his wife makes a request possibly related to events in his history. These unpleasant feelings may be alleviated when he raises his voice and she withdraws. Similarly, she may experience fear or shame when he raises his voice; his temper may trigger thoughts about events in her history. These painful thoughts and feelings may then subside as she withdraws and he stops shouting. Such avoidance of difficult private events on the part of both partners can lead to ineffective communication patterns in the relationship.

Trauma History and Posttraumatic Stress Symptomatology

Although the focus of this chapter is the treatment of survivor couples, therapists are strongly advised to routinely assess for trauma early in treatment and not to make assumptions about partners' histories. This type of assessment is best accomplished during individual interviews as many survivors may be reluctant to discuss traumatic events in the presence of their partners and may even feel hesitant to disclose such information with therapists. Therapists should ask questions about traumatic events openly and directly while recognizing and normalizing any difficult feelings that arise for the client. Once a client has disclosed a traumatic event, further assessment should include a complete understanding of how that event has affected the individual. There is no one constellation of symptoms experienced across survivors of CSA, so it is important that therapists not make assumptions about how a traumatic event has affected a client. An assessment for PTSD may be important to determine whether or not individual treatment is indicated, in addition to couple therapy.

Further assessment of the circumstances surrounding the traumatic event at the time it occurred (e.g., age of onset, frequency, duration, environmental responses, etc.) can help the therapist place the client's current functioning in context. For example, a survivor who received appropriate support in her environment for disclosing abuse as a child may, as an adult, have less difficulty trusting herself and others than a survivor who was blamed for the abuse or instructed to act as if the abuse did not occur. In the latter case, behaviors such as excessive acquiescence or chronic feelings of worthlessness may be easily understood. Therapists should regard thorough trauma assessment as an ongoing process that may span the course of treatment as survivors feel increasing emotional safety with their partners and therapists (Compton & Follette, 1998).

A number of other problems occur at significantly higher rates among sexually abused women compared to nonabused women. These include substance abuse, depression, suicide attempts, self-injurious behavior, and relationship violence (Polusny & Follette, 1995). Assessment of these behaviors should include a thorough exploration of the circumstances surrounding them in order to determine their function.

Individual and couple strengths. While survivor couples certainly present to treatment with a wide range of problems, they also bring with them a variety of strengths that have helped them cope with their difficult and challenging histories. Some survivors of CSA report that their traumatic experiences have made them stronger, enhanced their caring and compassion for others, and increased their willingness to recognize when they need support or treatment (Compton & Follette, 1998). Choosing to participate in treatment as a couple may be a strong indication of a couple's willingness to face problems in their relationship and make necessary changes. Highlighting specific strengths alongside targeted problem areas sets a validating therapeutic tone during assessment and provides a strong positive foundation from which to discuss commitment to treatment.

COMPONENTS OF TREATMENT

Acceptance and Commitment Therapy is composed of strategies for change and strategies for acceptance, founded on a clear understanding of the purpose of the therapy. It has several specific components.

Informed Consent and Treatment Commitment

Perhaps the most important component of treatment occurs even before treatment begins. Thorough informed consent and commitment to treatment are crucial to effective therapy with survivor couples. Both partners must be fully educated about the rationale and structure of treatment, including the importance of completing homework outside of sessions. Couples must also understand that treatment may make relationship problems appear worse before they get better, especially as partners face issues they may have been avoiding for some time. Therapists can help the couple anticipate likely barriers to treatment participation in an effort to reduce premature termination of therapy. Normalizing fears about treatment, hopelessness about problems improving, and thoughts about ending therapy when difficult issues come up can help couples' willingness to address rather than avoid those issues when they inevitably arise.

Values and Goals Clarification

The first task in treatment is to help clients identify individual and couple values. From these values, treatment goals can be more clearly specified. Values clarification work is essential in ACT with survivor couples for several reasons. The task of identifying values can be extremely challenging for both partners. Individuals are rarely asked to think about what they value in life as separate from what others expect of them. Engaging in this task often elicits intense emotion, especially when partners' current lifestyles and behaviors are not congruent with identified values. This provides a rich opportunity early in therapy to coach clients on how to identify and express those emotions effectively to each other in session. Some CSA survivors may be so skilled in experientially avoidant coping that they have difficulty identifying a sense of self from which to observe their own private experience, much less deciding on core life values. Initial attempts at identifying their values may be influenced by others, both past and present. For this reason, it is important for both partners to complete their values homework separately. Therapists can validate the difficulty of the task and reassure clients that they can shape and refine their values as they progress in therapy. Values clarification is a powerful tool for helping partners find common ground for both treatment targets and shared life goals. Some couples may need to clarify for themselves and each other that being in an intimate relationship is a valued life direction in and of itself. Discussing values in session also presents an early opportunity for couples to practice approaching, rather than avoiding, communication and emotional intimacy.

Behavior Change Strategies

While acceptance is an essential component of treatment, couples also learn alternative ways of communicating and interacting in the relationship. Without acquiring skills for behavior change, couples may be unable to fully engage in acceptance work or move in the direction of their values. Clarifying desired values and recognizing areas of avoidance can be a crucial first step toward making behavioral changes in the relationship. For this reason, treatment incorporates both traditional behavior change strategies and acceptance-based strategies in a nonsequential manner, alternating between the two as needed (Compton & Follette, 1998). Self-monitoring, behavior exchange, and skills training in a variety of domains are key behavior change strategies that are incorporated into ACT for work with survivor couples.

Self-monitoring. Self-monitoring using a daily diary card to track changes in treatment targets should be an ongoing part of therapy. Each partner can track both individual and couple targets on their own diary card (e.g., ratings of relationship satisfaction, frequency of flashbacks or nightmares, frequency and content of relationship conflict, ratings and frequency of avoidance behavior such as substance use or suicidal ideation, identification of specific emotions, etc.). Not only can self-monitoring serve as a basic intervention in and of itself, but diary card information can also be used to set the agenda for each session, track treatment gains over time, revise treatment plans, and evaluate treatment progress.

Behavior exchange. Behavior exchange (BE) is a standard technique used in behavior couple therapy (Jacobson & Christensen, 1996; Jacobson & Holtzworth-Munroe, 1986). In its most basic form, BE involves each partner in generating lists of behaviors in which they could engage and that would increase their partner's day-to-day relationship satisfaction. Couples are then asked to engage in as many of these behaviors as possible and to notice when their partners perform these behaviors. BE is a useful strategy for facilitating collaboration and trust between partners early in treatment, issues that are particularly salient in this population. Because trust can be tremendously difficult for CSA survivors, BE exercises present regular, graduated opportunities to take risks in the relationship and build trust over time (Compton & Follette, 1998). The participation of both partners in BE homework also fosters an environment of collaboration between partners and shared responsibility for relationship satisfaction.

As with any skills practice, BE homework may expose skill deficits in communication and provide rich opportunities for assessment, coaching, and practice in more specific skill sets. CSA survivors may have skill deficits in both interpersonal and intrapersonal spheres (i.e., communication with others and identification and regulation of their private experience). Instruction in basic communication and problem-solving skills (e.g., listening, paraphrasing, using "I" statements, etc.), as well as emotional expression and validation, are effective avenues for increasing interpersonal skills between partners. Teaching couples to express their emotions and validate each other is an essential step in building trust and intimacy. Given that some CSA survivors experienced family environments characterized by significant invalidation, they may have learned that much of their private experience (e.g., thoughts, feelings, needs, sense of self) is unimportant, inaccurate, or worthless (Compton & Follette, 1998).

Validation and emotional expression skills strengthen the relationship, but individual skills that foster identification and effective regulation of emotion are also important in order to facilitate the survivor's acceptance and experience of difficult thoughts and feelings. Dialectical Behavior Therapy (DBT; Linehan, 1993) offers a comprehensive set of skills that emphasize experience of (rather than escape from) difficult emotion, along with effective action toward a life worth living. For couples with difficulties identifying, regulating, and expressing their emotions, the DBT skills of validation (Fruzzetti, 1996), mindfulness, distress tolerance, emotional regulation, and interpersonal effectiveness (Linehan, 1993) are useful skills modules to incorporate into treatment.

Acceptance Strategies

Acceptance is an important concept to introduce early in treatment as part of commitment to therapy. Acceptance can be broken down for couples into separate treatment categories: (a) acceptance of private events, (b) acceptance of one's history, (c) acceptance of self, and (d) acceptance of others (Follette & Pistorello, 1995).

Acceptance of private events. Acceptance of private events refers to the willingness and effort to observe all thoughts, feelings, and memories without engaging in attempts to avoid or escape their presence. This domain of acceptance is the foundation of acceptance of history, self, and others and is the avenue through which clients can ultimately make changes in their lives. When survivors are no longer invested in controlling their private experience, they are free to choose and commit to their own valued life directions.

Acceptance of history. Survivors' efforts to avoid difficult thoughts and feelings are often related to more global attempts to forget or get rid of their abuse histories. Some survivors may engage in behaviors aimed at convincing themselves of their worth as human beings (e.g., perfectionistic behavior or excessive involvement in work) in an effort to correct or negate their abuse histories. Other survivors may take extreme measures to avoid any reminders of the abuse (e.g., abstaining from intimate relationships). Some survivors may even seek treatment for help in forgetting the abuse. These behaviors make sense when considered in the context of a culture that explains behavior in terms of personal history (Follette & Pistorello, 1995). Because the current social context supports the idea that people do what they do because of events in their past, it is hardly surprising that some people look to the past to solve current problems ("If I could just forget about what happened, I could have a normal relationship"). ACT takes the perspective that it is the avoidance of one's history, not the history itself, which leads to problematic behaviors. Treatment works to help clients control their responses to their abuse histories while accepting that the abuse itself is unchangeable.

Acceptance of self. Some survivors of CSA may be so skilled in experientially avoidant coping that they have difficulty identifying a sense of self from which to observe their own private experience. Kohlenberg and Tsai (1991) have suggested that traumatic events can significantly contribute to problems of the self, explaining that an environment which fails to reinforce (or which punishes) expression of private experience may inadvertently bring private experience under the control of public stimuli. The presence of problems of the self in some survivors of CSA suggests the need for treatment components that foster an awareness of self from which individuals can begin to focus on acceptance of private experience.

In ACT, an effort is made to distinguish *self as content* from *self as context* and to help the client act from a *self as context* perspective as a route toward acceptance of private events (Follette & Pistorello, 1995). When faced with a painful private experience, a survivor of CSA may have difficulty distinguishing herself as separate from the memory or feeling. For example, while engaging in sexual intimacy with her partner, a survivor may experience an intrusive image of her abuse, may feel as if she is reliving the event, and may respond accordingly by pushing away her partner. In this case, the survivor is acting from a *self as content* perspective, unable to observe the intrusive image from a consistent, self-referenced point of view. In contrast, when acting from a *self as context* perspective, the survivor is able to observe herself experiencing the flashback while recognizing that the event is not actually occurring in real time. The survivor can then choose to respond in ways that move her in the direction of her values rather than in ways that reinforce avoidance.

Experiential exercises and metaphors are used to strengthen the *self as context* perspective. One powerful metaphor is that of a chessboard: the black and white chess pieces representing all aspects of private experience (thoughts, feelings, memories, etc.) and the board representing the self. The board (self) provides the context in which the chess pieces (private experiences) occur so that regardless of the configuration of the pieces, the board itself remains separate and free to move in any direction (Follette & Pistorello, 1995; Hayes et al., 1999).

Acceptance of others. For survivor couples, acceptance of others often involves acceptance of each other's histories. Acceptance of others does not mean approval of others or the condoning of another's behavior, but rather the acceptance of individual private events associated with another person. For example, one partner may ask the other to forget about or move on from her abuse, reminding her that he is not at all like the perpetrator. While he may be well-intentioned, such comments only perpetuate avoidance behavior in his partner and may actually function as a way for him to avoid his own discomfort with his partner's history (Follette & Pistorello, 1995). For both partners, acceptance of all aspects of each other's histories is an important part of building emotional closeness and intimacy. Over the course of treatment, couples learn to observe their own thoughts and feelings about each other while engaging in behaviors that function to increase relationship goals and values.

Acceptance and CSA Survivors

Walser and Hayes (1998) explain that in treating CSA survivors, it is very important to clarify the ACT concepts of acceptance and responsibility. Acceptance does not mean survivors are being asked to like their abuse histories or understand them as acceptable, but instead to experience the thoughts and emotions associated with those histories for what they are—memories and thoughts that, while painful, can inform rather than drive behavior. In addition, responsibility does not mean survivors are being blamed for their abuse, but instead refers to survivors' *response-ability*, the ability to respond to thoughts and feelings about the abuse using effective behavior.

Therapists must ensure that survivors do not feel as though their efforts to control their private experiences are wrong. Follette (1994) emphasizes that control is an important issue for CSA survivors; they had no control over the sexual abuse they experienced and thus may have learned to control their psychological experience of the trauma by numbing themselves or dissociating. Great care should be taken by the therapist to validate survivors' use of experiential avoidance as children to cope with the abuse in order to survive. The therapist can then help clients examine how well that coping strategy is working in their lives currently.

Common Treatment Issues

Sexual dysfunction. Sexual issues will likely arise when treating survivor couples, even though few couples will initially present for treatment specifically to address such problems (Compton & Follette, 1998). Types of sexual dysfunction may vary across couples, and sexual difficulties may be experienced by one or both partners. For partners of CSA survivors, sexual problems are particularly troubling, often contributing to feelings of inadequacy, rejection, or frustration when the survivor avoids sexual intimacy (Compton & Follette, 1998). A more traditional, structured approach to treating sexual dysfunction that involves graduated exposure to arousal, intimacy, and sexual contact (Wincze & Carey, 1991) may be incorporated into ACT (Follette & Pistorello, 1995). However, given the close association between sexual intimacy and communication, and the possibility that low sexual desire may function for some survivors as avoidance of closeness and intimacy (Compton & Follette, 1998), the treatment components of acceptance, emotional expression, and validation may effectively address sexual issues without a more structured approach. Thorough assessment of sexual dysfunction will help the therapist determine the most effective direction of treatment when sexual issues are present.

Flashbacks and dissociation. Flashbacks are highly distressing, intrusive, and disorienting experiences that occur for some survivors of CSA and can significantly interfere with effective functioning. Flashbacks usually occur in response to an environmental stimulus that reminds the survivor of the abuse including, but not limited to, sexual intimacy in the context of the relationship. Partners of survivors who experience flashbacks can be instrumental in helping their partner feel safe and remain grounded after experiencing a flashback (Follette & Pistorello, 1995). During a flashback, partners can gently orient the survivor to time and space and provide reassurance of her safety. Over time, this basic supportive strategy may help the survivor recognize the onset of a flashback and reduce her level of disorientation.

The extent to which both partners share their thoughts and feelings in the aftermath of a flashback varies from couple to couple. As couples develop their emotional expression and validation skills, they may find that discussing their respective reactions with each other increases their closeness and intimacy and helps the survivor cope more effectively with these distressing experiences. For other couples, more basic forms of support and less emotional processing may be the most effective way partners can help survivors cope with flashbacks. In either case, emphasis should be placed on the use of acceptance as opposed to avoidance strategies in response to flashbacks. Even in cases where the CSA survivor has not experienced flashbacks, it may be useful to prepare the couple for the possibility of flashbacks as treatment progresses (Follette & Pistorello, 1995).

Some survivors of CSA may also experience dissociation, either in response to flashbacks (Follette & Pistorello, 1995) or other aversive stimuli. Involving the survivor's partner in the ways discussed above can be effective interventions for dissociation when associated with flashbacks. However, thorough assessment of the function of a flashback will help guide effective treatment when it occurs in response to a variety of stimuli. Dissociation often functions as a form of escape from unpleasant thoughts, feelings, memories, or aversive environmental circumstances. Acceptance work, paired with increased skill acquisition in the areas of validation and emotional expression between partners, will help the survivor tolerate and accept difficult thoughts, emotions, and memories without engaging in escape behavior. As with any avoidance behavior, particularly one that functioned as a survival strategy, the couple must be helped to understand the behavior while recognizing its current ineffectiveness.

Guilt and blame. Additional problems that frequently occur in couples with an identified patient involve issues of guilt and blame. It is not uncommon for partners of CSA survivors to view their role in therapy as merely to support the survivor's individual growth and to blame the survivor or the survivor's trauma history for the problems in their relationship (Follette, 1991). Some CSA survivors may even share this view, believing their individual problems are to blame for relationship difficulties. We have called this the "benevolent blame" in that it is often not meant to be mean-spirited. However, such blame may still exacerbate posttraumatic symptomatology by perpetuating survivors' feelings of shame and stigmatization (Compton & Follette, 1998). Therapists must consistently highlight the transactional nature of relationship problems. By alternating treatment emphasis from one partner to the other and shifting between historical issues and current relationship functioning, the therapist can convey mutual responsibility for relationship issues throughout the treatment process (Follette & Pistorello, 1995).

Treatment Evaluation

As in all treatment approaches, ACT with survivor couples should include ongoing assessment to test hypotheses about the function of various behaviors and provide information about treatment progress. Videotaped sessions, brief self-report measures of treatment targets, and daily diary cards can be used consistently throughout treatment to track changes over time. Information obtained through regular assessment allows therapists and clients to make informed decisions about modifications in treatment, including when to continue or terminate therapy. In cases where couples are having difficulty complying with treatment demands or when difficult relationship issues appear to be getting worse before getting better, regular assessment provides clear, indisputable data that both therapists and clients can examine together. Observing interaction patterns in videotaped therapy sessions or noting small steady changes in self-report measures of treatment targets can be a motivating factor for couples who feel "stuck" in treatment.

Orienting clients to their long-term goals and shared relationship values throughout treatment can also provide an anchoring point for clients at times when relationship problems feel overwhelming. It is very important to remind clients that treatment often appears to make problems feel worse before they feel better. Helping clients anticipate these feelings and outline strategies for dealing with them when they arise may help prevent premature termination when treatment inevitably becomes difficult. When therapists establish open discussion of the difficulties of treatment and potential barriers to treatment compliance in the beginning of therapy, these issues are easier to revisit with clients as needed throughout treatment.

Final Thoughts

In closing, it seems fitting to address experiential avoidance and acceptance on the part of the therapist. Hayes et al. (1999) remind ACT therapists that "harmful moments in ACT can occur when the therapist is raising issues of acceptance and commitment and at the same time modeling a lack of these behaviors" (p. 277). Working with survivor couples can be both extremely challenging and intensely rewarding. The treatment process may engender internal struggles for therapists as they listen to clients disclose detailed descriptions of their abuse histories and the powerful emotions associated with those experiences (Follette, 1994). It is crucial that therapists address their own desires to avoid painful thoughts and feelings surrounding clients' disclosures during the course of therapy, just as they help the partners of survivors deal with their avoidance of partners' abuse histories. Therapists must be willing to do what they ask of their couples—to hear everything partners want to share and to experience and respond to the intensity of partners' feelings. Therapists are advised to carefully monitor their own experiential avoidance so as not to find themselves avoiding certain topics.

Follette (1994) stresses the importance of clinical supervision or consultation as a component of any treatment for CSA survivors. Supervision can provide therapists with a safe and appropriate place to express their thoughts and emotions associated with what they experience over the course of treatment. Finally, therapists should remember that working with couples in which one member has an abuse history presents many of the dialectics that can be observed in trauma therapy, including the dialectic of uniqueness and similarity. Couples with trauma histories have a great many commonalities with other distressed couples, and in addressing their unique concerns the therapist should not forget those similarities.

REFERENCES

Baucom, D. H., & Hoffman, J. A. (1986). The effectiveness of marital therapy: Current status and application to the clinical setting. In N. S. Jacobson & A. S. Gurman (Eds.), *Clinical handbook of couple therapy* (pp. 597–620). New York: Guilford.

Beach, S. R. H., Sandeen, E. E., & O'Leary, K. D. (1990). *Depression in marriage: A model for etiology and treatment.* New York: Guilford.

Briere, J. (1988). The long-term clinical correlates of childhood sexual victimization. *Annals of the New York Academy of Sciences, 528,* 327–334.

Briere, J. (1992). *Child abuse trauma: Theory and treatment of the lasting effects.* Newbury Park, CA: Sage.

Briere, J. N., & Runtz, M. (1991). The long-term effects of sexual abuse: A review and synthesis. In J. Briere (Ed.), *Treating victims of child sexual abuse* (pp. 3–13). San Francisco: Jossey-Bass.

Browne, A., & Finkelhor, D. (1986). The impact of child sexual abuse: A review of the research. *Psychological Bulletin, 99,* 66–77.

Compton, J. S., & Follette, V. M. (1998). Couples surviving trauma: Issues and interventions. In V. M. Follette, J. I. Ruzek, & F. R. Abueg (Eds.), *Cognitive-behavioral therapies for trauma* (pp. 321–352). New York: Guilford.

Davis, J. L., & Petretic-Jackson, P. A. (2000). The impact of child sexual abuse on adult interpersonal functioning: A review and synthesis of the empirical literature. *Aggression and Violent Behavior, 5,* 291–328.

DiLillo, D. (2001). Interpersonal functioning among women reporting a history of childhood sexual abuse: Empirical findings and methodological issues. *Clinical Psychology Review, 21,* 553–576.

Epstein, N., & Baucom, D. H. (1988). *Cognitive-behavioral marital therapy.* New York: Brunner/Mazel.

Fisher, P. M., Winne, P. H., & Ley, R. G. (1993). Group therapy for adult women survivors of child sexual abuse: Differentiation of completers versus dropouts. *Psychotherapy, 4,* 616–624.

Follette, V. M. (1991). Marital therapy for sexual abuse survivors. In J. Briere (Ed.), *Treating victims of child sexual abuse.* San Francisco: Jossey-Bass.

Follette, V. M. (1994). Survivors of child sexual abuse: Treatment using a contextual analysis. In S. C. Hayes, N. S. Jacobson, V. M. Follette, & M. J. Dougher (Eds.), *Acceptance and change: Content and context in psychotherapy* (pp. 255–268). Reno, NV: Context Press.

Follette, V. M., Alexander, P. C., & Follette, W. F. (1991). Individual predictors of outcome in group treatment for incest survivors. *Journal of Consulting and Clinical Psychology, 59,* 150–155.

Follette, V. M., & Pistorello, J. (1995). Couples therapy. In C. Classen & I. D. Yalom (Eds.), *Treating women molested in childhood. The Jossey-Bass library of current clinical technique* (pp. 129–161). San Francisco: Jossey-Bass.

Fruzzetti, A. E. (1996). Causes and consequences: Individual distress in the context of couple interactions. *Journal of Consulting and Clinical Psychology, 64,* 1192–1201.

Gottman, J. M., & Krokoff, L. J. (1989). Marital interaction and satisfaction: A longitudinal view. *Journal of Consulting and Clinical Psychology, 57,* 47–52.

Hahlweg, K., & Markman, H. J. (1988). The effectiveness of behavioral marital therapy: Empirical status of behavioral techniques in preventing and alleviating marital distress. *Journal of Consulting and Clinical Psychology, 56,* 440–447.

Hahlweg, K., Schindler, L., Revenstorf, D., & Brengelmann, J. C. (1984). The Munich marital therapy study. In K. Hahlweg & N. S. Jacobson (Eds.), *Marital interaction: Analysis and modification.* New York: Guilford.

Hayes, S. C., Barnes-Holmes, D., & Roche, B. (2001). *Relational frame theory: A post-Skinnerian account of human language and cognition.* New York: Plenum.

Hayes, S. C., Strosahl, K., & Wilson, K. G. (1999). *Acceptance and commitment therapy: An experiential approach to behavior change.* New York: Guilford.

Hayes, S. C., Wilson, K. G., Gifford, E. V., Follette, V. M., & Strosahl, K. (1996). Experiential avoidance and behavioral disorders: A functional dimensional approach to diagnosis and treatment. *Journal of Consulting and Clinical Psychology, 64,* 1152–1168.

Herman, J. L. (1992). *Trauma and recovery: The aftermath of violence—from domestic violence to political terror.* New York: Harper Collins.

Jacobson, N. S., & Christensen, A. (1996). *Integrative couple therapy: Promoting acceptance and change.* New York: Norton.

Jacobson, N. S., Dobson, K., Fruzzetti, A. E., Schmaling, K. B., & Salusky, S. (1991). Marital therapy as a treatment for depression. *Journal of Consulting and Clinical Psychology, 59,* 547–557.

Jacobson, N. S., Follette, W. C., & Pagel, M. (1986). Predicting who will benefit from behavioral marital therapy. *Journal of Consulting and Clinical Psychology, 54,* 518–522.

Jacobson, N. S., & Holtzworth-Munroe, A. (1986). Marital therapy: A social learning-cognitive perspective. In N. S. Jacobson & A. S. Gurman (Eds.), *Clinical handbook of marital therapy* (pp. 29–70). New York: Guilford.

Jacobson, N. S., Holtzworth-Munroe, A., & Schmaling, K. B. (1989). Marital therapy and spouse involvement in the treatment of depression, agoraphobia, and alcoholism. *Journal of Consulting and Clinical Psychology, 57,* 5–10.

Jacobson, N. S., & Margolin, G. (1979). *Marital therapy: Strategies based on social learning and behavior exchange principles.* New York: Brunner/Mazel.

Johnson, S. M. (1989). Integrating marital and individual therapy for incest survivors: A case study. *Psychotherapy, 26,* 96–103.

Kohlenberg, R. J., & Tsai, M. (1991). *Functional analytic psychotherapy.* New York: Plenum.

Linehan, M. M. (1993). *Cognitive-behavioral treatment of borderline personality disorder.* New York: Guilford.

Pistorello, J., & Follette, V. M. (1998). Childhood sexual abuse and couples' relationships: Female survivors' reports in therapy groups. *Journal of Marital and Family Therapy, 24,* 473–485.

Polusny, M. A., & Follette, V. M. (1995). Long-term correlates of child sexual abuse: Theory and review of the empirical literature. *Applied and Preventive Psychology, 4,* 143–166.

Reid, K. S., Taylor, D. K., & Wampler, R. S. (1995). Perceptions of partner involvement in the therapeutic process by patients who experienced sexual abuse as children. *Journal of Sex Education and Therapy, 21,* 36–45.

Rind, B., Bauserman, R., & Tromovitch, P. (1998). A meta-analytic examination of assumed properties of child sexual abuse using college samples. *Psychological Bulletin, 124,* 22–53.

Russell, D. E. (1986). *The secret trauma: Incest in the lives of girls and women.* New York: Basic Books.

Saxe, B. J., & Johnson, S. M. (1999). An empirical investigation of group treatment for a clinical population of adult female incest survivors. *Journal of Child Sexual Abuse, 8,* 67–88.

Stuart, R. B. (1980). *Helping couples change: A social learning approach to marital therapy.* New York: Guilford.

Walser, R. D., & Hayes, S. C. (1998). Acceptance and trauma survivors: Applied issues and behaviors. In V. M. Follette, J. I. Ruzek, & F. R. Abueg (Eds.), *Cognitive-behavioral therapies for trauma* (pp. 257–277). New York: Guilford.

Wincze, J. P., & Carey, M. P. (1991). *Sexual dysfunction: A guide for assessment and treatment.* New York: Guilford.

Index